# The Economy of Ghana

## Analytical Perspectives on Stability, Growth & Poverty

Edited by
**ERNEST ARYEETEY**
**ISSER, University of Ghana**
**&**
**RAVI KANBUR**
**Cornell University**

**JAMES CURREY**

**WOELI PUBLISHING SERVICES**

James Currey www. jamescurrey.co.uk
is an imprint of Boydell & Brewer Ltd
PO Box 9, Woodbridge, Suffolk IP12 3DF, UK
www.boydell.co.uk
and of Boydell & Brewer Inc.
668 Mt Hope Avenue, Rochester, NY 14620, USA
www.boydellandbrewer.com

Woeli Publishing Services
P.O. Box NT 601
Accra New Town
Ghana

**British Library Cataloguing in Publication Data**
The economy of Ghana: analytical perspectives on stability, growth & poverty
1. Ghana — economic conditions — 1957–1979
2. Ghana — economic conditions — 1979–
I. Aryeetey, Ernest, 1955–
II. Kanbur, S. M. Ravi                                330.9'66705

ISBN 978-1-84701-003-2 James Currey (Hardback)
ISBN 978-9988-626-82-2 Woeli (Paperback)

Typeset in 10/12 pt Times by Woeli Publishing Services
Printed and bound in Great Britain by CPI Antony Rowe, Chippenham

# Contents

# List of Contributors

**Frank Agbola,** School of Policy, University of Newcastle, UK
**David O. Andah,** Ghana Microfinance Institutions Network
**Elizabeth N. Appiah,** United States Agency for International Development (USAID)
**Kojo Appiah-Kubi,** Institute of Statistical, Social and Economic Research (ISSER)
**Ernest Aryeetey,** Institute of Statistical, Social and Economic Research (ISSER)
**Felix A. Asante,** Institute of Statistical, Social and Economic Research (ISSER)
**Joseph R. A. Ayee,** Faculty of Social Studies, University of Ghana
**Theresa Blankson,** Monetary Policy Division, Bank of Ghana
**Neils-Hugo Blunch,** George Washington University
**Thierry Buchs,** State Secretariat for Economic Affairs (SECO), Swiss Economic Ministry
**Harold Coulombe,** Consultant
**Augustin Fosu,** United Nations Economic Commission for Africa
**David L. Franklin,** Sigma One Corporation, North Carolina
**Kwabena Gyimah-Brempong,** Department of Economics, University of Florida
**Charles Jebuni,** Centre for Policy Analysis (CEPA) Accra
**Ravi Kanbur,** Department of Economics, Cornell University
**Tony Killick,** Overseas Development Institute, London
**Stephen Kyereme,** GDCON
**Johan Mathiesen,** International Monetary Fund (IMF)
**Andy McKay,** Department of Economics and International Development, University of Bath, UK
**N. N. N. Nsowah-Nuamah,** Institute of Statistical. Social and Economic Research (ISSER)
**Abena Oduro,** Centre for Policy Analysis, (CEPA), Accra.
**G. B. Overbosch,** Centre for World Food Studies, SOW-VU, Vrije University, Netherlands
**Daniel Bruce Sarpong,** Department of Agricultural Economics and Agribusiness, University of Ghana
**Bernadin Senadza,** Economics Department, University of Ghana
**Nii K. Sowa,** Centre for Policy Analysis (CEPA), Accra.
**William F. Steel,** Senior Adviser, World Bank
**Anthony Tsekpo,** Institute of Statistical, Social and Economic Research (ISSER)
**Peter Quartey,** Institute of Statistical. Social and Economic Research (ISSER)
**Susanna Wolf,** Department of Agricultural Economics and Agribusiness, University of Ghana
**Curtis E. Youngblood,** United States Agency for International Development (USAID)
**G. J. M. van den Boom,** Centre for World Food Studies, SOW-VU, Vrije University, Netherlands

# Acronyms

| | |
|---|---|
| AFRC | Armed Forces Revolutionary Council |
| ARB | Association of Rural Banks |
| BECE | Basic Education Certificate Examination |
| BoG | Bank of Ghana |
| CBO | Community-Based Organization |
| CDD | Centre for Democratic Development |
| CPI | Consumer Price Index |
| CSO | Civil Society Organization |
| CU | Credit Union |
| DA | District Assembly |
| DACF | District Assemblies Common Fund |
| DCE | District Chief Executive |
| DMBs | Domestic Money Banks |
| ERP | Economic Recovery Programme |
| GCB | Ghana Commercial Bank |
| GDP | Gross Domestic Product |
| GLSS | Ghana Living Standards Survey |
| GoG | Government of Ghana |
| GPRS | Ghana Poverty Reduction Strategy |
| GTZ | German Technical Cooperation |
| HDI | Human Development Index |
| IMF | International Monetary Fund |
| ISSER | Institute of Statistical, Social and Economic Research |
| JSS | Junior Secondary School |
| LDC | Less Developed Country |
| MFEP | Ministry of Finance and Economic Planning |
| MFI | Micro Finance Institution |
| MLGRD | Ministry of Local Government and Rural Development |
| NADMO | National Disaster Management Organization |
| NBFI | Non-Banking Financial Institutions |
| NBSSI | National Board for Small-Scale Industries |
| NDC | National Democratic Congress |
| NDPC | National Development Planning Commission |
| NGOs | Non-governmental organizations |
| NPP | New Patriotic Party |
| NRC | National Redemption Council |
| PAMSCAD | Programme of Actions to Mitigate the Social Costs of Adjustment |
| PNDC | Provisional National Defence Council |
| PRSP | Poverty Reduction Strategy Paper |
| PUFMARP | Public Financial Management Reform Programme |
| RCBs | Rural and Community Banks |
| RMFIs | Rural and Micro Finance Institutions |
| S&Ls | Savings and Loans Companies |
| SAP | Structural Adjustment Programme |
| SMC | Supreme Military Council |
| SSCE | Secondary School Certificate Examination |
| SSS | Senior Secondary School |
| TOR | Tema Oil Refinery |
| UNDP | United Nations Development Programme |
| UNICEF | United Nations Children's Emergency Fund |
| USAID | United States Agency for International Development |
| WAEC | West African Examination Council |

# I Overview

# 1 Ghana's Economy at Half-Century: An Overview of Stability, Growth & Poverty*

ERNEST ARYEETEY
& RAVI KANBUR

## 1. Introduction

Ghana experienced its first half-century as an independent nation in March 2007. However, the early promise of democracy combined with economic and social development that hailed the new era in 1957 led to disappointments in the first three decades of independence. While democracy has now been restored, with the peaceful transfer of one civilian administration to another in 2001, and while there has been some recovery from the earlier economic collapse, the challenge of economic and social transformation looms large.

Indeed, the last two decades have seen steady and significant economic growth in spite of considerable instability in macroeconomic performance and a growing dependence on aid and other foreign inflows. An average of 4.9% GDP growth and a per capita GDP growth of about 2.9% have been recorded for the best part of that period. While the growth performance may not be exceptional it has been significantly above average by African standards. In their study of the 'Drivers of Change' in Ghana, Booth et al. (2004) identify economic liberalization in the 1980s and political liberalization in the 1990s as the key factors behind the fairly decent growth performance. It is important to observe that, since 2001, the macroeconomic policy situation has improved considerably, and the environment is less subject to policy reversals and deviations from agreed policies.

But the relationship between economic growth and the most important social concern, poverty, has been unclear. The perception is that the number of people living below the poverty line has not changed in tandem. Thus, despite the sustained per capita growth accompanied by some measured reduction in income poverty,

* The papers in this volume were selected from those presented at the 'Ghana at the Half-Century' conference in Accra; 18–20 July 2004 organized by the Institute of Statistical, Social and Economic Research, University of Ghana, and Cornell University. We are grateful to USAID for financial support through its SAGA project.

levels of poverty remain high. The reduction in income poverty has been fairly reasonable and the changes in the non-income dimensions are not insignificant. But there are indications also that there have been significant movements in and out of poverty, and the perception that poverty is worsening prevails strongly (Oduro et al., 2004). Most important, the ability of the economy to generate employment has definitely not been strengthened following economic reforms in which private investments have hardly been significant. In the final analysis, the perception that social conditions have not improved significantly in twenty years is quite strong.

Related to the issue of growth and poverty is the question of structural change throughout this period. In the policy discussions of the last few years there has been the question of how an economy that has been able to achieve fairly decent growth rates over a long period remains unable to sustain that achievement with acceptable changes in its structure. It is not clear that this is simply a consequence of the chosen macroeconomic policies and their implementation, even though these clearly have contributed to the situation. There is the growing view that the absence of structural change is due to lack of clear direct effort to achieve such change (Aryeetey and McKay 2004). And the absence of the commitment to this change is considered to be largely political (Killick in this volume; and 2000).

The political transformation that Ghana has experienced, resulting in the historic transfer of power from one elected government to another, is definitely significant. While governance issues are still considered to be problematic, there is increasing openness in the discussion of economic policy. This is reflected in the institution of the annual national economic dialogue and the growing participation of civil society in policy discussions.[1] Like economic reforms, the process of democratization has been encouraged by donor agencies and governments. There is always the danger of a political reform process being dominated by external influences. But we recognize the fact that there have been some domestic influences also. Indeed, the need for democratic institutions and the process for achieving them have been both demand-driven and highly popular (Booth et al., 2004). In effect, powerful domestic concerns played useful roles alongside the external pressures in assisting the process of change.

Analyses of the economy's more recent performance indicate that, despite the relative macroeconomic stability achieved, private investment has not responded to this, employment has contracted, and agricultural performance outside of cocoa and key export crops has been poor (ISSER, 2004). Many studies have identified a number of key areas that need to be addressed. These include (i) discipline in control of the fiscal deficit through effective public expenditure management; (ii) the development of an efficient and competitive financial sector which can meet the needs of a developing private sector (iii) enhanced effectiveness of public service delivery; and (iv) policies to transform the agricultural sector, beginning with the land-tenure question. All of these involve difficult political choices and institutional reform (Booth et al., 2004).

---

[1] In May 2001, a workshop organized by the Institute of Statistical, Social and Economic Research, University of Ghana and Cornell University led to the issue of a memorandum on 'Economic Growth, Macroeconomic Stability and Poverty Reduction' by 40 independent economists as input for the National Economic Dialogue for that year.

The problem with the fiscal deficit and its management has attracted considerable attention from analysts over the years. The central issue has been the trade-off between fiscal deficits and growth. Reducing the fiscal deficit has often been seen to be important in enabling lower inflation and interest rates, and more real exchange-rate stability. And these are all important for private sector production and investment. It is important that the stability of these key variables is perceived to be permanent and institutionalized in order to have beneficial macroeconomic impacts. When the credibility of government, in terms of maintaining an appropriate fiscal stance, is judged to be weak, particularly given the influence of elections on levels of public spending, this poses a problem for reform. It is still not clear if Ghana is out of the woods, despite more impressive fiscal balances since 2001. Indeed, improvements have often been due to larger than expected external inflows, and lately some improvements in revenue collection. Thus, in 2004 there was a higher than expected outturn for receipts. Total receipts, including donor grants, foreign loans and Heavily Indebted Poor Countries (HIPC) relief for 2004 amounted to ¢28,736.8 billion, which was about ¢3,883.7 billion above the budget projection of ¢24,853.1 billion. Domestic resources made up 67.1% of this figure, with donor assistance contributing the remaining 32.9%. Disbursements and external grants reached a record level of ¢4,940.3 billion, equivalent to 6.2% of GDP in 2004 (See Table 1.1).

The financial sector, and what it can do to generate investment by the private sector, has also been the subject of considerable study over the years (Aryeetey, 1996). The reforms in the sector have not led to significant restructuring, thus leaving the sector incapable of leading private sector development. While the problems of the sector are partially related to the fiscal problems already mentioned, there are also indications that the inability to develop more innovative and competitive approaches to dealing with demand for financial services is another major obstacle. What is crucial is for the sector to respond to the changing environment in order to make a more meaningful impact on growth and development.

Dissatisfaction with public service delivery has been at the core of assessments made by many donor agencies of the difficulties of the Ghanaian economy (Aryeetey and Peretz, 2005). This explains the frequent calls by donors for public sector reform, which they consider to be a key requirement for raising the growth rate. While such a reform is in general politically sensitive, the expected poverty impact, as more poor people benefit from improved service delivery and better public expenditure management, is judged to be immense. Previous attempts at civil service reform are judged to have been largely unsuccessful due to lack of political support (Booth et al., 2004). It is clear, however, that in the absence of major public sector reform the constraints on private sector development will remain. Moreover, in the absence of private sector investment and also financial sector development, there appears to be little scope for significant employment creation.

Structural transformation is closely associated with agriculture and its relationship to the more modern sectors. Various studies have illustrated the low productivity associated with Ghanaian agriculture and provided explanations for this (Nyanteng and Seini, 2000). Aside from the technological problems linked to the little application

**Table 1.1**    **Performance of the Ghanaian Economy, 2003–4: Selected Economic Indicators**

| Indicator | 2003 | 2004 | 2004 | Difference | Difference |
|---|---|---|---|---|---|
| (% unless otherwise stated) | Actual (C1) | Target (C2) | Actual (C3) | C3-C1 | C3-C2 |
| **National GDP** | | | | | |
| Nominal GDP (¢ bn) | 65,262 | 77,620 | 79,803.7 | 14,541.70 | 2,183.70 |
| Real GDP Growth | 5.2 | 5.2 | 5.8 | 0.60 | 0.60 |
| Real Per Capita GDP Growth | 2.5 | | 2.7 | 0.2 | |
| **Sectoral Growth Rates** | | | | | |
| Agriculture | 6.1 | 6.0 | 7.5 | 1.40 | 1.50 |
| Industry | 5.1 | 5.2 | 5.1 | 0.00 | −0.10 |
| Services | 4.7 | 4.7 | 4.7 | 0.00 | 0.00 |
| **Fiscal Indicators** | | | | | |
| Domestic Revenue/GDP | 21.4 | 22.4 | 23.8 | 2.40 | 1.40 |
| Domestic Expenditure/GDP | 18.8 | 20.7 | 23.7 | 4.90 | 3.00 |
| Tax Revenue/GDP | 19.6 | 20.9 | 21.8 | 2.20 | 0.90 |
| Primary Balance/GDP | 2.5 | 1.7 | 0.7 | −1.80 | −1.00 |
| Overall Balance/GDP | −3.4 | −1.7 | −3.2 | 0.20 | −1.50 |
| Net Domestic Financing/GDP | −0.004 | −2.2 | 0.5 | 0.50 | 2.70 |
| **Monetary/Financial Indicators** | | | | | |
| Broad Money Supply Growth | 35.6 | | 26.0 | −9.60 | |
| Reserve Money Growth | 28.2 | | 18.77 | −9.43 | |
| M2+/GDP | 0.3 | | 0.34 | 0.04 | |
| Inflation (Year-on-Year) | 23.6 | 10 | 11.8 | −11.80 | 1.80 |
| Inflation (Yearly Average) | 26.7 | 17 | 12.6 | −14.10 | −4.40 |
| Interest Rates | | | | | |
| Demand Deposits (Annual Av.) | 8.5 | | 7.50 | −1.00 | |
| Savings Deposits (Annual Av.) | 11.1 | | 9.50 | −1.60 | |
| Time Deposits (Annual Av.) | 14.3 | | 13.25 | −1.05 | |
| Lending Rates (Annual Av.) | 34.9 | | 28.75 | −6.15 | |
| 91-Day Bills (End Period) | 18.7 | | 17.0 | −1.70 | |
| Lending Rates (End Period) | 32.8 | | 28.75 | −4.05 | |
| Depreciation (¢/$) | | | | | |
| Inter-Bank Rate | 8,852.30 | | 9,051.26 | 198.96 | |
| Forex Bureau Rate | 9,130.43 | | 9,222.73 | 92.30 | |
| **External Sector Indicators ($ m)** | | | | | |
| Merchandise Exports | 2063.9 | 2314.0 | 2297.1 | 487.50 | 2,784.60 |
| Merchandise Imports | 2705.1 | 3168.1 | 2969.3 | −7,266.60 | −4,297.30 |
| Trade Balance | −641.2 | −854.1 | −672.2 | −840.40 | −1,512.60 |
| Current Account | 15.6 | −130.9 | 40.8 | −276.50 | −235.70 |
| Balance of Payments | 39.8 | −76.9 | 367.3 | −367.30 | 0.00 |
| Gross International Reserves (GIR) | 601.2 | 811.0 | 1425.6 | 16,306.40 | 17,732.00 |
| GIR in Months of Imports | 2.5 | 2.2 | 3.9 | −0.10 | 3.80 |
| Net International Reserves | 130.86 | 130.0 | 657.7 | 196.00 | 984.54 |

*Source:*    Bank of Ghana and Budget Statements

of capital in agricultural production, there are the issues of land-tenure arrangements which fail to provide adequate incentive for injecting capital into agriculture and other structural and institutional problems. There is the general perception that the political transformation that has been observed in Ghana has not necessarily facilitated the development of institutions that make structural transformation feasible. The politics behind winning elections is not necessarily one that promotes efficiency in public service delivery and supports difficult land-tenure reforms.

As policy-makers have struggled to identify the most practical ways of bringing about improvements in policy and its implementation, so also it has become necessary to encourage researchers to provide information on the state of the economy and views on what policies and institutional developments would be most appropriate for tackling the problems identified. This essay is an introduction to a volume of papers that seek to achieve this objective. Based on these papers, and on the literature in general, it provides an overview of economic stability, growth and poverty in Ghana as the nation enters its second half-century.

## 2. Growth and Macroeconomic Performance

As seen earlier, macroeconomic conditions in Ghana have been relatively stable since 2001, even if somewhat mixed for a number of indicators. This stability contrasts quite considerably with performance in the preceding decade. In 2004, two of the five 'key macroeconomic targets' were met, namely real GDP growth and gross international reserves. The targets set for the domestic primary balance, inflation and the overall budget deficit were not achieved. But more important is the fact that, to a very large extent, the performance is still driven by external factors. In that sense, not much has changed after almost five decades of independence.

### *The Growth Record*

Fig.1.1 shows how the growth rate appears to have settled around the 5% level for two decades, with some improvement in 2004 at 5.8%. As in the past few years, the growth has been led by the agriculture sector which grew by 7.5% in 2004 compared with 6.1% in 2003. The sector contributed 46.7% of overall 2004 growth, which may be compared to 41.4% in 2003. Cocoa was the driving force in the sector's growth, with a 29.9% increase in the sub-sector. The industrial sector grew by 5.1% contributing 22.1% to overall growth in 2004, with the highest growth being in construction which experienced a 6.6% growth, having risen from 6.1% in 2003. The services sector grew by 4.7%, contributing 24.3% to overall growth.

But there is a sometimes traumatic history to the growth story. We have suggested that over the past two decades Ghana's fairly decent growth performance has compared favourably with that in many other sub-Saharan African countries. This has been achieved in an environment that was often unstable and which then impacted on households in a manner that was different from expected. Fosu and Aryeetey (in this volume) present that growth experience. The growth record shows considerable unevenness, particularly in the 1970s. With reasonably high GDP growth in the 1950s and early 1960s, the Ghanaian economy began to experience a slowdown in GDP

Growth in 1964. Growth was turbulent during much of the period after the mid-1960s and only began to stabilize by 1984. There have been several years of negative growth, which were often years that saw changes in government and explosive policy reversals. The lowest ever growth of –14% was experienced in 1975, coinciding with the oil price shock as well as a policy reversal from a market-oriented stance to an inward-looking protectionist regime. The period of turbulence, however, also had positive growth episodes, with the highest peak rate reaching 9% in 1970 and 1978.

**Fig. 1.1: Real GDP and Real Per Capita GDP Growth (1970–2005)**

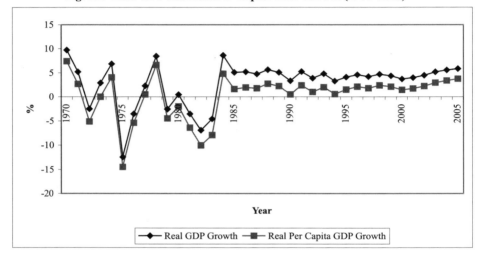

*Source:* World Bank (2007)

The significance of policy regimes for growth performance has depended, to a large extent, on how those policies led to the infusion of new capital into the economy. Significant growth was recorded in the early 1960s under import-substitution policies, so long as the state could find the resources to invest. In the 1980s, the liberal reform programme or Economic Recovery Programme (ERP), with major support from the International Monetary Fund (IMF) and the World Bank, was intended to halt the downward economic spiral. Starting in 1986, the second phase of reform saw the ERP being supplemented with the Structural Adjustment Programme (SAP), geared toward correcting a number of structural imbalances in order to engender sustained healthy economic growth. The economy definitely responded positively to the ERP/SAP soon after its inception, recovering from its negative growth rate of about –5% in 1983 to a hefty positive rate of 8% in 1984. The favourable rate of growth has continued since that time, with relatively little variance, even if there has been a slight slowdown since the mid-1990s and a little faster growth since 2001.

The growth record, based on *per capita* income, is similar to that of GDP. Indeed *per capita* GDP growth closely tracks that of GDP, suggesting that population growth has been fairly stable, though the larger gap between them since the 1980s suggests an acceleration of population growth over this period.

Sustained economic growth would normally be accompanied by major structural transformation of the economy. The current and historical pattern of the Ghanaian economy portrays hardly any structural changes. This finding is supported by the analysis of Killick (2000) and Round and Powell (2000). The structure of the economy in the 1990s indicated a shift in dominance from agriculture to services, with little change in the share of industry.

## *Growth in an Unstable Environment*
Fosu and Aryeetey (this volume) offer explanations as to why the measured growth in Ghana often raised questions in the minds of the people. They do this by showing that most of the growth has been driven by public investments of questionable productivity, the returns on which have been sometimes misallocated. Aryeetey and Tarp (2000) had earlier argued that the growth of the 1980s came about as a result of the expansion of capital application, largely as a consequence of increased aid inflows, which was similar to the expansion that occurred in the 1960s financed largely through accumulated reserves from the 1950s. In neither case was the increased use of capital accompanied by significant improvements in total factor productivity (TFP). In both instances, the injection of capital came after long periods of relatively high capital depreciation. Again in both instances, the initial high growth rates could not be sustained into the medium term because the policies were not anchored in appropriate all-embracing development frameworks. The first attempt sought to deny the market its place, while the second attempt took place with weakened state structures that were unable to deliver outcomes in a timely and adequate manner.

Aryeetey and Fosu utilize the growth accounting results presented in O'Connell and Ndulu (2000) for the decomposition of *per capita* growth in Ghana during 1960–97, which showed that during this entire period, output per worker declined by 0.12%. At the same time, growth in factor accumulation, measured by physical capital per worker, accounted for 0.52%, and education per worker for 0.50%; however, this positive contribution by physical and human capital was more than offset by the negative contribution of total factor productivity (TFP), measured as the residual, of 1.15%. Thus, overall, the slow rate of *per capita* income growth in Ghana during 1960–97 seems to be attributed largely to productivity rather than to production inputs.

It would appear that, in the last two decades, the most unstable macroeconomic environment was in the 1990s, and this is reflected by the discussions of Youngblood and Franklin (this volume). They note that, despite the modest but steady economic growth throughout the 1990s, the monetary, exchange-rate and fiscal policies were inconsistent with one another. The fundamental problem, they argue, was the failure of the government to rein in spending and bring deficits down to levels that could be comfortably financed. Many public sector expenditures, including the Bank of Ghana's quasi-fiscal activities and the operations of state-owned enterprises, occurred outside the purview of central government, as public sector expenditures averaged nearly

27% of GDP during the 1990s, while revenue from all sources averaged only 20%. Instead of running a much smaller primary deficit in order to be consistent with the exchange-rate policy adopted in late 1997, the government continuously ran large deficits that had to be financed by printing money and borrowing both domestically and externally. According to Youngblood and Franklin, excessive reliance on printing money and domestic borrowing resulted in bouts of inflation, exchange-rate depreciation, and high nominal and real interest rates.

The inconsistency between monetary and fiscal policies reached its peak in 1997 with the decision to adopt the exchange rate as the nominal anchor without the fiscal restraint needed to support such a policy. The result was a speculative assault and a real depreciation of such a magnitude (174% nominal, 106% real) that Ghana was forced to seek relief under the HIPC programme. Youngblood and Franklin argue that policy-makers should have seen the risks that were increasing the likelihood of a speculative assault, in view of the availability of the extensive economic literature.

Ghana exhibited many of the risk factors present in these crises: a weak financial system over-exposed to foreign liabilities (e.g. borrowing to service external debt); constraints on the central bank's ability to respond to shocks and defend its policies; and a monetary policy that was inconsistent with the fiscal realities. The monetary and exchange-rate policies of the Bank of Ghana had created large and persistent deviations from interest-rate parity, that resulted in abnormally high returns to holders of domestic T-bills, returns that could not possibly be expected to last. Ultimately, Youngblood and Franklin explain that market forces, especially in the foreign-exchange market, accounted for the adjustments.

Interest in the macro environment that has fostered the growth experiences described is strong and varied in terms of focus. Using Ghana as a case study, Kyereme (this volume) examines the determinants of per person real output growth (a measure of economic growth), exchange-rate volatility, and price inflation — and their interactions and implications for economic development — using vector auto regression models. He argues that, while inflation leads to a weakening cedi, a declining cedi may only in part cause inflation, because physical and human capital constraints (and sub-optimal levels of complementary investments in infrastructure, research and development, etc.) hamper real output growth, as dynamic interrelationships between output and inflation are mostly insignificant. Hence, effective management of macroeconomic policies that relax the input constraints through time can lead to real output responding robustly to price and monetary shocks.

Arguing that, in the long run, the role of money exceeds that of price, Kyereme suggests that as Ghana's economy modernizes financially, access to bank credit must be improved (e.g. via innovative micro-finance schemes) for the majority rural population, most of whom rely on the informal sector for scarce credit at very high interest rates such that policies to combat inflation must restrain excessive growth of the money supply. He concludes that fiscal discipline and macroeconomic policies which boost per person real output growth can dampen inflation and strengthen the cedi.

In view of the fact that the foreign-exchange market is one that has seen considerable volatility, its effects on trade are certainly important. Agbola (in this volume) traces and examines the impact of devaluation on Ghana's trade balance from the 1970s to 2002, using the Johansen MLE multivariate co-integration procedure as well as the Stock-Watson dynamic OLS model (DOLS) to determine the relations between key determinants of that balance. Very few studies have assessed the impact of devaluation on Ghana's economy in recent times; Agbola therefore argues from the premise that devaluation will not succeed in improving its trade balance. Aside from serving as the death knell of most governments in post-colonial Ghana, devaluation, according to his empirical results, fails to improve the trade balance in the long run because the response in the balance to movements in the exchange rate appears to be characterized by an M-curve phenomenon. Specifically, the results indicate that the trade balance and the key determinants are non-stationary in levels; the Johansen MLE multivariate co-integration procedure suggests that the trade balance and the key determinants were cointegrated, and thus share a long-run equilibrium relationship. The Stock-Watson dynamic OLS (DOLS) modelling shows that the key determinants of Ghana's trade balance are real domestic and foreign income, domestic and foreign interest rates, nominal exchange rate, and real foreign money supply. Lastly, the results of this study indicate that devaluation of the cedi worsens the trade balance in the long run. To offset these problems, Agbola suggests the imposition of restrictions on less essential imports and foreign-exchange movements, cutting back on government spending, and a deregulation of the labour market.

## 3.    Sectoral Developments

The dominance of the agricultural sector in the economy of Ghana ensures that nearly 40% of GDP and 50% of all employment are derived from the sector. Agriculture's growth rate lagged behind the other sectors in most of the reform years, however largely due to inefficient farming practices, a strong dependence on rain-fed agriculture and poor transport and distribution channels. This trend saw some reversal in 2003, however, when agriculture once again became the fastest growing sector.

The declining share of agriculture after 1983 did not necessarily signal structural change in the economy. Much of the change observed in the data coincided with a poorly documented national accounts rebasing exercise in 1994, and so may be exaggerated. We also note that much of the increase in services was drawn from the relatively lower-order service sectors, notably wholesale and retail trade, and also restaurants and hotels. Again, while the share of construction in GDP has increased over the past decade, those of mining and manufacturing have not done so.

The external trade sector has seen only marginal changes in many years. The composition of exports was hardly changed until very recently. Since the mid-1980s, trade as a share of GDP has increased sharply due to more liberal trade and exchange-rate policies, the rehabilitation of cocoa and gold production, and an increase in the share of non-traditional exports — mostly agricultural or processed agricultural products, including pineapples, yams, wood products, cocoa products, canned tuna and oil palm products — in the total.

**Table 1.2    GDP by Sector at 1993 Constant Prices, 1997–2004 (% of Total)**

| Item | 1998 | 1999 | 2000 | 2001 | 2002 | 2003 | 2004 |
|---|---|---|---|---|---|---|---|
| **Agriculture** of which: | **36.7** | **36.5** | **36** | **35.9** | **35.9** | **36.1** | **36.7** |
| Agriculture and Livestock | 24.9 | 25 | 24.3 | 24.5 | 24.70 | 24.7 | 24.6 |
| Cocoa Production and Marketing | 3.6 | 3.4 | 3.5 | 3.3 | 3.27 | 3.5 | 4.2 |
| Forestry and Logging | 3.2 | 3.3 | 3.5 | 3.6 | 3.58 | 3.6 | 3.6 |
| Fishing | 5 | 4.9 | 4.6 | 4.5 | 4.35 | 4.4 | 4.3 |
| **Industry** of which: | **25.1** | **25.2** | **25.2** | **24.9** | **24.9** | **24.9** | **24.7** |
| Mining and Quarrying | 5.8 | 5.7 | 5.6 | 5.3 | 5.25 | 5.2 | 5.2 |
| Manufacturing | 9.1 | 9.2 | 9.2 | 9.1 | 9.15 | 9.1 | 9.0 |
| Electricity and Water | 2.5 | 2.6 | 2.8 | 2.89 | 2.56 | 2.5 | 2.5 |
| Construction | 7.7 | 7.8 | 7.9 | 7.9 | 7.96 | 8.0 | 8.1 |
| **Services** of which: | **29** | **29** | **29.7** | **29.9** | **30** | **29.8** | **29.5** |
| Transport, Storage and Communication | 4.6 | 4.7 | 4.8 | 4.8 | 4.87 | 4.9 | 4.9 |
| Wholesale & Retail Trade, Restaurants and Hotels | 6.7 | 6.8 | 6.8 | 7 | 6.96 | 7.0 | 6.9 |
| Finance, Insurance, Real Estate and Business | 4.2 | 4.2 | 4.3 | 4.4 | 4.33 | 4.3 | 4.3 |
| Government Services | 10.8 | 10.7 | 11.0 | 11.0 | 11.00 | 10.8 | 10.7 |
| Community, Social and Personal Services | 1.8 | 1.8 | 1.9 | 1.9 | 1.93 | 1.9 | 1.9 |
| Producers of Private Non–Profit Services | 0.9 | 0.9 | 0.9 | 0.9 | 0.89 | 0.9 | 0.9 |
| **Sub Total** | **90.8** | **90.8** | **90.9** | **90.7** | **90.7** | **90.9** | **90.9** |
| Indirect Taxes | 9.2 | 9.2 | 9.2 | 9.3 | 9.27 | 9.1 | 9.1 |
| **GDP in Purchaser's Value** | **100** | **100** | **100** | **100** | **100** | **100.0** | **100** |

*Source:* Bank of Ghana, *Statistical Bulletin.*

Considering that manufacturing remains the weakest link in Ghana's economic growth, it is not surprising that considerable attention is paid to the behaviour of firms in a difficult macroeconomic environment. This is analysed in this volume by Wolf and Sarpong who proceed from the hypothesis that firms that are successful exporters will invest more and that firms that invest more are more likely to export, such that a strong relationship between export performance and investment behaviour at the firm level is expected to complement market access in diversifying Ghana's exports. To test this proposition they use probit regressions, a simultaneous equation model on a 2003 survey of a stratified sample of 100 enterprises in Ghana to analyse the factors that influence the investment and exporting behaviour of firms. They also investigate the different factors that influence the investment and export decisions in different sectors. Their results are a mixed bag of findings. Contrary to the initial hypothesis, no significant positive relationship is established between exporting and investment. They explain the negative relationship they observe as due to difficult access to capital. On the other hand, they find that younger, larger firms and more efficient firms are more likely both to invest and export.

The issue of finance for development is definitely important in the campaign to change economic structure. According to Buchs and Mathisen (this volume), a competitive banking system is a prerequisite for ensuring that banks operate as credible forces for financial intermediation, channeling savings into investment and thereby fostering higher economic growth. They argue that the structure, as well as the other market characteristics, constitute an indirect barrier to entry into the Ghanaian banking system and thereby shield the banks' large profits . They present an overview of Ghana's sector in which the three largest banks account for 55% of the total assets of the banking system. Despite the tightening of monetary policy in 2001, domestic credit to the private sector remained at around 10% of GDP, which is regarded as low, even by African standards. In contrast, Ghanaian banks' pre-tax returns on assets and equity are rated among the highest in Africa (6.1% in 2002).

By applying panel data to variables derived from the Panzer and Rosse (1987) analytical framework, Buchs and Mathisen find evidence of a non-competitive (monopolistic) market structure in the Ghanaian banking system that hampers financial intermediation. They identify the following factors as key obstacles to competition: persistent financing of government needs, to the detriment of the private sector; high cost of investment; barriers to competition on interest revenues; and losses on the loan portfolio. Thus the key recommendations to improve financial intermediation include achieving effective fiscal adjustments and a rigorous enforcement of creditor rights by addressing institutional lapses in financial regulations and judicial reviews of Ghana's legal structures.

A different approach to discussing the financial sector, but one which leads to similar ideas about how to make the sector more effective is provided by Steel and Andah (this volume). In analysing and assessing how policy and regulatory frameworks for the sector have been affected and influenced by the development of rural and micro finance institutions (RMFIs) in Ghana, particularly in terms of the range of institutions and products available, and their financial performance and outreach, they argue that the adoption of business rules on a different tier basis reflects the Bank of Ghana's growing understanding of microfinance and non-bank financial institutions (MFIs and NBFIs). They discuss the extent to which a flexible regulatory environment can encourage innovation, while a diversity of RMFIs and products can serve different market niches not reached by commercial banks. They also consider the point at which special legislation may be needed, whether to facilitate commercialization and sustainability of the rural and micro finance (RMF) industry or to protect deposits and ensure the stability of the financial system. However, while Ghana's approach has fostered a wide range of both formal and informal RMFIs, it has not yet been very successful in achieving strong financial performance, significant scale, and true commercialization of microfinance. Steel and Andah observe that maintaining the different tier system requires substantial investment in the Apex

Bank, in supervision and training and in strengthening the capacity to make good use of the liquidity being released. In sum, the biggest hurdle lies in finding the right balance between ease of entry for greater outreach, prudential regulations to enhance sustainability and monitoring capacity.

The poor reach of financial services is further highlighted in a contribution on savings by Quartey and Blankson who discuss the issue of poor mobilization of resources in an unstable environment and argue that, despite the reform, including financial sector liberalization, Ghana still experiences low savings. They attribute this to a combination of micro and macroeconomic, as well as political, factors. Noting that very few studies have been conducted into savings behaviour in Ghana (most of them concentrating on aggregate savings with hardly any on households), Quartey and Blankson use data from the Ghana Living Standard Surveys (GLSS III and IV) to argue from the standpoint that macrofinancial policies have no significant effect on household savings in Ghana. They also use a descriptive approach to discuss broad developments in domestic saving and monetary policies, while they employ a logit regression analysis to estimate the coefficients of the determinants of household domestic savings and to compare the marginal effects of two time spans — 1991/92 and 1998/99. In general, they conclude that the macrofinancial sector policies pursued between 1991/92 and 1998/99 had no appreciable effects on household savings. Secondly, young persons and the aged on average had higher savings balances than the working population, contrary to the life-cycle hypothesis. Interestingly, while people living in own houses saved less than those in rented accommodation, the study also confirmed that households with a higher average propensity to consume save less. Lastly, the fact that the average propensity to consume has increased in Ghana after years of financial sector liberalization is seen to confirm the ineffectual nature of macro-financial sector policies over the years.

## 4.    Poverty and Social Development

The extent and depth of poverty are generally to be seen as outcomes of the absence of effort to change the structure of the economy over several decades (Aryeetey and McKay 2004). The absence of change has left Ghana quite dependent on its main resource endowments and with that has come the associated vulnerability. The rigid economic structure combined with a rapidly growing population may be expected to create problems for any economy, thus leading to poverty among the population.

There is currently a lot of data on poverty and inequality in Ghana after several surveys during the last two decades. Thus conventional administrative data have been supplemented with survey data and qualitative or participatory assessments of poverty. Some of the important qualitative sources are the participatory poverty assessment carried out in several rural and urban communities in 1994/95 (Norton et al., 1995) and the Ghana *Voices of the Poor* study (Kunfaa, 1999).

What both the qualitative and quantitative assessments indicate is a large number of people who are poor and deprived. There are some important patterns to poverty in Ghana, mainly by geographic location, with the worst cases of deprivation in the northern savannah region as compared with the south. The GLSS data of 1998/99 showed that 42.2% of all households in Ghana in the lowest income quintile were located in the rural savannah, even though this area accounted for only 20.6% of the total population. In the 1992–8 period, Aryeetey and McKay (2004) report that headcount income poverty fell from 51.7% of the population to 39.5%, with strong geographic and other patterns. Inequality as measured by the Gini coefficient increased slightly over the same period (see Table 1.3).

**Table 1.3    Summary Information on Changes in Income Poverty and Inequality at the National Level**

|  | 1991/92 | 1998/99 | Changes, 1991/92 to 1998/99 |
|---|---|---|---|
| Average value of income standard of living measure (from survey; millions of cedis per person per year, constant prices) | 1.44 | 1.78 | 3.1% p.a. |
| Change in real consumption per capita (national accounts) |  |  | 2.9% p.a. |
| Gini coefficient | 0.373 | 0.388 |  |
| Poverty headcount index (%) | 51.7 | 39.5 | −12.2 |
| Growth elasticity of poverty headcount index |  |  | 0.98 |

*Source:*   Aryeetey and McKay (2004).

The overall rate of poverty reduction over the period suggests a growth elasticity of poverty incidence of 0.98, a figure which is comparable with other African countries (Christiaensen et al., 2003). But there are pockets in southern Ghana with high levels of poverty and deprivation, particularly in the Central Region. The Ghana poverty map (Coulombe in this volume) also shows important variations within localities, so that less poor districts within the very poor northern regions and a number of poor districts in coastal areas in the south have comparable poverty levels. The data show a strong urban-rural differential in poverty indicators, with deprivation being substantially higher in rural areas. Poverty also has important gender dimensions, with most indicators showing that women face higher levels of deprivation compared with men, and levels of income poverty are higher among households with higher dependency ratios. Landlessness, historically not a major problem in Ghana, has become an increasingly important issue underlying poverty and insecurity in peri-urban areas (Government of Ghana, 2003). Few of the poor work in non-agricultural wage employment, with the large majority working in small-scale agriculture. The majority of the latter produce food crops, though there are also significant numbers producing cocoa and other export crops who are poor.

Coulombe's presentation of the poverty map (this volume) discusses the methodology extensively and documents the numerous advantages that both the

Ghana Census 2000 and the Ghana Living Standards Survey (GLSS IV) provide to users and policy-makers in developing poverty profiles and maps at district and sub-district levels. The methodology takes advantage of the detailed information found in the survey and the exhaustive coverage of the census which makes it possible to compute standard errors of the different poverty estimates and thus conveys a notion of the reliability of the estimates arrived at. Significantly, researchers could easily use it with some fair degree of accuracy to determine the relationship between poverty distribution in Ghana and different socio-economic outcomes.

Appiah-Kubi, Oduro and Senadza (this volume) provide a poverty profile of Ghana using mainly GLSS IV data and estimate the incidence of vulnerability using a cross-sectional approach. With various conceptualizations of vulnerability, they argue that Ghanaian households and individuals vulnerable to poverty include both poor and non-poor, and are estimated to amount to 49.5 % of the total population in 1998/99. They suggest the need for further investigation, both quantitative and qualitative, of the poverty dynamics in order to provide information for more rigorous analysis. They advocate the use of public policy to provide a stable macroeconomic policy framework within which agents can operate and provide safety nets (welfare-enhancing) for households and individuals experiencing shock (vulnerability) to fall into for recovery. In this light, they regard the Ghana Poverty Reduction Strategy (GPRS) as well-intentioned to address the plight of the vulnerable and excluded, but suggest that it falls short on providing assistance to food-crop farmers to enhance their production. A major step forward would be to take measures to enable food-crop farmers to cope with the perennial long dry season.

The practical link between macroeconomic policies and poverty may be looked at through the lens of inflation and how it affects the poor. The chapter by McKay and Sowa contends that, given the extent to which the vast majority of households in Ghana rely on the market for their purchase of key commodities including food (52% of household income), inflation, which has averaged 25% per annum since 1983, is clearly important to both poor and non-poor persons. Whether or not it hits the poor harder depends on whether they are less able to hedge themselves against inflation compared with wealthier groups, and on whether they face a higher rate of inflation. Mckay and Sowa assert that, although the large majority of households in Ghana do not have ready access to conventional means of hedging against inflation through savings and investments, there is as yet no evidence that they face a systematically higher — or lower — inflation rate than the non-poor. They also suggest that, at the broad commodity category level, consumption baskets in Ghana are remarkably uniform across income groups, although there are some important differences in the composition at the individual commodity level. The initial calculations suggest that the choice of weighting method for computing inflation rates makes a difference. In the few cases considered, the authors conclude that there is no evidence to suggest that the poor face a systematically higher (or lower) inflation rate than the non-poor. They finally observe that in rural Ghana consumption of own production is important for many households and this provides them with some insurance against inflation as such transactions do not involve the exchange of money.

There is considerable discussion about whether government programmes to tackle poverty actually reach the poor. Tsekpo and Jebuni (this volume) explore the relationship between budget implementation and poverty reduction and observe that transfers to the local government sector show sensitivity to the poverty reduction agenda of central government. This is in spite of the fact that some budgetary allocations, commonly referred to as the District Assemblies Common Fund (DACF), are not necessarily directed at 'targeted' poor groups. There are further targeting problems, as some programmes of the Ghana Poverty Reduction Strategy (GPRS) benefit wealthier commercial farmers more than they do poor subsistence farmers. Even where the GPRS targets the poor, there are sometimes no funds for project implementation. Tsekpo and Jebuni also question the reliability of data which suggest a shift in spending from administration to capital expenditure, since a reclassification of expenditure items might have disguised the true picture. They point out, however, that data from the CWIQ 2003 survey results might be more useful in establishing that budgetary allocations may be moving increasingly in favour of the poor.

When the poor fail to secure access to public services, there is a greater likelihood that they will adopt survival techniques that may sometimes be costly to society. Self-medication is one such technique and it has been reported to be on the increase. Van den Boom et al. (this volume) find that the high prevalence of self-medication in Ghana (50%) may be attributed to the distance from health facilities and doctors (one in every four Ghanaians lives beyond a 15-km radius of a doctor) and the high cost of seeing a doctor ($10 compared with $1.5 for self-medication). With a current doctor/ population ratio of 1:16,000 (denominator reduces to 11,000 when private doctors are included), the authors' simulated utilization patterns indicate a possible demand of an additional 15–20% of doctors, which may further worsen the burden on conventional healthcare and pose a huge challenge. An option proposed is to improve the quality of self-medication through certification and training of chemical sellers, traditional healers, unsupervised druggists and medicine peddlers. Van den Boom and his colleagues suggest the exploration of innovative ways to encourage private contributions to augment Ghana's heavily subsidized health sector and thereby reduce self-medication.

## 5.  The State, Institutions and Socio-Economic Development

If we define the state as 'a set of institutions that possess the means of legitimate coercion, exercised over a defined territory and its population, known as society', then the role that each institution plays in bringing more rapid development to that society should be paramount. The state's role in development is changing throughout the world, with an increasing focus on effectiveness. The factors that influence the state's effectiveness vary from place to place, and similar structures may lead to different outcomes. But the fact that the state is central to the development process remains largely unchallenged. Economic and political reforms are redefining the role of the state, but the process often remains *ad hoc* in poor countries, including Ghana.

The use of policy as a tool for delivering the state's development output is challenged by the limitations of the state and its institutional capacities. Public policy must recognize this and adapt accordingly. The history of failed or failing states prior to reform in many countries prompted change, which itself is being questioned for possibly having gone too far.

In trying to offer explanations for why two decades of reform have failed to deal adequately with the problems of macroeconomic stability, Fosu and Aryeetey (this volume) argue that the problems could be attributed to the continuing presence of institutional constraints in the mobilization of resources and their allocation. The state and its institutions had been weakened by the many years of neglect, and the reforms did not deal adequately with these problems. While political instability may have been contained, this was achieved at some economic cost. Weak governments are more likely to experience slippages in macroeconomic programmes, as has been seen with vote-buying public expenditures in the past decade. Corruption and other institutional inadequacies increase the transaction cost for all economic endeavours, and this is seen clearly in Ghana. The end result was that policy reform slowed down in the 1990s and growth stagnated, although at a higher level than in most countries. The question then became what it would take for growth to accelerate once again and to be sustained. The answer from Fosu and Aryeetey is to continue with new programmes to strengthen the institutions that will support market reforms, mindful of complementarities in the public and private roles in bringing about investment and making such investment productive.

Killick (this volume) provides another angle to the discussion of the role of the state and its institutions. He argues that the economic achievements of the 1980s and 1990s were 'substantial and sufficient to refute any suggestion that existing inflexibilities make it impossible to achieve change'. But he observes major weaknesses and suggests that greater flexibility would have brought more rapid gains. The first reason he provides for the continuing difficulties is that the state sector remains large beyond its competence, illustrating this with the difficulties associated with the management of the budget. He sees the weaknesses of the civil service and the difficulty in its reform as further major obstacles to better growth rates. He maintains that successive governments have not been able to strengthen the public service and its ability to deliver on development promises because of the neo-patrimonial model of politics. He does not see democracy as the panacea, as 'the logic of competitive politics remains unfavourable to decisive action on public service reform'.

Killick suggests that many of the most important constraints on faster economic progress in Ghana go well beyond the confines of economics and require attention to improvements in political and social structures. Improvements in the democratic environment should be utilized to reform and strengthen the public service. He calls for major reductions in the economic role of the state, in view of the fact that the state has not shown an ability to deliver services and development in a sustained manner.

We recognize the growing perception in Ghana that, in order to reinvigorate state institutions with proper incentives, there must be effective rules and regulations, as indeed there should be greater competition for the state as well as increased citizen voice and partnership (Fosu and Aryeetey, this volume). The strengthened public sector will ensure that in order to achieve poverty reduction that does not compromise growth, poverty reduction is anchored within a clear macroeconomic framework. In recognizing the productivity problems facing the economy and society, human resource development institutions will have to respond to the changing demand for skills, without losing sight of the need to make the entire society literate. Monitoring mechanisms for public expenditures must be developed and strengthened to ensure that such expenditures reach their targets and generate the expected outputs. This requires that decentralization should lead to a more open system of governance and empower districts to generate additional resources from within.

In assessing the impact of decentralization on poverty reduction, Asante and Ayee (this volume) argue that poverty reduction was central to the decentralization programme in Ghana from its inception, as various initiatives such as the Programme of Action to Mitigate the Social Costs of Adjustment (PAMSCAD) in 1987, the Productivity and Income Generation Fund in 1996 and lately the Highly Indebted Poor Countries (HIPC) funds in 2002 and the Ghana Poverty Reduction Strategy (GPRS) in 2003 formed part of the programme. They note, however, that it is the poor implementation (function of decentralization) of the above poverty initiatives that accounts for the low impact of decentralization on poverty reduction. Moreover, even though they found that decentralization has an impact on poverty reduction, this impact is dependent on certain variables. It is not sufficient just to look at any type of decentralization, such as political decentralization, in isolation, when assessing the impact of decentralization on poverty reduction. Political, administrative and fiscal decentralization need to be considered simultaneously and the sequencing and pace of the different types of decentralization seem to play an important role. Asante and Ayee recommend an efficient local government that effectively combines strategies of political empowerment, resource mobilization and enhanced service delivery; addressing institutional bottlenecks that inhibit co-ordination between central and local government; and lastly, renewed political commitment by government to fully decentralize irrespective of its political and technical risks and trade-offs.

## 6.  Conclusion

As Ghana enters its second half-century, we are faced with a paradox. Despite a solid transition to democracy in the political sphere, despite recorded recovery in the last fifteen years from the economic malaise of the two preceding decades, and despite reductions in measured poverty, there is a widespread perception of failure of the economic and political system in delivering improving living standards to the population. We have argued in this chapter that policy-makers and analysts have to confront this perception and examine it. The papers in this volume call for a deeper examination of the macro-level data on growth and poverty. A sectoral and regional disaggregation reveals weaknesses in the levels and composition of private investment, in the generation of employment, in sectoral diversification, and in the distribution of the benefits of growth. Income poverty has declined, but inequality has increased in various dimensions. At the same time, the push for decentralization, and for better allocation, monitoring and implementation of public expenditure has raised more questions than it has answered. These are the challenges that Ghana faces if it is to fulfil the bright promise of its independence in 1957. The papers in this volume set out an analytical agenda that we hope will help in laying the groundwork for the path that the nation's policy-makers will have to steer on the road to 2057.

## References

Aryeetey, E. (1996) *The Formal Financial Sector in Ghana After the Reforms.* Working Paper 86, London: Overseas Development Institute.

Aryeetey, E. and Peretz, D. (2005) 'Monitoring Donor and IFI Support Behind Country-Owned Poverty Reduction Strategies in Ghana'. Legon: ISSER, University of Ghana (mimeo).

Aryeetey, E. and Harrigan, J. (2000) 'Macroeconomic and Sectoral Developments since 1970' in E. Aryeetey, J. Harrigan and M. Nissanke (eds), *Economic Reforms in Ghana, The Miracle and The Mirage.* Oxford: James Currey; Accra: Woeli Publishing Services and Trenton, NJ: Africa World Press.

Aryeetey, Ernest and McKay, Andrew (2004) 'Operationalising Pro- Poor Growth'. A Country Case Study on Ghana. A joint initiative of AFD, BMZ (GTZ, KfW Development Bank), DFID, and the World Bank.

Aryeetey E, and Tarp, F. (2000) 'Structural Adjustment & After: Which Way Forward?' in E. Aryeetey, J. Harrigan and M. Nissanke (eds), *Economic Reforms in Ghana, The Miracle & The Mirage.* Oxford: James Currey; Accra: Woeli Publishing Services and Trenton, NJ: Africa World Press.

Booth, David, Crook, Richard, Gyimah-Boadi, E., Killick, Tony and Luckham, Robin with Boateng, Nana (2004) *Drivers of Change in Ghana: Overview Report*, Final Draft, 25 May. London: Overseas Development Institute and Accra: Centre for Democratic Development.

Christiaensen, L., Demery, L. and Paternostro, S. (2003) 'Macro and Micro Perspectives of Growth and Poverty in Africa', *World Bank Economic Review*, Vol. 17: 317–47.

Government of Ghana (2003) *Ghana Poverty Reduction Strategy 2003–2005: An Agenda for Growth and Prosperity* Vol.1 Accra: Ghana Publishing Corporation, Assembly Press.

ISSER (2002) *The State of the Ghanaian Economy 2001.* Institute of Statistical, Social and Economic Research, University of Ghana, Legon.

ISSER (2004) *The State of the Ghanaian Economy 2003.* Institute of Statistical, Social and Economic Research, University of Ghana, Legon.

Killick, T. (2000) 'Fragile Still: The Structure of Ghana's Economy 1960-94', in E. Aryeetey, J. Harrigan and M. Nissanke (eds), *Economic Reforms in Ghana, The Miracle & The Mirage.* Oxford: James Currey; Accra: Woeli Publishing Services and Trenton, NJ: Africa World Press.

Kunfaa, E.Y. (1999) 'Consultations with the Poor: Ghana Country Synthesis Report', Kumasi: CEDEP, July.

Norton, A., Bortei-Doku Aryeetey, E., Korboe, D. and Dogbe, D. K. T. (1995) *Poverty Assessment in Ghana using Qualitative and Participatory Research Methods*, PSP Discussion Paper No. 83. Washington, DC: World Bank.

Nyanteng, V. and Seini, A. W. (2000) 'Agricultural Policy and the Impact on Growth and Productivity 1970–95' in E. Aryeetey, J. Harrigan and M. Nissanke (eds), *Economic Reforms in Ghana, The Miracle & The Mirage.* Oxford: James Currey; Accra: Woeli Publishing Services and Trenton, NJ: Africa World Press.

O'Connell, S. and Ndulu, B. (2000) 'Africa's Growth Experience: A Focus on the Sources of Growth'. Nairobi: AERC (mimeo).

Oduro, A. et.al. (2004) 'Understanding Poverty in Ghana: Risk and Vulnerability' Institute of Statistical, Social and Economic Research, University of Ghana, Legon, mimeo.

Panzer, L and Rosse, J. (1987) 'Testing for Monopoly Equilibrium', *The Journal of Industrial Economics,* Vol. 35, No. 4: 443–56.

Round, J. and Powell, M. (2000) 'Structure and Linkage in the Economy of Ghana: A SAM Approach' in E. Aryeetey, J. Harrigan and M. Nissanke (eds), *Economic Reforms in Ghana, The Miracle & The Mirage.* Oxford: James Currey; Accra: Woeli Publishing Services and Trenton, NJ: Africa World Press.

# 2 What Drives Change in Ghana? A Political-Economy View of Economic Prospects*

TONY KILLICK

## 1. Introduction

President Clinton famously had the slogan, 'It's the economy, stupid', hanging in the Oval Office as a constant reminder to himself of what his priority should be in order to keep the American electorate on his side. Giving priority to the population's economic well-being is good advice to all democratic politicians, but I shall argue that, if we want to understand the half-century of the Ghanaian economy's experiences, we should invert Clinton's priority and pay most attention to institutions and politics. The mantra for economists trying to understand the performance of Ghana's economy should be, 'It's the polity . . .' [readers to supply their own epithet].

Clark Leith's (2004) provides an excellent foundation on which my paper can build. Taking his review of the economic record as the starting point, the initial premises here are that:

- There has been real economic progress in Ghana since the early 1980s. The last two decades have produced the most sustained and consistent period of growth of the last half-century. This is no mean achievement, and there are no grounds for a habit of pessimism.
- But the progress made has been less than brilliant. Weaknesses have persisted. The economic structure has remained rather rigid. Much of the economy would

* This paper draws heavily on materials in a recent consultancy report on 'drivers of change' in Ghana prepared under the direction of David Booth of the Overseas Development Institute, London (Booth et al., 2004) and in a case study on the politics of the budget prepared in that connection (Killick, 2004). I should like to record my large debt to the co-authors of the general report, David Booth, Richard Crook, E. Gyimah-Boadi, Robin Luckham and Nana Boateng. I should also acknowledge the great assistance afforded by Seth Anipa and Kwamena Daisie in preparing the budget case study which is utilized below. I should stress, however, that what is presented here is my own interpretation, with which none of those just mentioned is necessarily in agreement.

still have to be described as pre-modern, and technological progress has been slow.

- Another negative has been the economy's inability to generate productive formal-sector jobs, to keep pace with the growth of the labour force. Wage employment has declined relative to total labour, and one of the consequences of this has been to keep successive governments under pressure to maintain a large public service — an important fact to which I shall be returning.
- So the overriding premise is that the economy could and should do better. Continuing the rate of progress of the recent past would leave Ghana classified as a low-income country for many years to come. It would mean that at least some Millennium Development Goal targets would be missed. Continuing the gradual pace of past development would fail to meet the aspirations of Ghanaians. The hunger for jobs would remain unsatisfied.

Business-as-usual would, therefore, be a second-best option, but improving upon it entails getting a better understanding of what has held the economy back. What needs to be explained is the only moderately successful record of improvement during the reform period: better than in the past but still inferior to what was achieved in other developing regions.

The remainder of this paper proceeds as follows. Section 2 draws attention to the persistence of a large but ineffectual state sector. Section 3 offers a political-economy interpretation of the observed facts, and this prepares the way for a consideration in Section 4 of what forces might produce an acceleration in the future pace of economic development, emphasizing the potential of democratization. Brief conclusions are set out in Section 5.

## 2. The Condition of the State Sector

### *The State-Private Balance*

If we look for explanations of the only moderate progress since the early 1980s, one obvious question to ask is whether the reform process has successfully re-balanced the respective roles of the public and private sectors. It was, of course, a central tenet of Nkrumah's approach to economic development that it should be led by a large and active state sector. In Killick (1978: 311–16) I argued that the immediately succeeding governments were ambivalent about substituting more market-oriented, private-sector-led policies for the Nkrumah model, so that in the later 1960s and early 1970s there was a lot more continuity than diminution in the role of the state. But what if we bring the story up to date? Has there not, since the beginning of the reforms in the early 1980s, been a decisive break with the state-led model? To some extent there clearly has, as symbolized by an active programme of privatizations. However, recent data show that the state sector remains large. Consider the following (IMF, 2003, Section III):

- As of 2003 the central government consisted of 36 ministries, with 250 departments and agencies operating under them.

- As of 2001 there remained 41 non-financial and 9 financial public corporations.
- The consolidated deficit of the five largest non-commercial public corporations averaged an extraordinary 9.25% of GDP in 1999–2001.
- In the same period the expenditures of the total public sector were equivalent to more than half of GDP. The consolidated deficit (i.e. dis-saving) of the sector was equal to no less than 17% of GDP.
- The public sector still accounts for about half of total recorded employment.

What about the relations of government with the private sector? These cannot be caught by statistics of the kind just provided. It is probably not controversial to say that the successive Rawlings administrations were ambivalent in their attitudes, but that this ambiguity to some extent reflected a lack of clarity in Ghanaian public opinion about the desirable balance between the private and public sectors. Although in many respects the political discourse today is quite different from that of the Nkrumah period, faith in a development process led by the state still finds reflection in this persistence of a large state sector.

Quite apart from questions of size, state interventionism appears to remain a large factor, again reflecting a legacy of the past as well as present-day political realities. Only to a limited degree does Ghana offer an 'enabling environment' to private businesses. Private investors continue to complain of shortages of credit, reflecting domination of bank credit by the needs of the public sector. They also complain about uncertain power supplies and high transportation costs, because of poor infrastructure. They complain of high and often-changing taxation, of continuing excessive regulation and bureaucratic delays, of problems of contract enforcement, of corruption at many levels, and of difficulties in accessing land with firm titles of ownership.

But surely the advent of the New Patriotic Party (NPP), with its promise of a Golden Age for Business, marks a decisive break? Perhaps it does; it is too early to form a conclusive judgement. There seems no doubt that, at a certain level, the present government would like to improve the operating environment for the private sector. But thus far there seems to have been a marked gap between its desire to improve the business environment and its actual achievements. The government's disappointing progress in this regard was decried by most of those we spoke to in connection with the 'drivers of change' study described in the opening note to this chapter.

There were complaints about the continued politicization of private business, meaning that some Ghanaian businesses have become associated with either the National Democratic Congress (NDC) or the NPP and that, when in office, each party favours its allies and discriminates against those of its opponents. The pattern of government-business relations remains very much in a patron-client mould, with organized business associations, such as the Ghana Federation of Industries, and individual entrepreneurs generally preferring to cultivate politicians to obtain protection or other special treatment, as distinct from governmental promotion of market competition. Ghanaian capitalism is thus less than full-blooded, and the drive to make it more so is weak on both sides of the government/private-sector relationship.

## The Management of the Public Finances

A government's ability to run its own budget is perhaps the most basic test of the capabilities of the state. How well does the contemporary Ghanaian state pass this test? The following paragraphs draw upon a recent short study of the politics of the budget (Killick, 2004) undertaken in connection with the 'drivers of change' project, which concluded that 'on the expenditure side the budgetary process is so weak as to be essentially ritualistic, with limited bearing upon reality . . .'. The evidence on which this was based is summarized below:

(a)   *Much information essential for budget monitoring and expenditure control does not exist in forms usable by policy-makers, or is very difficult to access.* For example, a major effort was necessary to compare budgeted and actual expenditures even for key ministries. These data were not publicly available and could only be obtained with difficulty and special access. Data were not available on a more disaggregated level, raising questions about the accuracy of ministry-wide data: of what are they aggregations?

(b)   *There are regularly large deviations between the estimates in the budget and the eventual actuals.* For the three ministries and development agencies (MDAs) for which we managed to get data the mean deviations were (percentages of original budget estimates, ignoring signs):

|                      |      |
|----------------------|------|
| Education (2000-03)  | ±42  |
| Health (2001–03)     | ±68  |
| NCCE (1999–2003)     | ±33  |

This evidence is reinforced by a joint IMF-World Bank report on the country's public expenditure management (IMF and World Bank, 2004: Table 5). Utilizing data for 16 MDAs, this confirms the occurrence of large discrepancies between budgeted and actual expenditures, with a mean deviation of ±27% in 2001–3 and with many discrepancies much larger than that.

There were strong systematic biases in the results just discussed.  In the great majority of cases, the budget underestimates spending on salaries and overestimates everything else. This is shown by the following figures of mean deviations, broken down by item number and observing the signs (percentages of original budget estimates):

|                      | *Salaries* | *Admin.* | *Services* | *Cap. Formation* |
|----------------------|:----------:|:--------:|:----------:|:----------------:|
| Education (2000–3)   | +45        | −26      | −39        | −56              |
| Health (2001–3)      | +76        | −48      | −67        | −80              |
| NCCE (1999–2003)     | +20        | −3       | −39        | −60              |

(c)   *There is evidence of large leakages in allocated funds between their release from the centre and arrival at the point of service delivery.* This observation is based on a pilot tracker study undertaken by two experienced World Bank economists who examined expenditures with respect to the Ministries of Education and Health in FY2000 (Ye and Canagarajah, 2002). Their main finding echoes that of (a) above — that the systems are not in place in Ghana to allow expenditures to be tracked. As a result, schools and clinics, let alone the local communities they are intended to serve, have little idea what they are supposed to receive in a given year. Ye and Canagarajah therefore had to undertake their own research in order to fill the informational gaps, arriving at disturbing results.

In the case of the Ministry of Education, Youth and Sports, they found that an average of only 51% of the non-salary resources which the Ministry thought had been allocated to a given primary school actually arrived there. The position in Health was worse, where there was a leakage of no less than 79% of non-salary allocations intended for clinics and health posts. Because of these shortfalls, those responsible for delivering health services were forced to augment their public funding by requiring patients to contribute more than half of the cost of their treatment, far more than was intended and expected by the ministry headquarters in Accra.

(d)   *The structure of expenditures is inflexible and non-developmental.* This becomes clear when expenditures are analyzed according to the ability of MDAs to allocate their monies in order to meet policy objectives and emerging demands. In addition to salaries, administration, services and capital formation there are statutory items of expenditure, such as interest payments on the public debt. To a major extent, wages and salaries should also be thought of as non-discretionary in practice, and a high proportion of capital formation expenditures are non-discretionary statutory obligations, leaving administration and services as the main discretionary elements. However, these in practice are only a small part of total spending. For example, in 2002 and 2003 the actual level of these items made up an average of only 11% of total government spending. It is only a slight exaggeration to say that the composition of spending in a given year is pre-determined and leaves MDAs with almost no capacity to use their budgets to pursue the government's developmental and social objectives.

It follows from this that the systematic biases reported in (b) above reflect the non-functional and anti-developmental nature of the way the budget works in practice, for it shows generally huge shortfalls in actual spending on those items which most influence the ability of MDAs to deliver services to the people, when, for macroeconomic purposes, the Ministry of Finance and Economic Planning (MFEP) seeks to control total spending by squeezing such items as are available for adjustment.

(e)   Lastly, *there is no clear evidence of an improving trend in the situation* described above. Examination of movements in the budget-actual deviations for the three MDAs listed earlier revealed no overall improvement; neither were improving trends evident in the skew away from development spending recorded in (b) nor in the inflexibility of expenditures recorded in (d).

To sum up, the alarming situation just described suggests that, on the expenditure side, the budget is largely a ritualized façade, bearing little relation to the actual pattern of state spending, reinforcing the claim by Aryeetey and Harrigan (2000: 29) to 'certain knowledge that the budget is not taken seriously . . .' In the most basic of its tasks — running its own budget — the state is revealed as extraordinarily incompetent, a defect which has persisted over successive governments. Given this fundamental failure, there must be a strong suspicion that the state similarly does not do well in many of its other economic functions.

In the case of the budget, it was not always so. The budget had greater meaning in earlier decades, so why might this deterioration have occurred?

## *The Public Service Problem*

The depleted condition of the civil service provides an obvious — if ultimately superficial — answer. Everyone seems to agree that the civil service has reached a low ebb, with the result that the ability of governments to implement reforms and new programmes is severely reduced. The *Ghana Poverty Reduction Strategy* (Government of Ghana, 2003: 119) accurately reflected this when referring to 'unacceptably poor conditions' in the public service and stating: 'Significant improvements to the latter represent a component without which the government reform programmes and the Ghana Poverty Reduction Strategy are unlikely to succeed.'

The numerous reviews and evaluations that have addressed the issue of public service reform in recent years agree on several diagnostic points. Incentive structures within the civil service actively discourage initiative and pro-activity; the way to move up the system is to avoid mistakes, maintain a low profile and let seniority work its magic. This results in a self-selection process in which those with initiative and drive either do not attempt to enter the public service or are driven out in frustration, often leaving only Dead Hands in place. Although there has been a large drain of talent out of the public service into the private sector or abroad, there do remain some good, dedicated people within the system; they are, however, frustrated by the absence of personnel management within the service, and by non-recognition of hard work and merit.

A recent examination of public sector reform by PricewaterhouseCoopers (2003) further illustrates the weaknesses. It describes the various reform efforts (pp. 1–2) as 'not as successful as may have been expected' and cites in evidence capacity gaps, lack of ownership, inability to institutionalize change, low morale in the public service, weak human resource management and 'Doubts about the relevance and worth of the reforms' — a rather comprehensive set of weaknesses! It reports 'capacity gaps in almost all critical posts in the service, due to the failure to address the fundamental issues of pay and conditions' (p.15) and refers to 'the extremely weak human resource management of what capacity . . . is left within the service' (p.16). It remarks of the Civil Service Performance Improvement Programme (CSPIP) that necessary 'high level political interaction was not forthcoming', and that the umbrella programme under which CSPIP falls 'had failed to provide the needed coordinating and oversight mechanism', leading to fragmentation and territorial disputes (pp. 20–21). Foster and Zormelo (2002) concur with this judgement, describing the reform agenda as 'too massive for effective co-ordination' (p.x).

Some of the reform efforts have been directed specifically at the MFEP, under the Public Financial Management Reform Programme (PUFMARP). This has ten components, no less. It too has produced disappointing results and its weaknesses have been similar to those of the wider range of public sector reforms. They have largely been the brain-children of various donors, with little governmental ownership, leading to the usual complaint of weak political commitment. They have been fragmented and ill co-ordinated. In aggregate, they have been too ambitious, exceeding the implementation abilities of the MFEP and other agencies involved. In order to avoid the difficulties of political commitment and of skill shortages, they have been biased in favour of technological fixes of doubtful sustainability.

Underlying all this, however, is a wider failure of successive governments to act decisively to restore the public service to something like its former condition, when it had the reputation of being the most efficient in sub-Saharan Africa. Since governments' prospects of re-election are strongly influenced by their ability to keep their promises and deliver public services, the question arises of why governments have been reluctant to act to raise their capacity to deliver. To understand this it is necessary to examine how politics works in Ghana, i.e. to move to a political analysis.[1]

## 3.    A Political Interpretation

### *The Politics of Clientelism and the Potential of Democratization*

Political scientists studying the state in Africa have made heavy use of the concept of the *neo-patrimonial state*, i.e. one in which there is little sense of the public good or of public service, and where the resources of the state are the estate of the ruler and his court (see, for example, Jackson and Rosberg, 1984; Sandbrook, 1985). In Ghana, the modern state has been described in this language, drawing attention to the way state resources — jobs, and the power to allocate rents, provide services, and to determine policies and their beneficiaries — are captured and 'owned' by personal or private networks in the hands of dominant patrons. According to this view, instead of the state being an instrument governed by explicit objectives and legal rules, it is effectively an apparatus serving the interests of the particular groups and individuals that control it. The prefix 'neo' is added to indicate that the state has a hybrid character: the most important parts of the patronage system are informal and unofficial, if not illegal. The mechanisms of patrimonialism are in conflict with, and not infrequently challenged by, formal commitments to 'legal-rational' or bureaucratic state operation.

The neo-patrimonial state is profoundly anti-developmental. It emphasizes the

---

[1] In the following paragraphs my intellectual debt to my colleagues on the drivers of change team is particularly large.

short-term appropriation and distribution of resources by the state, rather than growth and wealth creation. It is willing to ride roughshod over property rights. It leads to a personalized and unpredictable policy environment, highly inimical to the creation of a favourable investment climate. It favours the expansion of the state relative to the private sector, without reference to state capabilities. It is inward-looking and protectionist. It results in financial repression and the politicization of credit decisions, in order to have cheap loans to offer to supporters. To the extent that capitalist development occurs, it tends to be a protected crony capitalism based upon privileged access to public resources, rather than being based upon entrepreneurial talent and genuine risk-taking. In Ghana's recent history, the later years of the Acheampong regime probably represented the fullest flowering of the neo-patrimonial model. One of Ghana's most distinguished economists and public servants, the late Jonathan Frimpong-Ansah, was so affected by what he experienced and saw that he went beyond the neo-patrimonial model to label this as 'the vampire state' (Frimpong-Ansah, 1991). Remnants of that era linger on today.

This persistence is partly explained by what African political scientists have identified as a 'civic public', which does not apply in its attitudes to the state the morality that it observes in the private realm (Ekeh, 1975). That is to say, there is a discontinuity of moral principles between the social order and the state. This discontinuity has important and enduring implications and helps to explain, for example, the reluctance of Ghanaian governments to tackle the weaknesses of the public service described in the previous section. Among other things, it means that the basic obligation of powerful individuals to support their kin and other 'followers', and of the latter to show corresponding loyalty, has tended to prevail within the state, as well as outside it. Consequently, the state has limited ability to resist capture by patronage networks.

Admittedly, the working out of this model is increasingly modified or qualified by other forces. There were some sharp breaks in Ghana's first 25 years of history, and some of these (corruption in the Acheampong-Akuffo period, economic liberalization under Rawlings' military government in the 1980s) have had enduring effects on political fundamentals. Secondly, Ghana's various political traditions (Danquah-Busia, Nkrumah, Rawlings) have developed distinctive approaches, including different styles of patronage politics.

Above all, the emergence of genuinely competitive and democratic politics is a development of great importance. It is sometimes suggested that multi-party competition merely intensifies clientelism and corruption, at the same time providing incumbent regimes with a veneer of respectability and an enhanced capacity to pursue their political agendas, but in Ghana there are reasons for taking a more positive view. A vibrant mass media has already begun to raise the political costs associated with corruption and the more blatant forms of patronage politics, moderating the advantages of incumbency, intensifying pressures for improved accountability and increasing the probability that political leaders will be rewarded by voters for better management of the macroeconomy. So while the country's political system is still essentially patronage-based, it has become modified in important ways by other influences.

How does this melange of influences play out when it comes to improving the efficacy of the state as an economic agent? Let us first go back to the lamentable state of the budget.

## *Implications for the Efficacy of the State: (a) the Budget*

Although there have been some improvements, the budget process remains essentially closed and difficult to scrutinize. Getting hard information is still difficult. This compromises the ability of interested groups to make contributions during the preparation of the budget and its implementation. Those living outside the capital city are particularly at a disadvantage. Given the continuing poor levels of education within the population, there are also serious questions about people's ability to contribute meaningfully to processes of accountability, particularly in rural locations. This is not, in other words, a situation which is likely to generate strong in-built forces for self-improvement. Moreover, it should not be taken for granted that a government would feel moved to take action even in the face of criticisms. For example, when the reports of Parliament's Public Accounts Committee are submitted, remedial action is slow, at best.

It is no accident that the budget system retains these characteristics. The neo-patrimonial model predicts such an outcome. Consider the question, what kind of budget process is likely to be most agreeable to politicians working within the patrimonial tradition, in which public resources are used to reward supporters (and, by their withdrawal, to punish opponents) and for the pursuit of private advantage?

First, it will be a closed system, in which ministers and their aides retain as much discretionary control as possible and expose themselves to a minimum of public accountability. The less the general public and civil society organizations know about what decisions are being made and why, the easier it will be to utilize public resources for the exercise of patronage, and the less the risk of being held to account, of being exposed. This last is a particularly important consideration in present-day conditions, where it is difficult for governments to control the media to the extent that was possible in earlier periods.

Secondly, the system will be marked by ritualization. What is meant by this is a situation in which the formal processes of the budget's expenditure planning have limited bearing upon how public monies are spent in reality — precisely the situation described earlier. Maintaining the ritual, or the façade, is important so that taxpayers and others outside the process can believe that monies are being used in rational ways, and are accountable. In an aid-dependent situation, the façade is particularly important in order to satisfy donors and keep assistance flowing in. But the reality of ritualization is that ministers and high officials are able in practice (but within limits) to ignore what the budget says and to dispose of public monies according to quite other decision processes.

Democratization, with its concomitants of heightened transparency and accountability, is the enemy of such a model. *There is at present a democratic deficit in the country's budgetary system*, so that the further extension of democratization to the public finances — which has already made a beginning — has real potential for strengthening today's weak public expenditure management.

Analysis in terms of a patronage-based model of politics helps to explain another feature of the budgetary scene. We have noted earlier the inflexible structure of expenditures, with salaries and other personnel costs tending to have priority over expenditure categories which could permit MDAs to promote their policy objectives and the development of the economy. We have also seen systematic biases in comparisons of budgeted and actual expenditures, with salary expenditures consistently over budget, usually by large amounts, and the rest squeezed to accommodate this over-spending. The point here is that such biases are precisely what a patrimonial model of politics predicts: the giving of precedence to the award and protection of civil service jobs over the longer-term promotion of development. Here again, the gradual (and no doubt partial) replacement of clientelist politics by more democratically-based modes offers the best prospect for improvement, and for the emergence of a 'developmental state' with an expenditure structure to match.

### *Implications for the Efficacy of the State: (b) Public Service Reform*
What happens if we apply a similar mode of analysis to the all-important topic of public service reform? Here, the political logic is less encouraging. In this area, democratization may not result in a solution, for a number of reasons:

- Democratic politics geared to a four-year electoral cycle results in short time horizons. This places a premium on visible, quick-fix actions (new roads, clinics, etc.), as against longer-term, slower-acting structural reforms. This is all the more so when actions also bring visible short-term social costs.
- It seems likely that, because of the present levels of over-manning, an affordable civil service reform would have to include substantial retrenchments. With the civil service still a large employer, such actions are seen as likely to bring more pain than gain to ministers, an effect powerfully reinforced by social-network pressures which would be highly disapproving of giving such priority to efficiency-motivated norms.
- Despite the appalling pay and conditions, those left within the civil service constitute a powerful obstacle to change, as many of them have found ways of profiting from existing arrangements and many know that they would have difficulties in making their way within the private sector. Thus, any government wishing to tackle the problem seriously knows it will have a fight on its hands, raising the stakes and increasing the disincentives.

The deepening of democracy that has occurred in Ghana is thus not much help, with public service reform seen as a vote-loser, necessitating substantial political costs. For that reason, governments are unlikely to pursue it seriously for some time, however much donor pressure and funding it attracts, until the fundamental political logic changes. Politicians' incentives structures are at present too adverse.

The final step in this chapter is to look forward and to ask what forces might drive the economy forward on a faster developmental trajectory than in the past?

## 4. The Drivers of Change

Table 2.1 provides a summary statement of what can be seen as the key *economic* drivers of change. This will be taken as needing little elaboration. In the briefest terms, the view is that sustained acceleration of Ghana's development would have to be led by new private investment and by the penetration of new export markets. A strengthened state also has an important role to play but more as facilitating and responsive than as initiating. Table 2.1 lists four principal economic drivers of change:

- international trade and competition
- financial institutions
- foreign direct investment
- investment by Ghanaian entrepreneurs and the development of their businesses into substantial entities.

**Table 2.1    Possible Economic Drivers**

| Driver of change | Strengths | Likely obstacles | Releasing the potential |
|---|---|---|---|
| *International trade and competition* | Escape from domestic market. Raised efficiencies & productivities. Product & process innovations. | Sluggish world demand for commodities and price instability. Domestic protectionism. Present small scale. | Greater policy openness + domestic supporting measures (e.g. infrastructure). Implies policy autonomy and effective public service. |
| *Financial institutions* | Linking savers and investors; facilitating specialization; lowering transactions costs | Few competitive pressures. State-dominated (budget deficits). Ineffective supervision. | Higher taxes/lower spending to reduce government borrowing and debt (both unpopular). Increased competition. Strengthened supervision. |
| *Foreign direct investment* | Improved management, market & technical know-how; raised investment. | High transactions costs of investment; high perceived risks. Enclave nature (e.g. gold). | Improving the business environment, competition and market efficiency, & risk/reward calculus (e.g. via macro stability, property rights). |
| *Ghanaian entrepreneurship; small-to-large firm growth* | Extensive growth since 1984 provides a basis. Tapping the skills and savings of the diaspora | Rarely grow to large scale (the problem of trust). Unhelpful investment climate. Obstructive officialdom. | As for FDI. Also, improved infrastructure and credit availability. |

Note from the right-hand column of Table 2.1, on factors that will help the potential to be realised, two recurring themes: (a) raising competition and market efficiency, and (b) improving investors' reward/risk calculations.

Now what about *political* drivers of change, as summarized in Table 2.2? Here, we are concerned with whether political changes of the sort that can realistically be contemplated for Ghana will help build a developmental state which will deliver the kinds of policies and institutional shifts needed to enable the economic drivers of change to do their work. Three plausible candidates are suggested as key political drivers:

• intensified competition between political parties;
• the free flow of information, accompanied by an increasingly critical mass media and informed public opinion;
• an increased role in national political, as well as economic, life of the diaspora of Ghanaian emigrants.

The view argued above is that Ghana's political system is still essentially patronage-based, but modified in important ways by other influences. How does this melange of influences play out when it comes to improving the efficacy of the state as an economic agent? On an admittedly optimistic view, intensified competition for votes between political parties should result in a political debate that will little by little focus more on issues and less on pre-election sweeteners and promises of post-election patronage. 'Pork-barrel' politicking will continue, of course, as it does everywhere, but may increasingly take the form of providing widely shared collective goods, instead of special privileges to politicians' home areas and the like. In this case, the ability of a government to deliver promised services to voters will become electorally ever more important and that, in turn, would raise the incentives to reform the public service. No doubt, for some time pressure to build party 'war chests' will help to justify corruption but party competition will gradually make this a vote-loser.

Heightened party competition would not necessarily be neat and tidy, of course. But, assuming a relatively balanced party competition, with alternation in power as a real possibility, the result would be a more inclusive and democratic polity. This could also be good news for the less privileged regions, because no party can expect to win national power without making inroads into several regions other than its original heartland.

The second 'political' driver — the availability and quality of information about public affairs — is closely related to the first. Party competition strengthens issue-based politics only where ideas are accurately transmitted and analyzed, and this requires a mass media which is not only free but critical and technically capable. It also depends on the emergence of a public that is literate enough to make effective use of information. The gradual urbanization of the population and the spread of education, combined with the growth of communications technology, make these changes not only possible but to a degree inevitable. Information, backed by urbanization and education, therefore presents itself as a highly plausible driver of change.

**Table 2.2    Possible Political Drivers**

| Driver of change | Strengths | Likely obstacles | Releasing the potential |
|---|---|---|---|
| *Intensified party competition* | Long-term, encourages issue-based politics. Initially patronage may be intensified, but if corruption affects performance, this may become an issue. | Leaders must provide tangible benefits and avoid harm to influential interests — there is a short-run/long-run collective action problem. Opposition parties may be weakened without access to spoils of office. | Construction of a substantial and reliable funding base by several parties. The diaspora provides injections of funding and leadership that offset disadvantages of opposition. |
| *Free flow of information + critical mass media* | Quantity and quality of information sharpens demands for accountability — MDAs to the MFEP, executive to parliament, MPs to constituents, service providers to clients. A more urbanized and educated public increases the political salience of information. | Constitutional biases towards 'presidentialism', which protects incumbents regardless of performance. Official resistance to freedom of information; barriers to competition in media; elitist approaches to politics. | Constitutional reforms that strengthen parliamentary scrutiny and debate, and soften advantages of incumbency. A critical mass of business leaders benefiting from openness and scale economies is created and exercises influence. |
| *The Ghanaian diaspora — emigration and return processes* | Returnees often have money, management skills and enterprising attitudes. | Returnees who challenge traditional ways are ostracized; skills and money used to 'work the system' instead. | More deliberate and sustained efforts to attract and harness diaspora interests and build solidarity among returnees. |

The inclusion of *the Ghanaian diaspora* in a list of potential drivers is justified by its large size, its presence in a range of professional and occupational layers in countries of Europe and North America, and the fact that those emigrants who return can bring with them skills, financial capital and attitudes that are in short supply domestically. The potential seems clearly positive on balance.

## 5.    Conclusions

This study has argued that the economic achievements of the last two decades have been substantial and sufficient to refute any suggestion that existing inflexibilities make it impossible to achieve change. But major weaknesses remain and greater flexibility would have brought more rapid gains. Why has progress not been faster? A major reason, it is suggested, is that the state sector remains large beyond its competence — a feature we have illustrated by the deplorable state of budgetary management. A dominant but incompetent state sector is a formidable constraint on rapid economic progress. There is an urgent need to strengthen the apparatus of state, and the question posed is why it has not so far been reformed to make it more effective.

At a superficial level, it is suggested, an important part of the answer lies with the weaknesses of the civil service and the modest achievements of multiple attempts to reform it. But that explanation merely shifts the question a stage further back: why have successive governments not made more determined efforts to strengthen the public service, raising their ability to deliver on their promises to voters? To answer this question, a version of the neo-patrimonial model of politics has been invoked, but conditioned by specific features of the country's politics, most notably the development and deepening of democratic politics. Democracy is no panacea, however, so that the logic of competitive politics remains unfavourable to decisive action on public service reform.

Finally, three concluding observations suggest themselves:

1. Many of the most important constraints on faster economic progress in Ghana go well beyond the confines of economics and demand attention to the country's political and social structures. It is these which hold the key. We are here in agreement with a recent World Bank (2004) study of the lessons of global growth experiences in the 1990s, which emphasizes the central importance of institutions and country particularities. Growth they see as implying 'transformation of society, a break with past trends, behaviours, and institutions which reflect deep forces in societies and how they organise themselves' (p.1). Hence, they conclude on the need for 'a better understanding of non-economic factors in growth processes, such as history, culture and politics' (p.3). Hence the starting point of this chapter: 'It's the polity . . .'

2. As democratization proceeds, the ability of a government to deliver promised services to voters will become electorally ever more important. That, in turn, should raise the incentives to reform the public service. However, democratization alone may not give politicians sufficient incentive to grasp the public service nettle: determination and leadership are also needed. On the other hand, we have pointed out the existence of a 'democratic deficit' in budgetary processes, which have not caught up with advances in the conduct of public affairs elsewhere in the system. In this area, improvements ought to be achievable within the existing political milieu.

3. Above all, the analysis points up a pragmatic case for re-examining the desirable economic role of the state, whose reach still far exceeds its grasp. Deborah

Wetzel (2000:130) observes that 'The issues of the role of the state in economic development have been a matter of debate for decades. [But] The competing camps of "minimal state role" vs. "state planning" have to some extent come to a common ground in recent years. What is fundamental is to have an effective state; there is no point in the government playing a large role, if it can do nothing well.' We have shown that Ghana's state retains a central economic role but is not capable of 'doing it well'. There is thus an urgent need to strengthen the capabilities of the state sector. But, if the preceding paragraph is correct in suggesting that present-day political incentives are unfavourable to effective action in the short to medium term, this points to the desirability of further major reductions in the economic role of the state.

## References

Aryeetey, E., Harrigan, J. and Nissanke, M. (eds) (2000) *Economic Reforms in Ghana: The Miracle and the Mirage.* Oxford: James Currey; Accra: Woeli Publishing Services; Trenton, NJ: Africa World Press.

Aryeetey, Ernest and Harrigan, Jane (2000) 'Macroeconomic and sectoral developments since 1970.' in Aryeetey et al., chapter 1.

Aryeetey, Ernest and Tarp, Finn (2000) 'Structural adjustment and after: which way forward?' In Aryeetey et al., chapter 18.

Booth, David, Crook, Richard, Gyimah-Boadi, E., Killick, Tony and Luckham, Robin with Boateng, Nana (2004) 'Drivers of Change in Ghana: Overview Report.' Accra: Center for Democratic Development and London: Overseas Development Institute (mimeo), May.

Coulombe, Harold and McKay, Andrew (2003) 'Selective poverty reduction in a slow growth environment: Ghana in the 1990s.' University of Bath, September (mimeo).

Ekeh, Peter P. (1975) 'Colonialism and the Two Publics in Africa: A Theoretical Statement,' *Comparative Studies in Society and History,* Vol. 17.

Foster, Mick and Zormelo, Douglas (2002) *How, Why and When Does Poverty Get Budget Priority in Ghana?* Working Paper 164. London: Overseas Development Institute. April.

Frimpong-Ansah, Jonathan (1991) *The Vampire State in Africa: The Political Economy of Decline in Ghana.* London: James Currey.

Fukuyama, Francis (2004) *State Building: Governance and World Order in the Twenty-First Century.* Ithaca, NY: Cornell University Press.

Government of Ghana (2003) *Ghana Poverty Reduction Strategy, 2003–05: An Agenda for Growth and Prosperity.* Accra: Government of Ghana, February.

International Monetary Fund (2003) 'Ghana: Selected Issues and Statistical Appendix.' Washington, DC: IMF, 14 April. Available from IMF web-site.

International Monetary Fund and World Bank (2004) 'Public expenditure management country assessment and action plan: Ghana.' Washington, DC: IMF and World Bank. 14 May (Draft).

Jackson, Robert H. and Rosberg, Carl G. (1984) 'Personal Rule: Theory and Practice in Africa', *Comparative Politics*, Vol. 16, No. 4, July.

Killick, Tony (1978) *Development Economics in Action: A Study of Economic Policies in Ghana.* London: Heinemann Educational Books.

Killick, Tony (2004) 'The Democratic Deficit and the Politics of Ghana's Budgetary System.' Accra: Center for Democratic Development and London: Overseas Development Institute. June 2004 (mimeo).

Leith, J. C. (2004) 'What Have We Learned?' Paper prepared for 'Ghana at the Half Century' Conference, Institute of Statistical, Social and Economic Research, University of Ghana and Cornell University, Accra, 18–20 July.

Leith, J.C. and Söderling, L. (2003) *Ghana: Long-term Growth, Atrophy and Stunted Recovery.* Uppsala: Nordiska Afrikainstitutet Research Report No. 125.

PricewaterhouseCoopers Ltd. (2003) 'Public sector reform: towards a future strategic framework. Final report.' Accra: Government of Ghana. July (mimeo).

Sandbrook, Richard (1985) *The Politics of Africa's Economic Stagnation.* Cambridge: Cambridge University Press.

Wetzel, Deborah (2000) 'Promises and Pitfalls in Public Expenditure', in Aryeetey et al., chapter 6.

World Bank (2004) 'The Growth Experience. What have we learned from the 1990s?'. Washington, DC: World Bank (PREM), June (mimeo).

Ye, Xiao and Canagarajah, Sudharsham (2002) 'Efficiency of Public Expenditure Distribution and Beyond. A report on Ghana's 2000 public expenditure tracking survey in the sectors of primary health and education.' Washington, DC: World Bank. February (mimeo).

# 3 Ghana's Post-Independence Economic Growth: 1960–2000

AUGUSTIN K. FOSU
& ERNEST ARYEETEY

## 1.    Introduction

When Ghana became the first African nation to achieve independence from colonial rule on 6 March 1957, there was much jubilation and hope that it would pioneer the way toward rapid growth and development for Africa as a continent. Indeed, Ghana experienced reasonably high growth soon thereafter, but by 1965 per capita growth was already negative, and when the coup d'état overthrew the Nkrumah regime in February 1966, per capita income was below its value at the time of independence. Conditions appeared to improve significantly during the late 1960s and early 1970s. However, the mid-1970s saw the beginning of significant deterioration, so that, by the early 1980s, per capita GDP had reached its nadir in the history of Ghana's post-independence. While economic conditions have improved markedly since then, the growth rate has failed to accelerate significantly, and per capita income has yet to reach its level in 1957.

In 1993 Ghana set itself the target of becoming an upper middle-income country by 2020, requiring an estimated GDP growth rate of about 8% per annum. In the five years since the inception of the set targets, however, the economy showed no capacity to move towards it. Whereas GDP was expected to grow by between 7.1% and 8.3% in the period 1996–2000, actual growth was between 4.2% and 5.0%. In 1999, for example, all macroeconomic targets were off by quite substantial margins, and the trend continued into 2000. These targets included a real GDP growth rate of 5.5%, an end-of-period inflation of 9.5%, an overall budget deficit of 5.2% of GDP, a primary budget surplus of 3.8% of GDP, and a current account surplus of US$60 million. The overall growth target was based on a projected growth of 5.6% in agriculture, 6.3% in industry following full availability of energy and 5.3% in the services sector. However, the growth rate for GDP turned out to be a more modest 4.4%, with the agricultural sector growing by only 3.9%, industry by 4.9% and services by only 5%. Inflation at the end of the year was 13.8%, significantly higher than expected, and the budget deficit amounted to 8.2% of GDP. The primary balance was only 1.8% of GDP, while the current account balance showed a deficit, not a surplus, of $93.5 million. Indeed, by the end of 2000, inflation stood at 40.8% compared with the end-of-year target of less than 10%.

So, what went wrong? The present chapter is intended to help answer this question. The chapter will first present an account of the historical macroeconomic performance of Ghana following independence. It will then provide a thematic framework for understanding the observed pattern of performance. It will attempt to explain why growth seems to have collapsed by the mid-1960s, why there were recoveries following reforms, and why the growth seems stuck at a modest rate following the reforms of the mid-1980s. Special attention will be paid to the micro-level evidence of policy outcomes involving microeconomic agents of households and firms, markets, and the political economy. This approach is expected to provide a more in-depth analysis of the micro factors underpinning the macro picture of the generally dismal economic growth record during the pre-1983 period and the improved but stagnant performance following the reforms.

The chapter is structured as follows. Section 2, discusses 'macroeconomic policies and economic growth', presenting the growth record of Ghana and attempting to explain it using a growth-accounting methodology. It also discusses the macroeconomic policies for the various sub-periods. To provide a more in-depth explanation of the growth record based on micro factors underlying the macro structure, Section 3 divides the economic history into two distinct sub-periods reflecting major policy regimes, that is, *interventionist* and *liberal*: 1960-83 and post-1983. Consistent with the Growth Project of the African Economic Research Consortium (AERC),[1] the analysis entails a consideration of specific policies and how they affected the market structure and institutions of the economy. This includes the political economy underlying policies and their outcomes. Section 4 concludes.

## 2.   Macroeconomic Policies, Economic Growth and Structure

Major reviews of economic performance in Ghana (see, for example, Aryeetey et al., 2000) have attributed the recent growth following reform to the rapid expansion of capital after years of little accumulation, with some inconsistent role assigned to productivity growth. Our analysis here based on the growth-accounting framework of Collins and Bosworth (1996) suggests that total factor productivity (TFP) was by far the major contributor to growth initially, but then its importance waned considerably, and the contribution of capital has become more salient in recent years. This outcome might be attributable to the fact that the growth of capital came largely from public sources, at least initially during the reform, a fact that has significant implications for its productivity. However, there appear to be considerable increasing rates of private investment as well. In this section, we first consider the growth record, including any changes in the structure of the economy; then attempt to explain it using growth-

---

[1] For a description of the AERC Growth Project, see, for example, Fosu and O'Connell (2006).

accounting methodologies; and then sketch the macroeconomic policies underlying the record for specific sub-periods.

### An Overview of Long-Run Economic Performance

#### The Growth Record
The growth record of Ghana has been one of unevenness, as Figure 3.1 clearly indicates. With reasonably high GDP growth in the 1950s and early 1960s, the economy began to experience a slowdown in 1964. Growth was turbulent during much of the period after the mid-1960s and only began to stabilize by 1984. In 1966, 1972, 1975–6, 1979, 1981–3, the growth rate was actually negative. The years in which negative growth was experienced generally coincided with changes in government and sometimes with policy changes or reversals.

**Fig 3.1 Real GDP Growth and Per Capita Growth (1960-2005)**

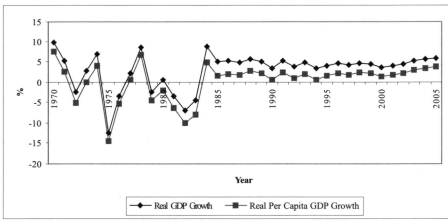

*Source:* World Bank (2007)

Negative growth was first recorded at the time of the first coup d'état in 1966, with a forceful transfer of authority from the Nkrumah regime to the military. The lowest growth of –12% was experienced in 1975, coinciding with the oil-supply shock, as well as a policy reversal from a market-oriented stance to an inward-looking protectionist regime. The period of turbulence, however, also had positive growth episodes, with the peak rate of 10% in 1970 during the time of the relatively liberal Busia civilian administration.

The first phase of reform, marked by the adoption of a stabilization programme, the Economic Recovery Programme (ERP), with major support from the International Monetary Fund and the World Bank, was instituted in April 1983, with implementation over the period 1983–6. The ERP, a market-oriented programme, was intended to halt the downward economic spiral. Starting in 1986, the second phase of reform saw the ERP being supplemented with the Structural Adjustment Programme (SAP), geared towards correcting a number of structural imbalances in order to engender sustained healthy economic growth.

The economy definitely responded positively to the ERP/SAP soon after its inception, recovering from its negative growth rates in 1981–3 to a hefty positive rate of 9% in 1984. The favourable trend has continued since that time, with relatively little variance; however, growth appears to have settled down to a rate around 5%.

Per capita GDP growth closely tracks that of GDP (Figure 3.1), suggesting that population growth has been rather stable. However, the larger gap between them since the 1980s, until more recently, implies acceleration in population growth over this period.

*Per Capita Income*

Per capita income generally maintained its value of about $300 (constant 2000 US$) at the time of independence, despite several dips, until about 1975 when its downward trend began, hitting a low of $185 in 1983 (Figure 3.2). It began a steady rise in 1984, however, after the initiation of the ERP, reaching nearly $276 in 2003. While this is still lower than its previous peak of $302 in 1971, it is nearly $100 above its nadir in 1983. It is important to remember, as observed above, however, that the actual value is considerably less than that required for achieving the national growth objectives.

**Figure 3.2:  Real per Capita GDP in US$ 2000**

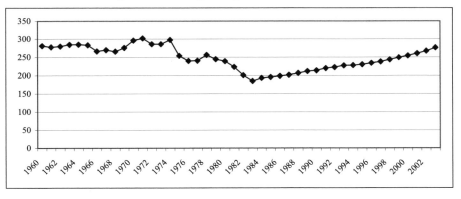

*Source:*  World Bank (2005).

*Structure of the Economy*

Sustained growth would normally be accompanied by a significant structural transformation of the economy. The overall historical pattern of the Ghanaian economy since independence portrays hardly any structural changes, however (Killick (2000); Round and Powell, 2000). As Table 3.1 shows, there was a slight shift from agriculture towards industry between the1960s and the early 2000s, while the share of services has barely increased. What is remarkable, though, is that at about the time of the ERP in the early 1980s, the industrial share had declined to 10%, one-half of its value in the

1960s. By the 2000s, however, this share had more than doubled to 25% (Table 3.1.A). Thus, the reforms may have succeeded in reversing the course of de-industrialization. The data also show, however, that much of the industrial growth was attributable to non-manufacturing (mining and quarrying, construction, and electricity and water), for while industry grew on the whole by an average of 4.3% per annum during 1986–2003, the growth of manufacturing averaged only 1.4% per annum over the same period (Table 3.1.B). Nonetheless, the share of manufacturing in value-added GDP rose from 3.9% in 1983 to 8.5% in 2003 (World Bank, 2005). Hence, the importance of manufacturing has been increasing following the reforms, though not sufficiently to signal a real structural change since independence.

**Table 3.1    Trends in the structure of the Ghanaian economy**

**A. Sectoral distribution of real GDP, period averages (%)**

|  | 1965 | 1966–1970 | 1971–1975 | 1976–1980 | 1981–1985 | 1986–1990 | 1991–1995 | 1996–2000 | 2001–2003 |
|---|---|---|---|---|---|---|---|---|---|
| Agriculture, (% of GDP) | 43.5 | 43.5 | 47.7 | 57.1 | 52.9 | 48.4 | 40.8 | 36.7 | 35.9 |
| Industry, (% of GDP) | 18.6 | 19.3 | 18.7 | 14.2 | 9.9 | 16.7 | 21.7 | 25.1 | 24.8 |
| Services, etc., (% of GDP) | 37.9 | 37.2 | 33.5 | 28.7 | 37.3 | 34.9 | 37.6 | 38.3 | 39.3 |

**B. Growth rates of industry and manufacturing (annual %)**

|  | 1966–1970 | 1971–1975 | 1976–1980 | 1981–1985 | 1986–1990 | 1991–1995 | 1996–2000 | 2001–2003 |
|---|---|---|---|---|---|---|---|---|
| Industry | 5.3 | 1.9 | –4.0 | –3.7 | 7.2 | 1.0 | 4.8 | 3.9 |
| Manufacturing | 9.8 | 2.4 | –4.6 | –2.7 | 6.5 | –7.4 | 5.0 | 1.6 |

**C. Manufacturing exports (% merchandise exports)**

| 1961–65 | 1966–70 | 1971–75 | 1976–80 | 1981–85 | 1986–90 | 1991–95 | 1996–2000 | 2001–2003 |
|---|---|---|---|---|---|---|---|---|
| 1.0 | 0.6 | 1.6 | 1.3 | 0.7 | – | – | 14.7 | – |

*Source:*    World Bank (2005).

## Manufacturing Exports and Diversification

While the above trends since independence may not be encouraging in terms of structural shifts towards manufacturing, there appears to be a silver lining in the manufacturing exports data, possibly pointing to the increased competitiveness of Ghana's slimmer manufacturing sector. For example, note that the manufacturing share of total exports has risen significantly over time, from about 1% in the 1960s to 15% in the latter part of the 1990s (Table 3.1.C). This finding appears to reflect 'market selection', whereby as inefficient manufacturing firms wither away in the face of increased international competition from trade liberalization, the remaining firms become more competitive exporters (Gunning and Mengistae, 2001). Note also that manufacturing exports comprise: chemicals and related products, basic manufactures, machinery and transport equipment, other manufactured articles and goods not elsewhere classified, excluding non-ferrous metals. Thus gold is not included in this classification, and the observed phenomenal increase in the share of manufacturing exports cannot be attributed to the dramatic increase in gold exports since the mid-1980s, for example.

Apparently, therefore, despite the lack of structural shift towards manufacturing in the general economy of Ghana, there appears to be an element of burgeoning manufacturing competitiveness. Perhaps that activity is embryonic, but if the increasing share of manufacturing in exports is sustained or improved, it should bode well for a sustained growth of the economy, given the potency of manufacturing exports in raising GDP growth in developing economies (Fosu, 1990).

## *Accounting for Ghana's Growth*

To shed light on the relative contributions of physical and human capital, as well as 'total factor productivity' (TFP), to growth, we use the Collins and Bosworth-type growth-accounting framework.[2] Results presented in Ndulu and O'Connell (2003) on the decomposition of per worker growth in Ghana during 1960-2000 are reported in Table 3.2 for Ghana, and comparatively for SSA (in brackets). During the overall 1960–2000 period, output per worker declined by 0.16% in Ghana. At the same time, growth

**Table 3.2    The Collins and Bosworth growth accounting-based decomposition of sources of growth, Ghana vs. [SSA]**

| Period | Growth in Real GDP per worker | Contribution of | | |
| --- | --- | --- | --- | --- |
| | | Physical capital per worker | Education per worker | Residual |
| **1960–1964** | 0.62 [1.33] | 1.90 [0.53] | 0.37 [0.12] | −1.64 [0.68] |
| **1965–1969** | −0.26 [1.74] | 0.65 [0.80] | 1.06 [0.20] | −1.97 [0.75] |
| **1970–1974** | 1.54 [2.33] | −0.28 [1.05] | 0.43 [0.22] | 1.39 [1.06] |
| **1975–1979** | −3.74 [0.19] | −0.06 [0.74] | 0.25 [0.24] | −3.92 [−0.79] |
| **1980–1984** | −4.17 [−1.70] | −1.19 [0.16] | 0.18 [0.29] | −3.17 [−2.16] |
| **1985–1989** | 1.52 [0.45] | −1.28 [−0.22] | 0.15 [0.34] | 2.65 [0.33] |
| **1990–1994** | 1.05 [−1.74] | 0.05 [−0.08] | 0.15 [0.30] | 0.85 [−1.95] |
| **1995–2000** | 1.77 [1.51] | 1.17 [−0.12] | 0.15 [0.26] | 0.44 [1.37] |
| **Total: 1960–2000** | −0.18 [0.51] | 0.10 [0.36] | 0.34 [0.25] | −0.62 [−0.09] |

*Source:* Ndulu and O'Connell (2003).

---

[2] The estimates are based on an aggregate production function that assumes capital and human capital ratios of 0.35 and 0.65, respectively.

in factor accumulation, measured by physical capital per worker, accounted for 0.10%, and education per worker for 0.34%; however, these positive contributions by physical and human capital were more than offset by the negative contribution of TFP, measured as the residual, of –0.62%. Thus, diminishing productivity seems to have played an important role in retarding the growth of the Ghanaian economy during post-independence.

Comparatively for SSA as a whole, output per worker during 1960–2000 increased by 0.51%, of which physical capital and education contributed 0.36% and 0.25%, respectively, while TFP's contribution was negative at –0.09%. Thus, over the entire period, per capita growth was much smaller in Ghana than in SSA as a whole, with the contribution to growth by physical capital smaller, and productivity declines substantially larger in Ghana. The only dimension where Ghana apparently performed better than SSA was in the area of education, where the contribution to growth was slightly larger. This outcome may be attributable to the comparatively large investment in education made by Ghana after independence.

As Table 3.2 further indicates, the half-decade decompositions suggest a non-uniform pattern over the period. While the periods 1960–64, 1970–74, and 1985–2000 show considerably positive per capita growth rates, growth was substantially negative for 1975–84. This pattern differs somewhat for SSA as a whole, however, according to Table 3.2. For example, in 1965–69, Ghana's growth was negative, compared with a substantially positive rate for SSA; however, during the more recent 1990–94 period, Ghana exhibited a positive growth rate, while SSA's growth was substantially negative. In effect, explanations for Ghana's growth performance are likely to differ from those of SSA as a whole.

The relatively strong growth in Ghana during the earlier 1960-64 period was explained mainly by physical capital accumulation, while that in 1970-74 was due to TFP. The decline in growth in 1975–84 was accounted for primarily by TFP; however, there was some disinvestment as well. When growth picked up during 1985–9, again the explanation was a positive TFP growth. Indeed, the contribution by physical capital was substantially negative over this period and was almost zero during the subsequent 1990–94 period. However, it took over during 1995–2000, while the role of TFP, though still positive, waned considerably. Meanwhile, the contribution of education seems to be uniformly positive; it was particularly substantial during 1965–9, though it has been diminishing over time. Comparatively, Ghana appears to have performed worse than the SSA average during the earlier 1965–84 period, but better in the more recent 1984–2000 period, especially in terms of per-worker output growth and TFP.

### Global Comparative Evidence

The above analysis shows in an absolute sense how Ghana's growth performance since independence is attributable to the various factors of production. How might Ghana's record be compared with those of other countries globally over roughly the same period? Based on Hoeffler's (1999) augmented Solow model, O'Connell and Ndulu (2000) present growth-accounting comparative results, relative to both OECD and non-OECD countries, for a number of SSA countries. Those for Ghana are reported in Table 3.3. We note that the growth and residual patterns over 1960–97 are generally similar to those presented earlier based on the results reported in Table 3.2;[3] however, the use in Table 3.3 of the logarithmic difference between the *initial* and *final* years of the period alters the current pattern somewhat, as the values differ for certain sub-periods compared with the previous estimates, which were based on the half-decade *averages*.

We find that the overall 1960-97 average per capita GDP growth is less than the average for the global sample of countries by as much as 1.64 percentage points. It is interesting to note that the only periods when Ghana's growth rate exceeded the sample average were in 1965–9 and 1985–9, though the estimate for the more recent 1990–7 period was about the same as the sample average. The result for the earlier period is likely attributable to the substantial increase in growth following the economic liberalization undertaken in the late 1960s following the coup of 1966. The latter positive differential, albeit small, is coincident with the period of structural adjustment. In contrast, the periods 1960–64, 1970–74 and 1980–84 exhibited rather large negative growth differentials: –2.2%, –4.9% and –6.1%, respectively. These periods roughly corresponded to control, petroleum-supply shock, and control regimes, respectively.

The results from Table 3.3 also reveal that, over the entire period, under-investment consistently explained the greatest portion of the growth differential between Ghana and other countries. Meanwhile, income convergence, as represented by Ghana's smaller initial income, consistently lowered the growth differential. Replacement investment also contributed to a widening in the gap. TFP's contribution was negative in the early 1960s and early 1970s, but seems to have reduced the gap somewhat, with much of that occurring in the most recent decade of structural adjustment. Meanwhile, except for the earlier decade when its relative contribution was negative, initial educational attainment exhibited little explanation of the growth differential, suggesting that Ghana's educational attainment became increasingly comparable to that of the other countries.

Ndulu and O'Connell (2000) also estimate a pooled conditional model, where political instability and policy variables as well as base variables (life expectancy, age dependency, labour force, terms of trade, etc.) serve as explanatory variables in a comparative set of regressions as in Table 3.3. The estimates for Ghana are shown in Table 3.4.[4] Unfortunately, a large number of the predicted values are missing, as a result of unavailable values for several periods for one or several of the explanatory variables. Consequently, only limited evidence can be gleaned. Nevertheless, what is clear is that the decade spanning the latter part of the 1970s and the early 1980s was characterized by substantial negative growth rates, as observed earlier. In addition, given its attributes, Ghana under-performed in the early periods. In particular, the decade 1975–84 appears to be a particularly bad period for Ghana's performance. This

---

[3] Unfortunately, the sample period was not updated to 2000, unlike the earlier Collins and Bosworth growth accounting reported in Table 3.2. Nonetheless, any potential change in the analysis due to this three-year difference is likely to be too small for concern.

[4] Note that half-decadal averages are used, so that the growth rates are similar to those in Table 3.2 but differ from those of Table 3.3 in some cases due to the two differing methods of computation.

**Table 3.3    Fits and residuals from SYS-GMM estimation of Hoeffler's augmented Solow model, Ghana**

| Period | $^a$In | Actual growth | Predicted growth | Residual | Actual deviation of growth from sample mean | Estimated contribution of: | | | | | |
| --- | --- | --- | --- | --- | --- | --- | --- | --- | --- | --- | --- |
| | | | | | | Initial income | Investment | Initial educational attainment | Replacement investment term | Time dummies | Residual |
| 1960–64 | 1 | −0.25 | 2.34 | −2.59 | −2.18 | 3.02 | −1.88 | −0.28 | −1.03 | 0.60 | −2.61 |
| 1965–69 | 1 | 3.64 | 2.29 | 1.34 | 1.70 | 3.06 | −3.15 | −0.25 | 0.09 | 0.63 | 1.32 |
| 1970–74 | 1 | −2.94 | −0.69 | −2.26 | −4.88 | 2.51 | −4.28 | 0.00 | −0.76 | −0.06 | −2.28 |
| 1975–79 | 1 | 1.31 | 0.39 | 0.92 | −0.62 | 2.95 | −5.01 | 0.00 | 0.27 | 0.26 | 0.90 |
| 1980–84 | 1 | −4.18 | −4.93 | 0.75 | −6.11 | 2.76 | −6.79 | 0.01 | −1.37 | −1.44 | 0.73 |
| 1985–89 | 1 | 2.60 | −1.14 | 3.74 | 0.67 | 3.39 | −5.14 | 0.02 | −1.43 | 0.10 | 3.72 |
| 1990–97 | 0 | 1.91 | −0.07 | 1.98 | −0.02 | 2.99 | −4.76 | 0.02 | −0.84 | 0.60 | 1.96 |
| Total | .9 | 0.30 | −0.26 | 0.56 | −1.64 | 2.95 | −4.43 | −0.07 | −0.72 | 0.10 | 0.53 |

Note  a)  Equals 1 if the observation is in the regression sample, 0 if otherwise.
*Source:*  O'Connell and Ndulu, 2000.

**Table 3.4　Pooled conditional model-based results, Ghana**

| Period | Fits and Residuals | | | Actual and predicted growth deviation | | | | | | |
| --- | --- | --- | --- | --- | --- | --- | --- | --- | --- | --- |
| | Actual growth | Fitted growth | Residual | Actual growth deviation from sample mean | Contribution to predicted Growth deviation | | | Breakdown of policy contribution by variable | | |
| | | | | | Base variables | Political instability | Policy | Inflation (>500%) | Black Mkt premium (>500%) | B/L gov't spending |
| 1960–64 | 0.37 | 3.25 | -2.88 | -1.83 | 0.25 | -0.06 | 0.35 | 0.04 | -0.14 | 0.44 |
| 1965–69 | -0.51 | 2.41 | -2.91 | -2.70 | 0.44 | 0.07 | -0.34 | 0.03 | -0.51 | 0.14 |
| 1970–74 | 1.75 | 2.94 | -1.19 | -0.45 | 0.01 | 0.13 | -0.01 | 0.02 | -0.08 | 0.05 |
| 1975–79 | -3.23 | -0.32 | -2.91 | -5.43 | 0.10 | 0.07 | -2.90 | -0.21 | -2.16 | -0.53 |
| 1980–84 | -4.01 | | | -6.21 | -1.28 | -0.06 | | -0.23 | | -1.15 |
| 1985–89 | 1.70 | | | -0.50 | 1.31 | 0.20 | | -0.04 | -0.36 | |
| 1990–97 | 1.40 | | | -0.80 | 0.52 | 0.20 | | -0.06 | 0.14 | |
| Total | -0.36 | 2.07 | -2.47 | -2.56 | 0.19 | 0.08 | -0.73 | -0.07 | -0.52 | -0.21 |

*Source:* Ndulu and O'Connell (2000).

period shows the country's negative per capita growth differential with the other OECD and non-OECD countries in the sample to be the largest during this sub-period at nearly 6 percentage points per annum, compared with an average of about 1 percentage point over the other periods.

According to Table 3.4, policy, much of it exemplified by an overvaluation of the domestic currency, seems to have been a major culprit in Ghana's underperformance, increasing the differential by some 2 percentage points annually. High inflation and excessive government spending during 1975–84 appear to have also contributed to this underperformance. Though the country's negative growth differential appears to have narrowed during the latter decade of 1985–97, the full ramifications of the structural adjustment programme during this period cannot be gleaned from the results reported in Table 3.4, due to missing data.

### Investment

Investment is the most robust explanatory variable in the growth equation of developing countries (Levine and Renelt, 1992). In 1965, for example, gross investment was 18% of GDP (Figure 3.3).[5] It fell to 13% about the time of the first coup in 1966, declined slightly further and then recovered, reaching 14% in 1971, but then fell precipitously to 7% in 1972 when the second coup occurred. It then became unstable, but tended downwards, reaching its nadir of about 3% by the time of the ERP in 1983. Since 1983, however, it has increased steadily, reaching 23% of GDP in 2003. While the upward trend seems to have ended in 1994, the ratio has averaged 20% since then. Thus, the evidence supports the view that gross domestic investment has increased substantially since the reforms. In addition, though choppy, private investment also appears to be rising, reaching 14.4% of GDP in 2003 from its very low value of 2.0% in 1986. Indeed, private investment has generally mirrored gross investment since the mid-1980s, suggesting that it has kept up with rising public investment.

### External Aid and Debt

The current thinking is that external aid promotes growth in a sound policy environment (Burnside and Dollar, 2000). Ghana is considered to be among those SSA countries with relatively good policies, that is, since the mid-1980s following the ERP. We therefore examine the flow of external aid to Ghana. For example, is the above positive investment merely being driven by external aid, and can this be sustainable?

Paying particular attention to the period of reform since the mid-1980s when investment has been on the rise, we note that the ODA/GDI ratio rose substantially during the late 1980s but then tended downwards as of 1989 until about the late 1990s, when a slight upward trend seems apparent (Figure 3.4). However, these latest increases are considerably lower than those experienced in the 1980s and early 1990s. Furthermore, the ODA/GDP ratio shows a steady rise until about 1989 and then levels

---

[5] This figure was only slightly less than the average value according to IMF data, which averaged 19% during 1957–64. According to those data, the ratio was about 16 percent immediately following independence.

off. Given the further observation above that the GDI/GDP ratio has been rising steadily while ODA/GDI has been falling as of the late 1980s, coupled with a reasonably stable public to private investment ratio, it appears that the role of external aid is no longer a dominant feature in the observed public investment record.

**Figure 3.3: Gross and Private Domestic Investment to GDP Ratios (%)**

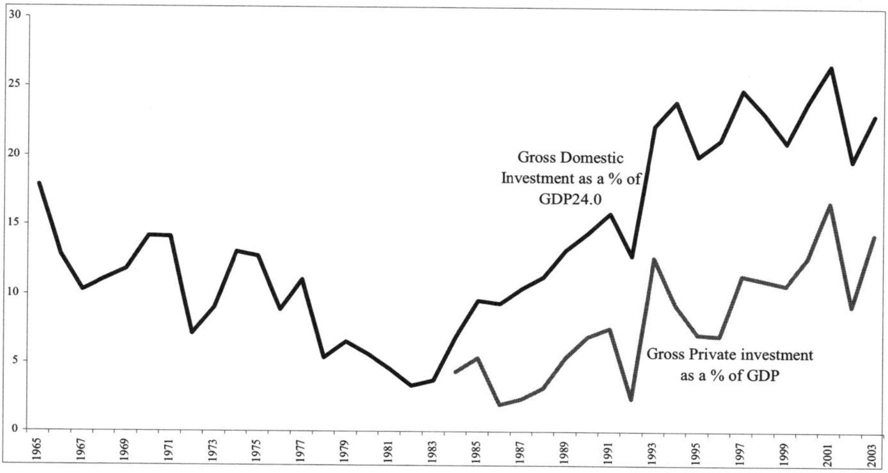

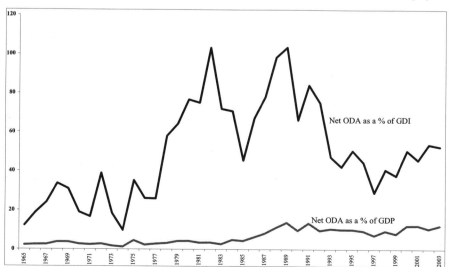

*Source:*    World Bank (2005).

**Figure 3.4: Net ODA from all Donors as Share of Ghana's GDI and GDP (%)**

*Source:*    Ibid.

Related to aid flows is the question of Ghana's external as well as domestic debt. As a proportion of exports, Ghana's external debt grew significantly from the late 1970s, from 80% in 1976 to nearly 350% in 1983; the growth slowed down from the time of the ERP in 1983 and became negative as of 1993 (Figure 3.5). Although still higher in 2003, for example (241%), than the levels of the 1970s, there is no doubt that the debt-service ratio has been tending downwards since 1993. If this trend continues, it will bode well for growth, as among SSA countries very high levels of external debt tend to be deleterious to growth (Fosu, 1996, 1999).

**Figure 3.5: External Debt as % of Exports and GDP**

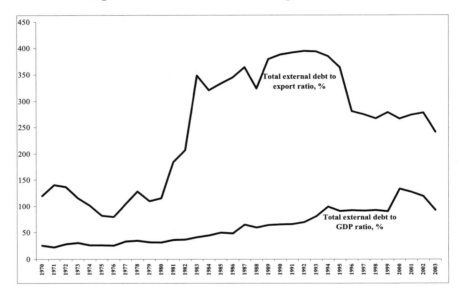

*Source:*    Ibid.

## Trends in Macroeconomic Policies

What macroeconomic policies might have engendered the above macroeconomic record? Four sub-periods of economic policy-making can be identified in Ghana. The first was from independence in 1957 until the coup of 1966; the second, after the coup when liberalization measures were initiated, till the second coup in 1972; the third, from the second coup until the ERP reform in 1983; the fourth, the period since the reform.

### 1957–66

Ghana attained independence from British colonial rule in 1957 under the leadership of Kwame Nkrumah and his Convention People's Party (CPP). At independence, Ghana was the world's leading producer of cocoa and its per capita income was amongst the highest in sub-Saharan Africa. Partly as a backlash to the colonial policies and partly in line with current thinking at the time on economic development, the CPP embarked on a policy of import-substituting industrialization (ISI). The constitution of the CPP indicated the establishment of 'a Socialist State in which all men and women shall have equal opportunity and where there shall be no capitalist exploitation'. Its Manifesto promised free education up to the age of 16, a free national health service, the mechanisation of agriculture, and rapid industrialization.

The Nkrumah government embarked on a Seven-Year Development Plan: 1963/4–1969/70, which was aimed at modernizing the economy through industrialization. It is therefore not surprising to observe that physical capital accumulation during the early period was the most significant contributor to output growth (Table 3.1).

At the macroeconomic level, however, the economy was in decline. The estimated fall in TFP of 1.6 percentage points per year during 1960–64 (Table 3.1) was a precursor to the decline. It suggests that the higher input growth was not efficiently allocated. The external reserve position deteriorated considerably between 1957 when net reserves stood at US$269 million, and 1966 when they were negative at –US$391 million (Frimpong-Ansah, 1991). This outcome reflected a deteriorating balance-of-payments position and also the poor credit rating accorded the country. The saving/GNP ratio fell from 18% in 1958 to only 8% in 1966 (ibid.). Ghana registered three consecutive years of zero or negative growth in per capita GDP between 1964 and 1966 (Table 3.1). Inflation increased from 1% in 1957 to 23% in 1965 (Frimpong-Ansah, 1991).

## 1967–72

The deteriorating economic situation with the attendant fall in living standards was the pretext on which a group of army and police officers, constituted as the National Liberation Council (NLC), overthrew the Nkrumah government in February 1966. The NLC subsequently handed over power in 1969 to the civilian elected Progress Party (PP) government of Dr K. A. Busia.

The ideological stance of these two governments was pro-private capital and opposed to Nkrumah's 'socialist' policies. They introduced IMF-sponsored monetary reforms, devalued the currency and liberalized the external sector (Frimpong-Ansah, 1991). Under the NLC, disinflationary policies aimed at stabilizing the macroeconomy were implemented. There was a reduction in (public) domestic investment, tighter control over import licences and a devaluation of the Cedi (Killick, 1978).

As Figure 3.1 shows, the objective of stabilization was largely achieved. GDP growth increased from –4.3% in 1965 to 6.0% by 1969 and averaged 7.0 % during 1969-71. The balance of trade moved into surplus and the current account and government budget deficits were also reduced (Killick, 1978; Ewusi, 1986). Inflation fell from 22.7% in 1965 to 6.5% by 1969, and to 3.0% by 1970 (Frimpong-Ansah, 1991). Nonetheless, note also that TFP continued to decline during 1965–9 by about the same amount as in the previous 1960–64 period of about 2 percentage points per year, while the contribution of physical capital to growth fell substantially from that of the previous period (Table 3.1).

By 1972, the economy found itself in a similar position, in some respects, as it was in 1965 with reduced growth and increasing fiscal and current account deficits (Frimpong-Ansah, 1991; Ewusi, 1986; Killick, 1978). The government responded with a devaluation of the Cedi at the end of 1971. The devaluation, together with preceding economic difficulties, provided the pretext for another coup d'état in January 1972, which ended Ghana's second democratic experiment.

## 1973–83

As noted earlier, the period between 1974 and 1983 saw the most significant decline in GDP growth per worker, with the fall in TFP being the most significant contributory factor (Table 3.1). What went wrong?

The above period was one of a sustained deterioration in the economy under five 'different' governments. By no means did these governments pursue the same policies. However, for the most part, the policies of the period emphasized import substitution, underpinned by a restrictive foreign-exchange regime, quantitative restrictions upon imports and price controls, with the state playing a major role as producer.

The dramatic contraction between 1970 and 1983 entailed a decline in GDP per capita by more than 3% a year, in industrial output by 4.2% a year and in agricultural output by 0.2% a year (Tabatabai, 1986). The main foundation of the economy — cocoa, mineral and timber production — was on the decline. Cocoa exports fell from 382,000 metric tonnes in 1974 to 159,000 metric tonnes in 1983 (World Bank, 1987a). Mineral exports declined from an index value of 100 in 1975 to 46 by 1983. Production of starchy staples fell from 7,988,000 tonnes in 1974 to 3,657,000 tonnes by 1983 (ibid.)

Although in 1983 food production was affected by the worst drought in the country's history, the decline was mainly due to the massive migration suffered by the rural sector. This exodus was partly a result of the deteriorating economic conditions and also of the 1973/4 oil boom in Nigeria (a crisis for Ghana), which induced more than two million Ghanaians to leave in search of greener pastures in Nigeria. Inadequate food prices intensified the demand for food imports, and the diminishing capacity to import deprived agriculture as well as other sectors of inputs, the shortage of which hampered production still further.

Particularly hard hit was the government's tax base, as those activities that provided it with the bulk of its revenues shrank disproportionately. Central government revenues, which amounted to 21% of GDP in 1970, fell to only 5% of a smaller GDP in 1983 (Tabatabai, 1986). The revenue collapse increased the reliance on the banking system to finance expenditures. Between 1974 and 1983 the monetary base expanded from ¢697 million to ¢11,440 million (IMF, 1987). The loss of monetary control accelerated inflation, which increased from 18.4% in 1974 to 116.5% by 1981 in the midst of a regime of controlled prices (ibid.) .The period of decline was also characterized by negative real interest rates, and domestic savings and investment decreased from 12% and 14% of GDP, respectively, to less than 4% (ibid.).

In the meantime, successive governments continued the policy of overvaluing the Cedi, quietly cognizant of the fate that befell the Busia government's attempt at devaluation in 1972. Between 1974 and 1983 the Cedi was devalued only once, in 1978 (from ¢1.15 to ¢2.75 to $US 1), despite a hundred-fold increase in domestic prices.

Indeed, by 1982 the parallel exchange rate of the Cedi was 22 times that of the official rate (World Bank, 2005). The current account deficit of US$ 2.7 million in 1975 increased to US$ 294 million by 1983 (IMF, 1987). The current account deficits not only depleted gross official foreign reserves but also involved an accumulation of external debts. Arrears amounted to the equivalent of 90% of annual export earnings in 1982 (ibid.).

Successive governments responded with import controls, which fell disproportionately on consumer goods. Perhaps more importantly, the fall in per capita GDP by more than a third between the early 1970s and 1983 (Figure 3.2) was a strong indication of the severe economic decline in Ghana. The continuing decline was, once again, the pretext on which Flt Lt Jerry John Rawlings staged a coup d'état in December 1981, establishing the Provisional National Defence Council (PNDC).

The initial economic policies of the PNDC were interventionist. The PNDC sought to reduce 'the stranglehold of privatization' on the economy and to increase state control of essential services as a means of protecting people from the so-called unscrupulous local and foreign capitalists. Price controls, import duties and tariffs were imposed on certain commodities produced in or imported into the country. The PNDC was hostile toward the prescriptions of Western financial institutions such as the International Monetary Fund (IMF) and World Bank.

A combination of a severe Sahelian drought, sporadic bush fires, the flight of capital from the country, and the continuing miserable performance of the economy threatened the very existence of the regime early in 1983. This precarious situation was compounded by the mass expulsion of over one million Ghanaians from Nigeria in the same year. In the absence of a realistic alternative, the regime turned to the World Bank and IMF for help. The April 1983 budget signalled the government's change of course. This budget contained a significant devaluation of the Cedi and an increase in the prices of basic foodstuffs. It marked the beginning of Ghana's reforms.

## 1984 to the Present

The first phase of reforms was instituted in April 1983 and was marked by the adoption of a stabilization programme, the ERP, with major support from the IMF and the World Bank. The full implementation, however, spread over 1983–6. The ERP, a market-oriented programme, was intended to halt the downward economic spiral. Starting in 1986, the second phase of reform saw the ERP being supplemented with the Structural Adjustment Programme (SAP), geared toward correcting a number of structural imbalances in order to engender sustained healthy economic growth. Under the ERP and SAP various sectors of the economy were liberalized. Exchange-rate policy, fiscal and monetary policies, privatization, and trade policies all saw dramatic changes with increased liberalisation of the economy.

As Figures 3.1 and 3.2 and Table 3.1 above clearly indicate, there is a marked contrast in the growth performance of the Ghanaian economy in the pre- and post-1983 periods. The economy recorded a remarkable recovery following the institution of the ERP in 1983. Since then, GDP growth rates have averaged 5% per annum, with the output of cocoa, minerals and timber recording significant increases. And inflation has fallen from the very high pre-reform levels (123% in 1983), to 10 % in 1992 (Figure

3.6). Though the rate seems to have risen since then, the current rate is certainly much lower than in the early 1980s (ibid.). Overall gross domestic investment also rose from less than 5% of GDP in 1983 to over 20% since 1993, with private domestic investment also recovering strongly (Figure 3.3).

**Figure 3.6  Inflation (1965-2005)**

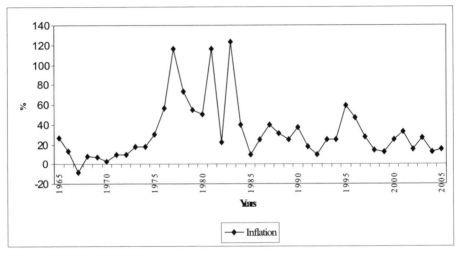

*Source:* World Bank (2007)

## *Fiscal Policy/Internal Balance*
The internal balance, measured as the government budget exclusive of grants as a proportion of GDP, remained negative by 2003 at –7%, compared with –3% in 1984 (Figure 3.7). Indeed, the deficit reached its highest value of 15% in 2001. Fortunately, the balance has been improving since then. External grants from ODA have helped fill the gap, to the point that by 2003 the deficit inclusive of grants was only 0.6%, compared with a deficit of 6.8% exclusive of grants (ibid.).

Reducing these deficits is important, for they tend to discourage private investment and, hence, growth in developing countries (Mlambo and Oshikoya, 2001), perhaps because their financing tends to crowd-out private investment. The gap not funded by external grants would require financing via external debt, which has already been discussed above; or money creation, a likely inflationary process; or via the flotation of government bonds, which tends to raise interest rates and increase the domestic debt, which could in turn crowd-out private investment.

These two latter forms of financing the budget gap were indeed quite prevalent in the economy in the 1990s. Regarding money creation, the government's demands on the Bank of Ghana (BoG) have been the main source of excess liquidity in the economy since the 1990s. For instance, broad money M2 as a proportion of GDP increased from 16% in 1991 to 31% in 2002 (World Bank, 2005).

**Figure 3.7: Internal Balance**

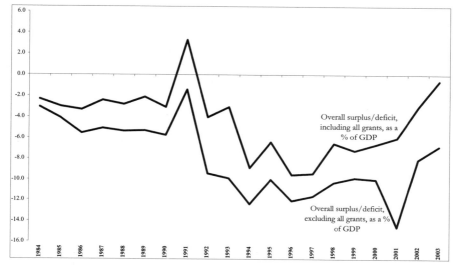

*Source:* Ibid.

Issuing domestic debt has become the main source of finance since 1997. The stock of real domestic debt stood at ¢1,404 billion at the end of 1996, for instance. This represented a growth of about 115% from 1990, and as much as 62% from 1995 alone (ISSER, 1997). In addition to raising interest rates, the continued rise in domestic debt poses a serious burden on future budgets, since increased budgetary allocations would be required for debt servicing in subsequent years. The extent of this fiscal constraint on the budget was evident particularly in the financial year 1996, when the interest payments on domestic debt rose by 87%, from ¢233 billion in 1995 to ¢435 billion (ISSER, 1997). Even though domestic debt accounted for only 11% of the total national (domestic plus external) debt in 1996, interest payments on the domestic debts constituted over 75% of the total interest payments (ISSER, 1997).

With closer monitoring of government expenditure and more effective management policies, the Ghana government budget deficits were stabilized at about 5% of GDP during 1986–91 and even fell to 1% of GDP in 1991 (Figure 3.7). However, the government recorded huge deficits subsequently on account of wage increases to the civil service and public corporations and costs incurred during the transition to democratic rule. Consistent with the electoral cycle, a similar phenomenon occurred in 1996.

## Exchange-Rate Policy/External Balance

The global setting is important for SSA economic growth (Fosu, 2002a). In particular, misalignment in the real exchange rate was a major source of the dismal growth record during 1975–83 (Table 3.4; see also Ghura and Greenes, 1993 for the SSA evidence).

As part of the economic reforms, Ghana has liberalized its exchange system. Although there was traditionally a difference between the inter-bank exchange rate and the average Forex rate, the two rates invariably moved together, with the inter-bank being the lower of the two; by the late 1990s these two rates were virtually the same, and the parallel premium had disappeared (World Bank, 2005).

Due to the balance-of-payment problems that prevailed in the latter part of the 1970s and early 1980s, one of the primary objectives of the ERP was that Ghana should attain a viable balance-of-payments (bop) position in the medium to long term. This was to be achieved through increased export earnings and foreign direct investments. Although exports have grown substantially since the reforms, imports ＿wn even faster, so that both trade and current account balances have ＿d to show persistent deficits and worsening trends (ibid.). Indeed, the worst ＿ccount deficit in history occurred in 1997 with a magnitude of 17% of GNI, ＿＿＿ ＿＿＿ ＿ext highest of 12% back in 1981 (Figure 8). What is clear is that current account deficits have exhibited a significant upward trend since the reforms. While there appears to be a slight downward trend in these deficits since 1997, the magnitude was still 8% of GNI in 2003, still higher than the 6% value in 1983. What these data suggest is that Ghana has been relying more and more on external sources to fund its external budget deficits resulting from its inability to produce as much for the external market as it imports. This situation cannot continue into the long run, however, and accelerated efforts to increase exports are required if the standard of living is to be at least maintained.

**Figure 3.8 External Balance: Current Account as % of GNI (1967-2005)**

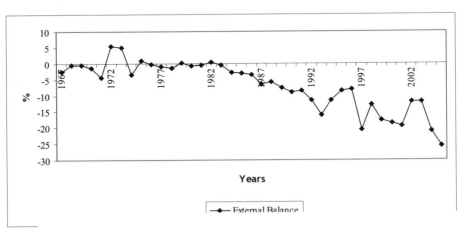

*Source*

## 3. Pre-liberalization (1960–83) and Reform (1984-) Economic Policy, Environment and Performance: The Control and Reform Regimes

The 1960–83 pre-liberalization period was one of state control of the economy, which has been found to be adverse to growth in SSA countries (Fosu and O'Connell, 2006). For example, the occurrence of a 'regulatory syndrome' of state controls, as opposed to a 'syndrome-free' regime, could reduce growth by as much as 1.8 percentage points of annual per capita growth (ibid.: Table 7, column (5)). This estimate is quite huge, given that SSA's per capita growth since 1960 has averaged 0.5% annually and Ghana's –0.2% (Table 3.2).

As observed above, capital accumulation and application were particularly erratic during the 1960–83 period (and also most recently since 1993) (Figure 3.3). This does not bode well for growth, as capital (investment) instability in SSA tends to reduce growth.[6] Meanwhile, improvements in TFP have been difficult to sustain. These stylized facts are the consequences of both policy and the institutional environment. It is important to link these conditions to the situation of markets and the institutions that govern them.

The reform period has exhibited remarkable economic stability. The annual GDP growth rate since 1984 has seldom deviated from 5% (Figure 3.1), and per capita GDP has tended almost linearly upward (Figure 3.2). Meanwhile, the investment/GDP ratio has moved steadily upward with relatively little variance, except for the more recent period after 1993. As observed above, however, the growth seems stuck at about 5%, despite the slight upwards tendency most recently. Nor has the economy shown any real structural transformation characteristic of a take-off.

The present section, therefore, discusses the workings of the economy through the functioning of market institutions under controls and reform macro regimes. It is important to observe that the period 1960–83 (except for the brief sub-period of 1968–72) was one in which the state sought to replace the market in allocating productive resources. This state allocation was felt in the markets for various production inputs, particularly for credit, labour and other agricultural inputs. The state also played a major role in price determination for many goods and services, imported as well as locally produced. We discuss here the functioning of the labour market, credit market, the land market, and the market for finished goods and services under different political regimes in the period 1960–83. The objective is to show the pervasive role of the state and the bottlenecks it created for capital accumulation and improvements in TFP.

The pursuit of liberal economic reforms beginning in April 1983 with the ERP was not simply the consequence of poor domestic economic policies. While the downward slide of the economy and political instability reflected the corruption and poor economic management, there were a number of disastrous exogenous shocks as well that were experienced prior to reform. They included (i) the 1983 drought, which was the worst in decades, and the subsequent need to import large quantities of food on commercial terms and the negative impact on the production of hydroelectric power;

---

[6] Using an augmented production function framework, Fosu (1991), for example, finds that capital instability has a negative impact on growth in a cross-country sample of SSA countries.

(ii) the return in 1983 of more than a million Ghanaians, who had been working in Nigeria during the oil boom; and (iii) a drastic fall in the international terms of trade in the late 1970s and early 1980s due to the drop in cocoa prices and gargantuan rises in oil prices.

Perhaps what prompted the society to take note was the fact that income per capita reached its lowest point in 1983, more than $100 below its peak in the 1970s (Figure 3.2). Both agricultural and industrial production were in conspicuous decline, and gross domestic investment averaged no more than 5% of GDP during the early 1980s (Figure 3.3). Government revenue had fallen from about 20% of GDP in 1970 to less than 5% (World Bank, 2005), making it impossible for the state to offer any meaningful social services. The macro situation was therefore literally begging for reform. Thus, in spite of previous populist/Marxist leanings, the Rawlings government recognized that it had little choice in the matter and that 'fighting corruption in the context of extreme scarcities and distortions was essentially a lost cause' (Leechor, 1994). The government proceeded to reactivate negotiations with the IMF and the World Bank. Subsequently, the first stage of the ERPstabilization and structural adjustment programme was quickly agreed on in April of 1983.

As already observed above, the economy reacted positively to the reforms and began to reverse course, showing impressive gains at least at the initial stages of the reforms. However, despite considerable policy reform, particularly in the period 1983–91, the structure of the economy has not improved sufficiently to differ significantly from the two decades before the reform (Aryeetey and Harrigan, 2000; Killick, 2000).

Ghana's situation is not unlike what Easterly (2001) finds for developing countries in general, however. He writes: 'For whatever reasons, the response of developing country growth rates to the policy reforms of the '80s and '90s has not been what could have been expected from previous empirical work on growth. Zero *per capita* growth is a disappointing outcome whatever the cause' (p.7). He notes that in the period 1980–98, median per capita income growth was 0.0% when it had been 2.5% in 1960–79. This happened despite the improvements in policies on financial depth and overvaluation of currencies. It was also at a time when the initial conditions of health and education, as well as fertility and infrastructure, generally improved. Easterly speculates that other developments in the world, such as the structure of OECD interest rates, the debt situation, the slowed growth of OECD countries, and the skill-biased technical change, may account for the relatively poor growth in developing countries generally.

Below, we discuss the roles of market institutions and microeconomic agents and the political economy underlying the economic performance during the control and reform regimes. Although the period 1968-72 could be classified as one of liberalization, it was not long enough to be properly analyzed in terms of changes in the institutional environment. Hence, we shall simplify the analysis by considering only two periods: 1960–83 (control regime) and 1984-present (reform regime).

## *Market Institutions and their Functioning under Controls and Reform*

The discussion of market institutions is limited to the labour, credit, land and goods and services markets. We shall attempt to show that the state had a distinct role in the performance of these markets, except for the land market, which has structural problems of its own.

## Labour Market Performance under Control and Reform Regimes

*Employment.* An important characteristic of the labour market during the control regime is the extent to which different governments went to ensure that employment grew. Thus, the structure of the market (in terms of the regional and sectoral distribution of the labour force), the extent of unemployment, and the level of real wages all experienced remarkable changes: from a situation of geographical immobility and shortage of all kinds of labour to one of great mobility and surplus of many types of labour. Some researchers (e.g., Boateng, 1997) have attributed the growing fiscal deficits in the 1960s and 1970s to considerable featherbedding of the formal sector. With this, formal sector employment grew significantly but with very little attention paid to productivity.

The main instrument used by government to control the supply and demand for labour has been the minimum wage policy. A minimum wage policy was first adopted in Ghana in 1963. The objective was to raise the income levels of unskilled workers within a social policy context. Since then minimum wages have been used as an instrument to effect across-the-board increases in salaries in the public sector. Ghana applies two main concepts of minimum wages, namely, the daily minimum wage fixed for the civil service, and the statutory minimum wage below which it is illegal to employ. Usually the daily minimum wage is first established[7] and then upward adjustments are made to other levels in the salary structure according to some agreed criteria. This practice, together with attempts to compress wages, introduced significant downward rigidities in the earnings structure of the public sector.[8]

Aside from the minimum wage, the relatively rapid rise in formal employment in the 1960s was a consequence of the expansion of the public sector itself. The 1960s saw the creation of more and more state enterprises of different sizes in almost every sector of the economy. It had the effect of attracting not only skilled labour into the modern sectors but also of expanding the informal and unskilled urban labour class to support the more formal sector. The public sector consequently became both the most significant employer and trend-setter in the determination of wages as well as the regulator. This is a role that has not changed significantly despite the reforms of later years, and underlies many of the macro trends emanating from both the fiscal and monetary sides. The size of the public sector wage bill, together with how it was financed, has been for many years the most important issue in national economic management.

---

[7] Based on the statutory minimum wage fixed in consultation with the Tripartite Committee of government, employers and organized labour.

[8] The Ghanaian labour market is highly imperfect, exhibiting strong labour supply and demand inelasticity as well as wage rigidities due to the strong influences of labour market institutions. The unionization rate within the formal sector is about 68%, implying that at least two-thirds of formal sector jobs are subject to collective bargaining agreements. Due to the system of pattern bargaining, relative wages among sectors of the economy tend to be inflexible (Boateng and Fine, 2000).

A major development affecting the labour market during the reform period was the retrenchment and redeployment of large numbers of public service workers. The size of the Cocoa Board's payroll staff, for example, was slated to decline from 100,000 to 50,000. The civil service lost 36,000 jobs by the same token. What is particularly interesting about the reforms and retrenchment is the fact that organized labour did not react to the radical changes that were taking place. Jeffrey Herbst (1991) describes the reaction of labour as the outcome of a 'politics of acquiescence'. Political acquiescence is explained by the support the government lent to revolting trade unionists to usurp authority in the unions, thereby absorbing them into the political fold. Thus, being part of the structure that developed policies, labour lost its clout as a market operator.

*Formal Sector Employment and the Private Sector.* Formal sector employment, defined as recorded employment in establishments employing five or more workers, grew steadily from 332,900 in 1960 to 483,500 in 1976 (Boateng, 1997). It remained stagnant between 1976 and 1979, and began to decline between 1980 and 1982. It rose to a new height in 1985 and began a long descent thereafter, reaching a low 186,300 in 1991 under the liberal regime. Formal sector employment in 1991 was 44% less than in 1960, representing an average annual decrease of 1.4% compared with an average annual growth rate of the urban labour force of 5.3% between 1960 and 1990. Thus the importance of the formal sector as a source of employment declined from 3.6% to 2.5% between 1981 and 1991, as shown in Table 3.5.

**Table 3.5    Formal Sector Employment 1960–91 ('000)**

|      | Private Sector | Public Sector | All Sectors | Share of Private Sector % |
|------|----------------|---------------|-------------|---------------------------|
| 1960 | 149            | 184           | 333         | 44.7                      |
| 1965 | 118            | 278           | 396         | 29.8                      |
| 1970 | 110            | 288           | 398         | 27.6                      |
| 1975 | 137            | 318           | 455         | 30.1                      |
| 1980 | 48             | 291           | 337         | 13.6                      |
| 1985 | 67             | 397           | 464         | 14.4                      |
| 1986 | 66             | 347           | 414         | 15.9                      |
| 1987 | 79             | 315           | 394         | 20.0                      |
| 1988 | 55             | 252           | 307         | 17.9                      |
| 1989 | 38             | 177           | 215         | 17.7                      |
| 1990 | 34             | 189           | 229         | 17.5                      |
| 1991 | 30             | 156           | 186         | 16.1                      |

*Source:*   Boateng (1997)

The pre-reform era was one of mass employment in the public sector and was the consequence of a policy objective of employment maximization supported by a broad-based regime of state controls on all major aspects of the Ghanaian economy: from price and exchange-rate controls to state ownership of manufacturing and distributive trade centres. The private sector was a victim in this process, as apparent in Table 3.5. Private sector employment, which stood at about 149,000 in 1960, fell to 48,000 in 1980, representing only 14% of total employment in 1980, a tumble from 45% in 1960. Unfortunately, this private sector share had not changed much by 1991, standing at 16% and with employment of only 30,000.

The period of mass formal employment ended in 1985 during the early stages of the reform; however, the decline of the private sector in formal employment began before that, and continued through at least the 1980s. While the reform period appears to have halted the slide of the share of the private sector in employment, both private and public sector levels of employment continued to fall substantially, with the latter falling even faster thanks to the public sector retrenchment beginning in 1987 during the reform period.

In response to the substantial fall in formal employment, informal employment grew rapidly. The share of the informal sector in the total non-agricultural labour force is estimated to have increased from 70% to over 90% between 1970 and 1990 (Boateng, 1997).

*Wages.* Faltering output growth has generally led to sharp declines in real wages, especially between 1975 and 1980 when real earnings fell to less than one-third of their value (Table 3.6). Since nominal wages have always moved up sharply, however, the erosion in real wages was attributable to high inflation (Figure 3.6). The decline seems to have been reversed since 1986, however, coincidental with the reform period. By the late 1980s, the level of real earnings was about twice that in 1985 (ibid.).

**Table 3.6    Nominal and Real Average Monthly Earnings per Employee (cedis)**

|  | Nominal earnings | Real earnings | Index of earnings | |
|---|---|---|---|---|
|  |  |  | Nominal | Real |
| 1960 | 33.00 | 5.538 | 15 | 255 |
| 1965 | 38.97 | 3.828 | 18 | 176 |
| 1970 | 54.99 | 4.035 | 25 | 186 |
| 1975 | 102.69 | 3.473 | 47 | 160 |
| 1980 | 460.22 | 1.147 | 212 | 53 |
| 1985 | 3633.00 | 0.996 | 1671 | 46 |
| 1986 | 7433.00 | 1.636 | 3419 | 75 |
| 1987 | 10524.00 | 1.657 | 4841 | 76 |
| 1988 | 13805.00 | 1.655 | 6351 | 76 |
| 1989 | 24257.00 | 2.321 | 11159 | 107 |
| 1990 | 30056.00 | 2.096 | 13827 | 96 |
| 1991 | 35212.00 | 2.080 | 16199 | 96 |

*Source:* Ibid.

*Productivity.* Labour productivity in manufacturing (average value-added per worker deflated by the manufactures wholesale price index) declined by about 43% between 1977 and 1981 (World Bank, 1985). This downward trend was largely due to constraints in laying off redundant labour, despite low capacity utilization rates. The low wages, relative to the urban cost of living, provided little incentive to work. The compressed wage structure offered little reward to greater skills and productivity, especially in the public sector, and may have contributed to the huge decrease in TFP during 1975–84 (Table 3.2).

In contrast, TFP growth became substantially positive during at least the beginning of the reform period 1985–9. The higher productivity in the early reform years is attributed to increases in capacity utilization (Steel and Webster, 1991), which slowed down subsequently due to low demand, contributing to the subsequent lower productivity (Collier et al., 1999). Moreover, based on a 1992/3 survey of 70 large and medium-scale manufacturing enterprises, labour productivity rose following the introduction of the ERP, due mainly to: the restructuring of firms, increased capacity utilization, retraining of labour, re-organization of labour to undertake new tasks, and increased capital per worker.

## Credit Markets under Control and Reform Regimes

The small private domestic investment, as shown above, is often linked to the relatively small formal credit market. It was in an attempt to expand this credit market that the control regimes were instituted.

To deal with what was regarded as a market failure, which denied people access to credit and other financial services, the interventionist approach began under 'self-rule' in 1953 with the establishment of the Ghana Commercial Bank for both political and economic objectives.[9] Subsequently, to address the financing needs of specific sectors, state-owned development banks were established: the National Investment Bank (1963), the Agricultural Development Bank (1965), and the Bank for Housing and Construction (1973). The Bank of Ghana was founded in 1957 to supervise all other banks (replacing the role of the West African Currency Board). Direct intervention of state institutions in channelling credit paralleled the *statist* approach to investment.

Government interest in small clients during the 1970s fostered another generation of specialized banks: the Co-operative Bank, the National Savings and Credit Bank, the Social Security Bank, and unit rural banks.[10] They were all charged with directing credit to specific groups. The emphasis on directed credit was consistent with the approaches of international agencies at the time, particularly as a means of satisfying

---

[9] The two foreign banks at the time were seen to favour well-established foreign firms and to neglect indigenous farmers and small entrepreneurs in granting loans and advances.

[10] First launched in 1976, 128 were eventually established, owned and managed by members of the local community. Many became financially distressed or inoperative, but with rehabilitation efforts in the 1990s, 60 were ranked by the Bank of Ghana in 1996 as performing satisfactorily and another 47 as mediocre. Their primary success has been in savings mobilization, accounting for 27% of total formal deposits mobilized in 1993 (Nissanke and Aryeetey, 1998).

the basic needs of low-income households and providing them with opportunities for self-enhancement. Government intervention to overcome the perceived slow pace of private banking also took the form of pressure on state-owned banks to increase the number of branches. The total number of bank branches more than doubled in the 1970s, reaching 466 (including rural banks) by 1985.

Financial policies became very repressive following the 1972 change in government. Controls on all sectors of the economy were substituted for the market and tightened as weak macroeconomic management fostered rising inflation. For the management of bank portfolios, the largely state-owned banking system was directed to channel credit to 'the productive sectors' of the economy, using a mix of interest rates and selective credit controls and ceilings. Credit management policies were dictated by the concern that many productive sectors were not receiving credit (Bank of Ghana, 1980). The Bank of Ghana instituted some eleven borrower categories for the sectoral distribution of loans and advances for the purpose of prioritization.

The interventionist policies in the credit market resulted in a reduction in the size of financial market activity, limiting competition in the financial system and making the financial market respond more to the needs of the state than to those of the productive agents. Even though the number of financial institutions and their branches increased rapidly in the 1960s and 1970s, that did not lead to the efficient mobilization of resources for growth and development. In addition, the system failed in its role to support the development of the monetary sector.

The negative impact of repressive policies on financial sector development is illustrated by the halving of financial depth, measured by the M2/GDP ratio, from over 25% in 1977 to only 12% in 1984 (Figure 3.9). Between 1977 and 1984, most other indicators of the development of the financial system declined in size (measured as a percentage of GDP); demand deposits fell from 11.6% to 4.6%; savings and time deposits from 7.1% to 2.6% and domestic credit declined from 38.8% to 15.6% (Aryeetey 1996). The decline in financial development may have contributed to the slide in GDP growth during the period.[11]

**Figure 3.9: Indicators of Financial Deepening in Ghana**

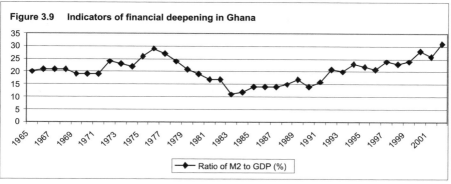

*Source:* World Bank (2005).

---

[11] See, for example, a review by Khan and Senhadji (2003), who conclude that there is a positive relationship between financial development and growth.

*Reform*. The major financial reform was the liberalization of interest rates, whereby banks were permitted to set lending and deposit rates in response to credit demand and supply conditions. Banks were also restructured and re-capitalized under the Financial Sector Adjustment Programmes (FINSAP). In addition, state-owned banks underwent privatization, with the Ghana Commercial Bank and the Social Security Bank, for example, selling less than 40% of the shares to ordinary Ghanaians. Support was also provided to informal finance and micro-finance institutions, via the Ghana Micro-finance Institutions Network (GHAMFIN), for instance. This has helped raise the growth of micro-finance in Ghana (Nissanke and Aryeetey, 1998).

By the M2/GDP measure, there appears to have been substantial financial deepening since the reform, with the measure rising from 11% in 1983 to 31% in 2002 (Figure 3.9). Nonetheless, financial product development continues to be slow and narrow; savings mobilization efforts have yielded only modest outcomes; credit delivery remains inadequate; and failing and distressed banks persist. While the reforms opened up the financial market, they also exposed weaknesses in the regulatory infrastructure.

## Land Markets under Control and Reform Regimes
One of the important characteristics of the investment profile of Ghana during the pre-reform era was been the low investment in agriculture, despite the fact that agriculture was for long the major income earner and source of employment. Thus, even though agricultural land constituted 57% of the total land area, only 20% of this has been cultivated (Nyanteng and Seini, 2000). The main reason for this rather paltry cultivation rate is that agricultural investment, at 2% of GDP, has always been too small (ibid.). What, then, are the constraints in the land market that often discourage investment in the improvement of land?

Benneh's work (1971) in the savannah-forest zone of Central Ghana, for example, showed that, while access to land under traditional systems was still relatively easy as an entitlement, there were growing signs of pressure as a result of the introduction of cash crops. Where economic activity was gathering pace, communities tended to be reluctant to permit the release of large tracts of land for commercial farming. An important conclusion is that the tenure system in Ghana was under considerable pressure, torn between social equity and the efficient use of land.

In the changing environment for land acquisition, the state in the 1960s used its powers of acquisition to acquire land, largely for state farms and other public economic activities, with only token (non-market) compensation paid to the communal/family owners. In using its authority to acquire land for various ventures, the state hardly affected the price of land, as a land market never really existed. This was largely because the state implicitly discouraged the development of a commercial land market. In the case of corporate bodies seeking land for their ventures, the state sometimes acquired communal lands that were leased to the investors at non-market rates. It also sometimes encouraged communal owners to make transfers of land directly to investors, a practice that Benneh (1971) saw as problematic, since it tended to create conflicts between public and private interests. The consequence has been that the land market is poorly developed and the use of land as an asset is often uneconomical.

*Reform.* The land market in both rural and urban areas, especially for agricultural purposes, has not changed in structure since the economic reform programme began. This is largely due to the fact that there is no free land market, mainly as a result of the land-tenure arrangements. The decision to put land on the market is often unrelated to demand and supply conditions. Even in the case of non-agricultural land in the urban areas, there is a tendency not to sell land outright from communal property, but instead to provide long-term leases of about 99 years. While these arrangements do not seem problematic in the short run, they may indeed represent ticking time bombs associated with property inheritance in the longer run as the leases become due.

## Goods and Services Markets under Control and Reform Regimes

Ghana began its march towards growth and development after independence focusing on industrialization, which was viewed as the key factor in modernization and development. The explicit objectives of industrialization were to exploit natural domestic resources, to form a base for developing other economic sectors, to satisfy the basic needs of the population, to create jobs, and to assimilate and promote technological progress and modernize society. The industrial strategy at the time was characterized by: (a) an emphasis on import-substitution through high levels of effective protection; (b) a reliance on administrative controls rather than market mechanisms to determine incentives and resource allocation; and (c) the use of large-scale, public sector investment as the leading edge in industrial development.

*Industry and Agriculture.* As observed above, there was a major push for expansion in manufacturing capacity in the 1960s. During the brief attempt at liberalization between 1966 and 1971, the establishment of state-owned enterprises slowed down. With the subsequent adoption of the principle of self-reliance and the desire to capture the 'commanding heights of the economy', however, the state-led import-substituting industrialization (ISI) strategy was revived in the 1970s. In addition to expansion in manufacturing production and capacity through ISI, policy statements also emphasized an expansion in manufactured exports. Even though export diversification was considered necessary if the foreign-exchange constraint on the economy was to be relieved, this was never actively pursued. The choice of an inward-oriented trade strategy was motivated by export pessimism at the time, in relation to the limited ability of primary exports to generate the necessary foreign exchange required for rapid growth. Unlike the East Asian Tigers that were able to make the transition from ISI to an outwardly oriented strategy, however, Ghana became stuck at the ISI stage, thanks to an anti-export bias orientation (Bates, 1981).

That the ISI push was unsuccessful is illustrated by Steel (1972: 226–7): 'Ghana's industrialization and IS policies were extremely unsuccessful in establishing a structure and level of manufacturing output which could efficiently reduce foreign exchange requirements and stimulate growth of GNP.' He points to massive capacity under-utilization, which he attributes to inappropriate foreign-exchange policies and high levels of effective protection that stimulated the domestic production of final-stage 'non-essential' activities. Killick (1978: 204–5) was also very critical of the strategy of ISI pursued by Ghana, arguing that '... a wide-ranging set of conditions conspired to limit the efficiency of the industrialisation drive', including over-optimism about the future growth of the economy, unselective and arbitrary protection, a variety of biases favouring capital intensity and processes with few linkages with other sectors, a deteriorating quality of investment decisions, and sub-standard performance by state enterprises.

The early industrial policies stimulated rapid growth of manufacturing output (averaging 13% per annum) and employment (averaging 8% per annum) during the 1960s (World Bank, 1984). By 1970, manufacturing as a share of GDP had risen to 13%. Total industrial output as a percentage of GDP peaked at 21.5% in 1977, when the industrial sector began to lose its momentum. Between 1975 and 1979, the manufacturing sector declined at an annual average rate of –2.5%, worsening to –12.3% between 1980 and 1982 (World Bank, 2005). The decline in manufacturing output prior to the ERP was mainly attributable to the serious difficulties experienced in the balance of payments, beginning in the mid-1970s. With most physical and raw materials imported, industrial capacity was critically dependent on import capacity, which was in turn determined principally by the level of exports, since capital inflows were negligible. Export earnings relied predominantly on cocoa and to a lesser extent on timber, gold and diamonds, all of which showed a downward trend. The sharpest decline in cocoa and gold production took place at a time when the world prices were favourable (1976–9). Due to their high dependence on imports of raw materials, spare parts and equipment, manufacturing industries suffered heavily from the decline in import capacity.

In the area of agriculture, the pronounced role of the state was again exhibited in the immediate post-independence period. The policies placed emphasis on the modernization of agriculture and expansion through major capital investments controlled by the state. This led to the establishment 'state farms', covering large tracts of land in all regions and using huge amounts of labour to operate them. Marketing boards, the one for cocoa being the most prominent, were set up as monopolies for the distribution of products.

Unfortunately, liberalization experiments in the late 1960s and early 1970s following the overthrow of the Nkrumah regime were short-lived. The military takeover in 1972 of the Busia civilian government led to the dismantling of the open-market policies initiated in the late 1960s and a command economy was re-instituted. Comprehensive import controls were resorted to, the scope of price controls was widened, and some imported consumer goods were subsidized. A monopoly system of cocoa purchasing (unitary buying system) was reintroduced in 1977.

The period 1972-82 saw the most intense regulation of prices for consumer goods and services, even though some controls existed for most of the 1960s. The military regime instituted in 1972 a wide-ranging set of prices for consumer items, covering food, household items, transportation, rent, etc. The Prices and Incomes Board became, in the 1970s, the institution for determining the purchase price of most consumer items, imported as well as domestically produced. Indeed, what most Ghanaians associate with the economic problems prior to the institution of reforms in 1983 was the shortage of most consumer items from the goods markets and the disappearance or decline of many basic social and economic services.

At the same time, there was considerable interest in raising agricultural production to self-sufficiency. The Acheampong government instituted the Operation Feed Yourself (OFY) and the Operation Feed Your Industries (OFYI) programmes after 1972. These programmes were to spearhead the campaign to raise food and agricultural raw material production. Among the objectives was the increase in small farm production through acreage expansion (Killick, 1978). The OFY emphasized the production of cereals, mainly maize and rice, while the OFYI encouraged the production of cotton, kenaf, and sugarcane.

*Reform.* Among the major reforms taking effect in the mid- and early 1980s were: (i) trade policy reform to achieve greater openness; (ii) support to industrial sector development; and (iii) support to agricultural sector development. Exchange rates were adjusted downward to reduce and eventually eliminate overvaluation, which has been a major growth deterrent in SSA countries generally (Ghura and Greenes, 1993) and in Ghana in particular (Table 3.4); the import licensing system was abolished; and the foreign-exchange retention scheme was liberalized to allow a greater retention of earnings and to relax restrictions in their use. Tariffs on both consumer and producer goods were also reduced and rationalized.

In support of industry, the regulatory framework was improved by repealing the 1971 Manufacturing Industries Act, the 1974 Price Control Decree, and the 1976 Control of Sale of Specific Goods Decree. A new Investment Code was enacted to encourage foreign direct private investment, and measures introduced to streamline investment procedures. Privatization of the state-owned enterprises has also been applied to stop the flow of government resources to loss-making enterprises, and to improve the environment for private sector participation.

The objectives for the agricultural sector under the ERP were to: revitalise the export crop sector; achieve self-sufficiency in the production of cereals; maintain adequate levels of buffer stocks of grains, particularly maize and rice; ensure price stability and the provision of maximum food security against unforeseen crop failure and other natural hazards; and increase foreign-exchange earnings from agriculture through incentives to cocoa farmers. The main feature of agricultural policy was the increase in output prices, with the highest increases for cocoa. Subsidies on input prices, particularly fertilizers, pesticides and farm equipment, were eliminated. Reform of public agricultural institutions led to the reduction in budgetary costs to the government of the large parastatal sector and a drastic redundancy programme for the Ghana Cocoa Marketing Board. The Agricultural Services Rehabilitation Project (ASRP) was implemented, with the main aim of enhancing the achievement of government policy objectives in agriculture.

In the second phase of reforms launched in 1986, agriculture received considerable attention. The programme emphasized increased productivity and internal price stability. The government actively promoted cereal production in pursuit of food security objectives. It also raised the guaranteed minimum price for maize and rice every year and subsidies on farm inputs such as fertilizers, machinery and other agricultural chemicals continued, though on a much reduced scale.

Institutional reforms were also intensified in the cocoa sector during this phase. The Cocoa Sector Rehabilitation Project was implemented with World Bank financing, the main objective being to increase efficiency with respect to production and marketing. This involved reduction in the size of the Cocoa Board and the transfer of a greater share of the world price of cocoa to producers.

*Results from Reform: Manufacturing Sector.* After years of steady decline, real manufacturing GDP saw positive growth from 1984, but at a decreasing rate after 1988 (Asante et al., 2000). As Table 3.7 shows, while the 1971–83 pre-reform period was characterized by a fall in manufacturing GDP of 4.3% per year, the 1984–95 post-ERP period experienced growth of 6.6%. However, the initial growth was not sustained and came from a low base, falling from 14.5% in 1984–7 to 2.6% in 1988–95. The growth of manufacturing lagged behind that of GDP, leading to a falling share of manufacturing in GDP, from 11.2% during pre-reform to 8.7% for the post-ERP period, and therefore to a lack of inter-sectoral structural change of the type usually associated with development (Nixson, 1990). The decline in the manufacturing growth rate between 1988 and 1995 has been attributed to the fact that, while competitive industries continued to grow, uncompetitive ones began to decline or fold up in the more liberalized environment. The slowdown in the growth of the manufacturing sector was reflected in the growth rate of the whole industrial sector, with industrial growth declining from 12.1% between 1984 and 1987 to 4.4% between 1988 and 1995.

**Table 3.7    Mean Output, Shares, and Growth Rates in Manufacturing Sector, 1971–95**

| | Real GDP | Ind. GDP | Man. GDP | SHARES | | Growth Rates | | | |
|---|---|---|---|---|---|---|---|---|---|
| | | | | Ind/GDP | Man/GDP | Man/Ind | Ind. | Man | GDP |
| *Period (m. 1975 Cedis)* | | | | | | | | | |
| 7179 | 5492.0 | 1043.8 | 671.8 | 9.0 | 12.3 | 64.5 | 2.0 | 1.1 | 0.4 |
| 8083 | 5126.2 | 695.5 | 462.8 | 13.5 | 8.9 | 65.7 | 9.6 | 12.0 | 3.4 |
| 8487 | 5563.7 | 726.9 | 475.6 | 13.0 | 8.5 | 65.2 | 12.1 | 14.5 | 6.0 |
| 8895 | 7386.5 | 1053.9 | 641.4 | 14.3 | 8.7 | 61.1 | 4.4 | 2.6 | 4.6 |
| *Pre-ERP* | | | | | | | | | |
| 7183 | 5379.5 | 936.6 | 607.5 | 17.3 | 11.2 | 64.9 | 4.3 | 4.5 | 0.8 |
| *Post-ERP* | | | | | | | | | |
| 84–95 | 6778.9 | 944.9 | 586.2 | 13.9 | 8.7 | 62.5 | 7.0 | 6.6 | 5.0 |
| T-Stat | 4.6[a] | 0.1 | 0.5 | 3.7[a] | 4.1[a] | 1.6 | 3.4[a] | 2.6[b] | 3.5[a] |

Notes: a)   Significant at the 1% level;  b) significant at the 5% level.
*Source:*   Statistical Service, *Quarterly Digest of Statistics,* various issues.

The slowdown in the growth of real manufacturing GDP after 1988 has been worrying. It has been interpreted to mean that, while appropriate trade and macroeconomic policies are necessary to support the performance of the manufacturing sector, they are by no means sufficient for sustained high performance in an environment of significant structural constraints. Output growth performance has, however, differed among sub-sectors of the manufacturing sector. Those with significantly diminished output include textiles, wearing apparel and leather goods, where high-cost, overprotected firms have had difficulty competing with liberalized imports. Those whose output has increased significantly include sawmill and wood products, and beverages that are domestic-resource-based (Asante et al., 2000).

Nevertheless, the manufacturing sector seems to have been revived since the mid-1990s. For example, its growth averaged 5% a year during the period 1996–2000, the same as for total industry, and 2% in 2001–3, one-half that of industry (Table 3.1.B).

Thanks in great part to the increased profitability of exporting resulting from the large devaluations accompanying the ERP, a flurry of export activities has been reported among several firms in Ghana, including agricultural equipment, beverages, furniture and aluminium products (Hettige et al., 1991). Indeed, as observed above, the share of manufacturing in total merchandise exports has increased from 1% in 1961–65 and in 1976–85 to 15% in 1996–2000 (Table 3.1.C). This is a hopeful sign of increasing competitive manufacturing in Ghana. Altogether, while in the right direction, the post-ERP performance of manufactured exports has arguably not been as impressive as could have been expected, especially given the substantial improvements in price incentives, implying the importance of other non-price factors.

Teal (1995) has argued that labour regulations, price controls and other obstacles to manufacturing expansion have constrained output and export growth, especially in the case of wood products, the major manufacturing export sub-sector. More generally, he postulates that government-induced market failure explains the failure to develop manufacturing exports. Structural adjustment and liberalization are not complete in Ghana and government policy continues to have an adverse effect on the output of firms in the exportable sector, in particular. (For a recent study that analyzes factors responsible for the dismal performance of manufacturing and suggests policies to improve manufacturing competitiveness in SSA, see Fosu et al., 2001).

*Results from Reform: Agricultural Sector.* The period 1990–95 exhibited a direct relationship between the overall performance of Ghana's economy and agricultural growth, especially given that the sector represented slightly over 40% of GDP. For instance, as observed above, there appeared to be a stagnant but relatively volatile GDP growth during this period. GDP grew by the relatively low rate of 3.3% in 1990 due to the catastrophic growth of agriculture in that year of –2.0%. When agricultural growth improved to 4.7% in the following year, so did GDP growth to 5.3% (CEPA, 1996). Similarly, a dismal performance of agriculture in 1992, when it grew by –0.6 %, resulted in GDP growth of only 3.9%. With significant improvement in food and livestock production, agricultural output in 1993 increased by about 2.8%, leading to an overall growth in real GDP of 5.0%. However, flooding as well as the disruptive effects on agricultural activities of ethnic conflicts in the Northern Region and unfavourable climatic conditions during the harvest season, brought about decreases in agricultural output in 1994, resulting in GDP growth of only 3.3%. And, when agricultural growth rebounded to more than 4.0% in 1995, GDP growth also improved by about 1 percentage point over the previous year's rate.

The fluctuations in agricultural growth primarily reflect volatility in weather, particularly rainfall (Nyanteng and Seini, 2000). The same trend is associated with cocoa, the main cash crop. Thus, the agricultural supply response has been weak, mainly as a result of other exogenous factors. While exchange-rate reforms and increases in producer prices initially helped to increase earnings from cocoa, these responses have stagnated (Sowa, 1996), and other measures to stabilize agricultural production are required if fluctuations in GDP growth are to be minimized.

## *The Political Economy of the Control Regime and Reform*

Why did Ghana adopt the control regime of the 1960s and continue with this in different forms into the 1980s before starting serious reform? Leith and Lofchie (1993) examined three theses to explain the policy choices made, the *urban bias* (Bates, 1981); the *dominant development ethos* (Killick, 1978; Aryeetey, 1989); and finally the *transaction and agency costs*. These theses derived from the new institutional economics, on the premise that the government was aware of the institutional inadequacies and hence opted for policies whose implementation minimized transaction costs in the short run.

Instead of examining each of the theses in turn, the discussion in the present section focuses on the roles played by the structure of political institutions in the formulation of economic policy. This is weighed against other external influences like the presence of pressure groups (e.g., via strikes), and the possibility of a direct assault on the state and government (e.g., via coups d'état). The role of corruption as a way of escaping from the legitimate influence of the state in the organization of economic activity is also discussed.

## *The Structure of Political Institutions and Economic Policy*

According to Apter (1975), for example, there was basic difficulty in entrenching democratic institutions into Ghanaian political life in view of the social and political tensions that erupted soon after independence. These tensions had been brewing in the run-up to independence; the Nkrumah government's reaction led to the demise of democratic structures, with their replacement by a single party. Faced with the development realities and difficulties of a young nation, and in order to hold on to power, the opposition had to be crushed, and this was done with relative ease. The ruling Convention People's Party (CPP) had to recreate itself in a manner that allowed it to dominate all social, economic and political life in Ghana, a process that made ideology emphasizing the role of the new secular state paramount. The process also led to the removal of moderate thinking from the party machinery. With moderates and 'capitalists' practically out of government by the early 1960s, the stage was set for state control of all production processes.

Most institutions associated with secular democracy were deliberately crushed in order to promote the party above all. The legal system in particular was weakened through the enactment of controversial laws that compromised the liberties of individuals and reduced the prospect for using the court system for resolving disputes in a transparent manner. The civil service was also weakened largely through intimidation, while organized labour was highly politicized and made an appendage of the ruling party. Free enterprise could not be encouraged and the system for national economic management saw to that. A five-sector economy was instituted: (i) state enterprises; (ii) enterprises owned by foreign private interests; (iii) enterprises jointly owned by the state and foreign private interests; (iv) co-operatives; and (v) small-scale Ghanaian private enterprises. Nkrumah's government was not in the mood for large private Ghanaian ventures and did everything to discourage this. Indeed, Nkrumah argued that the 'there was no bourgeois class among Ghanaians to undertake large-scale investments'.

It was the lack of results from economic endeavours at a time when political repression had taken root in Ghanaian life that provided widespread support for the military overthrow of the Nkrumah government in 1966. While the change of government was popular, it did not lead to a restoration of democratic institutions for a long time to come. The period from 1966 to 1983 saw a mixture of civilian and military governments that essentially worked with the same institutions, which the Nkrumah government had erected albeit with minor modifications in approach. Democracy was seldom an important feature of national governance, though there was a credible attempt under the elected government of Dr Busia (1969-72). The absence of democracy may be regarded as having fuelled the political instability that characterized Ghanaian political and economic life in the first three decades after independence.

*Reform.* Did the decision to embrace liberal reforms lead Ghana to develop an effective programme for addressing the economic problems of the times? Questions are still being raised about the 'ownership' of the reform (Aryeetey and Cox, 1997). What seems clear is that, while the government might have owned these reforms, in that it engaged in negotiations with the Bretton Woods institutions and reached certain agreements, this conclusion may not be extrapolated to the citizenry, especially given the non-representative nature of the military government dominated by Jerry Rawlings.

Perhaps more importantly, Ghana became a new democracy in 1992, almost a decade after the reforms began, with new institutions, including a parliament and a strengthened civil service as well as the development of a new civil society. However, it was not until the subsequent elections of 1996, 2000 and 2004 that these institutions could be considered as approaching some form of maturity.

## The Role of Pressure Groups

In most democratic societies, it is the strength of civil society or various pressure groups that dictates the nature and extent of influences on policy-making. Apter (1975) has argued that in the period before independence in Ghana, the traditional authorities symbolized the alternative source of authority to the colonial government.

This was achieved through *indirect rule* and the alliances that the chiefs developed with the educated elite groups and other professionals. Soon after independence, one of the strategies used by the Nkrumah government to strengthen its own position was slowly but steadily to chip away at the power bases of traditional authority. Secular agencies took over the roles of chiefs in all national institutions, and even in local government. Through charismatic leadership or intimidation, the authority of ethnically based institutions that were linked with chieftaincy was eroded; religious institutions were eclipsed through intimidation; academic institutions were slowly but steadily compromised; and the labour unions were absorbed into the party structure.

*Reform.* Despite considerable difficulty with the political Left and the left leanings of Jerry Rawlings himself, as well as opposition from the urban population, the Rawlings government was able to implement the economic reforms. This was mainly due to the fact that there appeared to be no realistic alternative, given the dismal fiscal condition of the country, with little expectation of a bailout (Aryeetey and Cox, 1995). For example, appeals to socialist countries during the drought of 1983 reaped little reward, thus 'revealing the lack of alternative to embracing the capitalist system' (ibid.). The Programme of Action to Mitigate the Costs of Adjustment (PAMSCAD) also helped, and so did the passive stance of the Trades Union Congress, as well as the use of the World Bank's imposed conditionalities as a scapegoat.

## Political Instability

'The distinct political instability that was aggravated by poor economic conditions throughout the 1960s and 1970s was reflected in high levels of corruption, policy reversals and a general lack of direction' (Aryeetey and Tarp, 2000). As the growth in the role of the state became pervasive, it branched into many spheres of economic activity that yielded relatively little economic return and contributed significantly to the macroeconomic instability. Indeed, one characteristic of the political economy of Ghana has been the high incidence of coups d'états and their association with economic conditions and sometimes with specific economic policies. Existing evidence suggests that, among African countries, Ghana has been among the foremost of those with the largest indicator of this form of 'elite' political instability (McGowan, 2003), which has been found to contribute substantially to the observed dismal economic growth performance among SSA countries (e.g., Fosu, 1992, 2002b).

Political instability and economic instability tend to reinforce each other (Apter, 1975). And they may both be growth-inhibiting as well.[12] Writing about the first coup, Apter (1975: 387) states:

> The specific reasons for the coup are many. What is clear is that Nkrumah's political method of creating new alternatives without foreclosing others could not go on indefinitely. The restrictions of political opposition and personal freedom, rising prices,

---

[12] See, for example, Fosu (2001) for an analysis of the relative roles of export, investment and import instabilities on growth.

higher taxes, and other economic burdens, exaggerated by an inadequate administrative and inefficient managerial infrastructure (under the form of state capitalism which passed for socialism) all contributed. Everyone in the end was affected.

Despite the unassailable evidence of foreign instigation of the coup, there is every indication that it was generally popular in the aftermath of failed policies.

The military government that overthrew Nkrumah in 1966 stayed in power until 1969, pursuing a set of economic policies, and indeed putting in place a 2-year development plan, that were never clear in their overall direction. While the government emphasized an anti-socialist ideology, its position on the state-owned enterprises was far less clear and the import of free market principles was never well established. While it denationalized some of the SOEs, it also set up new ones. It devalued the Cedi and discussed ways for renegotiating Ghana's growing debt and attracting private capital.

The two-and-half-year civilian administration that followed from 1969 to 1972 had an equally hard time trying to establish a direction for the economy. While its neo-liberal intentions were obvious, it never seemed to get to grips with tackling the daunting task in the wake of the Nkrumah government. Thus, while it continued with the divestiture of some SOEs, it failed to significantly reduce the size of government. Despite the dismissal of 568 public servants, public expenditures continued to rise. The attempt to pursue liberal economic reforms in the midst of mounting macroeconomic instability was its undoing. The liberal reforms were deemed harsh, particularly the devaluation of the Cedi, which provided a major pretext for the military to overthrow the Busia government in 1972.

Throughout the second military regime of 1972–9, economic policy-making could, at best, be described as an experiment in how to 'muddle through'. This was the period that was characterized by *kalabule,* a local expression for extortion and signifying 'the survival of the fittest' in an economic jungle. It has also been referred to as *kleptocracy* in the political science literature (Leith and Lofchie 1993). While the majority of Ghanaians were enduring dismal economic conditions, the relative affluence of the army caused demonstrations, and brutal repression became the order of the day. The gravity of the vicious circle or state of collapse in which Ghana found itself in the late 1970s and early 1980s was clearly apparent.

The situation therefore appeared to present itself for some shock political therapy, and that is what happened, beginning from 1979 when Flt Lt Jerry Rawlings overthrew the military government and summarily executed several of the current and previous leaders. Unfortunately, the political instability continued under the early Rawlings regimes in 1979 and 1981, interspersed with a brief period of civilian government that was marked by a rather passive economic programme.

In sum, Ghana has suffered severe bouts of political instability that can be closely associated with macroeconomic instability. The poor economic policies often resulted in political chaos that became self-perpetuating and drew inspiration from a number of sources to achieve a forced change of government. It would appear that, after the bold and yet wrong experiments of Nkrumah, other regimes failed to take the initiative and simply allowed the economy to drift.

*Reform.* The early reform years were difficult for the ruling group. Aside from innate opposition from ideologues, there were a number of attempted coups to replace Rawlings in October and November 1982 and June 1983. What these attempts did was to force Rawlings to purge the institutional structures for governing, making them weaker against his authority. As a result, those structures that had been intended to ensure accountability in the society became partially crippled. These included the People's and Workers' Defence Committees that had been created earlier to defend the 'revolution'.

While it is difficult to describe the coup attempts as having destabilized the government in any way, there is no doubt that they created a sense of urgency to find solutions to the myriad economic problems. Indeed, the response was to crush all possible sources of political instability. The fact that the coup attempts happened at all, however, helped to create a sense of vulnerability around the reform measures and led to questions about sustainability. While there were no significant policy reversals, there was always a question mark over how far the government could hold out against opposition (Aryeetey, 1994). There was also the question of whether the policies would change if there should be a change of government.

Under the current democratic dispensation there is a strong and growing perception that the political instability associated with coups is a thing of the past, thus giving fresh hope that radical changes to the liberal policies are unlikely in the near future.

## Corruption

To what extent did corruption contribute to the mismanagement that has characterized Ghana's economic history of the pre-reform era? And has this changed since the reform?

It was unsurprising that the hard-control regime spawned a great deal of corruption by providing rent-seeking opportunities. Indeed, the history of independent Ghana is replete with cases of corruption in all the regimes, both civilian and military. As economic incentives, these rent-seeking opportunities were likely to have contributed to the prevalence of elite political instability in Ghana, which in turn influenced economic policy-making. For example, the foreign-exchange controls led to overvaluation of the Cedi, while the accompanying quantity-rationing mechanisms provided the rent-seeking incentives that induced political instability.[13] Meanwhile, the fear of being replaced by another government would reduce the propensity of the sitting government to devalue the Cedi (Fosu, 1992).

Thus, a vicious circle is created, and corruption creates its own dynamics, becoming the most visible measure of failed policies. Since the public perception of corruption in high places is likely to lead to active support for change in the political leadership, it has always provided the immediate rationalization for forced changes in government. For every forced change of government, corruption has been listed as one of the major reasons (Collier, 2000).

---

[13] See Fosu (2003) for empirical evidence on SSA for the direct effect of real exchange-rate misalignment on political instability.

*Reform.* Has the corruption issue changed since the reforms? For a while in the 1980s, there was a general consensus among Ghanaians that corruption among policy-makers and senior government officials had diminished considerably. This was based on a perceived good example from the leadership in government. There were hardly any allegations in public about government officials demanding and taking bribes on government contracts. This was partly due to the harsh methods that the PNDC instituted, described by Gyimah-Boadi and Jeffries (2000: 41) as 'an anti-corruption drive which included vetting of lifestyles and investigation into sources of income and wealth — through newly created extra judicial bodies such the Public Tribunals, Citizens Vetting Committee and the National Investigations Committee'.

After the late 1980s, however, all that changed. Allegations at all levels of public life began to increase. A survey of 1500 households in August 2000 yielded the result that 75% saw corruption as a major problem in Ghana. And 82% believed that corruption was more prevalent than three years earlier (CDD, 2000). The study showed that many Ghanaians considered corruption to be widespread, and commonest in the Police Service and among Customs officials. Many regarded politicians also to be relatively corrupt. They suggested that corruption permeated the entire society.

It is difficult to link the relatively poor performance of the economy since 1992 directly to corruption. There is, however, evidence of politically corrupt behaviour leading to what may be described as political business cycles, surfacing with democratization in Ghana. This is quite similar to what Block (2002) identifies for many emerging African democracies. The corrupt behaviour has seen periodic attempts 'to buy votes' from the population with 'development projects' that lead to dramatic expansions of public expenditure and the fiscal deficit, the financing of which has always led to significant inflation and rapid depreciation of the Cedi — one general sense in which 'corrupt' policies hurt the economy.

At another level, the corruption of civil servants, customs officials and policemen enormously affects the transaction costs of doing business and pushes up prices of goods and services. In the CDD survey, about 66% of households earning more than a million Cedis (approximately $200) a month indicated that about 10% of their incomes were used to make unofficial payments to public officials.

## 4.  Conclusion

With independence there were great expectations that Ghana would experience significant growth to better its people. Unfortunately, as we have observed above, these expectations were never realized. The socialist mode of development adopted, accompanied by hard controls by the state, only produced major inefficiencies that hobbled growth and development. What became clear, sooner or later, was that a major reform was required if the country was to reverse its direction.

The economic reforms beginning in 1983 provided an opportunity for Ghana to change course. They have helped improve policies, which have helped generate substantial growth. As noted above, a good part of this growth was attributable to TFP improvements, suggesting that inefficiencies caused by at least two decades of controls were being attenuated. However, neither the growth rates nor the TFP improvements could be sustained. Apparently, more is required at the micro level to ensure that the appropriate institutional reforms are in place to enhance the proper functioning of markets and the responsiveness of the economic agents of firms and households, and to ameliorate the political environment in support of enduring improvements in economic performance.

Required measures include those that remove human capacity constraints in the labour market. While Ghana has historically been a leader in SSA in educating its people, it is also true that it has lost much of its investment through emigration. Just as important, technological investments have not been adequate, in great part because the private sector has not been the main source of investment, nor has public investment provided the requisite basic infrastructure. The absence of technological investments can in turn be linked to the weak credit market. It may also, to some degree, be associated with a land market characterized by uncertainties emanating from ambiguities.

As the first SSA country to have a smooth civilian-to-civilian transfer of government in 2000, Ghana has once again taken the lead, this time in setting the agenda for multi-party democracy. Concomitant with this important development is the maintenance of a relatively high level of political stability during the reform period, a break with the pre-reform past when the country had the dubious distinction of being a leader in the incidence of elite political instability. With appropriate support for the continued strengthening of institutions, it is hoped that this innovation will provide the requisite framework for faster growth and development in Ghana.

## References

Apter, D. (1975) *Ghana in Transition,* Princeton. NJ: Princeton University Press.

Aryeetey E. (1985) *Decentralizing Regional Planning in Ghana,* Dortmunder Beitraege zur Raumplanung 42, Dortmund.

Aryeetey E. (1989) 'Africa in Search for an Alternative Development Path', in *Planning African Growth and Development; Some Current Issues,* A Joint ISSER/UNDP Publication. Accra: ISSER.

Aryeetey, E. (1994) 'Private Investment Under Uncertainty in Ghana', *World Development,* Vol. 22, No. 8: 1211–21.

Aryeetey, E. (1996) *The Formal Financial Sector in Ghana after the Reforms,* Working Paper No. 86, London: Overseas Development Institute.

Aryeetey E. and Cox, A. (1997) 'Aid Effectiveness in Ghana' in J. Carlsson et al. (eds). *Foreign Aid in Africa.* Uppsala: Nordiska Afrikainstituet.

Aryeetey, E. and Harrigan, J. (2000) 'Macroeconomic and Sectoral Developments since 1970' in E. Aryeetey, J. Harrigan and M. Nissanke (eds), *Economic Reforms in Ghana, The Miracle and the Mirage.* Oxford: James Currey and Accra: Woeli Publishing Services.

Aryeetey, E., Harrigan, J. and Nissanke, M. (eds) (2000) *Economic Reforms in Ghana, The Miracle and the Mirage.* Oxford: James Currey and Accra: Woeli Publishing Services.

Aryeetey E, and Tarp, F. (2000) 'Structural Adjustment & After: Which Way Forward?' in Aryeetey et al., chapter 18.

Asante, Y, Nixson, F. and Tsikata, G. K. (2000) 'The Industrial Sector Policies and Economic Development', in Aryeetey et al.

Bank of Ghana (1980) *Annual Report.* Accra:Bank of Ghana.

Bates, Robert H. (1981) *Markets and States in Tropical Africa: The Political Basis of Agricultural Policies.* Berkeley, Los Angeles and London: University of California Press.

Benneh, G. (1971) 'Land Tenure and Sabala Farming System in the Anlo Area of Ghana: A Case Study,' *Research Review,* Vol. 7. Institute of African Studies, Legon.

Block, S. A. (2002), 'Political Business Cycles, Democratization and Economic Reform', *Journal of Development Economics,* Vol. 67: 205–28.

Boateng, K. and Fing, B. (2000) 'Labour and Employment under Structural Adjustment,' in Aryeetey et al.

Boateng, K. (1997) *Institutional Determinants of Labour Market Performance in Ghana.* Accra: Centre for Economic Policy Analysis, Research Paper, March.

Burnside C. and Dollar, D. (2000) Aid, *Policies and Growth.* Washington DC: World Bank, Policy Research Department.

Centre for Democratic Development (CDD-Ghana) (2000) *The Ghana Governance and Corruption Survey: Evidence from Households, Enterprises and Public Officials.* Commissioned by the World Bank and conducted by the Ghana Centre for Democratic Development, August.

CEPA (1996) *Macroeconomic Review and Outlook.* Accra: Center for Economic Policy Analysis.

Collier, P. (2000) 'How to Reduce Corruption', *African Development Review,* Vol. 12, No. 2: 191–205.

Collier, P., Hoeffler, P. and Patillo, C. (1999) *Flight Capital as a Portfolio Choice.* Policy Research Paper No. 2066. Washington, DC: World Bank.

Collins, S. and Bosworth, B. (1996) 'Economic Growth in East Asia: Accumulation versus Assimilation', *Brookings Papers on Economic Activity* 2: 135–203.

Easterly, W. (2001) 'The Lost Decades: Developing Countries' Stagnation in Spite of Policy Reform 1980–1998'. Washington, DC: World Bank (mimeo).

Ewusi, K. (1986) *The Dimension and Characteristics of Rural Poverty in Ghana.* Accra: ISSER Technical Publication.

Fosu, A. K. (1990) 'Export Composition and the Impact of Exports on Economic Growth of Developing Economies', *Economics Letters,* Vol. 34, No. 1: 67–71.

Fosu, A. K. (1991) 'Capital Instability and Economic Growth in Sub-Saharan Africa,' *Journal of Development Studies,* Vol. 28, No. 1: 74–85.

Fosu, A. K. (1992) 'Political Instability and Economic Growth: Evidence from Sub-Saharan Africa', *Economic Development and Cultural Change,* Vol. 40: 829–41.

Fosu, A. K. (1996) 'The Impact of External Debt on Economic Growth in Sub-Saharan Africa', *Journal of Economic Development,* Vol. 21, No. 1: 93–118.

Fosu, A. K. (1999). 'The External Debt Burden and Economic Growth in the 1980s: Evidence from Sub-Saharan Africa', *Canadian Journal of Development Studies*, Vol. 20, No. 2:307–18.

Fosu, A. K (2001) 'Economic Fluctuations and Growth in Sub-Saharan Africa: The Importance of Import Instability', *Journal of Development Studies*, Vol. 37, No. 3:71–84.

Fosu, A.K (2002a) 'The Global Setting and African Economic Growth', *Journal of African Economies*, Vol. 10, No. 3:282–310.

Fosu, A.K (2002b) 'Political Instability and Economic Growth: Implications of Coup Events in Sub-Saharan Africa', *American Journal of Economics and Sociology*, Vol. 61, No. 1:329–48.

Fosu, A. K. (2003) 'Political Instability and Export Performance in Sub-Saharan Africa', *Journal of Development Studies*, Vol. 39, No. 4:68–82.

Fosu, A. K, Nsouli, S. M. and Varoudakis, A. (2001) (eds), *Policies to Promote Competitiveness in Manufacturing in Sub-Saharan Africa*. Paris: OECD.

Fosu, A. K. and O'Connell, S. A. (2006) 'Explaining African Economic Growth: The Role of Anti-growth Syndromes', in Francois Bourguignon and Boris Pleskovic (eds), *Annual Bank Conference on Development Economics (ABCDE)*. Washington, DC: World Bank.

Frimpong-Ansah, J. (1991) *The Vampire State in Africa: The Political Economy of Decline*. Oxford: James Currey.

Ghura, D. and Greenes, T. J. (1993) 'The Real Exchange Rate and Macroeconomic Performance in Sub-Saharan Africa', *Journal of Development Economics*, Vol. 42: 155–74.

Gunning, J. and Mengistae, T. (2001) 'Determinants of African Manufacturing Investment: The Microeconomic Evidence,' *Journal of African Economies*, Supplement, Vol. 10: 47–79.

Gyimah-Boadi, E. and Jeffries, R. (2000) 'The Political Economy of Reform', in Aryeetey et al.

Herbst, J. (1991) 'Labor in Ghana under Structural Adjustment: The Politics of Acquiescence', in D. Rothchild (ed.), *The Political Economy of Recovery*. Boulder, CO: Lynne Rienner.

Hettige, H., Steel, W. F. and Wayen, J. A. (1991) 'The Impact of Adjustment Lending on Industry in African Countries'. Washington, DC: World Bank Industry and Energy Department (mimeo).

Hoeffler, A. (1999) *The Augmented Solow Model and the African Growth Debate*. Oxford: Centre for the Study of African Economies, Oxford University.

IMF (1987) *Theoretical Aspects of the Design of Fund-Supported Adjustment Programs*, Occasional Paper No. 55. Washington, DC: International Monetary Fund.

ISSER (1996) *State of the Ghanaian Economy Report 1995*, University of Ghana, Legon.

ISSER (1997) *State of the Ghanaian Economy Report 1996*. University of Ghana, Legon.

Khan, M. S. and Senhadji, A. S. (2003) 'Financial Development and Economic Growth: A Review and New Evidence', *Journal of African Economies*, supplement 2: 89–110.

Killick, T. (1978) *Development Economics in Action: A Study of Economic Policies in Ghana*. London: Heinemann Educational Books.

Killick, T. (2000) 'Fragile Still: The Structure of Ghana's Economy 1960–94', in Aryeetey et al.

Leechor, C. (1994) 'Ghana: Frontrunner in Adjustment', in Ishrat Husain and Rashid Faruque (eds), *Adjustment in Africa: Lessons from Case Studies*. Washington, DC: World Bank.

Leith, C. and Lofchie, M. (1993) 'The Political Economy of Structural Adjustment in Ghana', in R. H. Bates and A. O. Krueger (eds), *Political and Economic Interaction in Economic Policy Reform*. Oxford: Blackwell.

Levine, R and Renelt, D. (1992) 'A Sensitivity Analysis of Cross-Country Growth Regressions', *American Economic Review*, Vol. 82, No. 4.

McGowan, P. (2003) 'African Military Coups d'Etat, 1956–2001: Frequency, Trends and Distribution', *Journal of Modern African Studies*, April.

Mlambo, K. and Oshikoya, T. W. (2001) 'Macroeconomic factors and Investment in Africa', *Journal of African Economies*, Vol. 10, Supplement 2, Oxford.

Ndulu, B. J. and O'Connell, S. A. (2003) 'Revised Collins/Bosworth Growth Accounting Decompositions' (mimeo).

Nissanke, M., and Aryeetey, E. (1998) *Financial Integration and Development in Sub-Saharan Africa*. London and New York: Routledge.

Nixson, F. (1990) 'Industrialization and Structural Change in Developing Countries', *Journal of International Development*, Vol. 20, No. 3: 310–33.

Nyanteng, V. and Seini, A. W. (2000) 'Agricultural Policy and the Impact on Growth and Productivity 1970–95' in Aryeetey et al.

O'Connell, S. A. and Ndulu, B. (2000) 'Africa's Growth Experience: A Focus on the Sources of Growth'. Nairobi: AERC (mimeo).

Round, J. and Powell, M. (2000) 'Structure and Linkage in the Economy of Ghana: A SAM Approach' in Aryeetey et al.

Sowa, N. K. (1996) *Policy Consistency and Inflation in Ghana*. Research Paper 43. Nairobi: African Economic Research Consortium, March.

Steel, W. F. (1972) 'Import Substitution and Excess Capacity in Ghana', *Oxford Economic Papers*, Vol. 24: 212–40.

Steel, W. F. and Webster, L.M. (1991) *Small Enterprises in Ghana: Responses to Adjustment*. Industry Series Paper No. 33. Washington, DC: World Bank Industry and Energy Department.

Tabatabai, H. (1986) *Economic Decline, Access to Food and Structural Adjustment in Ghana*, Working Paper No. WEP 10-6/WP80. Geneva: ILO.

Teal, F. (1995) *Does 'Getting Prices Right' Work? Micro Evidence from Ghana*. WPS/95–19. Oxford: Centre for the Study of African Economies, Institute of Economics and Statistics, University of Oxford.

World Bank (2005) 'World Development Indicators', CD ROM. Washington, DC: World Bank.

World Bank (1987a) *Ghana: Policy Framework Paper*. Washington, DC: World Bank.

World Bank (1987b) *Ghana: Policies and Issues of Structural Adjustment*, Report No. 6635-GH, Washington, DC: World Bank.

World Bank (1985) *Ghana: Growth, Private Sector and Poverty Reduction*. Washington, DC: World Bank.

World Bank (1984) *World Development Report 1984*. New York: Oxford University Press for the World Bank.

# II Macroeconomy, Trade & Finance

# 4

## Persistent Public Sector Deficits & Macroeconomic Instability in Ghana*

CURTIS E. YOUNGBLOOD
& DAVID L. FRANKLIN

## 1. Introduction

Over the decade of the 1990s Ghana was considered an example among African countries regarding the pace and extent of the economic reforms affecting its trade regime, its financial sector, and the conduct of its fiscal and monetary policy (Kapur et al., 1991). This reputation was earned in the latter half of the 1980s when the government instituted a series of policy measures to rescue the economy from the depths of its most severe crisis in the post-colonial period. The Economic Recovery Programme (ERP) placed Ghana on a path of modest economic growth: from a per capita GDP of $309 in 1983,[1] per capita income grew at an average rate of 1.8% per year to $371 in 1993. Despite this early promise, Ghana's economic growth has continued to be moderate; per capita incomes grew at only 1.5% per year from 1993 through 2000 to reach $411. At this rate, per capita income will double in 50 years. This is a far cry from the ambitious growth rates envisioned in official growth plans such as Vision 2020, which was predicated on per capita growth rates of 5–7% per annum. Yet, it was perplexing to most observers that in March 2001 the recently elected government of the New Patriotic Party (NPP) sought relief under the Highly Indebted Poor Countries (HIPC) initiative, as it dealt with the aftermath of a severe currency crisis.[2]

Over the period of the late 1980s and 1990s, fiscal policy was characterized by persistently large ex-post primary deficits which were financed by domestic borrowing,

---

* This work was done while working for the United States Agency for International Development Mission to Ghana under the Trade and Investment Reform Program — Contract No. 641-C-00-98-00229. The opinions expressed herein are those of the authors and do not necessarily reflect the views of the US Agency for International Development. The authors gratefully acknowledge the comments on an earlier version of this paper from Clark Leith, Patrick Conway, and Martin Brownbridge, which resulted in substantial revisions.

[1] This contrasts with the high water mark for per capita GDP of $485 in 1971.

[2] Ghana sought relief under HIPC after the newly elected government discovered a fiscal gap of 6.9% of GDP ($367 million) for 2001, resulting from its obligations to service external debt.

external borrowing, and printing money. One consequence of financing these large deficits has been macroeconomic instability: high rates of high-powered money growth, inflation, exchange-rate depreciation, and high nominal interest rates (see Table 4.1).

**Table 4.1     Budget Deficits and Selected Indicators of Macroeconomic Instability**

|  | Broad budget deficit (% of GDP) | Base money growth (% per year) | Inflation (% per year) | Nominal interest rate (% per year) | Exchange-rate depreciation (% per year) |
|---|---|---|---|---|---|
| 1990 | −2.1 | 16.5 | 37.3 | 23.1 | 20.9 |
| 1991 | −1.4 | −4.0 | 18.0 | 31.5 | 12.7 |
| 1992 | −8.7 | 32.2 | 10.1 | 20.4 | 18.8 |
| 1993 | −7.4 | 44.4 | 25.0 | 33.5 | 48.5 |
| 1994 | −3.8 | 35.4 | 24.9 | 29.8 | 47.4 |
| 1995 | −4.0 | 53.1 | 59.5 | 38.8 | 25.5 |
| 1996 | −8.4 | 43.7 | 46.6 | 46.5 | 36.4 |
| 1997 | −10.1 | 41.9 | 26.0 | 47.9 | 25.2 |
| 1998 | −8.1 | 25.6 | 16.4 | 37.6 | 12.9 |
| 1999 | −5.1 | 28.5 | 12.4 | 28.2 | 14.4 |
| 2000 | −7.4 | 59.0 | 25.2 | 39.3 | 101.0 |
| Average | −6.1 | 34.2 | 27.4 | 34.2 | 33.1 |

*Sources:*  Broad budget deficits from IMF Staff *Country Report*: Statistical Annex, various years. Nominal interest rates on 91-day Treasury bills from Bank of Ghana, *Quarterly Economic Bulletin.* Other indicators computed from IMF, *International Financial Statistics* on CD-ROM and Bank of Ghana.

This chapter demonstrates that the fundamental source of this instability is the government's persistent spending in excess of revenues. Public sector expenditures averaged nearly 27% of GDP for the 1990–2000 period, whereas revenues from all sources averaged 20% of GDP. The result was a string of broad public sector deficits averaging 6% of GDP during the 1990–2000 period (see Table 4.1). This figure understates the true size of the public sector, because many public sector activities occur outside the purview of the central government, for example the operations of state-owned enterprises (SOEs) which are not explicitly funded in the government's budget. The Bank of Ghana (BoG) also engages in quasi-fiscal activities, notably transactions with the International Monetary Fund on behalf of the government and lending to SOEs.

These activities can be captured in a *consolidated* public sector budget framework, which nets out the claims of the central government on the central bank and vice versa, thereby revealing the liabilities of the consolidated public sector to the rest of the economy and the world. This framework also explicitly highlights the role of money creation as a financing source, along with domestic and external borrowing. In Section 2 we present the framework, apply it to Ghana, and calculate the financing burden of the consolidated public sector on the economy over the period 1987–2000. The resulting financing burden is shown to be almost 2 percentage points of GDP larger on average than the traditional measure of the public sector deficit.

In Section 3 we show how the use of the nominal exchange rate as a policy instrument to achieve multiple and inconsistent objectives *in the presence of unsustainably large deficits* laid the foundation for the speculative assault on the currency in 2000. In late 1997, with inflation running at 26% per year, the Bank of Ghana began using the exchange rate as the nominal anchor for the economy. While this did slow the rate of depreciation and inflation, the fiscal stance was inconsistent with the exchange-rate anchor policy. Broad budget deficits averaged 8% of GDP during 1996–9, whereas the government should have been running a much smaller primary deficit (before interest payments) to be consistent with the exchange-rate policy. The speculative assault, during which the exchange rate depreciated by 100% in 2000, was triggered by a downturn in the terms of trade.

We use a simple open economy rational expectations framework to assess not only the size of the primary deficit that would have been consistent with the nominal anchor policy but also to demonstrate that the speculative assault was predictable and could have been prevented, either by significantly tightening fiscal policy or by letting the exchange rate float. Section 4 concludes.

## 2.   Analytical Framework

Fiscal deficits are financed through domestic borrowing, external borrowing and money creation; each source of financing has a cost. Borrowing from financial markets requires servicing of the resulting debt at the prevailing real rate of interest. Financing through money creation generates inflation and its concomitant social costs. In addition, inflationary finance can lead to expectations of future inflation and a higher social burden to finance a current fiscal deficit. When deficits persist, monetary policy can be ineffective in reducing the rate of inflation. Sargent and Wallace (1986) show that if the real rate of interest exceeds the economy's real growth rate, the monetary authority faces an unpleasant choice: inflation now or inflation later. If the central bank chooses low inflation now as an objective, the deficits must be financed by issuing additional interest-bearing debt. This current borrowing at real rates of interest that exceed economic growth will ultimately require higher rates of money growth to finance the future deficits and the increasing debt-servicing requirements.

This occurs because eventually the real stock of interest-bearing debt either consumes all of the savings in the economy or reaches some threshold value representing the maximum holdings of debt that are willingly held by the private sector. At this point, the fiscal authority can raise taxes, reduce spending, or do both in order to generate surpluses and pay off the real stock of government debt.[3] Failing that, the monetary authority has no choice but to issue base money to finance the

---

[3] A balanced budget would not suffice since the real interest rate exceeds the rate of real economic growth; even rolling over an existing stock of debt would entail raising additional revenues merely to meet the real interest payments.

deficit. As Sargent and Wallace point out, the larger the value at which the real debt stock is stabilized, either the tighter subsequent fiscal policy has to be or the greater future monetary expansion (and inflation) has to be. If the monetary authority chooses to avoid this outcome by financing more of today's deficits by issuing high-powered money, then the consequence is high inflation today rather than in the future.[4]

Krugman (1992) shows what happens when the government runs persistent deficits and pegs the exchange rate. In his model, the deficit can be financed either by issuing high-powered money or by running down international reserves. He shows that a speculative attack on the currency, in which the private sector acquires all of the government's reserves by exchanging domestic currency for foreign currency, is not a matter of 'if' but of 'when'. The timing of the attack is determined by the initial stock of reserves: the bigger the stock of reserves with which the government can defend the exchange rate, the greater the delay in the timing of the speculative attack, but the greater the increase in the private sector's net wealth after it makes the attack. In other words, the depreciation of the currency will be greater the longer the attack is postponed by the central bank's intervention in the foreign-exchange market.

These two models capture salient features of how policy-makers in Ghana have managed fiscal, monetary and exchange-rate policy since 1987. These insights serve to illustrate that the ultimate failure of monetary policy to stabilize the Ghanaian economy was predictable. In our opinion, the currency crisis of 2000 could have been avoided had the Bank of Ghana not used the nominal exchange rate as an anchor during 1997–9, although the cost would have been continued macroeconomic instability.

To illustrate this point, we use an accounting framework for the public sector that incorporates the activities of any entity or institution that undertakes a fiscal activity, whether that institution is formally classified as part of the central government or not. This *consolidated* public sector framework includes the fiscal consequences of SOE operations that are not explicitly budgeted for, as well as the quasi-fiscal activities of the BoG.

The accounting framework consists of an equality constraint, with uses of funds (spending) on one side and sources of funds (financing) on the other. Because Ghana has experienced high and variable rates of inflation and nominal depreciation, nominal values of items in the budget obscure critical distinctions between the uses and sources of funds. Accordingly, all variables in the financing constraint are corrected for the effects of inflation and real exchange-rate changes. This properly accounts for the accelerated amortization of debt induced by inflation and the capital gains and losses caused by real exchange-rate changes as financing items rather than as expenditure items. Finally, each expenditure and financing item is expressed as a share of GDP, as follows:

$$\delta + (r-q)\,\beta + (r^*+\hat{e}-q)\,\phi = (q-\theta+\pi)\,\mu + \beta + (\beta^*-f^*)$$

---

[4] Actually, Sargent and Wallace show that, in a model in which the demand for base money depends on expected inflation, the monetary authority's choice of tighter money today means not only higher money growth rates and inflation in the future, but also higher inflation today.

The variables are defined in Box 4.1. A dot over a variable denotes the derivative with respect to time.

The equality is the consoli-dated public sector's budget constraint, and thus serves as a criterion for judging fiscal performance. This framework has been used primarily to judge the consistency of monetary and fiscal policy in meeting selected macroeconomic targets (Anand and van Wijnbergen, 1989; Catsambas and Pigato, 1989). Macroeconomic targets, such as a target inflation rate or a desired debt-to-output ratio, impose restrictions on the financing sources, as Anand and van Wijnbergen point out. The restrictions on financing in turn lead to a primary deficit that is consistent with the targets. If the actual deficit is greater than the one consistent with the targets, one or more of the macroeconomic targets cannot be met. Riesen (1989) uses the framework to trace the fiscal impact of a change in the real exchange rate and calculates the degree of fiscal discipline needed to sustain a significant real depreciation and to achieve a low rate of inflation. Amoako-Tuffour (1999) applied this framework to Ghana for the 1983–95 period and found that the consolidated public sector deficit exceeded the central government operational deficit on average by 1.2% of GDP.

---

**Box 4.1   Budget Constraint Variable Definitions**

$\delta$   real primary deficit (non-interest expenditures net of revenues from all sources)

r   real rate of interest on domestic debt

q   real GDP growth rate

$\beta$   real stock of domestic debt

r*   real rate of interest on external debt

$\hat{e}$   proportional deviation of the real exchange rate from purchasing power parity

$\varphi$   real stock of net external debt $= (\beta* - \int*)$

$\theta$   proportional change in the income velocity of base money

$\pi$   proportional change in the GDP deflator

$\mu$   real monetary base

$\beta*$ real stock of gross external debt

$\int*$ real stock of foreign assets held at the BoG

---

The key building blocks of the accounting framework are presented in Table 4.2. The first two columns are the growth-adjusted real domestic interest rate and the stock of domestic debt as a percentage of GDP. As the growth-adjusted real interest rate turned significantly positive from 1997 onwards, the real stock of domestic debt rose from 10 to 16% of GDP, an increase of more than 50%. This is one of the conditions in the Sargent and Wallace model that sets the stage for inflationary financing of the deficit, as the stock of domestic debt reaches unsustainable levels because real interest rates exceed the growth rate of the economy and the government does not run a primary surplus to offset this.

The last three columns relate to external debt servicing and debt levels. Gross debt levels as a percent of GDP ($\beta*$) are offset by the gross foreign assets held at the BoG ($\int*$). The net indebtedness of the consolidated public sector to the rest of the world is the difference between gross external debt and foreign assets held at the BoG (denoted as $\varphi$ in the equation). For much of the 1990s, net external indebtedness was relatively stable at around 70% of GDP. The speculative assault in 2000 boosted net external indebtedness to over 100% of GDP.

**Table 4.2   Debt Levels and Servicing Requirements**

|  | Growth-adjusted real interest rate<br>$r - q$<br>(%) | Real stock of domestic debt<br>$\beta$<br>(% of GDP) | Cost of servicing external debt<br>$r^* + \hat{e} - q$<br>(%) | Gross stock of external debt<br>$\beta^*$<br>(% of GDP) | Stock of foreign assets at BoG<br>$\int^*$<br>(% of GDP) |
|---|---|---|---|---|---|
| 1990 | −12.0 | 4.6 | −9.6 | 57.9 | 6.5 |
| 1991 | 6.4 | 4.6 | −2.7 | 61.3 | 8.4 |
| 1992 | 3.9 | 6.3 | 5.2 | 63.4 | 8.2 |
| 1993 | −4.6 | 7.6 | 9.0 | 76.1 | 6.4 |
| 1994 | −3.9 | 10.9 | 10.7 | 91.5 | 9.7 |
| 1995 | −13.6 | 10.2 | −15.7 | 80.1 | 10.0 |
| 1996 | −4.5 | 9.6 | −3.5 | 77.0 | 10.4 |
| 1997 | 13.5 | 11.3 | 2.1 | 81.4 | 8.5 |
| 1998 | 14.5 | 13.0 | −6.5 | 78.2 | 6.8 |
| 1999 | 7.1 | 15.9 | −1.6 | 75.1 | 6.0 |
| 2000 | 1.7 | 15.6 | 35.2 | 116.7 | 7.6 |

*Sources:* Interest payments from Budget Statements of the Government of Ghana, various years. Domestic and external debt stocks from Bank of Ghana's *Quarterly Economic Bulletin,* various years. Real exchange rates, US interest rates, and BoG foreign assets from IMF, *International Financial Statistics* on CD-ROM.

The external debt-servicing term in the third column captures the effects of international real interest rates,[5] real economic growth and real exchange-rate changes. Real interest rates were either zero or slightly negative throughout the 1990s. When real growth rates are netted out, the burden of external debt servicing is consistently negative throughout the period. That is, a given stock of external debt, and even increases in that stock, could be serviced without increasing the share of expenditures relative to the size of the economy.

In many years, this benefit of concessional lending by the international community was more than offset by a depreciating real exchange rate that resulted from exchange-rate and trade-policy reforms. Thus, the terms at which Ghana had to convert domestic resources into external claims in order to service its external debt increased by more than the difference between the real concessional interest rate and economic growth. However, a real appreciation of 10% in 1995 further reduced the negative growth-adjusted real interest rate, and the modest depreciation in the following year was not sufficient to make this interest-rate differential positive. Accordingly, in 1995 and 1996, external debt servicing shrank as a share of GDP. The same phenomenon occurred in 1998 and 1999 as exchange-rate movements were repressed as a consequence of the use of the exchange-rate as a nominal anchor for the economy.

These real exchange-rate effects are present in the external debt stocks as a share

---

[5] The implied nominal interest rate was computed by dividing annual external interest payments by the average stock of external debt for the year. The US CPI was used as the deflator.

of GDP, which rise with a real depreciation and fall with a real appreciation. Throughout the period, however, the trend in the gross external debt stock is increasing; it averaged 74% of GDP from 1990 to 1999. Offsetting these claims by the rest of the world on Ghana are the foreign assets at the BoG (last column of Table 4.2). These increase from 6.5% of GDP in 1990 to over 10% in 1996 and decline thereafter. It is likely that this build-up of foreign assets to more than 10% of GDP contributed to the decision to adopt the exchange-rate anchor in 1997.

### The Primary Deficit and Debt Servicing

The primary deficit, δ, is non-interest expenditures net of tax and non-tax revenues, including grants from international donors, as well as SOE divestiture receipts.[6] We calculated each item in the financing constraint separately and summed them to get total expenditures and total financing. For every year except 1996, total financing exceeded total spending. Other investigators have chosen to adjust different items in the constraint to impose equality. For example, Catsambas and Pigato (1989) calculated domestic borrowing as a residual. However, an important element of our paper is to estimate the primary balance of the consolidated public sector. Accordingly, we treat this as the residual, because the primary balance calculated from the Government of Ghana's budget statements does not reflect the net spending of the large SOE sector. We therefore used the estimate of total financing as the true size of the operational deficit (the primary deficit plus all interest expenditures). This reflects the notion that net positive financing is observed when there is excess spending, whether or not this is captured in the official budget statistics. We then calculated the broad primary deficit by subtracting domestic and international interest payments from total financing (Table 4.3).

The average of the operational deficits during 1990-2000 is 7.9% of GDP, or 1.8 percentage points larger than the average conventional broad deficit (see Table 4.1). There were very large primary deficits in 1993 and 1994, followed by a more restrained fiscal stance in 1995 and 1996. However, significant primary deficits reappeared during the 1997–2000 period and provided one of the building blocks for the speculative assault.

Domestic interest payments did not add to the financing burden on the economy until the late 1990s. From 1997 onwards, they became more sizeable as a result of highly positive real interest rates on government securities and the build-up in the stock of domestic debt, as discussed above.

External interest payments exhibited much more volatility over this period. This volatility arose almost entirely from the behavior of the real exchange rate. During

---

[6] This concept of the primary deficit differs significantly from the *domestic* primary deficit reported by the Government of Ghana in its budget statements and reproduced in IMF publications. The domestic primary deficit excludes both grants and divestiture receipts from revenues, and foreign capital expenditures and arrears clearance from expenditures. Since the excluded expenditure items are usually much larger than the excluded revenue items, the domestic primary balance often shows a surplus, whereas the consolidated primary balance we calculate shows either a deficit or a much smaller surplus. The consolidated primary balance is a more complete measure of the financing burden that the economy must support.

periods of depreciation such as occurred between 1992 and 1994, interest payments claimed between 3% and 9% of GDP. During periods of real appreciation, the burden of servicing the external debt shrank. This illustrates a trade-off between external debt servicing and the need to maintain a competitive real exchange rate to support export-led growth. Ghana's net external indebtedness has been large, averaging 70% of GDP from 1990 to 2000. For given real international interest rates and GDP growth, a real depreciation will increase the burden of servicing the external debt and this burden will have to be financed. One way to finance it is to borrow more to service the debt, which is what Ghana did in 1993 and 1994. But this adds to the stock of external debt that will have to be serviced in the future. Another way is to tighten fiscal policy and run a primary surplus that would support a real depreciation, i.e., to make the adjustment on the expenditure rather than the financing side. This is the point of Riesen (1989).

**Table 4.3**   **Expenditures and Financing of the Consolidated Public Sector (% of GDP)**

| | Expenditure Categories | | | Financing Items | | | |
|---|---|---|---|---|---|---|---|
| | Primary deficit payments | Domestic interest payments | External interest | Money creation | Domestic borrowing | Gross external borrowing | Change in BoG foreign assets |
| | (1) | (2) | (3) | (4) | (5) | (6) | (7) |
| 1990 | 0.9 | −0.4 | −0.7 | 0.5 | 0.2 | | |
| 1991 | 2.7 | 0.3 | −1.4 | −0.2 | 0.2 | 3.4 | 1.8 |
| 1992 | 2.3 | 0.2 | 2.9 | 1.3 | 1.7 | 2.1 | −0.2 |
| 1993 | 11.6 | −0.3 | 6.3 | 1.8 | 1.3 | 12.7 | −1.8 |
| 1994 | 8.6 | −0.4 | 8.7 | 1.5 | 3.3 | 15.4 | 3.3 |
| 1995 | 2.0 | −1.4 | −11.0 | 2.1 | −0.7 | −11.4 | 0.3 |
| 1996 | 0.4 | −0.4 | −2.3 | 1.8 | −0.6 | −3.0 | 0.4 |
| 1997 | 6.9 | 1.5 | 1.5 | 2.0 | 1.7 | 4.3 | −2.0 |
| 1998 | 4.4 | 1.9 | −4.6 | 1.4 | 1.7 | −3.1 | −1.6 |
| 1999 | 2.5 | 1.1 | −1.1 | 1.6 | 2.9 | −3.1 | −0.9 |
| 2000 | 4.7 | 0.3 | 38.9 | 3.3 | −0.3 | 41.6 | 1.6 |

*Notes:*   (col. 1) Calculated as total financing (columns 4 + 5 + 6 − 7) less domestic and external interest payments (columns 2 + 3). A positive sign implies a deficit; a negative sign implies a surplus. (Col. 7) Positive sign = increase in foreign assets and consequent decrease in net external borrowing.

*Sources:*   Interest payments from Budget Statements of the Government of Ghana, various years. Domestic and external debt stocks from Bank of Ghana's *Quarterly Economic Bulletin*, various years. Real exchange rates, US interest rates, and BoG foreign assets from IMF, *International Financial Statistics* on CD-ROM.

## *Financing the Consolidated Public Sector: Money Creation*

The financing alternatives available to the consolidated public sector are money creation, domestic borrowing and international borrowing. The tax base for money creation is the real monetary base as a share of GDP, $\mu$. The public sector captures revenues by taxing this base through inflation, p. As inflation induces flight from the domestic currency, the yield of the inflation tax will be lower. The public sector also captures seignorage revenues, $(q - q)m$, that are generated as the net demand for base money rises with increases in real GDP. From 1991 to 1999, inflationary finance through money creation averaged 1.5% of GDP per year, well below its average of nearly 5% of GDP annually during the period 1972–8. During this time, however, the monetary base accounted for 15% of GDP on average. For 1991–9, the monetary base had been eroded to 6% of GDP because of the persistent use of this source of financing. This much smaller tax base made this financing option more unstable — a given injection of base money has greater inflationary consequences than if the real base were much larger — and perhaps explains why the authorities have relied on domestic and external borrowing as financing alternatives in more recent times. In 2000, in line with the predictions of the Sargent and Wallace and Krugman models, the government was forced to monetize the deficit; base money increased nearly 60% that year, more than double the growth rates of the preceding two years, and as a consequence money creation to finance the deficit more than doubled to 3.3% of GDP.

### *Financing the Consolidated Public Sector: Domestic Borrowing*
Domestic borrowing is measured as the change in the real stock of domestic debt instruments held by the private sector, $\beta$. The main instruments issued by the government were Treasury securities with maturities of 91 days, 182 days, 1 year and 2 years.[7] In the early 1990s, the share of short-term (ST) instruments (91- and 182-day Treasury bills) fell sharply from 80 to 40% as significant reductions in the rate of inflation occurred (Fig. 4.1). As inflation began increasing in 1993 and accelerated to

**Figure 4.1:  Share of ST Instruments and the Inflation Rate**

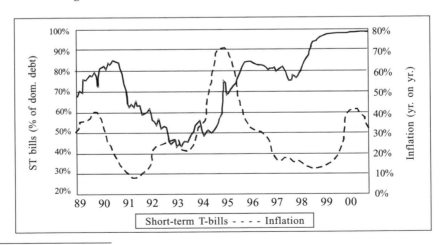

[7] Interest rates on 2-year bonds were not reported after October 1998. Bank of Ghana data show a sharp drop in the outstanding value of these instruments between August and October 2000, indicating that they were no longer issued, or were issued only in very small amounts from October 1998 onward.

70% per year in 1995, the share of ST instruments climbed to more than 80%.

This relationship changed in 1996 and 1997 as inflation declined; the share of ST instruments remained stable at around 80%. More surprisingly, as inflation continued to fall during 1998 and the first half of 1999, the share began to rise, eventually reaching 98% of the total. This shift occurred well before the severe exchange-rate depreciation in the last quarter of 1999, which led to a resurgence in inflation in 2000.

What precipitated the rapid switch to holding only ST financial instruments? To answer this question we looked at the real returns to following two alternative investment strategies, a short-term strategy of holding 91-day T-bills and a 'long-term' strategy of holding 1-year Treasury notes.[8] The returns to the long-term investing strategy are persistently and significantly below the returns to the short-term strategy. Also, the returns to the long-term strategy were negative from August 1999 through August 2000. Short-term instruments yielded on average 11 percentage points more in real terms than the 1-year instrument from 1997 through the first half of 2001. The share of ST instruments did not fall as inflation declined during the latter part of the 1990s because the expected returns to the short-term strategy were simply too lucrative.

The resulting concentration of domestic debt at very short maturities increased the financing costs of the public sector. This occurred not only because of high interest rates, but also because the existing stock of debt had to be rolled over at increasingly higher interest rates. This is the condition in Sargent and Wallace (1986) that will ultimately lead to monetization of the deficit, unless the government tightens fiscal policy.

### *Financing the Consolidated Public Sector: External Borrowing*
External borrowing by the consolidated public sector is measured as the change in the real stock of external debt[9] as a share of GDP, $\beta*$, less the change in the foreign assets held by the BoG, $\int *$.[10] Ghana was a 'darling of the donors' throughout the late 1980s and the first part of the 1990s. As a result, external debt rose from $2.1 billion in 1985 to $5.8 billion in 2000. But, as discussed above, significant changes in Ghana's debt burden arose through a price effect caused by real exchange-rate changes. The speculative attack of 2000 raised the stock of debt relative to GDP from 70% to 110%.

## 3.    The 1999/2000 Speculative Assault
The decision in late 1997 to adopt the exchange rate as the nominal anchor for the economy came after the Inflation Management Round Table in May 1996 which was led by the late Michael Bruno. Bruno (1989, 1991) had helped design a similar strategy to reduce inflation in Israel.[11] The Bank of Ghana would intervene in the foreign-

---

[8] The material in this section is taken from Youngblood et al. (2002).

[9] The stocks of short-, medium-, and long-term debt held or guaranteed by the public sector, including borrowings from the IMF.

[10] Hence, this measure will differ from the commonly reported external debt statistics for Ghana by the amount of foreign assets held by the BoG.

[11] One reviewer of an earlier draft of this paper expressed doubts that Bruno would have supported the use of an exchange-rate anchor without a tightening of fiscal policy to support the anchor.

exchange market to repress depreciation to meet multiple policy objectives. One objective was to lower the current period's cost of servicing the external debt in order to reduce pressure on the budget. Also, lower rates of depreciation would translate into smaller increases in the prices of tradable goods in the consumer price index, thereby reducing the inflation rate, and would signal to external and domestic agents that the monetary authority was achieving its strategy for stabilizing the Ghanaian economy.

There were some immediate benefits. The nominal rate of depreciation slowed dramatically (during 1998 it depreciated by only 3%), and the inflation rate was halved, falling from 33% in 1996 to 16% in 1997.[12] Inflation remained relatively stable at about 15% per year during 1998 and 1999.

However, real interest rates became highly positive once again, as discussed earlier. They averaged 15% per year, while the real economy grew at 4.5% per year. Combined with a low rate of nominal depreciation, this created powerful incentives for wealth to be held in domestic interest-bearing assets. Government 91-day Treasury bills yielded an average premium of nearly 12% per year over US T-bills, as shown by the deviations from interest-rate parity (Fig. 4.2).[13] As a result, domestic debt swelled from 10% of GDP in 1996 to 16% in 1999. This persistent subsidization of domestic debt-holders

**Figure 4.2: Deviations from Interest Rate Parity, 1987–2000**

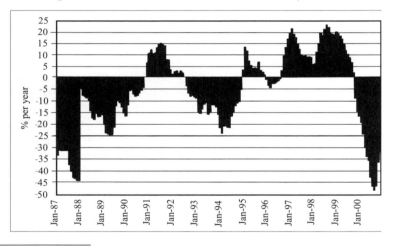

(11 cont.) This is undoubtedly true. Our belief is that policy-makers 'cherry picked' from among their set of options. The authorities opted for an exchange-rate anchor because it was easy to do and, thinking only of the very short run, perceived an immediate pay-off in the form of lower inflation without having to make painful and difficult choices about reducing government expenditures.
[12] Rates measured on a year-to-year basis using December values of the exchange rate and CPI.
[13] Interest-rate parity equilibrates nominal interest rates between two countries, adjusted for exchange-rate movements, when there is perfect capital mobility and the two assets on which interest is paid are perfect substitutes. It is given by $[(i - \rho)/(1 + \rho)] = i'$, where $i$ and $i'$ are domestic and international nominal interest rates and $\rho$ is the expected depreciation in the nominal exchange rate.

was unsustainable because of its dependence on the continued availability of foreign exchange which the BoG needed to repress the depreciation of the currency. As the government serviced its domestic debt at real interest rates well above the economy's growth rate, the BoG ran down its stock of scarce foreign-exchange reserves to maintain the nominal anchor, from over 10% of GDP in 1996 to 6% in 1999 (Table 4.2).

In addition to the foregoing conditions, considerable uncertainty was generated by the upcoming election in 2000. The previous two election cycles (1992 and 1996) had been marked by large fiscal excesses that produced bouts of inflation and exchange-rate depreciation. There was a sharp increase in 2000 in expenditures on public sector salaries, payment of arrears, and development projects. The elements of a speculative attack on the currency were now in place, and needed only a catalyst to start the reaction. This was provided by a sharp downturn in the terms of trade, which declined by 65% from 1999:Q1 through 2000:Q2, as a result of decreases in the price of cocoa and gold and an increase in the price of petroleum (Fig. 4.3). With an important source of the BoG's supply of foreign exchange threatened, individuals and institutions recognized the unsustainability of the situation and switched out of domestic assets into the safe haven offered by dollars. The cedi depreciated sharply. From June 1999 to the end of 2000, the cedi depreciated in nominal terms by 174% and in real terms by 106% (Fig. 4.3).[14]

**Figure 4.3:  Terms of Trade and Real Exchange Rate (1995=1.0)**

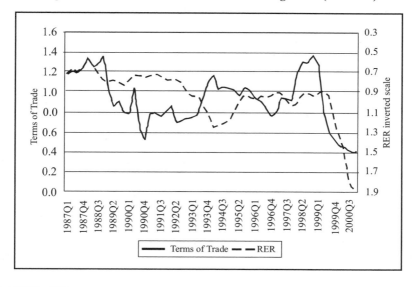

---

[14] Ghana had suffered a similar decline in its terms of trade in the past, without precipitating a speculative assault. For example, from 1988Q4–1990Q4, the terms of trade declined by 61%, while the real exchange rate was essentially unchanged. Thus, it was not only the decline in the terms of trade that caused the speculative assault, as an IMF representative who read an earlier draft of this paper maintained.

## Speculative Attack or Severe Depreciation?

What distinguishes this event, aside from the size of the depreciation, from the sharp depreciations of the currency (nearly 50% per year) that occurred in 1993 and 1994? In other words, what makes the 2000 event a speculative assault and the earlier episodes 'merely' large drops in the value of the currency? To answer this question we construct an index of exchange-market pressure (Eichengreen et al., 1997, and Kaminsky et al., 1998).

Pressure in the exchange market may be manifested as a tendency for the exchange rate to appreciate or depreciate. But the monetary authorities may choose to resist an incipient depreciation by selling foreign exchange and running down reserves. As Eichengreen et al. (1997) point out, interest-rate policy can also be used as a countervailing measure against pressure on the exchange rate to fall. The index of exchange-market pressure combines movements in the nominal exchange rate, gross international reserves (less gold) at the Bank of Ghana, and interest rates on 3-month Treasury bills:

$$EMP_t = \frac{1}{\sigma_E^2} \Delta\%E_t - \frac{1}{\sigma_R^2} \Delta\%R_t + \frac{1}{\sigma_i^2} i_t$$

where $EMP_t$ = value of the exchange-market pressure index at time t, $\Delta\%E_t$ = 12-month percentage change in the nominal exchange rate at time t, $\Delta\%R_t$ = 12-month percentage change in international reserves, $i_t$ = annualized interest rate on 91-day Treasury bills issued by the government of Ghana, and $\sigma_j^2$ = the variances of the respective series.

Weighting the components in this way offsets the differences in volatility of the component series and makes the conditional variance of the index with respect to each series equal. We use monthly data from January 1987 to August 2002.

The resulting values of the index (Fig. 4.4) serve as a useful summary measure for conditions in the exchange market, much as the inflation rate is a useful measure of excess demand conditions in the goods market. We can use extreme positive values of the index to define a crisis in the market for foreign exchange. We define our extreme values as those falling more than 2 standard deviations above the mean of the EMP index.[15]

Based on this definition, we find a currency crisis of 10 months duration, beginning in July 2000 and ending in May 2001.[16] The crisis was the culmination of a sharp rise in the EMP which began in late 1999. After the crisis, the newly elected government of Ghana chose to apply for Highly Indebted Poor Country (HIPC) relief because of unsustainably high debt-servicing costs. The unsustainability was manifested in

---

[15] Kaminsky et al. (1998) apply a stricter criterion of 3 standard deviations, while Eichengreen et al. (1997) use a looser standard of 1.5 standard deviations.
[16] Despite two dips of the index below the threshold during this period, we treated the entire period as a single crisis.

inadequate levels of foreign-exchange reserves and the significantly higher cost of acquiring more as a result of the sharp depreciation of the cedi. The attack also boosted the inflation rate to 41% at the end of 2000 through its effect on the prices of tradable goods in the CPI. To stem the attack, the authorities raised the nominal interest rate 20 percentage points, from 26% to 46%, in an attempt to make domestic assets more attractive.

**Figure 4.4:    Exchange-Market Pressure and the Crisis Threshold**

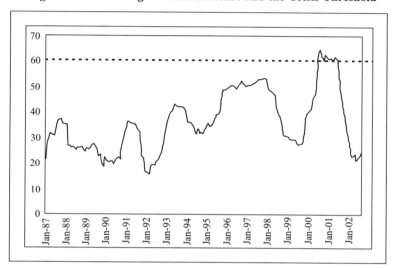

## *A Consistent Fiscal Policy*

In order for fiscal policy to be consistent with the nominal exchange-rate anchor, the government should have been running a very restrained fiscal policy. The amount of restraint can be calculated by using the public sector budget constraint and making some assumptions about the values of some key variables. We use the budget constraint to estimate the size of the primary deficit that would be consistent with *no increase in debt*, since it was the sharp increase in the debt-to-GDP ratio that contributed to Ghana's eligibility for HIPC relief. Thus, no financing is raised by issuing domestic or external debt — the last 2 terms on the right-hand side of the budget equation are zero. After making assumptions about the other variables in the budget constraint, we calculate the amounts required to service the domestic and external debt (the last 2 terms on the left-hand side of the budget constraint) and the revenues that can be raised by money creation. The primary deficit consistent with the nominal anchor policy is then solved by adding the debt-servicing payments (with a change of sign) to the revenues from money creation.

The assumed values of the variables, and the consequent values of the remaining items in the budget equation, are presented in Table 4.4. Real GDP growth and the change in the income velocity of base money are set at their average values for 1997–

9. Domestic debt to GDP, net external debt to GDP, and base money to GDP are set at their 1996 values and are assumed to remain constant. We use a real domestic interest rate of 5%, about half of the average value of 10% over the 1997–9 period. Since the government in this scenario is not having to place as much debt as it did in reality, it seems reasonable to assume that real interest rates would be lower. Another key assumption is that inflation, measured as the percentage change in the GDP deflator, would be 13% per year, which was about the rate observed in 1999. This lower inflation rate means that less revenues are generated from money creation; this implies that the primary deficit would have to be smaller to support the lower inflation rate and the exchange-rate anchor.

**Table 4.4    Elements of a Fiscal Policy Consistent with the Exchange-Rate Anchor**

| | |
|---|---:|
| **Domestic debt servicing** | |
| Real domestic interest rate (%) | 5.0 |
| Real GDP growth (% per year) | 4.4 |
| Domestic debt (% of GDP) | 9.6 |
| Interest payments on domestic debt (% of GDP) | 0.1 |
| **External debt servicing** | |
| Real foreign interest rate (%) | 0.0 |
| Change in real exchange rate (%) | 2.3 |
| External debt (% of GDP) | 66.6 |
| Interest payments on external debt (% of GDP) | −1.4 |
| **Revenue from money creation** | |
| Inflation (% change in GDP deflator) | 13.0 |
| Change in income velocity of base money (%) | 1.6 |
| Monetary base (% of GDP) | 6.0 |
| Money creation (% of GDP per year) | 1.0 |
| **Consistent primary deficit (% of GDP)** | 2.3 |
| **Actual primary deficit (% of GDP)** | 4.6 |

The primary deficit that would have been consistent with the exchange-rate policy was 2.3% of GDP, half the size of the actual deficit. This large divergence between what was needed and what occurred on the fiscal front was the fundamental reason that the exchange-rate policy failed, culminating in the speculative assault on the currency.

## 5.    Conclusion

Throughout the 1990s, Ghana's monetary, exchange-rate and fiscal policies were inconsistent with each other. The fundamental problem was the failure of the government to rein in spending and bring deficits down to levels that could be comfortably financed. Instead, the government continuously ran large deficits that have had to be financed by printing money, borrowing domestically and borrowing externally. Excessive reliance on the first two sources resulted in bouts of inflation, exchange-rate depreciation, and high nominal and real interest rates.

The inconsistency between monetary and fiscal policies reached its zenith in 1997 with the decision to adopt the exchange rate as the nominal anchor, without the fiscal restraint needed to support such a policy. The result was a speculative assault and a real depreciation of such a magnitude that Ghana was forced to seek relief under the HIPC programme. Policy-makers in Ghana should have seen the risks that were increasing the likelihood of a speculative assault. The Chilean crisis of 1981 was well documented in the economics literature (Edwards, 1996). The Mexican crisis of 1994 was also well understood by 1997 (Edwards, 1996; 1997; Sachs et al., 1995), and the Asian currency crisis of 1998 was well under way. Ghana exhibited many of the risk factors that were present in these crises: a weak financial system overexposed to foreign liabilities; constraints on the central bank's ability to respond to shocks and defend its policies; and a monetary policy that was inconsistent with the fiscal realities. The monetary and exchange-rate policies of the BoG had created large and persistent deviations from interest-rate parity that resulted in abnormally high returns to holders of domestic T-bills. These returns were so high that they could not possibly be expected to last. The authorities were aware of these risk factors and of the experiences of other countries that had suffered currency crises, but chose to do nothing to mitigate them. Ultimately, market forces, especially in the foreign-exchange market, made the adjustments.

## References

Amoako-Tuffour, J. (1999) 'Ghana Government Fiscal Deficits: How Small or How Large?', *Journal of African Economies*, Vol. 8: 1–30.

Anand, R. and van Wijnbergen, S. (1989) 'Inflation and the Financing of Government Expenditures: Introductory Analysis with an Application to Turkey.' *The World Bank Economic Review*, Vol. 3, January: 17–38.

Bawumia, M. (2000) *Monetary Growth, Exchange Rates and Inflation in Ghana.* Accra: Research Department, Bank of Ghana.

Bruno, M. (1989) 'Econometrics and the Design of Economic Reform.' *Econometrica*, Vol. 57, No. 2: 275–306.

Bruno, M. (1991) *High Inflation and the Nominal Anchors of an Open Economy.* Essays in International Finance No. 183. Princeton, NJ: Princeton University Press.

Catsambas, T. and Pigato, M. (1989) *The Consistency of Government Deficits with Macroeconomic Adjustment: An Application to Kenya and Ghana.* Policy, Planning, and Research Working Paper 287. Washington DC: World Bank, Africa Technical Department, October.

Edwards, S. (1996) *A Tale of Two Crises: Chile and Mexico.* Working Paper 5794. Cambridge, MA: National Bureau of Economic Research, October.

Edwards, S. (1997) *The Mexican Peso Crisis: How Much Did We Know? When Did We Know It?* Working Paper 6334. Cambridge, MA: National Bureau of Economic Research, December.

Eichengreen, B., Rose, A. and Wyplosz, C. (1997) *Contagious Currency Crises.* London: Centre for Economic Policy Research, March.

Fischer, S. and Easterly, W. (1990) 'The Economics of the Government Budget Constraint.' *World Bank Research Observer*, Vol. 5, No. 2: 127–142.

Gockel, A. F. (2000) 'The Bank of Ghana's Role in Providing Liquidity to the Financial Markets Versus Using the Nominal Exchange Rate as an Anchor for the Price Level.' Background paper prepared for Bank of Ghana and funded by Sigma One Corporation. Legon: University of Ghana.

Kaminsky, G., Lizondo, S. and Reinhart, C. M. (1998) 'Leading Indicators of Currency Crises.' *IMF Staff Papers*, Vol. 45, No. 1: 1–48.

Kapur, I., Hadjimichael, M. T., Hilbers, P., Schiff, J. and Szymczak, P. (1991) *Ghana: Adjustment and Growth, 1983–91.* Occasional Paper No. 86. Washington, DC: International Monetary Fund.

Krugman, P. R. (1992) 'A Model of Balance-of-Payments Crises.' in Paul R. Krugman. *Currencies and Crises,* Chapter 4. Cambridge, MA: MIT Press.

Research Department, Bank of Ghana (1996) 'Inflation Management by Bank of Ghana: The Strategies, the Difficulties and the Way Forward.' Paper presented at the Inflation Management Round Table, Akosombo, 20–21 May.

Riesen, H. (1989) *Public Debt, External Competitiveness, and Fiscal Discipline in Developing Countries.* Princeton Studies in International Finance No. 66. Princeton, NJ: Princeton University Press.

Sachs, J., Tornell, A. and Velasco, A. (1995) *The Collapse of the Mexican Peso: What Have We Learned?* Working Paper No. 5142. Cambridge, MA: National Bureau of Economic Research, June.

Sargent, T. J. and Wallace, N. (1986) 'Some Unpleasant Monetarist Arithmetic,' in Thomas J. Sargent (ed.), *Rational Expectations and Inflation,* Chapter 5. New York: Harper & Row.

Youngblood, C. E., Dordunoo, C. K., Larrain, F., Younger, S. D. and Greenes, T. J. (1992) 'Ghana: Macroeconomic Environment for Export Promotion.' Paper prepared for USAID/Ghana, Contract No. CO-641-0000-C-00-1026. Research Triangle Park, NC: Sigma One Corporation.

Youngblood, C. E. (2000) 'Instruments of Monetary Policy in Ghana.' Paper prepared for USAID/Ghana, November.

Youngblood, C. E., Gockel, A. F. and Bawumia, M. (2002) 'The Government Bond Market: Fiscal and Monetary Policy Linkages.' Paper presented at the National Workshop on Debt Markets for the Golden Age of Business, July.

# 5

## Effects of Exchange-Rate Volatility & Changes in Macroeconomic Fundamentals on Economic Growth in Ghana

STEPHEN KYEREME

## 1. Introduction

This study explores the determinants of per person real output growth, exchange-rate volatility, and price inflation — and their interactions and implications for economic development — as well as the roles of money and interest rates in price and output determination in Ghana. The interrelated problems of inflation, exchange-rate instabilities and unstable output (or economic) growth afflict many countries. In the less developed countries (LDCs), high inflation is induced in part by excessive money-supply growth often resulting from easy fiscal policy, with uncertain effects on real output growth. Inflation is a problem because, *ceteris paribus,* it lowers real incomes, discourages savings, makes productive inputs more expensive — and may act as a disincentive to hard work, thereby leading to sub-optimal per person real output growth (or economic development).

Unstable exchange rates disrupt international trade and investment (on which many LDCs depend for essential capital inputs and consumer goods) because agents are uncertain about the specific exchange rates to use for transactions (Hodrick, 1989: 433–459). LDCs with overvalued fixed exchange rates (and thriving black markets) may use periodic devaluations to realign their currencies, contributing in part to unstable output growth. Other LDCs (e.g., Ghana, Nigeria) which have shifted to flexible exchange-rate regimes experience asymmetric exchange-rate volatility (reflected by continuous currency weakness). Hence, exchange-rate policy would be expected to influence a developing country's trade balance, net capital inflows, prices and output growth.

Ghana's economy depends on key imports — capital inputs and essential consumer goods. In 1995, for example, imports made up 32.81% of Ghana's GDP, and exports 24.5% (IMF, 2000). Capital (physical and human) scarcities constrain the production of high valued-added goods, hence these goods are imported with scarce foreign exchange. In 1995, for instance, private gross fixed capital formation made up 21% of Ghana's GDP. Currency depreciation, *ceteris paribus*, may increase net exports, thereby increasing the supply of foreign exchange. It may also be argued that by replacing a fixed exchange-rate regime (and black currency markets) with a flexible regime which permits private 'forex' bureaux to buy and sell foreign exchange at market equilibrium prices, the supply of foreign exchange (by Ghanaians living abroad and foreign investors) would be expected to expand to meet rising demand, thereby increasing net capital inflows (Johnson, 1987) and boosting Ghana's economic growth. However, via insights from endogenous growth theory, the above-average rates of return on foreign investment possible from a LDC like Ghana with a low capital-labour ratio may not attract the desired level of such investment because of sub-optimal levels of complementary investments in infrastructure, human capital and research and development (Lucas, 1990). Further, sub-optimal incentive and institutional structures may hamper investments and hence real output growth. Asymmetric cedi volatility,[1] high inflation and high interest rates have existed in an environment of (on average) easy fiscal and monetary policies in Ghana. Hence, overall, a correct macroeconomic policy environment is crucial in fostering optimal per person real output growth in Ghana.[2] This justifies the macro variables used in this study. Analysis of the above issues (particularly the determinants of inflation, the exchange rate and output growth, and how these variables interact) to help formulate effective macroeconomic and development policies in Ghana justify this study.

In sum, country-specific studies which forecast systems of the time series variables described above and analyze the dynamic effects of random shocks and controls on the systems can provide useful information with which to formulate appropriate policies to deal with the above problems. This should improve average economic welfare, which is a function of average real output growth. Using time series data[3] on Ghana and vector autoregression models, the main objectives of this study are to: (i) study the factors that determine inflation, exchange-rate variation, and economic growth through time to help forecast and monitor these variables for effective policy formulation; (ii) examine the nature of dynamic interrelationships that exist among the growth rates of the variables, to include the effects of money and interest rates in price and output determination; (iii) discuss alternative policies and their implications for price stability, currency stability, and economic growth. Furthermore, the cointegration technique is used to test for the existence of long-run relationships between pairs of the above macroeconomic variables of interest.

The next section discusses the vector autoregression models used, followed by a discussion of the empirical results and policy implications, and conclusions.

---

[1] Periods of socialist-leaning regimes (with fixed exchange rates and black markets) include: 1961–6; 1972–7; 1979–82. Periods of free-market regimes include 1967–71 and 1983–5 (fixed exchange rates and black markets); and 1986-date (freely floating exchange rates). Hence, if the economic and political weights are directly proportional to the observations, then a weight of about 68% may be assigned to the fixed exchange-rate period.

[2] The World Bank's (1993) East Asian Miracle Report found that macro stability was a clear source of the East Asian region's success. Hence, improved macroeconomic policies can help boost Ghana's economic development, justifying this study's focus on macroeconomic variables.

[3] Time series data (1960–95 and 1970–2000) from IMF, *International Financial Statistics and Yearbook* (various issues).

## 2. Vector Autoregression (VAR) Models

A VAR is a system of equations in which each endogenous variable is a linear function of its past values, past values of other endogenous variables in the system, exogenous variables that help determine the endogenous variables, and other non-random parts like constant terms or polynomial functions of time (Todd, 1990: 1). Even though VARs, over the past decade, have become popular among economists as forecasting tools, their use to test economic theories is controversial because empirical results are not necessarily stable or robust (ibid.).

Instability implies that VAR statistics may be sensitive to arbitrary modifications[4] in the VAR's random and non-random parts. Hence, checking for possible instability is desirable, even though it is not easy or cheap to do so using current techniques (ibid.: 35).

Adapting the general VAR approach used by Sims (1980) to study the dynamic interrelationships among interest rates, money, prices, and output (assuming this causal chain from interest rates to output), this study postulates a causal chain among the endogenous variables as follows: currency exchange rate to money to the general price level to per person real output. The basic VAR model used in this study is formulated, using annual data from 1960 to 1995 and one-year lags, as a system of four equations:

$$(1) \quad C_t = K_c + b_{1c}C_{t-1} + b_{1m}M_{t-1} + b_{1p}P_{t-1} + b_{1q}Q_{t-1} + b_{1r}R_t + e_{1t}$$

$$(2) \quad M_t = K_m + b_{2c}C_{t-1} + b_{2m}M_{t-1} + b_{2p}P_{t-1} + b_{2q}Q_{t-1} + b_{2r}R_t + e_{2t}$$

$$(3) \quad P_t = K_p + b_{3c}C_{t-1} + b_{3m}M_{t-1} + b_{3p}P_{t-1} + b_{3q}Q_{t-1} + b_{3r}R_t + e_{3t}$$

$$(4) \quad Q_t = K_q + b_{4c}C_{t-1} + b_{4m}M_{t-1} + b_{4p}P_{t-1} + b_{4q}Q_{t-1} + b_{4r}R_t + e_{4t}$$

where: t is time; C, M, P, and Q are the natural logarithms of the cedi per dollar exchange rate, Ghana's money supply, price level, and per person real output respectively; and R is the natural logarithm of Ghana's interest rate, the exogenous variable (initially); 'K' and 'b' terms are coefficients that determine how the variables interact; and 'es' are the random error terms, which reflect the annual unexplained or surprise movements in the four endogenous variables. The logarithmic transformations of the data lead to percent changes, which were found (using unit root tests via the Augmented Dickey Fuller t-statistic) to be stationary processes, as opposed to the actual levels of the data (Babula et al., 1990: 13–21). In logs or first differences, the exchange rate, price, and interest rate were found to be stationary at 1%, and money and output at 5%.

Estimated coefficients are hard to interpret, so the impulse response functions and variance decompositions of the system are used to draw implications about a VAR.

---

[4] Modifications that may cause instability include adding a time trend, switching from monthly to quarterly or annual data, adding more lagged values of variables, and using alternative measures of variables {see, for example, Spencer (1989); Runkle (1987)}.

Based on Sims (1980), the *impulse response* depicts how an endogenous variable responds over time to a single surprise increase in itself or in another variable, thereby suggesting evolutionary effects for each variable. If the error terms are uncorrelated, then each depicts the surprise movement (or innovation) in the corresponding dependent variable. But they are correlated to some degree, so they have a common part which is not unique to any given variable. A widely used, somewhat arbitrary method of attributing common effects is the Choleski decomposition, in which the errors are orthogonalized so that the covariance matrix of the resulting surprise movements is lower triangular. This implies a recursive chain of causality among the surprise movements in any given year, so that effects flow only downward, from variables earlier in the causal chain to those later (Todd, 1990: 23).

The *forecast error (FE)* of variance decomposition of a variable can suggest that forces associated with one variable are major influences on the evolution of another variable. For example, if money's share of the forecast error of inflation were relatively large, then the basic determinants of monetary volatility would seem to be relatively important sources of inflation. Hence, FE depicts how much of the average squared forecast error the model makes is caused by surprise movements associated with each of the variables in the model (Todd, 1990: 22). FE is used to interpret the VAR results.

To check for possible model instability, arbitrary modifications made to the basic VAR model summarized by equations (1) to (4) are: (a) including a linear trend variable and (b) re-specifying the interest rate as an endogenous variable. Each modification is compared with the basic model for significant differences.

## 3.  Empirical VAR Results

To estimate the VAR model, specific variable measures for the sample years (1960–95) used are described below. Actual cedi per dollar exchange rates ($C_t$ or CPDE) are based on year-end values. The price level ($P_t$) is represented by the consumer price index (CPI), using 1980 as the base year. Per person real output ($Q_t$) is reflected by per person real gross domestic product (PPRGDP), a measure of economic growth or development. Total money supply (M)[5] is depicted by $M_2$ and/or $M_1$, while the discount rate of interest is the measure of interest rate (R) used. The correlation between $M_1$ and $M_2$ was found to be 0.999, hence each measure can represent M, since savings and time deposits (or quasi-money) make up a relatively small part of $M_2$ (when compared with the US and UK, for example). Both measures of money are used in this study, with no significant difference in the results. Hence, results are reported for $M_1$.

---

[5] LDCs in general have less developed financial systems in which: officials may arbitrarily alter interest rates with little regard to macroeconomic fundamentals;  currency is the main form of money; and modern financial instruments may not exist. In 1992, for example, $M_2$ in Ghana was made up of 36% currency, 31% quasi-money (savings and time deposits), and 33% demand deposits. The corresponding figures for the UK were 3.14%, 57.71%, and 39.15%; and for the USA, 7.54%, 57.93%, 20.82% and 13.73% money market instruments. R,  the only interest rate with values for all sample years, is about the same as the rate commercial banks use in rewarding savers or the rate on Ghana government securities.

M and R are determined to some extent by the Bank of Ghana (BoG),[6] but while R is assumed to be exogenous in this study, M is assumed to be partially endogenous. That is, even though the BoG controls M, the fact that the BoG is not independent (often reacting to what is happening to other variables like exchange rates, prices, output growth, employment, deficits, etc.) causes the controlling actions of the BoG to be partially endogenous. The linear trend variable used is a series starting from 10 (1960) and ending at 45 (1995). The one-year lag used is consistent with the data since longer lags were insignificant.[7]

Table 5.1 provides summary statistics on key variables. Coefficient of variation (CV) values depict the volatility of variables in percentage terms, thereby making possible the comparison of different variables in terms of their year-to-year changes. The highest volatility is exhibited by nominal $M_1$ (CV of 210%), closely followed by nominal $M_2$ (206%), given excessive money supply growths in easy monetary policy regimes for the periods: 1960–66; 1972–82; and 1992–5, which make up 23 of the sample of 35 years. Next in high volatility is the price level (197%), followed by the exchange rate (158%), the inflation rate (121%), and the real interest rate (95%). The lowest variability is exhibited by per person real output or PPRGDP (11%), followed by real $M_1$ (26.5%), and real $M_2$ (26.6%). Hence, based on these volatilities, it appears that most increases in nominal $M_1$ or $M_2$ are reflected in price increases (with average inflation of 32.6% per year). This result may be described in terms of rational expectations. Using the expectations adjustment framework, it follows that if real output growth is stagnant (as depicted by PPRGDP) and unemployment is high (in part due to human and physical capital limitations), then expected changes in the stock of money through time are reflected essentially in price changes. That is, monetary policy (which most people perceive to be expansionary most of the time in Ghana) may have insignificant effects on real output (i.e. as expectations change, short-run aggregate supply and demand adjust along a vertical long-run real output line), but may significantly affect inflation. Using PPRGDP as an imperfect welfare indicator, it may be concluded that, in real terms, average economic welfare has been relatively stable in the sample period. Finally, nominal interest-rate volatility is the fourth lowest and reflects the general tendency for officially determined interest rates to remain fixed for long time-spans.

Table 5.2 presents simple correlations between pairs of variables. The highest correlation of 0.999 is between $M_1$ and $M_2$. There is above-average negative correlation between economic welfare (reflected by PPRGDP) and the exchange rate, and a high positive correlation of 0.94 between the cedi/dollar rate and the price level. Ghana's excessive money supply growth (particularly before 1983) is consistent with the very high correlation of 0.97 between $M_2$ and the price level, and 0.95 between $M_2$ and the cedi/dollar rate. There is positive correlation (0.72) between the cedi/dollar rate and the interest rate. The positive correlation of 0.81 between the price and interest-rate levels indicates that high inflation exists in an environment of high interest rates.

---

[6] Since independence in 1957, one-party socialist (1957–66) and military (1966–9; 1972–9; 1982–92) regimes have directly controlled money supply through the Bank of Ghana. This implies fiscal and monetary policies were inter-linked.

[7] Using the autoregressive model: $Y_t = f(Y_{t-s})$, s =1, 2,......,5

**Table 5.1    Summary Statistics on Variables**

| VARIABLE | MEAN | SD | CV (%) |
|---|---|---|---|
| Per person real GDP (cedis) | 6070.80 | 674.22 | 11.11 |
| Cedi/Dollar rate (actual) | 29.39 | 46.41 | 157.91 |
| Price level (CPI, 1980=100) | 958.84 | 1887.27 | 196.83 |
| Inflation (% change in CPI) | 32.60 | 39.44 | 120.98 |
| Nominal interest rate (%) | 11.73 | 6.92 | 58.99 |
| Real interest rate (%) | 0.62 | 0.59 | 95.16 |
| Nominal $M_1$ money supply (billion cedis) | 11.00 | 23.13 | 210.27 |
| Real $M_1$ (billion cedis) | 7.93 | 2.10 | 26.48 |
| Nominal $M_2$ money supply (billion cedis) | 14.27 | 29.39 | 205.96 |
| Real $M_2$ (billion cedis) | 9.16 | 2.44 | 26.64 |

SD = Standard Deviation; CV = Coefficient of Variation = (SD/ MEAN) *100.

**Table 5.2    Correlations Between Selected Variables**

| VARIABLE-1 | VARIABLE-2 | CORR |
|---|---|---|
| Cedi/Dollar rate | Per person real GDP | −0.57 |
| Cedi/Dollar rate | Price level (CPI) | 0.94 |
| Cedi/Dollar rate | Interest rate | 0.72 |
| Cedi/Dollar rate | $M_2$ money supply | 0.95 |
| Price level (CPI) | $M_2$ money supply | 0.97 |
| Price level (CPI) | Interest rate | 0.81 |
| $M_1$ money supply | $M_2$ money supply | 0.99 |

CORR = Correlation coefficient

## Impulse Responses

In sum, the impulse responses (which reinforce the variance decomposition results) suggest significant dynamic interrelationships between the exchange rate and inflation. While high price inflation leads to a weakening cedi, a declining cedi in part causes price inflation. Interrelationships between PPRGDP and CPI are not significant. Money responds insignificantly to all the four shocks, while price responds most to monetary shocks. Interrelationships between real output and the exchange rate are slightly significant. That is, effective exchange-rate policy (e.g. liberalized via private 'forex' bureaux) could play an important role in determining real output growth in Ghana, as discussed in the Introduction. Also, as physical and human capital (and complementary input and policy) constraints are relaxed through time, real output could respond robustly to price and monetary shocks — subject to continuous improvements in incentive and institutional structures.

## Forecast Error Decompositions

To check for model instability, one modification made to the basic VAR model is the inclusion of a linear trend variable to capture the time-dependent effects not of direct relevance to this study.[8] Table 5.3 compares the four-year forecast error of variance decompositions of the basic model and the same model with a linear trend variable. Overall, no significant differences in forecast error (FE) values result from adding linear trends. However, in a few cases, there are significant differences in the percent contributions to FE by the endogenous variables as a result of trend. The trend coefficients in the estimated VAR equations have t-values less than 1 and can be considered insignificant.[9] Because the addition of a linear trend variable does not lead to significant changes in the FE and percent contributions, it may be concluded that the basic VAR model is reasonably robust. Given this stability, useful inferences may be drawn from the percent contributions.

**Table 5.3     Comparison of VAR Models for Instability Using Variance Decompositions[a]**

| VARIABLES/MODELS | % CONTRIBUTION OF EACH SHOCK TO EACH VARIABLE'S 4-YEAR FE[b] | | | | |
| | SOURCES OF SHOCKS | | | | |
| | FE | CPDE % | $M_1$ % | CPI % | PPRGDP % |
| Variance Decomposition (VD) of CPDE | | | | | |
| Basic Model | 0.540 | 93.60 | 0.45[c] | 5.53 | 0.425 |
| Basic Model with Trend | 0.520 | 94.01 | 0.78 | 4.70 | 0.518 |
| VD of $M_1$ | | | | | |
| Basic Model | 0.293 | 5.50[c] | 94.08 | 0.028[c] | 0.389 |
| Basic Model with Trend | 0.230 | 1.79 | 97.19 | 0.623 | 0.399 |
| VD of CPI | | | | | |
| Basic Model | 0.334 | 29.59 | 51.21 | 19.18 | 0.020[c] |
| Basic Model with Trend | 0.313 | 28.13 | 51.15 | 20.69 | 0.030 |
| VD of PPRGDP | | | | | |
| Basic Model | 0.168 | 58.29 | 9.24[d] | 16.59[d] | 15.89 |
| Basic Model with Trend | 0.170 | 59.13 | 12.48 | 13.39 | 15.00 |

*Notes:* (a) Using the Time Series Processor (TSP) command VARSTAT with the 'variance decomposition' option. All variables are in natural logarithms. Use of 8-year FEs did not lead to significantly different conclusions.
(b) FE = Forecast Error of Variance Decomposition
(c) Significant difference at 5%
(d) Significant difference at 10%

[8] Sims (1989: 444) argues that adding a linear trend variable with no clear economic meaning adds uncertainty to the estimation of long-run effects. But his critics {for example: Spencer (1989); Todd (1990); Runkle (1987)} believe robustness can be checked by adding trend variables. Todd (1990) argues that quadratic trend models tend to make money's impact on output strongly negative; hence they are excluded from this study.
[9] True t-value less than one (see Feldstein, 1973). F-tests for structural shifts in the parameters suggest no significant structural shifts in (both intercepts and slopes) for the periods 1960–79,

Table 5.4 and Appendix 5A present the percent contributions of each endogenous variable to a given variable's forecast errors of variance decomposition for up to four and eight years, respectively, using the four equation basic VAR model described earlier.

Variance decomposition of CPDE suggests that CPDE itself, and hence factors influencing it, account for about 93.6% of its estimated fourth year FE of 0.54. The CPDE contribution declines from 100 in year 1 to 81.1% in year 8 (see Appendix A for year 8 results). Next, CPI accounts for about 5.5% of CPDE's fourth-year forecast error, followed by $M_1$ (0.45%) and PPRGDP (0.43%). The CPI contribution steadily increases from 0 in year 1 to 9.7% in year 7, and then declines to 9.3% in year 8. Money's contribution rises from 0 in year 1 to 9.3% in year 8, suggesting a long-run relatively reasonable role of money in exchange-rate determination that equals that of price. The insignificant contribution of output remains below 0.5% up to the eighth year.

Variance decomposition of $M_1$ suggests that $M_1$ itself, and hence factors influencing it, account for about 94% of its fourth-year FE of 0.29, followed by CPDE (5.5%), PPRGDP (0.39%) and CPI (0.03%). In the eighth year, money's share falls to 87.7% while CPDE's share rises to 11.5%, with output and price each still contributing less than 0.5%. However, in the decomposition of CPI's fourth-year variance, $M_1$ accounts for the biggest share (51.2%), followed by CPDE (30%), CPI (19.2%) and PPRGDP (0.02%). In the eighth year, money's share rises to 57.9%, followed by CPDE (35.7%), while CPI's share falls to 6.4% and output's share remains about constant at 0.02%. Money's dominant role in price determination is consistent with the easy monetary policy and weak cedi environments that have existed in Ghana (most of the period from 1960 to 1982 and 1992–5). Hence, easy monetary policy (linked to easy fiscal policy) is the main determinant of inflation in Ghana, followed by CPDE.

Finally, CPDE and factors influencing it contribute about 58.3% to PPRGDP's fourth year FE of 0.17, followed by CPI (16.6%), PPRGDP (15.9%), and $M_1$ (9.2%). In the eighth year, CPDE's share rises to 62.4%, followed by money (18.4%), while CPI's share falls to 10.3%, followed by output (8.9%). Hence, in the short and medium terms, $M_1$ shocks have no significant impact on real output growth due mainly to physical and human capital constraints and input price inflation discussed earlier, while price and output shocks play fairly reasonable roles in output growth. However, in the long run, $M_1$ shocks play a relatively reasonable role in output determination in Ghana, while exchange-rate shocks are the dominant determinants of output changes in the short, medium, and long terms (which is consistent with exchange rate's role discussed in the Introduction).

## Money and Interest Rates

To determine the roles of money and interest rates in price and output determination

([9] cont.) 1980–88, and 1983–93. Observations for the economic restructuring or adjustment period (1983–93) are not enough to provide the dominance needed to make the calculated F-values greater than the critical F-values at the 5% significance level, but there is weak significance at 10%.

in Ghana based on Sims' VAR methodology,[10] the original VAR model is modified by excluding CPDE and including interest rate (R) as an endogenous variable. Table 5.5 and Appendix 5B summarize the percent contributions of the variables to four and eight years, respectively, of forecast errors of the variance decompositions. The direction of causation is as shown in the table, from interest rate to money to prices to real output (to be consistent with Sims' procedure).

**Table 5.4    Exchange Rate, Money, Price, and Output Interrelationships[a]**

| VARIABLES | % CONTRIBUTION OF EACH SHOCK TO EACH VARIABLE'S FORECAST ERROR FOR FOUR YEARS | | | | |
|---|---|---|---|---|---|
| | SOURCES OF SHOCKS | | | | |
| | YEAR | FE[b] | CPDE % | $M_1$ % | CPI % | PPRGDP % |
| Variance Decomposition (VD) of CPDE | | | | | | |
| | 1 | 0.373 | 100.00 | 0.00 | 0.00 | 0.000 |
| | 2 | 0.474 | 98.30 | 0.37 | 1.11 | 0.224 |
| | 3 | 0.521 | 96.03 | 0.48 | 3.12 | 0.369 |
| | 4 | 0.540 | 93.60 | 0.45 | 5.53 | 0.425 |
| VD  of  $M_1$ | | | | | | |
| | 1 | 0.144 | 0.09 | 99.91 | 0.000 | 0.000 |
| | 2 | 0.201 | 1.04 | 98.72 | 0.036 | 0.205 |
| | 3 | 0.249 | 3.11 | 96.51 | 0.039 | 0.336 |
| | 4 | 0.293 | 5.50 | 94.08 | 0.028 | 0.389 |
| VD  of  CPI | | | | | | |
| | 1 | 0.118 | 6.08 | 28.71 | 65.22 | 0.000 |
| | 2 | 0.180 | 9.25 | 41.94 | 48.81 | 0.002 |
| | 3 | 0.254 | 20.98 | 48.31 | 30.69 | 0.014 |
| | 4 | 0.334 | 29.59 | 51.21 | 19.18 | 0.020 |
| VD  of  PPRGDP | | | | | | |
| | 1 | 0.078 | 7.35 | 3.91 | 37.75 | 50.99 |
| | 2 | 0.110 | 31.29 | 4.37 | 31.70 | 32.63 |
| | 3 | 0.141 | 48.87 | 6.42 | 22.91 | 21.80 |
| | 4 | 0.168 | 58.29 | 9.24 | 16.59 | 15.89 |

*Notes:*  (a)  All variables are in natural logarithms.
(b)  FE = Forecast Error of Variance Decomposition.

---

[10] Sims's monist theory or monism (Todd, 1990), a version of monetarism, assumes that: (a) monetary policy, or its instability, is the main cause of business cycles; (b) the time path of money in circulation is a good indicator of monetary policy; (c) at least in the short run, changes in the stock of money cause, lead to, and are positively related to changes in output; and (d) at least in the long run, changes in the money stock lead to, are positively related to, and are the main determinants of changes in the price level. The last two points, common to most forms of monetarism but not directly listed by Sims, have been listed by other monetarists such as Friedman and Schwartz (1963) and Poole (1978).

Interest rate (R) and factors influencing it account for about 71.7% of its estimated fourth year FE of 0.20, followed by $M_1$ (24.8%), PPRGDP (3.5%) and CPI (0.01%). In the eighth year, R's share falls to 51.3%, while money's share rises to 43.6%, and output's insignificant share rises to 5.1%, with CPI's negligible share still below 0.5%. Sims obtained a monetary share of 30% for the US implying that monetary policy shocks to interest rates are much more important there than to Ghana in the short and medium terms. However, in the long run, money's share in Ghana exceeds Sim's 30%. In the long run, in the case of Ghana, the result is consistent with the reality that high levels of money supply co-exist with or contribute to high interest rates. That is, the effects of easy fiscal and monetary policies are countered by high interest rates, which result in the government (via higher yielding T-bills) crowding out some private firms in the credit market. In 1993, for instance, based on IMF (1995), government spending made up 13% of Ghana's GDP, while private investment made up 13.6%, depicting the competition between government and the private sector for limited resources.

The variance decomposition of $M_1$ suggests, as before, that $M_1$ shocks contribute about 96% to changes in $M_1$, followed by PPRGDP (3%), R (0.9%) and CPI (0.03%). In the eighth year, money's dominant share falls slightly to 93.7%, output's insignificant share rises slightly to 5.8%, while R's negligible share falls to 0.5%, followed by CPI (0.01%). Sims found interest rate's share to be over 50% for the US. Hence, interest rate's insignificant share in Ghana suggests that monetary policy relying solely on interest-rate changes may not work there, as it would in the US. In other words, in Ghana, rising interest rates do not necessarily lead to significant reductions in borrowing activities so as to reduce money supply as is usually the case in the US. In Ghana, over 70% of the population live in rural areas and have insignificant access to bank credit, relying instead on money-lenders who demand no collateral but tend to charge very high interest rates (some as high as 100%). Also, in Ghana where interest rates are repressed, the inflation rate (which is computed by Ghana's Statistical Service to reflect the whole country, as opposed to the capital city) may capture some of the opportunity cost of money. With time, interest-rate shocks would be expected to play significant roles in influencing money supply as the economy modernizes financially (e.g., improvements in the recently introduced stock exchange) and fiscal policy, which is inter-linked with monetary policy, becomes less easy.

In the decomposition of CPI's fourth-year variance, as before, $M_1$ accounts for the biggest share (67.3%), followed by PPRGDP (16.5%), CPI (15.8%) and R (0.43%). In the eighth year, money's dominant share rises to 76.2%, followed by output (17.8%), while CPI's share falls to 5.5%. Interest rate's negligible share rises slightly to 0.5%. Hence, money plays a big, dominant role in price determination in Ghana in the short, medium, and long terms — followed by real output, while the interest rate plays the smallest, insignificant role. *Ceteris paribus,* real output scarcities would be expected to lead to higher prices, and vice versa.

Finally, in the variance decomposition of PPRGDP, given that CPDE is absent, PPRGDP itself accounts for about 54.2% of its fourth-year FE of 0.20, followed by $M_1$ (26.1%), CPI (19.1%) and R (0.6%). In the eighth year, output's dominant share falls slightly to 50%, money's share rises to 37%, CPI's share falls to 12%, while R's insignificant share rises to 1%. Hence, interest rate's insignificant role in output determination is less than that of money (Sims found an opposite result for the US). The relatively reasonable role of money in output determination in Ghana disagrees with Sims' conclusions (he found money's share to be 4% in the US, assuming significant parameter shifts have not taken place). Hence, monetarism's idea that monetary policy is a key cause of fluctuations in output growth may hold to some reasonable extent in Ghana, as suggested by this model which excludes the exchange rate. But money's role in output determination is dramatically reduced if the exchange rate is included in the model (see Table 5.4) — in which case the exchange rate becomes the dominant determinant of output (as explained earlier). In price determination in Ghana, however, the evidence strongly suggests that monetary policy plays an important role. To promote stable real output growth in Ghana, monetary policy that makes money supply grow in proportion to real output growth

**Table 5.5 The Importance of Money and Interest Rates in Price and Output Determination[a]**

| VARIABLES | % CONTRIBUTION OF EACH SHOCK TO EACH VARIABLE'S FORECAST ERROR FOR FOUR YEARS | | | | | |
| --- | --- | --- | --- | --- | --- | --- |
| | SOURCES OF SHOCKS | | | | | |
| | YEAR | FE[b] | R (%) | $M_1$ (%) | CPI (%) | PPRGDP (%) |
| Variance Decomposition (VD) of R | | | | | | |
| | 1 | 0.165 | 100.00 | 0.00 | 0.00 | 0.00 |
| | 2 | 0.176 | 88.55 | 9.89 | 0.0009 | 1.56 |
| | 3 | 0.186 | 79.26 | 18.05 | 0.0014 | 2.69 |
| | 4 | 0.196 | 71.66 | 24.83 | 0.0050 | 3.50 |
| VD of $M_1$ | | | | | | |
| | 1 | 0.147 | 4.93 | 95.07 | 0.000 | 0.00 |
| | 2 | 0.226 | 2.10 | 97.00 | 0.015 | 0.88 |
| | 3 | 0.295 | 1.27 | 96.76 | 0.024 | 1.94 |
| | 4 | 0.359 | 0.91 | 96.08 | 0.025 | 2.98 |
| VD of CPI | | | | | | |
| | 1 | 0.133 | 2.84 | 27.46 | 69.70 | 0.00 |
| | 2 | 0.234 | 1.32 | 52.24 | 38.44 | 8.00 |
| | 3 | 0.336 | 0.64 | 62.17 | 23.67 | 13.52 |
| | 4 | 0.435 | 0.43 | 67.27 | 15.81 | 16.48 |
| VD of PPRGDP | | | | | | |
| | 1 | 0.096 | 0.83 | 7.06 | 43.02 | 49.09 |
| | 2 | 0.140 | 0.43 | 15.24 | 31.17 | 53.15 |
| | 3 | 0.174 | 0.46 | 21.37 | 23.82 | 54.35 |
| | 4 | 0.201 | 0.58 | 26.11 | 19.13 | 54.18 |

*Notes:* As for Table 5.4.

should be consistently adhered to, in a stable exchange-rate and macro environment.

As stated earlier, the use of VARs to test theories is controversial because empirical results from estimated VARs are not necessarily robust (Todd, 1990: 1). Even though the simple model modifications discussed earlier depict reasonable robustness in the VAR results of this study, the forecast error of variance decomposition of a variable can only suggest that forces associated with one variable are major influences on the evolution of another variable. Unlike VARs, structural econometric models ignore the dynamic properties of the interrelationships, or at best treat them in an ad hoc manner if the model is not correctly specified. However, because the impulse responses focus on the total final effect of one endogenous variable on another, a structural model like the simultaneous equation model that decomposes the effects into direct and indirect ones may be used to describe the mechanics of the interrelationships. Structural models tried (results not reported here because of space limitations) reinforce the VAR results. Future research may focus on alternative models and time spans.

## 4.    Cointegration Tests

The Johansen (1995, 1991) cointegration procedure is used to test for the existence of long-run relationships between pairs of variables of interest (i.e. between the exchange rate and real output growth, between the exchange rate and price inflation, and between the real interest rate and the exchange rate), based on time series data from 1970 to 2000. The test statistic is the Likelihood Ratio (LR). Insignificance implies that the null hypothesis that *there is no cointegration* for the pair of variables making up the cointegrating vector is not rejected (which means the test statistic is less than the critical values at 5% and at 1%). However, the null hypothesis is rejected (which implies there is significant cointegration) if the test statistic is greater than the critical values (at 5% and at 1%). Cointegration test results suggest: (a) a significant long-run relationship between real output growth and the exchange rate at 5% and 1%; (b) a significant long-run relationship between price inflation and the exchange rate at 5%; and (c) an insignificant long-run relationship between the real interest rate and the exchange rate at 5% and also at 1%. These results reinforce the vector autoregression results discussed above.

## 5.    Conclusions

This study explores the determinants of price inflation, exchange-rate volatility and real output growth — and their interactions and implications for economic development — as well as the roles of money and interest rates in price and output determination in Ghana. Impulse responses suggest significant dynamic interrelationships between the exchange rate and inflation. While inflation leads to a weakening cedi, a declining cedi in part may cause inflation. However, in part because physical and human capital constraints (and sub-optimal levels of complementary investments in infrastructure, research and development, etc.) hamper real output growth, dynamic interrelationships between output and inflation are mostly insignificant. Hence, effective management of macroeconomic policies that relax the input constraints through time can lead to real output responding robustly to price and monetary shocks.

Variance decompositions suggest that: (a) the cedi/dollar exchange rate and factors influencing it account for most of its forecast error, followed by the price level, money, and real output; (b) money is the most important determinant of price inflation, followed by the cedi/dollar rate, price itself, and then output; (c) the cedi/dollar rate and factors influencing it contribute most to output's forecast error, followed by price, output itself, and then money. In the long run, however, money's role exceeds that of price. Capital and complementary input constraints increase the demand for imports of capital inputs and essential consumer goods. Hence, exchange-rate policy can affect Ghana's trade balance, net capital inflows, and hence real output or economic growth. This may explain the exchange rate's strong role in output determination. Price shocks, however, are less important in determining output, due in part to scarce capital and complementary inputs.

Overall, money shocks explain money itself and price, suggesting that easy monetary policy is a key source of inflation. Comparing Sims' (1980) results with this study suggests that monetary policy shocks to interest rates are much more important in the US than in Ghana in the short and medium terms, but not in the long run. Hence, in the short and medium terms, monetary policy relying solely on interest rates may not work in Ghana as it would in the US. To make such a policy work, as the economy modernizes financially, access to bank credit must be improved (e.g. via innovative micro-finance schemes) for the majority rural population, most of whom rely on the informal sector for scarce credit at very high interest rates.

The fairly reasonable role of money in output determination in Ghana, unlike Sims' conclusion for the US, weakly supports the core idea of monetarism that monetary policy is a key cause of fluctuations in output growth. However, money plays a major role in price determination in Ghana, which strongly supports monetarism. Hence, policies to combat inflation must avoid excessive growth in the money supply. Fiscal discipline and macroeconomic policies which boost per person real output growth (i.e. economic growth or development) can dampen inflation and strengthen the cedi.

Finally, cointegration tests suggest: (a) a significant long-run relationship between real output growth and the exchange rate; (b) a significant long-run relationship between price inflation and the exchange rate; and (c) an insignificant long-run relationship between the real interest rate and the exchange rate. These results reinforce the vector autoregression results discussed above.

Policy-makers, researchers, and future research may find insights from this study useful.

## References

Babula, R. A., Bessler, D. A. and Schluter, G. E. (1990) 'Poultry-related Price Transmissions and Structural Change since the 1950's,' *The Journal of Agricultural Economics Research,* Vol. 42: 13–21.

Doan, Thomas A. and Litterman, R. B. (1986) *Regression Analysis of Time Series Version 2.11.* Minneapolis, MN: VAR Econometrics.

Feldstein, Martin (1973) 'Multicollinearity and Mean Square Error of Alternate Estimators', *Econometrica,* Vol. 41: 337–46.

Friedman, Milton, and Schwartz, A. J. (1963) *A Monetary History of the United States, 1867–1960,* Princeton, NJ: Princeton University Press.

Hodrick, R. J. (1989) 'Risk, Uncertainty, and Exchange Rates,' *Journal of Monetary Economics,* Vol. 23: 433–59.

IMF, *International Financial Statistics Yearbook, 1994–2000,* various issues. Washington, DC: IMF.

Johansen, S. (1991) 'Estimation and Hypothesis Testing of Cointegration Vectors in Gaussian Vector Autoregressive Models,' *Econometrica,* Vol. 59: 1551–80.

Johansen, S. (1995) *Likelihood-based Inference in Cointegrated Vector Autoregressive Models.* Oxford: Oxford University Press.

Johnson, Omotunde E. G. (1987) 'Currency Depreciation and Imports,' *Finance & Development,* June: 18-21.

Kloek, T. and Dijk, Van H. K. (1978) 'Bayesian Estimates of Equation System Parameters: an Integration by Monte Carlo,' *Econometrica* Vol. 46: 1–20.

Lucas, R. B. (1990) 'Why Doesn't Capital Flow from Rich to Poor Countries?' *AEA Papers and Proceedings,* Vol. 80: 92–6.

Poole, William (1978) *Money and the Economy: A Monetarist View,* Reading, MA: Addison-Wesley.

Runkle, David E. (1987) 'Vector Autoregressions and Reality,' *Journal of Business and Economic Statistics,* Vol. 5: 437–42.

Sims, Christopher A. (1980) 'Comparison of Inter-war and Postwar Business Cycles: Monetarism Reconsidered,' *American Economic Review,* Vol. 70: 250–57.

Sims, Christopher A. (1989) 'Models and their Uses,' *American Journal of Agricultural Economics,* Vol. 71: 489–94.

Spencer, David E. (1989) 'Does Money Matter? The Robustness of Evidence from Vector Autoregressions,' *Journal of Money, Credit, and Banking,* Vol. 21: 442–54.

Todd, Richard M. (1990) 'Vector Autoregression Evidence on Monetarism: Another Look at the Robustness Debate,' *Quarterly Review,* Vol. 14: 19–37.

World Bank (1993) *The East Asian Miracle: Economic Growth and Public Policy,* New York: Oxford University Press for the World Bank.

**Appendix 5A     Exchange Rate, Money, Price, and Output Interrelationships[a]**

| VARIABLES | YEAR | FE[b] | % CONTRIBUTION OF EACH SHOCK TO EACH VARIABLE'S FORECAST ERROR FOR YEARS 5 to 8 | | | |
|---|---|---|---|---|---|---|
| | | | SOURCES OF SHOCKS | | | |
| | | | CPDE (%) | $M_1$ (%) | CPI (%) | PPRGDP (%) |
| Variance Decomposition (VD) of CPDE | | | | | | |
| | 5 | 0.549 | 90.95 | 0.85 | 7.76 | 0.433 |
| | 6 | 0.559 | 87.97 | 2.37 | 9.24 | 0.418 |
| | 7 | 0.577 | 84.63 | 5.29 | 9.68 | 0.394 |
| | 8 | 0.603 | 81.10 | 9.30 | 9.27 | 0.364 |
| VD of $M_1$ | | | | | | |
| | 5 | 0.335 | 7.69 | 91.87 | 0.039 | 0.404 |
| | 6 | 0.374 | 9.44 | 90.06 | 0.092 | 0.405 |
| | 7 | 0.410 | 10.71 | 88.69 | 0.186 | 0.405 |
| | 8 | 0.443 | 11.55 | 87.73 | 0.315 | 0.409 |
| VD of CPI | | | | | | |
| | 5 | 0.413 | 34.19 | 53.06 | 12.74 | 0.018 |
| | 6 | 0.485 | 36.09 | 54.67 | 9.22 | 0.013 |
| | 7 | 0.548 | 36.37 | 56.27 | 7.35 | 0.012 |
| | 8 | 0.601 | 35.71 | 57.87 | 6.41 | 0.017 |
| VD of PPRGDP | | | | | | |
| | 5 | 0.191 | 62.45 | 12.10 | 12.88 | 12.58 |
| | 6 | 0.208 | 63.67 | 14.66 | 11.00 | 10.67 |
| | 7 | 0.220 | 63.39 | 16.76 | 10.30 | 9.55 |
| | 8 | 0.228 | 62.43 | 18.38 | 10.28 | 8.91 |

*Notes:* (a)  All variables are in natural logarithms.
       (b)  FE = Forecast Error of Variance Decomposition.

**Appendix 5B    The Importance of Money and Interest Rates in Price and Output Determination[a]**

| VARIABLES | YEAR | FE[b] | % CONTRIBUTION OF EACH SHOCK TO EACH VARIABLE'S FORECAST ERROR FOR YEARS 5 TO 8 | | | |
|---|---|---|---|---|---|---|
| | | | SOURCES OF SHOCKS | | | |
| | | | R (%) | $M_1$ (%) | CPI (%) | PPRGDP (%) |
| Variance Decomposition (VD) of  R | | | | | | |
| | 5 | 0.205 | 65.32 | 30.58 | 0.012 | 4.09 |
| | 6 | 0.214 | 59.95 | 35.51 | 0.020 | 4.52 |
| | 7 | 0.223 | 55.32 | 39.82 | 0.029 | 4.84 |
| | 8 | 0.232 | 51.27 | 43.62 | 0.038 | 5.07 |
| VD of $M_1$ | | | | | | |
| | 5 | 0.421 | 0.73 | 95.35 | 0.022 | 3.91 |
| | 6 | 0.481 | 0.63 | 94.68 | 0.017 | 4.68 |
| | 7 | 0.539 | 0.57 | 94.12 | 0.014 | 5.30 |
| | 8 | 0.595 | 0.53 | 93.67 | 0.012 | 5.78 |
| VD of CPI | | | | | | |
| | 5 | 0.529 | 0.40 | 70.46 | 11.30 | 17.85 |
| | 6 | 0.616 | 0.42 | 72.76 | 8.52 | 18.30 |
| | 7 | 0.696 | 0.46 | 74.60 | 6.73 | 18.21 |
| | 8 | 0.769 | 0.50 | 76.15 | 5.52 | 17.83 |
| VD of  PPRGDP | | | | | | |
| | 5 | 0.221 | 0.71 | 29.82 | 16.11 | 53.36 |
| | 6 | 0.237 | 0.83 | 32.76 | 14.14 | 52.27 |
| | 7 | 0.248 | 0.92 | 35.12 | 12.86 | 51.10 |
| | 8 | 0.257 | 0.99 | 37.04 | 12.02 | 49.96 |

*Notes:* As for Appendix 5A.

# 6 Ghana's Exchange-Rate Reform & its Impact on the Balance of Trade

FRANK W. AGBOLA

## 1. Introduction

Since the breakdown of the Bretton Woods Accord in 1973, and the advent of floating exchange rates, there has been renewed interest in the effect of devaluation on the trade balance of both developed and developing countries. Developing countries facing balance-of-payments problems due to expansionary financial policies, a deterioration in the terms of trade, price distortions, higher debt servicing or a combination of these factors, have often resorted to devaluing their currencies (Nashashibi, 1983). The aim of such a policy is to promote export-oriented growth by liberalizing their markets. As pointed out by Katseli (1983), 'it is by now well understood that the use of the extended facility of the International Monetary Fund or approval of standby loans involves the undertaking of comprehensive programs of adjustment that include policies required to correct structural imbalances . . .' (p.359). The standby agreements, Katseli notes, require severe tightening of expenditure through contractionary fiscal and monetary policy measures such as the imposition of ceilings on net government borrowing and/or net domestic assets of the central bank or an upward adjustment of nominal interest rates in cases where rates are fixed by the government. Katseli further notes that the approval of funds also involves an 'understanding' with the IMF on exchange-rate policy and exchange-rate arrangements whereby devaluation becomes a component of a restrictive package for improving a country's balance of payments and its foreign-exchange reserve position.

Exchange-rate devaluation which is an essential component of IMF conditionality, under what have become known as the Structural Adjustment Policies (SAP), was implemented reluctantly by developing countries. Musila and Newark (2003) attribute this to the 'fear that the dismal performance may not cover the cost of imports resulting from currency depreciation' (p.340). However, proponents of the flexible exchange-rate regime argue that deregulation of the financial system serves to balance the country's international trade by making prices of internationally traded goods and services flexible. Although the structural adjustment programme is capable of delivering benefits to developing countries, there are heated debates on its impact on economies in sub-Saharan Africa (see Musila and Newark, 2003).

Nashashibi (1983) summarizes the main criticisms of the use of exchange-rate policies to facilitate adjustment within an economy. Most of the reforms under the structural adjustment programme have been associated with reduced economic growth and increased unemployment, and, in countries with an active public sector, have been linked to undermining public sector investment and development strategies. These reforms have also been associated with a rise in the cost of living and the redistribution of income, shifting the burden of adjustment, in most cases, to the lower income groups who are least able to afford it. Another criticism of Nashashibi (1983) is the ineffectiveness of devaluation; devaluation is capable of increasing inflation without sufficiently improving the external balance-of-payments position, which eventually induces another devaluation and plunging the country into an inflation-cum-devaluation spiral. While the main criticism is the failure of the scheme to achieve its intended goal of economic growth and development, proponents of the SAP attribute its failure to the incomplete and incoherent implementation of policies (see Musila and Newark, 2003).

The Ghanaian economy, with its longstanding tradition in international trade, has experienced severe stress in the past three decades and has undergone major macroeconomic and trade policy reforms. In the early 1980s, Ghana was faced with severe competition in international markets for domestically produced primary goods. Coupled with this was political instability. In a climate of declining export values and rising imports, the balance-of-payments position was dislocated, resulting in the widening of the current account deficit. In response to the persistent adverse trade balance and disequilibrium in the balance of payments, the government accepted stringent IMF and World Bank loan conditions under the Structural Adjustment Programme launched in 1983. As part of the reform process, the policies implemented included fiscal stringency, devaluation of the cedi, and liberalization of trade and financial markets. The Government of Ghana and the World Bank have argued that there has been an appreciable upswing in macroeconomic indicators, such as the relatively high annual growth rate and the reduction in the level of inflation and the improvement in services resulting from the structural adjustment policies. In the early 1990s, Ghana's economic recovery was geared towards the export rather than the domestic market. Gross Domestic Product has risen by an average of 5% per year since 1984, inflation decreased to about 20%, and export earnings reached US$1 billion. In 1990, mineral exports also increased by about 23% over the previous year (Anonymous, 2004). Ghana's SAP experience is admired by most in the developed and developing world and generally regarded by the IMF as a success story. Nevertheless, the adjustment programmes have been found to have had a negative impact on employment generation and the welfare of the populace (Boafo-Arthur, 1999).

Does devaluation improve the trade balance? Although economic theory posits that devaluation of a country's currency will probably improve its trade balance, there is conflicting empirical evidence on this. According to proponents of the elasticity approach, the nominal devaluation of a country's currency changes the real exchange rate (a relative price) and thus improves the global competitiveness of its tradable goods through its impact on relative prices, thereby improving the trade balance. It has been argued by monetarists that the devaluation of a country's currency will cause an increase in the price level by the same percentage points and, given that the real balance effect is not present, Dornbusch (1973) argues that '. . . then it might stand to reason that the effects of devaluation are negligible, not that there must be other powerful avenues through which it exerts its effects' (p.883). This argument is based on the assumption that goods and assets are perfect substitutes and prices are exogenously determined for a small country, and that wages and prices are flexible in both nominal and real terms. Although a plethora of theoretical and empirical studies have been undertaken both at the multi-country and individual country level, there is still controversy about how devaluation affects the trade balance.

The purpose of this paper is to add to the understanding of the adjustment of trade flows to the exchange-rate stimuli of a small developing economy, by empirically investigating the quantitative impact of devaluation of the Ghanaian cedi on the trade balance for the period 1970-2002. A simple model is specified and estimated in order to examine relationships between the trade balance and the structural characteristics of the domestic and foreign economy and variables relating to the currency risk. In the present author's view, very few studies have examined the impact of devaluation on the Ghanaian economy. This paper attempts to address this imbalance by shedding some light on the controversial question in Ghana's macroeconomic policy reform process: Does devaluation improve the trade balance? The hypothesis to be tested is that devaluation will not succeed in improving the trade balance in Ghana. In other words, a positive relationship exists between the trade balance and exchange rates in the long run.

We draw upon some of the latest advances in econometric time-series modelling and use these techniques to reassess linkages between the trade balance and key determinants. In particular, we adopt tests for unit root of Dickey and Fuller (1979) and Phillips and Perron (1988), and a more robust test for multivariate co-integration provided by Johansen (1988, 1991). Extending the analysis, we estimate Stock-Watson (Stock and Watson, 1993) dynamic OLS (DOLS) models of Ghana's trade balance. This paper contributes to the existing literature by taking a broader perspective in investigating the impact of devaluation — using annual data — on Ghana's trade balance. Its findings provide useful information for policy formulation and implementation in Ghana.

The rest of the paper is organized as follows. Section 2 provides a snapshot of Ghana's foreign-exchange system, outlining the evolution of policies and the arguments and evidence that the economy needs to devalue its currency, and the role of the International Monetary Fund. Section 3 briefly reviews theories and empirical evidence on the impact of devaluation on the trade balance. Section 4 describes the model employed in the analyses, the description and sources of data employed being presented in the Appendix. Section 5 presents the empirical results of our study, and Section 6 concludes by rejecting the null hypothesis that the devaluation of the cedi during the period 1970-2002 has improved the position of Ghana's trade balance.

## 2.   A Snapshot of the Ghanaian Exchange-Rate System

Before Ghana gained its independence from Britain in 1957, the economy appeared to be stable and prosperous. At the start of independence, President Kwame Nkrumah pursued a policy of diversification and expansion, with the cedi fixed to the US dollar. Zhang (2002) argues that a fixed exchange-rate regime only serves to act as an accounting tool in the allocation of resources. Using cocoa revenue as security, Nkrumah took out loans to establish industries that would produce import substitutes as well as processing many of Ghana's exports. Unfortunately, the price of cocoa collapsed in the mid-1960s, destroying the fundamental stability of the economy and making it impossible for Nkrumah to continue his plans. Coupled with this was the pervasive corruption, which exacerbated the problems.

The effect of devaluation on Ghana's economic and political instability has to be seen in historical context. In May 1965, the Nkrumah government approached the International Monetary Fund and the World Bank for assistance. Their prescriptions were non-inflationary borrowing and drastic reduction of government spending (Boafo-Arthur, 1999), which were seen as counter-productive because, as Boafo-Arthur put it, 'this will mean placing a cap on the expansionist development programmes of the government that has become a distinctive trademark of the government at the time' (p.2). On 24 February 1966, Nkrumah's government was ousted in a military coup headed by General Kotoka. Although Nkrumah was overthrown before the IMF package of reforms, including devaluation, spelled out by Ghana's international creditors was implemented, Younger (1992) points out that the devaluation of the cedi was seen by many as the trigger of the coup. In April 1967, General Kotoka was killed in an abortive coup attempt.

In September 1969, the second civilian government of the Progress Party headed by Dr Kofi Abrefa Busia, came to power. The Busia government undertook protracted negotiations with the IMF and the World Bank due to the divergent views on policy direction (Boafo-Arthur, 1999). On 27 December 1971, Busia signed an agreement with the IMF, which included, *inter alia* the devaluation of the cedi from 1.02 to 1.82 cedis per US dollar. Seven days after the implementation of the IMF policies the Busia government was overthrown. The military government, the National Redemption Council, headed by Col. Ignatius Kutu Acheampong, cited the general dissatisfaction of Ghanaians after the implementation of the IMF conditionality as the reason for the overthrow, despite his own admission of having planned the coup long before the implementation of the IMF policies (Boafo-Arthur, 1999). As highlighted by Boafo-Arthur , this seems to suggest that the coup was not directly caused by the devaluation of the cedi, most of which the NRC rolled back, revaluing upwards by about 21.4% to 1.15 cedis to the dollar. During the NRC reigime, IMF and World Bank pressures were vigorously resisted.

Following the palace coup of July 1978, the Supreme Military Council (SMCII), headed by General Fred Akuffo, succumbed to IMF pressures and introduced a structural adjustment programme, the stabilization measures of which included devaluation of the cedi by 58% against the US dollar. This culminated in another coup on 4 June 1979 that brought Flight Lieut. Jerry John Rawlings and the Armed Forces

Revolutionary Council (AFRC) into power, with the new government effectively terminating the structural adjustment programme of the SMC II (Boafo-Arthur, 1999). As correctly put by Younger (1992: 372), 'the devaluation of the Ghanaian cedi has come to be seen as the death knell for governments'. The exchange rate as such was changed only once (in 1978) between 1973 and 1983, despite a rise in the CPI of over 5,000% during the same period. At this time, the Ghanaian cedi was considered to be overvalued and was perceived as taxing exports and subsidizing imports, with the result that cocoa prices suffered, dampening cocoa production and resulting in the smuggling of the cocoa crop to neighbouring countries (Anonymous, 2004).

By 1980, the Ghanaian economy was in a state of collapse. Economic indicators were lacklustre. The GDP had fallen by 3.2% a year from 1970 to 1981, cocoa production fell by about 50% between the mid-1960s and the late 1970s, gold production declined by about 47%, and inflation rose by 50% a year between 1976 and 1981, hitting a high of 116.5% in 1981 (Economic Inquiry, 1994). In an attempt to reverse this trend, a military government the Provisional National Defence Council, PNDC, took power on 31 December 1981. With a severe drought in 1983, and in a climate of declining export values and rising imports, the balance-of-payments position was dislocated, resulting in a widening of the current account deficit. In response, the military government, the PNDC headed by Rawlings, accepted stringent IMF and World Bank loan conditions, which included fiscal stringency, devaluation of the currency and liberalization of the financial market under the Economic Recovery Programme (ERP).

On 19 June 1983 an abortive coup attempt was crushed by government troops. Throughout the 1980s, following the PNDC's assumption of power, a number of attempts were made to overthrow the government without success. The PNDC, under pressure from Western donor nations and opposition groups to restore a multi-party civilian government, announced the launch of a national discussion on the country's political future. On 2 November 1992 the PNDC, now transformed as a political party, the National Democratic Congress (NDC) won the presidential election, and on 29 December 1992 gained almost all the seats in the new parliament following a boycott by the opposition parties. On 7 January 1993, the Fourth Republic was proclaimed. The party went on to win another general election in 1996. However, it lost the 2000 elections to the New Patriotic Party led by John Agyekum Kufour. Over the course of the 1990s and early 2000s, there have been a number of macroeconomic and trade policy reforms, including devaluation of the cedi.

## 3.    Devaluation and the Trade Balance: Theory and Empirics

*Theory*: There are heated debates in the economic and econometric literature on the impact of devaluation on the trade balance. Several theories have been advanced in this regard, the most common being the elasticity, monetary and absorption approaches. The elasticity approach, put forward by Robinson (1947) and Metzler (1948) and popularized by Kreuger (1983), posits that transactions under contract completed at the time of devaluation or depreciation may dominate a short-term change in the trade balance. As pointed out by Upadhyaya and Dhakal (1997: 343), such a devaluation of the currency would cause the trade balance to deteriorate in the short run. Over time, export and import quantities adjust and this causes the elasticities of exports and imports to increase, tending to reduce the foreign price of the devaluing country's exports and raise the price of imported goods. This causes the demand for imports to decline, with a consequent improvement in the trade balance. Clearly, the effect of devaluation on the trade balance depends on the elasticity of exports and imports. Williamson (1983) is critical of the elasticity approach, arguing that the higher import prices, caused by devaluation, could stimulate increases in the domestic prices of non-traded goods. If this causes inflation to rise, this could potentially reduce the benefits of devaluation as manifested in the increase in the trade balance, under the elasticity approach.

The monetarist approach to exchange-rate determination (Mundell, 1971; Dornbusch, 1973; Frenkel and Rodriguez, 1975) is based on the argument that devaluation reduces the real value of cash balances and/or changes the relative price of traded and non-traded goods, thus improving both the trade balance and the balance of payments (Miles, 1979). As pointed out by Upadhyaya and Dhakal (1997: 343), this implies that devaluation or depreciation decreases the real supply of money, resulting in an excess demand for money, the effect being hoarding and a decrease in demand for goods, thereby resulting in an increase in the trade balance. From the monetary perspective, the role of relative prices in the analysis of devaluation is of little importance in explaining the impact of devaluation on the trade balance.

Proponents of the absorption approach argue that devaluation may change the terms of trade by increasing production, switching expenditure from foreign to domestic goods, or generally by reducing domestic absorption relative to production, and thus improve the trade balance. Himarios (1989) cites the work of Laffer (1977) to argue that the links in the chain postulated in the elasticity approach are less likely to hold in reality. Himarios identifies the core of the debate as lying in the effectiveness of nominal devaluation in affecting the real exchange rate and the importance of real exchange rates in influencing trade flows.

In summarizing the theories for analyzing the impact of devaluation on the trade balance, we quote Buluswar et al. (1996: 429) as follows: 'The elasticity approach focuses on the exchange rate as the major determinant of the trade balance. The monetary approach focuses on the exchange rate by isolating relative money supplies, with excess demand for money and the desire to hoard cash lowering a trade balance. The absorption approach to the trade balance stresses that an increase in real domestic income relative to foreign income would lower the trade balance due to the increased demand for imports.'

*Empirical studies.* Despite extensive research on the impact of exchange-rate adjustment on an economy, empirical studies have not resolved the debate over the impact of devaluation on the trade balance. Cooper (1971) studied the effect of 24 devaluation episodes in 19 developing countries over the period 1959–66, and found that, overall, devaluation improves the trade balance and the balance of payments. Musila and Newark (2003) criticize Cooper's findings on the ground that the methodology used was unsound, arguing that it is not possible to distinguish between the effects of devaluation and macroeconomic factors on the trade balance in the estimated model. Kamin's (1988) study of devaluation and macroeconomic performance found that devaluation does improve the trade balance because it stimulates exports. Salant (1977) found that devaluation improves the balance of payments, if not the trade balance. Gylfason and Risager (1984) reach similar conclusions. In contrast, the studies of Laffer (1977) and Miles (1979) find that devaluation does not improve the trade balance. Himarios (1985) criticized the work of Miles (1979) on the ground that there are serious deficiencies in the methodology and tests used, and by accounting for these deficiencies the results are reversed.

Other extensions of the traditional approach include the use of a macro-simulation modelling framework. Authors who have used this approach include Gylfason and Risager (1984), Branson (1986), Solimano (1986), Roca and Priale (1987), Horton and McLaren (1989) and Gylfason and Radetzki (1991). As Musila and Newark (2003) note, apart from Gylfason and Risager (1984) and Gylfason and Radetzki (1991), the other studies conclude that devaluation worsens the trade balance and the balance of payments. Musila and Newark find that it improves the trade balance. In recent times, a number of studies have extended the work of earlier authors in this area by examining the impact of devaluation on the trade balance in a time-series theoretical framework. Studies using this approach include Himarios (1989), Edwards (1989), Mataya and Veeman (1997), Buluswar et al. (1996), Upadhyaya and Dhakal (1997), Musila (2002) and Musila and Newark (2003), among others.

Although a number of studies have investigated empirically the effects of devaluation on the trade balance, few of these studies have been conducted on Ghana. Rawlins and Praveen's (2000) study examined the impact of devaluation on the trade balance of certain selected African countries, including Ghana. Following the work of Kreuger (1983), Rawlins and Praveen specified and estimated an Almon Distributed lag process of the trade balance with a set of monetary and fiscal policy variables and using annual data for the period 1960–89. They found that the real exchange-rate depreciation did not have any impact on Ghana's trade balance in the year of the devaluation and concluded that the J-curve effect appears not to be significant in the case of Ghana.

Younger (1992) studied the linkage between devaluation and inflation in Ghana for the period 1976–86 using a time-series theoretical approach. He finds that the highly regulated economy, with extensive trade and exchange-rate restrictions, has meant that the nominal devaluation has had very little impact on domestic prices. In other words a 100% increase in the exchange rate causes prices to rise by 5–10%. He argues that there is scope for African countries, such as Ghana, to pursue a policy of devaluing the currency since it has very little impact on inflation and has the ability to redistribute income from importers to the government, assuming that exporter's prices are not adjusted in line with the devaluation. Younger concludes that, given that devaluation improves the government's fiscal position, there is scope to use such a policy instrument to reduce the growth rate of the money supply, and hence inflation.

From the above it is clear that neither theoretical nor empirical studies have definitely established whether the devaluation of a country's domestic currency would improve its trade balance. Understanding the long-run relationship between exchange-rate devaluation and the trade balance is important for policy formulation and implementation in developing countries, such as Ghana.

## 4.    The Model

To reiterate, the central theme of this paper is to examine the impact of devaluation on the trade balance. Economic theory posits a number of key variables that have a significant effect on imports and exports and hence the trade balance. Now, let the trade balance of an economy be defined as export revenue $X$ minus import expenditure $M$. Let us also make a small country assumption. Then, the trade balance of Ghana can be expressed, following Buluswar et al. (1996), as

$$TB = X - M = P_X Q_X \left( \frac{P_X}{e}, Y^* \right) - eP_M^* Q_M \left( eP_M^*, Y \right) \qquad (1)$$

where $TB$ is the trade balance, $X$ is exports revenue, $M$ is import expenditure, $P_X$ is the cedi price of exports, $Q_X$ is the quantity of exports, $P_M$ is the foreign currency price of imports, $Q_M$ is the quantity of imports, $e$ is the value of foreign currency in terms of the Ghanaian cedi, $Y$ is domestic national income, and $Y^*$ is foreign income.

The monetary model postulated here is based on the Ghanaian economy. Following Buluswar et al. (1996: 430), 'the monetary model of exchange rates is built on money market equilibrium', and is specified as

$$\frac{M_s}{P} = L(Y, e) \qquad (2)$$

where $M_s$ is the nominal money supply, $P$ is the domestic price level, $L$ represents the demand for money, $e$ is the value of foreign currency in cedis, and $Y$ is domestic real income.

The expression in Equation (2) postulates that the money market is in equilibrium and this ensures that the real money supply is determined by the demand for money and the exchange rate in terms of the domestic economy. The original inspiration for this modelling can be found in Johnson (1972), Dornbusch (1973, 1975) and Frenkel and Rodriguez (1975). From Equation (2) it can be deduced that a higher $e$ would reduce the purchasing power of the cedi, and this will increase the demand for money to maintain imports. An increase in $M_s$ would increase the supply of money and this causes the domestic residents to spend their cash balances. In Ghana, this will result in a decrease in cash balances and consequently a worsening of the trade balance. As pointed out by Buluswar et al. (1996), there is some ambiguity, however, about the effect of real balances, $M_s/P$, on the trade balance. Higher $M_s$ could raise $P$ and lower the effective exchange rate, thereby causing the trade balance to rise in the long run. A higher price level $P$ could also lower the real money supply, $M_s/P$, causing hoarding (Dornbusch, 1973), and consequently improving the trade balance. A higher domestic income could also lead to excess money demand and hence an increase in imports, causing the trade balance to worsen.

Now, interest rates affect the trade balance through their effect on demand for money and other monetary assets. This means that changes in the domestic interest rate influence savings and consumption (and hence imports). On the one hand, a rise in interest rate would generate an excess money supply, thereby causing the trade balance to deteriorate. On the other hand, an increase in the domestic interest rate could create an excess demand for bonds, which in turn would improve the trade balance, given that the demand for imports will fall. As emphasized by Himarios (1985), the impact of changes in the interest rate depends on the competing income and substitution effects. If the income effect dominates the substitution effect, an increase in interest rates would cause the trade balance to deteriorate. If the substitution effect dominates the income effect, then the trade balance will improve, with an increase in interest rates.

The empirical model used in this study is dictated by the typical formulation postulated by economic theory. Following Himarios (1985, 1989), Bahmani-Oskooee (1985, 1989) and Buluswar et al. (1996), a linear empirical model incorporating the basic variables is specified as

$$TB = a_0 + a_1 Y_D + a_2 Y_W + a_3 M_D + a_4 M_W + a_5 IR_D + a_6 IR_W + \sum_{i=0}^{5} NER_{t-1} + \varepsilon_t \qquad (3)$$

where $TB$ is the trade balance, $Y_D$ ($Y_W$) is real domestic (foreign) income, $M_D$ ($M_W$) is the real domestic (foreign) money supply, $IR_D$ ($IR_W$) represents the domestic (foreign) interest rate, $NER$ is an index of trade-weighted nominal effective exchange rates, and $e_t$ is the error term which satisfies all the classical assumptions of OLS. The time subscripts are dropped for simplicity.

In summarizing the approaches to explaining the determinants of the trade balance, Buluswar et al. (1996) emphasize that proponents of the absorption approach argue that a higher real domestic income is associated with a rise in the quantity of imports $Q_M$ and this lowers the trade balance, while a higher real foreign income causes exports to rise and consequently leads to an increase in the trade balance. The underlying premise of the elasticity approach is that the exchange rate is the key determinant of the trade balance. The elasticity approach predicts a short-run negative effect of the exchange rate on the trade balance and a positive effect in the long run to give what has become known as the *J*-curve.

The *J*-curve is a time path showing the response of a country's trade balance to exchange-rate changes. This response consists of two parts, namely, the price effect and the quantity effect. The price effect relates to the change in the terms of trade (or relative prices), while the quantity effect is due to a change in the volume of real goods and services. Although economic theory posits that the quantity effect from devaluation dominates the price effect resulting in instantaneous adjustment, in the real world adjustments are not instantaneous. Consequently, in the short run, as a country devalues its currency, the price effect dominates, with a rise in the import price and a fall in the export price causing the trade balance to worsen. In the long run, the adjustment of economic agents within the country devaluing its currency causes exports to rise and imports to fall, causing the trade balance to improve. Arguably, the rise in prices caused by inflation may cause an increase in the real exchange rate and this could diminish the potential increase in the trade balance in the long run (see Williamson, 1983). This indicates that the estimated sign of the effects of devaluation on the trade balance is ambiguous. Hence, this analysis will provide an insight into which theory dominates the adjustment process in Ghana.

The empirical analysis uses annual time-series data spanning the period 1970–2002. Data used in the analyses were obtained from the International Monetary Fund's *International Financial Statistics CD-Rom* and *Direction of Trade Statistics CD-Rom*. A description of variables employed in the analyses is provided in the Appendix.

## 5.   Empirical Results

### *Unit Root Test Results*
This study follows recent advances in the econometric literature of time-series analysis to investigate the long-run relationship between the time-series variables. To avoid spurious results, unit root tests of augmented Dickey-Fuller (ADF) (Dickey and Fuller, 1979) and Phillip-Perron (PP) (Phillips and Perron, 1988) were performed to determine the time-series properties of the data employed in the analysis. The auxiliary regression is run with an intercept and is specified as

$$\Delta y_t = \alpha_0 + \alpha_1 y_{t-1} + \sum_{j=1}^{p} \gamma_j \Delta y_{t-j} + \varepsilon_t \tag{4}$$

where $y_t$ is the variable whose time-series properties are being investigated, $\Delta$ is the difference operator, and $\varepsilon_t$ is the random error term with $t = 1 \ldots n$ assumed to be Gaussian white noise.

The augmentation terms are added to convert the residuals into white noise without affecting the distribution of the test statistics under the null hypothesis of a unit root. As Alba (1999) notes, the ADF and PP tests have a null of unit root against the alternative of trend stationary. The usefulness of the PP test over the ADF is that it allows for the possibility of heteroscedastic error terms (Hamilton, 1994). For the PP test, the maximum lag length was chosen based on the Newey-West criteria (Newey and West, 1994). Table 6.1 reports the ADF and the PP test results of variables in levels and first difference. The ADF test reveals that all the variables are non-stationary in levels for the ADF and PP tests. For the ADF test, with the exception of the trade balance variable, all other variables are stationary in first difference. For the PP test, all variables are stationary in first difference. Given that the PP test is superior to the ADF test, we proceed to use the PP test results as the basis for investigating the co-integrating relationship between the variables.

### *Multivariate Co-integration Test Results*
In this section, we investigate the possible co-integrating relationship(s) between

**Table 6.1    Unit Root Test Results**

| Variable | ADF[a] | | PP[a] | |
|---|---|---|---|---|
| | Levels | First Difference | Levels | First Difference |
| TB | 4.099 | −0.161 | −0.274 | −5.879 |
| $Y_D$ | 0.488 | −4.254 | 0.264 | −4.254 |
| $Y_W$ | 2.142 | −3.822 | 3.337 | −3.827 |
| $M_D$ | 0.127 | −6.037 | −2.232 | −15.309 |
| $M_W$ | 1.569 | −5.470 | 2.650 | −5.471 |
| $IR_D$ | −1.735 | −6.463 | −1.631 | −7.982 |
| $IR_W$ | −2.828 | −4.108 | −1.974 | −3.908 |
| NER | −1.298 | −4.159 | −1.373 | −4.112 |

*Note:* a)    Critical values are −4.273, −3.558 and −3.212 at the 1%, 5% and 10% levels respectively.

variables in Ghana's trade balance function. Two or more variables are said to be co-integrated, i.e., they exhibit long-run equilibrium relationship(s), if they share common trend(s). The co-integration among variables rules out the possibility of the estimated relationships being 'spurious'. Although Engle and Granger's (1987) two-step approach for testing for co-integration is used extensively in the literature, this study adopts the Johansen-Juselius multivariate MLE co-integration testing procedure (Johansen, 1991, 1995). As Masih and Masih (2000) note, unlike the Engle-Granger approach, the Johansen procedure does not, *a priori*, assume the existence of at most a single co-integrating vector; rather it tests for the number of co-integrating relationships. Furthermore, unlike the Engel-Granger procedure, which is sensitive to the choice of the dependent variable in the co-integrating regression, the Johansen procedure assumes all variables to be endogenous.

The study adopts the Johansen test procedure for testing for co-integrating relationship(s) between the trade balance and key determinants. The Max-eigenvalues test is used. This test compares $H_0(r\text{-}1)$ with the alternative $H_1(r)$. The Akaike's Final Prediction Error criteria (FPE) (see Cuthbertson et al., 1992, and for a survey, Muscatelli and Hurn, 1992) is used to determine the lag length of the vector error correction model and to evaluate the robustness of the empirical results. The Johansen test results of co-integration between the variables in Equation (3) are reported in Table 6.2. Based on the maximum Eigen-value statistics and corresponding critical values, due to Osterwald-Lenun (1992), the null hypothesis of no co-integration between the trade balance and the key determinants of interest is rejected, while the hypothesis that there is at most 2 (3) co-integrating equation(s) could not be rejected at the 1 (5)% significance level. The results confirm the existence of an underlying long-run stationary steady-state relationship between the trade balance and the key determinants. Given that there is at least one co-integrating vector in the trade balance model, the equation can be estimated in levels.

**Table 6.2    Johansen's Co-integration Test Results of the Trade
Balance Function for Ghana**

| Hypothesized No. of CE(s) | Max-Eigen Statistic | 5% Critical Value | 1% Critical Value |
|---|---|---|---|
| None | 62.302[a,b] | 51.42 | 57.69 |
| At most 1 | 52.118[a,b] | 45.28 | 51.57 |
| At most 2 | 40.138[b] | 39.37 | 45.10 |
| At most 3 | 17.115 | 33.46 | 38.77 |
| At most 4 | 12.605 | 27.07 | 32.24 |
| At most 5 | 7.182 | 20.97 | 25.52 |
| At most 6 | 6.625 | 14.07 | 18.63 |
| At most 7 | 2.034 | 3.76 | 6.65 |

*Note*: *a* and *b* denote rejection of the hypothesis at the 1% and (5%) level.

## *The Estimation of Co-integrating Coefficients*

When sets of variables are co-integrated, then there exists an adjustment process of the variables towards the long-run equilibrium. The OLS estimator of the coefficients of the co-integrating regression is consistent, although it has a non-normal distribution, and tests carried out result in invalid statistical inference. To overcome this, a number of estimators have been proposed in the econometric literature to estimate co-integrating coefficients. This study adopts the dynamic OLS (DOLS) estimator (Stock and Watson, 1993). The DOLS estimator of the co-integrating regression equation includes all variables in Equation (3) in levels, leads and lags of values of the change in the explanatory variables. The usefulness of this approach is that it allows for simultaneity bias and introduces dynamics in the specification of the model (Masih and Masih, 2000).

The current study estimates the following DOLS (Stock and Watson, 1993):

$$Y_t = \beta_0 + \beta_i X_t + \sum_{j=-p}^{p} \delta_j \Delta X_{t-j} + u_t \tag{5}$$

where $Y_t$ is the trade balance, $X_t$ is a vector of explanatory variables and D is the lag operator.

To ensure that the standard errors of the co-integrating regression equation have a standard normal distribution, we estimated the model using OLS estimation procedure and the standard errors were derived using the Heteroscedastic and Autocorrelation Consistent (HAC) covariance matrix estimator (see Newey and West, 1987). These robust standard errors facilitate valid inferences being made about the coefficients of the variables entering the regressors in levels. The coefficients of the explanatory variables in levels in Equation (5) denote the long-run cumulative multipliers, that is, the long-run effect on *Y* of a change in *X*.

Before proceeding to discuss the empirical it is important to discuss two empirical issues. The first relates to the relationship between nominal exchange rate (NER) and real exchange rate (RER). The decision to use the nominal exchange rate is based on the fact that economic agents in developing countries are more concerned about changes in nominal exchange rates rather than real exchange rates. In addition, the correlation coefficient between nominal and real exchange rate is very high, estimated to be 0.96. Inclusion of the real exchange rates in the estimated models did not improve the empirical results significantly. The results of the models using RER are available from the author. Consequently, the models with NER are discussed. A test for structural change using CUSUM testing procedure was also performed. The results revealed that the parameters of the model were stable during the study period.

Table 6.3 reports the Stock-Watson DOLS parameter estimates of Ghana's trade balance regression equation using EViews version 4.1 econometric package. Considering the small sample size, the equation was estimated including up to one period lead and lag of the change in the explanatory variables. The final model was chosen based on the signs, significance and behaviour of the parameter estimates.

**Table 6.3**    **Regression Results of Trade Balance Model for Ghana**

| Variable | Stock-Watson DOLS model | | Traditional TB model | |
|---|---|---|---|---|
| | Coefficient | *t*-statistic | Coefficient | *t*-statistic |
| Constant | 19121.63 | 4.181 | 18415.61 | 5.803 |
| $Y_D$ | −4.516 | −3.563 | −1.757 | −1.427 |
| $Y_W$ | −3.654 | −2.579 | −3.716 | −3.441 |
| $M_D$ | −0.245 | −1.020 | −0.215 | −0.864 |
| $M_W$ | 1.351 | 0.328 | 5.287 | 1.893 |
| $IR_D$ | 324.177 | 4.860 | 54.215 | 1.698 |
| $IR_W$ | 123.266 | 1.915 | 192.181 | 3.988 |
| NER | −0.147 | −3.821 | −0.186 | −4.998 |
| NER (−1) | − | − | 0.013 | 0.387 |
| NER (−2) | − | − | −0.068 | −2.233 |
| NER (−3) | − | − | 0.0193 | 0.677 |
| NER (−4) | − | − | −0.077 | −1.408 |
| $DY_D$ | 3.858 | 2.118 | − | − |
| $DY_W$ | 0.812 | 0.592 | − | − |
| $DM_D$ | 0.203 | 2.122 | − | − |
| $DM_W$ | 5.798 | 0.831 | − | − |
| $DIR_D$ | 90.938 | 0.832 | − | − |
| $DIR_W$ | 0.062 | 1.852 | − | − |
| DNER | −251.137 | −3.416 | − | − |

The most satisfactory empirical result of the estimated model with one period lag of explanatory variables is discussed. The high $R^2$-adjusted (goodness-of-fit) measure of 0.92 indicates a good fit of the data set. The calculated $F$-statistic of 27.57 is statistically significant at a 1% level, indicating that the explanatory variables are jointly significant in influencing Ghana's trade balance. The Breusch-Pagan LM test for autocorrelation is 0.191 ($p$-value = 0.67) and reveals no presence of first order autocorrelation at a 1% significance level.

The coefficient of the real domestic income variable, $Y_D$, is negative and statistically significant at a 1% level. The result indicates that, *ceteris paribus,* an increase in real domestic income increases imports and this in turn causes the trade balance to deteriorate. It is interesting to note, however, that the coefficient of the real foreign income, $Y_W$, captured by the real gross domestic product of Ghana's major trading partners, is also negative and statistically significant at a 1% level.

The coefficient of the real domestic (foreign) money supply variable, $M_D$ ($M_W$) is negative (positive) but statistically non-significant at a 10% level. This implies that both domestic and foreign money supply have no effect on the trade balance. It should be noted, however, that the negative sign of the coefficient of the domestic money supply variable in the trade balance equation is consistent with the argument that an increase in domestic money supply would lead to an increase in the level of real balances. Now, if individuals perceive the rise in the level of real balances as a rise in their wealth, this will cause the level of expenditure to increase relative to income, resulting in the trade balance deteriorating (see Johnson, 1972). Furthermore, as pointed out by Johnson (1977: 263), '. . . a preliminary test of the monetary approach can be conducted by testing whether the coefficient of the real money balance is negative and statistically significant'. Given that the coefficient of the real domestic money supply variable is statistically non-significant, this implies that the monetary approach is not the major channel by which adjustment takes place in Ghana. For $M_W$, the positive sign of the coefficient, although not significant, is consistent with *a priori* expectations. *Ceteris paribus*, an increase in foreign money supply would lead to an increase in the level of real balances. Proponents of the absorption approach argue that devaluation may change the terms of trade by increasing production, switching expenditure from foreign to domestic goods, or generally by reducing domestic absorption relative to production, and thus improve the trade balance.

The coefficient of the domestic interest-rate variable, $IR_D$, is positive and statistically significant at a 1% level. The result indicates that an increase in the interest rate causes the trade balance to improve. The result of this study suggests that the substitution effect dominates the income effect. That is, an increase in the domestic interest rate causes savings to rise rather than an increase in consumption, the effect being a decrease in imports and hence an improvement in the trade balance. The foreign interest-rate variable, $IR_W$, also has a positive impact on Ghana's trade balance. This indicates that an increase in the foreign interest rate causes the trade balance to improve. This could be interpreted from the standpoint of the income effect which dominates the substitution effect. As interest rates rise in foreign economies this causes an increase in consumption relative to savings. The impact is an increase in demand for Ghana's exports and consequently an improvement in Ghana's trade balance. It should also be noted that the positive sign of both the domestic and the foreign interest-rate variable reflects the response of economic variables in Ghana to conditions in world credit markets.

Now, we turn to the central theme of this paper: does devaluation improve the trade balance of Ghana? The coefficient of the exchange-rate variable, NER, which captures the impact of devaluation on Ghana's trade balance, is negative. As pointed earlier, the coefficient of the exchange-rate variable, NER, in levels in the DOLS model captures the long-run multiplier effect on the trade balance of the change in NER. The coefficient of the NER variable is negative and statistically significant at a 1% level. This indicates that devaluation of the cedi worsens the trade balance of Ghana in the long run.

Under the J-curve, the coefficients of lags of the exchange-rate variable would be negative initially, followed by positive signs (Buluswar et al., 1996). Now, incorporating the lag of the exchange-rate variable in the DOLS model is theoretically inconsistent because of the presence of the first difference of the explanatory variables. To overcome this problem, a traditional trade balance (TB) model, as specified in Equation (3), is estimated with lags of the NER variable. The most satisfactory empirical result of the maximum likelihood estimation is reported in Table 6.3 and discussed. The $R^2$-adjusted (goodness-of-fit) measure of 0.61 indicates a relatively good fit of the data set. The calculated $F$-statistic of 4.42 is statistically significant at a 1 percent level, indicating that the explanatory variables are jointly significant in influencing Ghana's trade balance.

The results of the TB model indicate that the dynamics of the adjustment path in the Ghanaian economy does not follow the traditional J-curve effect. Ignoring the significance of the coefficients of the lagged NER variables, the sign of the contemporaneous coefficient is positive, and the sign of every other lag of the exchange-rate variable changes. The result can be described as an M-curve. This finding appears to be consistent with those of Buluswar et al. (1996). The results indicate that there is no immediate effect of devaluation on the trade balance of Ghana; it does not cause the trade balance to deteriorate. In the following year, the negative effect of the devaluation takes hold. This may be due to an increase in the quantity of imports which causes the trade balance to deteriorate. This is followed by a positive impact on the trade balance, possibly due to the decreased domestic income which discourages demand for imports and thereby causes the trade balance to improve. Finally, the market adjusts in the second year towards the long-run equilibrium. The long-run effect, captured by the sum of the lagged coefficients, is negative, implying that devaluation has not improved Ghana's trade balance during the study period. This is consistent with the results from the DOLS model. The perverse effect of devaluation of the exchange rate on Ghana's trade balance has also been reported in the studies by Bahmani-Oskooee (1985) and Himarios (1989). It should be noted that the positive but statistically non-significant coefficient of the NER variable suggests that traders in Ghana have not adjusted adequately to the changing economic conditions of devaluation of the cedi, thereby causing the trade balance to worsen in Ghana.

Before concluding, it is important to compare the results reported here with previous studies, in general, and Ghanaian studies, in particular. First, the finding that devaluation of the Ghanaian cedi does not follow the traditional J-curve is consistent with the findings of Rawlins and Praveen (2000). The impact of devaluation of the cedi on the trade balance appears to exhibit an M-curve effect. This finding is similar to those by Buluswar et al. (1996) who also found that the impact of devaluation of the Indian Rupee exhibits an M-curve effect. Secondly, although previous Ghanaian studies by Rose and Yellen (1989), Rose (1990) and Rawlins and Praveen (2000) find that devaluation has no effect on Ghana's trade balance, the present study finds to the contrary; devaluation does cause the trade balance to deteriorate in the long run. Thirdly, taking the values in parenthesis of Table 6.3 of Rawlins and Praveen's (2000) study to denote *t*-values, this means that the positive impact, although statistically non-significant, of the foreign money supply reported in this study is consistent with that reported by Rawlins and Praveen (2000). No other statistically significant coefficient was found by Rawlins and Praveen, while this study finds that domestic and foreign real income and the monetary variables of interest rates, foreign money supply, and exchange rates are key determinants of Ghana's trade balance.

## 6.    Summary, Conclusions and Implications

This chapter analyzes the long-run relationships between Ghana's trade balance and real domestic and foreign income, real money supply, interest rates and the exchange rate, using annual data for the period 1970-2002. The key findings are summarized. First, the most recent techniques for unit root and co-integration testing were employed to investigate the stationary of the series. The results indicate that the trade balance and the key determinants are non-stationary in levels. Secondly, the Johansen MLE multivariate co-integration procedure reveals that Ghana's trade balance and the key determinants are co-integrated, and thus share a long-run equilibrium relationship. Thirdly, the Stock-Watson dynamic OLS (DOLS) modelling, which is superior to a number of alternative estimators finds that the key determinants of Ghana's trade balance are real domestic and foreign income, domestic and foreign interest rates, the nominal exchange rate, and real foreign money supply. Fourthly, the results of this study indicate that devaluation of the Ghanaian cedi worsens the trade balance in the long run.

Given that devaluation is costly, it is important that the benefits and costs of devaluing the currency are well understood before it is implemented. This is because the devaluation of a currency increases the domestic currency debt-servicing burden of external loans denominated in foreign currency (see also Nashashibi, 1983). Another devastating impact of devaluation is its impact on the interest burden which, as Nashashibi points out, tends to absorb resources that could be employed in current production and spending. Now, if wages are tied up with the Consumer Price Index and are enforced via social pressures rather than formal contracts, as is the case with Ghana, a rise in wages causes the terms of trade to fall such that working capital rises (see Nashashibi, 1983). The effect is a decrease in output resulting in a rise in the level of unemployment as observed in Ghana during the 1980s and 1990s.

The above discussion raises questions about the efficacy of devaluation in achieving the intended goal of economic growth and development of a country that devalues its currency. An alternative policy to devaluation is the imposition of restrictions on less essential imports and foreign-exchange movement. Nashashibi (1983) emphasizes that the success of such a policy depends on the ability of the government to encourage technological innovation, remove structural bottlenecks and rigidities, ensure the efficient allocation of resources and encourage investment in labour-intensive production techniques, given that the devaluation of a currency tends to bias production towards capital-intensive techniques. In terms of restricting foreign-exchange movement, Nashashibi argues that such a policy could potentially encourage expansion of the black market for foreign exhange, causing a divergence in private and public rates, the consequence being capital flight.

The Ghana government's policy of establishing the Forex Bureau is in the right direction, because it will ensure that foreign-exchange movement can be monitored and supervised. A cut-back in government spending is also capable of reducing the negative impact of devaluation on the trade balance in the long run, because it lowers wages and prices and thereby improves the profitability of firms. However, such a policy could cause a rise in the level of unemployment, because nominal wages and prices are sticky downwards and therefore would not fall enough to bring about equilibrium in the labour market. This means that the cut-back in government spending should also be accompanied by deregulation of the labour market and the removal of structural bottlenecks and rigidities within the economy. Clearly, the impact of any such policy on Ghana's trade balance is an empirical one worth investigating.

To sum up, the information provided in this study is particularly useful for policy-makers who want to anticipate future changes in the trade balance in response to devaluation of the Ghanaian cedi and other monetary variables. The results indicate that, despite the deregulatory reforms, the Ghanaian economy is still rather weak to respond to market signals so as to use the exchange-rate policy reforms to manage its external balance. While monetary and fiscal variables in domestic and foreign economies do influence Ghana's trade balance, exactly how changes in economic variables, such as interest rates, impact on bonds, savings and investment behaviour, and hence the trade balance, needs to be explored. Future research would attempt to disentagle the dynamics inherent in this process in order to gain a better understanding of the Ghanaian economy so that these impacts can be incorporated into monetary and fiscal policy formulation for it to be most effective in achieving the intended objectives of sustained economic growth and development in Ghana.

## References

Alba, J. D. (1999) 'Are there Systematic Relationships between China's and Southeast Asia's Exchange Rates? Evidence form Daily Data', *Asian Economic Journal*, Vol. 13, No. 1: 73–92.

Alexander, S. S. (1952) 'The Effect of a Devaluation on a Trade Balance', *IMF Staff Papers*, Vol. 2, No. 2: 263–78.

Anonymous (2004) 'Country Studies: Ghana — The Economy's Historical Background', *Country Studies*, Country Studies/Area Handbook Program, Federal Reserve Division of the Library of Congress, USA. http://www.country-studies.com/ghana/the-economy-historical background. html (accessed 3 March 2004)

Bahmani-Oskooee, M. (1985) 'The Effects of Devaluation on Trade Balance: A Critical View and Reexamination of Miles's New Results', *Journal of International Money and Finance,* Vol. 4: 553–63.

Bahmani-Oskooee, M. (1989) 'Do Devaluations improve Trade Balance? The Evidence Revisited', *Economic Inquiry*, Vol. 27: 143–68.

Boafo-Arthur, A. (1999) 'Ghana: Structural Adjustment Democratisation and Politics of Continuity', *African Studies Review*, Vol. 42, No. 2: 41–72.

Branson, W. H. (1986) 'Stabilisation, Stagflation and Investment Incentives: The Case of Kenya 1979–80', in S. Edwards and L. Ahamed (eds), *Economic Adjustment and Exchange Rates in Developing Countries*. Chicago, Il: Chicago University Press.

Buluswar, M., Thompson, H. and Upadhyaya, K. P. (1996) 'Devaluation and the Trade Balance in India: Stationarity and Cointegration', *Applied Economics,* Vol. 28: 429–32.

Cooper, R. N. (1971) 'An Assessment of Currency Devaluation in Less Developed Countries', in G. Ranis (ed.). *Government and Economic Development*. New Haven, CT: Yale University Press.

Cuthbertson, K., Hall, S. G. and Taylor, M. P. (1992) *Applied Economic Techniques*. Ann Arbor, MI: University of Michigan Press and New York: Simon and Schuster.

Dickey, D.A. and Fuller, W.A. (1979) 'Distribution of the Estimators for Autoregressive Time Series with a Unit Root', *Journal of the American Statistical Association*, Vol. 74: 427–31.

Dornbusch, R. (1973) 'Devaluation, Money and Non-Traded Goods', *American Economic Review*, Vol. 63: 871–80.

Dornbusch, R. (1975) 'A Portfolio Balance Model of an Open Economy', *Journal of Monetary Economics*, Vol. 1: 3–20.

Edwards, S. (1989) 'Structural Adjustment in Highly Indebted Countries', in J. Sachs (ed.), *Developing Countries' Debt and Economic Performance,* Vol. 2. Chicago, IL: University of Chicago Press.

Engle, R. F. and Granger, C. W. J. (1987) 'Co-integration and Error Correction: Representation, Estimation, and Testing', *Econometrica*, Vol. 55: 251–76.

Frenkel, J.A. and Rodriguez, C. (1975) 'Portfolio Equilibrium and the Balance of Payments: A Monetary Approach', *American Economic Review*, Vol. 65, No. 4: 674–88.

Gylfason, T. and Risager, O. (1984) 'Does Devaluation Improve the Current Account?' *European Economic Review*, Vol. 25: 37–64.

Gylfason, T. and Radetzki, M. (1991) 'Does Devaluation Make Sense in the Least Developed Countries?', *Economic Development and Cultural Change*, Vol. 40: 1–25.

Hamilton, J. D. (1994) *Time Series Analysis*. Princeton, NJ: Princeton University Press.

Himarios, D. (1985) 'The Effects of Devaluation on Trade Balance: A Critical View and Re-Examination of Miles's New Results', *Journal of International Money and* Finance, Vol. 4: 553–63.

Himarios, D. (1989) 'Do Devaluations Improve the Trade Balance? The Evidence Revisited', *Economic Inquiry*, Vol. 27: 143–68.

Horton, S. and McLaren, J. (1989) 'Supply Constraints in the Tanzanian Economy: Simulation Results from a Macroeconometric Model', *Journal of Policy Modelling*, Vol. 11: 297–313.

Johansen, S. (1988) 'Statistical Analysis of Cointegration Vectors', *Journal of Economic Dynamics and Control*, Vol. 12: 231–54.

Johansen, S. (1991) 'Estimation and Hypothesis Testing of Cointegration Vectors in Gaussian Vector Autoregressive Models', *Econometrica*, Vol. 59: 1551–80.

Johansen, S. (1995) *Likelihood-based Inference in Cointegrated Vector Autoregressive Models*. Oxford: Oxford University Press.

Johnson, H. G. (1967) 'Towards a General Theory of the Balance of Payments', in *International Trade ad Economic Growth: Studies in Pure Theory*. Cambridge, MA: Harvard University Press.

Johnson, H. G. (1972) 'The Monetary Approach to the Balance of Payments Theory', *Journal of Financial and Quantitative Analysis*, Vol 7: 1555–71.

Johnson, H. G. (1977) 'The Monetary Approach to Balance of Payments Theory and Policy: Explanation and Policy Implications', *Economica*, August: 217–29.

Kamin, S. B. (1988) *Devaluation, External Balance and Macroeconomic Performance: A Look at the Numbers*. Study in International Finance No. 62. Princeton, NJ: Princeton University.

Katseli, L.T. (1983) 'Devaluation: A Critical Appraisal of the IMF's Policy Prescriptions', *American Economic Review*, Papers and Proceedings, May: 359–63.

Kreuger, A.D. (1983) *Exchange Rate Determination*. Cambridge: Cambridge University Press.

Laffer, A. B. (1977) 'Exchange Rates, the Terms of Trade and the Trade Balance', in Clarke et al. (eds), *The Effects of Exchange Rate Adjustments*. Washington, DC: OASIA Research Department of the Treasury.

Masih, R. and Masih, A.M.M. (2000) 'A Reassessment of Long-run Elasticities of Japanese Import Demand', *Journal of Policy Modelling*. Vol. 22, No. 5: 625–39.

Mataya, C. S. and Veeman, M. M. (1997) 'Trade Balance and the J-Curve Phenomena in Malawi', in A. K. Rose et al. (eds), *Issues in Agricultural Competitiveness: Markets and Policies*. International Association of Agricultural Economists Occasional Paper, No, 7. London: Dartmouth, pp. 279–89.

Metzler, L. (1948) 'The Theory of International Trade', in S. E. Howard (ed.), *A Survey of Contemporary Economics*. Vol. 1. Philadelphia, PA: Blakiston.

Miles, M.A. (1979) 'The Effects of Devaluation on the Trade Balance and Balance of Payments: Some New Results', *Journal of Political Economy*, Vol. 87: 600–20.

Mundell, R. (1973) 'International Monetary Reform and Exchange Rate Issues: Discussions', in E. Hinshaw (ed.), *Key Issues in Monetary Reform*. New York: Marcel Dekker.

Muscatelli, V.A. and Hurn, S. (1992) 'Cointegration and Dynamic Time Series Modes', *Journal of Economic Surveys*, Vol. 6, No. 1: 1–43.

Musila, J. W. (2002) 'Exchange Rate Changes and Trade Balance Adjustmets in Malawi', *Canadian Journal of Development Studeis,* Vol. 23, No. 1: 69–85.

Musila, J.W. and Newark, J. (2003) 'Does Currency Devaluation Improve the Trade Balance in the Long Run? Evidence from Malawi', *African Development Review*, Vol. 15, No. 2: 339–52.

Nashashibi, K. (1983) 'Devaluation in Developing Countries: The Difficult Choice', *Finance and Development*, March: 14–17.

Newey, W. and West, K. (1994) 'Automatic Lag Selection in Covariance Matrix Estimation', *Review of Economic Studies*, Vol. 61: 631–53.

Osterwald-Lenun, M. (1992) 'A Note with Quantiles of the Asymptotic Distribution of the ML Co-integration Rank Test Statistics', *Oxford Bulletin of Economics and Statistics*, Vol. 54: 461–72.

Phillips, P. C. B. and Perron, P. (1988) 'Testing for a Unit Root in Time Series Regression', *Biometrika*, Vol. 75: 335–46.

Rawlins, G. and Praveen, J. (2000) 'Devaluation and the Trade Balance: The Recent Experience of Selected African Countries', Centre for Economic Research on Africa, School of Business, Montclair State University, NJ (mimeo).

Robinson, J. (1947) 'The Foreign Exchanges', in *Essays in the Theory of Employment*. Oxford: Blackwell.

Roca, S. and Priale, R. (1987) 'Devaluation, Inflation Expectations and Stabilisation in Peru', *Journal of Economic Studies*, Vol. 14: 5–33.

Rose, A.K. and Yellen, J.L. (1989) 'Is there a J-Curve?' *Journal of Monetary Economics*, Vol. 2, No. 1: 53–68.

Rose, A. K. (1990) 'Exchange Rates and the Trade Balance: Some Evidence from Developing Countries', *Economic Letters*, Vol. 34: 271–5.

Salant, M. (1977) 'Devaluations Improve the Balance of Payments Even If Not the Trade Balance', in Clarke et al. (eds), *The Effects of Exchange Rate Adjustments*. Washington, DC: OASIA Research Department of the Treasury.

Solimano, A. (1986) 'Contractionary Devaluation in the Southern Cone: The Case of Chile', *Journal of Development Economics*, Vol. 23: 135–51.

Stock, J. H. and Watson, M. W. (1993) *Introduction to Econometrics*. Boston, MA: Pearson Education Inc.

Upadhaya, K. P. and Dhakal, D. (1997) 'Devaluation and the Trade Balance: Estimating the Long Run Effect', *Applied Economic Letters*, Vol. 4: 343–5.

Williamson, J. (1983) *The Open Economy and the World Economy*. New York: Basic Books Inc.

Younger, S. D. (1992) 'Testing the Link between Devaluation and Inflation: Time-series Evidence from Ghana', *Journal of African Economies*, Vol. 1, No. 3: 369–94.

Zhang, Z. (2002) 'China's Exchange Rate Reform and Its Impact on the Balance of Trade and Domestic Inflation', *Asia Pacific Journal of Economics and Business*, Vol. 3, No. 2: 4–22.

## Appendix 6.1

*Data definitions and sources*

All data are annual from 1970 to 2002 and are in real terms where applicable, and are taken from various issues of the International Monetary Fund's *International Financial Statistics CD-ROM 2004* and *Direction of Trade Statistics 2004.*

TB $\quad=\quad$ Ghana's trade balance, derived as export revenue minus import expenditure;

$Y_D$ $\quad=\quad$ the real annual gross domestic product of the Ghanaian economy in local currency (cedi);

$Y_W$ $\quad=\quad$ the real annual gross domestic product of foreign economy in US dollars, derived as M1 of Ghana's major trading partners, the Netherlands, the United States, the United Kingdom, Germany and France, (a proxy for world income);

$M_D$ $\quad=\quad$ Ghana's real money supply, derived as high-powered money (i.e. claims on the Ghana government by the central bank);

$M_W$ $\quad=\quad$ Real money supply, derived as M1 of the US, a proxy for the money supply in the rest of the world;

$IR_D$ $\quad=\quad$ the Treasury bill rate, a proxy for the interest rate of the Ghanaian economy;

$IR_W$ $\quad=\quad$ the US interest rate, a proxy for rest of the world's interest rate;

NER $\quad=\quad$ the nominal exchange rate of the cedi with the US dollar (cedi/US$), with devaluation of the cedi being an increase in NER.

# 7 Export Performance & Investment Behaviour of Firms in Ghana*

SUSANNA WOLF
& DANIEL BRUCE SARPONG

## 1. Introduction

After two decades of macroeconomic stabilization policies, Ghana still has a low GDP per capita and is highly dependent on commodity exports. Specifically, it is one of the countries with the lowest proportion of exporting manufacturing firms in sub-Saharan Africa. To change this situation, a shift towards non-traditional exports with higher demand growth and less price volatility is a precondition. However, the declining terms of trade and external shocks have an impact on macroeconomic variables such as exchange and interest rates and therefore reduce the prospects for investment and growth (UNCTAD, 2004). Therefore at the macro level export and investment performance are closely linked.

From previous studies and theoretical considerations, a strong relationship between export performance and investment behaviour at the firm level is also expected (Collier and Pattillo, 2000; Rankin et al., 2002, Söderbom and Teal, 2003). Because of the fixed costs of marketing and access to foreign markets, a certain scale of operations is needed for a firm to be a successful exporter. Furthermore, firms need to invest in equipment and technology, to produce goods of the required quality for exporting, and to exploit economies of scale to produce goods more cheaply. On the other hand, profits from good export performance might be used for subsequent investment, as many firms depend on internally generated funds.

In the literature, evidence is mixed on whether export activities cause an increase in size and productivity which is associated with investment or vice versa. In this paper the main question is whether this relationship runs in both directions for the Ghanaian

* Support for this research has been provided by the Alexander von Humboldt Foundation (Germany). The study has been carried out in collaboration with the Department of Agricultural Economics and Agribusiness of the University of Ghana. The authors want to thank participants at the ISSER/University of Cornell conference for useful comments, Nicholas Nikoi Abossey, Theodora Tettey, and Richard Tweneboah-Kodua for excellent research assistance and especially the managers of the firms that participated in the survey for sharing their time and experiences.

agricultural and manufacturing sectors. The hypothesis is that firms that are successful exporters will invest more and that firms that invest more are more likely to export.

After an overview of recent trends in investment and exports in the commercial agricultural and manufacturing sectors, the investment and export patterns of private firms drawn from a survey of 100 enterprises in Ghana are described. On the basis of this survey, the factors that influence the investment and exporting behaviour of firms are analyzed using a simultaneous equation model to allow for the endogeneity of investment and exporting. However, no significant positive relationship between exporting and investment could be found. There seems rather to be a negative association, which might be explained by constraints on the access to capital.

## 2.     Growth, Investment and Export Performance in Commercial Agriculture and Manufacturing

After difficult times for business in 1999 and 2000 because of macroeconomic instability — especially high inflation — the situation improved in 2001. The cedi stabilized after 2001 but the decline in the external value of the cedi in 1999/2000 led to a depreciation of the real exchange rate, which meant that exports became more competitive, whereas imports became relatively more expensive than domestically produced goods (Wolf, 2003). This was reflected by an increase in the growth rates of the manufacturing sector from 3.8% and 3.7% in 2000 and 2001 respectively to 4.8% in 2002. This growth was partly driven by an expansion of non-traditional exports that picked up again in 2001 and 2002 after stagnation from 1998 to 2000 (ISSER, 2003; GoG, 2004). However, in 2003 inflation was higher than the depreciation of the cedi which might lead again to some problems for exporters.

One of the major constraints of the private sector in Ghana is its limited access to finance. High real interest rates make it more attractive to buy government bonds than to invest in risky businesses. In recent years a number of special credit programmes were put in place, especially in the area of micro-credit, but so far they are not sufficient to meet the demand (Aryeetey et al., 2000). Bank lending to the private sector has not improved much in real terms from 2000 to 2002. The share of credits from Deposit Money Banks (DMB) to the manufacturing sector declined from 28% in 2000 to around 20% between 2001 and 2003. Also for the agricultural sector the share declined from 12% in 1999 to around 9.5% thereafter. Most of the credits to the private sector went into services. After a decline between 1999 and 2001 the share of the private sector in credits to all enterprises rose again (see Figure 7.1). In 2003 the real value of credits to private enterprises also increased by around 10% (BoG, 2004).

Overall, the development of foreign direct investment follows a similar pattern to that of credit to the private sector. In the services sector, which accounts for the highest share of FDI, investment is associated with lower sunk costs and shorter turnover periods, which makes investment more flexible and reversible.

From 1999 to 2002 the dollar amounts of FDI declined further and only in 2003 was an increase to US$118.38 million observable, although the 2000 levels were not achieved again. The share of capital invested in the manufacturing sector was around 20%, whereas agriculture played only a minor role for foreign investors with less than 10% of invested capital, except in 2002 when it increased to more than 30% (see Figure 7.2).

**Figure 7.1:  Sectoral Allocation of DMB Credit, 1999–2003 (%)**

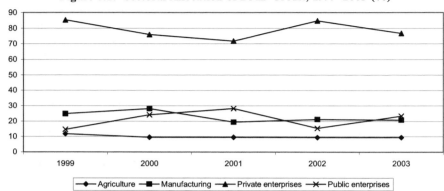

*Source:*   ISSER (2003) and BoG (2004).

**Figure 7.2:  FDI, 2000–2003, Total in Million US$, Manufacturing, Agriculture and Services in %**

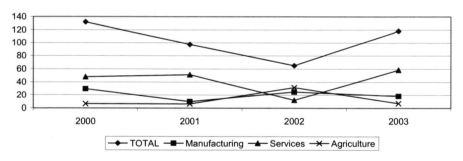

*Note:*     GIPC figures do not include investment in the mining sector.
*Source:*   GIPC (2004).

Since 1990, the value of non-traditional exports (NTE) in nominal US$ terms has increased by a factor of 8, so that overall the NTE sector can be regarded as a success story. The value of NTE started from a relatively low level of US$62.3 million and reached US$504.3 million in 2002, which represents around one-third of total export earnings in recent years (ISSER, 2003). However, from 1998 to 2000, the value of NTE stagnated, despite a massive devaluation of the cedi during that period. In 2001 and 2002, export growth picked up again, with increases of 14.7% and 9.7% respectively. The number of exporting firms grew at a much slower pace from 1,729 enterprises in 1990 to 3,083 enterprises in 2002, which is an increase of 78%. In 2002 the bulk of NTE comprised processed and semi-processed products, mainly wood products (21% of the total, mainly builders woodwork and sliced veneers), prepared foods and beverages (17% of the total, mainly canned tuna), aluminium products (6.5% of the total) and other processed and semi-processed products (33% of the total, mainly cocoa products, cotton sheets and cut pineapples), which together constituted more than 80% of the total. It has to be noted that the last category includes approximately 23% (of the total) of processed agricultural products. Other NTE are agricultural products with 17%, where pineapples and yams make the bulk of exports. Handicrafts constituted only 2% (see Figure 7.3). For many of these exports Ghana enjoys preferential access to the European Union — its main market — under the Cotonou Convention. Overall it can be assumed that the outward-oriented trade policy, with reductions in export and import taxes since 1983, has contributed to the increase in exports and output (Sarpong, 1998).

**Figure 7.3: Non-traditional Exports by Sector, Value in US$ m. 1986–2002**

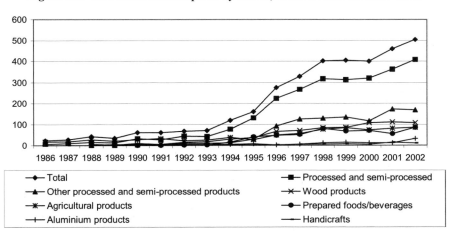

*Source:* GEPC (1987–2003).

## 3. Characteristics of Sample Firms

A survey of 100 agricultural and manufacturing firms in Ghana that was administered in 2003 is used for the analysis. As the focus of the study is on investment behaviour and export performance, a stratified sampling approach (that over-samples larger firms and firms that do export) was used, and only formally registered enterprises are included.[1] To capture the dynamic aspects of firm performance, most questions were asked regarding the years 2000, 2001 and 2002. The firms in the sample cover most sectors that are relevant in Ghanaian manufacturing and non-traditional agricultural export products.

In the enterprise sample, the agricultural sector consists mainly of pineapple and pawpaw producers as well as producers of cassava, yam, and pepper, but no cocoa

---

[1] A stratified sample is appropriate if firms within groups are relatively similar but there are significant differences between groups, especially in size categories. The main lists from which enterprises were drawn are the list of non-traditional exporters in 2002 from GEPC and the list of agricultural and manufacturing companies with foreign investment between 1994 and 2000 from GIPC.

producers, as the focus of the study is non-NTE. In the agricultural processing sector, there are a number of beverage producers (beer and soft drinks) as well as producers of vegetable oil, dairy products, etc. In the wood and furniture sector, no producers of raw timber are included and the sample consists mainly of furniture companies. The textiles and garments and handicraft sectors are aggregated, as the textiles sector includes batik and kente weaving which is often categorized as a handicraft. In the aluminium sector, producers of roofing sheets, louvre blades and cooking utensils are included. The plastic and rubber sector covers producers of both packaging materials and household goods. Other manufacturing is a residual category and captures salt, cosmetics, and other metal products among others.

Of the 100 firms, 68 are located in Accra, 13 in Tema, 11 in the Northern Region (mainly agricultural, agricultural processing and textiles) and 8 in other regions.[2] Some of the surveyed enterprises have been operating for quite a long time — roughly one quarter of them before the beginning of the Economic Reform Programme in 1983. These older firms were often started as state-owned enterprises or taken over by the state and (partly) privatized later on. The majority of firms have only been registered over the past decade. This reflects the relatively high exit rate especially of small and medium enterprises, which cannot be captured by this type of survey.

## *Investment Behaviour*

Overall only 43% of the enterprises did any new investment in a given year (see Table 7.1), an observation that is in line with previous findings of private firms in Ghana (Rankin et al., 2002). The propensity to invest was highest in agricultural processing, which also has a high capital intensity. In general, the propensity to invest increases significantly with size. The large proportion of big enterprises and subsidiaries of multinational firms in the agricultural processing sector explains the higher percentage of firms that invest, as access to finance is less problematic for these firms. However, due to loans denominated in foreign currencies, some firms experienced high exchange-rate losses, especially in 2000 when the cedi depreciated heavily. Most of the smaller firms reported that they finance investments from profits.

The amount of investment a firm makes, if it invests at all, is on average 18% of its total capital stock. This level is also comparable with the results of other studies (Rankin et al., 2002). In the agricultural sector the high investment rate is driven by one relatively newly established firm. Also in the plastic and rubber sector, which is relatively capital-intensive, investment rates are relatively high, which is mainly driven by the growth of medium-sized enterprises.

Small and medium-sized enterprises have on average a higher investment rate than large enterprises if they invest, but they are less likely to invest at all, which is consistent with earlier studies (Pattillo, 1998; Rankin et al., 2002). This reflects the problems of access to credit for small enterprises. They can only invest if they have

---

[2] Because of time restrictions other commercial centres, especially Kumasi and Takoradi, could not be included in the study. However, previous studies of Ghana's manufacturing sector did not find any location-specific effects (see Rankin et al., 2002).

accumulated enough profits. In addition, small firms are constrained by the fact that investment in office equipment, machines or vehicles has to be made in one large sum, as leasing is not very widespread.

**Table 7.1     Propensity to Invest and Investment Rates (%) by Size and Sector, av. 2000–2002**

| Propensity to invest[a] | size category (number of employees) | | | |
|---|---|---|---|---|
| | *less than 20* | *20 to 75* | *more than 75* | *Total* |
| agricultural | 0.17 | 0.42 | 0.47 | 0.34 |
| agricultural processing | 0.47 | 0.46 | 0.72 | 0.60 |
| textiles/garments + handicraft | 0.15 | 0.31 | 0.60 | 0.28 |
| wood and furniture | 0.43 | 0.25 | 0.33 | 0.38 |
| aluminium | 0.47 | 0 | 0.46 | 0.42 |
| plastic and rubber | 0.25 | 0.38 | 0.36 | 0.36 |
| other manufacturing | 0.29 | 0.80 | 0.50 | 0.50 |
| All | 0.31 | 0.40 | 0.52 | 0.43 |
| **Average investment rate[b]** | | | | |
| agricultural | 96 | 13 | 9 | 24 |
| agricultural processing | 21 | 32 | 14 | 19 |
| textiles/garments + handicraft | 16 | 9 | 2 | 8 |
| wood and furniture | 5 | 3 | 55 | 21 |
| aluminium | 29 | – | 14 | 18 |
| plastic and rubber | 1 | 53 | 16 | 23 |
| other manufacturing | 16 | 16 | 1 | 7 |
| All | 23 | 25 | 14 | 18 |

*Notes:* a)  investment propensity means the likelihood that a firm in a specific sector invests.
b)  amount invested divided by the total capital stock if a firm invests.

## Characteristics of Exporting Firms

In total, 62% of the firms in the sample were engaged in exporting (see Table 7.2). This clearly is a higher percentage than the average for all firms in Ghana, due to the sampling procedure used. Of the total GEPC lists, only 215 manufacturing enterprises, 27 handicraft producers and 178 agricultural producers were actively exporting in 2002 (GEPC, 2003). On average 36% of all exports are targeted towards other ECOWAS member countries. However, it is likely that a significant proportion of exporting to other countries in the region is done by informal traders and therefore not reported, as the producers do not know its extent.

A clearly positive relationship exists between size and the likelihood to export, as can be seen from Table 7.2. Less than half of the small firms are engaged in exporting, but 73% of the large firms export.[3] On average, exporting enterprises have approximately

---

[3] As exporting firms are over-sampled the share of exporting firms does not represent a national average; there is evidence from other studies that less than 20% of all manufacturing firms in Ghana export (Rankin et al., 2002).

twice the number of employees of non-exporters. However, if small firms export, they tend to export a higher fraction of their production than larger firms. On average, exporting firms export around half of their output, which is comparable with other studies (Rankin et al., 2002). The positive relationship between size and exporting could be explained by different factors. Small exporters have a relatively high share of exports in total output. This observation is compatible with the high fixed costs of exporting, for example establishing contacts, acquiring market information or specific product design for overseas markets. Exports are thus only profitable for smaller firms, if a large proportion of output is exported. On the other hand, larger firms may be better able to finance these costs and are therefore more likely to export.

**Table 7.2    Propensity to Export and Export Intensity (%) by Size and Sector,
Average 2000–2002**

| Propensity to export[a] | size category (number of employees) | | | |
|---|---|---|---|---|
| | *less than 20* | *20 to 75* | *more than 75* | *All* |
| agricultural | 0.94 | 0.85 | 0.83 | 0.88 |
| agricultural processing | 0.21 | 0.65 | 0.60 | 0.54 |
| textiles/garments + handicraft | 0.70 | 1.00 | 1.00 | 0.85 |
| wood and furniture | 0.00 | 0.00 | 0.67 | 0.21 |
| aluminium | 0.45 | 0.00 | 0.65 | 0.53 |
| plastic and rubber | 0.67 | 0.50 | 0.92 | 0.81 |
| other manufacturing | 0.00 | 0.00 | 0.67 | 0.35 |
| All | 0.46 | 0.65 | 0.73 | 0.62 |
| **Export intensity if a firm exports[b]** | | | | |
| agricultural | 94 | 70 | 86 | 84 |
| agric. processing | 60 | 67 | 40 | 50 |
| textiles/garments + handicraft | 57 | 95 | 32 | 66 |
| wood and furniture | – | – | 54 | 54 |
| aluminium | 72 | – | 18 | 33 |
| plastic and rubber | 5 | 5 | 35 | 30 |
| other manufacturing | – | – | 40 | 40 |
| All | 71 | 71 | 41 | 56 |

*Notes:* a) export propensity means the likelihood that a firm in a specific category exports. If it is 1.00 all firms in this category export, if it is 0.50 half of all firms export and if it is 0.00 no firm exports.

b) percent of output that is exported if a firm exports.

*Source:* Author's calculations

The huge differences in export shares of the different sectors are due to various factors. For some sectors, transport costs are prohibitively high so they can only export to neighbouring countries (e.g. mattresses and beverages). Aluminium products and plastic and rubber articles are predominantly exported to other ECOWAS countries. This explains the relatively small percentage of exports in these sectors, which is hampered by the slow implementation of the free trade area. By contrast, almost all commercial agricultural enterprises in the sample produce to some extent for the export market and almost all in the textiles, garments and handicrafts sectors. These sectors export a high percentage of their output to Europe and the US, which indicates a high degree of specialization.

In general, firms with some foreign participation tend to export less, which means that their main reason for producing in Ghana is not so much to exploit the Ghanaian comparative advantages, such as cheap labour, but rather to penetrate the Ghanaian market. This corresponds with the relatively high percentage of foreign investors in the agricultural processing and plastics sectors, both of which mainly serve the domestic and regional market.

As regards a number of other characteristics, exporters differ from non-exporters. For example, exporters employ considerably more women, have a higher rate of capital utilization and use more modern, imported machines. These factors might contribute to lower costs of production and higher productivity.

On average, the percentage of firms that exported increased from 61% in 2000 to 65% in 2002, whereas the share of exports in total output for exporters declined from 61% in 2000 to 57% in 2002, although the differences are not significant. This means that the export intensity has declined over the period. As the real value of output has increased over the same period, this is not necessarily associated with a decline in absolute exports and is therefore compatible with the overall picture of Ghanaian non-traditional exports. As inflation and depreciation were high in 2000, firms were forced to export relatively more as domestic demand was restricted. This is in line with the lower perception of insufficient demand as a major business obstacle on the part of exporting enterprises compared with non-exporters. However, aspects like access to domestic raw materials, inappropriate industrial policies, high interest rates and shortage of skilled labour are perceived as more problematic by exporters.

**Table 7.3     Export and Investment Categories, Average 2000–2002**

| | | | investment category | | Total |
|---|---|---|---|---|---|
| | | | no | yes | |
| exporting category | no | % of exporting category | 56.3 | 43.8 | 100.0 |
| | | % of investment category | 37.3 | 35.3 | 36.4 |
| | yes | % of exporting category | 54.1 | 45.9 | 100.0 |
| | | % of investment category | 62.7 | 64.7 | 63.6 |
| | Total | % of exporting category | 54.9 | 45.1 | 100.0 |
| | | % of investment category | 100.0 | 100.0 | |

*Note:* The figures in the upper lines add up horizontally, whereas the figures in the lower lines add up vertically. For example the first figure in the first line means that 56.3% of those enterprises that do not export also do not invest.

The differences in investment behaviour between exporting and non-exporting enterprises in the sample are smaller than expected. However, more of the exporting enterprises also invest and more of the investing enterprises also export (see Table 7.3). However, these differences are not statistically significant at the 5% level.

### *Efficiency of Enterprises*

For the analysis of exporting and investment decisions, a measurement of firm efficiency is useful. In this paper technical efficiency is measured as the time invariant residual from a Cobb-Douglas production function using random effects panel regressions. Value added (VA) is expressed as a function of capital (K) and labour (L) (equation 1). Capital is measured as the replacement value of equipment, land and buildings. Labour is measured as wage expenditure to capture different skill levels, as the education indicator is not available for a number of firms. Firm age (also squared) is entered as a control to capture the experience of the firm, but is not significant. The production function is reported below with standard errors in parenthesis.[4]

$$\ln (VA) = 2.020 + 0.156* \ln(K) + 0.800** \ln (L) + 0.033\ age - 0.0003\ age^2 \qquad (1)$$
$$\quad\ [0.016]\ \ [0.074] \qquad\quad [0.106] \qquad\quad\ \ [0.029] \quad\ [0.0005]$$
(Figures in parenthesis are standard errors)

In the estimation, year and sector dummies are used as controls. A test for the sum of coefficients being equal to one leads to acceptance, so it can be concluded that in the overall sample there are no economies of scale.

## 4.    The Decision to Export and the Decision to Invest

### *Methodology*

As the direction of the relationship between exporting and investment is not very obvious, the methodology that is used to capture the possible endogeneity of export performance and investment behaviour is a simultaneous-equation model. As a significant proportion of firms do not invest and/or export in a given period, the decisions to invest and export are estimated using probit regressions. The share of investment in total capital and the share of exports in total output are then modelled in a next step conditional on the decision to invest and the decision to export respectively, using a two stage least-square approach.

As the decision to export and the decision to invest are made at the same time, a simultaneous equations approach is used. Whether or not a firm exports does not change from year to year, so it will depend more on long-term development, whereas

---

[4] A random effects specification is used, although the Hausman test rejects the assumption that the variables and the unobserved firm effect are not correlated. One reason is that otherwise time invariant factors (especially sector) cannot be included in the regressions. When separate regressions are run for each sector the Hausman test does not reject the assumption that the variables and the unobserved firm effect are not correlated.

the decision to invest in a given year varies much more. Therefore the following model is used:

$$P(I=1) = G(z\delta_1 + á_1 E + u_1) \tag{2}$$

$$P(E=1) = G(z\delta_2 + v_1) \tag{3}$$

where I is an investment dummy, E is an exporting dummy, z is a vector of explanatory variables such as firm age, share of FDI in capital, firm size (measured as number of employees), importing, use of business services, technical efficiency and sector, which are mostly used in similar analysis (Pattillo, 1998; Bigsten et al., 1999; Rankin et al., 2002). G is the standard normal distribution.

The Rivers-Vuong approach was used to test for the exogeneity of E (see Wooldridge, 2002: 473ff). The test did not reject the null hypothesis that E is exogenous, so equation (3) was also estimated with a simple probit regression.[5]

As a specific interest of this study is the differences in exporting and investment between sectors, not only sector dummies are included but the firm characteristics are also interacted with the sector dummies. The firm characteristics are all treated as exogenous in both regressions, although past export and investment performance might have an influence on some of them, for example profits from exporting might impact on firm growth and investment. Therefore the regression results cannot be interpreted as causal relationships, strictly speaking.

## Determinants of the Decision to Export

First, the factors that are associated with the decision to export are determined. Table 7.4 reports the results of two probit regressions with and without interaction terms as explanatory variables.

Although the significance is not robust for the inclusion of different control variables, the likelihood to export first decreases and then increases with firm age. This partly confirms the learning effects that are necessary for exporting. In the aluminium sector an increase in age is directly positively associated with exporting.

In all specifications the coefficient for firm size is positive and significant, which is in line with the observations in Table 7.2 and with findings of other studies of Ghana's exporting firms (see Rankin et al., 2002; Söderbom and Teal, 2003). There are a number of possible explanations for the positive association of exporting with size. It might be related to the high fixed costs of exporting. Higher quality standards, like constant delivery of products and the ability to meet large orders, are more easily achieved by larger firms. Larger firms might also have better access to credit and lower capital costs, which might be more important for exports than domestic sales (see Bigsten et al., 1999).

---

[5] For binary regressions the two-stage approach cannot be used (Wooldridge, 2002: 478). Although panel data are used for the analysis, in the binary regressions it is assumed that there are no firm-specific fixed effects and therefore simple probit regressions can be used. Under the assumption that the model is dynamically complete this is a valid procedure (see Wooldridge, 2002).

**Table 7.4     Probit Regression of Decision to Export, exporting = 1, marginal effects**

|  | [1] | | [2] | |
| --- | --- | --- | --- | --- |
| Firm age | −0.007 | | −0.011 | |
|  | (0.008) | | (0.005) | ** |
| Firm age$^2$ | 0.0002 | | 0.0002 | |
|  | (0.0001) | | (0.0001) | * |
| % of FDI | −0.007 | | | |
|  | (0.002) | *** | | |
| Import intensity | −0.003 | | −0.004 | |
|  | (0.001) | ** | (0.002) | *** |
| ln firm size | 0.239 | | 0.235 | |
|  | (0.049) | *** | (0.047) | *** |
| Index business services | 0.076 | | 0.105 | |
|  | (0.041) | * | (0.033) | *** |
| Firm efficiency (value added) | −0.040 | | 0.072 | |
|  | (0.048) | | (0.034) | ** |
| FDI* agric. processing | | | −0.010 | |
|  | | | (0.002) | *** |
| FDI* plastic | | | −0.020 | |
|  | | | (0.005) | *** |
| imports*textiles etc. | | | 0.005 | |
|  | | | (0.002) | ** |
| imports * aluminium | | | 0.008 | |
|  | | | (0.0029 | *** |
| age * agric. processing | | | 0.004 | |
|  | | | (0.006) | |
| age * aluminium | | | 0.012 | |
|  | | | (0.007) | * |
| Agriculture | −0.391 | | −1.844 | |
|  | (0.206) | * | (0.462) | *** |
| Agric processing | −1.056 | | −2.176 | |
|  | (0.194) | *** | (0.497) | *** |
| Textiles/garments + handicrafts | −0.233 | | −1.693 | |
|  | (0.221) | | (0.432) | *** |
| Wood and furniture | −1.336 | | −2.443 | |
|  | (0.236) | *** | (0.575) | *** |
| Aluminium | −0.922 | | −2.668 | |
|  | (0.222) | *** | (0.632) | *** |
| Other manufacturing | −1.446 | | −2.785 | |
|  | (0.355) | *** | (0.654) | *** |
| No. of observations | 164 | | 164 | |
| % correctly predicted | 81.71 | | 90.24 | |
| Pseudo R$^2$ | 0.4244 | | 0.5899 | |
| Log likelihood | −59.4 | | −42.3 | |

*Notes:*     level of significance: * 10%, ** 5%, *** 1%; heteroskedasticity-robust standard errors in parenthesis (using Huber/White corrections).

*Source:*     Author's calculations

The percentage of raw materials that are imported seems to have a negative effect on the probability that a firm exports. This is contrary to the assumption that imported inputs are of higher quality and would therefore facilitate exporting. It rather seems to be the case that imported inputs are more expensive, especially as there was a major depreciation of the cedi in 2000 which reduced the competitiveness of firms that are dependent on imports. However, this effect is overcompensated in the agricultural processing and plastic sectors where the percentage of imported inputs has a positive impact on exporting. In agricultural processing, packaging material, that is often not available locally, is a crucial input, and in the plastic sector 98% of all inputs are imported.

Also the firms with more foreign ownership tend to be less export-oriented but rather serve the domestic market, in particular in the agricultural processing and plastic sectors. This is contrary to the expectation that firms with foreign ownership, that already have some links to foreign countries, face lower costs of exporting (Bigsten et al., 1999).[6]

As stated earlier, the likelihood to export increased from 2000 to 2002 but the coefficients of the year dummies are not significant and are therefore dropped from the final regressions. The insignificance of the time dummies can be interpreted as that changes in macroeconomic policies and business climate were either not very big or had no strong association with the decision to export. Many general managers of the sampled firms saw little improvement in the business environment.

The use of various business services, such as accounting, feasibility studies and marketing, is positively associated with exporting. The indicator used reflects the intensity of use of services in 4 categories (never, rarely, sometimes, regularly). The relationship between exporting and use of business services could run in both directions, as firms that want to enter into exporting might use more business services.

Whereas in regression [1] the efficiency parameter derived from the value-added specification of the production function is not significant, in regression [2] it is positively associated with exporting, which means that firms with higher efficiency are more likely to export. As was already seen in Table 7.2, the likelihood to export is highest in agriculture and textiles and handicrafts as compared with the other sectors.

## Determinants of the Decision to Invest

Theoretically a firm will make an investment if the expected present value adjusted by risk aversion is greater than the investment costs. The expected pay-off cannot be measured directly, but it can be assumed that past efficiency and firm size are used as a basis for investment decisions. Indicators such as firm age and foreign ownership are assumed to have an impact on attitude to risk and access to finance, which in turn influences investment costs. Unfortunately, variables that capture the risk attitude of entrepreneurs and the uncertainty of the environment directly were not available (see Pattillo, 1998). The goodness of fit of the models is not very high, probably because no dynamic effects could be included as the available time periods are very short.

---

[6] A dummy for subsidiaries of multinational firms was introduced to distinguish them from firms with foreign ownership that mainly operate in Ghana, but this dummy is not significant (not reported).

Table 7.5 reports the results of two probit regressions, with and without interaction terms as explanatory variables, in the decision to invest.

**Table 7.5    Probit Regression of Decision to Invest, investing = 1, marginal effects**

|  | [1] |  | [2] |  |
|---|---|---|---|---|
| Firm age | −0.009 |  | −0.014 |  |
|  | (0.005) | ** | (0.006) | ** |
| % of FDI | 0.003 |  |  |  |
|  | (0.002) | * |  |  |
| Export dummy | −0.006 |  | 0.075 |  |
|  | (0.125) |  | (0.139) |  |
| ln (firm size) | 0.143 |  | 0.110 |  |
|  | (0.053) | *** | (0.055) | ** |
| ln (capital per worker) | −0.046 |  | −0.067 |  |
|  | (0.027) | * | (0.033) | ** |
| Firm efficiency (value added) | 0.133 |  | 0.115 |  |
|  | (0.057) | ** | (0.068) | * |
| Female owner dummy | −0.019 |  | 0.041 |  |
|  | (0.147) |  | (0.192) |  |
| FDI* plastic |  |  | 0.052 |  |
|  |  |  | (0.005) | *** |
| exports*agriculture |  |  | −0.006 |  |
|  |  |  | (0.004) |  |
| ln (size) * textiles etc. |  |  | 0.353 |  |
|  |  |  | (0.106) | *** |
| age * agric. processing |  |  | 0.012 |  |
|  |  |  | (0.007) | * |
| Agriculture | 0.063 |  | 2.063 |  |
|  | (0.265) |  | (0.558) | *** |
| Agric processing | 0.443 |  | 1.928 |  |
|  | (0.256) | * | (0.476) | *** |
| Textiles/garments + handicrafts | −0.161 |  |  |  |
|  | (0.262) |  |  |  |
| Wood and furniture | 0.309 |  | 1.941 |  |
|  | (0.263) |  | (0.477) | *** |
| Aluminium | 0.294 |  | 1.958 |  |
|  | (0.258) |  | (0.474) | *** |
| Plastic and rubber | −0.098 |  | −3.142 |  |
|  | (0.696) |  | (0.122) | *** |
| Other manufacturing |  |  | 1.754 |  |
|  |  |  | (0.538) | *** |
| No. of observations | 157 |  | 157 |  |
| % correctly predicted | 52.23 |  | 49.68 |  |
| Pseudo R squared | 0.2348 |  | 0.3463 |  |
| Log likelihood | −82.6 |  | −70.5 |  |

*Notes:*    level of significance: * 10%, ** 5%, *** 1%; Heteroskedasticity-robust standard errors in parenthesis (using Huber/White corrections).
*Source:*   Author's calculations.

The likelihood to invest seems to decrease with firm age. However, in the agricultural processing sector an increase in age is positively associated with investing, and the negative effect is therefore partly offset. The fact that older firms invest less frequently than younger firms implies that the older firms have come closer to their optimal size, whereas new firms build up their business over a number of years and do not jumpstart operations. One reason for this observation might be the widespread credit constraints. On the other hand, there is evidence that entrepreneurs start small to test the market for their product and only increase operations once they have developed an accepted product. From the general investment pattern it can be concluded that younger firms will use newer machinery and equipment, which is associated with more current technology (see Rankin et al., 2002).

Firms with more foreign ownership tend to be more likely to invest, which is mainly due to their easier access to finance. This effect is especially strong in the plastics and rubber sector, where most enterprises are foreign-owned. The fact that a firm does export does not have a significant relationship with investing.

In both specifications the coefficient for firm size is positive and significant, which is in line with the observations in Table 7.1 and previous studies (Pattillo, 1998; Rankin et al., 2002). Larger firms have been more successful and therefore have higher expectations for future investments. They also have better access to finance. Furthermore, for small firms, even the purchase of one machine might be beyond their means, so they invest less frequently due to the indivisibility of investment goods. More efficient firms seem also more likely to invest, as they also expect higher pay-offs in the future.

By contrast, the coefficient of capital per worker is negative and significant for both specifications, which means that more capital-intensive firms are less likely to invest. This could indicate that some firms are too capital-intensive and therefore do not make the optimal allocation of labour and capital. The coefficients of the year dummies, that could capture changes in the uncertainty of the environment, are not significant and are therefore dropped from the final regressions. This indicates that the investment frequency has not changed over the period.

The likelihood to invest is highest in commercial agriculture. This might be due to the fact that investment in agricultural machines is more easily reversible than investments in other sectors, as there are no installation costs and there are alternative possibilities for using the machines in the large Ghanaian agricultural sector (see Pattillo, 1998). Other factors being equal, firms in agricultural processing, wood and furniture, and aluminium production are also more likely to invest as compared with the other sectors.

So far no relationship between exporting and investment could be found. However, some factors work in the same direction for both decisions. For example, firm age has a negative association with both the likelihood to export and the likelihood to invest, whereas firm size and efficiency are positively associated with both decisions. On the other hand, the share of foreign ownership has a negative effect on the likelihood to export and a positive effect on the likelihood to invest. For further investigation of the issue, the export and investment intensities are analyzed.

## 5.    Export Intensity and Investment Ratio

### *Methodology*

The basic model considered here allows for the endogeneity of export and investment intensity. Therefore a two-stage least squares approach is used with the following simultaneous equation model:

$$\text{Exp} = \alpha_{1,0} + \alpha_{1,1} \, \text{Inv} + \beta_1 \, X_1 + u_1 \tag{4}$$

$$\text{Inv} = \alpha_{2,0} + \alpha_{2,1} \, \text{Exp} + \beta_2 \, X_2 + u_2 \tag{5}$$

where Exp is the share of output exported, Inv is the investment ratio and $X_1$ and $X_2$ are different sets of exogenous variables, such as firm age, share of FDI in capital, firm size (measured as number of employees), importing, use of business services, technical efficiency, sector and year.

To control for self-selection into exporting and investment the Heckman procedure is used to estimate the determinants of export and investment intensity (Greene, 2000; Wooldridge, 2002). To estimate equations (4) and (5) the inverse Mills ratios that are obtained from regression [1] in Table 7.4 and regression [1] in Table 7.5 are used to control for sample selection bias.[7]

### *Export Intensity*

For the analysis of the factors associated with export intensity, random effects panel regressions are used. From the descriptive statistics, it is already known that larger firms are more likely to export, but their export intensity is lower than that for small firms. This leads to the assumption that the factors associated with export intensity might differ from those associated with the decision to export. The results are reported in Table 7.6.

In contrast to the decision to export, firm age seems to have no effect on the export intensity once the firm has entered the export market. Only for wood and furniture producers does the export intensity increase, whereas for other sectors the coefficients of the interaction terms are not significant and are therefore dropped from the regression. Size is again positively associated with export intensity, which is contrary to other findings.

Firm efficiency is also positively associated with the export intensity, so more efficient firms are not only more likely to export but also to export a bigger share of their production. The coefficient of the capital: labour ratio is not significant and is therefore dropped.

The investment ratio (which has been instrumented) seems to be also negatively associated with export intensity. This is contrary to the theoretically positive

---

[7] To be able to include time invariant determinants of export intensity, especially the sector dummies, random effects panel regressions are used for the estimation of the determinants of export shares and investment ratios. As the inverse Mills ratios differ for the two equations, no identification problem occurs.

relationship between exporting and investment discussed earlier. However, in order to investigate this relationship in more detail, time lags would have to be considered. Given the constraints in the capital market, additional investment could lead to the reduction of working capital, which makes it difficult to meet export orders unless they are pre-financed by the customer.

**Table 7.6 Random Effects Regression of Export Intensity, with Correction for Sample Selection**

| | [1] | | [2] | |
|---|---|---|---|---|
| Investment ratio[a] | −23.685 | | −25.424 | |
| | (13.054) | * | (15.296) | *** |
| Firm age | | | −0.058 | |
| | | | (0.268) | |
| Share of regional exports | −101.516 | | −99.881 | |
| | (19.494) | *** | (21.007) | *** |
| ln firm size | 3.206 | | 3.273 | |
| | (1.530) | ** | (1.569) | ** |
| Firm efficiency (value added) | 13.061 | | 13.217 | |
| | (4.695) | *** | (4.783) | *** |
| Index education | −4.679 | | −4.740 | |
| | (8.453) | | (8.528) | |
| FDI * other manufact. | | | 3.969 | |
| | | | (1.354) | *** |
| Age * wood | | | 4.422 | |
| | | | (1.510) | *** |
| Agriculture | 98.248 | | 99.124 | |
| | (17.850) | *** | (18.428) | *** |
| Agric processing | 86.076 | | 86.925 | |
| | (23.325) | *** | (23.824) | *** |
| Textiles and handicrafts | 81.764 | | 82.865 | |
| | (18.010) | *** | (18.837) | *** |
| Wood and furniture | 102.472 | | | |
| | (34.258) | *** | | |
| Aluminium | 138.859 | | 138.892 | |
| | (29.569) | *** | (29.809) | *** |
| Plastic | 110.211 | | 109.591 | |
| | (26.953) | *** | (27.336) | *** |
| Other manufacturing | 116.484 | | | |
| | (38.432) | *** | | |
| Lambda (inv. Mills ratio) | −4.196 | | −4.325 | |
| | (5.103) | | (5.165) | |
| No. of observations | 83 | | 83 | |
| $R^2$ overall | 0.7006 | | 0.6982 | |

*Notes:* level of significance: * 10%, ** 5%, *** 1%; a — instrumented using all independent variables in equations (4) and (5), standard errors in parenthesis.

*Source:* Author's calculations.

Again certain firm characteristics have different effects on the export intensity in different sectors. Firms with a higher share of FDI in capital in other manufacturing and older wood processing firms seem to export more.

The coefficients for the sector dummies are all significant in both regressions. Especially in aluminium processing the share of exports in total output is higher than the average for the whole sample, after controlling for other factors.

Other factors that might be associated with export intensity like education of the workforce, giving training to workers, and the rate of capacity utilization are not significant and are not reported here.

## The Investment Ratio

For the analysis of the factors associated with the investment ratio, random effects panel regressions are again used. The Hausman test was in favour of random effects regressions.

From the descriptive statistics it is known that larger firms are more likely to invest, but their investment ratio is lower than that for small firms. This leads to the assumption that the factors associated with the investment ratio might differ from those associated with the decision to invest. The results are reported in Table 7.7.

In contrast to the decision to invest, firm age seems to have no effect on the investment ratio once the firm has decided to invest, and age was therefore dropped from the regression. The same holds for FDI. These findings are again in line with findings from other studies (Pattillo, 1998; Rankin et al., 2002).

In line with the descriptive statistics in Table 7.1, size is negatively associated with the investment ratio in contrast to the decision to invest, which can be explained by the indivisibility of investment. Firm efficiency is not significant in the investment ratio regressions, although more efficient firms are more likely to invest. The capital: labour ratio is negatively associated with the investment ratio and the decision to invest, which means that firms with a high capital: labour ratio try to reduce their investment.

The export share (which has been instrumented) seems to be also negatively associated with the investment ratio. This confirms the results from the regressions with the export share as dependent variable (see Table 7.6). To achieve an increase in exports might incur extra costs so that less capital for investment is available, given the constraints in the capital market.

The share of imports in raw materials has a negative association with the investment ratio. This might be due to the higher costs of imported inputs that leave less profit available for investment. The use of imported inputs is also associated with higher risk, as the delivery of domestic inputs might be more regular and might have a shorter planning period as compared with imported inputs which are subject to border delays (see Söderbom, 2000).

The growth of the workforce (from the previous to the current year), which captures some dynamic effects of firm performance, is not significant. An increase in the workforce might lead to greater capital utilization instead of more investment, and a decrease in the workforce might not be associated with the rationalization of investment. The fact that a firm gives training to its workers is positively associated with the investment ratio, as trained workers are better able to use new machinery.

**Table 7.7    Random Effects Regression of Investment Ratio, with Correction for Sample Selection**

|  | [1] |  | [2] |  |
|---|---|---|---|---|
| Export intensity[a] | −0.013 |  | −0.013 |  |
|  | (0.006) | ** | (0.006) | ** |
| ln firm size | −0.245 |  | −0.245 |  |
|  | (0.077) | *** | (0.077) | *** |
| ln (capital/labour) | −0.072 |  | −0.072 |  |
|  | (0.036) | ** | (0.036) | ** |
| Growth of labour | −0.0003 |  | −0.0003 |  |
|  | (0.0004) |  | (0.0004) |  |
| Import intensity | −0.002 |  | −0.002 |  |
|  | (0.001) | * | (0.001) | * |
| Dummy training | 0.657 |  | 0.657 |  |
|  | (0.376) | * | (0.376) | * |
| Firm efficiency (value added) | −0.088 |  | −0.088 |  |
|  | (0.079) |  | (0.079) |  |
| Imports * other manufact. |  |  | −0.022 |  |
|  |  |  | (0.013) | * |
| Agric processing | −0.959 |  | −0.959 |  |
|  | (0.365) | *** | (0.365) | *** |
| Textiles and handicrafts | −0.627 |  | −0.627 |  |
|  | (0.298) | * | (0.298) | * |
| Wood and furniture | −1.738 |  | −1.738 |  |
|  | (0.570) | *** | (0.570) | *** |
| Aluminium | −0.962 |  | −0.962 |  |
|  | (0.407) | ** | (0.407) | ** |
| Plastic | −0.766 |  | −0.766 |  |
|  | (0.423) | * | (0.423) | * |
| Other manufacturing | −0.648 |  |  |  |
|  | (0.391) | * |  |  |
| Year 2001 | 4.079 |  | 4.079 |  |
|  | (1.231) | *** | (1.231) | *** |
| Year 2002 | 4.128 |  | 4.128 |  |
|  | (1.234) | *** | (1.234) | *** |
| Year 2003 | 4.190 |  | 4.190 |  |
|  | (1.241) | *** | (1.241) | *** |
| Lambda (inv. Mills ratio) | −1.049 |  | −1.049 |  |
|  | (0.364) | *** | (0.364) | *** |
| No. of observations | 63 |  | 63 |  |
| $R^2$ overall | 0.4143 |  | 0.4143 |  |

*Notes:*    As for Table 7.6.
As the change from the dummy of other manufactures to the interactive term dummy of other manufactures * percentage of imported inputs only affects very few observations, the other coefficients remain unaffected.

*Source:*    Author's calculations.

As in the case of export shares, only a few of the interaction terms were significant, so, apart from sector dummies, the other investment determinants seem to have the same effects in all sectors. Only the imports of raw materials seem to have a bigger negative effect in the other manufacturing sector.

The coefficients for the sector dummies are all significant in both regressions. In agriculture, which is the omitted sector, the investment ratio is highest, whereas in the wood and furniture sector it is lowest. Likewise the year dummies are all significant and indicate that the investment ratio was lowest in 2000, whereas there was not much difference thereafter. This might be explained by the higher macroeconomic instability in 2000.

For other factors that might be associated with the investment ratio, like education of the workforce, the ratio of sunk investment, and the rate of capacity utilization, too few observations are available, so they could not be included in the regressions.

## 6.   Conclusions

Contrary to the initial hypothesis, no positive association between exporting and investment could be found in the survey of private enterprises in Ghana for the period 2000–2003. This result might be due to limitations of the time period, that does not allow long-term effects to be captured. The time lag from an increase in investment to the production of more exports could be longer than a year. The depreciation of the cedi in 1999 stimulated the non-traditional export total immediately, whereas firms seem to have delayed bigger investment decisions, waiting for the outcome of the 2000 elections and the performance of the new government. Only in 2003 did both credits from domestic banks to the private sector and FDI start to pick up. The bulk of the increased exports might therefore have been produced by greater capital utilization, not by new investment.

On the other hand there is some evidence of a short-term trade-off between exporting and investment. In order to export, firms usually need more working capital to produce higher quality goods and to pre-finance shipment, so that less capital is available for investment. Most entrepreneurs rate access to finance and high interest rates as the major business obstacles. Hence, better access to finance could improve both exporting and investment. Initiatives like the establishment of the Export Development and Investment Fund (EDIF), that provides investment capital for exporters, are likely to contribute to the performance of exporters. However, the limited funds that are allocated to the EDIF and the difficulties for smaller firms to access funds restrict its impact severely.

The empirical analysis has confirmed the assumption that different factors have an impact on exporting and investment in different sectors. For example, enterprises that import a higher share of raw materials are less likely to enter into exporting, whereas in the textiles and handicraft and aluminium sectors they are more likely to export. This means that while for some sectors the high costs of imports reduce their competitiveness, for others the use of high quality inputs facilitates exporting or firms that export a larger share of output need a larger share of imported inputs to meet quality standards. For many agricultural and agro-processing goods, packaging plays a major role in being successful as an exporter. However, there are still significant shortages of adequate packaging material from Ghana, although the situation has improved. This is reflected by the perception of exporters that access to domestic inputs is a bigger problem as compared with non-exporters. Likewise, the availability of laboratory services as well as transport and storage infrastructure (which could partly be financed privately) are crucial for exporters, especially of high value agricultural products and agricultural processing.

The decision to export as well as the share of output that is exported by the sample firms seems to be unchanged over the period of analysis. This is in line with Figure 7.3 which reports increases in exports only for the aluminium sector and other processed and semi-processed goods, the latter being insufficiently captured in the survey. The stagnation of exports for most sub-sectors means that the business environment has not changed much in favour of exporting. However, positive changes in export performance might occur only over a longer period, as a lot of information has to be gathered and contacts have to be established before exports can take place. Although the decision to export was also unchanged over time, the investment ratio has increased since 2000, which shows a small positive effect of macroeconomic stabilization with respect to inflation, the exchange rate and interest rates.

With respect to the provision of business services and information, an awareness problem still persists, although users of business services are more likely to export. Firms are not aware of the potential benefits from external services, and if they are looking for services, they have difficulties in finding the most appropriate provider as a large number of small private commercial and donor-funded agencies exist. Since it is difficult for enterprises with little experience to assess the quality of service providers, transparency could be increased by means of export promotion agencies and business associations. General business services and training of entrepreneurs should have a high priority in private sector development, as efficiency is positively related to the decisions to export and invest as well as the export intensity.

Strengthening the competitiveness of Ghana's NTE does not mean that the traditional export sectors should be neglected. However, private and public revenues from cocoa production and gold mining should be used to diversify the economy and to improve the overall business environment. Focusing too much on direct incentives for exporters, instead of reducing overall distortions and improving the infrastructure, is likely to benefit mainly firms that are already exporting. The effect on current non-exporters might be very weak, as evidence from other African countries shows (Adenikinju et al., 2002).

## References

Adenikinju, Adeola, Söderling, Ludvig, Soludo, Charles and Varoudakis, Aristomene (2002) 'Manufacturing Competitiveness in Africa: Evidence from Cameroon, Côte d'Ivoire, Nigeria and Senegal,' *Economic Development and Cultural Change,* Vol. 50, No. 3: 643–665.

Aryeetey, E., Nissanke, M. and Steel, W. F. (2000) 'Intervention & Liberalization: Changing Policies & Performance in the Financial Sector' in E. Aryeetey, J. Harrigan and M. Nissanke (eds), *Economic Reforms in Ghana — The Miracle & the Mirage.* Oxford: James Currey; Accra: Woeli Publishing Services; and Trenton, NJ: Africa World Press, pp. 209–226.

Bank of Ghana (BoG) (2004) *Statistical Bulletin,* Accra, April.

Bigsten, A., Collier, P., Dercon, S., Fafchamps, M., Gauthier, B., Gunning, J. W. , Habarurema, J., Isaksson, A., Oduro, A., Oostendorp, R., Pattillo, C., Söderbom, M., Teal, F. and Zeufack, A. (1999) 'Exports of African Manufactures: Macro Policy and Firm Behaviour', *Journal of International Trade and Development,* Vol. 8:53–71.

Collier, P. and Pattillo, C. (2000) 'Investment and Risk in Africa', in P. Collier and C. Pattillo (eds), *Investment and Risk in Africa.* New York: St Martins Press, pp. 3–30.

Ghana Export Promotion Council (GEPC) (1987–2003) *Comparison of Export Performance of Non-traditional Products,* Accra: GEPC, various issues (photocopy).

Ghana Export Promotion Council (GEPC) (2003) 'List of Active Non-Traditional Exporters', Accra: GEPC (photocopy).

Ghana Investment Promotion Centre (GIPC) (2004) *Cumulative and Yearly Sector Breakdown and Investment Cost of Projects,* Accra: GIPC

Government of Ghana (GoG) (2004) *The Budget Statement and Economic Policy of the Government of Ghana.* Accra: Government of Ghana.

Greene, William H. (2000) *Econometric Analysis.* 4th edn. Upper Saddle River, NJ: Prentice Hall.

ISSER (2003) *The State of the Ghanaian Economy 2002.* Accra: Institute of Statistical, Social and Economic Research, University of Ghana, Legon.

Pattillo, C. (1998) 'Investment, Uncertainty, and Irreversibility in Ghana'. *IMF Staff Papers No. 45,* Washington, DC: IMF.

Rankin, Neil, Söderbom, Mans and Teal, Francis (2002) *Ghanaian Manufacturing Enterprise Survey 2000.* CSAE, University of Oxford. http://www.economics.ox.ac.uk/csaeadmin/reports (accessed 15 January 2004).

Sarpong, Daniel B. (1998) *Ghana Integrated to the World Economy: Focus on Ghana-UK-Germany Trade Linkage Model.* HWWA Diskussionspapier No. 58, Hamburg: HWWA.

Söderbom, Mans (2000) *Managerial Risk Attitudes and Firm Performance in Ghanaian Manufacturing,* CSAE-UNIDO Working Paper No. 3. CSAE, Univeristy of Oxford.

Söderbom, Mans and Teal, Francis (2003) 'Are Manufacturing Exports the Key to Economic Success in Africa?', *Journal of African Economies,* Vol. 12, No. 1:1–29.

UNCTAD (2003) *Economic Development in Africa, Trade Performance and Commodity Dependence,* New York and Geneva: UNCTAD.

Wolf, Susanna (2003) *Private Sector Development and Competitiveness in Ghana.* ZEF Discussion Paper No. 70. Zentrum für Entwicklungsforschung, University of Bonn.

Wooldridge, Jeffrey M. (2002) *Econometric Analysis of Cross Section and Panel Data.* Cambridge, MA: MIT Press.

# 8 Household Savings in Ghana: Does Policy Matter?

PETER QUARTEY
& THERESA BLANKSON

## 1. Introduction

Savings, a necessary engine of economic growth, have been very low in Ghana. Gross Domestic Savings as a percentage of GDP in Ghana have been low compared with many other African countries, averaging, between 1980 and 2001, 6.4% in Ghana, 37.4% in Botswana, 21.4% in Cameroon, 21.6% in Nigeria, 13.9% in Kenya and 7.3% in Malawi (World Bank, 2003). The apparent low saving rate in Ghana has been due to a combination of micro and macroeconomic and political factors. In order to overcome the problem of low savings in Ghana, various monetary and fiscal policies have been pursued over the years, but these have not yielded the required results postulated by the Mckinnon-Shaw hypothesis (Quartey, 2002; Zorklu and Barbie, 2003). This raises a number of issues for consideration: why do people find financial savings less attractive? Which age group or occupational category saves in Ghana? Do females hold financial savings as compared with their male counterparts? These and a few other issues which have been of major concern to policy-makers in Ghana will form the focus of this paper. It will critically examine the reasons for the relatively low savings in Ghana despite the numerous macro-financial policies pursued in the 1990s.

Following a consideration of the literature in Section 2, Section 3 outlines the monetary policy instruments used in Ghana since the Economic Recovery Programme was launched in 1983. A section on the methodological approach follows this. Section 5 provides a descriptive analysis of GLSS 3 and 4, and Section 5 contains concluding remarks and suggests directions for further research.

## 2. Savings and Macro-financial Policy

Examining the reasons for the relatively low savings in Ghana would require a critical look at the determinants of savings and whether macro-financial policy has a role to play. The determinants of savings in Ghana have been examined at the aggregate level, but there has not been any substantive work on the effects of macro-financial policy on household savings behaviour in developing countries, particularly in Ghana.

**153**

Testing for the effects of macro-policy changes on household savings is an empirical matter, on which limited work has been done. Nevertheless, a considerable amount of theoretical reviews or studies have been carried out, but the literature on the effects of financial market policies on savings is mixed. Whereas some are of the view that liberalizing financial market policies would make no significant changes to private savings, others hold a contrary view. For example, a study of personal money demand and savings in China identified that the demand for money did respond to shifts in the policy regime (Ma, 1993). Browning and Lusardi (1996), in an article which examined the effects of policy changes on consumption, especially of durables, when social security payments increases were paid, rather than when they were announced six weeks earlier, found that these policy changes had positive effects. This finding supports the work of Wilcox (1989) and also suggests myopia, binding liquidity constraints, or substantial credit market transaction costs or changes in credit restrictions as factors (Alessi et al., 1993).

The literature discussed so far is concerned with policy effects on household savings behaviour in the presence of liquidity constraints, but they run counter to what is predicted by the standard life-cycle model (Ando and Modigliani, 1963). Examining changes in savings behaviour due to changes in policy events enables us to distinguish between the effects of a one-off change in policy and the effects of policy changes over time. Thus, other studies have examined the impact of policy changes on savings over time. Gregory et al. (1999), using longitudinal household survey data, found that, despite the upheavals of transition, Russian households saved much the same in the 1990s, which was higher than savings in 1976. This finding is contrary to expectations, since there is widespread belief that savings were actually relatively high in the Soviet era because of shortages of consumption goods (a form of forced saving) and that saving became lower with price liberalization. In contrast, Liu and Xu (1997), in a study of Shanghai households, found a change in savings behaviour after economic reform. After the economic reforms in Shanghai, not only did household savings grow, but there was also a diversification into new financial instruments. The reforms which have impacted on health and pension provision did encourage households to increase saving. These findings suggest that it is important to distinguish between financial sector and other sectoral policy changes when examining policy effects on household financial behaviour.

Some studies have used panels of countries and aggregate data to test for the relationships between key variables and saving and the effects of policy on saving. Loayza et al. (2000) find that there are long lags between policy changes and changes in private saving behaviour, and that financial liberalization reduces private saving rates. They also find no positive relationship between financial deepening and saving or between higher real interest rates and saving. They do, however, find a positive relationship between income growth and saving and this is in line with the findings of Attanasio et al. (2000). Maimbo and Mavrotas (2001), in a case study of Zambia, also find that financial reforms have not resulted in an increase in savings rates, partly because of poorly functioning institutions, which, as in Russia, result in people holding their financial assets in hard currency. Hussain et al. (2002) examined the impact of financial liberalization on resource mobilization and investment in 25 African countries, including Ghana, and found that the real interest rate does not seem to be an important factor as a determinant of financial saving and total saving, but that the activities of the informal financial market are an important determinant of financial savings.

Other studies have examined the determinants of savings across developed and developing countries, and in particular whether monetary policy effects on savings in developing countries differed from those of developed countries. For instance, Masson et al. (1998), in an attempt to discover the determinants of private savings across a large number of developed and developing countries over time, found that the interest rate is a significant explanatory variable for developed countries in determining savings rates. However, this is not the case in developing countries. They found that growth in income was associated with higher rates of saving, but, beyond a certain point, as income increases savings ratios fall.

There have been few studies on Ghana to ascertain the impact of policy on savings behaviour. The most recent study by Zorklu and Barbie (2003) examined the impact of financial sector reform on private financial savings. Its results show that financial sector reform did not achieve its intended goal of enhancing private financial savings. This is because the inflationary pressures in Ghana during the reform period resulted in negative real deposit interest rates and, as a result, the savings response was weak. This corroborates the findings of earlier studies (Aryeetey and Gockel, 1991; Brownbridge and Gockel, 1998; Akoena and Gockel, 2002). A major lesson from Ghana's experience is that financial sector reform undertaken in countries with high inflationary pressures has a reduced chance of increasing savings mobilization.

Despite the relevance of the findings made by the above studies, they suffer from major drawbacks. The first is that most of them have been focused on developed countries, but the determinants of savings in developing countries may be different from those of developed countries, as revealed in Masson et al. (1998). Secondly, as far as Ghana is concerned, there has not been any formal empirical analysis of the effects of macro-financial policies on household savings behaviour. Such macro-micro relationships have very useful policy relevance. Finally, studies on savings in Ghana have used aggregate savings data. As pointed out by Schmidt-Hebbel et al. (1992), the use of national aggregate savings data in empirical work is flawed in cases where private savings account for a predominant part of total savings. Schmidt-Hebbel and his colleagues argued that aggregate savings can be used as a proxy for household savings only if the Ricardian equivalence holds and private and public savings can thus be substituted, and household savings are a perfect substitute for private corporate savings. Thus, unless a formal test of the Ricardian equivalence is carried out, the use of aggregate savings as a proxy for household savings will give different results. It is against this background that the present study intends to use micro data to test for the effects of macro-financial policies on household savings behaviour in Ghana.

It must be emphasized that although studies have attempted to ascertain the determinants of savings in Ghana (Brownbridge and Gockel, 1988; Zorklu and Barbie,

2003), these studies have used national savings and little attempt has been made to ascertain the impact of macro-financial policy on household savings. However, it is of great importance to ascertain the factors that influence changes in household savings as this will assist in formulating policies to stimulate savings and investment — two important factors necessary for sustained economic growth. However, the absence of earlier work on the impact of macro-financial policies on household savings presents a challenge to this study, as there are no existing results with which a comparison can be made.

## 3.   Monetary Policy in Ghana

Significant changes have been observed in the conduct of monetary policy in Ghana, particularly with regard to the type of instruments used, though the primary objective of price stability has remained unchanged since independence and through to the launching of the Economic Recovery Programme (ERP) in 1983. Ensuring price stability by improving the monetary policy instruments has been particularly necessary to boost confidence in the financial system within both the national and the international community in order to increase financial flows. At present the instruments of monetary policy have been improved and made more indirect relative to the instruments used prior to the ERP. Before the ERP, the main instruments adopted were direct controls in the form of credit ceilings on commercial banks' credit to the private sector and the regulation of interest rates. This system of monetary management, though implemented with ease, had several disadvantages. All the Bank of Ghana had to do was to determine growth in the money supply for the year based on economic growth and inflation objectives, determine the credit growth among banks based on set criteria, and then monitor the banks' compliance with the guidelines (Addison, 2001). High reserve requirements were also imposed during that era. This method of monetary management was thus seen to be simple and straightforward.

With high unremunerated reserve requirements, however, coupled with credit ceilings, excess liquidity was accumulated in the banking sector with no avenue for investing these funds. As a result, the banks had no incentive to mobilize savings. In addition, interest rates became negative in real terms as a result of ceilings on lending rates often kept low in order to keep the cost of borrowing low, especially to the government; this was a further disincentive to savings. The system of direct controls therefore contributed to the deterioration in the banking system by increasing transaction costs, discouraging financial intermediation and leading to misallocation of resources.

The instruments currently used by the Bank of Ghana include reserve requirements, open market operations (OMO), and repurchase agreements. In recent times, the government has set up the Monetary Policy Committee (MPC) with the onerous responsibility of setting the prime rate — another monetary policy instrument which gives signals to the financial institutions about the BoG's assessment of monetary conditions. Other monetary policy instruments used in Ghana include moral suasion and reverse repo (a repurchase agreement and banking perspective under which the borrower provides a collateralized loan to the creditor, in this case the Bank of Ghana).

## Primary Reserve Requirements

Ghana has a long history of using reserve requirements for both prudential and monetary management purposes. During the period of direct controls, they were used as a supplement to credit controls. The central bank continued to use reserve requirements after the introduction of indirect monetary control. However, the ratios, base and method of calculation have evolved over the years. Prior to March 1990, the ratios discriminated between types of deposit; those applied to demand deposits were higher than those for savings and time deposits (quasi money), the idea being to encourage commercial banks to mobilize long-term funds, which could be channeled into long-term lending. After 1990, the two ratios were merged into a single ratio on all deposits (demand, time and savings deposits).

The coverage has been extended to include foreign-exchange deposits since 1997. This was in response to the central bank's decision to target the broader definition of money supply, M2+, which also includes foreign currency deposits (Bank of Ghana, *Annual Report,* 1997). In this way, the central bank would have better control over the money supply, while at the same time levelling the playing field for the mobilization of both domestic and foreign currency deposits. The level of the ratio itself fluctuated over the years, reflecting liquidity conditions in the banking system, and reaching its highest level of 27% in 1990. Thereafter the ratio was progressively lowered until it reached its lowest point of 5% in 1993. The reserve ratio was again raised to 10% in 1996 and lowered to 8% in 1997 when foreign currency deposits were included in the total deposit base for the calculation of reserves. In July 2000, in response to rising inflation and the sharp depreciation of the cedi, the ratio was raised to 9% where it continues to remain (BoG, *Annual Report,* 2000).

## Reserves against Foreign Currency Deposits

There are two main issues that frequently come up with foreign currency deposits: whether the reserves against these deposits should be held in foreign or domestic currency, and whether foreign currency deposits should be included in the monetary target. Generally, when reserves against foreign currency deposits are held in the domestic currency, banks are likely to be exposed to foreign currency risks. However, Hardy (1997) points out that denominating some reserves in foreign currency can complicate the implementation of monetary policy by removing some of the central bank's control over base money. The second issue of whether foreign currency deposits should be included in the monetary target is an empirical issue, depending on the substitutability of foreign and domestic currencies. Reserve requirements against foreign currency deposits were introduced in Ghana in 1997 with the main aim of levelling the playing field for the mobilization of domestic and foreign currency deposits. As in the case of cedi deposits, the requirements for foreign currency deposits are currently fixed at 9% and are not remunerated.

However, the BoG requires banks to keep reserves against foreign currency deposits in cedis for a number of reasons. First, keeping them in foreign currency would be operationally difficult because the central bank would have to monitor the banks' various nostro accounts in different currencies. Also, there was a need at the time to tighten liquidity further in order to sustain the downward trend in inflation. This measure apparently provided an avenue for the central bank to tighten liquidity conditions without appearing to increase overall reserve requirements. It is important to note here that, in the application of this policy, banks with large foreign currency deposits have found themselves increasingly having to augment their reserve requirements at the Bank of Ghana as a result of the depreciation of the domestic currency. The problem was more pronounced in 2000 with the sharp depreciation of the cedi following the external sector shocks that adversely affected the economy. This led to calls for a review of the policy by banks that had been hard hit. In summary, the Bank of Ghana has used reserve requirements extensively to support its monetary management.

The methodology the BoG follows generally conforms to acceptable norms in terms of base, method of computation and conformity in the treatment of all types of reserves. However, the level of the ratio is still considered high at 9%. It is generally accepted that the optimal level should be close to the level of reserves kept by banks for clearing purposes, which in Ghana is estimated at between 2% and 3%. Because of the continued existence of excess liquidity in the system, it is unlikely the ratio will be reduced immediately. Effective on 23 September 2002, the domestic money banks were allowed to maintain the primary reserve requirement of their foreign currency deposits in foreign currency. Hitherto, they had been required to keep primary reserves on both cedi and foreign currency deposits in cedis. It was expected that the new policy would improve market liquidity (Bank of Ghana, *Annual Report, 2001*).

## *Measurement of Reserve Requirements*

Addison (2001) reiterates that reserve requirements are more effective if they are observed contemporaneously, both for monetary targeting and prudential purposes. However, for developing countries where there are significant lags in reporting, it may be convenient to have lags between the base and the maintenance period. Hardy (1997) also points out that an averaging method is preferable to a day-to-day maintenance method, since the latter compels banks to hold excess reserves and thus affects the stability of the multiplier and further complicates the conduct of monetary policy. In Ghana, the contemporaneous observance and daily maintenance of reserve requirements were used until 1994, when this was replaced by a one-week lagged observance. The seven-day week averaging method also replaced the daily observance at the same time. In terms of coverage, two items are usually included in the definition of reserves, namely cash in the tills of banks (vault cash) and balances with the central bank. A third item, which is sometimes included, is call money in the interbank market. In 1986, the Bank of Ghana included all three items in the definition. In 1989, call money was dropped and finally in 1996 the definition was narrowed to include only balances with the central bank. This was done to avoid the difficulty of monitoring compliance when the cash in the tills of banks is included in the definition.

## *Open Market-type Operations*

In implementing monetary policy, the Bank of Ghana intervenes mainly through the primary auction of Treasury bills and BoG bills, a process also referred to as open market-type operations. The system has undergone several transformations. Originally, weekly auctions of Treasury and BoG bills were held on Fridays, with the amount offered being based on the difference between projected and targeted reserve money, maturing bills as well as the government's borrowing requirements (PSBR). The weekly auctions were initially open to banks and also to the non-bank public, although the non-bank public had to submit their bids through their bankers. Pricing at the auction is based on the multiple price auction system, where bids are arranged in descending order and the higher prices are allotted first until the offer is exhausted. Each bidder pays the price he quotes. Investors could also purchase on tap directly from the BoG between tenders (auctions) at the weighted average price declared at the preceding auction. The tap was supposed to be open only when targets had not been met, but was, in practice, always open in view of the large liquidity overhang. The tap between tenders was closed to all banks in March 1996, but remained open to the non-bank sector. This situation discouraged the development of the secondary market, and therefore in 1997 the BoG abolished the tap for the non-bank sector as well. Tap sales continue to operate, however, at the BoG's regional branches.

## The Primary Dealer System

In March 1996, the Bank of Ghana introduced the wholesale auction system. Tenders became restricted to primary dealers comprising commercial banks, discount houses and four brokerage firms. A well-functioning primary dealer system should help to develop the secondary market. The primary dealers should be able to underwrite the whole issue at the tender. They should also be leaders in the market and should act as market makers in government and central bank securities. In this regard, primary dealers should stand ready to give firm price quotations. In return, the dealers are offered certain privileges such as access to special financing arrangements. In Ghana, the system has not worked well. The auctions are often under-subscribed and the primary dealers make no effort to promote secondary market activity. The Bank of Ghana has in a way contributed to the problems by continuing to maintain a window for the discount of government securities. The tap continues to be open to the non-bank sector in parts of the country. There also seems to be a lack of expertise on the part of the market participants, including the central bank.

## Money Market Instruments

The main instruments over the years have not changed significantly, although there has been a recent shift in composition from BoG bills to Treasury bills. In the 1990s the proportion of BoG bills in the total stock increased from 34% to a peak of 80% in 1994 and then fell sharply to less than 4% in March 1998. This followed a deliberate central bank policy of replacing BoG bills with Treasury bills, apparently because of the government's increasing concerns about interest payments on these instruments. Thus, from 1996, Treasury bills became the main instrument of intervention, while at the same time serving the purpose of the government's debt management. The process of conversion was largely completed by March 1998, with the remaining stock comprising 30-day bills and 3-year and 5-year bonds, but the last two were not actively traded on the market. At present the debt instruments used include 91-day bills, 182-day bills and the 1-year notes categorized as Treasury bills. In addition to 2-year notes/bonds categorized as bonds, the Government of Ghana 3-year Indexed-Linked Bonds (GGLIBs) were also introduced in 2001.

## Monetary Market Rates

While a lot has been achieved in laying down the infrastructure for market intervention, there has not been much success in achieving money-supply and inflation targets. Again, the main problem has been the continued presence of the government in the market, as well as the inability of the central bank to vary rates to achieve the desired targets. Between January 1995 and December 1996 the Bank Rate remained relatively stable, although market conditions (as measured by the inflation rate) fluctuated during the period. For the whole of 1997, the monthly average rate remained at 42.8% in spite of a declining inflation rate. In 1995 and 1996, the real Treasury bill rate was negative for long periods.

The Ghanaian experience has revealed that market participants respond only to the central bank's actions, which come either through movements in the Bank Rate or the results of preceding auctions. Thus, even if all other indicators (inflation, growth, etc.) point to a change in rates, the market participants appear to wait for signals from the central bank before reacting. Addison (2001) indicates one possible explanation of such inertia on the part of the market participants, namely the long history of controls (especially regulated interest rates) which renders them dependent on the central bank in order to develop their own expertise in this area. The central bank therefore appears to have a major role to play in removing this inertia, and encouraging banks to follow market trends. The central bank previously made use of the Bank Rate in signalling its policy stance. However, it was limited in its ability to use it effectively, given cost considerations, and therefore allowed the rate to remain stable for long periods while the underlying macroeconomic conditions changed. Previously, the cost of intervention was mainly financed by the government, which mostly resisted interest-rate increases to the levels necessary to clear the market. Therefore, as a necessary condition for improvements in money market performance, there was an increasing need for the government's borrowing requirement to decline significantly (Addison, 2001). Secondly, there was also the need for the Bank of Ghana to intensify the use of secondary instruments rather than primary issues for monetary intervention so as to reduce the financial burden on the government.

The phasing out of BoG bills brought into focus the issue of the over-financing of the deficit, with the difference between the deficit and the actual issue representing the central bank's monetary intervention. The BoG has addressed this issue by opening a separate account called OMO-T bills into which the proceeds from intervention are put and sterilized. This procedure, however, raises the problem of reconciliation between the stock of bills in the register and what actually goes to finance the budget, a situation which may raise questions about transparency. In spite of the problems, the BoG's decision to switch to Treasury bills appears justified in view of the government's increasing concerns about the interest cost. Addison (2001) argues that there was the danger that in future the government might decide to stop paying the interest cost on BoG bills, an action that might affect the profitability of the central bank and potentially compromise the conduct of monetary policy. Addison suggests that, in addressing this issue, there was the need for the central bank to introduce secondary instruments, such as repos, for its monetary policy intervention. This would require the central bank to take prior action to develop the secondary market by putting in place the framework and instruments, establishing a book entry system, and acquiring a portfolio of assets for use on the market. This system was expected ultimately to eliminate the cost to the government of the BoG's monetary intervention.

**Figure 8.1: Trends in Interest Rates**

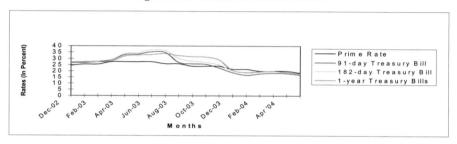

*Prime Rate*

The Monetary Policy Committee (MPC) has been established for the purpose of setting the prime rate, which gives a signal to financial firms about the prevailing market conditions. The prime rate, which basically replaces the Bank Rate, operates alongside the other instruments of monetary policy mentioned above. The MPC sets the prime rate, given the balance of risks in the macroeconomic outlook. From the onset the prime rate was positioned at 24.5% in November 2002, reaching its highest point in March 2003 when the MPC decided to increase it from 25.5% to 27.5%, as a result of exaggerated price developments following the rationalization of the price of fuel. From June 2004, however, the rate has witnessed substantial declines, given the downward trends in inflation, and now stands at 18.5% due to the substantial decline in the rate of inflation to 11.2% in April 2004. This goes to confirm the fact that market participants are quite dependent on signals from the BoG because of the long history of controls. Fig. 8.1 illustrates trends in interest rates between December 2002 and May 2004.

## 4. Methodology

The principal objective of the present study is to investigate the impact of 'macro-financial policy changes on household savings behaviour' between 1991/2 and 1998/9. It aims specifically to address the following issues:

(i) to examine whether monetary policies affect savings behaviour in Ghana, and

(ii)   to ascertain whether household savings are influenced by demographic factors, such as age, occupation, level of education and ethnic background.

The principal hypothesis of the study is that macro-financial policies have no significant effect on household savings in Ghana. In testing this hypothesis, two approaches will be followed. First, a descriptive approach in which the broad developments in domestic saving and monetary policies will be discussed. The second approach will employ quantitative techniques to estimate the coefficients of the determinants of household domestic savings and to compare the marginal effects between the two dates (1991/2 and 1998/9). This is done against the background that the financial sector was more liberalized in 1998/9 than it was in 1991/2.

## *The Model*

In order to ascertain the impact of policy changes on household savings behaviour, a linear model will be estimated. The estimation technique will involve both a classical linear regression technique and a logistic regression approach. Both approaches will be used to compare the policy effects on savings under the two separate models. A typical classical linear regression technique can be specified as

$$Y = \beta_0 + \beta_1 X_{i1} + \beta_2 X_{i2} + \beta_3 X_{i3} + \beta_4 X_{i4} + \ldots\ldots\beta_k X_{ik} + \varepsilon_i \tag{1}$$

where Y is the dependent variable, in this study 'household savings', and the Xs are the independent or explanatory variables, which would include income, remittances, level of education, household size and other demographic variables.

The second estimation technique, namely, the logistic regression analysis, can be used in models in which the dependent variable is a discrete outcome, that is, a 'Yes or No' decision. For example, 'yes' when an individual saves and 'no' when the individual does not. In such a case, the conventional regression methods are inappropriate. The method of estimation is Maximum Likelihood and assumes that the optimality properties of the Maximum Likelihood Estimators (MLEs) are met (Amemiya, 1981; Maddala, 1983; Greene, 2000). Thus, our savings equation will be formulated in terms of probabilities such that

$$\text{Prob} (Y=1) = F(B'X) \ldots\ldots\ldots\ldots\ldots (2)$$
$$\text{Prob} (Y=0) = F(B'X) \ldots\ldots\ldots\ldots\ldots (3)$$

The set of parameters $\beta$ reflect the impact of changes in X on the probability. A linear regression can be derived from equations (2) and (3) as

$F(X,B) = \beta'X$
Since $E(Y/X) = F(X,B)$, a regression model can be constructed as
$Y = E[Y/X] + (Y - E[Y/X])$
$Y = \beta'X + \varepsilon$

## Definition of Variables
The following variables are the principal determinants of savings to be used in the analysis.

### a. Income
The Keynesian Savings function and the Permanent Income of Friedman postulate a positive relationship between savings and income. According to the permanent income hypothesis, which distinguishes between permanent and transitory components of income, households will spend mainly the permanent income while the transitory income is channelled into savings with a marginal propensity to save from this income approaching unity. The positive relationship postulated by the Keynes savings function and Friedman's permanent income hypothesis has been confirmed by empirical studies (Rossi, 1988; Gupta, 1987; Koskela and Viren, 1982; Avery and Kannickel, 1991). In addition to permanent and transitory income components, the rate of growth in income is used as an additional explanatory variable in empirical studies on savings. Increased growth rates in income are expected to have a positive effect on household savings (Collins, 1989).

### b. Wealth
Whichever definition of wealth is used, wealth is expected to have a negative effect on savings through a reduction in savings from permanent income (Schmidt-Hebbel et al., 1989). This study adopts the view that monetary asset holdings can be used to measure wealth, because monetary assets reduce the dependence on current income, especially when it declines temporarily (also see Muradoglu and Taskin, 1996).

### c. Inflation
The direction of the effects of inflation on household savings is ambiguous in the theoretical literature. The Tobin-Mundell effect suggests that higher inflation leads to lower real interest rates and causes a portfolio adjustment from real money balances towards real capital. Thus, anticipated increases in inflation would be expected to lead to increased investment. However, given the limited portfolio choices available in Ghana, such anticipated increases in inflation will lead to portfolio adjustment from real money balances to real assets (land, livestock, foreign currency, and consumer durables). Thus, higher anticipated inflation could reduce household savings in Ghana. The empirical literature provides ample evidence in support of both views. Gupta (1987) found that, in a group of Asian countries, both expected and unexpected components of inflation had a positive effect on savings, but the work of Lahiri (1988) had inconclusive results. Zorklu and Barbie (2003) also found that the inflationary pressures in Ghana during the reform period resulted in negative real deposit interest rates and, as a result, the savings response was weak.

### d. Rates of Return
The direction of the effect of interest-rate changes on savings is inconclusive. Due to inter-temporal consumption decisions, an increase in the real interest rate can adversely

affect savings. This viewpoint is supported by Balassa (1992), where he argued that the effect of the real interest rate on savings is positive for developing countries. Similarly, Koskela and Viren (1982) observed that savings increase as the real rate of interest increases. It is worth noting that the effect of the interest rate may also be explained by the inflation effect, that is, assuming that nominal rates of interest are constant and a rise in the inflation rate lowers the real cost of borrowing, which in turn increases consumers' expenditure and lowers savings.

An empirical study by Ouliaris (1981) found that real interest rates in Australia exert a negative influence on the savings ratio; hence a decline in the real interest rates leads to a rise in the savings ratio. Giovannini (1985) in an empirical study found that, in most countries, the response of savings growth to real rates is no different from zero. He argued that, in developing countries, assumptions about elasticity of substitution may not hold because a significant proportion of the population may not be able to borrow even at black market rates.

### e. Foreign Inflows
Foreign savings are commonly used as a determinant of national savings in some empirical studies. Access to foreign borrowing in international markets is expected to supplement domestic resources and fill in the savings gap. Thus foreign inflows are expected to reduce national savings. Giovannini (1985) observed a significant negative effect of foreign savings, but Gupta (1987) observed a positive effect of foreign savings. However, foreign inflows are expected to influence national aggregate savings and not household savings. Rather, private remittances would be an important decision parameter for household savings.

### f. Demographic Variables
The life-cycle hypothesis postulates that demographic variables affect savings rates (Ando and Modigliani, 1963). The dependency ratio[1] is the most common demographic variable. The young and the elderly are expected to consume out of past savings, while those within working age are expected to accumulate savings. A developed capital market as well as the number of children in the family has been seen as an alternative means of maintaining income in old age. Hence, as a country develops its age structure is likely to change and people will save more rather than rely on the benefits expected from children. However, Cornia and Jerger (1982), using ILO statistics, found that household size contributes to savings only for middle-income economies and does not have any significant effect in developing countries.

### Data Sources
The study will mainly use household survey data, namely, Ghana Living Standards Survey (GLSS) 3 and 4 available at the Ghana Statistical Service. The GLSS contains information, such as whether an individual household member holds a savings account

---

[1] Defined as the share of the population under age fifteen or over sixty-five.

or participates in Susu,[2] the current value of savings, additions and subtractions during the past 12 months, whether a household member has received remittances, the amount of remittances received, etc. It also has demographic information on households, and this will be complemented with indexes of macro-financial policy to ascertain whether policy changes do affect household savings in Ghana.

## 5.   Statistical Analysis

A statistical description of household asset choices using GLSS 3 and 4 shows very interesting results. First, the proportion of households owning furniture, a sewing machine, a stove or a radio increased between 1991/2 and 1998/9. For instance, the proportion of households that owned furniture increased by 3.1 percentage points, while those with a radio also increased by 2.46 percentage points. Similarly, the proportion of households which owned means of transport (bicycles, motor cycles or cars) also increased and, in particular, the proportion of households with cars increased by 9.7 percentage points. Ironically, the proportion of households that own houses, land or plots declined significantly between 1991/2 and 1998/9. Although not surprising, the proportion of households that owned shares declined by 0.63 percentage points. This ties in perfectly with the monetary policies pursued at the time. The interest rate on Treasury bills was as high as 40% and households or investors found the risk-free asset a better form of investment than shares.

**Table 8.1   Mean Savings Account Balances**

|  | GLSS 3 (1991/2) | | | GLSS 4 (1998/9) | | |
|---|---|---|---|---|---|---|
|  | < 18 yrs | 18–60 years | > 60 years | < 18 yrs | 18–60 years | > 60 years |
| 1. Proportion with savings accounts or Susu | 53.1% | 40.5% | 6.4% | 53.8% | 39.5% | 6.8% |
| 2. Mean current value of savings (including Susu) | ¢62,838 | ¢45,310 | ¢69,947 | ¢479,053.2 | ¢410,887.9 | ¢355,482.7 |

*Source:* GLSS 3 & 4.

In terms of household savings with formal and informal institutions (including Susu), an interesting pattern emerged. First, the GLSS 3 data show that 11.74% of the

---

[2] A form of informal savings in which Susu collectors take regular fixed deposits from individual clients and return the accumulated amount at the end of each month less a day's contribution (commission).

sample size held savings accounts or Susu, of which 48.2% were males and 51.8% females. Sons and daughters of the head of household were the majority (47%) followed by heads of households (25.5%), spouses of household heads (13.1%) and grandchildren of household heads (7.4%). Similarly, the GLSS 4 data revealed that 12.1% of the total sample saved or held savings accounts, of which 46.5% were males and 53.5% females. Thus, the proportion of males with savings accounts declined for the 1998/9 period relative to the 1991/2 period. Of the total that held savings accounts, again the majority were sons and daughters of household heads (48.5%), followed by the household heads themselves (23.8%), then by spouses of household heads (11.8%) and grandchildren of household heads (9.5%). Three main issues can be gleaned from the descriptive statistics above. First, it appears that the proportion of households that held savings accounts between the two data periods (1991/2–1998/9) had not changed significantly, and was still low. Secondly, children formed over 60% of those with savings accounts and the number of people in this category increased between the two periods.

Table 8.1 also confirms the earlier findings that household members aged below 18 years account for a greater proportion of households with savings accounts (including Susu). Whereas the proportion of household members who saved and were below 18 years of age increased between 1991/2 and 1998/9, those aged 18–60 declined over the same period. Meanwhile, the proportion of household members aged over 60 but holding savings accounts increased during the period under consideration. Thus, it can be concluded that the proportion of households with savings accounts and within the working age group had declined between 1991/2 and 1998/9. Another interesting observation is that the mean savings account balance increased from ¢56,203 in 1991/2 to ¢443,766.5 in 1998/9 (¢1538.96 in 1991/2 and ¢2065.7 in 1998/9 in real terms — an increase of 34.2% over the two periods). In terms of the three age categories, they all recorded increases in savings account balances during the period under consideration. However, those aged 60 and above had the highest mean savings balance, followed by household members aged below 18 years. The working population had the lowest mean savings account balance. This finding contradicts the Life Cycle Hypothesis, namely, that the working population accumulates savings while the young and the old consume out of past savings. What accounts for this savings pattern?

In terms of numbers, the majority of households that save are engaged in agriculture but the mean savings of this group of households was low (Table 8.2). Households engaged in finance, insurance, real estate and business services had the highest mean current value of savings (¢889,038). This is followed by household members with occupations such as restaurants, hotels and food selling. Agriculture ranks seventh among the group of occupations; livestock farmers saved more than food-crop farmers, while cash-crop farmers saved the least among the occupations (apart from construction). It is not surprising food-crop farmers saved more than cash-crop farmers; the latter receive income over a shorter period as compared with the latter.

In order to further explain the savings pattern observed above, a logistic regression approach is used to estimate the micro-determinants of savings in Ghana. Table 8.3 provides the regression results where the dependent variable is the probability that the individual saves. The independent variable includes level of education, type of accommodation (captures wealth effect), household size, age composition of household, gender and average propensity to consume. The average propensity to consume (APC) is defined as $1 - APS$, where average propensity to save (APS) is the current value of savings divided by income. Income here comprises income from employment, agricultural income, gross non-farm self-employment income, actual and imputed rental income, income from remittances and other income.

**Table 8.2    Occupational Profile of Savers (GLSS 4)**

| Industry | No. of savers | Mean current value of savings ($¢$) | Rank |
|---|---|---|---|
| Finance/Insurance/Real Estate and Business Services | 22 | 914,227 | 1 |
| Restaurants/Hotels and Food Sellers | 37 | 889,038 | 2 |
| Transport/Storage/Communications | 21 | 795,761 | 3 |
| Community/Social and Personal Services | 47 | 595,829 | 4 |
| Mining/Quarrying | 1 | 500,000 | 5 |
| Wholesale/Retail Trade | 165 | 472,399 | 6 |
| Agriculture (Livestock)[a] | 31 | 443,467 | 7 |
| Agriculture (Food) | 547 | 441958 | 8 |
| Manufacturing/Processing | 98 | 352,540 | 9 |
| Agriculture (Cash Crops) | 84 | 331,997 | 10 |
| Construction | 21 | 242,403 | 11 |

*Note*    a)  Total savers working within the agricultural sector rank 7th with a mean value of current savings amounting to $¢428,076$.
*Source:*    Computed from GLSS 4

The regression results present interesting findings on household savings behaviour. First, higher levels of education (tertiary) would significantly increase the probability of savings in 1991/2 but that cannot be said for 1998/9; the probability of savings increases as one attains tertiary education, but the marginal effect was not significant. Secondly, the probability of savings is also dependent on the type of accommodation the household has; households living in rented or rent-free accommodation are likely to save more than those living in their own houses. Moreover, the marginal effects increased over the two periods. Thus, it can be concluded that households living in rented accommodation are more likely to have financial savings perhaps to pay for rent advance (deposit[3]) or to put up their own houses than those

---

[3] This can range from 6 months to 3 years depending on the landlord's time preference.

living in their own houses. Those living in own houses may have used their savings to put up houses — a form of savings, particularly in a country where real interest rates are low and sometimes negative.

**Table 3  Logistic Regression Results (GLSS 3 & 4)[a]**

| Regressors | GLSS 3 Marginal Effects | | GLSS 4 Marginal Effects | |
|---|---|---|---|---|
| **Level of Education** | β | P > \| t \| | B | P > \| t \| |
| Basic Education | −0.12 | 0.00 | −0.43 | 0.00 |
| Secondary School | −0.09 | 0.00 | −0.13 | 0.00 |
| Post-secondary | −0.15 | 0.00 | −0.07 | 0.00 |
| Tertiary | 0.05 | 0.00 | 0.003 | 0.39 |
| | | | | |
| **Type of Accommodation** | | | | |
| Owner Occupier | 0.20 | 0.00 | 0.51 | 0.00 |
| Renting | 0.38 | 0.00 | 0.55 | 0.00 |
| Rent-free | 0.36 | 0.00 | 0.55 | 0.00 |
| | | | | |
| **Other Demographic Variables** | | | | |
| Females | −0.003 | 0.49 | 0.001 | 0.61 |
| Children | 0.005 | 0.32 | 0.02 | 0.00 |
| Aged | 0.012 | 0.32 | 0.03 | 0.00 |
| Household Size | 0.002 | 0.00 | 0.0002 | 0.43 |
| | | | | |
| **Economic Factors** | | | | |
| Average Propensity to Consume | −0.045 | 0.00 | −0.050 | 0.00 |
| | | | | |
| F | 350.12 | | 2009.7 | |
| Prob > FR | 0.000 | | 0.000 | |
| $R^2$ | 0.26 | | 0.48 | |

*Note:* a) The OLS regressions gave inconsistent estimates and therefore the results are not reported here.

Also, children and the aged were more likely to save in 1998/9 than previously. This confirms the results from the descriptive statistics above. Household size significantly increased the probability of saving in 1991/2 rather than in 1998/9. This is contrary to the view that households tending to have more children to act as a form of savings for the future are no longer significant and it is supported by the findings of Cornia and Jerger (1982). Finally, higher average propensity to consume reduced the probability of saving in both 1991/2 and 1998/9 but the marginal effect on saving is higher in 1998/9 than in 1991/2.

## 5. Conclusion

The study sought to investigate whether macro-financial policies can explain savings behaviour in Ghana over the period 1991/2 and 1998/9, the period covered by the Ghana Living Standards Survey (GLSS) 3 and 4. The approach involved using both descriptive and logit regression analysis to ascertain how household savings behaviour has been influenced by the various macro-financial policies during the period under review. The study found that the financial sector witnessed more liberal policies towards the end of the period under consideration than at the beginning of the period. Also, whereas evidence on the effects of financial sector liberalization on savings is mixed, the study believes that a well liberalized financial sector will significantly enhance savings mobilization.

A statistical analysis of GLSS 3 and 4 provides mixed results on household asset choices. The proportion of households that owned certain consumer durables such as sewing machines, stoves, furniture, radio, cars, bicycles and motor cycles increased between 1991/2 and 1998/9, but the proportion of households that held landed property such as houses and plots of land declined significantly between the two periods — perhaps an indication that the rising cost of building materials and land has put landed property out of the reach of many households. Similarly, the proportion of households that owned shares declined over the period, and this may be attributed to the high interest rate and low risk on Treasury bills as compared with shares. Moreover, the proportion of households with a savings account or Susu did not increase significantly between the two periods. Interestingly, although the mean savings balance of households increased significantly (in real terms) over the two periods, on average, children and the aged had higher savings balances as compared with the working population. This finding is contrary to the life-cycle theory. Moreover, people working in occupations such as finance, insurance, real estate and business services had the highest mean value of savings, followed by those engaged in hotels, restaurants and food selling businesses. Also, people living in their own houses saved less than those living in rented accommodation. Last but not least, household size significantly increases household savings. Finally, the study confirms the theory that households with higher average propensity to consume save less, and the analysis revealed that average propensity to consume has increased over the two periods — a clear indication that the liberalization of the financial sector has not improved household savings habits over the two periods.

In conclusion, the financial sector reforms in Ghana have not led to any significant improvement in savings mobilization, owing to inherent weaknesses or inertia within the financial system. For instance, whereas interest on credit remains high, interest on savings has been extremely low and the real interest rate on savings has sometimes been negative; it is therefore not surprising that the working population are saving less. These revelations suggest that real incomes have declined and that policy should be directed towards improving the income-earning capacity of households in order to improve their livelihood and their savings habits. Secondly, the proportion of shares held by households declined over the two periods which clearly signals that households found other forms of investment, especially Treasury bills, more attractive than shares, thus confirming the notion that the government was crowding out the private sector, a necessary engine of economic growth. The study suggests that interest rates on Treasury bills would need to be reduced in order to enable the Ghana Stock Exchange to raise sufficient capital for the private sector.

One would have expected that in a country where interest on savings is less attractive, households would hold savings in the form of land or buildings. However, the proportion of households owning these assets declined over the two periods. This suggests two things: households are disposing of their landed property in order to meet their consumption needs and/or the increase in the price of land and building materials, not to mention land litigation, has put these assets beyond the reach of some households. The study therefore proposes that the government should pursue polices which will increase incomes and also minimize the cumbersome procedures involved in land acquisition. Finally, it was evident that the demand for consumer durables increased over the two periods. Again, the macro-financial policies pursued did not discourage households from consuming these items but rather increased their average propensity to consume. This calls for a critical examination of the macro-financial policies pursued over the period in order to address the problem of relatively low savings in Ghana.

# References

Addison, E. K. Y. (2001) 'Money Management in Ghana', Paper presented at Conference on Monetary Policy Framework in Africa, Pretoria, South Africa, September.

Akoena, S. and Gockel, F. A. (2002) *Financial Intermediation for the Poor: Credit Demand by Micro Small and Medium Enterprises in Ghana: A Further Assignment for Financial Sector Policy.* IFLIP Research Paper No. 6. Geneva: ILO.

Alessi, M., Devereux, P. and Weber, G. (1997) 'Intertemporal Consumption, Durables and Liquidity Constraints: A Cohort Analysis', *European Economic Review,* Vol. 41, No. 1: 37–59.

Amemiya, T. (1981) 'Qualitative Response Models: A Survey', *Journal of Economic Literature,* Vol. 19: 481–536.

Ando, A. and Modigliani, F. (1963) 'Life Cycle Hypothesis of Saving: Aggregate Implications and Tests', *American Economic Review,* Vol. 53, No. 1.

Aryeetey, E. and Gockel, F. (1991) *Mobilising Domestic Resources for Capital Formation in Ghana: The Role of Informal Financial Sectors.* AERC Research Paper No. 3. Nairobi: AERC.

Attanasio, O. P., Picci, L. and Scorcu, A. E. (2000) 'Saving Growth and Investment: A Macroeconomic Analysis Using a Panel of Countries', *Review of Economics and Statistics,* Vol. 82, No. 2.

Attanasio, O. P. and Banks J. (2001) 'The Assessment: Household Saving — Issues in Theory and Practice', *Oxford Review of Economic Policy,* Vol. 17, No. 1.

Avery, R. B. and Kannickel, A. B. (1991) 'Household Savings in the US', *Review of Income and Wealth,* Series 37, No. 4, December.

Balassa, B. (1992) 'The Effects of Interest Rates on Savings in Developing Countries', *Banca Nazionale del Lavoro Quarterly Review,* No. 172, March.

Baline, Tomas J. T. and Zamaloa, L. M. (1997) (eds) *Instruments of Monetary Management: Issues and Country Experiences.* Washington, DC: International Monetary Fund.

Bank of Ghana *Annual Reports,* various issues.

Bank of Ghana Monetary Policy Committee Reports, various issues.

Binswanger, H. P. and Khandker, S. R. (1995) 'The Impact of Formal Finance on the Rural Economy of India', *Journal of Development Studies,* Vol. 32, No. 2: 234–62.

Brownbridge, M. and Gockel, F. A. (1998) 'The Impact of Financial Sector Reforms since Independence' in M. Brownbridge, F. A. Gockel and C. Harvey (eds), *Banking in Africa,* Oxford: James Currey.

Browning, M. and Lusardi, A. (1996) 'Household Saving: Micro Theories and Micro Facts', *Journal of Economic Literature,* Vol. 34, No. 4.

Collins, S. M. (1989) 'Savings Behaviour in Ten Developing Countries', Paper presented at the NBER Conference on Savings, Cambridge, MA.

Cornia, G. and Jerger, G. (1982) 'Rural versus Urban Saving Behaviour: Evidence from an ILO Collection of Household Surveys', *Development and Change,* Vol. 13, No. 1.

Ewusi, K. (1997) *The Determinants of Price Fluctuations in Ghana.* ISSER Discussion Paper. Institute of Statistical, Social and Economic Research, University of Ghana, Legon.

Giovannini, A. (1985) 'Savings and the Real Interest Rate in LDCs', *Journal of Development Economics,* Vol. 18, No. 2–3, August.

Greene, W. H. (2000) *Econometric Analysis,* 4th edn. Upper Saddle River, NJ: Prentice Hall.

Gregory, P., Mokhtari, M. and Schrettl, M. (1999) 'Do the Russians Really Save That Much? — Alternate Estimates from the Russian Longitudinal Monitoring Survey', *Review of Economics and Statistics,* Vol. 81, No. 4.

Gupta, K. L. (1970) 'Foreign Capital and Domestic Savings: A Test of Haavelmo's Hypothesis with Cross-country Data: A Comment', *Review of Economics and Statistics,* Vol. 52, No. 2.

Gupta, K. L. (1987) 'Aggregate Savings, Financial Intermediation and Interest Rate', *Review of Economics and Statistics,* Vol. 69, No. 2.

Hardy, Daniel C. (1997) 'Reserve Requirements and Monetary Management: An Introduction', in Baline and Zamaloa.

Hussain, M., Mohammed, N. and Kameir, E. (2002) 'Resource Mobilization, Financial Liberalization, and Investment: the Case for some African Countries' in T. Mkwandire and C. Soludo (eds), *African Voices on Structural Adjustment, A Companion to Our Continent, Our Future.* Ottawa: IDRC; Dakar: CODESRIA; and Trenton, NJ: Africa World Press.

Koskela, E. and Viren, M. (1982) 'Savings and Inflation: Some International Evidence', *Economic Letters,* Vol 9, No. 4.

Lahiri, A. K. (1988) *Dynamics of Asian Savings: The Role of Growth and Age Structure.* IMF Working Paper No. 88/49. Washington, DC: International Monetary Fund.

Liu, J-C, and Xu, L. (1997) 'Household, Savings and Investment: The Case of Shanghai', *Journal of Asian Economics*, Vol. 8, No. 1.

Loayza, N. Schmidt-Hebbel, K. and Servén, L. (2000) 'What Drives Private Savings Across the World?', *The Review of Economics and Statistics,* Vol. 82, No. 2: 165–81.

Ma, G. (1993) 'Macroeconomic Disequilibrium, Structural Changes, and the Household Savings and Money Demand in China', *Journal of Development Economics*, Vol. 41: 115–36.

Maddala G. S. (1983) *Introduction to Econometrics,* 2nd edn. London: Macmillan.

Maimbo, S. M. and Mavrotas, G. (2001) 'Financial sector Reforms and Savings Mobilisation in Zambia', Conference paper, Manchester, April.

Masson, P. R., Bayoumi, T., and Samiei, H. (1998) 'International Evidence on the Determinants of Private Saving', *World Bank Economic Review,* Vol. 12, No. 3: 483–501.

Muradoglu, G. and Taskin, F. (1996) 'Financial Liberalisation from Segmented to Integrated Economies', *Journal of Economics and Business,* Vol. 55, No. 6.

Ouliaris, S. (1981) 'Household Savings and the Rate of Interest, Economic Record', Vol. 57, September.

Quartey, P. (1997) 'The Effects of Non-Bank Financial Intermediaries on Money Demand and Monetary Policy in Ghana'. MPhil. Thesis, University of Ghana, Legon.

Quartey, P. (2002) 'Finance and Small and Medium Enterprise Development in Ghana', PhD Thesis, University of Manchester.

Rossi, N. (1988) 'Government Spending, the Real Interest Rate and the Behaviour of Liquidity Constrained Consumers in Developing Countries', *IMF Staff Papers,* Vol. 35, No. 1, March.

Schmidt-Hebbel, K., Webb, S. B. and Corsetti, G. (1992) 'Household Savings in Developing Countries: First Cross-Country Evidence', *World Bank Economic Review,* Vol. 6, No. 3.

Wilcox, D. (1989) 'Social Security Benefits, Consumption, Expenditure and the Life Cycle Hypothesis', *Journal of Political Economy,* Vol. 97, No. 2: 288–304.

World Bank (2003) *World Development Indicators.* Washington, DC: World Bank.

Zorklu, S. Q. and Barbie, W. (2003) 'Financial Sector Reforms and Financial Savings in SSA', *Savings and Development,* Vol. 1.

# 9 Banking Competition & Efficiency in Ghana

THIERRY BUCHS
& JOHAN MATHIESEN

## 1. Introduction

Financial systems tend to evolve around a banking sector seeking to achieve economies of scale in order to offset the costs of collecting and processing information designed to reduce uncertainty, thereby facilitating a more efficient allocation of financial resources. However, a competitive banking system is required to ensure that banks are effective forces for financial intermediation, channelling savings into investment fostering higher economic growth.

This paper assesses the level of competition in the Ghanaian banking sector. At first sight, the very high profit ratios and high cost structure of Ghanaian banks could indicate a monopolistic banking structure. This is partly corroborated by the findings of this study. By deriving variables from a theoretical model and using a 1998-2003 panel data set, we find evidence for a non-competitive market structure in the Ghanaian banking system, possibly hampering financial intermediation. The study argues that the structure, as well as the other market characteristics, constitute an indirect barrier to entry, shielding the large profits in the Ghanaian banking system.

## 2. Overview of the Ghanaian Banking System

### Structure of the Banking Sector

The Ghanaian banking system is rather diverse. Of the 17 banks operating in the country, there are 9 commercial banks, 5 merchant banks, and 3 development banks (Table 9.1).[1] The three largest commercial banks account for 55% of the total assets of the banking sector, which is relatively moderate compared with other countries in the region. However, about 25% of total assets and 20% of deposits are held by a single

---

[1] Commercial banks engage in traditional banking business, with a focus on universal retail services. Merchant banks are fee-based banking institutions, mostly engaging in corporate banking services. Development banks specialize in the provision of medium- and long-term finance.

**Table 9.1  Structure of the Banking Sector[a]**

| | Ownership (%) | | Total Assets (Bns of cedis) | As % of GDP | No. of Branches | Share of Total (%) | | |
|---|---|---|---|---|---|---|---|---|
| | Ghanaian | Foreign | | | | Total assets | Net lending | Deposits |
| Banking system | | | 18,668 | 38.2 | 309 | 100.0 | 100.0 | 100.0 |
| Commercial banks | | | 13,055 | 26.7 | 229 | 69.3 | | |
| Ghana Commercial Bank Ltd | 97 | 3 | 4,624 | 9.46 | 134 | 24.8 | 16.9 | 20.8 |
| SSB Bank Ltd | 46 | 54 | 1,713 | 3.50 | 38 | 9.2 | 10.2 | 8.8 |
| Barclays Bank of Ghana Ltd | 10 | 90 | 2,710 | 5.55 | 24 | 14.5 | 18.1 | 16.9 |
| Standard Chartered Bank | 24 | 76 | 3,011 | 6.16 | 23 | 16.1 | 16.3 | 18.8 |
| The Trust Bank Ltd | 39 | 61 | 470 | 0.96 | 6 | 2.5 | 2.1 | 2.6 |
| Metropolitan and Allied Bank | 53 | 47 | 128 | 0.26 | 4 | 0.7 | 0.6 | 1.0 |
| International Commercial Bank | 0 | 100 | 120 | 0.25 | 3 | 0.6 | 0.3 | 0.8 |
| Stanbic Bank Ghana Ltd | 9 | 91 | 230 | 0.47 | 1 | 1.2 | 0.5 | 1.2 |
| Unibank | 100 | 0 | 49 | 0.10 | 1 | 0.3 | 0.3 | 0.3 |
| Merchant banks | | | 2,875 | 5.9 | 18 | | | |
| Merchant Bank Ghana Ltd | 100 | 0 | 751 | 1.54 | 5 | 4.0 | 4.8 | 5.4 |
| Ecobank Ghana Ltd | 6 | 94 | 1,325 | 2.71 | 4 | 7.1 | 8.2 | 6.2 |
| CAL Merchant Bank | 34 | 66 | 409 | 0.84 | 3 | 2.5 | 2.1 | 2.6 |
| First Atlantic Bank | 71 | 29 | 286 | 0.59 | 2 | 1.5 | 1.5 | 2.0 |
| Amalgamated Bank | 100 | 0 | 104 | 0.21 | 1 | 0.6 | 0.4 | 0.7 |
| Development banks | | | 2,738 | 5.6 | 62 | | | |
| Agricultural Development Bank | 100 | 0 | 1,847 | 3.78 | 42 | 0.0 | 11.2 | 8.4 |
| National Investment Bank | 100 | 0 | 538 | 1.10 | 14 | 0.0 | 3.8 | 2.0 |
| Prudential Bank | 100 | 0 | 352 | 0.72 | 6 | 0.0 | 1.9 | 2.0 |

*Note*  a)  As of December 2002. The housing bank established in 2003 has been excluded from this study.
*Source*:  IMF (2003).

state-owned commercial bank, the Ghana Commercial Bank (GCB). Foreign investors hold about 53% of the shares in 8 commercial banks, which is below the average for sub-Saharan Africa (Table 9.2), and 3 banks are state-owned. The banking penetration ratio, at one bank branch per 54,000 inhabitants, is relatively high, but formal banking reaches only 5% of the population and the coverage varies widely. This reflects the fact that 35% of bank branches are in the Greater Accra region, even though this region represents less than 13% of the country's population. About half of all bank branches in the interior belong to the GCB.

As measured by the aggregated total-assets-to-GDP ratio, the banking sector grew rapidly between 1996 and 2000, reflecting partly financial deepening as well as loose monetary conditions. After reaching 44% in 2000, the ratio dropped to 38% in 2001 and further to 31% at end-2003, reflecting tightened monetary conditions. The same trend characterized the share of commercial banks' foreign operations: the share of bank assets denominated in foreign currency reached 35% in 2000 and then declined to 30% in 2001, probably reflecting the increased stability of the cedi exchange rate.

Following the tightening of monetary policy in 2001, domestic credit to the private sector has remained at around 10% of GDP, which is low even by African standards (Table 9.2). This essentially reflects a typical crowding-out effect, as most of the banks' resources are absorbed by the public sector, either in the form of loans to state-owned enterprises or holdings of government securities. As shown in Figure 9.1, increasing government financing requirements led to very high real Treasury bill yields, especially in periods of tight monetary policy, and by extension, to high lending rates. During 1998–2003, net loans averaged 34% of total assets (peaking at 43% in 2001), as banks preferred to invest their resources in liquid, low-risk assets, such as government securities, the latter constituting about 25% of total assets during the period.[2]

**Figure 9.1:  Nominal Interest Rates, Government Debt, Real Growth of Private Sector Credit, Private Sector Credit, 1998–2003**

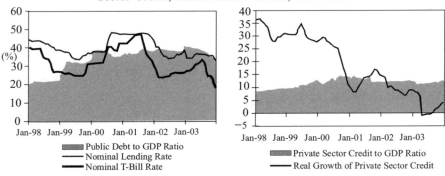

*Source:*  Bank of Ghana.

---

[2] Apart from the financing constraints imposed by Ghana's large fiscal deficits, the banks' holdings of government securities are also sustained by high secondary reserve requirements that require banks to hold 35% of their deposit liabilities in such securities.

**Table 9.2   International Comparison of Selected Banking and Institutional Indicators (% unless otherwise indicated)**

| | Ghana | Kenya | Mozambique | Nigeria | South Africa | Tanzania | Uganda | Zambia | SSA Average |
|---|---|---|---|---|---|---|---|---|---|
| **Size of financial intermediaries** | | | | | | | | | |
| Private credit to GDP | 11.8 | 26.8 | 16.7 | 14.4 | 147.2 | 4.9 | 4.0 | 7.5 | 15.2 |
| M2 to GDP | 19.0 | 43.8 | 5.1 | 25.8 | 87.2 | 18.3 | 13.0 | 16.9 | 24.8 |
| Currency to GDP | 10.5 | 13.2 | 15.6 | 10.8 | 28.4 | 8.5 | 8.8 | 6.4 | 13.9 |
| **Banking industry** | | | | | | | | | |
| No. of banks | 17 | 53 | 10 | 51 | 60 | 29 | 15 | 16 | – |
| Net interest margin | 11.5 | 5.0 | 5.9 | 3.8 | 5.0 | 6.5 | 11.6 | 11.4 | 8.3 |
| Overhead costs | 7.3 | 3.7 | 4.5 | 7.4 | 3.7 | 6.7 | 4.6 | 11.2 | 5.7 |
| Foreign bank share (assets) | 53 | 4.8 | 98 | 11.0 | 0.6 | 58.7 | 89.0 | 66.6 | – |
| Bank concentration (3 banks) | 55.0 | 61.6 | 76.6 | 86.5 | 77 | 45.8 | 70.0 | 81.9 | 81.0 |
| Non-performing loans (share of total loans) | 28.8 | 41.0 | – | 17.3 | 3.9 | 12.2 | 6.5 | 21.8 | – |
| **Capital markets** | | | | | | | | | |
| Stock market capitalization (% of GDP) | 10.1 | 9.2 | – | 10.9 | 77.4 | 4.3 | 0.6 | 6.0 | 21.3 |
| **Contract enforcement** | | | | | | | | | |
| No. of procedures | 21 | 25 | 18 | 23 | 16 | 26 | 14 | 1 | 29 |
| Duration (no. of days) | 90 | 255 | 540 | 730 | 99 | 207 | 127 | 188 | 334 |
| **Bankruptcy** | | | | | | | | | |
| Time in years | – | 4.6 | – | 1.6 | 2.0 | 3.0 | 2.0 | 3.7 | 3.5 |
| **Credit market** | | | | | | | | | |
| Credit rights index (0 is weakest)[a] | 1 | 1 | 3 | 1 | 2 | 3 | 1 | 2 | 2 |
| **Entry regulations** | | | | | | | | | |
| No. of procedures | 10 | 11 | 16 | 9 | 9 | 13 | 17 | 6 | 11 |
| Duration (no. of days) | 84 | 61 | 153 | 44 | 38 | 35 | 36 | 40 | 72 |
| Cost (% of GNI per capita) | 111 | 54 | 100 | 92 | 135 | 9 | 199 | 24 | 255 |

*Note:* a) The index is based on four powers of secured lenders in liquidation and reorganization. A minimum score of 0 represents weak creditor rights and the maximum score of 4 represents strong creditor rights. For a description of the methodology, see http://rru.worldbank.org/DoingBusiness/Methodology/CreditMarkets.aspx.

*Sources:* IMF, *International Finance Statistics*; BankScope; World Bank, *World Development Indicators*; Doing Business Indicators Database; and *Tanzania: Financial System Stability Assessment*, IMF Staff Country Report No 03/241. Washington, DC: IMF (2003): Table 2. Banking statistics and capital market indicators are for 2001. All institutional indicators are for 2003.

In addition, state-owned enterprises have attracted sizeable amounts of lending from commercial banks recently, thereby exacerbating the crowding-out effect (Figure 9.2). As a result, during the last few years, bank lending to the public sector has typically absorbed more than half of total available resources, while about 30% of total assets were channelled towards the private sector. With the exception of the Tema Oil Refinery (TOR), which is the sector's largest exposure,[3] no single borrower amounts to 10% of the financial sector's total equity.

**Figure 9.2  Investment and (Gross) Lending of the Banking Sector (1996–2003)**

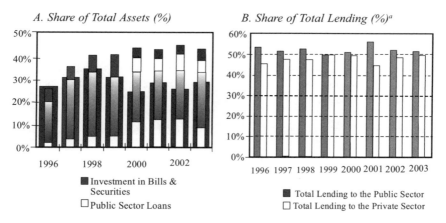

*A. Share of Total Assets (%)*

■ Investment in Bills & Securities
□ Public Sector Loans

*B. Share of Total Lending (%)[a]*

■ Total Lending to the Public Sector
□ Total Lending to the Private Sector

*Note:* a) Total lending includes loans, overdrafts and investments.
*Source:* Bredenkamp et al. (2003: Section II); Bank of Ghana.

## Financial Performance of the Banking Sector

Financial performance indicators portray a mixed picture. Although the average capital adequacy ratio (CAR) was about 13.4% in 2002 and 9.3% at end-2003, well above the minimum 6% required by law, there was significant dispersion among the banks. In addition, as a result of the negative macroeconomic developments in 1999–2000, the asset quality of the banks' loan portfolio appears to have deteriorated. Past-due/non-performing loans soared from 16.2% in 2000 to an eight-year high of 28.6% of total loans in 2001 and 2002 before declining slightly to 24.4 % in 2003 (Table 9.3). Note, however, that these costs are below those reported in Nigeria and Zambia (Table 9.2). The overall impact of this sizeable increase on the banking system has been partially softened by the relatively prudent lending of the two largest foreign-owned banks, however. The system is also characterized by high overhead costs. The five largest banks incur on average overhead costs of 7% for average assets, which is similar to the sector as a whole but substantially higher than the sub-Saharan African average

---

[3] Even though a large portion of TOR's short-term debt was restructured into medium-term government bonds in 2001 and 2002, TOR exposure still exceeded 75% of the GCB's equity capital as of June 2003.

**Table 9.3** **Financial Soundness Indicators for the Banking Sector, 1997–2003**
(% at year's end, unless otherwise indicated)

| | 1997 | 1998 | 1999 | 2000 | 2001 | 2002 | 2003 |
|---|---|---|---|---|---|---|---|
| **Capital adequacy** | | | | | | | |
| Regulatory capital to risk-weighted assets[a] | 15.2 | 11.1 | 11.5 | 11.6 | 14.7 | 13.4 | 9.3 |
| % of banks greater or equal to 10% | 87.5 | 75.0 | 60.0 | 62.5 | 64.7 | 52.9 | 66.7 |
| % of banks below 10 and above 6% minimum | 6.3 | 12.5 | 40.0 | 37.5 | 35.3 | 35.3 | 27.8 |
| % of banks below 6% minimum | 6.3 | 12.5 | 0.0 | 0.0 | 0.0 | 11.8 | 5.6 |
| Capital (net worth) to assets | 13.4 | 12.2 | 12.2 | 11.9 | 13.1 | 12.6 | 12.5 |
| **Asset quality** | | | | | | | |
| Foreign-exchange loans to total loans[b] | 25.6 | 28.5 | 33.4 | 35.3 | 34.1 | 33.8 | – |
| Past-due loans to gross loans | 24.6 | 18.9 | 20.1 | 16.2 | 28.0 | 28.6 | 24.4 |
| Non-performing loans | 21.6 | 17.2 | 12.8 | 11.9 | 19.6 | 22.7 | 18.3 |
| Watch-listed loans | 3.0 | 1.7 | 7.3 | 4.3 | 8.4 | 5.9 | 6.0 |
| Provision as % of past-due loans | 78.0 | 89.4 | 67.2 | 58.6 | 46.4 | 63.6 | 64.4 |
| **Earnings and profitability** | | | | | | | |
| Net profit (before tax)/net income | 51.5 | 39.2 | 61.2 | 52.4 | 45.9 | 43.4 | 39.2 |
| Return on assets[c] | 8.0 | 8.6 | 8.5 | 9.7 | 8.7 | 6.8 | 6.4 |
| Return on equity[d] | 39.9 | 48.9 | 48.8 | 65.7 | 49.7 | 36.9 | 54.0 |
| Expense/income | 44.0 | 42.2 | 44.3 | 38.2 | 40.2 | 47.3 | 36.0 |
| **Interest-rate spread (deposit money banks)** | | | | | | | |
| Lending rates minus demand deposit rates | 37.0 | 33.8 | 32.5 | 30.5 | 30.5 | 30.5 | 23.3 |
| Lending rates minus saving deposit rates | 16.3 | 22.0 | 23.5 | 29.3 | 29.5 | 25.5 | 23.0 |
| **Liquidity** | | | | | | | |
| Actual reserve ratio (as % of total deposits) | 60.1 | 64.8 | 61.8 | 49.9 | 62.4 | 66.0 | 66.1 |
| Excess reserve ratio[e] | 17.1 | 21.8 | 18.8 | 5.9 | 18.4 | 22.0 | 22.1 |
| Loan/deposit | 42.2 | 48.7 | 59.0 | 64.0 | 63.9 | 50.1 | 56.1 |
| Foreign-exchange liabilities/total liabilities[b] | 24.9 | 21.1 | 29.7 | 36.2 | 27.0 | 27.4 | – |
| **Sensitivity to market risk** | | | | | | | |
| Net foreign-exchange assets (liabilities) to shareholders' funds[b] | 62.9 | 48.1 | (7.6) | (9.4) | 22.9 | 24.3 | – |

*Notes* a) The method for calculating CAR is different from that of Basel CAR and is likely to be more conservative than the Basel method.

b) No comparable estimate available for 2003 as commercial banks' foreign assets and liabilities were reclassified.

c) The ratio of net profit before tax to two-year annual average assets.

d) The ratio of net profit after tax to two-year annual average shareholders' funds.

e) The actual reserve ratio in excess of the minimum requirement ratio.

*Source:* IMF (2003) and Bank of Ghana.

of 5.7%. The high costs could partly reflect substantial investments in banking infrastructure, notably in the telecommunications sector, which still suffers from interconnectivity problems.[4] However, one key element in the total overhead costs is the staff expenditure component (about 3.7% for average assets), which constitutes roughly half of total overhead costs. This high ratio suggests both a low level of assets per employee and a relatively high average staff cost per employee.

On the other hand, profitability indicators indicate that, despite high overhead costs and sizeable provisioning, Ghanaian banks' pre-tax returns on assets and equity are among the highest in sub-Saharan Africa (Table 9.2) — a situation that reflects very wide interest margins. On an adjusted basis, the return on assets (RoAA) was 6.1% in 2002, which is remarkable even by African standards, and the same applies to both net interest revenue and non-interest revenue which are, respectively, 10% and 6.4% of average assets. The decline in interest rates in 2002 reduced the banks' income from government securities and led to a slight narrowing of interest-rate spreads, but the latter remain between 20 and 30%. The combination of wide interest margins, sizeable overhead costs, and an ample supply of relatively low-risk, high-return government paper, has resulted in high costs of intermediation. Since the large interest margins also reflect the non-performing loan problem, the poor quality of banks' loan portfolios is a major source of concern for the stability of the system. Most banks would indeed be vulnerable in the event of a major credit risk shock (IMF, 2003).

## Possible Factors Explaining Bank Profitability and the Efficiency of Intermediation

At least three factors may have prevented further financial deepening in Ghana so far, and these may be relevant for the interpretation of both profitability and efficiency indicators of the banking system. The first factor is the high degree of uncertainty associated with Ghana's unstable macroeconomic environment, which may have negatively affected both the size and the quality of financial intermediation. This assumption is supported by the low level of overall savings and investment, the absence of long-term savings and the short-term maturities of Treasury bills. A second possible factor is the risky lending environment prevailing in Ghana, as reflected in the high level of past-due/non-performing loans. This is largely due to the significant losses of some state-owned companies, but also reflects broad institutional factors. For instance, as shown in Table 9.2, the enforcement of creditors' rights is weak compared with the sub-Saharan African average.

It is important to note that, although non-performing loans have some substantial provisioning implications, provisioning standards are lower in Ghana than in most African countries.[5] Depending on loan classification practices (and potential rollover

---

[4] For example, Barclays has set up a direct satellite network to bypass the Ghana Telecom network altogether.

[5] In Ghana, non-performing loans are defined based on a minimum of 180 days in arrears; loans are classified as 'substandard' when they are in arrears for 90 to 180 days, as 'doubtful' when they are in arrears for 180 to 540 days, and as 'loss-making' when arrears exceed 540 days. Full provisioning is required for loss-making, whereas substandard loans required a 50% provisioning.

**Table 9.4  Profitability Indicators (% of average assets)**

| | Net interest | Non-interest income | Overheads | Provisions | RoAA | RoAE | RoAA | Deflated RoAE |
|---|---|---|---|---|---|---|---|---|
| Ghana[a] | 10.0 | 6.4 | 7.0 | 2.2 | 6.1 3 | 6.9 | 5.3 | 22.3 |
| Ghana Commercial Bank Ltd[a] | 12.2 | 4.4 | 6.4 | 3.2 | 6.0 | 46.1 | 5.3 | 31.5 |
| Barclays Bank of Ghana Ltd[a] | 10.8 | 6.7 | 6.2 | 0.5 | 9.7 | 64.3 | 8.4 | 49.6 |
| Standard Chartered Bank[a] | 10.7 | 6.1 | 7.4 | 0.2 | 7.3 | 53.8 | 6.3 | 39.1 |
| Median | | | | | | | | |
| CFA franc zone[b] | 4.6 | 0.6 | 4.8 | 1.0 | 1.8 | 17.7 | 1.8 | 15.0 |
| Large SSA economies[b] | 5.9 | 2.5 | 5.4 | 1.2 | 1.4 | 16.3 | 1.3 | 10.5 |
| Small SSA economies[b] | 5.9 | 1.2 | 4.6 | 0.6 | 2.8 | 30.1 | 2.6 | 20.2 |
| SSA[b] | 5.7 | 1.2 | 4.8 | 0.8 | 1.9 | 27.9 | 1.9 | 15.0 |

*Note:*  a) 2002; b) 1998–2001 averages.
*Sources:*  IMF, *International Financial Statistics*; banks' financial statements, and authors' estimates.

of debt), this may suggest that the asset quality of banks' loan portfolio is somewhat overestimated, which may act as a further disincentive to engage in financial intermediation. A third factor that may account for low and inefficient financial intermediation in Ghana is the presence of an uncompetitive market structure. Although bank concentration appears to be moderate by regional standards, the GCB enjoys substantial market power, with 20% of total deposits and 44% of total branches — a situation that may influence price setting among banks and distort competition. Another potential piece of evidence is the fact that the GCB invariably records the widest interest margin among the commercial banks (12.2% in 2002; see Table 9.4).

However, beyond anecdotal evidence, more analysis is needed to draw some firm conclusions about the nature of the market structure in Ghana and the extent to which it offers a plausible explanation of the sector's profitability. The next section therefore introduces a basic analytical framework to assess the nature of competitive conditions.

## 3.   Analytical Framework and Econometric Estimation

The concept of market *contestability* has spanned a large theoretical and empirical literature covering many industries. The basic idea of market contestability is that, on the one hand, there are several sets of conditions that can yield competitive outcomes, with a competitive outcome possible even in concentrated systems. On the other hand, collusive actions can be sustained even in the presence of many firms. The most commonly used models for testing for the degree of competition are Bresnahan (1989) and Panzar and Rosse (1987). The Panzar and Rosse model investigates the extent to which a change in factor input prices is reflected in (equilibrium) revenues earned by a specific bank in the context of a Chamberlinian equilibrium model, and allows us to estimate the degree of competition. The advantage of this model is that it uses bank-level data, allows for bank-specific differences in the production function, and permits an analysis of the differences between types of banks in terms of size and ownership.

### *The Panzar and Rosse Analytical Framework*

Consider the following structural demand and cost relationship facing a particular firm $i$:

$$R_i = R_i(y_i, n, z_i) \tag{1}$$

$$C_i = C_i(y_i, p_i, x_i), \tag{2}$$

where $R$ = total revenue, $C$ = total costs, $y$ = output, $n$ = number of firms, $z$ = exogenous variable affecting revenue, $p$ = input prices and $x$ = other exogenous variables, with all variables expressed in logarithms,

Profits are defined as $\pi = Ri(y_i, n, z_i) - C_i(y_i, p_i, x_i)$, implying that the firm maximizes its profits where marginal revenue equals marginal costs (equation 3). This means that in equilibrium, the zero profit constraint holds at the market level as well:

$$\frac{\partial R_i}{\partial R_i \ (y_i, n, z_i)} - \frac{\partial C_i}{\partial C_i \ (y_i, p, x_i)} = 0 \tag{3}$$

Profit-maximizing output is defined as equation (4), with an asterisk (*) representing equilibrium values. Substituting (4) into (1), and assuming that $n$ is endogenously determined in the model, yields equation (5), which is the reduced form of the revenue function.

$$y^*_i = y^*_i \ (z_i, p, x_i \tag{4}$$

$$R^*_i = R^*_i \ (y^*_i (z_i, p_i, x_i), n^*, z_i) = R^* \ (z_i, p_i). \tag{5}$$

Note that market power is measured by the extent to which a change in factor input prices $(\partial p_i)$ is reflected in the equilibrium revenue $(\partial R^*_i)$ earned by firm i. Panzar and Rosse then define a measure of competition $H$ as the sum of the elasticities of equation (5) with respect to input prices, with i denoting a particular firm.

$$H = \sum_1 \frac{\partial R^*_i}{\partial pi} \frac{P_i}{R_i^*}. \tag{6}$$

According to Panzar and Rosse, it is not just the sign of the $H$-statistic that matters, but its magnitude as well. Under a monopolistic structure, an increase in input prices $P$ will increase marginal cost, thus reducing equilibrium output y* and revenue, thereby implying that the $H$-statistic value is less or equal to zero. In contrast, in a perfectly competitive setting in the long run, an increase in input prices $P$ will increase marginal cost as well as average costs by the same proportion, without — under certain assumptions — changing the equilibrium output of banks. As inefficient banks are forced to exit the market, the increased demand faced by the remaining firms leads to an increase in output prices and revenues in the same proportion as costs, thereby implying a value of the $H$-statistic equal to unity. In the case of monopolistic competition, described as the most plausible characterization of banks' interactions by Bikker and Haaf (2002b: 6), under certain assumptions an increase in input prices P will lead to a less than proportional increase in revenues, as the demand for banking facing individual banks is inelastic. In this case, the $H$-Statistic will lie between 0 and 1. The main discriminatory powers of the $H$-statistics, as discussed in the literature, are summarized in Table 9.5.

Note that the model is subject to several assumptions (see Gelos and Roldos, 2002 for a discussion of additional assumptions).

- banks are operating in (long-run) equilibrium;
- the performance of the banks is influenced by other participants' actions (except in the case of a purely monopolistic structure);

- the cost structure is homogeneous and the production function is a standard Cobb-Douglas function with a constant return to scale; and
- the price elasticity of demand is greater than unity.

**Table 9.5    Panzar and Rosse's *H*-Statistics**

| Values of *H* | Implied Market Structure |
|---|---|
| $H \leq 0$ | Monopoly<br>Colluding oligopoly, conjectural variations of oligopoly |
| $0 < H < 1$ | Monopolistic competition |
| $H = 1$ | Perfect competition<br>Natural monopoly in a perfectly contestable market |

However, the definition of equilibrium is not very clear in the Panzar and Rosse model. Given the internal logic of the model, it is best to think of equilibrium as a steady state, reflecting adjustments to shocks.

The Panzar and Rosse approach has been extensively used to analyze the nature of competition in mature banking systems, initially in North America[6] and subsequently in various European countries and Japan.[7] More recently, the approach has also been applied to emerging markets' banking systems[8] or in the context of large cross-country studies.[9] However, there is no published study that we are aware of that examines the case of African countries, except for Claessens and Laeven (2003), who do include Nigeria and South Africa in their sample of 50 countries.

In the empirical analysis, let us operationalize equation (5) as follows:

$$LogR_{it} = \lambda + \sum_{j=1}^{j} \mu_j \, logP_{it}^{\,j} + p\log Y_{it} + \sum_{k=1}^{k} \sigma_{it} \, \log Z_{it}^{\,k} + \varepsilon_{it} \,, \qquad (7)$$

with j=3 inputs, so that $P_{it}^{\,j}$ is a three-dimensional vector of factor prices. $Y_{it}$ is a scale variable, $Z_{it}^{\,n}$ is a vector of exogenous and bank-specific variables that may shift the revenue schedule (business mix), $\lambda$ is a constant term and $\varepsilon_{it}$ is the stochastic error term.

For the dependent variable *R*, various authors, Molyneux et al. (1994), Bikker and

---

[6] On the US banking system, see Shaffer (1989) and on Canada, see Nathan and Neave (1989).
[7] On European countries, see Molyneux et al. (1994) (France, Germany, Italy, Spain, UK), Vesala (1995) (Finland); Coccorese (2002) (Italy); De Brandt and Davis (2000) (France, Germany, Italy); Rime (1999) (Switzerland); Hondroyiannis et al. (1999) (Greece); Bikker and Groeneveld (1998) (15 EU countries); Hempell (2002) (Germany); and Maudos and Perez (2002) (Spain). On Japan, see Molyneux et al. (1996).
[8] See Gelos and Roldos (2002) (Central Europe and Latin America); Belaisch (2003) (Brazil); Yildirim and Philippatos (2002) (Central and Eastern Europe); Levi Yeyati and Micco (2003) (Latin America); and Zambrano Sequin (2003) (Venezuela).
[9] See, for example, Claessens and Laeven (2003) (50 countries) and Bikker and Haaf (2002a) (OECD countries).

Groeneveld (1998), Claessens and Laeven (2003), Levy Yeyati and Micco (2003), use the ratio of interest revenue (or alternatively total revenue) to total balance sheets, but, as noted by Vesala (1995), such a specification provides a price equation. Following Gelos and Roldos (2002), we prefer to estimate two reduced-form revenue equations, one for scaled total revenue, and one for unscaled total revenue. We also use both total revenue and interest revenue as the dependent variable to compare results.

$H$ is estimated for the whole sample t, and the H-statistic test is defined as:

$$H_i = \sum_{j=1}^{j} \mu_j = 0. \tag{8}$$

As noted previously, one of the crucial hypotheses of the Panzar and Rosse model is that the banking sector is assumed to be in equilibrium. As the $H$-statistics depend on industry-specific characteristics, cross-country comparisons may be misleading. In practice, researchers have usually overcome this problem by focusing on and testing for the change in $H$ over time, or by formally testing the equilibrium hypothesis, even if the definition of what constitutes an equilibrium in the banking sector remains elusive (see Shaffer (1982), Molyneux et al. (1996), and Claessens and Laeven (2003)).

### Description of the Data and Definitions of Variables
Annual individual bank balance sheets and income statements from 20 banks in operation during (part of) 1998–2003 have been used to construct the data set. For econometric estimations, banks that closed (4) or commenced operations (2) during the period have been omitted, along with one small bank due to data unavailability, leaving 65 observations for each explanatory variable. Moreover, given that the data used in this estimation concern institutions operating in the same field of business within the same country, a common effect specification was chosen for the estimates presented in this study.[10] Finally, panel regressions were run on pooled cross-sections for each year, as well as over the whole sample period to pick up the time-series components of the data.[11]

The variables are defined as follows (all in natural logs):

$$UPL = \frac{\text{Personnel Expenses}}{\text{Total Loans \& Deposits}}$$

$$UPF = \frac{\text{Interest Expenses}}{\text{Total Deposits}}$$

---

[10] Fixed-effect and random-effect models were, however, also estimated, yielding similar results.
[11] However, the time series is insufficient to test for stationarity in the summed residuals.

$$UPC = \frac{\text{Other Expenses}}{\text{Fixed Assets}}$$

$TA$ = Total assets (scale variable)

$$\text{Risk component 1 } (RC1): \frac{\text{Past-Due Loans}}{\text{Total Loans}}$$

$$\text{Risk component 2 } (RC2): \frac{\text{Total Loans}}{\text{Total Assets}}$$

In addition, we have included a dummy variable (*dum1*) for public ownership (=1) and another (*dum2*) for foreign ownership (=1). Finally, the Treasury bill rate in nominal (*NTBR*) and real (*RBTR*) terms has been included, as well as inflation (*INFL*).

## *Estimation Results*

Prior to the formal estimation of the model and following the existing literature (see Molyneux et al. (1996) and Claessens and Laeven (2003) among others), the market equilibrium test E defined in equation (10) was carried out on the basis of equation (9).

$$Log(1 + ROA_{it}) = \lambda + \sum_{j=1}^{j} \mu_j P_{it}^j + \rho \log Y_{it} + \sum_{n=1}^{n} \sigma_n Z_{it}^n + \varepsilon_{it} \qquad (9)$$

$$E_i = \sum_{j=1}^{j} \mu_j = 0 \qquad (10)$$

where ROA is the pre-tax return on assets.[12] The equilibrium test E is computed as a standard F-test, the intuition being that, in equilibrium, returns on assets should not be statistically correlated with input prices. The results of the equilibrium tests for the pooled data over the whole period, not reported here but available upon request from the authors, show that the market equilibrium condition cannot be rejected at the 5% level over the whole period.

As regards market structure, the results (Table 9.6) suggest that the Ghanaian banking sector is characterized by monopolistic competition according to the Panzar and Rosse classification. Irrespective of model specification, the *H*-statistic consistently lies between 0 and 1, with a value of 0.56 on average. Note that there seems to be some volatility in the *H*-statistics, especially in the scaled regressions, as

---

[12] As ROA can take on negative values on occasion, the dependent variable is simply computed as *ln(1+ROA)* for convenience. Although this approximation does slightly change the mathematical properties of the regression by reducing the size of the elasticities of the right-hand-side coefficients, the results did not seem to be affected by this approximation.

shown in Table 9.6. This is not unusual, as evidenced by other recent studies using the same methodology with different specifications (see Gelos and Roldos (2002), and Yildirim and Philippatos (2002)). However, the unscaled specification appears to display more stable results, and allowed for better assessing the crucial role of the scale variable.

**Table 9.6    *H*-Statistics Values for the Banking System in Ghana[a]**

|  | All Specifications | Unscaled Specifications | Scaled Specifications |
|---|---|---|---|
| Average *H*-statistic | 0.555 | 0.627 | 0.482 |
| Median *H*-statistic | 0.569 | 0.626 | 0.481 |
| Standard deviation | 0.092 | 0.038 | 0.064 |

*Note:*  a) The H-statistics are computed at the 5 percent significance level.

The market structure identified in Ghana — monopolistic competition — and score appears to be similar to that of comparable countries in the region (Table 9.7). Although cross-country comparison results should be treated with caution, it appears that Ghana's market structure is only slightly less competitive that of Nigeria and Kenya, even though the Nigerian banking sector operates with much narrower interest margins and less foreign penetration than Ghana's (Table 9.2). Note also that the market structure of South Africa is believed to be significantly more competitive, including by international standards.

**Table 9.7    Banking Sector Market Structure in Selected Countries**

| Country | Period | *H*-statistic | No. of banks | No. of observations |
|---|---|---|---|---|
| Ghana | 1998–2003 | 0.56 | 13 | 65 |
| **Sub-Saharan Africa** | | | | |
| Kenya | 1994–2001 | 0.58 | 34 | 106 |
| Nigeria | 1994–2001 | 0.67 | 42 | 186 |
| South Africa | 1994–2001 | 0.85 | 45 | 186 |
| North America (median) | 1994–2001 | 0.67 | 3 countries covered | |
| South America (median) | 1994–2001 | 0.73 | 12 countries covered | |
| East Asia (median) | 1994–2001 | 0.67 | 6 countries covered | |
| South Asia (median) | 1994–2001 | 0.53 | 3 countries covered | |
| Western Europe (median) | 1994–2001 | 0.67 | 14 countries covered | |
| Eastern Europe (median) | 1994–2001 | 0.68 | 7 countries covered | |

*Sources:*  Authors' calculations (Ghana); and Claessens and Laeven (2003; Table 2).

**Table 9.8  Regression Results***

| | Total Revenue (TR) | | Total interest revenue (TIR) | | Total Revenue (TR/TA) | | Total interest revenue (TIR/TA) | |
|---|---|---|---|---|---|---|---|---|
| C | 0.238 | -0.171 | -1.085** | -1.395** | 0.172 | 0.483 | 0.014 | -0.253 |
| t-statistic | 0.634 | -0.436 | -2.763 | -3.305 | 0.653 | 1.908 | 0.048 | -0.822 |
| UPL | 0.254** | 0.253 | 0.293** | 0.293** | 0.239** | 0.243** | 0.233** | 0.234** |
| t-statistic | 4.265 | 4.274** | 4.676 | 4.601 | 4.109 | 4.179 | 3.499 | 3.433 |
| UPF | 0.235** | 0.248 | 0.361** | 0.373** | 0.196** | 0.195** | 0.189** | 0.199** |
| t-statistic | 3.850 | 4.117** | 5.633 | 5.778 | 4.730 | 4.668 | 3.930 | 4.094 |
| UPC | 0.108** | 0.091** | 0.056 | 0.045 | 0.093** | 0.108** | 0.057 | 0.050 |
| t-statistic | 3.658 | 2.969 | 1.798 | 1.382 | 3.041 | 3.670 | 1.676 | 1.390 |
| TA | 1.025** | 1.033** | 1.112** | 1.116** | – | – | – | – |
| t-statistic | 36.909 | 36.511 | 38.156 | 36.717 | – | – | – | – |
| RC1 | 0.011 | 0.013 | 0.003 | -0.001 | 0.011 | 0.012 | 0.006 | -0.005 |
| t-statistic | 0.650 | 0.683 | 0.190 | -0.045 | 0.575 | 0.684 | 0.319 | -0.203 |
| RC2 | 0.318** | 0.294** | -0.012 | -0.026 | 0.341** | 0.352** | 0.147 | 0.141 |
| t-statistic | 4.234 | 3.864 | -0.155 | -0.320 | 5.283 | 5.468 | 1.990 | 1.869 |
| DUM1 | -0.090 | -0.094 | -0.225** | -0.221** | -0.076 | -0.078 | -0.181** | -0.169** |
| t-statistic | -1.277 | -1.327 | -3.027 | -2.895 | -1.088 | -1.128 | -2.273 | -2.081 |
| DUM2 | 0.100** | 0.100** | 0.075 | 0.076 | 0.111** | 0.108** | 0.115** | 0.117** |
| t-statistic | 2.177 | 2.208 | 1.553 | 1.551 | 2.487 | 2.415 | 2.246 | 2.237 |
| RTBR | – | 0.104** | – | 0.091** | – | 0.103** | – | 0.099** |
| t-statistic | | 3.326 | | 2.726 | | 3.283 | | 2.703 |

**Table 9.8** (*cont'd.*)

|  | Total Revenue (TR) | Total interest revenue (TIR) | Total Revenue (TR/TA) | Total interest revenue (TIR/TA) |
|---|---|---|---|---|
| NTBR | 0.348** — | 0.395** — | 0.368** — | 0.490** — |
| t-statistic | 3.511 | 3.797 | 3.818 | 4.439 |
| INFL | — 0.192** | — 0.235** | — 0.215** | — 0.311** |
| t-statistic | 2.759 | 3.149 | 3.229 | 3.984 |
| (**) *Statistically significant at the 5% level* | | | | |
| **Memorandum items:** | | | | |
| $R$-squared | 0.988 | 0.986 | 0.691 | 0.634 |
| Adjusted $R$-squared | 0.986 | 0.982 | 0.647 | 0.582 |
| S.E. of regression | 0.145 | 0.158 | 0.145 | 0.166 |
| $F$-statistic | 486.9 | 317.9 | 15.657 | 12.126 |
| Prob (F-statistic) | 0.000 | 0.000 | 0.000 | 0.000 |
| Mean dependent var. | 11.7 | 11.2 | -1.611 | -1.956 |
| S.D. dependent var. | 1.208 | 1.196 | 0.244 | 0.256 |
| Sum squared resid. | 1.157 | 1.055 | 1.173 | 1.541 |
| Durbin-Watson stat. | 1.864 | 1.097 | 1.883 | 1.464 |
| **Market structure Wald test** | | | | |
| Ho: $H=0$ (Monopolostic) | Rejected | Rejected | Rejected | Rejected |
| Ho: $H=1$ (Perf. competition) | Rejected | Rejected | Rejected | Rejected |
| Ho: $0<H<1$ (Mon. competition) | Not | Not | Not | Not |
|  | Rejected | Rejected | Rejected | Rejected |
| $H$-statistic | 0.597 | 0.654 | 0.546 | 0.422 |

*Note:* a)  Market structure tests at the 5% level.
*Source:*  Authors' calculations.

## *Interpretation of the Coefficients*

In interpreting the coefficients in Table 9.8, the following results should be underscored:

- The unit price of labour (*UPL*) is significant in all specifications and with similar positive coefficients. This result appears to confirm that personnel costs are as important as overhead costs, which are notoriously high in Ghana, as discussed in Section 2.

- The unit cost of funds (*UPF*) is significant in all specifications and greater than zero. Moreover, as expected, the cost of capital has a higher impact on interest revenue than other revenue. The elasticities of the scaled specifications of the model are much lower, giving further support to a presence of economies of scale as the relative interest expense depends on asset size.

- The unit cost of fixed assets (*UPC*) is positively correlated with total revenue, but not related to total interest revenue. The positive relationship could reflect Ghana's reliance on a very high level of private transfers, many of which are associated with costs exacerbated by the lack of a reliable telecommunications network. It could also be due to investment costs for which revenues are also fee-based. The lack of correlation with interest revenue might further indicate a lack of competition between banks, perhaps because of the high costs of exiting a relationship with a bank or other measures that hamper the effectiveness of, for example, marketing campaigns or other efforts by banks to attract this type of business.[13]

- The scale variable (*TA*) is strongly significant and positive in all models, which implies that size is a major determinant for total as well as interest revenue. All things being equal, the larger the bank, the higher the revenues, confirming the results of earlier studies (Bossone and Lee, 2002). This denotes a strong economies-of-scale effect, which not only indicates that the profitability structure of the banking sector in Ghana is skewed towards the larger banks, but also implies that small banks suffer a definite disadvantage in the system. This could indicate scope for greater consolidation in the sector in the future, especially if government securities were to evaporate as a relative high-yield, risk-free source of income for the banks.

- The risk variables (*RC1* and *RC2*) require some careful interpretation. The past-due loan ratio does not appear to be significant, and its coefficient is positive at times, which would seem to be counter-intuitive. However, this could well reflect the definition problem of past-due loans in Ghana, as discussed in Section 2. Given the over-exposure of the banking system to financially weak, state-owned enterprises, the non-relevance of the loan ratio for interest revenue is certainly plausible. As regards its contribution to total revenue, this could well reflect the

---

[13] See http://www.bog.gov.gh/notices/notice03/chgintrates0603.htm.

fact that the loan recipients are paying a sizeable share of commissions and fees.

- The dummy for state-ownership (*DUM1*) is consistently negative and statistically significant in all interest-revenue model estimations. This may capture the fact that state-owned banks have embarked on extensive lending to public enterprises which are prone to defer interest payments. Interestingly, the dummy is not significant when it comes to total revenue model estimations.

- Foreign ownership (*DUM2*) is consistently positive and statistically significant in all total revenue model estimations. This result appears to confirm that foreign banks are more effective than public institutions in generating non-interest income, notably through the extensive use of commissions and fees. As regards total interest revenue, the foreign ownership is positive and statistically significant in most of the regressions, which is consistent with other measures indicating that foreign banks tend to be more profitable across the board. This last result may be explained both in terms of efficiency in generating revenue and in terms of overall more cautious lending policy, as reflected in lower provisioning for bad loans (Table 9.3). The results presented in Table 9.8 also illustrate the potentially positive influence of foreign ownership on competition in Ghana's banking sector.[14]

- The results show that nominal (*NTBR*) and real (*RTBR*) have strong positive effects on both total and interest revenues and this holds true even when controlled for inflation. This offers further confirmation of the private sector crowding-out effect, fuelled by the large financing needs of the government, and may even indicate that competition and efficiency in the banking sector have an important fiscal dimension in Ghana. One possible interpretation is that both the banking sector and the government are trapped in a codependency scheme. On the one hand, the persistence of domestic financing needs[15] puts the larger banks in a possible price-maker position regarding interest rates, while the limited competition among these banks tends to affect their bidding behaviour, which is apparent from the chronic undersubscription at Treasury bill auctions and results in higher interest rates.

- On the other hand, the banking sector's profitability is highly dependent upon high interest rates, which dampens financial intermediation, widens interest spreads at the expense of the private sector, possibly exacerbates the loan quality problem, and ultimately restricts competition.

- Finally, as expected, inflation is positive and significantly correlated with revenues.

---

[14] Internationally, however, the empirical evidence is still mixed. On the one hand, Claessens and Laeven (2003) found a positive correlation between foreign banks' presence and competition (defined as measured by the H-statistic) in 53 countries, and Gelos and Roldos (2002) reached the same conclusion in 8 countries of Latin America and Europe. On the other hand, Levy Yeyati and Micco (2003) found that foreign bank presence actually weakened competition in Latin America.
[15] Assuming no access to foreign capital markets and limited recourse to inflation financing.

Other macroeconomic variables, such as the nominal exchange rate and banking system credit to the government, were not significant.

## 4.   Conclusions

The main finding of this study is that banks in Ghana appear to behave in a non-competitive manner that could possibly hamper financial intermediation. This result is consistent with their seemingly high profitability, which seems to indicate a persistently low level of market contestability. Several factors are believed to affect banks' behaviour, either because they constitute indirect barriers to entry or because they tend to limit competition among banks. The main factors are as follows:

• **Decisive role of size.** Our results show that scale matters substantially in the Ghanaian banking system. In addition, the very small savings base prevents smaller banks from emerging quickly, and thus size could act as a serious constraint on market entry.

• **Persistent financing needs of the government.** Our results indicate that the persistent domestic financing needs of the government have fostered inefficiency in the banking system as holdings of government securities have become the driving force in the revenue function for the banks. Thus, the banks' reliance on government securities as a source of large steady profits appears to have limited competition between banks. In addition, large deficit financing through the issuance of Treasury bills has not only crowded out the private sector in capturing banks' investments, but may also have put pressure on interest rates, thereby making access to bank lending even more difficult for the private sector and hampering private sector development.

• **High investment costs.** A third impediment to stronger competition among banks could be the high investment costs that are needed to overcome the current telecommunication problems prevailing in Ghana. Our results show that a sizeable portion of total bank revenue is fee-based, and thus dependent upon heavy technology investment, which might further deter potential new entrants.

• **Barriers to competition on interest revenue.** The lack of correlation among costs other than on personnel, funding, and interest revenue — traditionally the main source of revenue for banks — is clearly an indication that competition is stifled in the Ghanaian banking system. This could be due to the non-transparent fee structure of the banks, which helps to shield the bank market structure from competition.

• **Losses on the loan portfolio.** One further explanation for the lack of contestability is the past-due loans element, which does not seem to be related to either revenues or returns. This may suggest some serious definition problems and, hence, a lack of adequate provisioning, which may in turn signal high lending risks to potential entrants. Domestic banks might be more prone to this behaviour, as foreign banks appear to be more profitable and the quality of their portfolio tends to be better; however, domestic and foreign banks are equally effective in generating revenue.

Probably the most important policy recommendation arising from this analysis is that achieving effective fiscal adjustment may be a necessary condition for deepening and increasing the efficiency of the Ghanaian banking system. This is evidenced by the positive impact of the fiscal effort initiated in 2002/3 on domestic interest rates; in particular, T-bill rates have declined steeply, reflecting the reduction in public financing requirements, but the decline in lending rates has been more modest. Sustained fiscal adjustment — a key precondition for further declines in interest rates and higher domestic investment — would reduce the dependence of banks upon government securities as a source of low-risk, high-yielding assets. This would lead to increased competition, as banks would have to identify new lending opportunities and expand their customer base in order to generate income. In turn, increased competition could foster some efficiency gains through consolidation in the banking system. Notwithstanding the importance of maintaining a prudent fiscal stance, other factors contributing to high banking spreads may also need to be addressed. For example, facilitating more transparency in the fee structure of banks and improvements in telecommunications may prove very useful in addressing the high investment costs. In addition, addressing the losses on the loan portfolio, particularly in the domestic banks, seems highly desirable. Such an action would not only require that bank regulation and supervision be further strengthened, but also that key institutional issues affecting investors be addressed at the legal and judicial levels, most notably in terms of creditor rights.

## References

Belaisch, A. (2003) *Do Brazilian Banks Compete?*, IMF Working Paper WP/03/113. Washington, DC: International Monetary Fund, May.

Bikker, J. A. and Groeneveld, J. M. (1998) *Competition and Concentration in the EU Banking Industry*, Research Series Supervision No. 8. Amsterdam: De Nederlandsche Bank.

Bikker, J. A. and Haaf, K. (2002a) 'Measures of Competition and Concentration in the Banking Industry: A Review of the Literature', *Economic and Financial Modelling*, Vol. 9: 53–98.

Bikker, J. A. and Haaf, K. (2002b) 'Competition, Concentration and Their Relationship: An Empirical Analysis of the Banking Industry', *Journal of Banking and Finance*, Vol. 26: 2191–2214.

Bossone, Biagio and Lee, Jong-Kun (2002) *In Finance, Size Matters*, IMF Working Paper WP/02/113. Washington, DC: International Monetary Fund, June.

Bredenkamp, Hugh, Enrique G. de la Piedra and Osa Ahinakwah (2003) 'Reforming Ghana's Financial Sector.' Ghana: Selected Issues. Washington, DC: IMF Working Paper. WP/05/17.

Bresnahan, T. F. (1989) 'Empirical Studies of Industries with Market Power', in R. Schmalensee and R. D. Willig (eds), *Handbook of Industrial Organisation*, Vol. II: 1012–55. The Hague: Elsevier Science Publishers.

Cetorelli, N. (1999) 'Competitive Analysis in Banking: Appraisal of the Methodologies', *Economic Perspectives* (Federal Reserve Bank of Chicago), Issue Q1: 2–15.

Claessens, S. and Laeven, L. (2003) *What Drives Bank Competition? Some International Evidence*, World Bank Policy Research Paper No. 3113. Washington, DC: World Bank, August.

Coccorese, P. (2002) *Competition among Dominant Firms in Concentrated Markets: Evidence from the Italian Banking Industry*, Working Paper No. 89. Salerno: Università degli Studi di Salerno, October.

De Brandt, O. and Davis, P. (2000) 'Competition, Contestability and Market Structure in European Banking Sectors on the Eve of EMU', *Journal of Banking and Finance*, Vol. 24: 1045–66.

Gelos, G. and Roldos, J. (2002) *Consolidation and Market Structure in Emerging Market Banking Systems*, IMF Working Paper WP/02/186. Washington, DC: International Monetary Fund, November.

Hempell, H. S. (2002) *Testing for Competition among German Banks*, Deutsche Bank Discussion Paper 04/02. Frankfurt: Deutsche Bank.

Hondroyiannis, G., Sarantis, L. and Papapetrou, E. (1999) 'Assessing Competitive Conditions in the Greek Banking System', *Journal of International Financial Markets, Institutions and Money*, Vol. 9, No. 4, November: 377–91.

IMF (2003) 'Ghana: Financial System Stability Assessment Update', Country Report No. 03/396 http://www.imf.org/external/pubs/cat/longres.cfm'sk=17098.

Levy Yeyati, E. L. and Micco, A. (2003) 'Concentration and Foreign Penetration in Latin American Banking Sector: Impact on Competition and Risk', Universidad Torcuato Di Tella, August (mimeo).

Maudos, J. and Pérez, F. (2002) 'Competencia versus poder de marcado en la banco española', Universitat de Valéncia, October (mimeo).

Molyneux, P., Thorton, J. and Lloyd-Williams, M. (1994) 'Competitive Conditions in European Banking', *Journal of Banking and Finance*, Vol. 18: 445–59.

Molyneux, P., Thorton, J. and Lloyd-Williams, M. (1996) 'Competition and Market Contestability in Japanese Commercial Banking', *Journal of Economics and Business*, Vol. 48: 33–45.

Nathan, A. and Neave, H. (1989) 'Competition and Contestability in Canada's Financial System', *Canadian Journal of Economics*, Vol.22: 576–94.

Panzar, L. and Rosse, J. (1987) 'Testing for Monopoly Equilibrium', *The Journal of Industrial Economics*, Vol. 35, No. 4, June: 443–56.

Rime, B. (199) 'Mesure du degré de concurrence dans le système bancaire suisse à l'aide du modèle de Panzar et Rosse,' *Revue Suisse d'économie politique et de statistique*, Vol. 135, No.1: 21–40.

Shaffer, S. (1982) 'A Nonstructural Test for Competition in Financial Markets' in *Bank Structure and Competition*, Conference proceedings, Chicago, IL: Federal Reserve Bank of Chicago.

Shaffer, S. (1989) 'Competition in the US Banking Industry', *Economic Letters*, Vol. 29, No. 4: 349–53.

Vesala, J. (1995) 'Testing competition in banking: behavioral evidence from Finland', *Bank of Finland Studies E:1.*: 1–206.

Yildirim, S. and Philippatos, G. (2002) 'Competition and Contestability in Central and Eastern European Banking Markets', University of Saskatchewan, September (mimeo).

Zambrano Sequin, L. Z. (2003) 'Competencia Monopolística y Sistema Bancario en Veneruela', Asamblea Nacional, April (mimeo).

# 10 Rural & Microfinance Regulation in Ghana: Implications for Development of the Industry*

## WILLIAM F. STEEL
## & DAVID O. ANDAH

This study assesses how the policy, legal and regulatory framework has affected, and been influenced by, the development of rural and microfinance institutions[1] (RMFIs) in Ghana, especially in terms of the range of institutions and products available, and their financial performance and outreach. The potential of microfinance to reach large numbers of the poor is well understood (Robinson, 2001). Questions for regulation are the extent to which a flexible regulatory environment can encourage innovation and a diversity of RMFIs and products serving different market niches not reached by commercial banks, and at what point special legislation may be needed, whether to facilitate the commercialization and sustainability of the rural and microfinance (RMF) industry or to protect deposits and ensure the stability of the financial system.

Ghana is particularly interesting because its tiered system of different laws and regulations for different types of institutions has evolved largely in response to local conditions, and because so many of its institutions are savings-based. The resulting system resembles the tiered approach recommended by the World Bank's 1999 study of microfinance regulation (Van Greuning et al., 1999) and more recently adopted by

* A previous (longer) version of this study was issued as World Bank Africa Region Working Paper No. 49 (June 2003). The authors are grateful for comments on earlier drafts from peer reviewers Joselito Gallardo and Rich Rosenberg, as well as from Kwaku Addeah, Stefan Staschen, Andreas Thiele, Antony Thompson, and participants in conferences on the World Bank and Ghana. They also appreciate information and inputs provided by Ken Appenteng Mensah, Edmund Armah, Eyob Tesfaye, Amha Wolday, the Association of Rural Banks, the Bank of Ghana, the Ghana Co-operative Credit Union Association, and the Ghana Microfinance Institutions Network.
[1] 'Microfinance' refers to small financial transactions with low-income households and microenterprises (both urban and rural), using non-standard methodologies such as character-based lending, group guarantees, and short-term repeat loans. 'Rural finance' includes other instruments and institutions specifically intended to finance rural activities, both farm and off-farm. The common elements are that the clients being served typically lack the characteristics (e.g., titled property as collateral) required by commercial banks or are located beyond the reach of commercial bank branches, and that innovative methods and specialized products or institutions are needed to reach these markets.

Uganda.[2] While Ghana's approach has fostered a wide range of both formal and informal RMFIs, it has not as yet been so successful in achieving strong financial performance, significant scale, and true commercialization of microfinance.

## 1.    Structure and Performance of the Rural and Microfinance Industry

The financial system in Ghana falls into three main categories — formal, semi-formal, and informal:

* Formal financial institutions are those incorporated under the Companies Code 1963 and licensed by the Bank of Ghana (BoG) under either the Banking Law 1989 or the Financial Institutions (Non-Banking) Law 1993 (NBFI Law) to provide financial services under Bank of Ghana regulation. Rural and Community Banks (RCBs) operate as commercial banks under the Banking Law, except that they cannot undertake foreign-exchange operations, their clientele is drawn from their local catchment area, and their minimum capital requirement is significantly lower. Among the nine specified categories of non-bank financial institutions (NBFIs), the Savings and Loans Companies (S&Ls), which are restricted to a limited range of services, are most active in micro and small-scale financial intermediation using microfinance methodologies.

* Non-governmental organizations (NGOs) and Credit Unions (CUs) are considered to be semi-formal — legally registered but not licensed by the Bank of Ghana. NGOs are incorporated as companies limited by guarantee (not for profit) under the Companies Code. Their poverty focus leads most of them to provide multiple services to poor clients, including micro credit, though mostly on a limited scale. They are not licensed to take deposits from the public and hence have to use external (usually donor) funds for micro credit. Credit Unions are registered by the Department of Co-operatives as co-operative thrift societies that can accept deposits from and give loans to their members. Although credit unions are nominally included in the NBFI Law, the Bank of Ghana has allowed the apex body, the Ghana Co-operative Credit Union Association, to continue to regulate the societies pending the introduction of a new Credit Union Law.

* The informal financial system covers a range of activities known as *Susu*, including individual savings collectors, rotating savings and credit associations, and savings and credit 'clubs' run by an operator. It also includes money-lenders, trade creditors, self-help groups, and personal loans from friends and relatives. Money-lenders

---

[2] Uganda's Microfinance Deposit-taking Institutions Act (2002) provides for central bank licensing of specialized microfinance institutions that wish to mobilize savings and use them for lending, while leaving credit-only NGO MFIs and small member-based organizations to operate outside direct regulation. This approach stands in contrast to the approaches of countries such as Ethiopia, which allows only one category of licensed RMFI.

are supposed to be licensed by the police under the Money-lenders Ordinance 1957.[3]

The commercial banking system is dominated by a few major banks (among the 17 total) and reaches only about 5% of households, most of which are excluded by high minimum deposit requirements. With 60% of the money supply outside the commercial banking system, the RCBs, S&Ls, and the semi-formal and informal financial systems play a particularly important role in Ghana's private sector development and poverty reduction strategies. The assets of the RCBs are nearly 4% of those of the commercial banking system, with S&Ls and CUs adding another 2%. While 'RMFIs' is used to refer collectively to the full range of these institutions, they use different methodologies to reach different (albeit overlapping) clienteles among farmers, rural households, the poor, and microenterprises, and hence different regulatory and supervisory instruments may be appropriate.

## *Rural and Community Banks*[4]

RCBs are unit banks owned by members of the rural community through the purchase of shares and are licensed to provide financial intermediation. They were first initiated in 1976 to expand savings mobilization and credit services in rural areas not served by commercial and development banks.[5] The number expanded rapidly in the early 1980s, mainly to service the government's introduction of special cheques instead of cash payment to cocoa farmers — though, with adverse consequences for their financial performance (Nissanke and Aryeetey 1998). Through a combination of rapid inflation, currency depreciation, economic decline, mismanagement of funds and natural disasters, combined with weak supervision, only 23 of the 123 RCBs qualified as 'satisfactory' in 1992 (Table 10.1).

The obvious need for re-capitalization and capacity-building was addressed during 1990–94 under the World Bank's Rural Finance Project, with half of them achieving 'satisfactory' status by 1996. The combination of very high (62%) primary and secondary reserve requirements imposed by the Bank of Ghana in 1996 and high Treasury bill rates helped to reduce the risk assets and increase net worth, further improving their financial performance. The number of RCBs reached a peak of 133 in 1998, but fell to 111 in 1999 with the closure of 23 distressed banks and the

---

[3] The apparent motivation of the Ordinances was to register these agents both to give them a legal basis for recovery of debt and as a form of restraint on usurious practices.

[4] While the Agricultural Development Bank has played an important role in making finance available for agriculture, poor economic conditions in the 1970s and early 1980s, poor repayment and other problems resulted in negative net worth by the end of the 1980s and restructuring in 1990. Furthermore, 'the share of smallholder credit in ADB's total lending declined to 15% in 1992, while the share of lending to agriculture fell to 30%', and short-term loans accounted for some 80% of lending (Nissanke and Aryeetey, 1998: 63). The share of smallholders has since risen to 24% in 1999 and the share of agriculture loans to 51%.

[5] The concept was extended to an urban Community Bank in 1987. There is no limit on the number of shares an individual can own. 'RCBs' is used to refer to the entire category (since 1987); 'RBs' is used to refer solely to Rural Banks.

commissioning of one new bank. These closures sent a strong signal to the remaining rural banks to maintain or improve their operations in order to achieve satisfactory status. Between 1999 and 2001 there was a 64% increase in the number of satisfactory banks.

**Table 10.1  Classification of Rural Banks** (number)

| Category | 1981 | 1986 | 1992 | 1995 | 1998 | 1999 | 2001 | 2003 |
|---|---|---|---|---|---|---|---|---|
| 'Satisfactory'[a] | – | – | 23 | 53 | 52 | 53 | 87 | 114 |
| Mediocre | – | – | 82 | 54 | 58 | 56 | 27 | 1 |
| Distressed[b] | – | – | 18 | 18 | 23 | 2[c] | 0 | 0 |
| Total | 29 | 106 | 123 | 125 | 133 | 111 | 115[d] | 117[e] |

*Notes:* a)  Based on compliance with a 6% capital adequacy ratio (a relatively low standard for RMFIs).
  b)  Based on solvency.
  c)  Allowed only to handle workers' salary payments.
  d)  Includes 1 licensed at the end of the year.
  e)  Includes 2 for which data are not yet available.
*Source*:   Addo, 1998: 27–9. BoG, *Annual Reports,* Banking Supervision Department.

Originally, RBs made standard commercial loans to individuals or groups, often related to agriculture, but the term loans tended to result in portfolio performance problems, as borrowers had difficulty making balloon payments and RBs had weak follow-up capacity. During the 1990s, some more progressive RCBs adopted a more commercial approach and innovative programmes, often in collaboration with NGOs that offered proven microfinance methodologies, such as Freedom From Hunger's Credit with Education (FFH/CWE) programme (see Box 10.1).[6] Some RCBs have tried to develop linkages with *susu* collectors (GHAMFIN, 2001), introduced mobile banking to reach rural markets on a weekly basis, or served community-based organizations (CBOs) associated with donor programmes.

A few RCBs have succeeded in expanding to over 20,000 clients and reaching high levels of operational and financial sustainability. The total number of recorded depositors in all RCBs is 1.2 million, with about 150,000 borrowers (some of them groups of 5 to 35 members, so actual outreach is somewhat greater). On average, however, RCBs are relatively small compared even with African MFIs, especially in terms of lending — though they are relatively profitable, thanks in large part to past high reserve requirements and interest rates (Table 10.2).

---

[6] Loans of this type are generally short-term (4–6 months) with weekly repayment, averaging around $50-75 but ranging up to several hundred dollars, with compulsory up-front savings of 20% that is retained as security against the loan, complementing group or individual guarantees as the other principal form of security. Most donor-supported programmes also use these methodologies, often working through existing RCBs and NGOs.

---

**Box 10.1     Types of Group and Individual Savings and Credit Programmes**

*Group savings with credit*:  A group of members (whether pre-existing or formed for this purpose) open a joint bank savings account and mobilize initial savings deposits to qualify for a loan. Group savings may be used as security against loans and may be invested in T-bills. Groups usually are made up of 3-4 sub-solidarity groups.

*Group and individual savings with credit*:  Group members contribute to both a joint group account and their individual accounts. The group may be a 'village bank' of 25–40 members; or as small as 5 members. While both individual and group savings accounts are used as collateral, the individual account includes the member's additional personal savings. Loan repayments are made by individuals but handled through the group account.  Examples include Nsoatreman, Bosomtwe, and Lower Pra RBs.

*Individual savings with group credit*:  Individuals lodge their savings through the group, which receives a loan for distribution to members after a qualifying period, and they continue to save into their individual accounts as they repay the loan. The group handles the collection of savings and repayments, acts as the interface with the loan officer, and bears group responsibility for recovery (though the loans are made to individual members).  Example: Freedom from Hunger's Credit with Education programme, operated through Brakwa, Lower Pra, Nsoatreman and Nandom RBs, Bulsa Community Bank, and Women's World Banking Ghana (Quainoo, 1997).

*Individual savings with credit*: direct lending to individuals, either those who had established a credible history as a member of a group but who need larger or separate loans, or in cases where a group approach is not suitable. Examples: Lower Pra RB; Nsoatreman RB's District Assembly Poverty Alleviation Programme.

*Source*:    CHORD (2000).

---

**Table 10.2   Average Size of Ghana's Rural Banks and Credit Unions Relative to African MFIs**

| Indicator (average) | African MFIs[a] | Rural Banks | Credit Unions |
|---|---|---|---|
| Number of clients | 7374 | 8488 | 405 |
| Loan balance | $119 | $30 | $153 |
| Total loan portfolio | $690,027 | $251,924 | $65,180 |
| Total assets | $1,612,029 | $841,102 | $110,961 |
| Capital/assets | 60.3% | 2.6% | 3.5% |

*Note:*  a)  From the Micro-Banking Bulletin.
*Source*:    Sample survey data from Kowubaa (2000: 60). S&Ls were not sampled.

The Association of Rural Banks (ARB) was founded in 1981 as an NGO with voluntary membership 'to promote and strengthen the rural banking concept' through advocacy and training. The association initiated the proposal for the ARB Apex Bank, licensed in 2001 to perform apex financial services for RCBs (including the introduction of new products such as domestic money transfers) and, eventually, to take over some supervisory and training functions.

## Non-Bank Financial Institutions

Table 10.3 shows the rapid growth in the number of NBFIs following the passage of the new law in 1993. Except for finance houses, growth has stalled since 1998, in part because new applicants have been unable to keep up with increases in the minimum capital requirement.

**Table 10.3    Growth of Licensed NBFIs by Type since Passage of Law in 1993**

| Type of NBFI | 1994 | 1995 | 1998 | 2001 | 2003 |
|---|---|---|---|---|---|
| Savings & Loan[a] | 2 | 5 | 7 | 8 | 9 |
| Leasing & Hire Purchase | 0. | 5 | 6 | 6 | 5 |
| Finance Houses | 0. | 7 | 12 | 16 | 15 |
| Discount Companies | 1 | 2 | 3 | 3 | 3 |
| Building Societies | 1 | 2 | 2 | 2 | 2 |
| Venture Capital | 0 | 1 | 1 | 2 | 2 |
| Mortgage Finance[b] | 0 | 1 | 1 | 1 | 1 |
| Total (except CUs) | 4 | 23 | 32 | 38 | 37 |

*Notes:* a)  Two additional S&Ls have been licensed and began operations in 2004.
        b)  The mortgage finance company was re-licensed as a commercial bank in 2004.
*Source:*   Bank of Ghana. No acceptance house has been licensed.

## Savings & Loans Companies

Initial licensing of the new S&L category was difficult, as the Bank of Ghana grappled with how to implement the new law. The required minimum capital (¢100 million or US$150,000) initially posed a hurdle, but its real value was eroded by rapid inflation, and the number of S&Ls grew from 5 in 1995 to 7 by 1998. By 2002 the 8 S&Ls had over 160,000 depositors and 10,000 borrowers. Increases in the minimum capital requirement in 1998 and 2000 restored the dollar value through a ten-fold increase in the nominal value, and a further increase in 2001 to about US$2 million stalled the rate of new entry. Nevertheless, the S&L category has proved to be a flexible means of regularizing three types of MFIs:

• transformation of NGOs into licensed financial intermediaries;[7]

---

[7] The first license as an S&L went to Women's World Banking Ghana (WWBG) in 1994, representing the first transformation of an NGO into a licensed financial institution. Sinapi Aba Trust was licensed in 2004 as the second NGO to become an S&L. EMPRETEC, an NGO providing training

- formalization of actual or potential informal money-lending operations;
- establishment of small private banking operations serving a market niche.

The S&L category has also made possible the entry of private investment to serve a particular market niche on a smaller scale than would be required for a commercial bank, although providing a challenge to the supervisory authorities. A recent investment is Sikaman S&L Company Ltd., which is applying international best practices in microfinance to reach profitability within two years.

The S&Ls generally use the loan products described in Box 10.1. For example, First Allied S&L uses a group and individual savings with credit scheme with existing, registered occupation-based groups such as butchers, kente weavers, carpenters, and other associations (CHORD, 2000). S&Ls have also been leaders in innovating. Citi S&L has pioneered linkages with *susu* collectors and clubs, and offers a micro-leasing product to clients with at least two successful loan terms (Anin, 2000).[8]

## *Credit Unions*

Credit Unions are thrift societies offering savings and loan facilities exclusively to members. The first credit union in Africa was established in Northern Ghana in 1955 by Canadian Catholic missionaries. By 1968, when they were brought under legislation and the Credit Union Association (CUA) was formed as an apex body, there were 254 CUs (64 of them rural) with some 60,000 members (Quainoo, 1997). The number of CUs continued to grow to nearly 500 by the mid-1970s, but their financial performance was not particularly strong. High inflation in the late 1970s eroded their capital, and by the early 1990s, the number of CUs had fallen by half (Table 10.4). The weak financial performance of CUs has been due in large part to their organization as co-operative societies with a welfare focus, and in particular to their policy of low interest rates.

The CUA has 250 affiliates (2003) with 132,000 members (about a quarter of them Study Groups in the process of becoming full credit unions). Credit unions average about 400–500 members, and their average loan size of US$153 is well above that for African MFIs, as well as for RCBs[9] (Table 10.2).

The CUA has attempted to establish a financial reporting system for its members, but the quality data remain poor. Furthermore, many managers, as well as the Board and members, have little understanding of the business of financial intermediation. 'Over 70% of all Ghanaian credit unions were in an "unsatisfactory" situation as of April 1996, and 42% of them were placed in the worst category' (Camara, 1996). By the end of 2001, these ratings had improved to 60% and 15%, respectively, and the share given the top rating for financial soundness had improved significantly to 29% (CUA, 2002).

---

for micro and small-scale businesses, is also trying to meet the paid-up capital requirement for an S&L.

[8] Although leasing companies have substantial potential to assist SMEs by solving the collateral problem that makes it difficult for them to obtain loans, this market is only just emerging. One leasing company established a micro-lease department (mainly for SMEs) in 2001.

[9] This is probably because 59% of the CUs are workplace-based, with 71% of the membership serving a more middle-class salaried clientele than the community-based ones.

**Table 10.4   Growth in Credit Unions and Membership, 1968–2001**

| Year | Number | Membership |
|------|--------|------------|
| 1968 | 254 | 60,000 |
| 1972 | 204 | 27,405 |
| 1976 | 457 | 48,705 |
| 1980 | 310 | 49,103 |
| 1984 | 233 | 55,170 |
| 1988 | 330 | 65,052 |
| 1992 | 223 | 44,068 |
| 1996 | 228 | 51,423 |
| 2000 | 225 | 70,046 |
| 2002 | 253 | 123,204 |
| 2003 | 250 | 132,000 |

*Source*:   Ghana Credit Union Association (CUA).

Most CUs require borrowers to provide security, in addition to being in good standing with their deposits. Ideally, this can be in the form of a guarantee from another member of the credit union who has an adequate uncommitted savings balance. Some CUs use the *susu* method in the collection of deposits and loan repayments. The CUA is an innovator in providing both credit insurance (which pays off the outstanding loan balance in case of the death of a borrower) and a contractual savings programme (which matches savings, up to a limit, if held at death or to maturity) (Gallardo et al., 2002).

## Non-Governmental and Community-Based Organizations

NGOs have facilitated the development of good microfinance practices in Ghana by introducing internationally tested methodologies, often in partnership with RMFIs. These methodologies are often based on group solidarity methods, and have benefited from linkages with CBOs that have already 'come together on the basis of some kind of location, occupations, friendship, family ties, gender, or other grounds to serve a purpose at the community level' (CHORD, 2000). NGOs and CBOs are particularly important in making financial services available in the northern part of the country, where both commercial and rural banks are scarce — although they tend to be localized and donor-dependent.

Ghana has relatively few NGOs whose primary mission is microfinance and that have reached significant scale. Although some 50 NGOs have active microcredit programmes, they are generally multipurpose or welfare-oriented agencies (only four exceed 3,000 clients and total outreach is only about 60,000 clients (GHAMFIN, 2003). The principal exception is Sinapi Aba Trust (SAT, established 1994), which has 16 branches country-wide, offering both group-based and individual loans. SAT has reached financial and operational sustainability and sufficient scale to transform into a licensed S&L. The ability to take and intermediate savings would free it from its current reliance on RCBs and other intermediaries to handle clients' funds and on donor funds to finance its lending.

Box 10.1 described the models used by NGOs, often in collaboration with RCBs or other RMFI partners. 'Village banking' is a group and individual savings with credit methodology promoted most notably by Catholic Relief Services and the SNV/ Netherlands Development Programme; some are registering with the CUA as Study Groups. FFH/CWE uses individual savings with group credit to target women and provide accompanying education on health, nutrition, family planning, financial planning and budgeting, and microenterprise development. FFH trains the loan officers for partner RMFIs and the groups handle the bookkeeping, so the programme can be quite profitable — although, until recently, the high reserve requirement for RCBs prevented them from using their own mobilized savings.

## *Informal Finance*

### *Money-lenders*
Money-lenders were the first form of microfinance to be officially licensed in Ghana, and have long been an important source of emergency and short-term finance (after relatives and friends) for the vast majority of the population lacking access to commercial financing. By the mid-1960s, money-lending had become more of a part-time activity by traders and others with liquid funds rather than a full-time profession (Offei, 1965, cited in Aryeetey, 1994).[10] The importance, and certainly the registration, of individual money-lenders may have been reduced by the emergence of RCBs, CUs, *susu* associations and clubs, and especially S&Ls, which has enabled money-lending-type operations to become licensed. These days most individual money-lenders do not hold licences or operate full-time, and the Ordinance has ceased to be of any importance, although it remains on the statute book.

### *Susu Collectors, Associations, Clubs, Companies and Products*
The *susu* system (see Box 10.2) primarily helps clients accumulate their own savings over periods ranging from one month (*susu* collectors) to two years (*susu* clubs), although credit is also a common feature. In an effort to capitalize on *susu* collectors' intimate knowledge of their clients, several RCBs and S&Ls participated in a pilot programme to provide funds to *susu* collectors for them to on-lend to their clients (GHAMFIN, 2001), and some have continued with their own funds.

The *susu* collectors are the most visible and extensive form. Even though they mobilize savings, the central bank has refrained from attempting to regulate them, leaving them to try to improve the reputation and quality of the industry through self-

---

[10] 'Official statistics indicate that in 1972, there were 33 licensed money lenders in Accra Region. By 1988 the number has dwindled to 4' (Anin, 2000).

regulation.[11] Susu collectors who are registered with associations account for nearly a quarter of the estimated more than 4,000 collectors nationwide, collecting an average of US$15 a month from approximately 200,000 clients (GCSCA, 2003).

---

**Box 10.2    Types of *Susu* (Savings Collection) in Ghana**

Ghana has at least five different types of institutions known as, or offering products termed, *susu*:

- ***Susu* collectors**: individuals who collect daily amounts set by each of their clients (e.g., traders in the market) and return the accumulated amount at the end of the month, minus one day's amount as a commission.

- ***Susu* associations** or mutualist groups are of two types: (i) a *rotating* savings and credit association (ROSCA), whose members regularly (e.g., weekly or monthly) contribute a fixed amount that is allocated to each member in turn (according to lottery, bidding, or other system that the group establishes); (ii) *accumulating*, whose members make regular contributions and whose funds may be lent to members or paid out under certain circumstances (e.g., death of a family member).[12]

- ***Susu* clubs** are a combination of the above systems operated by a single individual, in which members commit themselves to saving towards a sum that each decides over a 50- or 100-week cycle, paying a 10% commission on each payment and an additional fee when they are advanced the targeted amount earlier in the cycle; they have existed at least since the mid-1970s, quite likely earlier.

- ***Susu* companies** existed only in the late 1980s as registered businesses whose employees collected daily savings using regular *susu* collector methodology, but promised loans (typically twice the amount saved) after a minimum period of at least six months.

- Some licensed financial institutions (commercial banks, insurance companies, RCBs, S&Ls, and credit unions) have offered a **systematic savings plan** termed '*susu*', sometimes hiring employees to go out and gather the savings in the manner of a *susu* collector. The State Insurance Corporation first introduced such a 'Money Back' product in the 1980s, including a life insurance benefit for clients as an additional incentive to mobilize savings, but the scheme was discontinued in 1999.

---

[11] The one type of *susu* institution that has come under formal regulation was the *susu* companies, whose guarantee of loans of double the amounts saved, combined with mismanagement of funds, made them unsustainable. Passage of the NBFI law essentially terminated this practice by registered businesses and required that they raise sufficient minimum capital and become registered as an S&L (which Women's World Banking Ghana did for its *susu* scheme).

[12] The accumulating type is usually larger; a 1993 survey found that they average 37 members, as against 12 for a typical monthly rotating *susu* group.

Some commercial banks have introduced savings products modelled on and advertised as *susu*. Likewise, some RCBs, S&Ls and NGOs have *susu* schemes, with daily collections carried out by salaried or commissioned agents. These methodologies have helped them to reach lower-income brackets and women, who constitute 65% to 80% of the clients of these *susu* schemes. Thus, the combination of specialized categories of licensed financial institutions and traditional methodologies has succeeded both in mobilizing savings from lower-income households and giving them access to financial services that are part of the formal, supervised system.

## Traders

A major component of rural finance in Ghana has always been the traders who operate between producers in rural areas and urban markets, and often provide credit in the form of inputs on supplier's credit or an advance against future purchase of the crop. Traders do not usually require collateral, but rather the agreement of the farmer to sell them the crop. The implicit interest rate can be as much as 50% of the principal for the farming season (Offei, 1965, cited in Aryeetey, 1994). Fish traders similarly use advances to lock in their suppliers at relatively low prices. While these middlemen are often regarded as exploitative in view of their monopsony power, for a large number of farmers and fishermen, access to financing depends heavily on the liquidity available from these traders — and hence, in turn, on the ability of traders to access funds.

## Government Credit Programmes

The government has launched a number of special credit schemes since 1989, usually at subsidized rates, reaching very few people and with extremely poor recovery rates. A partial exception has been Enhancing Opportunities for Women in Development (ENOWID), which in the early 1990s made over 3,500 relatively small loans (over 6 years) with a cumulative recovery rate of 96% using funds from the Programme of Action to Mitigate the Social Costs of Adjustment (PAMSCAD) (Quainoo, 1997). PAMSCAD, launched in 1989, directly reached only some 1,200 clients and struggled to achieve an average 83% cumulative recovery by 1996. None of the other four programmes being administered by the National Board for Small-Scale Industries (NBSSI) (which charges 20% interest) has achieved a 70% recovery rate or as many as 200 clients. As a result, these 'revolving funds' are steadily depleting, involve substantial costs to operate, and have negligible outreach.

The government has also entered into microcredit through poverty alleviation programmes and the District Assembly Common Fund. While in some instances this made wholesale funds available to local RMFIs for on-lending to clients whom they chose, more commonly it has been perceived and used as politically motivated, with negative consequences for repayment. The main threat to sustainable rural microfinance from these government programmes comes from the negative effects on the efforts of RMFIs to mobilize savings and collect from borrowers, whose willingness to repay is typically low when loans are known to come from government or donor funds at subsidized rates.

## 2.   Licensing and Regulatory Framework for Rural and Microfinance

Different tiers of Ghana's legally recognized, specialized RMFIs come under different legislation, adopted at different points in time in response to different circumstances and objectives:

- Money-lenders Ordinance (1940 and 1957 ) legally recognized an existing practice;

- Credit Unions developed under non-financial legislation (Co-operative Decree 1968), were nominally brought under the Bank of Ghana via the NBFI Law, and will eventually come under special legislation adapted to their dual situation as both co-operatives and financial institutions;

- Rural Banks emerged from special rules applied under an existing Banking Law (1970) and its subsequent amendments;

- The NBFI Law (1993) stimulated new types of financial institutions, in particular S&L companies, as well as bringing some existing ones under the regulatory framework.

These laws are summarized in Annex 10.1, Schedule 1. This section discusses the application of key regulations within this framework, focusing on prudential regulations — i.e., the standards and guidelines the financial institutions must meet to obtain or retain a licence from the central bank, which assumes responsibility for assuring the soundness of licensed institutions.

### *Evolution of Regulatory Norms*

The regulations governing NBFIs did not differentiate between different institutions according to the nature of their activities until 2001, when the Bank of Ghana issued new Business Rules for application of the NBFI law.[13] These Rules distinguish between deposit-taking and non-deposit-taking institutions; clarify the procedures for compliance with capital adequacy and solvency requirements (10% capital adequacy ratio for deposit-taking NBFIs and 10:1 gearing ratio for non-deposit-taking NBFIs); define individual and group-based loans for microfinance and small business, with single-borrower limits for individual microfinance loans; and establish criteria for classifying microfinance loans into current and delinquent, provisioning standards for delinquent loans, and liquidity reserve requirements.

Adoption of these Business Rules reflects growing understanding by the BoG of ways in which MFIs and other NBFIs differ from commercial banks and of the value of

---

[13] These new Business Rules group NBFIs into four categories of licensed institutions for differential treatment (excluding credit unions, for which a separate legal, regulatory and supervisory framework is being prepared): (i) deposit-taking institutions (other than discount houses); (ii) non-deposit-taking institutions in credit business; (iii) discount houses; and (iv) venture capital fund companies.

focusing regulation on the nature of the activities being undertaken. The Rules have clarified the prudential expectations of the BoG. Better understanding of the requirements by the NBFIs has led to more accurate reporting, and some have brought in well-qualified people for their management and boards. The BoG has since enforced penalties for breaches of regulatory requirements. NBFIs are required to provide action plans and a definite timeframe for the implementation of recommendations.

Deposit-taking institutions are more tightly regulated, through higher levels of minimum initial capital, capital adequacy standard and mandatory holding of liquid reserve assets. Since the Rules apply only to 'licensed institutions', they appear to leave the door open for non-financial NGOs to engage in credit activities using their own funds. However, they do block the mobilization of savings by other registered companies (such as the ill-fated *susu* companies of the 1980s, and, more recently, businesses operating pyramid schemes, which the BoG has actively shut down).[14]

## Minimum Capital Requirement

The old Banking Act (1970) specified a minimum paid-up capital of ¢0.75 million (US$0.65 million) for Ghanaian banks and ¢2 million (US$1.76 million) for foreign banks. After a period of rapid inflation and currency depreciation, changes in 1989, 2000 and 2001 brought the minimum capital requirements to ¢25 billion (US$2.8 million as of 2004) for Ghanaian banks, ¢50 billion (US$5.6 million) for foreign banks, and ¢70 billion (US$7.8 million) for development banks (Table 10.5).

**Table 10.5  Evolution of Minimum Capital Requirements, in Cedis and US$**

| Type | 1993 | 1998 | 2000 | 2001 | 2004 | 1993 | 1998 | 2000 | 2001 | 2004 |
|---|---|---|---|---|---|---|---|---|---|---|
| | Cedis (billion) | | | | | US dollars (million) | | | | |
| Comm'l banks: | | | | | | | | | | |
| Ghanaian[a] | 0.2 | 0.2 | 5.0 | 25 | 25 | 0.31 | 0.09 | 0.94 | 3.52 | 2.78 |
| Foreign | 0.5 | 0.5 | 8.0 | 50 | 50 | 0.77 | 0.22 | 1.5 | 7.04 | 5.56 |
| Dev't banks | 1.0 | 1.0 | 10.0 | 70 | 70 | 1.54 | 0.43 | 1.9 | 9.85 | 7.78 |
| Rural banks | 0.01 | 0.03 | 0.1 | 0.5 | 0.5 | 0.015 | 0.013 | 0.018 | 0.07 | 0.056 |
| NBFIs: | | | | | | | | | | |
| Deposit-taking | 0.1 | 0.5 | 1.0 | 15 | 15 | 0.15 | 0.22 | 0.19 | 2.1 | 1.7 |
| Non-deposit | 0.1 | 0.5 | 0.5 | 10 | 10 | 0.15 | 0.22 | 0.09 | 1.4 | 1.1 |

*Note:* a) 60% of shares owned by Ghanaians.
*Source:* 2000 from Gallardo (2002); 2001 from Addeah (2001) (updated). Average annual exchange rates (¢/$): 1989 – 270; 1993 – 649; 1998 – 2314; 2000 – 5322; 2001 – 7104; 2004 – 9000 (mid-year).

---

[14] As informal individual agents without corporate identity and business licence, *susu* collectors and operators of *susu* clubs, as well as *susu* groups (ROSCAs) appear to remain outside the law, and BoG officials have repeatedly indicated no interest in attempting to supervise them, but rather the need to observe their activities for possible infringement of the laws.

The already low minimum paid-up capital for RCBs was eroded steadily by inflation until 1998, when the Bank of Ghana responded to concerns about poor portfolios and non-compliance with capital adequacy ratios by raising the minimum capital requirement. It has since been adjusted twice, though not as drastically for RCBs as for other categories, standing at ¢500 million (US$56,000) as of 2004 (Table 10.5). Many RCBs have had difficulty raising additional capital to comply because of non-payment of dividends since their inception, shareholders' perception that they are entitled to loans, and local politics.

The Financial Institutions (Non-Banking) Law of 1993 prescribed a uniform minimum paid-up capital of ¢100 million for all categories of NBFIs, but the BoG has since differentiated the capital requirement of deposit-taking institutions from that of non-deposit-taking institutions. Increases in required minimum capital in 1998 and 2000 served mainly to restore the value to the 1993 level in dollar terms (Table 10.5). Nevertheless, this represented a tenfold increase in cedi terms, which only 3 of 8 S&Ls were able to achieve. Reasons for difficulties in compliance include: low initial paid-up capital; lack of additional funds among present shareholders; unwillingness of shareholders to cede some of their shares and dilute ownership; and poor operational performance and profitability.

In 2001, concerns about the health and under-capitalization of the majority of the S&Ls, as well as the rising number of applications relative to the limited supervision capacity, led the BoG to raise the minimum capital requirements for NBFIs substantially to ¢15 billion (over US$2 million) for deposit-taking institutions and ¢10 billion (US$1.4 million) for non-deposit-taking institutions. This increase was far more than necessary to adjust for the substantial depreciation of the cedi in 2000–01, and proportionately greater for NBFIs than for commercial banks, thus limiting the rate of entry and perhaps encouraging some consolidation. So far, the regulatory authorities have refrained from closing down existing S&Ls that cannot meet the new requirements.

## Liquidity Reserve Requirements

All banks and other deposit-taking commercial institutions are required to maintain a proportion of deposits in the form of liquidity reserves, consisting of primary reserves in cash and balances with other banks and secondary reserves in government and BoG bills, bonds and stocks.[15] In fact, the high returns on relatively risk-free secondary reserve assets (T-bill rates averaged 35% from 1993 to 2001, ranging from 24% to 43%) made the requirements virtually redundant, as they accounted for as much as 75% of the combined total deposits of commercial banks (Camara, 1996).

To help soak up liquidity and improve the solvency of RCBs, the BoG raised their secondary liquidity reserve requirement from 20% to 52% in 1996. While intended to strengthen poorly performing institutions, the regulations did not distinguish between

---

[15] The reserve requirements of 10% for primary and 15% for secondary have remained unchanged for S&Ls since 1993. The primary reserve requirement for commercial banks was reduced from 18% in 1996 to 9% in 2000, while the secondary reserve requirement was raised from 24% in 1996 to 35% in 1999.

stronger and weaker ones, thereby penalizing the more efficient RCBs by limiting their ability to pursue profitable lending opportunities. In 2002 the BoG lowered the reserve requirements to a total of 43%, including 8% primary and 30% secondary, as well as 5% placement with ARB Apex Bank (to facilitate cheque clearing).

## Interest Rates

Restrictive policies during the 1970s and early 1980s, such as government-controlled interest rates and sectoral allocation of credit, no doubt retarded the development of Ghana's formal financial system. Nevertheless, various forms of informal finance predated financially repressive policies in Ghana, and actually expanded after the financial markets were liberalized in 1987 (Aryeetey, 1994). Although interest rates have not been officially controlled since 1987, the government has nevertheless introduced a number of credit programmes targeted on small business development or poverty alleviation whose interest rates were pegged in 2001 at 20% (well below market-determined rates), and District Assemblies have been mandated since 1979 to provide 20% of their 'Common Fund' for micro and small enterprises at an interest rate of 75% of the commercial bank rate.

## Security

Licensed banks normally require that loans be secured by title to land or physical assets, deposit balances, or T-bills, following BoG guidelines. These options are clearly beyond the reach of poor households. Close co-ordination between the Ministry of Finance, the BoG and the Ghana Microfinance Institutions Network (GHAMFIN) has led to a better understanding of the characteristics of microfinance loans and the methodologies underlying high repayment rates (Gallardo, 2002: 14), and personal and group guaranteed loans are now recognized as secured microfinance loans.

## Delinquency and Provisioning

All licensed financial institutions are required to monitor and review their portfolio of credit and other risk assets at least quarterly. Assets of all banks, both major and rural, are classified into five grades of risk, for which the rate of provisioning increases from 10% for loans overdue by less than 30 days to 50% for 'doubtful' loans over 180 days and 100% beyond 540 days. For NBFIs, assets are classified into four grades of risk: (i) current; (ii) sub-standard; (iii) doubtful; and (iv) loss. Assets in risk grades (ii) to (iv) are considered non-performing and, therefore, no income may be accrued on them.

The BoG has specified prudential norms for microfinance and small business loans that take into account the characteristics of these activities and classify them as either (i) current or (ii) delinquent (i.e., scheduled payment not received as of the due date), on which no interest income may be accrued (Gallardo, 2002). Provisioning for delinquent microfinance and small business loans is made on a 'basket' basis, rather than an individual loan basis (i.e., the aggregate outstanding balances in each arrearage basket are grouped without regard to any security available for individual loans). The prescribed rate of provisioning increases steadily every 30 days of delinquency from 5% for under 30 up to 100% for over 150 days.[16]

## *Other Prudential Regulations*[17]
In supervising credit unions, the CUA applies the PEARLS system of the World Council of Credit Unions in order to evaluate **P**rotection, **E**ffective financial structure, **A**ssets quality, **R**ates of return and costs, **L**iquidity and **S**igns of growth, and to assess when a CU should be stopped from making further loans and given technical assistance to restore its financial health. Credit Unions seriously in breach of compliance and performing poorly are downgraded to Study Group status.

**Capital Adequacy:** Prior to the Banking Law (1989), banks were to maintain a minimum capital of 5% of total mobilized resources. Following international best practice, the Banking Law (1989) shifted the adequacy of capital from deposit-based to its relationship to risk-weighted assets (Asiedu-Mante, 1998). The Banking law prescribes the capital base at 6% of the adjusted asset base as the minimum capital adequacy ratio for the banks, which is being raised to 10% under the new Banking Law. The NBFI Law already prescribes the rate of 10% for S&Ls and other deposit-taking institutions. Likewise, Credit Unions are to maintain 10% of their total assets as capital (including shares).

**Credit Exposure:** Both the Banking Law and the NBFI Law limit unsecured loans to individual customers to 10% of net worth, with somewhat different limits for secured loans of 25% for banks and 15% for non- banks. Credit exposure is also severely limited with respect to loans to any firm in which any of the bank's directors or officials are connected as a partner or principal shareholder.

## *Supervision and Monitoring Mechanisms*
The Bank of Ghana has legal authority over all banking and credit institutions, whether

---

[16] In addition to the specific loss provisions for delinquent or non-performing microfinance and small business loans, the BoG requires licensed MFIs to maintain a general loss provision of 1% of the aggregate outstanding of all the standard class of loan assets. Financial institutions are also required to disclose separately, in their financial accounts and reports, the specific and general loss provisions made for non-performing delinquent loans and standard/current loan assets (Gallardo, 2002).

[17] Additional special regulations for RCBs include prohibition on paying dividends for 10 years after commencing business; the co-operative principle of one shareholder, one vote (irrespective of number of shares); and prior clearance by the BoG for loans of ¢2 million or above to a single party, as well as all loans to RCB directors or companies in which they have a financial interest. The BoG has restricted RCBs from operating agencies in urban areas, which some RCBs have undertaken to facilitate their rural customers making transactions in urban markets, where they sell their produce, as well as to mobilize savings through more convenient facilities than commercial banks offer. The BoG considers that operating such agencies without good MIS co-ordination between head office and agency opens up the potential for abuse or mismanagement, was getting some RCBs into large loans beyond prudential norms, and diverts the RCBs from their intended rural focus as the Chief Executives relocate in the urban areas. However, the BoG does not appear to object to such RCB agencies in rural or even peri-urban areas, if properly applied for and managed.

formal or informal (Addeah 2000). Functions stipulated by the Bank of Ghana Act 2002 include to 'regulate, supervise and direct the banking and credit system' and to 'license, regulate, promote and supervise non-banking financial institutions'. The NBFI Law gives the BoG the 'supervisory authority in all matters relating to the businesses of any non-bank financial institution licensed under the law'. The 1992 (current) Constitution empowers it 'to operate a banking and credit system to promote economic development in Ghana'. The BoG has used its authority to intervene and close down dubious and fraudulent financial practices such as pyramid schemes, as well as insolvent banks.

The BoG's supervisory functions have been carried out by the Banking Supervision Department (BSD) and the Non-Bank Financial Institutions Department (established in 1994 to oversee licensing of NBFIs under the new Law, supervise and regulate them, and provide advisory and promotional services), which were merged in 2002. Until 2002, a separate department was involved in promoting RCBs and, to some extent, following up on supervision issues.[18]

## Methods

Methods employed by the Bank of Ghana for its regulatory functions include:

- *Off-site examination* of prescribed reports to verify compliance and performance; on-going basis;

- *On-site examination* to assess the accuracy of the reports submitted and to review in detail compliance and performance (the Banking Law enjoins this assignment to be undertaken at least once a year for each bank, while the NBFI Law is silent on frequency); follow-up on-site visits may be undertaken to discuss supervisory concerns raised during examinations and to ensure compliance with recommendations;

- *Special assignments* have been established by the BoG to manage the risks from RCB managers staying on for years, using a special pool of 9 experienced commercial bankers to relieve RCB managers while they take their annual leave. Besides minimizing fraud and enhancing internal controls, these special assignments have helped raise the skills of RCB staff, improved credit administration and the submission of prescribed norms, restrained undue interference by Board members and local authorities, and raised customer confidence in RCBs.

---

[18] Prior to 1989 rural banks were supervised by the Rural Banking Department (later renamed Rural Finance Department). In 1989 the BoG transferred the research and supervisory functions of the Rural Finance Department to the Banking Supervision and Research Departments, respectively. The department's name was again changed to Rural Finance Inspection Department, and its responsibilities included follow-up on issues arising out of banking supervision reports and management audits as its primary function. The department also assisted rural banks through advice and resolution of problems. The department was later merged with the Development Finance Department to form the Rural and Development Finance Department, which in turn was itself abolished in 2002 and its functions assigned to Banking Supervision and other departments (and perhaps implicitly to the newly constituted ARB Apex Bank).

## Compliance

Enforcement mechanisms available to the BoG include fines, suspension, revocation of licence, criminal penalties and appointment of auditors and managers (Addeah, 2000). Twenty-three distressed RBs have had their licences revoked. The BoG has been concerned about irregular submission of prudential reports, and has begun applying fines for late returns and reporting non-compliance due to negligence of the executive to the RCB Board.[19]

The Credit Union Association serves as a self-regulatory apex body for the 250 CUs, and its norms must be met as a condition for full registration of a new credit union by the Department of Co-operatives.[20] The CUA applies prudential norms that are similar to the operating and financial standards of the World Council of Credit Unions (WOCCU). The BoG has refrained from applying the regulatory functions authorized by the 1993 NBFI Law. The proposed new Credit Union Law would help clarify the delegation of specific supervisory functions to the CUA, which will report to a Supervisory Board with BoG membership rather than to the Department of Co-operatives as at present. The CUA enforces its regulations by downgrading CUs that are seriously in breach of compliance to Study Group status.

The Ghana Co-operative Susu Collectors Association (GCSCA) imposes a number of regulatory barriers to entry as well as providing services to its members. A prospective member must be recommended by a zonal executive, provide two sworn guarantors, deposit ¢1 million (about US$110) into a security fund, save ¢5,000 a month, take a medical examination, and undergo a three-month training with an existing member. Other measures intended to improve public confidence in doing business with GCSCA members include wearing uniform colours, paying off clients' deposits from the security fund in case of the death or disappearance of a collector, and assisting in dispute arbitration. The entry requirements are sufficiently onerous that about half the *susu* collectors in the Greater Accra area are reported to be completely informal, i.e., not registered with the GCSCA. The GCSCA attempts to monitor the performance of the industry by collecting quarterly data from its zonal societies on the number of clients, amounts mobilized, problems encountered, and assistance given.

## Performance of the Supervision System

The costs of supervising a large number of small NBFIs and rural banks are high in both staff resources and transportation, and the BoG has struggled to perform regular on-site examination. Prior to 2000, only about two-thirds of NBFIs were examined, with a focus on those taking deposits. The 23 supervisory staff handling the 115 rural banks with total assets in 2001 of ¢1,275 billion compare with 30 supervisors assigned

---

[19] Well-performing banks tend to submit timely, accurate reports. S&Ls and RCBs with weak compliance invariably do not use the reports as tools for management information, regarding them simply as information the BoG seeks for its own use.

[20] In 2000 only 159 of the 219 credit unions registered by the Department of Co-operatives were considered by the CUA as full-fledged financial co-operatives; the remainder were undergoing a process of institutional and membership development in order to be certified by the CUA as full-service credit unions ready for registration.

to the 17 major banks with total assets of ¢25,395 billion (Table 10.6). The World Bank-supported NBFI Project in the late 1990s helped to strengthen the NBFI and BSD's supervision capabilities.[21] The BSD covered 97% of the rural banks in 2000 and 100% in 2001. The NBFI Department covered 100% of the S&Ls (with total assets of ¢199 billion) in 2000 and 2001.

The CUA's annual audit covered 92% of the CUs in 2001, and had reached 90% by the end of March 2002. Teams of two persons, consisting of a CUA staff member and another from the Department of Co-operatives, undertake the audits. Credit Unions pay the CUA ¢150,000 (US$20) per day for the annual audit, which takes a minimum of 4 days.[22] The amount is shared between the CUA and the Department of Cooperatives in the ratio of 3:1 (the CUA is responsible for all staff travel and transport costs). In 2002 CUA members ratified a resolution empowering the CUA to sanction CUs and their staff.

**Table 10.6  Selected Balance Sheet Items (end 2003) (¢ billion)**

|  | Rural Banks | S & Ls | Major Banks |
|---|---|---|---|
| Paid-up capital | 22.3 | 24.6 | 286.7 |
| Deposits | 949.2 | 160.9 | 16,251.6 |
| Borrowing, other liabilities | 147.5 | 10.9 | 6,315.1 |
| Investments | 524.7 | 65.8 | 7,823.2 |
| Loans & Advances | 348.4 | 72.8 | 8,892.1 |
| **Total Assets** | **1,275.4** | **199.1** | **25,395.3** |
| Average assets ($ million) | 1.3 | 2.6 | 175.7 |

*Note*:    Total assets of discount houses were ¢586.2 billion, or an average of US$21.7 million.
*Source*:  Bank of Ghana. Exchange Rate: US$1 = ¢8500.

## Strengths in Supervision

The Bank of Ghana's ability to supervise is well grounded in effective empowering laws and supported by a proactive judiciary. Supervision of RMFIs is simplified somewhat by the less cumbersome prudential reporting required of these categories, compared with countries whose laws and regulatory requirements do not distinguish between different types of financial institutions. Enforcement procedures are transparent. Holding briefing sessions before on-site examinations has helped to smooth the process, at least with those RMFIs capable of meeting the requirements.

The growing professionalization of RMFIs, supported by training programmes

---

[21] The Banking Supervision Department had previously benefited from capacity-building and technical assistance under the Financial Sector Adjustment Project, financed by the World Bank/IDA. Supervision of RCBs takes about 6 staff-weeks, S&Ls about 3–4 staff-weeks (no data are available on the monetary costs). Commercial banks, RCBs and NBFIs do not pay for supervision by the BoG, auditing fees for RCBs average around ¢10 million.

[22] 17% of the less well endowed CUs were allowed to pay less than the ¢600,000 minimum.

organized by the ARB, GHAMFIN and donor agencies, has raised the number of RMFIs with a qualified board, committed executive, and dedicated, trained staff. Where this does not apply, the BoG has demonstrated willingness to dissolve Boards and replace them with Interim Management Committees, and to replace managers against whom serious allegations have been made with BoG staff as supervising managers.

The BoG has also taken direct action to deal with long-standing problems, especially in 1999 when it closed 23 RBs, after giving them some time to improve operations, raise additional capital, and recover outstanding loans. The BoG provided resources to ensure that all depositors were paid, but the impact was minimal, given that these banks had been moribund for some time.[23] Given that the NBFI system is relatively young, the BoG has not yet intervened to close or take over management of NBFIs. Recently, however, it has begun fining S&Ls for delay in submission of prudential returns.

### Difficulties in Supervision

Nevertheless, many RMFIs remain difficult and costly to supervise because of: (i) lack of financial professionals such as accountants, bankers or economists on the Boards which results in weak understanding of the purpose and importance of management information and poor decisions; (ii) tendencies of RBs to take action without prior required BoG consultation (e.g., opening agencies); (iii) inadequate qualification or training of some staff; (iv) high turnover of qualified staff; (v) poor staff understanding of required information, resulting in inadequate reports and preparation for supervision; and (vi) entrenched leadership. Other difficulties encountered by BoG supervisors of RCBs and S&Ls (as well as CUA supervision teams) include wide dispersion, inadequate communication facilities and technological support, and lack of experience of some supervision teams with RMFIs.

## 3.    Assessment of the Impact of Regulation on the Evolution of Microfinance

Licensing and regulation of RMFIs can have effects ranging from stifling to promotional, depending on coverage, timing and restrictiveness. In Ethiopia, for example, introduction of a single legal format for MFIs (apart from savings and credit co-operatives under non-financial jurisdiction) forced NGOs out of direct microfinance activities and limited the flexibility in approaches to microfinance (Shiferaw and Amha, 2002). At the same time, it implied that microfinance should become more professional and commercial, establishing greater potential for long-run sustainability. In contrast, Uganda's Micro Deposit-taking Institutions Bill has stimulated leading MFIs (several with microfinance as their sole core business) to accelerate upgrading and capacity-building measures and donor agencies to mobilize support for this process, raising standards for the industry as a whole without imposing regulatory constraints on those RMFIs that do not wish to take and intermediate savings from the public.

---

[23] The refund of deposits was a one-time arrangement; there is no deposit insurance scheme.

Ghana has evolved different licensing and regulatory structures for different segments of the financial system, including RMFIs, and has administered them flexibly with periodic revisions of regulatory standards and relatively high tolerance for traditional financial mechanisms and NGOs that are not covered. Nevertheless, the Bank of Ghana has adopted these measures more in response to emerging situations than through several years of systematic study of, and consultation with, the RMF industry, as in Uganda. In part for this reason, regulation and supervision have not been as systematic in Ghana as appears likely to be the case in Uganda, and regulations have occasionally been tightened to deal with the imbalance between numerous weak institutions and inadequate supervision capacity.

## Advantages and Drawbacks of Ghana's Approach

### Adaptive Regime Fosters a Range of Institutions

The adaptive nature of Ghana's regulatory regime is indicated by the fact that each segment has evolved in a rather different way. The introduction of special rules permitting local unit RBs and the initial role of the Bank of Ghana in capitalizing them represented an active government response to a perceived developmental need that was not being served adequately by the existing financial institutions. Their poor performance, in turn, triggered a restrictive response in the form of higher reserve requirements, which gradually helped improve their financial position, but restricted their ability to achieve their mandate of increasing the availability of rural credit. The government has responded to this situation by means of a project to strengthen their capacities and create a new Apex Bank to better serve, develop, and eventually supervise them. Despite weaknesses in financial performance and direct financing of agriculture, RBs today constitute the backbone for the extension of financial services to rural areas.

Introduction of the NBFI Law led to the development of this emerging market by facilitating entry or the formalization of a wider range of financial intermediaries, many serving the micro and small enterprise sector and low-income households. Nevertheless, frequent increases in the minimum capital requirement have caused some delays and disruption to the institutions involved. Initially, the law was designed with large formal institutions in mind. But the minimum capital requirements were modest enough (at least after some erosion by inflation) and application of the regulations sufficiently flexible to permit licensing of a variety of S&L models (NGO, small bank, money-lending operations).

Ghana's process of encouraging entry and then adjusting regulation has fostered a wide range of RMFIs and products in formal, semi-formal and informal segments, including some suitable for microenterprises and lower-income households, with some linkages between segments. The strength of Ghana's system lies in a diversified structure of both institutions and regulatory regimes, well adapted to local economic circumstances. Nevertheless, outreach of the system has been fairly limited, particularly with respect to the rural poor. Most RMFIs serve only a local market, and only one high-performing MFI with a national client base has emerged.

*Balancing Prudential Supervision Capacity and Barriers to Entry*
A recurring problem of Ghana's strategy of allowing easy entry into promising new types of financial intermediaries — credit unions in the 1960s and 1970s; Rural Banks in the 1980s; and S&Ls in the 1990s — has been a substantial number of weak institutions that pose two dilemmas to regulators: (i) the disproportionate share of staff resources absorbed in the supervision of small institutions; and (ii) when authorities also have a promotional role, action to weed out weak institutions may be delayed.

The Bank of Ghana's response has been to use regulatory requirements to offset the limits of prudential supervision. High reserve requirements served as a rather blunt instrument to help restore many RBs to financial health. The 2001 increase in minimum capital requirements went well beyond adjusting for currency depreciation and assuring adequate capital to a restrictive level that few existing RCBs and S&Ls can hope to attain. Only 74% of RCBs and 63% of S&Ls had met the requirement even in 2000, and it was then raised five-fold and fifteen-fold, respectively, in 2001. While one S&L is reportedly preparing to float shares on the Ghana Stock Exchange, in general the high entry barrier appears likely to exclude those without foreign partners. On the positive side, two S&Ls have brought in foreign investment and one NGO is poised to do so.[24]

Regarding transformation of NGOs into licensed MFIs, Ghana's system now resembles Uganda's Micro Deposit-taking Institutions Bill (2002), which has a special category for large RMFIs that wish to mobilize and intermediate deposits. The minimum capital and prudential regulation requirements for Uganda's 'Tier 3' category are expected to limit entry to only two to four institutions in the first two years; but NGOs and other RMFIs that do not qualify can operate as unsupervised 'Tier 4' institutions, as long as they do not mobilize and intermediate savings from the public.

*High Interest Rates and Reserve Requirements Improve Soundness, Inhibit Outreach*
Throughout the 1990s, weak fiscal discipline, persistent double-digit inflation, and the use of monetary policies to restrain liquidity resulted in relatively high interest rates for Treasury bills (above 30% for seven years). Banks have had little incentive to lend, because they could make a good return (over much lower deposit rates)

---

[24] High minimum capital is a particular restraint on Ghanaian-owned S&Ls, whose microfinance methodologies and relatively poor clientele tend to make them relatively small and local. As deposit-taking NBFIs, S&Ls have to post the same minimum capital as discount houses, implying that they would be expected to book comparable risk assets. In reality, S&Ls' assets average only an eighth of those of discount houses, and only double those of RBs, despite having 30 times as much required minimum capital. Whereas efficient use of minimum capital of US$2 million would imply risk assets of the order of $18–20 million, S&Ls' actual average risk assets are only US$1.2 million, implying that the present capital requirement is misaligned with the type of business that S&Ls actually do. Consideration should be given to a lower requirement for small, local private MFIs that can efficiently serve a limited market niche, to avoid driving them underground and reversing the positive trends of both formalizing what were essentially money-lending operations and enabling successful NGOs to move into mobilizing and intermediating savings as a basis for greater outreach.

simply by investing excess liquidity in T-bills. Although the high reserve requirements (62% primary and secondary) imposed on Rural Banks have sometimes been blamed for the small amount of credit they provide, in fact they have generally maintained more than the required amount of reserves (for example, 28% in primary reserves in 1998 as against the 10% required; and 64–65% in 2000–01 in secondary reserves as against the 52% required). While these conditions have been largely responsible for improving the rating of a substantial number of RCBs, reduced interest-rate and reserve requirements are re-establishing conditions for them to fulfil their mandate to make credit available in rural areas. Successful lending will depend not only on improving management capacity and information systems in the RCBs, but also on improving the capacity of the Bank of Ghana and the ARB Apex Bank to implement an effective supervision system that distinguishes between well-performing RCBs and less capable ones, and on strengthening linkages between RCBs and MFIs or CBOs that can provide sound microfinance methodologies and deeper outreach to the rural poor.

## *Linkages between Tiers*

Ghana's flexible, multi-tiered system appears to have fostered some linkages between different segments, including: (i) licensed RCBs and S&Ls using informal agents or CBOs to mobilize or on-lend funds; (ii) NGOs using RCBs and S&Ls to handle the funds for their microfinance programmes; and (iii) *susu* collectors and clubs using commercial banks, RCBs and S&Ls to deposit funds.

## 4. Conclusion

Ghana's evolutionary approach to regulation appears to be moving toward a network of financially sound, licensed and supervised RMFIs that can reach a sufficient scale for self-sustainability (even if only in a local market) and also serve as the backbone for greater penetration in rural areas and to the very poor through linkages to (unregulated) NGOs, CBOs and informal agents that target these clients. Ghana's Rural and Community Banks have an important role to play in this approach, and distinguish it from most other African countries by providing a licensed banking institution located in rural areas as a basis for both outreach through linkages with MFIs and CBOs and integration with the formal financial system through the Apex Bank. Nevertheless, building up this system entails substantial investment in the Apex Bank, in supervision and training, and in strengthening their capacity to make good use of the liquidity being released through lower reserve requirements and interest rates on T-bills.

Transformation of NGOs into licensed RMFIs has been less of an issue in Ghana than in other countries in part because they have been able to work synergistically with RCBs. The S&Ls have provided a useful urban counterpart to RBs, offering convenient transactions for urban commerce and households through adaptations of traditional *susu* and money-lending methodologies.

Ghana's experience shows the value of opening up different tiers of formal, semi-formal and informal RMFIs that provide different products and services to different market niches. However, it is also clear that taking too promotional an approach and allowing too easy entry in the early stages tend to foster a number of weak institutions, especially when relatively new methodologies that are relatively untested in the local market are being used. This can both undermine the credibility of that category of institutions and drain scarce supervision resources — or foster benign neglect until the problems become severe. Nor has Ghana's approach succeeded as yet in reaching poor rural clients on a significant scale. Clearly, the biggest challenge in regulating RMFIs is finding the right balance between ease of entry for greater outreach, prudential regulations to promote sustainability, and supervision capacity.

## References

Addeah, Kwaku (2001) 'The Legal and Regulatory Framework of Micro and Rural Finance Institutions in Ghana', paper presented at the Rural Financial Services Project Launch Workshop, Agona-Swedru, Ghana, 8 November.

Addo, J. S., Consultants (1998) 'A Feasibility Study and Business Plan for the Establishment of an ARB Apex Bank', Accra: revised report for the Association of Rural Banks.

Anin, T. E. (2000) *Banking in Ghana*, Accra: Woeli Publishing Services.

Aryeetey, Ernest (1994) *A Study of Informal Finance in Ghana,* Working Paper 78. London: Overseas Development Institute.

Asiedu-Mante, E. (1998) 'Financial Markets in Ghana', in *Issues in Central Banking and Bank Distress*, Lagos: WAIFEM.

Bank of Ghana (2000) *Non-Bank Financial Institutions Business (BoG) Rules*. Accra: BoG.

Camara, Modibo Khane (1996) 'Microfinance Institutions in Ghana', Frankfurt: draft report for Internationale Projekt Consult and the World Bank.

CHORD (2000) 'Inventory of Ghanaian Micro-Finance Best Practices'. Accra: Report for Ministry of Finance, Non-Banking Financial Institutions Project.

Department of Co-operatives. *Annual Reports* 1999–2003, Accra.

Gallardo, Joselito (2002) *A Framework for Regulating Microfinance Institutions: Experience in Ghana and the Philippines.* Policy Research Working Paper No. 2755. Washington, DC: World Bank.

Gallardo, Joselito, Kalavakonda, Vijaysekar and Randhawa, Bikki (2002) *Developing Micro-Insurance Products: The Experience of Ghana and Bangladesh.* Washington, DC: World Bank.

Ghana Co-operative Credit Union Association (CUA) Ltd. (2002) 12th CUA Biennial Report (January 2000–December 2001. Accra: CUA.

Ghana Co-operative Susu Collectors Association (GCSCA) (2003) 'Delegation of Data Collection Activities by Ministry of Finance to Ghana Co-operative Susu Collectors Association'. Accra: GCSCA, draft.

Ghana Microfinance Institutions Network (GHAMFIN) (2003) 'Census of Micro Credit NGOs, Community-Based Organizations and Self Help Groups in Ghana'. Accra: GHAMFIN, draft report prepared by Asamoah & Williams Consulting.

GHAMFIN (2001) 'On-Lending to Savings Collectors in Ghana'. Africa Region Studies in Rural and Micro Finance No. 12. Washington, DC: World Bank.

Kowubaa Ltd. (2000) *Rural Finance Review Study,* Report prepared for Ministry of Finance/ World Bank NBFI Project.

Nissanke, Machiko and Aryeetey, Ernest (1998) *Financial Integration and Development.* London: Routledge Studies in Development Economics.

Offei, C. (1965) 'Rural Credit in Ghana', Master's thesis, University of Ghana, Legon.

Owusu Ansah, Mark (1999) *Nsoatreman Rural Bank — Ghana: Case Study of a Microfinance Scheme.* Africa Region Studies in Rural and Micro Finance No. 6. Washington, DC: World Bank.

Quainoo, Aba Amissah (1997) 'A Strategy for Poverty Reduction through Micro-Finance: Experience, Capacities and Prospects', Accra: draft report of a study commissioned by Government of Ghana, UNDP, African Development Bank, World Bank, August.

Quainoo, Aba Amissah (1999) 'Financial Services for Women Entrepreneurs in the Informal Sector of Ghana', World Bank, Africa Region Studies in Rural and Micro Finance No. 8.

Robinson, Marguerite (2001) *The Microfinance Revolution: Sustainable Finance for the Poor.* Washington, DC: World Bank.

Shiferaw, Bekele and Amha, Wolday (2002) *Revisiting the Regulatory and Supervision Framework of the Micro-Finance Industry in Ethiopia.* Report No. 13. Oslo: Drylands Co-ordination Group.

Steel, William F., and Aryeetey, Ernest (1995) 'Savings Collectors and Financial Intermediation in Ghana', *Savings and Development*, Vol. 19.

Van Greuning, Hennie, Gallardo, Joselito and Randhawa, Bikki (1999) *A Framework for Regulating Microfinance Institutions.* Policy Research Working Paper No. 2061. Washington, DC: World Bank.

**Annex 10.1 Summary of Laws and Regulations for RMFIs and Businesses**

**Schedule 1 Legal and Regulatory Requirements for Different Types of MFIs — Ghana**

| Country Institution | Type of Institution | Permitted Activities | Organizational Format | Requirements for Entry Required Minim. Capital | Capital Adequacy | Portfolio Quality | Liquidity Reserves | Area Restriction | External Regulation | Prudential Supervision |
|---|---|---|---|---|---|---|---|---|---|---|
| **Ghana** | | | | | | | | | | |
| Rural Banks | Specialized Bank | Limited banking services, savings, deposits, loans | Limited liability Co. Unit Bank | US$67,000 equivalent | 6% of risk asset | Provisioning 1% Current 5-100% Delinquent | 8% Primary 20-30% Secondary | Rural District | Co. Registrar; Bank of Ghana | BSD— Bank of Ghana |
| Savings & Loans Company | NBFIs | Limited banking services, savings, deposits, loans | Limited liability Company | US$ 2 million equivalent | 10%of risk asset | ditto | 10% Primary 15% Secondary | None | Co. Registrar; Bank of Ghana | NBFID— Bank of Ghana |
| ARB Apex Bank | Apex Fin. Inst. | Apex bank functions | Limited liability Company | US$133,000 equivalent | 6% of risk asset | ditto | " " | None | Co. Registrar; Bank of Ghana | BSD— Bank of Ghana |
| CUA | Apex Fin. Inst. | Wholesale loans/ deposits, central capital fund, training assessment | 2nd-tier members' co-operative association | Not applicable | Int'l(CCA-WOCCU) standards | Int'l(CCA-WOCCU) standards | Int'l(CCA-WOCCU) standards | None | Department of Co-operatives Bank of Ghana | Department of Co-operatives Bank of Ghana |
| Credit Unions | Credit Union | Deposits and loans to members only | Co-operative association | Not applicable | Int'l(CCA-WOCCU) standards | Int'l(CCA-WOCCU) standards | Int'l(CCA-WOCCU) standards | None (Common bond) | Department of Co-operatives Bank of Ghana | Credit Union Association Bank of Ghana |
| NGO-MFIs | NGO | Micro-credit | Company limited by guarantee (not-for profit Trust) | Not applicable | Not applicable | N/A | N/A | None | Registrar of Companies | None |
| National Ass'n of Susu Collectors | Co-operative Society | Deposits and loans to member collectors | Co-operative Association | Not applicable | Not applicable | N/A | N/A | None | Department of Co-operatives Bank of Ghana | None |
| Individual Susu Collectors | Informal | Collecting & safekeeping of clients' savings | Informal individual enterprise | Not applicable | Not applicable | N/A | N/A | N/A | N/A | N/A |

BSD — Banking Supervision Department
NBFID — Non-Bank Financial Institutions Department

**Schedule 2    Classification of Regulations According to Objective — Ghana**

| Primary Objective | Main Regulation | Specific Implementing Measures | Sector/Segment Intended to be Protected | Assessment of Effectiveness of Regulation |
|---|---|---|---|---|
| Credit risk | Minimum capital requirement Loan provisioning | Capital adequacy Adjustment to value of loans | Financial resource management Portfolio quality | Low compliance Fair compliance |
| Liquidity risk | Liquidity ratios | Reserve requirements | Solvency | Very effective |
| Market risk | Assets diversification | Exposure limits disclosures | Solvency portfolio quality | High compliance |

**Schedule 3    Legal Systems and Judicial Processes**

| Country | Legal System / Tradition | Regulation of Business Activities | Laws Covering Real and Personal Property Rights | | | | | | |
|---|---|---|---|---|---|---|---|---|---|
| | | | Fixed Assets | Movable Property | Registration System | Transfers Recording | Enforcement Processes | Accepted Negotiable Instruments | Central Credit Bureau |
| **Ghana** | English Common Law | Business permits; business names registration; corporate registration; licensing and prudential supervision | Mortgage law Land Title Registration Law | N/A | Central registry (manual) | Manual system of recording and registry | Courts Act Extra-judicial foreclosure not feasible | Warehouse receipts | None |

# III Poverty, Education & Health

# 11 Ghana Census-Based Poverty Map: District & Sub-District Level Results*

HAROLD COULOMBE

## 1. Introduction

This study documents the construction of a poverty map based on data from the fourth round *Ghana Living Standards Survey* (GLSS 4) and the *Housing and Population Census 2000*. Based on a recently developed methodology, it permits the calculation of poverty indicators at very low levels of aggregation, using the detailed information found in the survey and the exhaustive coverage of the census. Results at district level as well as at the town and area council level are presented and analyzed.

In the past decade poverty profiles have been developed into useful tools for characterizing, assessing and monitoring poverty. Based on information collected in household surveys, including detailed information on expenditures and incomes, these profiles present the characteristics of the population according to their level of — monetary and non-monetary — standard of living, help assess the poverty-reducing effects of some policies and compare poverty levels between regions, groups and over time.

While these household-based studies have greatly improved our knowledge of the welfare level of households in general and of the poorer ones in particular, the approach suffers from a number of constraints. In particular, policy-makers and planners have need of finely disaggregated information in order to implement their anti-poverty schemes. Typically they need information for small geographic units such as city neighbourhoods, towns or villages. Telling Ghanaian policy-makers that the neediest people are in the Savannah region would not be too impressive, as that

* This project was funded by the UK Department for International Development (DfID), along with some initial funding by the World Bank. The work was undertaken by Harold Coulombe (consultant) with full support from the Ghana Statistical Service staff, in particular Dr Grace Bediako, Dr Nicholas Nsowah-Nuamah, Dr K. A. Twum-Baah, Mr K. B. Danso-Manu and Ms Jacqueline Anum. Technical guidance from Peter Lanjouw, Berk Özler and Johan Mistiaen (World Bank) as well as full support from Richard Harris (World Bank, previously DfID) was also welcomed.The author can be reached at hcoulombe@videotron.ca

information is well known and not useful since it would be too vague; telling them in which villages or towns or even districts the poorest households are concentrated would be more convincing! Using regional-level information often hides the existence of poverty pockets in otherwise relatively well-off regions and this would lead to poorly targeted schemes. Having better information at local level would necessarily minimize leaks and therefore permit more cost-effective and efficient anti-poverty schemes. Poverty indicators are needed at a local level as spatial inequalities can be important within a given region.

This paper presents results at regional, district and council levels. The methodology used has been developed by Elbers et al. (2002, 2003) and should be seen as more sophisticated than other methods, as it uses information on household expenditure, is fully consistent with poverty-profile figures, and permits the computation of standard errors of these poverty indicators. Since these types of poverty maps are fully compatible with poverty profile results, they should be seen as a natural extension to the Poverty Profile, a way of operationalizing poverty profile results. The current poverty map would reach its full potential once a series of applications under consideration had been undertaken.

The remainder of this study is structured as follow. We first present the methodology in layman's words, followed by a description of the data used. The paper ends with a discussion of the results and further work to be undertaken. A more technical presentation of the methodology can be found in the annex, along with some detailed results.

## 2. Methodology

The basic idea behind the methodology is quite straightforward. First, a regression model of adult equivalent expenditure is estimated using GLSS survey data, limiting the set of explanatory variables to those which are common to both that survey and the latest Census. Next, the coefficients from that model are applied to the Census data set to predict the expenditure level of every household in the Census. And finally, these predicted household expenditures are used to construct a series of welfare indicators (e.g. poverty level, depth, severity, inequality) for different geographical subgroups.

Although the idea behind the methodology is conceptually simple, its proper implementation requires complex computations. These complexities mainly arise from the need to take into account spatial autocorrelation (expenditure from households within the same cluster are correlated) and heteroskedasticity in the development of the predictive model. Taking into account these econometric issues ensures unbiased predictions. A further issue making computation non-trivial is our willingness to compute standard errors for each welfare statistic. These standard errors are important since they will tell us how far we can disaggregate the poverty indicators. As we disaggregate our results at lower and lower levels, the number of households on which our estimates are based decreases as well and therefore yields less and less precise estimates. At a given level, the estimated poverty indicators would become too imprecise to be used with confidence. The computation of these standard errors will help us to decide where to stop the disaggregation process. The methodology used is further discussed in Annex 11.1.

## 3. The Data

The construction of such a poverty map is also very demanding in terms of data. The basic requirement is a household survey with expenditure modules and a population and housing census. If not already done, a monetary-based poverty profile would have to be constructed from the survey, using the household-level welfare index and the poverty line from such a poverty profile. Apart from household-level information, community-level characteristics are also useful in the construction of a poverty map, as differences in geography, history, ethnicity, access to markets, public services and infrastructure, and other aspects of public policy can all lead to important differences in standard of living, whether defined in monetary terms or not. Fortunately all that information was available in the case of Ghana.

### The Census

The latest Housing and Population Census was conducted in Spring 2000. The questionnaire is relatively detailed but does not contain any information on either incomes or expenditures. At the individual level, it covers demography, education and economic activities. At the household level, dwelling characteristics are well covered. The Census database comprises more than 18.9 million individuals grouped into 3.7 million households. The Census field work grouped households into around 26,800 enumeration areas (EAs) of 138 households each on average.

Along with the housing and population census a *facility census* was conducted in every single locality. These 'localities' range from tiny sub-EA settlements to large urban neighbourhoods with many EAs. There are around 89,000 'localities' in the facility census database. The information collected includes the existence in the locality of a post office, telephone, traditional healing centre, hospital, maternity/clinic, and primary, JSS and SSS schools. If any of these facilities was not found in the locality, the distance to the nearest one was requested.

### The GLSS 4 Survey

The fourth round of the Ghana Living Standard Survey is the latest national survey to have collected expenditure data at household level. Having been administered in 1998/91, it is also the most appropriate survey timewise. The survey dataset was also enhanced by including information from the facility census. This required a tedious matching exercise to link the Enumeration Areas (EAs) used as sampling units (clusters) in the GLSS — which were based on the 1984 Census — with the 2000 Census EAs.

The welfare index to be used in our regression models (expenditure per equivalent adult in real terms) is the same as the one used in the government-sponsored poverty profile based on GLSS 4. Using the same welfare index ensures full consistency between the latest poverty profile (GSS, 2000; Coulombe and McKay, 2003) and the new poverty map. It will also permit testing whether the predicted poverty indicators match those found in the poverty profile at stratum level, the lowest statistically robust level achievable in GLSS 4.

On the basis of the information collected in the latest Census, a number of GLSS4 localities have been reclassified from rural to urban; an urban location is one with 5,000 or more persons. However, the urban/rural variable used in GLSS4 was defined on the basis of information from the 1984 Census. Therefore many EAs (clusters) in GLSS4 had been considered rural, while they had certainly become urban by 1998/9 when GLSS4 was conducted. This phenomenon is illustrated by the figures in Table 11.1. Compared with the latest Census, the urban localities (outside Accra) are underrepresented in GLSS4, while the rural ones are overrepresented. The problem is particularly important in Coastal and Forest ecological zones. For the current study, 24 clusters have been redefined from rural to urban. The last column of Table 11.1 clearly shows that the new GLSS4 distribution of clusters across strata is much more similar to the Census one and therefore closer to the reality at the time of GLSS4, 1998/9.

**Table 11.1 Distribution of Households according to Strata and Ecological Zones GLSS4 and Census 2000 (%)**

|  | GLSS4 | | Census | Difference | |
|---|---|---|---|---|---|
|  | 1984 urban/rural definition | 2000 urban/rural definition | 2000 | 1984 urban/rural definition | 2000 urban/rural definition |
| *GLSS4 strata* |  |  |  |  |  |
| Accra | 10.51 | 10.51 | 9.86 | +0.65 | +0.65 |
| Urban Coastal | 8.55 | 13.44 | 14.07 | −5.52 | −0.63 |
| Urban Forest | 13.11 | 18.08 | 17.98 | −4.87 | +0.10 |
| Urban Savannah | 4.49 | 6.68 | 5.26 | −0.77 | +1.42 |
| Rural Coastal | 15.46 | 10.84 | 11.58 | +3.88 | −0.74 |
| Rural Forest | 30.55 | 24.61 | 26.07 | +4.51 | −1.46 |
| Rural Savannah | 17.33 | 15.84 | 15.18 | +2.15 | +0.66 |
|  |  |  |  |  |  |
| *Ecological zone* |  |  |  |  |  |
| Accra | 10.51 | 10.51 | 9.86 | +0.65 | +0.65 |
| Coastal | 24.02 | 24.28 | 25.65 | +0.34 | −1.37 |
| Forest | 43.66 | 42.69 | 44.05 | −2.37 | −1.36 |
| Savannah | 21.82 | 22.52 | 20.44 | +1.38 | +2.08 |
|  |  |  |  |  |  |
| Total | 100.0% | 100.0% | 100.0% | 0.0% | 0.0% |

*Sources:* Author's calculation based on GSS (2000) and Census (2000).

## *Administrative Layers*

Ghana is currently in the process of an important decentralization effort which formally started more than ten years ago. The Local Government Act of 1993 and the National Development Planning (Systems) Act of 1994 have defined the current local government structure. It consists of four tiers. The top tier is the Regional Co-ordinating Council, followed by the Metropolitan/Municipal/District Assemblies. The Town/Zonal/Urban/ Area Councils and the Unit Committees are the bottom two tiers. However, the implementation of this administrative structure was held back by limited financial and human resources (Awoosah et al., 2004). In practice, only regions and districts have been formally defined. In our study, we use the official definitions for the regions and the districts, as well as an unofficial definition of the different types of councils. No attempt was made to define the last tier. Table 11.2 presents some descriptive statistics on the size of these different administrative levels.

**Table 11.2   Descriptive Statistics on the Ghanaian Administrative Structure**

| Administrative | No. of | No. of Households | | | No. of Individuals | | |
|---|---|---|---|---|---|---|---|
| Unit | Units | Median | Minimum | Maximum | Median | Minimum | Maximum |
| Region | 10 | 355,263 | 80,573 | 680,419 | 1,810,044 | 574,918 | 3,590,511 |
| District | 110 | 24,852 | 9,912 | 364,805 | 133,154 | 51,918 | 1,647,202 |
| Council | 1,048 | 2,055 | 41 | 48,334 | 12,258 | 263 | 272,208 |

*Note*:    Although 263 individuals seem rather small for a council, only 8 councils (out of 1048) have less than 1000 people.
*Source*:    Author's calculation based on Census, 2000.

***Strata***: the GLSS4 sample design was based on seven strata defined in terms of agro-climatic zones (coastal, forest and savannah) and urban/rural breakdown. Although that level is not an administrative level, poverty estimates were made at this fairly aggregated level mainly to establish their statistical validity. These predicted figures can be compared with the actual figures found in the latest Ghana Poverty Profile and statistical tests performed on the equality of these indicators.

***Region***: the national territory is divided into 10 regions which are divided further down into districts. No districts overlapped two or more regions.

***District***: the lowest administrative level for which a formal geographical definition is currently available is the 110 districts. The importance of the District Assemblies in the on-going decentralization process makes district-level poverty figures fundamental. These poverty figures, presented in this report, are the first value-added product to emerge from the poverty map. In 2004, a district remapping yielded 28 new districts but unfortunately the information needed to perform the poverty map using this new district definition was not available in time for this study. Once an operational EA-based definition of the 138 districts becomes available, it would be easy to update the poverty map to reflect the new administrative realities.

***Council***: although district-level poverty estimates would certainly be useful, that level of politico-geographical breakdown could still be too aggregated to be used for more finely targeted interventions. Currently there is no properly mapped sub-district breakdown. Each District Assembly has created a series of sub-district councils, broadly defined — in words — in a series of Legislative Instruments (LI) from 1988, prior to the formal establishment of the current four-tier system. However, these councils do not have formally mapped boundaries. Based on these LI, a Ghana Statistical Service team from cartography and GIS departments was to establish the link between these 'councils' and the Census 2000 EAs. Although the definition of the councils was not made official, we believe it would be a very fair approximation to an on-going data collection exercise being undertaken by CERSGIS from the University of Ghana at Legon.[1] All together, we defined 1048 councils. These units would be small enough for most decision-making, while being large enough to enable a statistically robust poverty map to be computed.

## 4.    Results
In order to maximize accuracy we have estimated the model at the lowest geographical level for which the GLSS survey is representative. In the case of the fourth round of GLSS, that level is the sampling strata: Accra, Urban Coastal, Urban Forest, Urban Savannah, Rural Coastal, Rural Forest and Rural Savannah. A household-level expenditure model has been developed for each of these strata using explanatory variables which are common to both the GLSS and the Census. These variables do not need to be causal as we are only interested in their predictive power. The results are presented stage by stage.

### *Stage 1: Aligning the Data*
The first task was to make sure the variables deemed common to both the Census and the survey were really measuring the same characteristics. In the first instance, we compared the questions and modalities in both questionnaires to isolate potential variables. We then compared the means of those (dichotomized) variables and tested whether they were equal using a 95% confidence interval.[2] Restricting ourselves to these variables would ensure that the predicted welfare figures were consistent with the survey-based poverty profile. As noted above, that comparison exercise was done at strata level. The two-stage sample design of GLSS 4 was taken into account in the computation of the standard errors. The results are not presented here but are available on request.

### *Stage 2: Survey-based Regressions*
The table in Annexe 11.2 presents the strata-specific regression results based on GLSS 4. The ultimate choice of the independent variables was based on a backward

---

[1] The Centre for Remote Sensing and Geographic Information Services (CERSGIS) is working on a comprehensive project which involves exhaustive data collection and mapping, including the definition of the councils which will eventually be made official by the Government of Ghana. The project, called Establishing a Mapping and Monitoring System for Development Activities in Ghana (EMMSDAG), is co-sponsored by the Ministry of Finance and the European Union. Final results are not expected for a year.

[2] We also deleted or redefined dichotomic variables being less that 0.03 or larger than 0.97 to avoid serious multicollinearity problems in our econometric models.

stepwise selection model. A check of the results confirmed that almost all the coefficients are of expected sign. As mentioned earlier, these models are not for discussion. They are exclusively prediction models, not determinants of poverty models that can be analyzed in terms of causal relationships. In the models used for the poverty map we were only concerned with the predictive power of the regressions without regard, for example, to endogenous variables. At that stage, we attempted to control the location effect by incorporating a cluster average of some of the variables. We also ran a series of regressions using the base model residuals as dependent variables. Those results — not shown here — would be used in the last stage in order to correct for heteroskedasticity.

The $R^2$s of the different regressions vary from 0.27 to 0.60. Although they might appear to be on the low side, they are typical of survey-based cross-section regressions and can be favourably compared with results from other poverty maps. While these coefficients look 'credible', it is important to note that these models were purely predictive in the statistical sense and should not be viewed as determinants of welfare or poverty. The relatively low $R^2$s for some of the models are mainly due to four important factors. First, in many areas households are fairly homogeneous in terms of observable characteristics, even if their consumption varies relatively more. This necessarily yields low $R^2$. Second, a large number of potential correlates are simply not observable using standard closed-questionnaire data collection methods. Third, many good predictors had been discarded at the first stage, since their distributions did not appear to be identical. And finally, many indicators do not take into account the quality of the correlates. Not taking into account the wide variation in quality of the different observable correlates makes many of these potential correlates useless in terms of predictive power.

### *Stage 3: Welfare Indicators[3]*
Based on the results from the previous stage, we applied the estimated parameters[4] to the Census data to compute a series of poverty and inequality indicators: the headcount ratio $(P_0)$, the poverty gap index $(P_1)$, the poverty severity index $(P_2)$, the Gini Index, the mean log deviation and the Theil index.[5] Table 11.3 presents estimated poverty figures for each stratum and compares them with actual figures from the latest survey-based poverty profiles. For each stratum and poverty indicator, the equality of GLSS 4-based and Census-based indicators cannot be rejected (at 95%).[6] Apart the case of

---

[3] The computation of the welfare indicators has been greatly eased thanks to PovMap, a software especially written to implement the methodology used here. We used the February 2005 version developed by Qinghua Zhao (2005).
[4] Apart from regression models explaining household welfare level, we also estimated a model for the heteroskedasticity in the household component of the error. We also estimated the parametric distributions of both error terms. See Annexe 11.1 for further details.
[5] Because of space constraint, only the poverty figures are presented here. The inequality figures will be found in a forthcoming GSS report,which would be an extended version of the current paper.
[6] It is worth noting that the standard errors of the mean of the Census-based figures are systematically lower that the ones calculated from GLSS4.

Urban Forest where the census-based headcount ratio is 3.2 points higher, the gaps are always smaller than 1.5% and often minute. Although the census-based poverty figures can only be compared with those provided by the GLSS survey at stratum level, the equality of these poverty figures provided an excellent reliability test of the methodology used here.

**Table 11.3    Poverty Rates based on GLSS 4 (actual) and Census 2000 (predicted) by Strata**

|  | Headcount Incidence $(P_0)$ | | Poverty Gap Index $(P_1)$ | | Poverty Severity Index $(P_2)$ | |
|---|---|---|---|---|---|---|
|  | GLSS 4 (Actual) | Census (Predicted) | GLSS 4 (Actual) | Census (Predicted) | GLSS4 (Actual) | Census (Predicted) |
| Accra | 0.038 | 0.052 | 0.008 | 0.012 | 0.002 | 0.004 |
|  | *(0.017)* | *(0.009)* | *(0.004)* | *(0.002)* | *(0.001)* | *(0.001)* |
| Urban Coastal | 0.286 | 0.280 | 0.085 | 0.098 | 0.035 | 0.049 |
|  | *(0.040)* | *(0.020)* | *(0.016)* | *(0.009)* | *(0.008)* | *(0.006)* |
| Urban Forest | 0.176 | 0.208 | 0.047 | 0.074 | 0.018 | 0.037 |
|  | *(0.036)* | *(0.013)* | *(0.011)* | *(0.007)* | *(0.005)* | *(0.004)* |
| Urban Savannah | 0.518 | 0.510 | 0.162 | 0.183 | 0.067 | 0.088 |
|  | *(0.078)* | *(0.041)* | *(0.036)* | *(0.021)* | *(0.018)* | *(0.013)* |
| Rural Coastal | 0.485 | 0.471 | 0.152 | 0.163 | 0.065 | 0.076 |
|  | *(0.046)* | *(0.025)* | *(0.023)* | *(0.013)* | *(0.012)* | *(0.008)* |
| Rural Forest | 0.409 | 0.407 | 0.117 | 0.137 | 0.048 | 0.064 |
|  | *(0.025)* | *(0.021)* | *(0.012)* | *(0.010)* | *(0.007)* | *(0.006)* |
| Rural Savannah | 0.695 | 0.690 | 0.324 | 0.331 | 0.181 | 0.197 |
|  | *(0.054)* | *(0.023)* | *(0.036)* | *(0.018)* | *(0.024)* | *(0.015)* |

*Notes*:    Robust standard errors in parentheses. The poverty indicators based on GLSS 4 are slightly different from the ones already published by GSS since we used the new definition of the urban/rural breakdown (see Table 11.1).
*Source*:    Author's calculation based on GSS (2000) and Census (2000).

Using the same econometric results, the table in Annexe 11.3 presents poverty figures for each of the 10 regions and 110 districts, broken down into urban/rural areas. The standard errors are also presented and are — in most cases — relatively small, which makes the predicted poverty figures quite reliable. These district-level estimates are the first ever monetary-based poverty figures available in Ghana. Overall these figures seem to make sense and anecdotal evidences supports these results, although some results might raise questions at first sight. In particular, in a few districts the urban population are found to be poorer than the rural population. However, these districts tend to be isolated ones where the so-called urban population are likely to live in 'big' villages not having the infrastructure usually found in Ghanaian towns.

Council-level figures were also computed but space constraints do not permit their presentation here. These council-level results are available in an exhaustive companion report published by the Ghana Statistical Service. Nonetheless, some analysis concerning the relevance of these finely disaggregated estimates can be found in the following sub-section.

### *How Low Can We Go?*

Further examination of poverty estimates from the table in Annexe 11.3 reveals that the standard errors — in relation to their associated indicators — seem to indicate that our poverty estimates at district level are fairly precise. However, it is difficult to make an 'objective' judgement on the precision of these estimates without some kind of benchmark. To do so, Figure 11.1 presents the headcount incidence coefficients of variation (inverted) of the district- and council-level estimates and compares them with the ones computed from the GLSS4 survey. Hence, we use the precision of the GLSS 4-based headcount incidence as our benchmark, which is represented by the step curve. These steps represented the different inverted coefficients of variation associated with the different strata. The curves in Figure 11.1 clearly show that our district-level headcount incidence estimates do at least as well as the GLSS 4-based poverty estimates since the district-level curve lies on or below the GLSS4 one. Since council estimates are based on smaller samples, its curve shows that the council-level estimates are not as precise, although they compared favourably with the GLSS4 figures. How low can we go? If one takes the GLSS4 benchmark as a good one, it is clear that both district- and council-level poverty estimates would be good guides for policy-makers.

**Figure 11.1: Poverty Headcount Accuracy, by Disaggregation Level**

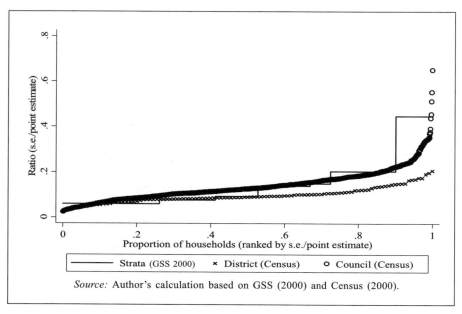

*Source:* Author's calculation based on GSS (2000) and Census (2000).

## *How Low Should We Go?*

Although we have just demonstrated that we can use the district and council headcount figures with some confidence about their level of precision, it might be the case that these disaggregated figures do not yield much information. Within a rather homogeneous region, it might be that the different districts are not statistically different from each other in terms of monetary poverty. The same question can be raised concerning the use of the council-level figures within a given district. To test whether additional information about the poverty level is gained when we disaggregate from regions to districts and from districts to councils, Table 11.4 gives the proportion of

**Table 11.4   Disaggregation and Change in Headcount Incidence, by Region**

|  | % of geographic unit | | % of population | |
|---|---|---|---|---|
|  | **Districts** different from their **Regions** | **Councils** different from their **Districts** | **Districts** different from their **Regions** | **Councils** different from their **Districts** |
| *Urban* | *43.4* | *19.8* | *66.0* | *15.0* |
| Western | 27.3 | 18.2 | 16.5 | 26.5 |
| Central | 16.7 | 16.7 | 21.5 | 9.7 |
| Greater Accra | 100.0 | 14.8 | 100.0 | 7.3 |
| Volta | 33.3 | 10.0 | 39.3 | 8.9 |
| Eastern | 40.0 | 14.7 | 48.9 | 10.7 |
| Ashanti | 82.4 | 26.9 | 87.7 | 22.2 |
| Brong Ahafo | 46.2 | 33.3 | 59.8 | 28.1 |
| Northern | 38.5 | 10.5 | 20.0 | 6.6 |
| Upper East | 25.0 | 50.0 | 5.5 | 49.2 |
| Upper West | 0.0 | 0.0 | 0.0 | 0.0 |
| *Rural* | *29.9* | *11.9* | *29.1* | *11.7* |
| Western | 30.0 | 3.4 | 27.2 | 1.7 |
| Central | 83.3 | 27.3 | 85.8 | 23.1 |
| Greater Accra | 25.0 | 42.1 | 16.4 | 54.5 |
| Volta | 0.0 | 14.0 | 0.0 | 15.3 |
| Eastern | 26.7 | 9.0 | 18.8 | 9.0 |
| Ashanti | 11.8 | 6.9 | 8.1 | 7.5 |
| Brong Ahafo | 7.7 | 9.4 | 8.9 | 9.7 |
| Northern | 53.8 | 15.8 | 62.2 | 12.9 |
| Upper East | 66.7 | 6.9 | 66.7 | 5.0 |
| Upper West | 0.0 | 10.9 | 0.0 | 14.7 |
| *Total* | *36.6* | *13.7* | *45.2* | *13.2* |

*Notes:*   Following Mistiaen et al. (2002), these percentages represent differences in headcount incidence that are statistically different (at 95% confidence interval) using the standard errors of the point estimates for the lower level of disaggregation.

*Sources:*   Author's calculation based on GSS (2000) and Census (2000).

districts (in terms of unit and of population) that are statistically poorer or richer than their associated regions. We also computed the relationship between districts and councils. Overall, some 36.6% of the different districts have a poverty headcount statistically smaller or higher than their own region. Similarly, 13.7% of councils are different poverty-wise from their own district. In terms of population the overall figures are significantly higher at 45.2% and 13.2% repetitively. As expected, these figures show that urban areas are less homogeneous than rural areas. At least in rural areas, it is also clear that the smaller the entities the more homogeneous they are. Urban areas are visibly more heterogeneous. Based on these results, it appears that using the results from councils on top of those from districts should improve the targeting efficiency of any allocation of resources aimed at reducing poverty.

## 5.   Concluding Remarks

This study has documented the construction of a regional-, district- and council-level poverty map for Ghana. The methodology developed by Elbers et al. (2003) has permitted us to obtain the first ever reliable poverty estimates at district and council levels. This map reports on 110 districts but it would be easy and straightforward to update it once we obtain the definition (in terms of EAs) of the recently redrawn districts. However, we acknowledge that the definition of the councils is our own and should not be regarded as official. These finely disaggregated poverty figures are fully compatible with the latest Poverty Profile (GSS, 2000; Coulombe and McKay, 2003).

One of the main advantages of the methodology used here is the possibility of computing standard errors of the different poverty estimates and therefore gives an idea of the reliability of these estimates. We considered that, using the precision level of the latest poverty profile as benchmark, both the district and council levels are precise enough to be useful to planners, policy-makers and researchers.

However interesting these results, they only acquire their full potential if they are used. How? Amongst others, they can be used to design budget allocation rules to be applied by the different administrative levels towards their subdivisions: the central government toward the districts, and the districts toward their councils. This map could become an important tool in support of the decentralization process currently being undertaken in Ghana. Obviously such monetary-based target indicators could be used in conjunction with some alternative measures of poverty based on education, health or infrastructure indicators. In particular, merging the poverty map with education and health maps would yield powerful targeting tools. Others uses of the poverty map would include the evaluation of locally targeted anti-poverty schemes (social funds, town/village development schemes), impact analysis, etc. And finally, researchers could use it in a multitude of ways, such as the study of the relationship between poverty distribution and different socio-economic outcomes.

# References

Awoosah, E. T., Agamah, J. C., Kwarteng, A. S., Oppong, B. M. and Owusu, F. (2004) 'Planning with the Area Council: Experience with CBP in Ghana', in Ian Goldman and Joanne Abbott (eds), *PLA Notes 49: Decentralisation and Community-based Planning.* London: International Institute for Environment and Development (IIED).

Coulombe, Harold and McKay, Andrew (2003) 'Selective Poverty Reduction in a Slow Growth Environment: Ghana in the 1990s' (mimeo).

Elbers, Chris, Lanjouw, Jean Olson and Lanjouw, Peter (2002) *Welfare in Villages and Towns: Micro-level Estimation of Poverty and Inequality.* Policy Research Working Paper No. 2911. Washington, DC: World Bank, DECRG..

Elbers, Chris, Lanjouw, Jean Olson and Lanjouw, Peter (2003) 'Micro-Level Estimation of Poverty and Inequality' *Econometrica*, Vol. 71, No. 1: 355–64

Ghana Statistical Service (GSS) (2000) *Poverty Trends in Ghana in the 1990s.* Accra: GSS, October.

Mistiaen, Johan, Ozler, Berk, Razafimanantena, Tiaray and Razafindravonona, Jean (2002) *Putting Welfare on the Map in Madagascar.* Africa Region Working Paper Series, No. 34. Washington, DC: World Bank.

Zhao, Qinghua (2005) 'User Manual for PovMap'. Washington, DC: World Bank, Development Research Group (mimeo).

# Annexe 11.1    Methodology

The basic idea behind the methodology developed by Elbers et al. (2002, 2003) is unchallenging. At first a regression model of the log of per capita expenditure is estimated using survey data, employing a set of explanatory variables which are common to both a survey and the census. Next, parameters from the regression are used to predict expenditure for every household in the census. And third, a series of welfare indicators are constructed for different geographical subgroups.

The term 'welfare indicator' embraces a whole set of indicators based on household expenditures. This note put emphasis on poverty headcount ($P_0$), but the usual poverty and inequality indicators can be computed (Atkinson inequality measures, generalized Entropy class inequalities index, FGT poverty measures and Gini).

Although the idea is rather simple, its proper implementation requires complex computation if one wants to take into account spatial autocorrelation and heteroskedasticity in the regression model. Furthermore, proper calculation of the different welfare indicators and their standard errors tremendously increases its complexities.

The discussion below is divided into three parts, one for each stage necessary in the construction of a poverty map. This discussion borrows from the original theoretical papers of Elbers et al. as well as from Mistiaen et al. (2002).

## First Stage

In the first instance, we need to determine a set of explanatory variables from both databases that are meeting some criteria of comparability. In order to be able to reproduce a poverty map consistent with the associated poverty profile, it is important to restrict ourselves to variables that are fully comparable between the census and the survey. We start by checking the wording of the different questions as well as the proposed answer options. From the set of selected questions we then build a series of variables which are to be tested for comparability. Although we might want to test the comparability of the whole distributions of each variable, in practice we restrict ourselves to testing only the means. In order to maximize the predictability power of the second-stage models, all analysis will be performed at the strata level, including the comparability of the different variables from which the definitive models would be determined.

The list of all potential variables and their equality of means test results is not presented in this note but can be obtained on request.

## Second Stage

We first model per capita household expenditure[7] using the limited sample survey. In order to maximize accuracy we estimate the model at the lowest geographical level for which the survey is representative. In the case of the fourth round of GLSS that level

---

[7] In our study we used the welfare index constructed for the GLSS4 poverty profile. Although that welfare index is defined in terms of equivalent adults, the demonstration remains unchanged.

is the sampling strata: Accra, urban coastal, urban forest, urban savannah, rural coastal, rural forest and rural savannah.

Let us specify a household-level expenditure $(y_{ch})$ model for household $h$ in location $c$, $\mathbf{x_{ch}}$ is a set of explanatory variables, and $u_{ch}$ is the residual:

$$\ln y_{ch} = E[\ln y_{ch} \mid \mathbf{x_{ch}}] + u_{ch} \qquad (1)$$

The locations represent clusters as defined in the first stage of typical household sampling design, which usually also represents census enumeration areas, although this is not necessary. The explanatory variables need to be present in both the survey and the census, and need to be defined similarly. The model also needs to have the _____ents in order to properly measure the different welfare indicators. The set ____ al variables had been defined in the first stage.

_____ linearise the previous equation, we model the household's logarithmic per _____ ꜱenditure as

$$\ln y_{ch} = \mathbf{x}_{ch}\,\beta + u_{ch} \qquad (2)$$

The vector of disturbances $u$ is distributed $F\,(0,\Sigma)$. The model (2) is estimated by Generalized Least Squares (GLS). To estimate this model we need first to estimate the error variance-covariance matrix $\Sigma$ in order to take into account possible spatial autocorrelation (expenditure from households within a same cluster are certainly correlated) and heteroskedasticity. To do so we first specify the error terms as

$$u_{ch} = \eta_c + \varepsilon_{ch} \qquad (3)$$

Where $\eta_c$ is the location effect and $\varepsilon_{ch}$ is the individual component of the error term.

In practice we first estimate equation (2) by simple OLS and use the residuals as estimates of the overall disturbances, given by $\hat{\mu}_{ch}$. We then decompose those residuals between uncorrelated household and location components:

$$\hat{\mu}_{ch} = \hat{\eta}_c + e_{ch} \qquad (4)$$

The location term $(\hat{\eta}_c)$ is estimated as a cluster means of the overall residuals and therefore the household component $(e_{ch})$ is simply deducted. The heteroskedasticity in the latest error component is modelled by regressing its squared $(e_{ch}^2)$ on a long list of all independent variables of model (2), their squared interactions as well as the imputed welfare. A logistic model is used.

Bo

to, $\hat{\Sigma}$

matrix permits us to estimate the final set of coefficients of the main model (2).

## Third Stage

To complete the map we associate the estimated parameters from the second stage with the corresponding characteristics of each household found in the census to predict the log of per capita expenditure and the simulated disturbances.

Since the very complex disturbance structure has made the computation of the variance of the imputed welfare index intractable, bootstrapping techniques have been used to get a measure of the dispersion of that imputed welfare index. From the previous stage, a series of coefficients and disturbance terms have been drawn from their corresponding distributions. We then, for each household found in the census, simulate a value of welfare index ($\hat{y}^r_{ch}$) based on the predicted values and the disturbance terms:

$$\hat{y}^r_{ch} = \exp(\mathbf{x}'_{ch}\tilde{\beta}^r + \tilde{\eta}^r_c + \tilde{\varepsilon}^r_{ch}) \tag{5}$$

This process is repeated 100 times, each time redrawing the full set of coefficients and disturbance terms. The means of the simulated welfare index become our point estimate and the standard deviation of our welfare index is the standard errors of these simulated estimates.

## Annexe 11.2   Survey-Based Regression Models

| Accra | | | Urban Coastal | | |
|---|---|---|---|---|---|
| No. of observations | 620 | | No. of observations | 799 | |
| No. of clusters | 31 | | No. of clusters | 40 | |
| $R^2$ (without location means) | 0.2444 | | $R^2$ (without location means) | 0.3924 | |
| $R^2$ (with location means) | 0.2659 | | $R^2$ (with location means) | 0.4179 | |

| Variable | Coeff. | | Variable | Coeff. |
|---|---|---|---|---|
| No. of boys aged 7–14 | –0.168 | | No. of boys aged 7–14 | –0.083 |
| | (4.93) | | | (2.66) |
| No. of girls aged 7–14 | –0.161 | | No. of girls aged 7–14 | –0.100 |
| | (6.51) | | | (2.70) |
| Head schooled (0/1) | 0.199 | | Proportion of members that | 0.414 |
| | (2.83) | | went to school | (3.38) |
| Head is self-employed, | 0.141 | | No. of people that went to | –0.107 |
| non-agro (0/1) | (3.25) | | school | (4.62) |
| Cement Roof (0/1) | 0.143 | | Other Christian (0/1) | 0.171 |
| | (2.25) | | | (3.36) |
| Has flush toilet (0/1) | 0.148 | | Protestant (0/1) | 0.160 |
| | (2.75) | | | (3.15) |
| Use coal for cooking (0/1) | –0.254 | | Head reads English and | 0.184 |
| | (7.00) | | Ghanaian (0/1) | (4.04) |
| Accra Metro Assembly | 0.147 | | Use electricity (0/1) | 0.189 |
| no. 5 (0/1) | (3.05) | | | (4.00) |
| Garbage collection | 0.281 | | Has flush toilet (0/1) | 0.352 |
| (EA average) | (2.53) | | | (5.36) |
| Use electricity (EA average) | 0.751 | | No. of pc weekly hours | 0.006 |
| | (2.30) | | worked | (3.89) |
| Has flush toilet (EA average) | –0.405 | | Eastern region (0/1) | –0.221 |
| | (2.40) | | | (2.60) |
| Constant | 14.107 | | Central region (0/1) | –0.280 |
| | (46.96) | | | (4.25) |
| | | | Western region (0/1) | –0.241 |
| | | | | (3.38) |
| | | | Shama 1 (0/1) | 0.391 |
| | | | | (4.05) |
| | | | Hours worked (EA average) | 0.014 |
| | | | | (3.87) |
| | | | Use water from wells (EA | 0.630 |
| | | | average) | (4.81) |
| | | | Use pipe water (EA average) | 0.514 |
| | | | | (5.61) |
| | | | Constant | 13.164 |
| | | | | (75.80) |

**Annexe 11.2 Survey-Based Regression Models (*cont'd*)**

| Urban Forest | | Urban Savannah | |
|---|---|---|---|
| No. of observations | 960 | No. of observations | 300 |
| No. of clusters | 48 | No. of clusters | 15 |
| $R^2$ (without location means) | 0.5749 | $R^2$ (without location means) | 0.5975 |
| $R^2$ (with location means) | 0.5855 | $R^2$ (with location means) | 0.5975 |
| Variable | Coeff. | Variable | Coeff. |
| No. of boys aged 7–14 | –0.065 | Household size (in log) | –0.478 |
| | (2.51) | | (11.35) |
| No. of girls aged 7–14 | –0.058 | Mole (0/1) | –0.212 |
| | (2.33) | | (2.99) |
| people that went to school | –0.079 | Islam (0/1) | 0.179 |
| | (6.09) | | (2.48) |
| Male head (0/1) | –0.104 | Thatch roof (0/1) | –0.258 |
| | (2.77) | | (5.14) |
| Head age | –0.022 | No toilet (0/1) | –0.224 |
| | (3.19) | | (2.70) |
| Head age squared | 0.000 | Use coal for cooking (0/1) | 0.154 |
| | (2.52) | | (2.55) |
| Head reads English (0/1) | 0.143 | Phone available in EA (0/1) | 0.550 |
| | (2.86) | | (6.58) |
| Head reads English and | 0.217 | Upper East region (0/1) | 0.149 |
| Ghanaian (0/1) | (4.86) | | (2.63) |
| Catholic (0/1) | 0.221 | Constant | 14.212 |
| | (3.42) | | (167.42) |
| Protestant (0/1) | 0.086 | | |
| | (2.48) | | |
| Head is self-employed, | 0.291 | | |
| non-agro (0/1) | (4.54) | | |
| Head does not work (0/1) | 0.169 | | |
| | (2.25) | | |
| Head is employed (0/1) | 0.336 | | |
| | (4.34) | | |
| pc weekly hours worked in | 0.011 | | |
| self agro | (4.81) | | |
| Use electricity (0/1) | 0.245 | | |
| | (3.64) | | |
| Has flush toilet (0/1) | 0.214 | | |
| | (3.46) | | |
| Use wood for cooking (0/1) | –0.312 | | |
| | (5.05) | | |

**Annexe 11.2    Survey-Based Regression Models** (*cont'd*)

| Urban Forest | | Urban Savannah |
|---|---|---|
| Post office in EA (0/1) | −0.383 | |
| | *(6.75)* | |
| Phone in EA (0/1) | 0.656 | |
| | *(8.28)* | |
| Volta Region (0/1) | 0.185 | |
| | *(4.27)* | |
| Western Region (0/1) | 0.231 | |
| | *(3.92)* | |
| Ashanti region (0/1) | 0.305 | |
| | *(8.42)* | |
| Bronga Afaho region (0/1) | 0.364 | |
| | *(8.21)* | |
| Kumasi Metro | 0.387 | |
| Assembly 1 (0/1) | *(4.83)* | |
| Use coal for cooking (EA | 0.380 | |
| average) | *(3.25)* | |
| Use electricity (EA average) | −0.173 | |
| | *(2.53)* | |
| Constant | 14.245 | |
| | *(68.51)* | |

**Annexe 11.2  Survey-Based Regression Models** (*cont'd*)

| Rural Coastal | | | Rural Forest | | |
|---|---|---|---|---|---|
| No. of observations | 699 | | No. of observations | 1680 | |
| No. of clusters | 35 | | No. of clusters | 84 | |
| R² (without location means) | 0.5156 | | R² (without location means) | 0.2819 | |
| R² (with location means) | 0.5300 | | R² (with location means) | 0.3011 | |

| Variable | Coeff. | Variable | Coeff. |
|---|---|---|---|
| household size (in log) | −0.494 | No. of boys aged 7–14 | −0.137 |
| | (9.68) | | (7.04) |
| No. of children aged 0–6 | 0.072 | No. of female adults | −0.147 |
| | (3.71) | aged 15–59 | (6.61) |
| Ga ethnic group (0/1) | 0.272 | Head reads English (0/1) | 0.085 |
| | (3.91) | | (2.84) |
| Head is unemployed (0/1) | 0.437 | Head is self-employed, | -0.167 |
| | (4.92) | agro (0/1) | (3.49) |
| pc weekly hours worked | 0.008 | pc weekly hours worked — | 0.013 |
| | (3.63) | formal sector | (4.83) |
| Use electricity (0/1) | 0.425 | pc weekly hours worked | 0.011 |
| | (3.91) | in self agro | (5.21) |
| No toilet (0/1) | −0.130 | Thatch Roof (0/1) | −0.096 |
| | (2.23) | | (1.96) |
| Junior secondary school (0/1) | 0.193 | Cement wall (0/1) | 0.110 |
| | (2.98) | | (2.63) |
| Central region (0/1) | −0.331 | Use coal for cooking (0/1) | 0.276 |
| | (4.73) | | (5.56) |
| pschool (EA average) | 0.887 | Post office in EA (0/1) | 0.214 |
| | (3.04) | | (3.02) |
| Cement wall (EA average) | −0.586 | Western region (0/1) | 0.292 |
| | (3.66) | | (4.34) |
| Use coal for cooking (EA | 1.102 | Central region (0/1) | 0.397 |
| average) | (3.71) | | (5.18) |
| Constant | 13.879 | Ashanti region (0/1) | 0.126 |
| | (67.39) | | (1.99) |
| | | Head reads English (EA | 0.406 |
| | | average) | (2.29) |
| | | No Toilet (EA average) | −0.582 |
| | | | (5.02) |
| | | Constant | 13.822 |
| | | | (127.64) |

**Annexe 11.2 Survey-Based Regression models** (*cont'd*)

### Rural Savannah

| | |
|---|---|
| No. of observations | 950 |
| No. of clusters | 47 |
| $R^2$ (without location means) | 0.2496 |
| $R^2$ (with location means) | 0.4400 |

| Variable | Coeff. |
|---|---|
| No. of girls aged 7–14 | –0.116 |
| | *(4.02)* |
| No. of boys aged 7–14 | –0.146 |
| | *(6.55)* |
| Head is employed — formal | 0.361 |
| sector (0/1) | *(3.16)* |
| pc weekly hours worked | 0.009 |
| | *(3.61)* |
| Upper East Region (0/1) | –0.305 |
| | *(4.51)* |
| pc weekly hours worked | 0.063 |
| (EA average) | *(4.92)* |
| No. of rooms (EA average) | –0.191 |
| | *(6.41)* |
| Hours worked (EA average) | –0.035 |
| | *(3.36)* |
| Constant | 14.255 |
| | *(70.79)* |

*Sources*: Author's calculation based on GSS (2000).

**Annexe 11.3 Regional and District Level Poverty Estimates, by Urban/Rural**

| ID | Name | District Population | Total P0 | Total P1 | Total P2 | Urban Population | Urban P0 | Urban P1 | Urban P2 | Rural Population | Rural P0 | Rural P1 | Rural P2 |
|---|---|---|---|---|---|---|---|---|---|---|---|---|---|
| **1** | **Western** | **1,919,212** | **0.325** *0.041* | **0.106** *0.018* | **0.049** *0.010* | **692,717** | **0.288** *0.039* | **0.102** *0.019* | **0.051** *0.012* | **1,226,495** | **0.346** *0.041* | **0.109** *0.017* | **0.048** *0.009* |
| 101 | Jomoro | 110,972 | 0.491 *0.047* | 0.176 *0.025* | 0.085 *0.015* | 32,685 | 0.412 *0.068* | 0.149 *0.035* | 0.075 *0.022* | 78,287 | 0.525 *0.038* | 0.188 *0.020* | 0.090 *0.012* |
| 102 | Nzema East | 142,523 | 0.446 *0.046* | 0.151 *0.023* | 0.071 *0.014* | 37,716 | 0.427 *0.071* | 0.157 *0.038* | 0.079 *0.023* | 104,807 | 0.452 *0.037* | 0.149 *0.018* | 0.068 *0.010* |
| 103 | Ahanta West | 94,826 | 0.378 *0.044* | 0.126 *0.020* | 0.058 *0.012* | 18,750 | 0.297 *0.072* | 0.095 *0.031* | 0.043 *0.017* | 76,076 | 0.398 *0.037* | 0.133 *0.018* | 0.062 *0.010* |
| 104 | Shama-Ahanta E | 366,215 | 0.264 *0.033* | 0.090 *0.015* | 0.044 *0.009* | 366,215 | 0.264 *0.033* | 0.090 *0.015* | 0.044 *0.009* | n/a | n/a | n/a | n/a |
| 105 | Mpohor-Wassa | 122,752 | 0.292 *0.045* | 0.089 *0.017* | 0.039 *0.009* | 15,664 | 0.187 *0.048* | 0.063 *0.020* | 0.030 *0.011* | 107,088 | 0.307 *0.044* | 0.093 *0.017* | 0.040 *0.009* |
| 106 | Wassa West | 231,952 | 0.222 *0.038* | 0.067 *0.014* | 0.030 *0.007* | 82,002 | 0.171 *0.036* | 0.056 *0.014* | 0.027 *0.008* | 149,950 | 0.250 *0.039* | 0.073 *0.014* | 0.031 *0.007* |
| 107 | Wassa Amenefi | 234,155 | 0.324 *0.044* | 0.101 *0.018* | 0.045 *0.009* | 30,996 | 0.357 *0.050* | 0.136 *0.027* | 0.072 *0.017* | 203,159 | 0.319 *0.043* | 0.096 *0.016* | 0.041 *0.008* |
| 108 | Aowin-Suaman | 118,978 | 0.350 *0.051* | 0.113 *0.022* | 0.052 *0.012* | 18,625 | 0.323 *0.047* | 0.122 *0.025* | 0.064 *0.016* | 100,353 | 0.355 *0.052* | 0.111 *0.022* | 0.049 *0.011* |
| 109 | Juabeso-Bia | 244,456 | 0.346 *0.049* | 0.111 *0.021* | 0.051 *0.011* | 16,940 | 0.589 *0.087* | 0.261 *0.058* | 0.151 *0.041* | 227,516 | 0.328 *0.046* | 0.100 *0.018* | 0.044 *0.009* |
| 110 | Sefwi Wiawso | 149,247 | 0.345 *0.048* | 0.113 *0.021* | 0.053 *0.012* | 34,669 | 0.384 *0.055* | 0.150 *0.030* | 0.080 *0.020* | 114,578 | 0.333 *0.046* | 0.102 *0.018* | 0.044 *0.009* |
| 111 | Bibiani | 103,136 | 0.315 *0.048* | 0.102 *0.021* | 0.047 *0.011* | 38,455 | 0.278 *0.044* | 0.097 *0.020* | 0.048 *0.012* | 64,681 | 0.337 *0.050* | 0.104 *0.021* | 0.046 *0.011* |
| **2** | **Central** | **1,581,482** | **0.448** *0.041* | **0.161** *0.020* | **0.078** *0.012* | **587,953** | **0.421** *0.039* | **0.163** *0.020* | **0.087** *0.013* | **993,529** | **0.465** *0.042* | **0.159** *0.019* | **0.073** *0.011* |
| 201 | Komenda | 109,940 | 0.514 *0.035* | 0.184 *0.019* | 0.087 *0.012* | 31,932 | 0.401 *0.040* | 0.145 *0.019* | 0.073 *0.012* | 78,008 | 0.561 *0.033* | 0.200 *0.019* | 0.093 *0.012* |

**Annexe 11.3  Regional and District Level Poverty Estimates, by Urban/Rural** (*cont'd*)

| District | | | Total | | | Urban | | | | Rural | | | |
|---|---|---|---|---|---|---|---|---|---|---|---|---|---|
| ID | Name | Population | P0 | P1 | P2 | Population | P0 | P1 | P2 | Population | P0 | P1 | P2 |
| 202 | Cape Coast | 114,142 | 0.273 | 0.085 | 0.038 | 78,358 | 0.275 | 0.088 | 0.041 | 35,784 | 0.268 | 0.079 | 0.034 |
| | | | *0.039* | *0.015* | *0.008* | | *0.039* | *0.016* | *0.009* | | *0.039* | *0.014* | *0.007* |
| 203 | Abura | 89,933 | 0.516 | 0.181 | 0.085 | 26,109 | 0.495 | 0.193 | 0.101 | 63,824 | 0.525 | 0.176 | 0.078 |
| | | | *0.042* | *0.022* | *0.013* | | *0.043* | *0.024* | *0.015* | | *0.042* | *0.021* | *0.012* |
| 204 | Mfantsiman | 152,965 | 0.473 | 0.168 | 0.081 | 76,107 | 0.424 | 0.155 | 0.078 | 76,858 | 0.521 | 0.181 | 0.083 |
| | | | *0.038* | *0.019* | *0.011* | | *0.040* | *0.020* | *0.012* | | *0.036* | *0.018* | *0.011* |
| 205 | Gomoa | 191,824 | 0.630 | 0.253 | 0.132 | 48,326 | 0.647 | 0.320 | 0.199 | 143,498 | 0.625 | 0.230 | 0.109 |
| | | | *0.038* | *0.026* | *0.018* | | *0.043* | *0.036* | *0.030* | | *0.036* | *0.022* | *0.014* |
| 206 | Awutu | 169,084 | 0.526 | 0.200 | 0.101 | 110,593 | 0.466 | 0.181 | 0.096 | 58,491 | 0.641 | 0.234 | 0.110 |
| | | | *0.042* | *0.024* | *0.016* | | *0.043* | *0.024* | *0.016* | | *0.040* | *0.025* | *0.016* |
| 207 | Agona | 158,358 | 0.471 | 0.168 | 0.080 | 102,562 | 0.363 | 0.126 | 0.062 | 55,796 | 0.669 | 0.244 | 0.114 |
| | | | *0.042* | *0.022* | *0.013* | | *0.040* | *0.018* | *0.011* | | *0.044* | *0.029* | *0.018* |
| 208 | Asikuma | 89,237 | 0.576 | 0.204 | 0.095 | 28,364 | 0.421 | 0.154 | 0.078 | 60,873 | 0.648 | 0.227 | 0.103 |
| | | | *0.053* | *0.029* | *0.017* | | *0.063* | *0.031* | *0.019* | | *0.049* | *0.028* | *0.017* |
| 209 | Ajumako | 91,976 | 0.541 | 0.188 | 0.087 | 16,246 | 0.426 | 0.153 | 0.077 | 75,730 | 0.566 | 0.196 | 0.089 |
| | | | *0.045* | *0.023* | *0.013* | | *0.045* | *0.022* | *0.013* | | *0.045* | *0.023* | *0.013* |
| 210 | Assin | 195,792 | 0.290 | 0.096 | 0.046 | 28,388 | 0.451 | 0.205 | 0.123 | 167,404 | 0.263 | 0.078 | 0.033 |
| | | | *0.056* | *0.022* | *0.012* | | *0.049* | *0.031* | *0.023* | | *0.057* | *0.021* | *0.010* |
| 211 | Twifu | 110,215 | 0.289 | 0.096 | 0.046 | 15,126 | 0.516 | 0.238 | 0.143 | 95,089 | 0.253 | 0.073 | 0.031 |
| | | | *0.057* | *0.023* | *0.013* | | *0.062* | *0.043* | *0.033* | | *0.056* | *0.020* | *0.009* |
| 212 | Upper Denkyira | 108,016 | 0.262 | 0.081 | 0.037 | 25,842 | 0.320 | 0.120 | 0.062 | 82,174 | 0.244 | 0.069 | 0.029 |
| | | | *0.054* | *0.021* | *0.011* | | *0.055* | *0.027* | *0.017* | | *0.054* | *0.019* | *0.009* |
| **3** | **Greater Accra** | **2,889,122** | **0.126** | **0.037** | **0.016** | **2,533,079** | **0.099** | **0.028** | **0.012** | **356,043** | **0.316** | **0.101** | **0.045** |
| | | | ***0.018*** | ***0.007*** | ***0.003*** | | ***0.016*** | ***0.006*** | ***0.003*** | | ***0.035*** | ***0.015*** | ***0.008*** |
| 301 | Accra | 1,647,202 | 0.052 | 0.012 | 0.004 | 1,647,202 | 0.052 | 0.012 | 0.004 | n/a | n/a | n/a | n/a |
| | | | *0.009* | *0.002* | *0.001* | | *0.009* | *0.002* | *0.001* | | | | |

**Annexe 11.3  Regional and District Level Poverty Estimates, by Urban/Rural** (_cont'd_)

| District | | | Total | | | Urban | | | | Rural | | | |
|---|---|---|---|---|---|---|---|---|---|---|---|---|---|
| ID | Name | Population | P0 | P1 | P2 | Population | P0 | P1 | P2 | Population | P0 | P1 | P2 |
| 302 | Ga | 549,049 | 0.237 | 0.076 | 0.035 | 400,960 | 0.215 | 0.069 | 0.033 | 148,089 | 0.297 | 0.094 | 0.042 |
| | | | _0.031_ | _0.014_ | _0.008_ | | _0.032_ | _0.014_ | _0.008_ | | _0.030_ | _0.013_ | _0.007_ |
| 303 | Tema | 503,627 | 0.154 | 0.044 | 0.019 | 445,372 | 0.153 | 0.044 | 0.020 | 58,255 | 0.164 | 0.044 | 0.018 |
| | | | _0.027_ | _0.010_ | _0.005_ | | _0.026_ | _0.009_ | _0.005_ | | _0.036_ | _0.011_ | _0.005_ |
| 304 | Dangbe West | 96,309 | 0.353 | 0.119 | 0.055 | 22,749 | 0.270 | 0.088 | 0.042 | 73,560 | 0.378 | 0.128 | 0.060 |
| | | | _0.043_ | _0.020_ | _0.011_ | | _0.036_ | _0.016_ | _0.009_ | | _0.045_ | _0.021_ | _0.012_ |
| 305 | Dangbe East | 92,935 | 0.387 | 0.126 | 0.057 | 16,796 | 0.289 | 0.096 | 0.046 | 76,139 | 0.408 | 0.133 | 0.060 |
| | | | _0.058_ | _0.025_ | _0.013_ | | _0.041_ | _0.018_ | _0.011_ | | _0.062_ | _0.026_ | _0.014_ |
| **4** | **Volta** | **1,629,523** | **0.495** | **0.185** | **0.093** | **436,925** | **0.431** | **0.170** | **0.090** | **1,192,598** | **0.519** | **0.190** | **0.093** |
| | | | _**0.040**_ | _**0.023**_ | _**0.015**_ | | _**0.046**_ | _**0.027**_ | _**0.018**_ | | _**0.038**_ | _**0.021**_ | _**0.013**_ |
| 401 | South Tongu | 64,613 | 0.493 | 0.178 | 0.087 | 7,213 | 0.388 | 0.138 | 0.068 | 57,400 | 0.506 | 0.183 | 0.089 |
| | | | _0.040_ | _0.022_ | _0.014_ | | _0.067_ | _0.033_ | _0.020_ | | _0.036_ | _0.021_ | _0.013_ |
| 402 | Keta | 132,800 | 0.458 | 0.164 | 0.080 | 70,780 | 0.427 | 0.153 | 0.077 | 62,020 | 0.494 | 0.177 | 0.084 |
| | | | _0.047_ | _0.025_ | _0.015_ | | _0.049_ | _0.025_ | _0.016_ | | _0.045_ | _0.024_ | _0.014_ |
| 403 | Ketu | 237,457 | 0.494 | 0.181 | 0.089 | 82,249 | 0.394 | 0.143 | 0.072 | 155,208 | 0.547 | 0.201 | 0.098 |
| | | | _0.044_ | _0.025_ | _0.015_ | | _0.043_ | _0.020_ | _0.012_ | | _0.044_ | _0.027_ | _0.017_ |
| 404 | Akatsi | 93,397 | 0.538 | 0.191 | 0.092 | 19,528 | 0.501 | 0.196 | 0.104 | 73,869 | 0.548 | 0.190 | 0.089 |
| | | | _0.043_ | _0.025_ | _0.015_ | | _0.045_ | _0.026_ | _0.018_ | | _0.043_ | _0.024_ | _0.014_ |
| 405 | North Tongu | 130,106 | 0.511 | 0.181 | 0.087 | 25,239 | 0.432 | 0.161 | 0.083 | 104,867 | 0.530 | 0.186 | 0.088 |
| | | | _0.044_ | _0.024_ | _0.015_ | | _0.053_ | _0.028_ | _0.017_ | | _0.042_ | _0.024_ | _0.014_ |
| 406 | Ho | 233,277 | 0.443 | 0.167 | 0.085 | 79,514 | 0.298 | 0.119 | 0.066 | 153,763 | 0.518 | 0.192 | 0.095 |
| | | | _0.043_ | _0.023_ | _0.015_ | | _0.047_ | _0.025_ | _0.016_ | | _0.040_ | _0.023_ | _0.014_ |
| 407 | Hohoe | 112,198 | 0.501 | 0.192 | 0.099 | 22,380 | 0.415 | 0.184 | 0.108 | 89,818 | 0.523 | 0.194 | 0.097 |
| | | | _0.042_ | _0.025_ | _0.017_ | | _0.047_ | _0.032_ | _0.024_ | | _0.040_ | _0.024_ | _0.015_ |
| 408 | Kpandu | 152,453 | 0.414 | 0.143 | 0.068 | 34,804 | 0.300 | 0.113 | 0.060 | 117,649 | 0.447 | 0.152 | 0.071 |
| | | | _0.046_ | _0.022_ | _0.012_ | | _0.049_ | _0.024_ | _0.015_ | | _0.045_ | _0.021_ | _0.012_ |

**Annexe 11.3 Regional and District Level Poverty Estimates, by Urban/Rural** *(cont'd)*

| District | | | Total | | | Urban | | | | Rural | | | |
|---|---|---|---|---|---|---|---|---|---|---|---|---|---|
| ID | Name | Population | P0 | P1 | P2 | Population | P0 | P1 | P2 | Population | P0 | P1 | P2 |
| 409 | Jasikan | 111,021 | 0.534 | 0.210 | 0.111 | 22,054 | 0.574 | 0.277 | 0.171 | 88,967 | 0.524 | 0.194 | 0.097 |
| | | | *0.042* | *0.026* | *0.018* | | *0.058* | *0.043* | *0.034* | | *0.038* | *0.022* | *0.014* |
| 410 | Kadjebi | 51,918 | 0.535 | 0.202 | 0.102 | 8,230 | 0.329 | 0.087 | 0.034 | 43,688 | 0.574 | 0.224 | 0.115 |
| | | | *0.046* | *0.024* | *0.015* | | *0.063* | *0.022* | *0.010* | | *0.043* | *0.025* | *0.016* |
| 411 | Nkwanta | 150,588 | 0.631 | 0.263 | 0.140 | 35,262 | 0.810 | 0.368 | 0.203 | 115,326 | 0.576 | 0.230 | 0.121 |
| | | | *0.046* | *0.034* | *0.024* | | *0.079* | *0.073* | *0.054* | | *0.036* | *0.022* | *0.015* |
| 412 | Krachi | 159,695 | 0.474 | 0.172 | 0.085 | 29,672 | 0.507 | 0.181 | 0.087 | 130,023 | 0.467 | 0.170 | 0.084 |
| | | | *0.041* | *0.021* | *0.012* | | *0.058* | *0.031* | *0.019* | | *0.037* | *0.018* | *0.011* |
| **5** | **Eastern** | **2,103,376** | **0.389** | **0.135** | **0.065** | **724,314** | **0.287** | **0.100** | **0.050** | **1,379,062** | **0.443** | **0.153** | **0.073** |
| | | | ***0.035*** | ***0.017*** | ***0.010*** | | ***0.034*** | ***0.015*** | ***0.009*** | | ***0.036*** | ***0.018*** | ***0.010*** |
| 501 | Birim North | 124,016 | 0.471 | 0.166 | 0.079 | 12,124 | 0.292 | 0.102 | 0.050 | 111,892 | 0.490 | 0.172 | 0.083 |
| | | | *0.042* | *0.021* | *0.013* | | *0.073* | *0.033* | *0.020* | | *0.039* | *0.020* | *0.012* |
| 502 | Birim South | 178,920 | 0.421 | 0.153 | 0.076 | 87,490 | 0.354 | 0.136 | 0.072 | 91,430 | 0.485 | 0.169 | 0.080 |
| | | | *0.035* | *0.019* | *0.012* | | *0.033* | *0.018* | *0.012* | | *0.038* | *0.020* | *0.012* |
| 503 | West Akim | 154,107 | 0.432 | 0.153 | 0.074 | 49,225 | 0.290 | 0.104 | 0.052 | 104,882 | 0.498 | 0.176 | 0.084 |
| | | | *0.040* | *0.021* | *0.012* | | *0.037* | *0.018* | *0.011* | | *0.042* | *0.022* | *0.013* |
| 504 | Kwaebibirem | 179,246 | 0.379 | 0.132 | 0.064 | 69,419 | 0.319 | 0.121 | 0.064 | 109,827 | 0.417 | 0.139 | 0.064 |
| | | | *0.037* | *0.018* | *0.011* | | *0.034* | *0.018* | *0.011* | | *0.039* | *0.018* | *0.010* |
| 505 | Suhum | 165,651 | 0.450 | 0.161 | 0.080 | 35,989 | 0.343 | 0.145 | 0.084 | 129,662 | 0.480 | 0.166 | 0.078 |
| | | | *0.042* | *0.022* | *0.013* | | *0.035* | *0.019* | *0.013* | | *0.044* | *0.023* | *0.013* |
| 506 | East Akim | 190,279 | 0.395 | 0.138 | 0.068 | 70,492 | 0.396 | 0.152 | 0.080 | 119,787 | 0.394 | 0.130 | 0.060 |
| | | | *0.036* | *0.018* | *0.011* | | *0.038* | *0.020* | *0.013* | | *0.036* | *0.016* | *0.009* |
| 507 | Fanteakwa | 86,708 | 0.465 | 0.166 | 0.081 | 15,906 | 0.443 | 0.170 | 0.089 | 70,802 | 0.471 | 0.165 | 0.079 |
| | | | *0.041* | *0.021* | *0.013* | | *0.041* | *0.022* | *0.014* | | *0.041* | *0.021* | *0.012* |
| 508 | New Juaben | 135,324 | 0.158 | 0.045 | 0.020 | 112,647 | 0.138 | 0.039 | 0.017 | 22,677 | 0.259 | 0.077 | 0.034 |
| | | | *0.026* | *0.010* | *0.005* | | *0.023* | *0.008* | *0.004* | | *0.040* | *0.016* | *0.008* |

**Annexe 11.3  Regional and District Level Poverty Estimates, by Urban/Rural (cont'd)**

| ID | Name | Total Population | P0 | P1 | P2 | Urban Population | P0 | P1 | P2 | Rural Population | P0 | P1 | P2 |
|---|---|---|---|---|---|---|---|---|---|---|---|---|---|
| 509 | Akwapim South | 115,049 | 0.290 | 0.088 | 0.039 | 52,553 | 0.181 | 0.052 | 0.023 | 62,496 | 0.382 | 0.118 | 0.052 |
|  |  |  | *0.035* | *0.015* | *0.008* |  | *0.029* | *0.010* | *0.005* |  | *0.041* | *0.018* | *0.010* |
| 510 | Akwapim North | 105,538 | 0.314 | 0.099 | 0.045 | 31,995 | 0.271 | 0.087 | 0.040 | 73,543 | 0.333 | 0.105 | 0.047 |
|  |  |  | *0.035* | *0.016* | *0.009* |  | *0.035* | *0.016* | *0.009* |  | *0.035* | *0.015* | *0.009* |
| 511 | Yilo Krobo | 85,724 | 0.242 | 0.068 | 0.029 | 15,319 | 0.190 | 0.056 | 0.025 | 70,405 | 0.253 | 0.071 | 0.029 |
|  |  |  | *0.041* | *0.015* | *0.007* |  | *0.033* | *0.013* | *0.007* |  | *0.043* | *0.015* | *0.007* |
| 512 | Manya Krobo | 153,990 | 0.431 | 0.147 | 0.069 | 61,358 | 0.291 | 0.074 | 0.028 | 92,632 | 0.524 | 0.195 | 0.097 |
|  |  |  | *0.044* | *0.020* | *0.011* |  | *0.056* | *0.019* | *0.008* |  | *0.037* | *0.020* | *0.012* |
| 513 | Asugyaman | 75,523 | 0.452 | 0.156 | 0.074 | 19,695 | 0.343 | 0.091 | 0.035 | 55,828 | 0.491 | 0.179 | 0.089 |
|  |  |  | *0.050* | *0.022* | *0.012* |  | *0.066* | *0.023* | *0.010* |  | *0.045* | *0.022* | *0.013* |
| 514 | Afram Plains | 135,854 | 0.462 | 0.166 | 0.081 | 6,885 | 0.339 | 0.092 | 0.036 | 128,969 | 0.469 | 0.170 | 0.083 |
|  |  |  | *0.041* | *0.019* | *0.011* |  | *0.079* | *0.030* | *0.015* |  | *0.039* | *0.019* | *0.011* |
| 515 | Kwahu South | 217,447 | 0.406 | 0.145 | 0.071 | 83,217 | 0.314 | 0.115 | 0.059 | 134,230 | 0.464 | 0.164 | 0.079 |
|  |  |  | *0.037* | *0.019* | *0.011* |  | *0.038* | *0.018* | *0.011* |  | *0.036* | *0.019* | *0.011* |
| **6** | **Ashanti** | **3,590,511** | **0.272** | **0.090** | **0.042** | **1,832,441** | **0.141** | **0.047** | **0.023** | **1,758,070** | **0.407** | **0.136** | **0.063** |
|  |  |  | ***0.024*** | ***0.011*** | ***0.006*** |  | ***0.013*** | ***0.006*** | ***0.003*** |  | ***0.035*** | ***0.016*** | ***0.009*** |
| 601 | Atwima | 237,600 | 0.343 | 0.112 | 0.051 | 49,219 | 0.170 | 0.055 | 0.026 | 188,381 | 0.389 | 0.127 | 0.058 |
|  |  |  | *0.036* | *0.016* | *0.009* |  | *0.029* | *0.012* | *0.007* |  | *0.037* | *0.017* | *0.009* |
| 602 | Amansie West | 108,679 | 0.437 | 0.146 | 0.068 | n/a | n/a | n/a | n/a | 108,679 | 0.437 | 0.146 | 0.068 |
|  |  |  | *0.039* | *0.018* | *0.010* |  |  |  |  |  | *0.039* | *0.018* | *0.010* |
| 603 | Amansie East | 224,830 | 0.380 | 0.121 | 0.055 | 27,253 | 0.259 | 0.086 | 0.041 | 197,577 | 0.397 | 0.126 | 0.056 |
|  |  |  | *0.037* | *0.016* | *0.009* |  | *0.030* | *0.014* | *0.008* |  | *0.038* | *0.017* | *0.009* |
| 604 | Adansi West | 229,061 | 0.225 | 0.071 | 0.032 | 136,172 | 0.122 | 0.037 | 0.017 | 92,889 | 0.376 | 0.121 | 0.055 |
|  |  |  | *0.024* | *0.010* | *0.005* |  | *0.015* | *0.006* | *0.003* |  | *0.036* | *0.016* | *0.009* |
| 605 | Adansi East | 129,249 | 0.446 | 0.151 | 0.071 | 9,616 | 0.248 | 0.078 | 0.036 | 119,633 | 0.462 | 0.157 | 0.074 |
|  |  |  | *0.038* | *0.018* | *0.010* |  | *0.036* | *0.015* | *0.009* |  | *0.039* | *0.018* | *0.010* |

**Annexe 11.3   Regional and District Level Poverty Estimates, by Urban/Rural** (*cont'd*)

| ID | Name | Population | Total P0 | P1 | P2 | Urban Population | P0 | P1 | P2 | Rural Population | P0 | P1 | P2 |
|---|---|---|---|---|---|---|---|---|---|---|---|---|---|
| 606 | Ashanti Akim S | 96,833 | 0.383 | 0.123 | 0.056 | 15,965 | 0.337 | 0.109 | 0.051 | 80,868 | 0.392 | 0.126 | 0.057 |
| | | | *0.042* | *0.018* | *0.010* | | *0.055* | *0.025* | *0.014* | | *0.039* | *0.017* | *0.009* |
| 607 | Ashanti Akim N | 125,817 | 0.341 | 0.116 | 0.056 | 70,055 | 0.316 | 0.114 | 0.058 | 55,762 | 0.371 | 0.118 | 0.053 |
| | | | *0.035* | *0.016* | *0.009* | | *0.028* | *0.014* | *0.009* | | *0.043* | *0.018* | *0.009* |
| 608 | Ejisu/Juaben | 123,761 | 0.328 | 0.105 | 0.048 | 32,881 | 0.265 | 0.088 | 0.042 | 90,880 | 0.351 | 0.111 | 0.050 |
| | | | *0.037* | *0.016* | *0.008* | | *0.033* | *0.015* | *0.009* | | *0.038* | *0.016* | *0.008* |
| 609 | Bosomtwi | 145,918 | 0.347 | 0.109 | 0.048 | 7,368 | 0.321 | 0.095 | 0.041 | 138,550 | 0.348 | 0.109 | 0.049 |
| | | | *0.039* | *0.016* | *0.008* | | *0.053* | *0.023* | *0.013* | | *0.039* | *0.016* | *0.008* |
| 610 | Kumasi | 1,162,408 | 0.077 | 0.022 | 0.009 | 1,162,408 | 0.077 | 0.022 | 0.009 | n/a | n/a | n/a | n/a |
| | | | *0.011* | *0.004* | *0.002* | | *0.011* | *0.004* | *0.002* | | | | |
| 611 | Afigya/Kwabre | 164,454 | 0.229 | 0.071 | 0.031 | 63,923 | 0.094 | 0.028 | 0.012 | 100,531 | 0.316 | 0.098 | 0.044 |
| | | | *0.029* | *0.011* | *0.006* | | *0.016* | *0.006* | *0.003* | | *0.036* | *0.014* | *0.007* |
| 612 | Afigya Sekyere | 118,775 | 0.403 | 0.138 | 0.066 | 42,041 | 0.402 | 0.144 | 0.072 | 76,734 | 0.404 | 0.135 | 0.063 |
| | | | *0.042* | *0.020* | *0.011* | | *0.040* | *0.020* | *0.012* | | *0.043* | *0.020* | *0.011* |
| 613 | Sekyere East | 156,969 | 0.430 | 0.153 | 0.075 | 52,738 | 0.343 | 0.116 | 0.056 | 104,231 | 0.474 | 0.172 | 0.084 |
| | | | *0.039* | *0.020* | *0.012* | | *0.040* | *0.018* | *0.011* | | *0.038* | *0.020* | *0.013* |
| 614 | Sekyere West | 142,126 | 0.418 | 0.158 | 0.081 | 54,827 | 0.336 | 0.139 | 0.077 | 87,299 | 0.469 | 0.169 | 0.083 |
| | | | *0.034* | *0.020* | *0.013* | | *0.025* | *0.017* | *0.013* | | *0.040* | *0.021* | *0.013* |
| 615 | Ejura/Sekyedu | 80,694 | 0.397 | 0.152 | 0.078 | 39,206 | 0.201 | 0.063 | 0.029 | 41,488 | 0.583 | 0.236 | 0.125 |
| | | | *0.038* | *0.021* | *0.014* | | *0.032* | *0.013* | *0.007* | | *0.044* | *0.029* | *0.020* |
| 616 | Offinso | 137,973 | 0.444 | 0.163 | 0.082 | 42,661 | 0.463 | 0.189 | 0.104 | 95,312 | 0.435 | 0.152 | 0.073 |
| | | | *0.037* | *0.020* | *0.012* | | *0.040* | *0.023* | *0.017* | | *0.036* | *0.018* | *0.011* |
| 617 | Ahafo Ano South | 133,508 | 0.434 | 0.147 | 0.069 | 12,313 | 0.543 | 0.236 | 0.133 | 121,195 | 0.423 | 0.138 | 0.063 |
| | | | *0.041* | *0.021* | *0.013* | | *0.065* | *0.051* | *0.038* | | *0.039* | *0.018* | *0.010* |
| 618 | Ahafo Ano North | 71,856 | 0.385 | 0.126 | 0.057 | 13,795 | 0.231 | 0.074 | 0.034 | 58,061 | 0.422 | 0.138 | 0.063 |
| | | | *0.042* | *0.019* | *0.011* | | *0.027* | *0.011* | *0.006* | | *0.045* | *0.021* | *0.012* |

**Annexe 11.3   Regional and District Level Poverty Estimates, by Urban/Rural** (*cont'd*)

| District | | Total | | | | Urban | | | | Rural | | | |
|---|---|---|---|---|---|---|---|---|---|---|---|---|---|
| ID | Name | Population | P0 | P1 | P2 | Population | P0 | P1 | P2 | Population | P0 | P1 | P2 |
| 7 | **Brong Ahafo** | **1,812,472** | **0.435** | **0.157** | **0.078** | **676,690** | **0.318** | **0.107** | **0.051** | **1,135,782** | **0.504** | **0.188** | **0.094** |
| | | | *0.037* | *0.019* | *0.012* | | *0.040* | *0.019* | *0.012* | | *0.036* | *0.019* | *0.012* |
| 701 | Asunafo | 174,096 | 0.433 | 0.149 | 0.070 | 49,293 | 0.257 | 0.079 | 0.036 | 124,803 | 0.502 | 0.176 | 0.084 |
| | | | *0.042* | *0.021* | *0.012* | | *0.048* | *0.020* | *0.011* | | *0.040* | *0.021* | *0.012* |
| 702 | Asutifi | 83,979 | 0.457 | 0.160 | 0.076 | 12,903 | 0.296 | 0.087 | 0.038 | 71,076 | 0.487 | 0.173 | 0.083 |
| | | | *0.039* | *0.019* | *0.011* | | *0.054* | *0.022* | *0.012* | | *0.036* | *0.019* | *0.011* |
| 703 | Tanoso | 123,084 | 0.393 | 0.132 | 0.062 | 53,078 | 0.287 | 0.087 | 0.039 | 70,006 | 0.472 | 0.166 | 0.079 |
| | | | *0.045* | *0.021* | *0.012* | | *0.049* | *0.020* | *0.011* | | *0.042* | *0.022* | *0.013* |
| 704 | Sunyani | 178,531 | 0.276 | 0.091 | 0.042 | 131,867 | 0.203 | 0.062 | 0.028 | 46,664 | 0.483 | 0.170 | 0.082 |
| | | | *0.038* | *0.017* | *0.010* | | *0.036* | *0.015* | *0.008* | | *0.045* | *0.024* | *0.014* |
| 705 | Dormaa | 150,050 | 0.426 | 0.147 | 0.070 | 46,785 | 0.280 | 0.092 | 0.044 | 103,265 | 0.492 | 0.172 | 0.082 |
| | | | *0.041* | *0.020* | *0.012* | | *0.043* | *0.020* | *0.011* | | *0.040* | *0.021* | *0.012* |
| 706 | Jaman | 147,686 | 0.629 | 0.273 | 0.152 | 46,725 | 0.617 | 0.253 | 0.133 | 100,961 | 0.635 | 0.283 | 0.161 |
| | | | *0.038* | *0.030* | *0.023* | | *0.051* | *0.045* | *0.033* | | *0.032* | *0.023* | *0.018* |
| 707 | Berekum | 93,978 | 0.332 | 0.112 | 0.052 | 51,723 | 0.202 | 0.061 | 0.027 | 42,255 | 0.492 | 0.174 | 0.083 |
| | | | *0.041* | *0.019* | *0.011* | | *0.033* | *0.014* | *0.007* | | *0.051* | *0.026* | *0.015* |
| 708 | Wenchi | 166,354 | 0.468 | 0.168 | 0.082 | 49,570 | 0.408 | 0.130 | 0.059 | 116,784 | 0.494 | 0.184 | 0.092 |
| | | | *0.043* | *0.021* | *0.012* | | *0.055* | *0.023* | *0.013* | | *0.038* | *0.020* | *0.012* |
| 709 | Techiman | 175,170 | 0.347 | 0.125 | 0.061 | 97,812 | 0.191 | 0.064 | 0.031 | 77,358 | 0.544 | 0.201 | 0.099 |
| | | | *0.036* | *0.019* | *0.011* | | *0.029* | *0.013* | *0.008* | | *0.045* | *0.026* | *0.016* |
| 710 | Nkoranza | 128,626 | 0.515 | 0.194 | 0.097 | 37,398 | 0.559 | 0.216 | 0.109 | 91,228 | 0.497 | 0.184 | 0.092 |
| | | | *0.043* | *0.026* | *0.017* | | *0.054* | *0.038* | *0.027* | | *0.038* | *0.020* | *0.012* |
| 711 | Kintampo | 146,206 | 0.491 | 0.180 | 0.089 | 39,019 | 0.475 | 0.171 | 0.084 | 107,187 | 0.497 | 0.184 | 0.091 |
| | | | *0.041* | *0.022* | *0.014* | | *0.046* | *0.027* | *0.018* | | *0.039* | *0.021* | *0.012* |
| 712 | Atebubu | 162,634 | 0.464 | 0.166 | 0.081 | 53,477 | 0.427 | 0.128 | 0.054 | 109,157 | 0.482 | 0.185 | 0.095 |
| | | | *0.046* | *0.022* | *0.013* | | *0.060* | *0.027* | *0.014* | | *0.038* | *0.020* | *0.012* |
| 713 | Sene | 82,078 | 0.442 | 0.156 | 0.075 | 7,040 | 0.397 | 0.116 | 0.048 | 75,038 | 0.446 | 0.160 | 0.078 |
| | | | *0.042* | *0.019* | *0.011* | | *0.081* | *0.031* | *0.015* | | *0.038* | *0.018* | *0.010* |

**Annexe 11.3  Regional and District Level Poverty Estimates, by Urban/Rural** (cont'd)

| District | | Total | | | | Urban | | | | Rural | | | |
|---|---|---|---|---|---|---|---|---|---|---|---|---|---|
| ID | Name | Population | P0 | P1 | P2 | Population | P0 | P1 | P2 | Population | P0 | P1 | P2 |
| **8** | **Northern** | **1,807,615** | **0.695** | **0.325** | **0.190** | **476,041** | **0.570** | **0.212** | **0.104** | **1,331,574** | **0.740** | **0.366** | **0.220** |
| | | | *0.034* | *0.027* | *0.021* | | *0.049* | *0.028* | *0.018* | | *0.028* | *0.027* | *0.023* |
| 801 | Bole | 127,188 | 0.648 | 0.285 | 0.159 | 15,604 | 0.440 | 0.132 | 0.055 | 111,584 | 0.677 | 0.306 | 0.174 |
| | | | *0.038* | *0.025* | *0.018* | | *0.072* | *0.031* | *0.016* | | *0.033* | *0.024* | *0.018* |
| 802 | West Gonja | 138,701 | 0.572 | 0.234 | 0.125 | 19,898 | 0.496 | 0.157 | 0.068 | 118,803 | 0.584 | 0.247 | 0.135 |
| | | | *0.041* | *0.023* | *0.015* | | *0.074* | *0.035* | *0.019* | | *0.036* | *0.021* | *0.015* |
| 803 | Wast Gonja | 174,566 | 0.551 | 0.220 | 0.116 | 23,881 | 0.463 | 0.142 | 0.061 | 150,685 | 0.565 | 0.232 | 0.125 |
| | | | *0.040* | *0.023* | *0.015* | | *0.068* | *0.030* | *0.016* | | *0.036* | *0.021* | *0.015* |
| 804 | Nanumba | 143,866 | 0.712 | 0.323 | 0.184 | 28,308 | 0.691 | 0.277 | 0.142 | 115,558 | 0.717 | 0.335 | 0.194 |
| | | | *0.039* | *0.030* | *0.023* | | *0.056* | *0.040* | *0.028* | | *0.035* | *0.028* | *0.021* |
| 805 | Sabsugu-Tatale | 79,036 | 0.684 | 0.298 | 0.164 | 16,720 | 0.760 | 0.322 | 0.171 | 62,316 | 0.663 | 0.291 | 0.162 |
| | | | *0.046* | *0.032* | *0.022* | | *0.059* | *0.047* | *0.033* | | *0.043* | *0.028* | *0.019* |
| 806 | Chereponi-Saboba | 93,471 | 0.752 | 0.351 | 0.202 | 6,144 | 0.866 | 0.410 | 0.231 | 87,327 | 0.744 | 0.347 | 0.199 |
| | | | *0.036* | *0.033* | *0.026* | | *0.066* | *0.073* | *0.057* | | *0.034* | *0.031* | *0.024* |
| 807 | Yendi | 128,387 | 0.718 | 0.333 | 0.192 | 43,889 | 0.629 | 0.236 | 0.117 | 84,498 | 0.764 | 0.383 | 0.231 |
| | | | *0.038* | *0.031* | *0.024* | | *0.056* | *0.035* | *0.022* | | *0.028* | *0.029* | *0.024* |
| 808 | Gushiegu-Karaga | 121,117 | 0.857 | 0.459 | 0.287 | 23,545 | 0.926 | 0.492 | 0.297 | 97,572 | 0.840 | 0.452 | 0.285 |
| | | | *0.037* | *0.044* | *0.038* | | *0.047* | *0.071* | *0.061* | | *0.034* | *0.038* | *0.033* |
| 809 | Savelugu-Nanton | 90,202 | 0.672 | 0.293 | 0.163 | 32,574 | 0.544 | 0.178 | 0.078 | 57,628 | 0.745 | 0.357 | 0.211 |
| | | | *0.045* | *0.032* | *0.022* | | *0.072* | *0.038* | *0.022* | | *0.030* | *0.028* | *0.023* |
| 810 | Tamale | 292,151 | 0.565 | 0.226 | 0.120 | 196,126 | 0.461 | 0.148 | 0.065 | 96,025 | 0.777 | 0.385 | 0.231 |
| | | | *0.048* | *0.029* | *0.019* | | *0.056* | *0.027* | *0.015* | | *0.031* | *0.033* | *0.027* |
| 811 | Tolon-Kumbungu | 131,791 | 0.835 | 0.453 | 0.289 | 20,532 | 0.660 | 0.238 | 0.112 | 111,259 | 0.868 | 0.492 | 0.322 |
| | | | *0.036* | *0.042* | *0.037* | | *0.076* | *0.047* | *0.029* | | *0.029* | *0.041* | *0.039* |
| 812 | West Mamprusi | 114,220 | 0.800 | 0.405 | 0.246 | 18,038 | 0.683 | 0.290 | 0.156 | 96,182 | 0.822 | 0.426 | 0.262 |
| | | | *0.035* | *0.037* | *0.031* | | *0.053* | *0.041* | *0.030* | | *0.032* | *0.037* | *0.032* |
| 813 | East Mamprusi | 172,919 | 0.861 | 0.470 | 0.299 | 30,782 | 0.739 | 0.314 | 0.167 | 142,137 | 0.888 | 0.504 | 0.327 |
| | | | *0.031* | *0.041* | *0.037* | | *0.050* | *0.042* | *0.031* | | *0.027* | *0.041* | *0.038* |

**Annexe 11.3   Regional and District Level Poverty Estimates, by Urban/Rural (*cont'd*)**

| | District | | Total | | | Urban | | | | | Rural | | |
|---|---|---|---|---|---|---|---|---|---|---|---|---|---|
| ID | Name | Population | P0 | P1 | P2 | Population | P0 | P1 | P2 | Population | P0 | P1 | P2 |
| **9** | **Upper East** | **914,016** | **0.715** | **0.337** | **0.197** | **141,885** | **0.511** | **0.182** | **0.088** | **772,131** | **0.752** | **0.365** | **0.217** |
| | | | *0.035* | *0.03* | *0.023* | | *0.049* | *0.026* | *0.016* | | *0.033* | *0.031* | *0.025* |
| 901 | Builsa | 75,246 | 0.575 | 0.224 | 0.115 | n/a | n/a | n/a | n/a | 75,246 | 0.575 | 0.224 | 0.115 |
| | | | 0.039 | 0.024 | 0.016 | | | | | | 0.039 | 0.024 | 0.016 |
| 902 | Kassena-Nankani | 148,719 | 0.611 | 0.246 | 0.128 | 23,245 | 0.532 | 0.194 | 0.095 | 125,474 | 0.626 | 0.255 | 0.134 |
| | | | 0.050 | 0.032 | 0.021 | | 0.059 | 0.035 | 0.023 | | 0.049 | 0.032 | 0.021 |
| 903 | Bongo | 77,768 | 0.706 | 0.299 | 0.160 | n/a | n/a | n/a | n/a | 77,768 | 0.706 | 0.299 | 0.160 |
| | | | *0.051* | *0.036* | *0.025* | | | | | | *0.051* | *0.036* | *0.025* |
| 904 | Bolgatanga | 227,725 | 0.647 | 0.276 | 0.150 | 48,472 | 0.395 | 0.115 | 0.047 | 179,253 | 0.716 | 0.319 | 0.178 |
| | | | 0.043 | 0.030 | 0.021 | | 0.066 | 0.028 | 0.014 | | 0.037 | 0.031 | 0.022 |
| 905 | Bawku West | 80,109 | 0.832 | 0.419 | 0.251 | 7,747 | 0.847 | 0.408 | 0.234 | 72,362 | 0.830 | 0.420 | 0.253 |
| | | | 0.038 | 0.043 | 0.036 | | 0.071 | 0.075 | 0.059 | | 0.035 | 0.040 | 0.033 |
| 906 | Bawku East | 304,449 | 0.821 | 0.443 | 0.282 | 62,421 | 0.552 | 0.201 | 0.098 | 242,028 | 0.891 | 0.506 | 0.329 |
| | | | 0.031 | 0.037 | 0.033 | | 0.051 | 0.028 | 0.017 | | 0.026 | 0.039 | 0.037 |
| **10** | **Upper West** | **574,918** | **0.758** | **0.385** | **0.236** | **100,458** | **0.379** | **0.112** | **0.047** | **474,460** | **0.839** | **0.443** | **0.276** |
| | | | **0.058** | **0.044** | **0.033** | | **0.123** | **0.049** | **0.024** | | **0.044** | **0.043** | **0.035** |
| 1001 | Wa | 223,424 | 0.677 | 0.319 | 0.187 | 66,364 | 0.361 | 0.104 | 0.043 | 157,060 | 0.811 | 0.410 | 0.248 |
| | | | 0.071 | 0.045 | 0.030 | | 0.124 | 0.047 | 0.023 | | 0.048 | 0.043 | 0.034 |
| 1002 | Nadawili | 83,013 | 0.855 | 0.452 | 0.280 | n/a | n/a | n/a | n/a | 83,013 | 0.855 | 0.452 | 0.280 |
| | | | 0.040 | 0.043 | 0.035 | | | | | | 0.040 | 0.043 | 0.035 |
| 1003 | Sissala | 84,707 | 0.801 | 0.432 | 0.275 | 8,839 | 0.385 | 0.116 | 0.050 | 75,868 | 0.850 | 0.469 | 0.301 |
| | | | 0.054 | 0.046 | 0.037 | | 0.130 | 0.054 | 0.028 | | 0.046 | 0.045 | 0.038 |
| 1004 | Jirapa-Lambussie | 96,602 | 0.754 | 0.377 | 0.229 | 13,296 | 0.402 | 0.121 | 0.051 | 83,306 | 0.810 | 0.418 | 0.257 |
| | | | 0.069 | 0.053 | 0.039 | | 0.132 | 0.054 | 0.027 | | 0.059 | 0.053 | 0.041 |
| 1005 | Lawra | 87,172 | 0.836 | 0.454 | 0.287 | 11,959 | 0.449 | 0.141 | 0.061 | 75,213 | 0.898 | 0.504 | 0.323 |
| | | | *0.046* | *0.044* | *0.036* | | *0.139* | *0.061* | *0.032* | | *0.032* | *0.041* | *0.037* |

*Sources:* Author's calculation based on GSS, 2000 and Census 2000.

# 12 Budget Implementation & Poverty Reduction in Ghana

ANTHONY TSEKPO
& CHARLES D. JEBUNI

## 1. Introduction

A critical instrument available to government in the pursuit of the poverty reduction objective is fiscal policy — budgetary allocation and disbursement of budgetary resources. In recent times, the Government of Ghana adopted the Ghana Poverty Reduction Strategy (GPRS), which serves as the overall framework document for medium to long-term development policy in Ghana. Budget and macroeconomic policies are therefore to be derived from the GPRS. The GPRS is broadly speaking one of the poverty reduction strategy papers demanded by the IMF and the World Bank, which describe the country's macroeconomic, structural and social policies and programmes over a three year or longer horizon to promote broad-based growth and reduce poverty, as well as the associated external financing needs and major sources of financing. The GPRS has poverty reduction as its focus, suggesting that resource allocation within the context of the budget will recognize expenditures that are more likely to have significant impact on the poor or sectors and activities where the poor are expected to benefit most. Reviews of the GPRS indicate that macroeconomic considerations dominated the programme (see Killick and Abugre, 2001).

The budgetary process entails the consolidation of micro-level proposals through consultation with different Ministries, Departments and Agencies (MDAs) in order to produce an aggregate revenue and expenditure projection for the year. Incidentally, there are various obstacles to making the budget system pro-poor. The scope for expenditure analysis may be limited by informational and capacity constraints, or the fractured structure of the budget. Incentives created within the budget system may cause managers and public agents to fail to translate policy decisions into the desired resource allocations within sectors and across spending categories. At this time it will be legitimate to acknowledge that the objective functions of the different groups involved in the process may differ. But this is not explicitly reflected in the GPRS. The different MDAs present projects that are only remotely relevant to the poverty

251

reduction agenda, because donors have indicated that the GPRS is to be the vehicle for the disbursement of aid to Ghana. More significantly since the budget is about bidding for resources, the poor who are often under-represented and voiceless are logically unable to attract resources towards the amelioration of their conditions. Indeed, the stabilization and growth objective of the budgetary framework over the year makes it more logical for policy-makers to talk of wealth creation instead of poverty alleviation. Despite this logically sound argument, which tends to suggest that poverty alleviation may not have the necessary resources devoted to it, there are legitimate reasons why poverty alleviation may be central to budgetary decision-making.

The 2001 *World Development Report* has demonstrated that it is not possible to separate issues of achieving growth from the overall pattern of social progress and distribution. Higher growth will translate into expanded economic opportunities for the poor and this will be reinforced by improvements along the complementary dimensions of increased empowerment and security of the poor. For example, the importance of education for poverty reduction is echoed by the microeconometric evidence from Ghana and elsewhere (Christiaensen et al., 2002).

It is on the basis of this understanding that the Ghana Living Standard Surveys (GLSS) try to provide a disaggregated understanding of who the poor are, where they live, and their sources of livelihood. This engenders an exploration of poverty determinants, which includes but is not limited to the social sectors.

The essence of this study is to examine the contribution of budgetary policy towards relieving poverty among the poor in their different locations and sectors. The rest of the paper is organized as follows. Section 2 details the poverty profile of Ghana; section 3 examines resource allocation within the framework of the GPRS and the budget; section 4 reviews transfers to the local government sector; section 5 outlines the trends in discretionary government expenditure; section 6 presents empirical evidence on the benefit incidence of public sector spending in the education and health sectors and also the share of the agricultural sector in government expenditure; and section 7 outlines the preliminary conclusions and the gaps that need to be researched further.

## 2. Poverty Profile

According to the GLSS 4, the incidence of poverty follows a geographic pattern, but also relates to the economic activities in which households are engaged. In 1998–9 in particular, poverty was highest among food-crop farmers. The contribution of food-crop farmers to the national incidence of poverty was much in excess of their population share. Indeed, at the national level around 58% of those identified as poor came from households for whom food-crop cultivation was the main activity. Other groups with a noticeable incidence of poverty included export farmers, private informal sector wage employees and the non-farm self-employed. The non-farm self-employed constituted a big group. In 1998/9, over 24% of the poor in Ghana were from households engaged primarily in non-farm self-employment. Table 12.1 shows the distribution of the poor by economic activity in 1998/9, whilst Figure 12.1 shows the incidence of poverty by geographical region.

In Figure 12.1 below, it is clear that the incidence of poverty is lowest in Greater Accra and highest in the three northern regions of the country, namely, the Northern, Upper East and Upper West Regions.

**Table 12.1  Indices of Poverty by Main Economic Activity, 1998/9**
**Poverty Line — 900,000 Cedis**

| | Pop'n share | Average welfare[a] | Poverty indices | | | | Contribution to national poverty | | |
|---|---|---|---|---|---|---|---|---|---|
| | | | $P_0$ | $P_1$ | $P_2$ | $P_1/P_0$ | $C_0$ | $C_1$ | $C_2$ |
| Public sector empl. | 10.7 | 1773.6 | 0.227 | 0.048 | 0.016 | 0.212 | 6.2 | 3.7 | 2.6 |
| Private formal empl. | 4.9 | 2211.5 | 0.113 | 0.024 | 0.007 | 0.214 | 1.4 | 0.9 | 0.5 |
| Private informal empl. | 2.9 | 1631.6 | 0.252 | 0.074 | 0.030 | 0.294 | 1.9 | 1.6 | 1.3 |
| Export farmers | 7.0 | 1234.4 | 0.387 | 0.103 | 0.039 | 0.266 | 6.9 | 5.2 | 4.2 |
| Food-crop farmers | 38.6 | 964.0 | 0.594 | 0.240 | 0.124 | 0.404 | 58.1 | 66.7 | 72.2 |
| Non-farm self-empl. | 33.8 | 1644.4 | 0.286 | 0.086 | 0.035 | 0.300 | 24.5 | 20.8 | 18.0 |
| Non-working | 2.1 | 2485.2 | 0.204 | 0.074 | 0.035 | 0.365 | 1.1 | 1.1 | 1.1 |
| All | 100.0 | 1412.1 | 0.395 | 0.139 | 0.066 | 0.352 | 100.0 | 100.0 | 100.0 |

*Note:*  a)  'Average welfare' denotes the mean value of the standard of living measure, expressed in thousands of cedis.
*Source:*  Ghana Statistical Service (2000a).

**Figure 12.1:  Indices of poverty by region, 1991/2 and 1998/9**

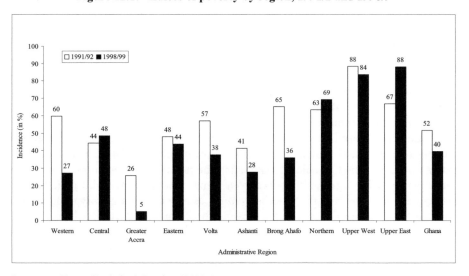

*Source:*  Ghana Statistical Service (2000a).

The GLSS 4 results also suggested that between 1991/2 and 1998/9, most groups experienced reductions in the incidence of poverty, but in differing degrees (see Table 12.1). Export farmers and wage employees in the private formal sector have experienced the largest reductions in poverty. Poverty levels fell among both wage employees in the public sector and the non-farm self-employed (though, over this period, the number in the former fell significantly, with a corresponding increase in the number working in non-farm self-employment). Among food-crop farmers, the incidence of poverty fell by 8.7 percentage points. This was quite a small change relative to other groups, and this is of concern, given the importance of this group and the very high level of poverty among such farmers. Food-crop farmers experienced a less than proportionate share in poverty reduction in Ghana.

The exception to the general reduction in poverty is with the non-working category. Though this group is small, and not disproportionately poor, it experienced a small increase in the incidence of poverty.

Overall, the GLSS4 results show that the declines in poverty were concentrated mostly in Western, Greater Accra, Volta, Ashanti and Brong Ahafo Regions. Some regions (Central, Northern, and Upper East) have experienced increases. Export farmers and wage employees in private employment enjoyed the greatest gains in their standard of living, while food-crop farmers, where poverty is the greatest, experienced the least gains.

## 3.    The Budgetary Process and the GPRS

In the GPRS, it was observed that in the past failure to allocate investment on the basis of a rational analysis of prevailing conditions led to very high deprivation in certain parts of the country, particularly the three northern regions and the Central Region. Capital investment in particular was skewed in favour of Accra, making opportunities, life style and quality of life in Accra much better than elsewhere in the country. The skewed capital investment also resulted in inadequate levels of economic infrastructure in Brong Ahafo, Volta and parts of Western Regions, for instance (Government of Ghana, 2003a: 31). Against this background the GPRS promises positive action to redress the imbalance, whilst acknowledging the limitations that can arise in the pursuit of such an objective within the context of a market-led economic regime.

Furthermore, the GPRS also recognizes the fact that sectoral and sub-sectoral allocations of government expenditure, including the donor components at the time the strategy was formulated, do not represent optimum distribution in support of poverty reduction and growth (ibid.: 41). Preparation of the GPRS was to a large extent undertaken by Ghanaian consultants. The process was touted as particularly participatory, with logistical support from some donors. Donors did their best to distance themselves from the process as much as possible, but history and practice point to the fact that donor influence cannot be completely avoided. The method suggested by the GPRS to tackle this problem is to integrate the prospective and medium-term planning which is statutorily located within the National Development and Planning Commission into the procedures for the Medium Term Economic Framework (MTEF) and the annual budget in order to produce a process jointly owned by the NDPC and the Ministry of Finance. The achievement of this objective will no doubt be affected by the institutional rivalry that appears to characterize the relationship between the NDPC and the Ministry of Finance (Killick and Abugre, 2001). The caveat is that there needs to be a timely release of funds to the MDAs to give meaning to the forward planning as envisaged under the MTEF.

Among the medium-term actions suggested to support long-term growth and poverty reduction, the GPRS is to target:

- a better sectoral composition of expenditure,
- a better balance between administrative and development costs, and
- a geographical distribution of expenditure that is sensitive to a rational assessment of the need for social protection and the potential for growth.

Specifically, the share of overhead (administrative) costs is expected to reach between 20 and 25% of total expenditure, with between 75 and 80% of total expenditure being applied to development costs. Between the social sector budget and the economic sector budget, the desired distribution of total expenditure is 60% and 40% respectively. These targets can only be achieved by consistent government efforts backed by donor co-operation.

**Table 12.2  Summary of Costs of GPRS Policy Actions and Programmes: 2003–5 (US$ m.)**

| Thematic Area | 2003 | 2004 | 2005 | Total | % of Total |
|---|---|---|---|---|---|
| Macroeconomic stability | 110 | 150 | 156 | 416 | 8 |
| Production and gainful employment | 434 | 491 | 503 | 1,428 | 27 |
| Human development and provision of basic services | 680 | 1,094 | 1,269 | 3,043 | 58 |
| Special programmes for the vulnerable and excluded | 66 | 61 | 40 | 168 | 3 |
| Governance | 75 | 75 | 77 | 228 | 4 |
| Total | 1,365 | 1,872 | 2,046 | 5,283 | 100 |

*Source:*  Government of Ghana (2003b: 15).

As part of its planning activities, the NDPC has calculated the estimated costs of the policy actions and programmes under the GPRS for the period 2003–5. Table 12.2 details the summary of the cost estimates as per thematic areas under the GPRS in the long term.

The challenge is to ensure that the planned medium-term expenditure begins the process of redressing the budgetary imbalance that led to the pattern of poverty observed across regions in the main economic activities outlined above. Thus, while the long-term programmes emphasize redistribution by allocating 58% of planned resources to human development and the provision of basic services, the costed medium-term priority programmes emphasize allocation of resources to production and gainful employment which is to receive 56% of all resources (i.e. US$1413 million out of US$2515.21 million budgeted) (see Government of Ghana, 2003b: 38).

It is important to observe that, as in the past, the cost of planned interventions far exceeds the financial resources available for realizing the objectives of the GPRS. Thus, despite the claims that current budget priorities fully reflect the GPRS, there is reason to believe that the constraints imposed by resource unavailability may induce re-prioritization by the Ministry of Finance and Planning which is responsible for determining the priorities, in consultation with sectoral groups within the context of the national budget and the resource envelope available to the public sector.

In addition, the implementation of the GPRS is meant to be decentralized. That is, the GPRS presents a general framework within which District Assemblies can develop their own plans that reflect local priorities. The NDPC co-ordinates plans developed at the level of the district assemblies and the regional co-ordinating councils. However, there are serious constraints and challenges at the district level that make co-ordination difficult. Often there is a lack of capacity and resources for formulating and implementing the district plans. Furthermore, programme implementation at the sectoral and the district levels frequently remains unsynchronized, as sector-wide approaches are often not incorporated in the district assembly budgets. Indeed, the central government budget and the district assembly budgets are independent of each other. Other resources that flow directly from donors, NGOs and other civil society organizations are more difficult to capture at the district assembly level. This presents serious difficulties in the implementation of the GPRS.

Furthermore, the medium-term priority programmes in production and gainful employment detailed in the GPRS appear to have very little direct effect on the lives of the poor. The programmes have the following objectives:

- modernizing agriculture based on rural development,
- promoting the development of agro-processing,
- increasing environmental protection through re-forestation,
- strengthening the private sector, and
- enhancing infrastructural development.

These objectives, targeted at the commercial farmers rather than the poor subsistence farmers, are clearly skewed towards promotion of the growth agenda. Growth is necessary, but undue emphasis on growth has a tendency to increase the incidence of poverty. The observation regarding the medium-term programmes may be adjusted by the annual programmes that are reflected in the budget. It is for this reason that we turn now to evaluate the performance of the budget as a reflection of the levels of transfers to the districts, the provision of social services and the allocation of resources to the agricultural sector as proxy for the provision of economic services to the poor.

## 4.    Transfers to District Assemblies

Public spending may influence poverty alleviation objectives at several levels including the overall spending plans of the government (aggregate fiscal policy), policy decisions funded in the budget and the flow of budgeted resources to MDAs' particular front-line service delivery institutions, whose activities directly impact the livelihoods activities of the poor. The overall framework document for guiding the medium to long-term policy decisions in Ghana is the GPRS. Thus, the budget and macroeconomic policy must flow from the GPRS. In this respect, the GPRS has identified three ways in which public spending programmes will benefit the poor and reduce poverty. These are:

(i)   expenditure targeted at providing basic social services to the poor and also assistance to enable the poor increase their production and productivity which ultimately affects the level of their incomes and assets;

(ii)  spending to improve the awareness and participation of the poor in the economy; and

(iii) spending to improve the performance of the public sector including institutions of governance.

Thus, examining spending levels relative to *ex ante* benchmarks for input use is fundamental to determining the cost-effectiveness of public expenditure. Unfortunately, constraints on data availability may not permit the conduct of such analysis. Analyzing the economic composition of spending within sectors can also expose problems of under-funding, especially on operations and maintenance spending in areas that are likely to help alleviate poverty. Planned spending can also be broken down by level of service and region to assess its distributional impact and equity.

Even if budget allocations reflect poverty reduction priorities, the actual flow of resources to front-line service delivery agencies (MDAs) determines the extent to which stated budget objectives are realized during budget execution. This flow of resources can only be understood within the overall incentive framework of the budget process and the public sector as a whole. If the budget document is not credible, or if hard budget constraints at the sectoral level are lacking, then it is likely that ad-hoc reallocations of fiscal resources will reduce the financing levels for poverty-focused programmes. More generally, the degree of flexibility within the budget process and institutions influences fiscal outcomes (Alesina et al., 1996).

The starting point of the analysis is therefore the position of statutory transfers vis-à-vis contractual obligations (personnel emoluments), debt service and amortization, and agreements with bilateral and multilateral organizations for the provision of counterpart funding for projects.

Statutory payments cover transfers to local government including the District Assemblies Common Fund (DACF), revenues earmarked for special funds (Road Fund, GET Fund), social security contributions, and welfare and pension entitlements. Contractual commitments, on the other hand, cover the payment of personnel (and pension entitlements), debt servicing and amortization and, in some cases, contracts for the delivery of goods and services that extend between budget periods, and sometimes agreements with bilateral and multilateral agencies for the counterpart financing for projects and programmes. For the purposes of this study, we assume that the direct impact of statutory payments on poverty reduction will be observed in the transfers to the local government. Consequently, we analyze the local government expenditure allocation to observe the extent to which it reflects deprivation of district assemblies.

Central Government transfers as a source of revenue to District Assemblies in Ghana may be broadly classified as Grants, Ceded Revenue, District Assemblies Common Fund (DACF), Recurrent Expenditure Transfers, and Specialized Transfers, including timber, minerals and stool lands royalties, revenue from donor agencies, etc.

### Grants
Grants, under the present-day local government system, are block monthly releases from the central government to local authorities for the payment of such recurrent expenditure as salaries of staff on the pay roll of local government units.

### Ceded Revenue
Ceded revenue constitutes another significant source of central government transfers to local authorities. Ceded revenue is income hitherto derived from taxes on entertainment casinos, betting, gambling income, registration of trade, business, profession or vocation, daily transport and advertisements and collected by the central government, which, in turn, is shared among the total collections to the District Assemblies. Items under ceded revenue are therefore centrally collected by the Internal Revenue Service (IRS), and all such collections in a year are transferred to the Ministry of Local Government and Rural Development which in turn, shares the total collections among District Assemblies, based on a formula agreed upon by Cabinet (Asibuo, 2000) and ratified by Parliament.

### District Assemblies' Common Fund (DACF)
To make additional funds available to the District Assemblies to support their numerous development projects, the District Assemblies' Common Fund (DACF) was created under section 252 of the Fourth Republican Constitution of 1992. This fund represents not less than 5% of the total revenue of Ghana — i.e. all revenues collected by or accruing to the central government other than foreign loans, grants, non-tax revenue and revenues already collected by or for District Assemblies under any enactment in force to the District Assemblies for development. The collection and subsequent disbursement of the Fund commenced in 1994, based on a formula approved annually by Parliament. The District Assemblies' Common Fund Administrator, who is responsible for the administration of the Fund, is expected, by legislation, to submit the sharing formula to Parliament for ratification and approval, based on the following disbursement considerations: Need factor — 35%; Equalizing factor — 30%; Responsive factor — 20%; Service pressure — 15%.

Under the GPRS, the sharing formula of the DACF has been modified to accommodate poverty reduction and sustainable development. According to the DACF Allocation Report 2002, the following factors are now employed in the disbursement of the DACF:

1. Need factor — 50% with the following corresponding weights: health facilities — 12.5%; doctor/population ratio — 7.5%; education facilities — 12.5%; teacher pupil ratio — 7.5%; and potable water coverage — 10%
2. Responsiveness — 5%. This represents the level of improvement in local revenue generation with respect to a selected base year.
3. Service pressure — 5%. This factor takes into account the population of the district and the effect of the population on the services available in the district.
4. Poverty status of the district — 5%. This takes into consideration indicators such as number of schools requiring major rehabilitation.
5. Equalization — 35%. This is the share of the DACF distributed equally among the 110 districts.
6. Reserve — 10%. This is the proportion of the DACF set aside for emergency situations, and allocations to Regional Co-ordinating Councils and Members of Parliament.

## Other Central Government Transfers
The central government further collects on behalf of some District Assemblies, such revenues as timber, stool-land and mineral royalties, which are later transferred to the respective District Assemblies.

## Grants from Development Partners
Also, donor agencies such as the UK Department for International Development (DfID), the Danish Development Agency (DANIDA), the European Union (EU), the Canadian International Development Agency (CIDA), German Technical Assistance (GTZ), etc. provide specific funds to District Assemblies to support development projects being sponsored by such agencies in various localities in the country.

The analysis of transfers to District Assemblies compared mean central government transfers to the 110 District Assemblies over the period 1997–2000. Items included in the transfers analyzed include grants in respect of wages, grants to the DACF including the MPs common fund, ceded revenue and other transfers. Table 12.3 shows the per capita transfers from the central government to the District Assemblies between 1997 and 2000. It indicates that the per capita transfers to the districts increased spectacularly over this period. Furthermore, it shows that there is a considerable spread between the district(s) receiving the smallest transfers in each year and those receiving the maximum transfers. The difference between the minimum and maximum transfers over the period was statistically significant with a *p-value of 0.001*. The skewedness is relatively stable and positive which suggests that per capita transfers are more to the right of the mean.

**Table 12.3   Per Capita Central Government Transfers to District Assemblies:
              1997–2000**

|            | Transfers 1997 | Transfers 1998 | Transfers 1999 | Transfers 2000 | Average 1997–2000 |
|------------|----------------|----------------|----------------|----------------|-------------------|
| Mean       | 6,282.02       | 10,250.83      | 11,445.65      | 12,080.06      | 10,014.64         |
| Median     | 5,865.48       | 9,299.47       | 10,435.69      | 11,049.43      | 9,357.10          |
| Minimum    | 1,994.67       | 1,728.74       | 2,262.44       | 2,893.54       | 2,615.59          |
| Maximum    | 13,451.42      | 21,886.11      | 25,303.54      | 26,980.41      | 20,203.46         |
| Range      | 11,456.75      | 20,157.38      | 23,041.10      | 24,086.87      | 17,587.87         |
| Skewedness | .811           | .822           | .851           | .844           | .853              |

As indicated earlier, one of the bases for the allocation of public expenditure to meet the poverty reduction objectives is to make sectoral, sub-sectoral and regional expenditure allocations reflect the level of deprivation across the country. Different exercises have been conducted to determine the level of deprivation. The Ministry of Local Government and Rural Development (MLGRD) computed an index of deprivation based on the availability of certain basic services in the district capitals, which are to serve as central places of influence for smaller settlements in the district. Eight (8) main services and the level of urbanization of the district capital, measured by size of population, were used in the assessment of the level of development, namely: political and administrative; posts and telecommunication; health; education; electricity; water; judicial (excluding police service); banking; and population of the district capital. As part of the exercise the MLGRD scored all the districts on a scale between 8 and 141, the most deprived scoring 8 points, whilst the least deprived, Accra, scored 141.

In the GPRS the various regions were ranked according to the level of deprivation using levels of consumption, health, social infrastructure, education, economic infrastructure, and household budget, with the most deprived region scoring zero and the least deprived region scoring 20. A statistical test performed on the MLGRD and the GPRS indices shows that the two classifications are consistent with each other, suggesting that not much had changed from the computation of the first index in 1989 to the time the GPRS was compiled in 2001.

The set of correlation coefficients presented in Appendix 12.1 shows that there is an inverse relationship between the deprivation indexes computed by the MLGRD and the GPRS, on the one hand, and the mean per capita transfers to the districts. However, the relationship was statistically significant only in 2 years, namely 1997 and 1998. What this suggests is that, while transfers to the local government sector were generally sensitive to the poverty reduction agenda, the allocations to the district assemblies became inconsistent with the poverty ratings of the districts over time. Ranking of the most recent cumulative disbursement of the District Assemblies' Common Fund (1999–2003) presented in Appendix 12.2 supports our argument that allocations have not been consistent with the incidence of poverty in the districts.

Appendix 12.2 reveals that a significant number of poor districts, particularly those in the 3 northern regions, are among the lowest recipients of the DACF. Whilst the statistical test suggests that a central government transfer to the local government sector is consistent with the poverty reduction agenda, some may argue that the evidence provided is a reflection of the allocations of the DACF. Because the DACF is an important component of the transfers to the local government sector, this argument cannot be dismissed outright. However, the fact that there exists an in-built mechanism to redress the inequality in the local government sector is a boost to the poverty reduction efforts of government.

## 5.    Trends in the Functional Distribution of Discretionary Expenditure MDAs

The composition of spending on projects and/or programmes promotes efficient service delivery and the redistribution of resources and services towards the poor. Discussion of government spending is limited to discretionary spending because the government may not have control over the level of statutory spending. For the purposes of this analysis discretionary spending was equated with non-statutory spending. There are pitfalls in such a broad categorization. Item 1 — personnel emoluments — is non-statutory but government can hardly have any discretion about the payment of wages and salaries in the short run; in the medium to long run government can plan on retrenchment and closure of departments to cut down on the wage bill. Similarly, other contractual obligations like arrears owed to businesses in respect of supplies and contracts executed for the government are non-statutory spending, but there can be little or no discretion about spending in respect of such items. Interest on government debt is another area where the government will have little discretion. Interest must be paid even if the debt stock is repackaged to change the payment terms.

Ideally, budget proposals would compete for financing at the sectoral level according to the government's overall policy objectives and also the impact of projects and programmes on poverty reduction. Thus, social sector programmes will generally form significant components of the effort, but actions to promote growth and capacity-building, and other sectors which expand incomes of the poor, such as rural development, local infrastructure, private sector development for jobs, action to reduce insecurity; will usually be of equal importance in an effective programme of action to tackle poverty in all its dimensions.

However, the constraints imposed by the budget will inform the choices made by the government. Thus it is assumed that the government evaluates the links between poverty outcomes, on the one hand, and levers for public action, on the other when it details the target distribution of discretionary expenditure in the GPRS. As observed earlier, the target is to limit the share of overhead (administrative) expenditure to between 20 and 25% of total expenditure with between 75 and 80% of total expenditure being applied to development expenditure.

The empirical evidence available with respect to the functional distribution of budgetary resources is presented in Figures 12.2 and 12.3. Figure 12.2 shows the allocation of discretional expenditure to MDAs from the government's own resources; Figure 12.3 presents the allocation of total discretionary expenditure to MDAs, i.e. resources from Government of Ghana (GoG) sources and those mobilized from donor sources. Figure 12.2 shows that discretionary allocations from government sources are on target with respect to the share of resources allocated to the administrative sector. Allocation to administration has successfully been reduced from approximately 40% of GoG resources in 2001 to about 20% in 2003. This reduction in allocations to the administrative sector resulted in an increased allocation to the social services sector, which expanded from approximately 40% of GoG discretionary resources in 2001 to about 55% in 2003. The public order and safety sector also experienced an expansion in its share of GoG discretionary resources from approximately 10% in 2001 to about 17% in 2003. However, there has been virtually no change in the share of GoG discretionary resources allocated to economic services and the infrastructure sectors since 2000.

**Fig. 12.2: Trends in MDA Discretionary Expenditure (GoG): 1998–2003**

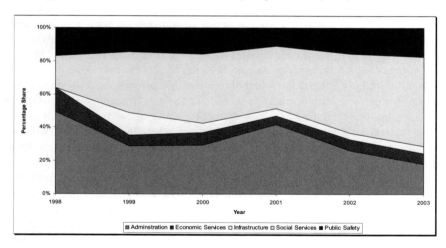

*Source:*   Various budget statements.

The redistribution of GoG discretionary resources suggests that the government has embarked on a consistent programme to provide essential services. The consensus on the impact of health and education spending outcomes on poverty is growing (see Christiaensen et al., 2002). The evidence from elsewhere suggests a direct link between public provision of these services and poverty outcomes. Indeed, community services like primary health care services, village water supply, and public drainage systems are critical in this respect, not only for their physical presence, but also the quality of these services, and, therefore, the institutional design of delivery mechanisms as well as funding (World Bank, 2000).

Figure 12.3 indicates the trends in the allocation of discretionary expenditure to

MDAs when all resources from GoG sources and Ghana's development partners were put together for disbursement. The figure shows that the share of the social services sector in total discretionary expenditure has been expanding since 2001, approaching approximately 40% in 2003. Similarly, the share of the infrastructure sector in total discretionary expenditure witnessed an increase in the flow of resources from approximately 10% in 2000 to about 14% in 2003. From Figure 12.3, it is also clear that the share of administrative costs in total discretionary expenditure declined from about 35% in 2000 to less than 20% in 2003. On the other hand, the share of the economic services sector in total discretionary expenditure expanded slightly between 2000 and 2002, but declined to approximately 10% in 2003. The question often asked is: how real are the observed shifts in public spending? It appears that the decline in spending on administration may be the result of a reclassification of expenditure items. Some of the expenditure classified under services and/or infrastructure may be directed towards the enhancement of the quality of work of public sector employees which may qualify as administrative expenditure. Examples of such spending may include expenditure on laptop computers, air conditioners, printers, fax machines, etc.,which are often applied to the personal businesses of public sector employees more than they are deployed in enhancing the quality of their official output.

**Fig. 12.3: Trends in MDA Total Discretionary Expenditure: 1998–2003**

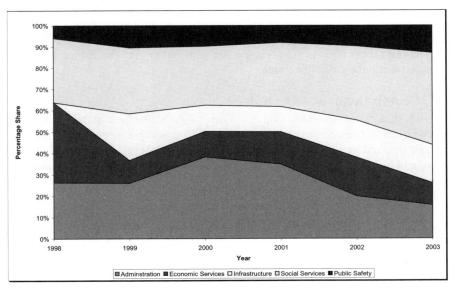

*Source:* Ibid.

The shifts observed in planned allocations may also be reversed as a result of the reallocation of resources during budget implementation. MDAs may re-prioritize their spending outcomes. Actual expenditure figures will not readily reveal the incidence of reallocation as they provide a snapshot of classified expenditure at the end of the financial year, without revealing the trajectory from allocation through reallocation within the budget to final figures. Audit reports which have not focused on the management of public funds are also unlikely to report on reallocations within the budget. A follow-up study to ascertain the degree of reallocation of resources within the budget would be ideal in a value-for-money evaluation of public sector spending.

It is important to highlight the disparity between the distribution of public spending when only GoG resources were analyzed, and that when total resources inclusive of donor funds were deployed. The proportion of public spending devoted to social services using only government resources expanded to 55% of total spending; however, when donor resources were pooled together with GoG resources, it increased to only 40% of the total. If the observed variation reflects donor preferences, then the composition of government spending may vary from time to time depending on the amount of donor resources that are available to support the government budget. This is a major challenge since donor pledges do not always materialize into actual resources.

Overall, the government appears to be on target with respect to a reduction in administrative expenditure while increasing social sector spending. However, the question is whether expenditure savings on administration and the expanded social sector expenditure really benefit the poor. Allocations as found in the budget are only indicative of government intentions. Actual spending outcomes may be more relevant in assessing the impact of government spending on poverty alleviation. Analysis of actual spending outcomes covering service delivery to locations and the distribution of spending across regions vis-à-vis income distribution, is certain to reveal more than planned budgetary allocations.

## 6.    Benefit Incidence Analysis

A review of service sector spending in the past suggests that the expanded allocation of resources to the sector may not necessarily be addressing poverty concerns. Canagarajah and Ye (2002) produce evidence to the effect that the regional subsidy per school-age child in the primary and junior secondary categories is lower than average in the three poorest regions of the country (see Figure 12.4).

It can be argued that the situation has not changed much since 1998. The Core Welfare Indicators Questionnaire for 2003 (GSS, 2004) shows a skewed distribution of access to primary schools. Access defined as the distance from households surveyed to the nearest primary school, may be considered as a proxy for the subsidy for primary education. At least the maintenance of school structures and teachers' wages are paid by the government in the majority of primary schools. The regional distribution of access presented in Figure 12.5 shows that more children in the poorest regions of Northern, Upper East and Upper West cover greater distances to access primary schools. The CWIQ 2003 also shows that more children in poor rural households are located further away from primary schools than all other children.

Canagarajah and Ye (2002) also observed that the distribution of classrooms and teachers did not favour the three poorest regions either. It was observed that the

**Figure 12.4: Regional Subsidy per School-age Child ('000 1998 Cedis)**

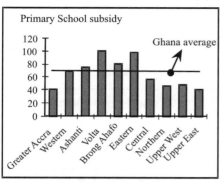
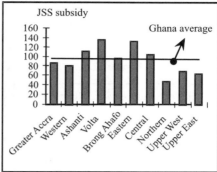

*Source:*Canagarajah and Ye (2002: 9–10).

**Figure 12.5: Distribution of Household Access to Primary Schools (in Minutes)**

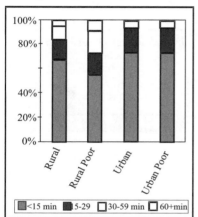
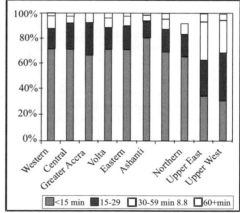

*Source:*Ghana Statistical Service (2004).

pupil-teacher ratio is high in the three poorest regions. Similarly, the number of school-age children per available classroom is relatively high in the three poorest regions compared with the other regions (see Figure 12.6).In the CWIQ 2003 there is evidence to suggest that the poorest regions are still disadvantaged as far as classrooms, availability of teachers and standard of teaching, supplies of books and other educational materials and of furniture and other facilities affecting education delivery are concerned. This is revealed in the percentage of children attending school who did not cite any problems whatsoever with school. As shown in Figure 12.7, the percentage of pupils who were satisfied with school at the time of the survey was lowest in the three northern regions. In the basic school system there were more dissatisfied students in Northern, Upper East and Upper West Regions than in the other regions. The level of dissatisfaction in the three northern regions was comparable only to the levels exhibited in the Volta Region which witnessed a significant decline in the incidence of poverty between 1991/2 and 1998/9.

Apart from the regional disparities in the distribution of teachers, classroom infrastructure and subsidies to the educational sector which suggest that the poorest

**Figure 12.6: Ghana: Teaching Capacity by Region**

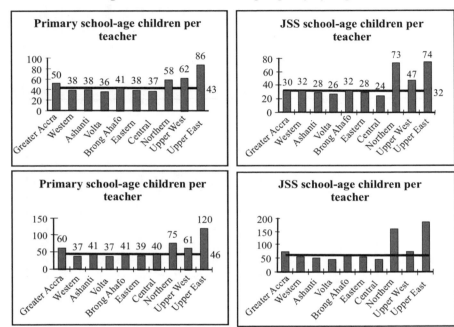

*Source:*    Canagarajah and Ye (2002: 9–10).

**Figure 12.7: Level of Satisfaction among School Pupils**

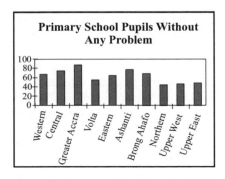
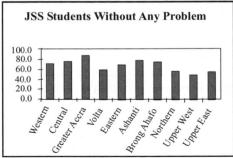

*Source:*    Ghana Statistical Service (2004).

regions benefited least from public spending, incidence analysis points to the fact that public spending benefited the rich more than the poor.

**Table 12.4   Allocation of Spending Subsidies 1989, 1992, and 1998**

| | % of subsidies captured Column share | | | | Share of subsidy to Share of children | |
|---|---|---|---|---|---|---|
| | 1989 | 1992 | 1998 | | 1992 | 1998 |
| *Primary education* | | | | | | |
| *Quintile* | | | | *Quintile* | | |
| *1* | 21.2 | 21.8 | 20.4 | *1* | 94 | 90 |
| *2* | 22.1 | 23.6 | 20.8 | *2* | 104 | 103 |
| *3* | 22.2 | 21.7 | 20.9 | *3* | 105 | 103 |
| *4* | 20.3 | 18.8 | 20.9 | *4* | 104 | 105 |
| *5* | 14.3 | 14.0 | 17.0 | *5* | 92 | 101 |
| *Total* | 100.0 | 100.0 | 100.0 | | | |
| *of which:* | | | | *of which:* | | |
| *Accra* | 6.3 | 5.3 | 7.4 | *Accra* | 74 | 82 |
| *Other urban* | 23.1 | 24.6 | 17.8 | *Other urban* | 102 | 101 |
| *Rural* | 70.6 | 70.1 | 74.8 | *Rural* | 102 | 102 |
| *Secondary education* | | | | | | |
| *Quintile* | | | | *Quintile* | | |
| *1* | 16.8 | 14.9 | 18.8 | *1* | 67 | 83 |
| *2* | 18.0 | 21.8 | 18.8 | *2* | 103 | 97 |
| *3* | 21.8 | 21.1 | 19.0 | *3* | 97 | 98 |
| *4* | 23.4 | 23.5 | 20.9 | *4* | 121 | 101 |
| *5* | 19.9 | 18.6 | 22.5 | *5* | 121 | 124 |
| *Total* | 100.0 | 100.0 | 100.0 | *Total* | | |
| *of which:* | | | | *of which:* | | |
| *Accra* | 11.1 | 12.0 | 14.9 | *Accra* | 135 | *121* |
| *Other urban* | 23.3 | 30.1 | 25.2 | *Other urban* | 110 | 119 |
| *Rural* | 65.6 | 57.8 | 59.9 | *Rural* | 91 | 90 |
| *Tertiary education* | | | | | | |
| *Quintile* | | | | *Quintile* | | |
| *1* | 7.7 | 6.0 | 12.5 | *1* | 39 | 66 |
| *2* | 3.8 | 9.5 | 10.9 | *2* | 56 | 56 |
| *3* | 19.2 | 19.0 | 21.1 | *3* | 100 | 109 |
| *4* | 19.2 | 20.2 | 19.2 | *4* | 91 | 95 |
| *5* | 50.0 | 45.2 | 36.4 | *5* | 170 | 165 |
| *Total* | 100.0 | 100.0 | | *Total* | | |
| *of which:* | | | | *of which:* | | |
| *Accra* | 42.3 | 27.4 | 41.8 | *Accra* | 258 | 318 |
| *Other urban* | 34.6 | 47.6 | 36.5 | *Other urban* | 178 | 156 |
| *Rural* | 23.1 | 25.0 | 21.6 | *Rural* | 40 | 34 |

*Source:*   Canagarajah and Ye (2002: Table 10, p.16).

Table 12.4, also adapted from Canagarajah and Ye (2002), shows the share of educational subsidy captured by population groups of different income levels and locations. It is apparent from the table that between 1992 and 1998, the benefit incidence of public primary school subsidies for the poor population (the bottom two quintiles) had either declined or stabilized, but had increased for the richest quintile. The authors concluded that, compared with other regions, Accra had greater gains proportionally in capturing the primary education subsidy, while the other regions remained the same. It was further observed that the primary education subsidies, while not particularly pro-poor, did serve more than three-fourths of children equitably. Public primary education has the most difficulty reaching the poorest of the poor, and had resulted in deterioration in the quality of the service in recent years. A similar bias against the poorest children in junior secondary schools was also observed.

It is more difficult to review the regional distribution of unit subsidies in the health sector but the little evidence seems to suggest that public spending on health services may not be affecting the poor in any significant way. The poor or rural population tend to use basic health-care facilities more than hospitals, although improvement in facilities between 1989 and 1998 was concentrated in the hospital sector which was more often patronized by the affluent rather than the poor (Canagarajah and Ye, 2002). According to the GLSS3 and GLSS4, the number of poor people who reported sick and attended health-care facilities actually declined between 1992 and 1998 compared with an increase in the attendance rate among the rich.

More significantly, however, the distribution of health subsidies among different income groups shows that the subsidy system favours the richest quintile, but with

**Table 12.5  Treatment Seeking among Self-reported Ill People**

| | % of | | | | | | | | |
|---|---|---|---|---|---|---|---|---|---|
| | Ill seeking no care | | | Ill seeking public health care | | | Ill seeking private modern health care | | |
| Expenditure quintiles | 1992 | 1998 | % change from 1992–8 | 1992 | 1998 | % change from 1992–8 | 1992 | 1998 | % change from 1992–8 |
| *1 — poorest* | 58.5 | 63.4 | 8.3 | 22.8 | 17.4 | −23.9 | 14.3 | 17.4 | 21.4 |
| *2* | 54.5 | 64.3 | 18.0 | 24.5 | 18.5 | −24.6 | 15.6 | 18.5 | 18.4 |
| *3* | 53.6 | 59.0 | 10.1 | 24.5 | 23.1 | −5.7 | 17.4 | 23.1 | 32.8 |
| *4* | 49.1 | 52.7 | 7.4 | 23.6 | 23.4 | −0.7 | 20.6 | 23.4 | 13.8 |
| *5 — richest* | 43.3 | 44.0 | 1.5 | 27.9 | 29.4 | 5.3 | 23.9 | 29.4 | 22.9 |
| *Urban* | 42.6 | 49.4 | 16.0 | 30.5 | 26.3 | −13.7 | 22.0 | 26.3 | 19.6 |
| *Rural* | 54.8 | 60.4 | 10.3 | 22.3 | 20.3 | −9.1 | 17.6 | 20.3 | 15.1 |
| Total | 50.8 | 57.6 | 13.4 | 25.0 | 21.8 | −12.8 | 19.0 | 21.8 | 14.8 |

*Source:*  Canagarajah and Ye (2002: Table 24, p.38).

a significant improvement in the middle expenditure group. In addition, rural areas gained significantly in their share of public subsidies between 1992 and 1998 (see Table 12.6).

Table 12.6    A Comparison of Benefit Incidence
of Public Health Subsidies

|  | 1989 | 1992 | 1998 |
|---|---|---|---|
| *1 — poorest* | 12.3 | 11.6 | 12.5 |
| *2* | 13.3 | 15.5 | 12.1 |
| *3* | 17.2 | 18.7 | 25.7 |
| *4* | 26.7 | 21.4 | 18.8 |
| *5 — richest* | 30.6 | 32.9 | 31.0 |
| *Urban* | 42.0 | 48.7 | 38.8 |
| *Rural* | 58.0 | 51.3 | 61.2 |

*Source*    Canagarajah and Ye (2002: Table 27, p.41).

The favourable change regarding rural residents is most likely the result of health reform programmes that promote basic health services in the rural areas. The authors concluded that the gains in the rural areas do not filter to the poorest of the poor. It should also be noted that, with a rural population of 70%, a 60% subsidy is still low. The observation that gains in the rural areas may not be reaching the poorest of the poor is significant. In 2003 the core welfare indicator questionnaire showed that only 38.5% of the rural poor consulted with public health service providers, compared with 45% among the urban poor and 41% of the entire population. However, the rural poor and rural residents in general consulted more with pharmacists and chemists who do not offer subsidized services (see Figure 12.8).

It is difficult to undertake incidence analysis for public spending in the economic services sub-sector. However, an examination of government expenditure on agriculture suggests that the sector, which embraces a high proportion of the poor, has witnessed a decline in the share of government spending (see Table 12.7). This decline is reflective of the stagnating expenditure on economic services as a whole. However, the recent efforts to assist cocoa farmers to improve crop yield and the support for the presidential initiatives on cassava and oil palm may lead to the recovery of government spending on agriculture.

It is important to point out that the kind of incidence analysis cited here to argue the case for the level of welfare distribution is constrained by the underlying assumption that there is no behavioural response on the part of recipients. Furthermore, evaluating a policy's impact requires assessing how different things would have been in its absence. But the counterfactual of no intervention is often tricky to quantify (see van de Walle, 1996).

**Figure 12.8:  Distribution of Health Consultations by Place of Residence**

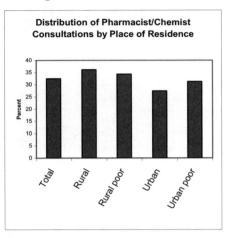

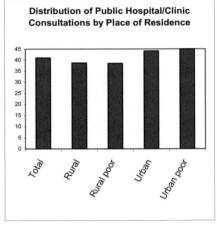

*Source:*   Ghana Statistical Service (2004)

**Table 12.7     Central Government Spending on Agriculture**

| Year | Agric as % of Total Expd. | Real Spending in Million Cedis |
|------|---------------------------|-------------------------------|
| 1983 | 10.4 | 586.5 |
| 1984 | 4.9 | 361.8 |
| 1985 | 4.2 | 419.0 |
| 1986 | 4.5 | 636.1 |
| 1989 | 0.5 | 790.8 |
| 1990 | 4.1 | 658.1 |
| 1991 | 3.6 | 661.2 |
| 1992 | 3.1 | 760.2 |
| 1993 | 2.8 | 769.4 |
| 1994 | 1.7 | 513.7 |
| 1995 | 1.7 | 455.1 |
| 1996 | 1.5 | 425.2 |
| 1997 | 1.9 | 785.1 |
| 1998 | 1.5 | 661.2 |
| 1999 | 1.3 | 536.7 |
| 2000 | 0.9 | 374.2 |

*Source:*   Oduro and Kwadzo (2003).

# 7.   Conclusions and Suggestions for Further Research

Due to data limitations, the conclusions as presented are preliminary in nature and may require further investigations. Two main conclusions stand out. First, there is an indication that transfers to the local government sector are sensitive to the poverty reduction agenda, although this conclusion may not be very robust as it is possible to argue that the evidence provided is a reflection of the allocation from the DACF. However, the fact that there exists an in-built mechanism to redress the inequality in the local government sector is a boost to the poverty reduction efforts of government.

Secondly, government resource allocation has also de-emphasized the allocation to administrative costs. In the same vein, allocation to the social sector has expanded considerably. These findings suggest that resource allocation is consistent with the long-term objectives of the GPRS and not the medium-term objectives, which seem to emphasize production and gainful employment. The caveat is that the reallocation we observe is not only a reclassification of expenditure but a real re-distribution in favour of activities that promote human development and give impetus to production and real growth of the economy.

It is also apparent that the expanded spending in the social services sector may not benefit the poor significantly, if past experience is taken as a guide. This assertion is supported by the preliminary results of the Core Welfare Indicators Questionnaire administered in 2003.

Overall, the analysis points to the fact that resource allocation is headed in the right direction but that people other than the poor enjoy the benefits. Ideally, the foregoing conclusions will be more relevant if it is possible to extend the coverage of the incidence analysis from 1998 to more recent times. The results of the CWIQ 2003 are indicative; however, the CWIQ is mainly a qualitative study and the results are not as robust when compared with the Ghana Living Standards Survey. Perhaps the most important task for researchers and policy-makers is to devise means to improve targeting in order to enable the poor to benefit more from the increased social sector spending.

One way in which the process of budget implementation will affect poverty reduction significantly is by improving the quality of public investment. If the quality of public investment has declined, the impact of the budget process on poverty reduction will be minimal. Apart from the evidence on the direction of public spending, a study of the productivity of public investment in Ghana is required to enable effective assessment of the impact of the budget on poverty reduction.

Beyond the productivity of public investments it is necessary to re-examine the incidence of regional inequality and how it affects the overall effort at poverty reduction. But more importantly researchers and policy-makers must investigate further how private sector investment can be stimulated to complement public sector investment in social services.

## References

Alesina, Alberto, Hausmann, Riccardo, Hommes, Rudolf and Stein, Ernesto (1996) *Budget Institutions and Fiscal Performance in Latin America.* NBER Working Paper 5586. Cambridge, MA: National Bureau of Economic Research.

Asibuo, S. K. (2000) 'Financial Capacities of District Assemblies' in W. Thomi, P. W. K. Yankson, and S. Y. Zanu (eds), *A Decade of Decentralisation in Ghana: Retrospect and Prospects.* Accra: Ministry of Local Government and Rural Development.

Canagarajah, Sudharshan and Ye, Xiao (2002) *Public Health and Education Spending in Ghana in 1992–1998: Issues of Equity and Efficiency.* Washington, DC: World Bank.

Christiaensen, Luc, Demery, Lionel and Paternostro, Stefano (2002) *Growth, Distribution and Poverty in Africa: Messages from the 1990s.* Washington, DC: World Bank.

Ghana Statistical Service (2000a) *Poverty Trends in Ghana in the 1990s.* Accra: GSS.

Ghana Statistical Service (2000b) *Ghana Living Standards Survey Report of the Fourth Round (GLSS4).* Accra: GSS.

Ghana Statistical Service (2004) *Core Welfare Indicator Questionnaire (CWIQ) 2003: Preliminary Results.* Accra: GSS.

Government of Ghana (2003a) *Ghana's Poverty Reduction Strategy 2003–2005: An Agenda for Growth and Prosperity,* Vol. 1 (Analysis and Policy Statement). Accra: Ghana Publishing Corporation.

Government of Ghana (2003b) *Ghana's Poverty Reduction Strategy 2003–2005: An Agenda for Growth and Prosperity,* Vol. 2 (Costing and Financing of Programmes and Projects), February. Accra: Ghana Publishing Corporation.

Government of Ghana (2003c) *The Budget Statement and Economy Policy of Government.* Accra: Ghana Publishing Corporation.

Government of Ghana (2002) 'Proposed Formula for Sharing the 2001 District Assemblies Common Fund'. District Assemblies Common Fund Administrator's Memorandum to Parliament, April.

Killick, Tony and Abugre, Charles (2001) 'Institutionalising the PRSP approach in Ghana'. Chapter 3, Final Report of PRSP Institutionalisation Study, submitted to the Strategic Partnership with Africa, 26 September.

Oduro, Abena D. and Kwadzo, George T-M. (2003) 'Impact of Agricultural Trade and Related Reforms on Domestic Food Security in Ghana'. A Paper Prepared for FAO, Rome, June.

van de Walle, Dominique (1996) *Assessing the Welfare Impacts of Public Spending.* Policy Research Working Paper No. 1670, Washington, DC: World Bank.

World Bank (2000) *Poverty Reduction Strategy Source Book.* Washington, DC: World Bank.

World Bank (2001) *World Development Report 2000/2001: Attacking Poverty.* Washington, DC: Oxford University Press for the World Bank.

## Appendix 12.1

### Correlations

|  |  | District Deprivation Index | Av. per capita Expenditure 1997–2000 |
|---|---|---|---|
| District Deprivation Index | Pearson Correlation | 1.000 | -.106 |
|  | Sig. (2-tailed) | – | .271 |
|  | N | 110 | 110 |
| Av. per capita Expenditure 1997–2000 | Pearson Correlation | -.106 | 1.000 |
|  | Sig. (2-tailed) | .271 | – |
|  | N | 110 | 110 |

### Correlations

|  |  | District Deprivation Index | Per capita Expenditure in 1997 |
|---|---|---|---|
| District Deprivation Index | Pearson Correlation | 1.000 | -.193 * |
|  | Sig. (2-tailed) | – | .043 |
|  | N | 110 | 110 |
| Per capita Expenditure in 1997 | Pearson Correlation | -.193 * | 1.000 |
|  | Sig. (2-tailed) | .043 | – |
|  | N | 110 | 110 |

\* Correlation is significant at the 0.05 level (2-tailed).

### Correlations

|  |  | District Deprivation Index | Per capita Expenditure in 1998 |
|---|---|---|---|
| District Deprivation Index | Pearson Correlation | 1.000 | -.190 * |
|  | Sig. (2-tailed) | – | .047 |
|  | N | 110 | 110 |
| Per capita Expenditure in 1998 | Pearson Correlation | -.190 * | 1.000 |
|  | Sig. (2-tailed) | .047 | – |
|  | N | 110 | 110 |

\* Correlation is significant at the 0.05 level (2-tailed).

### Correlations

|  |  | Av. per capita Expenditure 1997–2000 | Regional Deprivation Index |
|---|---|---|---|
| Av. per capita Expenditure 1997–2000 | Pearson Correlation | 1.000 | -.085 |
|  | Sig. (2-tailed) | – | .379 |
|  | N | 110 | 110 |
| Regional Deprivation Index | Pearson Correlation | -.085 | 1.000 |
|  | Sig. (2-tailed) | .379 | – |
|  | N | 110 | 110 |

### Correlations

|  |  | Regional Deprivation Index | Per capita Expenditure in 1997 |
|---|---|---|---|
| Regional Deprivation Index | Pearson Correlation | 1.000 | -.025 |
|  | Sig. (2-tailed) | – | .794 |
|  | N | 110 | 110 |
| Per capita Expenditure in 1997 | Pearson Correlation | -.025 | 1.000 |
|  | Sig. (2-tailed) | .794 | – |
|  | N | 110 | 110 |

### Correlations

|  |  | Regional Deprivation Index | Per capita Expenditure in 1998 |
|---|---|---|---|
| Regional Deprivation Index | Pearson Correlation | 1.000 | -.112 |
|  | Sig. (2-tailed) | – | .244 |
|  | N | 110 | 110 |
| Per capita Expenditure in 1998 | Pearson Correlation | -.112 | 1.000 |
|  | Sig. (2-tailed) | .244 | – |
|  | N | 110 | 110 |

**Appendix 12.1** *(cont'd)*

Correlations

| | | District Deprivation Index | Av. per capita Expenditure in 1999 |
|---|---|---|---|
| District Deprivation Index | Pearson Correlation | 1.000 | −.094 |
| | Sig. (2-tailed) | – | .327 |
| | N | 110 | 110 |
| Per capita Expenditure in 1999 | Pearson Correlation | −0.94 | 1.000 |
| | Sig. (2-tailed) | .327 | – |
| | N | 110 | 110 |

Correlations

| | | District Deprivation Index | Av. per capita Expenditure in 1999 |
|---|---|---|---|
| District Deprivation Index | Pearson Correlation | 1.000 | .018 |
| | Sig. (2-tailed) | – | .327 |
| | N | 110 | 110 |
| Per capita Expenditure in 2000 | Pearson Correlation | .018 | 1.000 |
| | Sig. (2-tailed) | .851 | – |
| | N | 110 | 110 |

Correlations

| | | Regional Deprivation Index | Per capita Expenditure in 1999 |
|---|---|---|---|
| Regional Deprivation Index | Pearson Correlation | 1.000 | −.048 |
| | Sig. (2-tailed) | – | .620 |
| | N | 110 | 110 |
| Per capita Expenditure in 1999 | Pearson Correlation | −.048 | 1.000 |
| | Sig. (2-tailed) | .620 | – |
| | N | 110 | 110 |

Correlations

| | | Regional Deprivation Index | Per capita Expenditure in 2000 |
|---|---|---|---|
| Regional Deprivation Index | Pearson Correlation | 1.000 | −.129 |
| | Sig. (2-tailed) | – | .178 |
| | N | 110 | 110 |
| Per capita Expenditure in 2000 | Pearson Correlation | −.129 | 1.000 |
| | Sig. (2-tailed) | .178 | – |
| | N | 110 | 110 |

## Appendix 12.2: Cumulative Allocation of DACF: 1999–2003

| DISTRICT | TOTAL | Rank | DISTRICT | TOTAL | Rank |
|---|---|---|---|---|---|
| Hohoe | 8,095,057,447.00 | 110 | Adansi East | 10,311,293,850.00 | 65 |
| Akuapem North | 8,382,832,311.00 | 109 | Akuapem South | 10,396,713,212.00 | 64 |
| Kpandu | 8,436,566,077.00 | 108 | Suh/Kra/Col. | 10,428,635,273.00 | 63 |
| Mpohor Wassa | 8,556,152,748.00 | 107 | Agona | 10,489,780,903.00 | 62 |
| Jasikan | 8,585,272,557.00 | 106 | Abura Asebu | 10,503,564,343.00 | 61 |
| Kadjebi | 8,603,010,338.00 | 105 | Gonja West | 10,516,758,170.00 | 60 |
| South Tongu | 8,691,546,709.00 | 104 | Nkwanta | 10,622,591,473.00 | 59 |
| Asi./Odo./Bra | 8,826,366,581.00 | 103 | Sekyere West | 10,639,647,068.00 | 58 |
| East Akim | 8,844,649,559.00 | 102 | Aowin Suaman | 10,666,812,947.00 | 57 |
| Sissalla | 8,848,676,300.00 | 101 | Jomoro | 10,715,060,695.00 | 56 |
| Domraa | 8,905,629,257.00 | 100 | Afigya Sekyere | 10,734,997,257.00 | 55 |
| North Tongu | 8,911,061,814.00 | 99 | Asanti Akim S. | 10,755,027,800.00 | 54 |
| Keta | 8,933,650,380.00 | 98 | Offinso | 10,776,473,802.00 | 53 |
| Jirapa Lambus | 8,961,443,166.00 | 97 | Awu.effu./Sen | 10,816,027,968.00 | 52 |
| U. Denkyira | 9,010,354,075.00 | 96 | Bole | 10,816,474,375.00 | 51 |
| Nadowli | 9,139,311,364.00 | 95 | Bosomtwi/Kwa | 10,843,175,899.00 | 50 |
| Wenchi | 9,154,260,110.00 | 94 | Kwaebibirim | 10,852,782,236.00 | 49 |
| Tano | 9,265,578,594.00 | 93 | Yendi | 10,866,470,021.00 | 48 |
| Wa | 9,296,510,050.00 | 92 | Kassena Nank. | 10,889,668,589.00 | 47 |
| Kwahu South | 9,343,963,625.00 | 91 | Ahafo Ano South | 10,892,210,968.00 | 46 |
| Twi/Hem/Low. D | 9,344,192,310.00 | 90 | Fanteakwa | 10,952,436,904.00 | 45 |
| Bib./Anw./Bek. | 9,360,641,222.00 | 89 | Assin | 11,013,850,614.00 | 44 |
| Ho | 9,367,616,753.00 | 88 | Afram Plains | 11,016,599,722.00 | 43 |
| Dangme West | 9,467,810,097.00 | 87 | Wassa West | 11,084,815,323.00 | 42 |
| Berekum | 9,526,762,422.00 | 86 | Sefwi Wiawso | 11,117,935,216.00 | 41 |
| Lawra | 9,534,990,541.00 | 85 | Kom/Edi/Egu/A | 11,129,554,605.00 | 40 |
| Amansie West | 9,565,370,809.00 | 84 | West Mamprusi | 11,137,629,793.00 | 39 |
| Manya Krobo | 9,600,787,226.00 | 83 | Akatsi | 11,183,014,498.00 | 38 |
| Asuogyaman | 9,604,941,400.00 | 82 | Amansie East | 11,225,957,998.00 | 37 |
| Busila | 9,691,714,522.00 | 81 | Asunafo | 11,253,779,779.00 | 36 |
| Jaman | 9,826,874,372.00 | 80 | Mfantsiman | 11,265,362,937.00 | 35 |
| Asanti Akim N. | 9,861,890,023.00 | 79 | Sene | 11,350,083,137.00 | 34 |
| Atebubu | 9,864,402,319.00 | 78 | Kwabre | 11,530,915,509.00 | 33 |
| Birim South | 9,867,562,516.00 | 77 | Zabzugu Tatal. | 11,560,834,817.00 | 32 |
| Krachi | 9,900,714,524.00 | 76 | Bawku East | 11,644,390,389.00 | 31 |
| Sekyere East | 9,979,494,792.00 | 75 | Dangme East | 11,704,359,633.00 | 30 |
| Kintampo | 10,026,572,078.00 | 74 | Techiman | 11,758,808,522.00 | 29 |
| Ej/Sekyedumasi | 10,039,781,452.00 | 73 | Birim North | 11,775,184,564.00 | 28 |
| Aju/Eny.essiam | 10,068,881,654.00 | 72 | Atwima | 11,851,873,260.00 | 27 |
| Savelugu Nan. | 10,108,273,819.00 | 71 | Wassa Amenfi | 11,962,143,886.00 | 26 |
| Sunyani | 10,155,450,004.00 | 70 | Bawku West | 12,006,213,380.00 | 25 |
| Ahanta West | 10,223,880,118.00 | 69 | Bongo | 12,132,420,715.00 | 24 |
| Nkoranza | 10,288,990,694.00 | 68 | Mamprusi East | 12,158,061,374.00 | 23 |
| Asutifi | 10,294,043,026.00 | 67 | | | |
| Soboba Cheri. | 10,307,236,400.00 | 66 | | | |

| DISTRICT | TOTAL | Rank |
|---|---|---|
| Gomoa | 12,190,974,671.00 | 22 |
| Adansi West | 12,209,157,957.00 | 21 |
| Gushiegu/Kara. | 12,313,875,948.00 | 20 |
| West Akim | 12,323,917,822.00 | 19 |
| Bolgatanga | 12,386,264,476.00 | 18 |
| Tamale | 12,479,218,942.00 | 17 |
| East Gonja | 12,610,659,327.00 | 16 |
| Nanumba | 12,701,868,687.00 | 15 |
| Ketu | 12,839,840,495.00 | 14 |
| Yilo Krobo | 12,871,530,607.00 | 13 |
| Ahafo Ano North | 13,135,227,284.00 | 12 |
| Nzema East | 13,197,035,084.00 | 11 |
| New Juaben | 13,326,886,814.00 | 10 |
| Juabeso Bia | 13,356,119,158.00 | 9 |
| Tolon Kumbu. | 13,532,330,991.00 | 8 |
| Cape Coast | 13,762,787,251.00 | 7 |
| Ejisu Juabeng | 14,062,554,179.00 | 6 |
| Shama Ahanta | 14,064,215,605.00 | 5 |
| Ga | 20,047,165,689.00 | 4 |
| Tema Munincipal | 20,141,566,681.00 | 3 |
| Kumasi Metro | 28,750,766,818.00 | 2 |
| Accra Metro | 30,671,611,204.00 | 1 |

# 13 Does Inflation in Ghana Hit the Poor Harder?*

ANDY McKAY
& NII K. SOWA

## 1. Introduction

One of the defining characteristics of the Ghanaian macroeconomy over the past 40 years has been its high, and often variable, rates of inflation. Inflation was particularly high and variable in the politically turbulent 1970s and early 1980s, but has persisted throughout the gradual economic recovery since 1983. Though it has been lower and less variable in the latter period, it still remains high in absolute terms and by comparison with many other countries.

High and variable inflation is typically seen as a symptom or indicator of macroeconomic instability. But it is also argued that macroeconomic instability in general, and inflation in particular, hits the poor hardest (Cardoso, 1992; Easterly and Fischer, 2001). There are two aspects of the suggested impact of inflation on the poor. First, poorer people typically have less flexibility in responding to adverse changes in their environment. The empirical evidence for this finding, however, is typically based on middle-income countries, notably in Latin America. Common rationales include the erosion of the value of savings and of the real value of minimum wages typically fixed in nominal terms, and the fact that the use of a variety of savings and investment means (including in foreign currency) for hedging against inflation is more easily available to richer groups. The applicability of these arguments to low-income African countries is less clear, however. Many of the poor may not hold their assets in financial terms, and few typically work in formal wage employment, and so do not benefit from minimum wage protection. Furthermore, many of the rural poor may obtain much of their consumption through non-market channels, notably from consumption of their own production.

A second respect in which inflation may hit the poor harder is that they may face higher rates of inflation. In general, changes in prices will vary by commodity and

* The authors are grateful for helpful comments from participants at the Ghana at the Half Century conference, especially those of their official discussant Dr Augustin Fosu.

location. Measures of inflation are by definition averages, relating to an average consumption basket; but the consumption basket typically varies significantly across the population, including by income level, while the prices of different commodities increase at different rates. Consequently the poor (especially perhaps the urban poor) may face a different inflation rate from that of the non-poor. In particular, a higher proportion of the consumption basket of the poor is likely to be devoted to necessities, including food. Responding to this concern, some African countries have constructed a separate inflation measure for low-income households, though this has not been the practice in Ghana in recent years.

For the reasons outlined above and discussed in more detail below, we regard the second set of issues as being more relevant for considering the differential impact of inflation on the poor in low-income African countries, including Ghana. The present study therefore focuses more on whether the inflation rate for the basket of purchases of the poor is higher than for the population as a whole. The remainder of the paper is structured as follows. The history and characteristics of inflation in Ghana over the past 45 years are discussed in section 2, including a brief discussion of explanations for these patterns. Section 3 then considers the first of the issues discussed above, the extent to which Ghanaians, poor and non-poor, are able to hedge themselves against inflation. The following two sections discuss the question of inflation rates for the poor, setting out the approach used to identify inflation for the poor in section 4 and presenting the results of its application in section 5. Section 6 concludes, including a discussion of ways in which future work can consider this issue in more detail.

## 2.   Inflation in Ghana and the Implications for Poverty

Inflation has remained one of the intractable problems the Ghanaian economy has faced for a very long time. Having registered low rates of inflation in the years immediately after independence, the country had its first taste of double-digit inflation in 1964. This was followed by a brief period of respite during 1967–71 with inflation below 10% per annum. Between 1972 and 1983 inflation was generally high, rising to 123% in 1983. Since then, there have been moderate rates of inflation averaging around 25% per annum.

Figure 13.1 illustrates the inflationary trend in Ghana since 1960. There are three distinctive characteristics about the trend: one relates to the three observable episodes of low, high and moderate rates of inflation; the second concerns the cyclical nature of the trend; and the last is the remarkable coupling of food and CPI inflation.

### *Different Inflationary Episodes*

From the period when Ghana was part of the West African Currency Board up to about 1972 inflation in Ghana was quite low. For most of the period the average rate of inflation was below 10%. Indeed, during the period of the Currency Board, quite characteristically the rate of inflation was below 1%. Following independence in 1957, the rapid pace of modernization and the development of import-substitution industries and infrastructure began to heat up the economy. Accumulated reserves from which the initial development was financed soon ran out; and with Ghana out of the Currency Board and having established its own central bank, deficit financing through the printing of money was an obvious option. In 1964 the stock of money increased by 37.2% causing inflation to jump into double digits at 15.8%. Even though the growth in money supply substantially slowed in the following years, the inflationary pressures, which had been generated in 1964, persisted for at least three years. One of the factors helping to sustain the pressure on prices was a severe foreign-exchange constraint faced by the country, which led to shortages of most consumer items and raw materials for the newly established industries.

**Figure 13.1: CPI Inflation and Food Inflation**

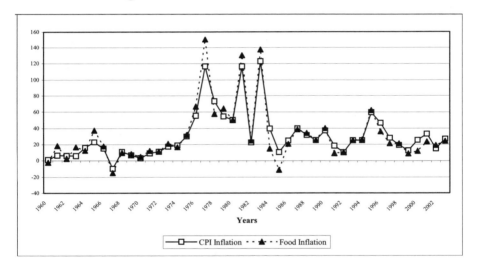

In 1966, Nkrumah's socialist government was overthrown in a coup d'état. The military government of the National Liberation Council (NLC) signed a stabilization package with the International Monetary Fund. Under the stabilization programme the new administration took measures to lower the high tempo of economic activity which characterized the preceding period. In particular, it cut back public spending and the use of bank financing. The extensive involvement of the state in the economy was curtailed and investments reduced, leading to large-scale economic retrenchment. Meanwhile, monetary policy was tightened through interest-rate increases and credit restrictions, among other things. The resultant effect of the new policy measures was deflation in 1967, followed by years of low rates of inflation but at the expense of economic growth.

This period of stabilization was followed, during 1969–71, by a marked boost in economic activity under the civilian administration of Prime Minister Busia. Government recurrent and investment outlays increased substantially, sustained, in part, by the use of foreign reserves and external borrowing. At the same time, private participation in the economy increased. The easing of the fiscal pressure coupled with a tight monetary policy kept inflation in check. Other contributory factors to holding inflation in single digits during 1969–71 were a combination of marked growth of domestic output and improved import supplies under a cocoa price boom in 1970 and a liberalized external trade policy. The latter policy, coupled with a downturn in cocoa prices in 1971, put enormous strain on Ghana's balance of payments, necessitating another devaluation (by 44%) in December 1971. This led to a coup d'état, which brought the military to power and set in motion the *second episode* of inflation in Ghana.

The 1972–82 period was characterized by the most expansionary phase of economic management in the country's history. This period witnessed a succession of regimes, largely military, which pursued highly expansionary fiscal programmes buttressed by monetary accommodation as widening budget deficits were financed by bank loans to government and parastatals. To contain the resultant inflationary pressure, extensive controls — of prices, the exchange rate, interest rates, etc. — were instituted. This led to extremely distorted relative prices, economic stagnation and severe shortage of goods, with attendant strong upward pressure (suppressed or otherwise) on prices.

A brief stabilization effort under IMF sponsorship from January 1979 fizzled out in June that year as a victim of another military intervention. Pervasive economic controls and restrictions from 1972 through 1982 bred a repertoire of malpractices, including smuggling, parallel-market activities in goods and foreign currencies, and corruption. Despite the widespread regime of price controls, however, inflation averaged as high as 50% per annum during 1972–82, with 1977 and 1981 recording the highest ever rates of 117% each.[1]

Clearly, pre-1983 Ghanaian inflation, especially during the period 1972–82, largely reflected excessive demand pressure sustained by excessive fiscal expansion and accommodating monetary growth. But it is equally true that the problem was made worse by inadequate growth of output and supplies, due to particular structural constraints faced by the economy.

Of utmost importance among these constraints was the severe scarcity of foreign exchange due, in large part, to over-reliance on highly erratic cocoa earnings. This severely constrained the capacity to supply essential imports for consumption and production, with potential inflationary consequences. Another important constraint was inadequate food production and supply. This was due to a catalogue of factors including: low productivity, poor storage and preservation facilities, unreliable weather conditions, inadequate marketing and distribution arrangements, fast growing population and urbanization, and pricing policies aimed at keeping down food prices. Food price inflation arising from supply gaps had immense economy-wide inflation effects.

Inadequate performance of the manufacturing sector also contributed to the worsening of the inflation problem. The problems of the sector included the persistence

---

[1] It is quite evident that if the inflation had been calculated on actual rather than official prices the rates would have been much higher.

of large excess capacities (due to lack of adequate imported inputs), outdated technologies and inefficient management. The erratic supply of consumer goods added to the upward pressure on prices.

As noted above, for most of the period under consideration, price controls and fixed exchange rates were extensively used in an attempt to contain inflation. But this only led to suppressed prices and incentives at the producer level without removing the causes of inflationary pressures in the economy. The price distortions accentuated structural constraints in the external trade sector and domestic production. As a result, by 1981 the economy was in very bad shape, with declining income per capita, mounting external deficits, and seriously run-down social and economic infrastructure. This *second episode* characterized by stagflation was at its apogee in 1983.

In April of 1983, faced with a near bankrupt situation, Ghana adopted an International Monetary Fund- and World Bank-supported Economic Recovery Programme (ERP). The ERP sought to minimize both external and domestic imbalances and put the economy on a path of sustainable growth. To this end, far-reaching measures were implemented over the years, including large exchange-rate corrections, price deregulation, trade liberalization, financial sector reforms and rehabilitation of the economic and social infrastructure.

Inflation control was a key objective under the ERP. Given the role of fiscal deficit financing in pre-1983 inflation, efforts were made to reduce budgetary deficits and minimise recourse to bank financing. There was marked improvement in revenue collection although government spending was also increased to kick-start the economy. Much of the increased expenditure was, however, supported by external donors. Thus although growth in the money stock continued to be high (averaging about 40% per annum during 1983–9, equal to the average growth rate recorded for 1972–82) the source of the expansion during the third episode did not lead to inflationary pressures of the same magnitude as during the second episode.

On average, inflation during the third episode has hovered around 25%. Although the government has been pushing for single-digit inflation, this is yet to become a sustainable reality.

## *Inflation Cycle*

Like output and monetary growth, inflationary trends in Ghana mimic a three-year business cycle. This cycle, which takes about eighteen months from peak to trough and another eighteen months to get back to peak, has never been adequately explained. Analysts have tried to explain it using the cocoa seasonal cycles, but it has been difficult to establish a clear and unambiguous link. Indeed, the difficulty in explaining this seasonality is made worse by another three-year jinx on the Ghana political scene: between 1948 and 1983, there was a major political change every three years.

With regard to inflation, the sinusoidal swings within an episode occur around a modal average. Except for the high inflationary episodes, the distributions within a cycle generally produced gentle kurtosis. The implication is that during the high inflationary episodes the variability of price changes is usually sharp.

## Food and CPI Inflation nexus

That consumer price inflation (CPI) and food inflation move in tandem is not surprising. Several household surveys have discovered that a large percentage of the average Ghanaian's expenditure is on food. The 1998/9 Ghana Living Standards Survey estimates that about 65% of the average Ghanaian's consumption expenditure (including consumption from own production) is on food. The CPI basket (based, of course, on market purchases) itself allocates about half of its weight to food. Given that the poor spend a higher proportion of their income on food, variability of food inflation is of immense interest in the analysis of inflation and poverty.

We turn now to a specific investigation of inflation as faced by the poor. First we consider the question of the extent to which Ghanaian households (poor and non-poor) are able to hedge themselves against inflation (section 3), and this is followed by an analysis of whether or not the poor do face a higher inflation rate in Ghana (sections 4 and 5).

## 3.    Hedging Against Inflation in Ghana

Inflation is an economic evil, as it eats into the purchasing power of consumers. Individuals on fixed income, such as wage-earners and pensioners, are usually worse-off in inflationary times. There are ways, however, that individuals can protect themselves against inflation. There are automatic hedges that are related to the consumption pattern of the individual. The other hedging forms, which we term 'traditional', normally involve investment in interest-bearing instruments that minimize the loss due to inflation.

Investigations into the causes of inflation in Ghana have put greater weight on supply inadequacies and bottlenecks (Sowa and Kwakye, 1993; Sowa, 1996), although Chhibber and Shaffic (1994) have maintained that inflation in Ghana has been largely a monetary phenomenon. On the supply side, food carries a greater weight as the Consumer Price Index itself assigns about half of its weight to food. Data from the latest Ghana Living Standards Survey, GLSS 4, show that those in the lower quintile classes devote, on average, about two-thirds of their expenditure (both actual and imputed) to food, while those in the higher quintile classes correspondingly devote about a half. However, if imputed food expenditure, as non-market expenditure, is not taken into account, the proportion of expenditure on food by all quintile groups comes out to be the same at 45% of total consumption expenditure (see Table 13.1). Thus as inflation is basically a market-place phenomenon, Ghanaian consumption patterns do not provide an automatic hedge against inflation for any quintile group.

In relation to the traditional forms of hedging, evidence from the developed countries demonstrates that the rich hedge better against inflation than the poor. The argument supporting this assertion is based on the availability of instruments that offer interest yields that minimize the loss due to inflation. For example, investment in stocks, bills, bonds and property has been a traditional way of hedging against inflation.

In Ghana, the dearth of financial instruments and the lack of sophistication in the behaviour of investors on both the money and capital markets raises suspicion regarding the hedging options for both the poor and the non-poor. On the money market, Government of Ghana Treasury bills offer the easiest opportunity to hedge against inflation. However, the available data point to only a small proportion of Ghanaians investing in Treasury bills. Institutional holdings of government paper far outweigh individual holdings (see Figure 13.2).

**Table 13.1 Components of Household Consumption Expenditure by Quintile (%)**

| Quintile | Component of Expenditure | | | | | Total | Food (actual & imputed) as %age of total |
| | Food | | Housing (actual & imputed) | Other Non-Food | | | |
| | Actual | Imputed | | Actual | Imputed | | |
|---|---|---|---|---|---|---|---|
| Lowest | 45.1 | 17.6 | 3.0 | 31.6 | 2.7 | 100.0 | 62.7 |
| Second | 45.1 | 16.6 | 2.0 | 33.2 | 3.1 | 100.0 | 61.7 |
| Third | 44.6 | 14.9 | 1.8 | 34.4 | 4.3 | 100.0 | 59.5 |
| Fourth | 45.7 | 11.1 | 1.9 | 35.9 | 5.2 | 100.0 | 56.8 |
| Highest | 45.6 | 6.1 | 1.9 | 38.1 | 8.3 | 100.0 | 51.7 |
| All | 45.4 | 10.3 | 2.0 | 36.1 | 6.2 | 100.0 | 55.7 |

*Source:* Ghana Statistical Service (2000, Table 9.6).

**Figure 13.2: Outstanding Stock of Government Securities by Holder (December 2003)**

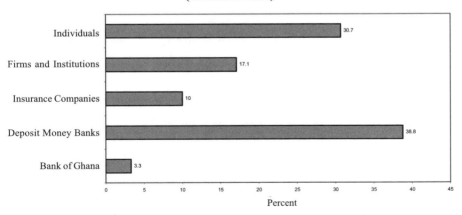

It is important to note that Government of Ghana Treasury bills are issued in 100,000-cedi lots. According to GLSS4, the income of the average Ghanaian in 1998–9 was less than one million cedis (281,000 cedis for the lowest quintile class) in March 1999 prices. Clearly very few Ghanaians have the opportunity to invest in Treasury bills as a hedge against inflation. Indeed, most Ghanaians could not even take advantage of simple bank savings accounts as a hedge. The minimum savings deposit balance that attracts interest ranges between 250,000 cedis and 5 million cedis, depending on the bank. GLSS4 data show that only a minority of households hold bank accounts (Figure 13.3).

**Figure 13.3: Proportion of Households Maintaining Savings Account by Locality, 1998–9**

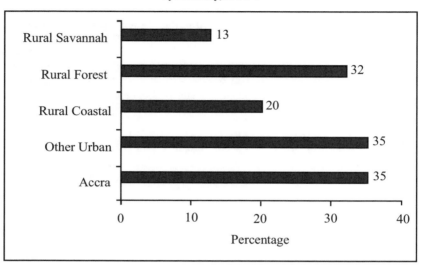

In conclusion, hedging opportunities in Ghana are quite limited for both the poor and the non-poor. Investment in Treasury bills, bonds, stocks and saving accounts as hedges against inflation must be undertaken by a few outliers within the highest quintile class. Thus if inflation has a differential impact on the poor, it must be because they face different rates of inflation.

## 4. Estimating Inflation Rates for the Poor

There are two main reasons why the poor in a country may face different inflation rates from the non-poor. One already discussed above is the differences in the consumption baskets they purchase. This may be due to differences in the composition of consumption baskets, or to differences in the extent to which specific commodities, generally foods, are supplied from own production as opposed to being purchased. But it may be also due to differences in the prices faced. Differences in prices can arise for several reasons, including if there are important regional differences (such as if prices are higher in remote areas — where poverty headcount ratios are often higher — due to transport costs) or if discounts are available for bulk purchases (more easily accessible to richer households for reasons of cash liquidity or ease of storage of perishable commodities). Potentially offsetting this, prices can vary depending on where the purchase takes place, with prices typically being cheaper in markets as compared with stores, but with the poor typically being more likely to purchase in markets.

For the purposes of this study we do not have information available on differences in prices paid by households for the same commodity. It is well known that prices do vary by location in Ghana. Coulombe and McKay (2003) show the extent of the difference in the price *level* between urban and rural areas, and between coastal, forest and savannah zones in rural areas, but the Consumer Price Index (CPI) is currently only disaggregated between Accra, urban areas and rural areas, thus not capturing any differences between different rural areas. While the raw price data collected for the CPI might be used to assess the extent of inflation differentials across regions, the number of observations by locality is likely to be a constraint on an accurate assessment.

This study therefore focuses on the impact of differences in the consumption basket in the Ghana CPI, considering the national level as well as the indices for rural areas, urban areas and Accra specifically. The price data are collected from market surveys, and the weights currently used for the index were computed from the expenditure data collected in the third round of the Ghana Living Standards Surveys (GLSS3) conducted in 1991–2. This was a nationally representative survey, so shares computed from this survey can be applied to the entire population of households in the corresponding category. The weights used for the nine main commodity groups are reported in Table 13.2. Note that, as appropriate for CPI calculations, these shares are based on purchases and exclude imputed consumption; thus the share of food and beverages in the budget here is around 52%. This differs from the share of purchased food reported in Table 13.1 mainly because the denominator for that calculation included imputed consumption as well.

**Table13. 2  Broad Commodity Weights Used in CPI (%)**

| CATEGORY | WEIGHT | | | |
|---|---|---|---|---|
| | National | Urban | Rural | Accra |
| Food and beverages | 51.9 | 51.37 | 52.38 | 50.27 |
| Alcohol and tobacco | 3.55 | 2.08 | 4.9 | 1.62 |
| Clothing and footwear | 9.58 | 9.2 | 9.92 | 10.23 |
| Housing and utilities | 9.24 | 11.11 | 7.52 | 13.20 |
| Household goods, operations and services | 7.3 | 6.95 | 7.62 | 7.35 |
| Medical care and health expenses | 4.25 | 3.51 | 4.94 | 2.63 |
| Transport and communications | 6.47 | 6.7 | 6.26 | 6.68 |
| Recreation, entertainment, education and cultural services | 4.9 | 5.79 | 4.09 | 5.36 |
| Miscellaneous goods and services | 2.81 | 3.29 | 2.37 | 2.66 |
| Combined | 100 | 100 | 100 | 100 |

*Source:*  Ghana Statistical Service, *CPI Newsletter,* February 2004.

These weights are computed across the entire relevant population as so-called plutocratic weights, in other words the sum of all expenditures on food and beverages in Ghana (for the national weights), divided by the sum of all expenditures on all categories. Thus, 51.9% of all purchases (note, not consumption) reported across all households in GLSS 3 were on food and beverages.

This is the standard procedure used for computing weights for a CPI, and is the appropriate procedure for summarizing the impact of inflation on national aggregate expenditure. However, it is not very suitable as a method for assessing the inflation faced by the poor, because the weights will be strongly influenced by richer households who will generally spend more on most commodities, as well as potentially having a different consumption pattern. In that sense it is not an average basket but rather one influenced disproportionately by the consumption patterns of richer households. An alternative procedure therefore is to compute expenditure share weights where each household contributes equally, so-called democratic weights. In the example of food and beverages above, this implies calculating for each individual household the share of this category in its total purchases, and then taking the average of this across all households. This is referred to as a democratic weight because each *household* counts equally in the determination of the overall weight.

The difference between the plutocratic and democratic weights can be represented mathematically as follows. If there are $H$ households indexed by $h$ ($h = 1, ..., H$) and $n$ commodities indexed by $i$ ($i = 1, ..., n$), and the expenditure of household $h$ on commodity $i$ is denoted by $x_i^h$, then the plutocratic weight is computed as follows:

$$w_i^p = \frac{\sum_{h=1}^{H} x_i^h}{\sum_{i=1}^{n}\sum_{h=1}^{H} x_i^h} \tag{1}$$

The democratic weight, however, is computed as follows:

$$w_i^d = \frac{1}{H}\sum_{h=1}^{H}\left(\frac{x_i^h}{\sum_{i=1}^{n} x_i^h}\right). \tag{2}$$

This difference between plutocratic and democratic weights is equivalent to the difference between the ratio of the means of two variables and the mean of the ratio of the same variables. While the plutocratic weight may still be the best overall macroeconomic measure of inflation, the democratic weight is more appropriate for present purposes. Thus a key focus of this study on the divergence between these two weights, and thus on the implications of this divergence for the estimate of inflation.

A study of this divergence in South Africa (Bhorat and Oosthuisen, 2003) found that there were systematic differences between plutocratic and democratic weights, with the plutocratic weight for food in urban areas, for example, being 22.5% while the democratic weight was 31.5%. This reflected a systematic change in consumption patterns by decile. Recomputing inflation using the democratic weights, however, showed only a very small change compared with the plutocratic weights (the overall inflation level was somewhat lower than in Ghana, but even in proportionate terms the effect was small).

In the next section we make an equivalent calculation for Ghana, focusing also on calculating the corresponding weight specifically for the poor.

## 5.   Alternative Measures of Inflation for Ghana

In this paper, we focus on the fourth round of the GLSS survey conducted in 1998–9, rather than the GLSS3 survey used for the CPI. In fact, the corresponding weights, computed on a plutocratic basis, are very similar to those used in the CPI (Table 13.3; and Annex Figure 13.A.1). At this level of aggregation there was little change in the consumption basket between 1991/2 and 1998/9.

**Table 13.3   Broad Commodity Weights Computed from GLSS4 Survey (Plutocratic basis)**

| CATEGORY | WEIGHT | | |
| --- | --- | --- | --- |
| | National | Urban | Rural |
| Food and beverages | 53.57 | 53.54 | 53.61 |
| Alcohol and tobacco | 2.31 | 1.49 | 3.20 |
| Clothing and footwear | 9.96 | 8.90 | 11.13 |
| Housing and utilities | 6.39 | 8.24 | 4.38 |
| Household goods, operations and services | 5.96 | 5.35 | 6.63 |
| Medical care and health expenses | 4.60 | 4.08 | 5.16 |
| Transport and communications | 5.63 | 5.83 | 5.40 |
| Recreation, entertainment, education and cultural services | 7.71 | 8.83 | 6.49 |
| Miscellaneous goods and services | 3.87 | 3.75 | 4.00 |
| Combined | 100 | 100 | 100 |

*Source:*   Authors' computation from GLSS 4 survey.

In practice computing the weights on a democratic rather than a plutocratic basis makes only a relatively small difference (Table 13.4 at national level and Annex Tables 13.A1 and 13.A2 for rural and urban areas respectively), much less so than the corresponding calculation in South Africa (Bhorat and Oosthuisen, 2003). For instance, the democratic weight for food and beverages is higher (as expected), but the difference is quite small in absolute terms. Making corresponding calculations for the lowest two quintiles (corresponding closely to the proportion identified as poor in GLSS4) also makes relatively little difference. Indeed, in this case the democratic weight for food and beverages is lower than the corresponding weight for the whole population, presumably because a greater share of the food consumption of the poor is supplied by own production, as will be confirmed below.

**Table 13.4  Alternative CPI Weights, National level**

| CATEGORY | WEIGHT | | | |
| --- | --- | --- | --- | --- |
|  | Plutocratic | Democratic | Plutocratic, bottom 40% | Democratic, bottom 40% |
| Food and beverages | 53.57 | 56.01 | 55.42 | 55.11 |
| Alcohol and tobacco | 2.31 | 3.21 | 3.56 | 4.81 |
| Clothing and footwear | 9.96 | 10.02 | 10.78 | 10.55 |
| Housing and utilities | 6.39 | 5.75 | 5.19 | 5.14 |
| Household goods, operations and services | 5.96 | 6.42 | 6.86 | 7.40 |
| Medical care and health expenses | 4.60 | 4.67 | 4.44 | 4.56 |
| Transport and communications | 5.63 | 4.51 | 3.60 | 3.34 |
| Recreation, entertainment, education and cultural services | 7.71 | 5.98 | 7.26 | 6.37 |
| Miscellaneous goods and services | 3.87 | 3.42 | 2.88 | 2.71 |
| Combined | 100 | 100 | 100 | 100 |

*Source:*  Authors' computation from GLSS 4 survey.

Distinguishing between urban and rural areas does show some difference, highlighted in Figure 13.4 for the share of food and beverages. In urban areas the weights do vary in a systematic and plausible manner according to how they are calculated, in that the democratic weight is larger than the plutocratic weight, and that

**Figure 13.4:  Share of Food and Beverages in Total Purchases under Different Weighting Schemes**

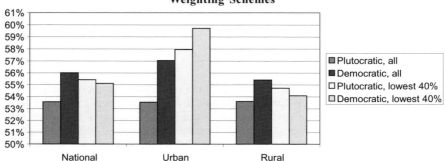

the weights for the bottom 40% are larger than those for the entire sample. The differences remain fairly modest, however, with the national plutocratic and democratic weights being 53.5 and 57 respectively.

In rural areas, the democratic share is larger than the plutocratic weight at the national level, but the democratic weight for the bottom 40% is lower. In other words, for the rural poor food accounts for a lower proportion of their purchases compared with the average rural household. Note again, though, that this relates to purchases rather than overall consumption. In each case, however, the differences between the different ways of calculating the weights are small, a point which also applies to the other broad expenditure categories as well.

Given these results, at this level of aggregation of commodity groups, alternative ways of computing the weights can be expected to make little difference to the computation of estimates of inflation, a fact confirmed by the results in Annex Table 13.A3. As expected from the discussion above, the largest difference is observed in the case of urban inflation, with differences in the estimate of inflation of up to 1.6% in 2000 depending on which estimate is chosen. But, as seen in Figure 13.5, there is no systematic pattern to this, according to the estimate chosen. Weights based on the consumption basket of the poorest 40% suggest slightly lower levels of inflation than those for the whole sample in 1999, 2000 and 2001, but the situation is reversed in 2002. In any case, the magnitudes of the differences are quite small. In rural areas the differences according to the method of calculation are even smaller, reaching a maximum of 0.75% in 2003.

**Figure 13.5: Estimates of Urban Inflation using Different Weights**

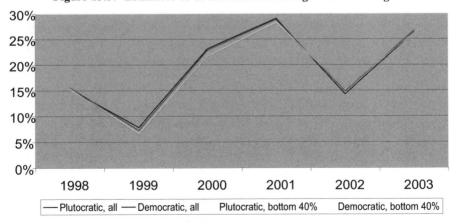

This insensitivity of the estimate of inflation to the manner of constructing the weights is clearly a consequence of the fact that expenditure patterns at this broad level of aggregation appear to differ little between the poor and the remainder of the population. Looking at the composition of expenditure by quintile, the very limited variation by quintiles is apparent (Annex Tables 13.A4, A5 and A6), especially so in rural areas where the share of food and beverages scarcely changes with the quintile group. As will be considered shortly, this may reflect a decreasing importance of own production as a source of consumption with increasing quintiles. In urban areas by contrast, there is a monotonic decline with the quintile in the share of food and beverages in total purchases as would be expected, but the difference between the lowest and highest quintiles remains small, at only 7 percentage points.

An important consideration here, however, is the detailed composition of these commodity groups. Thus while food and beverages might be thought of as being a consumption necessity, and therefore declining in relative importance with increasing income, in fact this large grouping is likely to include both necessity and 'luxury' commodities (in terms of the values of their income elasticities of demand). Moreover, the prices of individual commodities within a broad grouping may change at very different rates, a fact not captured above using the inflation indices for the broad commodity groupings. To consider the impact of this on the estimates of inflation requires the use of the raw price data collected for the CPI, in particular the month-by-month prices at the individual commodity level. This is beyond the scope of the present study, but is an issue we plan to follow up in co-operation with the Ghana Statistical Service (which has made individual price data available to us) in the short-term future.

**Figure 13.6:  Commodity Weights for Some Main Categories**

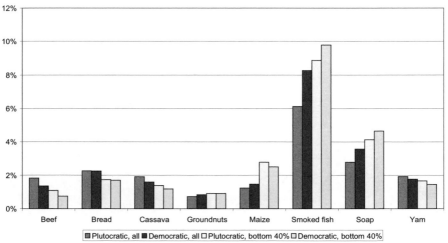

However, we present here a preliminary investigation to identify the likely importance of commodity-specific variations. Considering variations in budget shares at the individual commodity level according to the method of calculation (among the options discussed above), some important variations are apparent. Patterns for 8 main commodities (collectively accounting for between 18.8% and 22.9% of total purchases depending on how this is calculated) are presented in Figure 13.6. Several commodities are clearly much more important for the poor; for example, the share of smoked fish increases monotonically moving from left to right on the figure, in other words the calculated share is higher when more weight is placed on poorer households. A similar pattern applies to soap. By contrast the share of beef, bread, cassava and yams all decline monotonically from left to right, implying that they contribute relatively less to the basket of purchases for the poorest compared with the rest of the population. These detailed differences, some of which are quantitatively quite large, are lost in the much more aggregate approach adopted to date. However, whether these differences in the consumption basket matter for the estimation of inflation will also depend on the pattern of change of prices. This can only be judged based on commodity-specific price data. The greater variation in the weights at this level makes it more likely that it might have an impact compared with the broader categories used above.

At this stage we present an initial analysis of this question exploiting the information provided in selected *CPI Newsletters,* specifically the table which reports the specific contributions of the commodities accounting for the largest part of the overall change in the CPI in the month under consideration. This information was used for three selected *CPI Newsletters* chosen at random: May 2003, May 2004 and July 2004. In each case the contribution of the main commodities (typically around 25 commodities) to the overall month-to-month change in the index is reported. Based on the inflation rate for the month in question and the commodity-specific weights, it is possible to estimate approximately the commodity-specific price movements that underlay it. This can then be used to consider the impact of computing the weights on a different basis. For each of the three cases considered, the impact was quite small. For example, using the May 2003 *Newsletter,* the 26 main commodities accounted for an increase of 0.41% in the overall CPI (which increased by 1.17% on a month-to-month basis). Using the four alternative weights discussed above instead of those used in the CPI *Newsletter* implied contributions of these commodities to the overall CPI varying between 0.37% and 0.43%. While these numbers appear small, they are still quite large in relative terms, given the small magnitude of month-on-month inflation over this period. The differences were of similar orders of magnitude for the other two CPI *Newsletters* considered — but there was not a systematic pattern, according to how high the weights were computed, and no evidence based on this limited and very approximate method that inflation rates have been systematically higher (or lower) for poorer groups.

This, of course, is not generalizable, and is also done only at the national level — not distinguishing urban and rural areas, for example. But this preliminary and very approximate analysis is certainly sufficient to highlight the need for the question posed in this study to be addressed at the individual commodity level. We aim to address this question in subsequent work.

Finally, as repeatedly stressed here, measures of inflation concern purchases, whereas frequently households may obtain a significant proportion of their consumption from other sources including own production, gifts and barter exchange. In rural Ghana in particular, consumption from own production is important for many households, and this provides households with some insurance against inflation, because such transactions do not pass through markets (or equivalently households are simultaneously producers and consumers). Indeed, the extent to which households source their consumption from their own production as opposed to engaging in market transactions of selling and buying commodities is likely to be endogenous, with the extent and variability of inflation likely to be important factors influencing this. The more that poorer households rely on own production for their source of consumption, the more they are insured against the effects of inflation. But equally they are less able to exploit gains from trade.

**Table 13.5    Proportion of Food Purchased, by Quintile Group and Location**

| Quintile | Proportion of food purchased | | |
|---|---|---|---|
| | Urban | Rural | ALL |
| Lowest | 88.9 | 70.5 | 72.8 |
| Second | 90.7 | 72.0 | 76.0 |
| Third | 94.2 | 72.4 | 78.3 |
| Fourth | 93.6 | 75.2 | 82.9 |
| Highest | 97.3 | 80.3 | 90.2 |
| ALL | 94.9 | 74.0 | 81.7 |

*Source:*   Authors' computation from GLSS4 survey.

The extent to which households' food consumption is supplied by purchases disaggregated by quintile group is reported in Table 13.5, and in more detail in Annex Table 13.A.7. In urban areas unsurprisingly around 95% of food consumption is obtained through market purchases, and still around 90% among the poor (the two lowest quintiles). But even in rural areas, own production and other non-market sources account for only 26% of household food consumption by value. The contribution of purchases to food consumption in rural areas increases modestly with the quintile, but even in the poorest quintile 70.5% of food consumption is purchased in the market. The reliance on market purchases is higher in the rural areas of the coastal zone compared with the forest and savannah zones, but even in the savannah zone two-thirds of food consumption is purchased with no systematic variation by quintile (Annex Table 13.A7). Analogous calculations using GLSS3 show a similar pattern. Thus the vast majority of households are highly exposed to the effects of inflation, even those living in more remote rural areas.

## 6.    Conclusion

Given the extent to which the vast majority of households in Ghana rely on the market for their purchase of key commodities including food, inflation is clearly an issue of relevance to poor and non-poor alike. Whether or not it hits the poor harder depends on whether they are less able to hedge themselves against inflation compared with richer groups, and on whether they face a higher rate of inflation. On the former issue we argue that the large majority of households in Ghana do not have ready access to conventional means of hedging against inflation through savings and investments. Moreover, there is no evidence yet that the poor do face a systematically higher — or lower — inflation rate than the non-poor. In fact, at the broad commodity category level, consumption baskets in Ghana are remarkably uniform across income groups.

Both issues, however, merit further investigation in subsequent work. The question of hedging through savings and investment can be considered in more detail based on household-level data on asset holdings. In the case of the differential inflation rate, the key issue is to repeat the analysis in sections 4 and 5 of this study using price data at the individual commodity level. Important differences in the composition of the consumption basket become apparent at the individual commodity level. And initial calculations suggest that the choice of weighting method for computing inflation rates does make a difference. The few cases considered here do not provide evidence that the poor face a systematically higher (or lower) inflation rate than the non-poor. But this issue needs to be considered in future work on a systematic basis, using individual commodity price data over several years. We hope to pursue this, with the co-operation of the Ghana Statistical Service, in future work.

## References

Bhorat, H. and Oosthuizen, M. (2003) *The Differential Impact of Inflation on Poor South African Households*. Development Policy Research Unit Working Paper 03/72, University of Cape Town.

Cardoso, E. (1992) *Inflation and Poverty*. NBER Working Paper 4006. Cambridge, MA: National Bureau for Economic Research.

Chibber, A. and Shafik, N. (1990) *Exchange Reform, Parallel Markets and Inflation in Africa: The Case of Ghana*. Policy, Research and External Affairs Working Paper WPS 427. Washington, DC: World Bank.

Coulombe, H. and McKay, A. (2003) 'Selective Poverty Reduction in a Slow Growth Environment: Ghana in the 1990s' (mimeo).

Easterly, W. and Fischer, S. (2001) 'Inflation and the Poor', *Journal of Money, Credit and Banking*, Vol. 33, No. 2: 160–178.

Ghana Statistical Service (2000a) *Ghana Living Standards Survey Report of the Fourth Round (GLSS 4)*. Accra: GSS.

Ghana Statistical Service (2000b) *Poverty Trends in Ghana in the 1990s*. Accra: GSS.

Ghana Statistical Service, *CPI Newsletters*, various issues.

Sowa, N. K. (1996) *Policy Consistency and Inflation in Ghana*. Research Paper 25. Nairobi: African Economic Research Consortium.

Sowa, N. K. and Kwakye, J. K. (1994) 'Inflationary Trends and Control in Ghana'. Nairobi: African Economic Research Consortium (mimeo).

## Annex

### Figure 13.A1: Comparison of GLSS 3 and GLSS 4 Plutocratic Weights — National

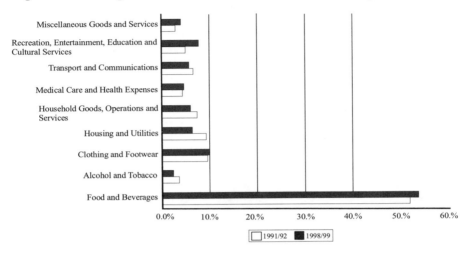

### Table 13.A1    Alternative CPI Weights, Rural Areas

| CATEGORY | WEIGHT | | | |
| --- | --- | --- | --- | --- |
| | Plutocratic | Democratic | Plutocratic, bottom 40% | Democratic, bottom 40% |
| Food and beverages | 53.61 | 55.41 | 54.73 | 54.08 |
| Alcohol and tobacco | 3.20 | 4.19 | 4.07 | 5.57 |
| Clothing and footwear | 11.13 | 10.83 | 11.47 | 11.07 |
| Housing and utilities | 4.38 | 4.26 | 4.18 | 4.46 |
| Household goods, operations and    services | 6.63 | 7.13 | 7.26 | 7.75 |
| Medical care and health expenses | 5.16 | 5.09 | 4.69 | 4.70 |
| Transport and communications | 5.40 | 4.20 | 3.83 | 3.52 |
| Recreation, entertainment,    education etc. | 6.49 | 5.47 | 6.83 | 6.07 |
| Miscellaneous goods and services | 4.00 | 3.41 | 2.95 | 2.78 |
| Combined | 100 | 100 | 100 | 100 |

*Source:*   Authors' computation from GLSS 4 survey.

**Table 13.A2    Alternative CPI Weights, Urban Area**s

| CATEGORY | Plutocratic | Democratic | Plutocratic, bottom 40% | Democratic, bottom 40% |
|---|---|---|---|---|
| Food and beverages | 53.54 | 57.04 | 57.96 | 59.71 |
| Alcohol and tobacco | 1.49 | 1.50 | 1.68 | 1.37 |
| Clothing and footwear | 8.90 | 8.63 | 8.27 | 8.24 |
| Housing and utilities | 8.24 | 8.34 | 8.88 | 8.22 |
| Household goods, operations and services | 5.35 | 5.21 | 5.38 | 5.84 |
| Medical care and health expenses | 4.08 | 3.94 | 3.52 | 3.95 |
| Transport and communications | 5.83 | 5.05 | 2.79 | 2.54 |
| Recreation, entertainment, education etc. | 8.83 | 6.85 | 8.87 | 7.73 |
| Miscellaneous goods and services | 3.75 | 3.44 | 2.65 | 2.39 |
| Combined | 100 | 100 | 100 | 100 |

*Source:* Authors' computation from GLSS4 survey.

**Table 13.A3    Estimated Inflation Rates Depending on Method for Computing Budget Weights (%)**

| Weighting basis | 1998 | 1999 | 2000 | 2001 | 2002 | 2003 |
|---|---|---|---|---|---|---|
| NATIONAL | | | | | | |
| Plutocratic, all | 15.2 | 12.2 | 23.4 | 30.6 | 15.4 | 26.1 |
| Democratic, all | 15.4 | 11.9 | 22.8 | 30.2 | 15.7 | 25.7 |
| Plutocratic, bottom 40% | 15.2 | 11.8 | 22.4 | 30.3 | 15.8 | 25.0 |
| Democratic, bottom 40% | 15.2 | 11.8 | 22.6 | 30.3 | 15.9 | 24.9 |
| | | | | | | |
| RURAL | | | | | | |
| Plutocratic, all | 14.9 | 16.3 | 23.1 | 31.7 | 16.6 | 27.1 |
| Democratic, all | 15.2 | 16.2 | 22.7 | 31.3 | 16.8 | 26.7 |
| Plutocratic, bottom 40% | 15.0 | 16.2 | 22.6 | 31.6 | 16.9 | 26.3 |
| Democratic, bottom 40% | 15.0 | 16.2 | 23.2 | 31.6 | 17.0 | 26.4 |
| | | | | | | |
| URBAN | | | | | | |
| Plutocratic, all | 15.3 | 7.8 | 23.1 | 29.0 | 14.3 | 26.3 |
| Democratic, all | 15.6 | 7.2 | 22.8 | 28.9 | 14.8 | 26.6 |
| Plutocratic, bottom 40% | 15.3 | 6.7 | 21.7 | 28.3 | 15.3 | 26.2 |
| Democratic, bottom 40% | 15.5 | 6.4 | 21.5 | 28.0 | 15.4 | 26.2 |

*Source:* Authors' computation from *CPI Newsletters* and GLSS4 survey.

**Table 13.A4    Composition of Household Purchases, Ghana (%)**

| CATEGORY | QUINTILE | | | | | |
| --- | --- | --- | --- | --- | --- | --- |
| | Lowest | 2nd | 3rd | 4th | Highest | All |
| Food and beverages | 55.18 | 55.55 | 54.64 | 53.97 | 52.59 | 53.57 |
| Alcohol and tobacco | 4.87 | 2.82 | 2.27 | 2.02 | 2.09 | 2.31 |
| Clothing and footwear | 10.83 | 10.76 | 10.25 | 9.92 | 9.68 | 9.96 |
| Housing and utilities | 4.99 | 5.30 | 6.00 | 6.81 | 6.65 | 6.39 |
| Household goods, operations and services | 7.60 | 6.45 | 6.36 | 5.69 | 5.72 | 5.96 |
| Medical care and health expenses | 4.02 | 4.68 | 4.73 | 4.67 | 4.57 | 4.60 |
| Transport and communications | 3.15 | 3.86 | 4.57 | 4.65 | 6.91 | 5.63 |
| Recreation, entertainment, education etc. | 6.97 | 7.43 | 7.39 | 8.29 | 7.67 | 7.71 |
| Miscellaneous goods and services | 2.38 | 3.16 | 3.80 | 3.98 | 4.12 | 3.87 |
| Combined | 100 | 100 | 100 | 100 | 100 | 100 |

*Source:* Authors' computation from GLSS 4 survey.

**Table 13.A5    Composition of Household Purchases, Urban (%)**

| CATEGORY | QUINTILE | | | | | |
| --- | --- | --- | --- | --- | --- | --- |
| | Lowest | 2nd | 3rd | 4th | Highest | All |
| Food and beverages | 59.34 | 57.50 | 56.36 | 55.12 | 52.27 | 53.54 |
| Alcohol and tobacco | 1.07 | 1.88 | 1.41 | 1.12 | 1.60 | 1.49 |
| Clothing and footwear | 8.65 | 8.14 | 7.91 | 8.51 | 9.20 | 8.90 |
| Housing and utilities | 8.45 | 9.03 | 9.65 | 9.28 | 7.67 | 8.24 |
| Household goods, operations and services | 5.50 | 5.34 | 5.17 | 4.84 | 5.53 | 5.35 |
| Medical care and health expenses | 3.57 | 3.50 | 3.87 | 3.93 | 4.20 | 4.08 |
| Transport and communications | 2.31 | 2.95 | 4.07 | 4.46 | 6.76 | 5.83 |
| Recreation, entertainment, education etc. | 8.88 | 8.87 | 8.29 | 8.99 | 8.85 | 8.83 |
| Miscellaneous goods and services | 2.24 | 2.79 | 3.28 | 3.75 | 3.91 | 3.75 |
| Combined | 100 | 100 | 100 | 100 | 100 | 100 |

*Source:* ibid.

**Table 13.A6    Composition of Household Purchases, Rural (%)**

| CATEGORY | QUINTILE | | | | | |
| | Lowest | 2nd | 3rd | 4th | Highest | All |
|---|---|---|---|---|---|---|
| Food and beverages | 54.44 | 54.90 | 53.76 | 52.92 | 53.24 | 53.61 |
| Alcohol and tobacco | 5.55 | 3.14 | 2.71 | 2.83 | 3.13 | 3.20 |
| Clothing and footwear | 11.22 | 11.63 | 11.45 | 11.22 | 10.67 | 11.13 |
| Housing and utilities | 4.37 | 4.06 | 4.13 | 4.54 | 4.53 | 4.38 |
| Household goods, operations and services | 7.97 | 6.81 | 6.97 | 6.47 | 6.13 | 6.63 |
| Medical care and health expenses | 4.10 | 5.07 | 5.17 | 5.35 | 5.34 | 5.16 |
| Transport and communications | 3.30 | 4.16 | 4.82 | 4.83 | 7.20 | 5.40 |
| Recreation, entertainment, education etc. | 6.63 | 6.95 | 6.93 | 7.65 | 5.20 | 6.49 |
| Miscellaneous goods and services | 2.41 | 3.28 | 4.06 | 4.19 | 4.56 | 4.00 |
| Combined | 100 | 100 | 100 | 100 | 100 | 100 |

*Source:*    ibid.

**Table 13.A7    Percentage of Food Purchased, by Location and Quintile**

| Quintile | Locality | | | | | All |
| | Accra | Other urban | Rural coastal | Rural forest | Rural savannah | |
|---|---|---|---|---|---|---|
| Lowest | 100.0 | 88.6 | 85.5 | 68.4 | 67.0 | 72.8 |
| Second | 98.2 | 90.3 | 81.0 | 68.9 | 68.7 | 76.0 |
| Third | 100.0 | 93.2 | 85.1 | 69.2 | 67.9 | 78.3 |
| Fourth | 98.9 | 91.0 | 84.7 | 73.8 | 63.1 | 82.9 |
| Highest | 99.2 | 96.2 | 91.0 | 78.9 | 62.6 | 90.2 |
| ALL | 99.1 | 93.3 | 85.6 | 72.4 | 66.6 | 81.7 |

*Source:* ibid.

# 14 Understanding Poverty in Ghana: Risk & Vulnerability

KOJO APPIAH-KUBI, ABENA ODURO
& BERNARDIN SENADZA

## 1. Introduction

Poverty, as a reflection of material, social or rights deprivation, is of concern in its own right, hence its reduction has been the focus of economic policy in both developed and developing countries. However, as pointed out by Gibson (2001), people may, in a given time period, be poor either because their mean quantitative proxy indicator for poverty, such as income, consumption expenditure or calories, falls below the national average (or poverty line) or because they have suffered a temporary shortfall in consumption or income. In other words, households or persons may be poor at a point in time either due to intertemporal variability in consumption or income, which is considered as 'transient', or because of the persistence of income or consumption expenditure below the poverty line, i.e. 'chronic poverty' (Jalan and Ravallion, 1998). Therefore, for effective poverty reduction programmes it is important to know not only those who are currently poor but also those who are vulnerable to poverty.

In participatory poverty assessments of rural and urban communities it was found that 'frequently local understandings of people in poor rural and urban communities of the key elements in sustaining their livelihoods concur more with the concept of "vulnerability" than that of poverty. The idea of a secure livelihood is frequently more important than the incentive to maximise income' (Norton et al., 1995). Participatory poverty assessments conducted in Ghana reveal that vulnerability is an important aspect of the perception of poverty.[1] Women in rural Ghana do not consider their households to be secure. They are of the opinion that the difference between poor and richer households lies in the ability of the latter to cope with the risks.

That vulnerability can be quantitatively important has been underscored by many analysts of poverty. For instance in the case of Indonesia, apart from having a

---

[1] Some researchers on poverty analysis advocate that risk and vulnerability should be conceptualized as a component of poverty (e.g. Sinha and Lipton, 1999).

**299**

headcount poverty rate of 20%, Pritchett et al. (2000) have estimated an additional 10-30% of households to be vulnerable to poverty (at even odds of at least one episode of poverty in three years). Thus, 30-50% of the population is vulnerable to poverty, with significant differences across groups. Indeed, since the last half-decade the need for better identification of the potential poor has also led to the broadening of the concept of poverty to include even vulnerability and exposure to risk — and voicelessness and powerlessness (World Bank, 2000), since considerations of risk and uncertainty are key to understanding the dynamics leading to and perpetuating poverty (Rosenzweig and Binswanger, 1993; Banerjee and Newman, 1994). According to the World Bank (2000) vulnerability analysis is crucial for understanding poverty insofar as it helps to identify the characteristics of those impoverished households that lack the means to ascend the economic ladder and to tailor human development policies to their specific needs. It also helps to quantify not only the existing poor but also those in danger of becoming poor in the future, and identifies a comprehensive set of sources of vulnerability of this group. In this way policy-makers can formulate better risk-management policies (including a mix of informal, market-based and public risk-management methods) to reduce the effect of these shocks in a cost-effective manner.

In Ghana very little work has been done in the area of vulnerability. This is largely because of the paucity of panel survey data which track the same households over time, suitable for analysis of poverty dynamics. The first attempt in 1987 at creating a panel data set was discontinued after only two data points, as the result of an inadequate household tracking system. Poverty analysis in Ghana has tended to focus on poverty at a point in time or else on poverty trends, i.e. changes in the incidence, depth and severity of poverty over time (Asenso-Okyere et al., 1997; Boateng et al., 1990; Canagarajah, et al., 1998; Glewwe and Twum-Baah, 1991; Seini et al., 1997). There has been very little done by way of analyzing poverty dynamics in Ghana, i.e. investigating the welfare movements of particular households or individuals over time. This study hopes to fill the vacuum. Using cross-sectional data from the fourth Ghana Living Standards Survey (GLSS 4) 1998/9, against the background of lack of longitudinal (panel) data, we attempt to provide additional information about poverty and vulnerability.

## 2.    Defining Risk and Vulnerability[2]

### *Vulnerability*

To some analysts poverty and vulnerability (to poverty) are two sides of the same coin, in that the observed poverty status of a household (defined simply by whether or not the household's observed level of deprivation is above or below a pre-selected poverty line) is the *ex-post* realization of a state, the *ex-ante* probability of which can be taken to be the household's level of vulnerability (Chaudhuri, 2000). This *ex-ante*

---

[2] Various disciplines have their respective views on the concept of vulnerability, even though there appear to be a lot of overlaps. In this context, however, we are concerned with vulnerability to poverty.

probability, on the one hand, connotes the *ex-ante* risk that a household that is currently not poor will fall below the poverty line and that a household that is currently poor will remain poor (Holzmann, 2001).[3] On the other hand, since poverty is a multi-dimensional construct, which reflects deprivation on multiple fronts, some analysts consider vulnerability to poverty in terms of exposure to adverse shocks, rather than to poverty (Cunningham and Maloney 2000; Glewwe and Hall 1998).[4] This view indeed considers vulnerability as the lack of capacity (of a household) to cope with (an adverse) shock or (a household's) resilience against a shock, that is, the likelihood that a shock will result in a decline in well-being of the household (Christiaensen and Subbarao, 2001; Alwang and Siegel, 2000). The Human Development Group of the World Bank in a report on social protection in Africa define vulnerability as '. . . the ability to manage risk, in other words, the ability of households to prevent major declines in their living standards or major variability in their consumption' (World Bank, 2000: 4).

Sen (2001) places the above definitions into differing perspectives by classifying vulnerability into 'risks-centric and rights-centric views'. To him the 'risks-centric view' refers to the *variability in the living standard* caused by consumption or income shocks, whilst the 'rights-centric perspective' is caused by the *lack of social and political rights*. He argues that both views are important when considering the implications of vulnerability for poverty reduction, because the risks-centric view tends to highlight transient poverty while the rights-centric view focuses on chronic poverty, though, admittedly, there is a considerable grey area between the two perspectives.

Alwang and Siegel (2000) conceptualize vulnerability as having four components: risk, exposure, response and outcome. Risk is the probability of an event happening. Exposure may be conceived as the value of the assets at risk or what will be lost from the realization of an uncertain event, and is a function of decisions and actions taken by households, for example, the choice of employment and asset portfolio. Response is the effort to mitigate and cope with risk and exposure. This will depend on the assets (physical, financial, human and social) available to the household or the individual. The type of assets that the household has at its disposal is critical to the nature of the response to the event. The assets must be liquid, i.e. readily convertible into cash at minimum cost and must not lose value in the face of the potentially poverty-reducing event (Dercon, 2000). Response will also depend on the extent to which the individual or household can gain access to credit to help smooth consumption as well as access to private transfers and/or public safety nets. Coping strategies such as increasing the supply of labour are other measures that the individual or household may adopt to respond to the crisis. Some actions that might

---

[3] Ellis (2000) notes that vulnerability has a dual aspect of external threats to livelihood security (e.g. climate, market collapse, theft) and internal risk management and coping capability (determined by access to a range of assets), and makes the important distinction between *ex-ante* risk-management strategies, and *ex-post* coping strategies.

[4] To Chaudhuri et al. (2002) the difference between the two definitions is substantive. They see the first to include among the vulnerable households that are currently poor and have a high probability of remaining poor even if they do not experience any large adverse welfare shocks.

be taken in response to the income-reducing or expenditure-reducing event might contribute to increasing the household's or individual's vulnerability to poverty, for example depleting assets for consumption purposes to such an extent that it will be difficult to attain previous levels. Outcome is the end-result of the impact of the shock and is the product of the interplay of risk, exposure and response.

On the basis of this conceptualization, the degree of vulnerability depends on the characteristics of the risks, exposure, and the ability to respond (Alwang and Siegel, 2000; Guillaumont, 1999).

The concepts of vulnerability presented here indicate that vulnerability is not static. Vulnerability to poverty of a household or individual can change over time as access to consumption-smoothing measures and the nature and size of the asset portfolio, for example, change over time. Vulnerability to poverty will change from one period to the next depending on what the nature of the risks is.

## *Risk*

Risk is the probability of an event occurring. The event may have a positive effect on consumption expenditure and/or income or it may have a negative effect (i.e. down-side risk). The discussion of risk within the context of poverty tends to focus on the down-side risks. A person's exposure to risk therefore refers to the probability of him/her being affected by an uncertain event (Christiaensen and Subbarao, 2001).

Dercon (2000) analyzes the sources of risk within the context of the security of assets and security of income. Assets are subject to risk and households can be vulnerable to poverty, based on the extent to which they are able to have a portfolio of assets that minimizes risk. The discussion of the riskiness of assets covers physical, financial, human and social capital (Dercon, 2000). Transformation of assets into income is subject to risk, as is the transformation of income into consumption. Thus, in assessing vulnerability it is not sufficient to quantify the number or value (if they can be given a numerical valuation ) of a household's assets. This is because the link between asset ownership and consumption, nutrition and/or health (different measures of welfare) is subject to risk.

There are various kinds of risks or shocks that households are exposed to. These may be classified as natural (for example, droughts, floods and pest invasion). The second source of risks is the result of human activity (i.e. conflicts, policy-induced (e.g. inflation), terms-of-trade shocks, illness and death). The war in the northern region of Ghana in 1993, the terms-of-trade shock suffered in late 1999 resulting in a sharp depreciation of the exchange rate, and the monetary shock of 2000 associated with the electoral cycle are all examples of this second source of risks. Bush fires, infertile land, snake bite and poor sanitary conditions were identified as some of the sources of risk amongst rural communities in Ghana (Kunfaa, 1999).

Risk may be classified on the basis of whether it is idiosyncratic or covariate. Idiosyncratic risks are those events that are specific to an individual or a household. Covariate risks tend to affect the community. Examples of this type of risk in Ghana are bush fires that destroy farms and the declining soil fertility that was perceived by participants in participatory poverty assessments conducted in 1995 and 1999.

The risks or shocks that households are exposed to may also be classified on the basis of the frequency of occurrence. Some risks or shocks may be seasonal or cyclical. Although risk is the probability of an event occurring, i.e. the event may or may not happen, households may face events that are predicted with certainty. An example of this is the long dry season in the northern part of the country. This period is associated with difficulty in accessing food and water. Certainty of the occurrence of this event will not necessarily reduce a household's or individual's vulnerability to poverty. This is because of the household's exposure to the event occurring and its limited ability to mitigate the effect of the event. In a participatory poverty assessment conducted in 1995 a group of men prepared a food availability calendar showing the times of the year when food is in short supply (Table 14.1). In a similar calendar constructed by women in Banyono, in five of the twelve months there was hunger. In addition, three of the remaining months of the year were described by the women as a situation of scarce food (Korboe, 1998).

**Table 14.1   Food Security Calendar of Beo Tankou**

| Month | Condition of Living Standards |
| --- | --- |
| November–December | There is food. Potatoes are sold for income. |
| January–February | Food is available but declining.Start eating flour water (fula). There are reduced sales. |
| March–April | Inadequate food resources and water shortage. Seeds are reserved for planting. Most people are out of cash. Poor people have no animals to sell. |
| May–June | Height of hunger period. All grain has been sown. Households now depend on fruits for consumption. |
| July–August | Improving food situation. Early millet is harvested. Some sales to pay for labour. |
| September–October | Improving food situation. Groundnuts and bambara beans are harvested. Some of the harvest is sold to pay debts and to buy animals for sacrifices. |

*Source:*   Norton et al. (1995).

The other category of risks may be random and cannot be predicted with certainty. The participatory poverty assessments identified another source of vulnerability to poverty that has a time dimension, namely, long-term trends arising from environmental degradation, for example declining soil fertility, declining access to water and declining availability of products from common property areas (Norton et al., 1995).

When households and individuals are classified on the basis of poverty and vulnerability to poverty, there may be some overlapping because some households will be poor and vulnerable to poverty. However, poverty is not a sub-set of vulnerability to poverty and vulnerability to poverty is not a sub-set of poverty. A classification of vulnerability to poverty developed by Dercon (2000) brings this out quite clearly. Vulnerable to poverty consists of four groups:

- the permanently poor;
- those becoming permanently poor because of trend events, for example erosion of assets that will take them below the poverty line;
- those likely to become poor because of predictable events; and
- those likely to become poor because of shocks or damaging fluctuations.

Thus households and individuals vulnerable to poverty include some of the poor and some of the non-poor.

## 3.    Measuring Risk and Vulnerability

During the last half-decade many analysts including Baulch and Hoddinott (2000), Dercon and Krishnan (2000), Jalan and Ravallion (2000a), McCulloch and Baulch (2000), Gunning et al. (2000) and Scott (2000), using different methods, have attempted to measure vulnerability and the welfare consequences of risk, and have thus provided additional evidence on the relationships between risk, vulnerability and poverty. Ideally measuring the incidence of vulnerability to poverty and identifying who are vulnerable and the risk factors should be conducted using either longitudinal data sets or qualitative data sets that include a historical perspective. Longitudinal (panel) data sets are a recent phenomenon for African countries. Indeed, many African countries did not have more than one cross-sectional data set on living standards prior to 2000. The Heavily Indebted Countries (HIPC) process has generated the need to obtain data on living standards. The first and second Ghana Living Standards Surveys were designed to include a panel component. Unfortunately there was a problem with identifiers, so the panel component of these data sets has not been exploited.

A number of participatory poverty assessments have been conducted in Ghana since 1995. These contain components that address the issues of vulnerability and risks. However, the reports do not provide enough information to classify groups of households on the basis of vulnerability to poverty, nor is it possible to analyze rigorously the link between different types of shocks and the probability of a household or individual experiencing a decline in consumption expenditure or income. However, the participatory poverty assessments, unlike the Living Standards Surveys that have been conducted so far, do provide some information on the types of shocks and risks facing households, in addition to information on coping strategies.

Several methodologies have been developed to measure vulnerability and identify groups vulnerable to poverty using cross-sectional quantitative survey data. Some of them exploit the panel data element within cross-sectional data sets, making use of the data that are collected during the different visits to the household in the course of the year. Ligon and Schechter (2003), for instance, have broken down vulnerability into four components: poverty, aggregate risk, idiosyncratic risk, and unexplained risk. Applying the methodology to Bulgaria, they found that poverty appears to be the largest single component of vulnerability, accounting for just over half. They also report several other sorts of risk accounting for the remaining vulnerability of households, with unexplained risk (which may include measurement error) being the most important source of vulnerability.[5] Chaudhuri (2000 and 2002) has developed a methodology for estimating vulnerability to poverty using cross-section data. This is the approach to be adopted in this paper to identify groups that are vulnerable to poverty in Ghana.[6]

## 4. Methodology for Estimating Vulnerability[7]

A household's vulnerability to poverty can be expressed as a probability statement reflecting its inability to attain a certain minimum level of consumption in the future (Christiaensen and Subbarao, 2001). Consider a household $h$. We may express the probability that such a household is vulnerable as:

$$v_{ht} = \Pr(c_{h,t+1} \leq z) \tag{1}$$

where $v_{ht}$ is the probability value associated with the household's vulnerability at time $t$, $c_{h,t+1}$ measures the household's per capita consumption at time $t+1$ and $z$ is an appropriate consumption benchmark (poverty line).

Following Chaudhuri et al. (2002), we specify the stochastic process generating the consumption of a household $h$ as:

$$\ln c_h = X_h \beta + e_h \tag{2}$$

where $c_h$ is per capita consumption expenditure, $X_h$ represents a bundle of observable household characteristics, such as household size, location, educational attainment of household head, etc., $\beta$ is a vector of parameters, and $e_h$ is a an error term that captures idiosyncratic factors (shocks) that contribute to differences in per capita consumption levels of households with the same characteristics.

By assuming that the variance of $e_h$ depends on household characteristics in some parametric way, we can specify the following simple functional form:

---

[5] They also report aggregate risks as being much more important than idiosyncratic risk, although the considerably larger unexplained risk may be largely made up of unobserved sources of idiosyncratic risk (Ligon and Schechter, 2003).

[6] Using Philippines data for 1997 Chaudhuri and Datt (2001) find that they are able to predict which households will be poor in 1998. Suryahadi and Sumarto (2001) have adopted this methodology to identify households that are vulnerable to poverty and to identify the chronic poor in Indonesia. They do this by making use of information on vulnerability to poverty based on current consumption, the estimated degree of vulnerability and the estimated expected consumption. Five categories of households are developed: poor, non-poor, high vulnerability to poverty, low vulnerability to poverty and the total vulnerable group. The total vulnerable group includes non-poor households. These are households that are currently non-poor but are expected to become poor in the future.

[7] This section draws extensively on the work of Chaudhuri (2000 and 2002).

$$\sigma^2_{e,h} = X_h \theta \tag{3}$$

Estimates for $\beta$ and $\theta$ are then obtained using a three-step feasible generalized least squares (FGLS) procedure proposed by Amemiya (1977).

To proceed we first estimate equation (2) by ordinary least squares (OLS). The residuals from equation (2) are used to estimate the following equation by OLS:

$$\hat{e}^2_{OLS,h} = X_h \theta + h_h \tag{4}$$

The predictions from equation (4) are used to transform the equation as follows:

$$\frac{\hat{e}^2_{OLS}}{X_h \hat{\theta}_{OLS}} = \left( \frac{X_h}{X_h \hat{\theta}_{OLS}} \right) \theta + \frac{\eta_h}{X_h \hat{\theta}_{OLS}} \tag{5}$$

Equation (5) is estimated by OLS to obtain an asymptotically efficient FGLS estimate, $\hat{\theta}_{FGLS}$. Note that $X_h \hat{\theta}_{FGLS}$ is a consistent estimate of $\sigma^2_{e,h}$, which is the variance of the idiosyncratic component of household consumption.

We then compute

$$\hat{\sigma}_{e,h} = \sqrt{X_h \hat{\theta}_{FGLS}} \tag{6}$$

and use it to transform equation (2) as follows:

$$\frac{\ln c_h}{\hat{\sigma}_{e,h}} = \left( \frac{X_h}{\hat{\sigma}_{e,h}} \right) \beta + \frac{e_h}{\hat{\sigma}_{e,h}} \tag{7}$$

Estimation of equation (7) by OLS yields a consistent and asymptotically efficient estimate of $\beta$. The estimates of $\beta$ and $\theta$ by the FGLS approach indicate how the various household characteristics determine the mean and the variance of consumption (Alayande and Alayande, 2004).

Using the estimates for $\beta$ and $\hat{\theta}$, the mean consumption and variance of consumption are obtained respectively as follows:

$$\hat{E}[\ln c_h \mid X_h] = X_h \hat{\beta} \tag{8}$$

$$\hat{V}[\ln c_h \mid X_h] = \hat{\sigma}^2_{e,h} = X_h \hat{\theta} \tag{9}$$

If we assume that consumption is log normally distributed, we obtain an estimate of a household's vulnerability level as:

$$\hat{v}_h = \hat{Pr} \ (\ln c_h < \ln z \mid X_h) = \phi \left( \frac{\ln z - X_h \hat{\beta}}{\sqrt{X_h \hat{\theta}}} \right) \qquad (10)$$

where $\phi$ is the cumulative density of the standard normal distribution.

## 5. Vulnerability to Poverty in Ghana

### Data

The data used for the analysis are taken from the fourth Ghana Living Standards Survey, a nation-wide household survey, conducted by the Ghana Statistical Service with technical assistance from the World Bank in 1998/9. The survey collected data for 5,998 households and some 25,000 household members in the ten regions of Ghana. It contains detailed information on the socio-economic and demographic characteristics of every household, including incomes and household expenditure patterns, education, occupation, age, sex and many other determinants of household welfare (Glewwe and Twum-Baah, 1991).

### Choice of Vulnerability Threshold

Determining the proportion of a population that is vulnerable to poverty involves dividing the population into two groups — those who are vulnerable and those who are non-vulnerable. This entails establishing a vulnerability threshold, $v$, such that a household is said to be vulnerable if its vulnerability coefficient is greater than or equal to the value $v$, i.e $v_h \geq v$. As noted by Chaudhuri et al. (2002), the choice of vulnerability threshold is ultimately quite arbitrary.[8] A common choice in the literature, which is also applied in this study, is a threshold of 0.5. In other words, households having vulnerability coefficients of 0.5 or higher are considered vulnerable. The choice of 0.5 is justified for two reasons. First, it makes intuitive sense to say that a household is vulnerable if it faces a 50% or higher probability of falling into poverty in the following period. Second, when a household whose current level of consumption is equal to the poverty line faces a zero mean shock, it has a one period ahead vulnerability of 0.5. In the limit, as the time horizon approaches zero, being currently poor and being vulnerable to poverty coincide (Pritchett et al., 2000)

---

[8] See Chaudhuri (2002) for a discussion of the various choices.

## *Results*

The consumption model is estimated in line with the specifications in section 4. The dependent variable was household real consumption expenditure per adult equivalent. The explanatory variables were: age, gender, level of education and socio-economic grouping of the household head.[9] Additional variables were location dummies and the size of the household (see Appendix 14.1 for regression results).

Vulnerability estimates for various households are obtained using equation (10). The poverty benchmark employed is the nutrition-based poverty line of ¢900,000 as estimated by the Ghana Statistical Service in the GLSS 4 Report of 2000. We then generated vulnerability headcount rates for the entire population as well as for various population characteristics using the threshold of 0.5. Table 14.2 presents the results.

As can be seen from the table, 49.5% of the population are vulnerable to poverty.[10] By extrapolation this implies that about 50% of the total population were vulnerable to poverty in 1998/9 and were likely to experience an episode of poverty in the future.

The vulnerability rate of 49.5% is significantly higher than the estimated poverty rate of 39.5% in Ghana. This indicates that the estimated probability of experiencing poverty in the near future was greater (25% more) than the average risk of poverty (equal to the observed incidence of poverty) in the population. These estimates appear to confirm the findings of Chaudhuri et al. (2002) that the observed incidence of poverty underestimates the fraction of the population that is vulnerable to poverty.

However, the above-mentioned results in the incidence of vulnerability to poverty mask wide gender disparities. The incidence of poverty amongst female-headed households was lower than that amongst male-headed households. A similar pattern prevails for the vulnerability to poverty in 1998/9. Approximately 54% of households headed by men were vulnerable to poverty compared with about 36% of households headed by women. That a lower proportion of households headed by women are vulnerable to poverty compared with male-headed households is surprising. This is because households headed by women are less endowed with assets compared with men. Half of the women heading households in 1998/9 had no formal education. A comparatively smaller proportion of adults in households headed by women in 1998/9 were engaged in wage employment. The mean value of non-farm business assets in households headed by women was also lower compared with that of households headed by men. Fewer households headed by women have financial savings compared with households headed by men. The mean value of financial savings held by female-headed households in 1998/9 was lower compared with that of men. On the other

---

[9] Education of the household head was measured using the highest level of education completed. Heads of household were classified into the following socio-economic groupings: public sector employee, private formal sector employee, private informal sector employee, export farmer, food-crop farmer, non-farm self-employed and not working.

[10] We varied the vulnerability threshold to ascertain its impact on the vulnerability headcount rate. It is worth noting that the vulnerability headcount is sensitive to the threshold chosen. For example, when thresholds of 0.6 and 0.7 were applied, the vulnerability rate decreased to 36.7% and 24.6% respectively. Lowering the threshold to 0.4 and 0.3 raised the vulnerability rate to 62.1% and 73.8% respectively. Detailed results of the sensitivity analysis are contained in Appendix 14.2.

**Table 14.2   Poverty and Vulnerability Profiles for Various Population Characteristics**

|  | Population share | Share of poor | Share of vulnerable | Poverty headcount | Vulnerability headcount | Vulnerability to poverty ratio |
|---|---|---|---|---|---|---|
| **Total** | **100** | **100** | **100** | **39.5** | **49.5** | **1.25** |
| **Region** | | | | | | |
| Western | 11.6 | 12.6 | 15.0 | 27.3 | 63.7 | 2.33 |
| Central | 8.9 | 12.0 | 8.0 | 48.5 | 44.6 | 0.92 |
| Greater Accra | 11.9 | 2.6 | 6.8 | 5.2 | 28.3 | 5.44 |
| Eastern | 11.6 | 12.2 | 12.9 | 43.7 | 54.9 | 1.26 |
| Volta | 12.4 | 17.1 | 5.7 | 37.7 | 22.6 | 0.60 |
| Ashanti | 16.8 | 15.1 | 11.9 | 27.8 | 35.1 | 1.26 |
| Brong-Ahafo | 8.7 | 11.8 | 8.6 | 35.8 | 48.6 | 1.36 |
| Northern | 10.2 | 9.6 | 15.8 | 69.2 | 76.3 | 1.10 |
| Upper West | 3.2 | 4.0 | 6.2 | 84.0 | 94.9 | 1.13 |
| Upper East | 4.5 | 3.1 | 9.1 | 88.2 | 100 | 1.13 |
| **Location** | | | | | | |
| Urban | 33.2 | 20.5 | 21.6 | 19.4 | 32.1 | 1.65 |
| Rural | 66.8 | 79.8 | 78.4 | 49.5 | 58.1 | 1.17 |
| **Gender of Household Head** | | | | | | |
| Men | 72.7 | 75.0 | 80.0 | 41.0 | 54.4 | 1.33 |
| Women | 27.3 | 25.0 | 20.0 | 35.2 | 36.3 | 1.03 |
| **Occupation of Household Head** | | | | | | |
| Public Sector | 10.7 | 11.2 | 16.0 | 22.7 | 73.8 | 3.25 |
| Private Formal | 4.9 | 2.6 | 1.8 | 11.3 | 18.6 | 1.65 |
| Private Informal | 2.9 | 2.1 | 0.9 | 25.2 | 14.8 | 0.59 |
| Export Farmers | 7.0 | 10.7 | 11.4 | 38.7 | 80.4 | 2.08 |
| Food crop | 38.6 | 44.3 | 48.1 | 59.4 | 61.7 | 1.04 |
| Non-farm | 33.8 | 28.1 | 21.7 | 28.6 | 31.7 | 1.11 |
| Non-work | 2.1 | 0.9 | 0.1 | 20.4 | 2.6 | 0.13 |
| **Education of Household Head** | | | | | | |
| None | 33.3 | 33.0 | 32.6 | 57.3 | 48.3 | 0.84 |
| Primary | 3.7 | 4.8 | 2.6 | 46.9 | 34.8 | 0.74 |
| JSS/Middle | 48.1 | 51.7 | 53.2 | 32.6 | 54.8 | 1.68 |
| Secondary | 11.8 | 8.7 | 10.6 | 18.6 | 44.7 | 2.40 |
| Tertiary | 3.1 | 1.8 | 15.7 | 24.6 | 15.7 | 0.64 |
| **Ecological Zone** | | | | | | |
| Coastal | 31.3 | 27.2 | 22.3 | 28.2 | 35.3 | 1.25 |
| Forest | 43.3 | 49.2 | 39.0 | 32.6 | 44.5 | 1.37 |
| Savannah | 25.4 | 23.6 | 38.7 | 65.0 | 75.4 | 1.16 |

*Source:*   Authors' computations.

hand, the lower incidence of vulnerability to poverty amongst households headed by women may be explained by the fact that women are usually part of mutual insurance schemes outside the family and the household, and therefore tend to have networks with other women (Goldstein et al., 2002). Participation in a mutual insurance scheme increases the opportunity for consumption smoothing.

As expected, vulnerability to poverty is higher amongst rural households. While about 67% of the population is rural, 78.4% of those estimated to be vulnerable to poverty live in rural areas compared with only 21.6% in urban areas, which harbour 33.2% of Ghana's population (Table 14.2). In terms of vulnerability headcount, about 58% of rural households are vulnerable as against 32.1% of urban households. This is similar to the findings of Chaudhuri et al. (2002) for Indonesia, who found that households located in urban areas are less likely than those in rural areas to suffer from shocks that plunge people into poverty and/or have a greater capacity to protect their consumption expenditures in the face of shocks.

Table 14.2 also reveals regional disparities in poverty and vulnerability rates. While vulnerability rates in general correlated positively with poverty rates, two regions, Volta and Central, have vulnerability rates lower than poverty rates, thereby posting vulnerability to poverty ratios at less than unity, i.e. 0.60 and 0.92 respectively. The most striking case is that of Volta Region, which ranks sixth in terms of poverty but is the least vulnerable region. Even though this is a surprising result, it could be plausibly explained in terms of lower consumption variance. In other words, a significant proportion of households in these two regions probably have mean consumption just below the poverty line with very little variability in consumption. Thus most of the households observed to be poor are only transitorily poor, and are highly likely to move out of poverty rather than remain in poverty in the near future. As expected, the three poorest regions — Northern, Upper West and Upper East — are also the most vulnerable regions, with the Upper East, the poorest of the three (88.2%), having all its population vulnerable to poverty (100%).

Besides the regional pattern, it is also important to relate poverty and vulnerability to poverty to the economic activities in which households are engaged. Our results show that even though poverty is highest by far among households headed by food-crop farmers (59.4%) and lowest among households headed by private formal workers (11.3%), the incidence of vulnerability to poverty appears to be highest among households headed by export farmers (80.4%) and lowest among households headed by persons who do not work (2.6%) (Table 14.2). It must be pointed out that, despite the high incidence of vulnerability among households headed by export farmers, only 11.4% of the total vulnerable belonged to this group. Another interesting picture that emerges from the comparison of observed poverty and the incidence of vulnerability to poverty is the low vulnerability incidence (2.6%) among non-working groups, despite their high poverty incidence (20.4%). The same applies to households headed by private informal workers (14.8% as against 25.2%). On the other hand, households headed by public sector workers, characterized by a relatively low poverty incidence (22.7%), seem to have high vulnerability incidence (about 74%). This phenomenon suggests that there is a high incidence of transient poverty amongst these three groups. Other groups, including households headed by non-farm self-employed workers, food-crop farmers and private formal sector employees, have relatively higher vulnerability rates compared with poverty rates.

In terms of vulnerability by level of education of household head, our results indicate that those with JSS/Middle School certificates are not only the most vulnerable group (54.8%), but also contribute the largest share of the total vulnerable (53.2%). The next group with a high incidence of vulnerability is households headed by persons with no education. The least vulnerable group is households headed by people with tertiary-level education, with a vulnerability rate (15.7%) lower than the observed poverty rate of 24.6%. An interesting picture that emerges from the comparison of poverty and vulnerability headcount rates in terms of level of education is that, while generally poverty rates decline with level of education, this trend is not observed for vulnerability rates.

A classification of poverty and vulnerability in terms of ecological zones shows that households located in the savannah belt are the poorest (65%) and the most vulnerable (75.4%). The coastal belt has the lowest incidence of poverty (28.2%) and vulnerability (35.3%).

In line with the traditional poverty analysis in Ghana, we apply two poverty lines to the distribution of the poverty and vulnerability to poverty measures. A lower poverty line of ¢700,000 per adult equivalent characterizes the very poor or extremely poor[11]. The second poverty line refers to those with income below an upper poverty line of ¢900,000 cedis per adult equivalent. As Table 14.3 illustrates, both the very poor and the poor are characterized by a high incidence of vulnerability to poverty.

**Table 14.3    Vulnerability Incidence According to Poverty Status**

| Poverty Status | Population share | Share of vulnerable | Vulnerability headcount |
|---|---|---|---|
| Very Poor | 26.9 | 38.8 | 71.5 |
| Poor | 12.6 | 15.5 | 60.8 |
| Non-Poor | 60.5 | 45.7 | 37.3 |

*Source:*  Authors' computations.

Over 71% and 60% of the very poor and poor respectively in 1998/9 were vulnerable to poverty. This gives a picture of the movement of people into and out of poverty over time, which also allows us to make some inferences about chronic and transient poverty in Ghana, even though it is difficult to estimate the incidence of chronic and transient poverty from one set of cross-sectional data or in the absence of longitudinal data sets. From Table 14.3 we find that of the almost 27% of the population who are

---

[11] According to the Ghana Statistical Service people in this category are extremely poor because, even if they allocated their entire budgets to food, they would not be able to meet their minimum nutrition requirements (if they consume the average consumption basket). This poverty line was 49.6% of mean consumption levels in 1998/9 (GSS, 2000).

estimated to be extremely poor, not everybody is vulnerable. Whilst an estimated 72% of the extremely poor are likely to remain in poverty, about 28% of this group are likely to move out of poverty. Against this background, it would not be far-fetched to characterize the 72% of the very poor that are vulnerable as the chronic poor, and the remaining 28% as the transient poor in Ghana. A similar picture can be deduced from the poor group, which has a vulnerability incidence of 60.8%. In this case, it is possible to refer to this section of the poor that are predicted to remain poor in the future as the chronic poor, whilst the rest can be referred to as transient poor. The proportions of the poor that are expected to remain poor are comparable to estimates that were obtained for Côte d'Ivoire in the period 1985/6 to 1987/8 using longitudinal data (Grootaert and Kanbur,1995). Using this rough rule of thumb we estimate the level of chronic poverty in Ghana to be about 27%. Interestingly, among the non-poor our findings reveal quite a large percentage (37.3%) of this group to be vulnerable to poverty, thus forming part of the transient poor.

## 6. Dealing with Risk and Vulnerability

Individuals and households have developed mechanisms to deal with risk and variability in income and expenditure. Risk-management strategies may be classified into three groups: risk reduction, risk mitigation and risk coping strategies (see Holzmann, 2001).

***Risk reduction strategies:*** These are actions that are taken to reduce the probability of a risky event occurring. In many communities, particularly the rural north of the country, out-migration has been a strategy used to reduce the risk of unemployment for extended periods of time. In the consultations that formed part of the preparation of the Ghana Poverty Reduction Strategy Paper another risk reduction strategy that was identified was treatment of water before drinking.

***Risk mitigation strategies:*** These are strategies taken prior to the occurrence of the risk event with the objective of reducing its impact when it occurs. Some of the risk mitigating strategies that have been adopted by individuals are shown in Table 14.4.

***Risk coping strategies:*** These are actions to reduce the impact of the risk event once it has occurred. Examples of these strategies that have been adopted by households in Ghana are to be found in Table 14.5.

A case-study of four villages conducted in 2001 in the Greater Accra, Ashanti and Upper East Regions of Ghana found that households went through periods when they had to reduce the number of meals consumed in a day.[12] The majority of

---

[12] One village, Obom, is located on the coast about 15 miles from Accra, the capital city. Two villages, i.e. Kasei and Kofikrom, are in the forest zone of the country. The fourth village, Kpikpira is situated in the savannah zone to the north of the country. Agriculture is the main activity in all of the villages. As is typical of farming in Ghana and the rest of Africa, the farmers do not tend to specialize. A wide range of crops is produced in each village. Although the main activity in the villages is agriculture, there are a number of non-farm activities.

households in the village in the Upper East Region had to reduce the number of meals consumed in a day (Table 14.6). Households were ranked on the basis of an asset index created using factor analysis. The percentage of households that had to reduce the number of meals consumed in a day due to hardship was highest amongst the bottom third of households in the ranking and was lowest amongst the top third of households in the asset wealth scale (Table 14.6).

**Table 14.4  Examples of Some Risk-Mitigating Strategies based on Discussions with the Communities**

| Northern Region | Volta Region | Central Region |
|---|---|---|
| • Engage in sheanut business (women) <br> • Undertake other jobs, e.g. blacksmithing, weaving <br> • Keep farm animals <br> • Practice mixed cropping as insurance against crop failure <br> • Provide communal labour <br> • Use animal manure <br> • Work as labourers for a fee <br> • Migration of young children and men | • Diversification of sources of income <br> • Petty menial jobs <br> • Migrate to do part-time jobs | • Migrate to do secondary jobs during the lean season <br> • Encourage early marriage |

*Sources:* Amadu, A, and Atua-Ntow, K. (2000) *Regional and District Level Consultations on Poverty Reduction: Northern Region.* GoG/UNICEF Collaboration on GPRS.
Nkum Associates and Ghartey Associates (2000) *Report on Poverty Reduction Consultations in the Volta Region.* National Development Planning Commission/German Technical Cooperation.
Nkum Associates and Ghartey Associates (2000) *Report on Poverty Reduction Consultations in the Central Region.* National Development Planning Commission/ German Technical Cooperation.

The risk-coping and risk-mitigating strategies adopted by households in Ghana have two features. The first is that the households use informal arrangements for risk management. The second is that some of the strategies that are adopted will perpetuate the condition of poverty and destitution.

***Risk-management arrangements:*** Informal arrangements dominate risk-management strategies in Ghana (Tables 14.4 and 14.5). This is largely because of limited, if any, public sector arrangements to manage risk as well as limited market-based instruments. Participatory poverty assessments revealed that 'Government safety nets were not mentioned by any informants as being in any way relevant for the poorest members of these communities' (Norton et al., 1995: 37). Data from the fourth Living Standards Survey conducted in 1998/9 show that only 27 households out of a sample of 5998 received social security flows. The coverage of the state pension scheme was no better; less than 50% of households with a member aged 60 or over were recipients of state pensions. The recipients of social security and state pensions are concentrated amongst non-poor households and in households headed by men. The limited coverage of the public sector arrangements is because provision is limited to mostly formal sector workers. In addition, there are no schemes such as unemployment benefit or child support. The option to use market-based strategies is determined by the stage of financial development that the country has attained, and whether in the instance that these insurance instruments exist they can be accessed by micro entrepreneurs and smallholder farmers, etc. The financial sector in Ghana provides instruments such as savings deposits, insurance and financial paper. However, the clientele of the institutions providing these instruments do not make up the group that is more likely than not to be vulnerable to poverty. The macroeconomic environment is also a critical factor in determining whether market-based instruments will be used for risk management. The macroeconomy is a source of shocks and can erode the value of, and returns to, financial assets.

**Table 14.5   Examples of Some Risk-Coping Strategies based on Discussions with the Communities**

| Northern Region | Volta Region | Central Region |
|---|---|---|
| • Borrow from friends and relatives<br>• Look for cheaper products<br>• Ration food/Take less food<br>• Withdraw children from school temporarily<br>• Ask for remittances from relatives<br>• Receive assistance from NGOs and other government agencies | • Depend on others for financial assistance<br>• Reliance on extended family for support<br>• Eat the same type of food e.g. Akple and hot pepper<br>• Withdraw wards from school<br>• Meeting needs through sub-standard means<br>• Selling and mortgaging property·<br>• Sell produce at low prices | • Depend on friends and relatives<br>• Secure loans at high interest rates<br>• Send children out as house help<br>• Eat once a day<br>• Sell produce at low prices<br>• Buy on credit |

*Sources:* Ibid.

**Table 14.6   Percentage of Households that Reduced the Number of Meals Consumed in a Day**

| Region | % of Households |
|---|---|
| Upper East | 94.12 |
| Ashanti | 37.25 |
| Greater Accra | 43.40 |
| **Asset Wealth Ranking** | |
| Bottom third | 72.55 |
| Middle third | 61.54 |
| Top third | 40.38 |

*Source:*   Survey of four villages.

Several of the informal arrangements that were identified as risk-coping strategies in the participatory poverty assessments were based on membership of groups, and on family and friendship ties (Table 14.7). In the case study of four villages located in three regions of the country, respondents were asked to identify individuals or groups they could confidently rely on for help. The most frequently cited groups of individuals were close family members, other family members and friends (Table 14.7).

**Table 14.7   Persons/Groups that Can be Relied on for Help**

| Person/Group | Frequency | Location of source of assistance | Frequency |
|---|---|---|---|
| Close relation (i.e. nuclear family member) | 73 | Within the village | 118 |
| | | Another village | 27 |
| Other relative | 20 | Large town | 47 |
| Friend | 51 | Accra | 5 |
| Money lender | 9 | Kumasi | 20 |
| Savings and credit union | 19 | Outside Ghana | 5 |
| Co-operative | 14 | | |
| Social group | 13 | | |
| Government/donor scheme | 9 | | |
| Other | 12 | | |

*Source:*   Survey of four villages.

The less frequently mentioned sources of assistance in time of need or crisis were the money-lender and government or donor schemes. The money-lender is unlikely to be the first point of call, since repayment is expected and most likely will have to be made with interest. Access to government or donor schemes is determined by whether such schemes exist in the village or in the district.

The potential sources of assistance tended to be located in the village, i.e in three-quarters of the cases (Table 14.7). Only 5 respondents in the sample indicated that they could depend on assistance from individuals or groups located outside the country. Dependence on support from within the village suggests that these risk-management arrangements will probably break down or not be effective to deal with covariate shocks or risks, since the whole community is likely to be affected.

Apart from family relationships and friendships, social capital can be built up through membership of co-operatives and social groups. The study of four villages found that there was greater participation in social groups, in particular religious-based groups, than in co-operatives. The low participation of respondents in co-operatives may be attributed to the obligation of having to pay a part of the produce as dues.

In the case of social groups, the obligations are mainly the payment of dues and attendance at meetings. In some instances the dues are about 1,000 cedis a month, which is less than US$2 per annum. Membership of social groups seems to be more geared towards dealing with risk than is membership of co-operatives (Table 14.8).

This may explain the larger membership of social groups compared with co-operatives in this set of villages.

**Table 14.8   Some Benefits from Membership of Social Groups in the Four Villages**

| Benefit or service | Frequency |
| --- | --- |
| Donate to members when bereaved | 18 |
| Receive financial help when needed | 13 |
| Receive counselling and prayers | 13 |
| Labour provided when needed | 5 |
| Receive food aid | 3 |
| Obtain credit | 2 |

*Source:*   Survey of four villages.

The strategies used by households and individuals to cope with shocks can contribute to making it difficult to attain previous levels of income, assets, and consumption, and can result in their remaining or declining further into poverty and destitution. Examples of such actions that emerged from the participatory poverty assessments that formed part of the preparation of the Ghana Poverty Reduction Strategy Paper are rationing of food, withdrawal of children from school and selling of assets (see Table 14.5).

All the participatory poverty assessments conducted in Ghana since 1995 find that, during the hunger season prior to the harvest, intake of nutrients can fall below the required minimum. This can have long-term detrimental effects on children. Evidence from Zimbabwe shows that the impact of the 1994/5 drought on children aged 12 to 24 months 'lowered annual growth rates of these children. Four years after the failure of the rains in 1994/95, these children remained shorter than identically aged children who had not experienced this drought at the 12 to 24 months range' (Hoddinot and Kinsey, 2001: 429). In Ghana the hunger season is a regular event. For those households that regularly reduce nutrient intake for two to three months at a time this can have detrimental effects on children. Studies from other countries have found that children with slow height growth perform less well in school.[13] There is also evidence of links between child height and adult productivity. Thus coping mechanisms that reduce nutrient intake of children erode their human capital and have long-term adverse implications for productivity and income. Erratic attendance at school is not beneficial to the child.

Failure to accumulate assets sufficient to maintain households at a level of well-being above the poverty line can cause a household to remain permanently poor.[14] Selling of assets results in the erosion of the physical and financial asset base of the household. Some households may find it difficult to rebuild the asset base, especially if they are regularly subjected to shocks.

[13] See Hoddinnot and Kinsey (2001) for a review of some of these studies.
[14] See Carter and May (2001) for a discussion of this.

## 7.    The Role of Public Policy

Households in Ghana are not able to insure themselves fully against risk. Some households are part of groups or networks that provide insurance to members, whilst some individuals do not have access to this form of insurance. In the absence of full insurance, consumption expenditures are reduced in the face of shocks and predictable fluctuations and in some instances the asset stock is reduced to dangerously low levels. In the face of shocks households or individuals may choose to invest in activities that have low but certain returns. These decisions can adversely impact on their ability to build up assets to move out of poverty and in the aggregate can put the economy on a lower growth trajectory than would otherwise be the case.

The public sector has two roles to play in assisting households, firms and individuals to deal with risk. The first is providing a stable macroeconomic and policy framework within which agents operate. Macro-level shocks from the economy (e.g. a sudden rise in the inflation rate due to a monetary shock) and the political sphere (e.g. conflict) must be minimized. A stable macroeconomy will encourage the development of financial instruments that can be used for insurance purposes. Sectoral policies are important in preventing and reducing the impact of shocks that households and economic agents might face.

The second function of the public sector is the provision of safety nets. The provision of safety nets that households and individuals are certain will be available if they should suffer a shock could bring about a change in behaviour that would be welfare-enhancing. It could encourage poor households to diversify into more productive but risky activities. Safety nets will also make it possible for the poor to maintain their consumption of food and other health-related expenditures at levels that will not impair their human capital. For those poor who are unable to take advantage of the relaxation of production constraints, safety nets are needed to maintain their consumption levels above the required minimum.

In designing public sector safety nets it is important that the potential beneficial effects outweigh any possible negative effects. Empirical evidence from developing countries produces a negative relationship between private transfers and social assistance. A simulation exercise using data from the Philippines finds that introducing an unemployment insurance scheme would not improve household income because of the accompanying decline in private transfers. Cash transfers to households below the poverty line intended to close the poverty gap would result in only a fraction of households moving above the poverty line (Cox and Jimenez, 1995). However, evidence from South Africa suggests that 'state actions may also "crowd in" other transfers' (Conway and Norton, 2002: 537). In South Africa it was found that, with the introduction of the universal state pension scheme, children who stopped transferring income to their parents used the money for their own children's education. Participation in mutual insurance schemes is not complete. Some individuals are not part of networks that can provide them with the type of insurance to protect them from shocks. Goldstein et al. (2002), in their sample of married couples in Akuapem, found that some individuals did not receive help when they approached others for it. In a country such as Ghana where there is really very little in the way of public or formal safety nets or ladders, the possible crowding-out effect of their introduction would probably be outweighed by the impact that increased coverage would have.

The Ghana Poverty Reduction Strategy addresses some of the issues of risk and vulnerability through its proposed programmes to improve access to and quality of health services and education particularly in the three northern regions. It also has strategies to improve the environment as a means of improving the health status of the population. The Strategy Paper also proposes direct state interventions for the vulnerable and excluded, such as expansion of social security schemes, slum upgrading, disaster management, coordinating service delivery and partnership programmes with non-governmental organizations. However, the proposal in the GPRS to expand coverage of the Social Security and National Insurance Trust to 500,000 is unlikely to apply to the bulk of the vulnerable who are food-crop farmers.

It has been estimated that approximately 50% of households in Ghana are vulnerable to consumption expenditure falling below the poverty line. Approximately 27% of the population may be chronically poor, with a large proportion of the chronic poor in extreme poverty. For developing countries such as Ghana, therefore, the challenge is that the need for safety nets and a social protection scheme is great, but the resources available to run an effective safety-net scheme are limited. Thus in designing a social protection programme several issues need to be addressed. It has to be decided clearly what the objective of the social protection programme is and the target group(s) must be clearly identified. The informal insurance arrangements need to be well understood so as to minimize the possible impact of crowding out with the introduction of the public sector schemes. As already mentioned, the macroeconomic framework should be so managed as to minimize the incidence of shocks emanating from the domestic economy. Education and health programmes should be designed to improve quality and coverage that includes the poor. Environmental degradation acts as a constraint on poor agricultural households improving upon agricultural incomes and contributes to making these households even more vulnerable to shocks that might hit them. Most if not all econometric analysis of the determinants of poverty do not include environmental variables that affect the quality of the natural resources households have to work with as explanatory variables. However, they constantly appear as factors that rural households perceive to be important as causes of poverty (Korboe, 1998; Kunfaa, 1999; Norton et al, 2000). Thus programmes to reverse the environmental degradation are a necessary component of any social protection scheme. In designing a social protection scheme it is important that there is information on the type of shocks to which households are susceptible. In the northern sector of the country it would appear (based on the participatory poverty assessments) that households are vulnerable to the predictable hunger period during which rainfall is below the average. Major headway in reducing vulnerability to poverty would be measures that would allow households to get through the long dry season without experiencing dramatic declines in income and being forced to reduce consumption expenditures.

## 8. Understanding Risk and Vulnerability in Ghana: The Way Forward

This study has made an attempt to estimate the incidence of vulnerability to poverty and to identify groups that are vulnerable to poverty in Ghana using cross-sectional data of 1998/9. The first criticism of this bold attempt is the age of the data set. Investigating risk and vulnerability in Ghana almost six years after the completion of GLSS 4 and after the economy has suffered the macro shocks of the third quarter of 1999, the monetary shock of 2000 and price shocks associated with the adjustment of petroleum prices in 2001 and 2003 would tempt one to ask of what relevance is the analysis. However, the analysis does provide some historical perspective of the groups that were vulnerable to poverty. It also clearly brings out the need for up-to-date data that are collected with the objective of addressing issues of poverty dynamics. The data set, out-dated as it is, cannot be used to explain or understand why some groups or households are vulnerable to poverty. There is no information on shocks that caused a decline in income and/or the reduction in the value of assets. There is no information on how households or persons responded to different types of shocks.

Thus a critical requirement for further understanding and investigation of poverty dynamics in Ghana is the availability of data sets (quantitative and qualitative) that provide the information needed to undertake more rigorous analysis. Knowing who the vulnerable to poverty are, what shocks they are subject to, the impact of the shocks on their stock of assets, income and consumption, and understanding how and why they respond to different shocks the way they do are critical for the design of social protection programmes to help households manage risk. Given the high incidence of vulnerability to poverty suggested by the GLSS 4 data set and the limited resources available to the public sector, it is important that programmes are designed that will be effective in helping households manage risk. The appropriate public safety-net and social protection measures should be put in place to evoke from households the behavioural responses that will shift them and the economy to a higher growth trajectory.

## References

Alayande, B. and Alayande, O. (2004) 'A Quantitative and Qualitative Assessment of Vulnerability to Poverty in Nigeria.' Paper presented at CSAE Conference on Poverty Reduction, Growth and Human Development in Africa, March.

Alwang, J. and Siegel, P. B. (2000) 'Towards Operational Definitions and Measures of Vulnerability: A Review of the Literature from Different Disciplines.' Paper prepared for the Social Protection Unit, Human Development Unit, World Bank, Washington, DC.

Amemiya, T. (1977) 'The Maximum Likelihood Estimator and the Non-linear Three Stage Least Squares Estimator in the General Non-linear Simultaneous Equation Model,' *Econometrica*, Vol. 45: 955–68.

Asenso-Okyere, W. K., Nsowah-Nuamah, K. N. N. and Alberson, P. (1997) 'Characterising the Poor in Ghana: A Logit Approach' in W. K. Asenso-Okyere, G. Benneh and W. Tims (eds), *Sustainable Food Security in West Africa.* Dordrecht: Kluwer Academia Publishers.

Banerjee, A. and Newman, A. (1994) 'Poverty, Incentives and Development,' *American Economic Review, Papers and Proceedings,* Vol.84, No. 2: 211–15.

Baulch, B. and Hoddinott, J. (2000) 'Economic Mobility and Poverty Dynamics in Developing Countries', *'Journal of Development Studies,* Vol. 88, No. 6: 1–24.

Bigsten, A. and Shimeles, A. (2003) 'The Dynamics of Poverty in Ethiopia.' Paper prepared for a WIDER Conference on 'Inequality, Poverty and Human Well-being', 30–31 May.

Boateng, E. O., Ewusi, K., Kanbur, R. and Mackay, A. (1990) *A Poverty Profile for Ghana 1987– 1988. Social Dimensions of Adjustment in Sub-Saharan Africa.* Working Paper No. 5. Washington, DC: World Bank.

Canagarajah, S., Mazumdar, D. and Ye, X. (1998) *The Structure and Determinants of Inequality and Poverty Reduction in Ghana, 1988–92.* Policy Research Working Paper. Washington, DC: World Bank.

Carter, M. R. and May, J. (2001) One Kind of Freedom: Poverty Dynamics in Post-Apartheid South Africa,' *World Development,* Vol. 29, No. 12: 1987–2006.

Chaudhuri S. (2000) 'Empirical Methods for Assessing Household Vulnerability to Poverty,' New York: Columbia University, Draft.

Chaudhuri, S. (2002) *Empirical Methods for Assessing Vulnerability to Poverty.* New York: University of Columbia, Department of Economics.

Chaudhuri S. and Datt, G. (2001) 'Assessing Household Vulnerability to Poverty: A Methodology and Estimates for the Philippines.' Washington, DC: World Bank, Draft.

Chaudhuri, S.,Jalan, J. and Suryahadi, A. (2002) *Assessing Household Vulnerability to Poverty from Cross-sectional Data: A Methodology and Estimates from Indonesia.* New York: Columbia University, Department of Economics Discussion Paper Series No. 0102–52.

Christiaensen, L. J. and Subbarao, K. (2001) *Towards an Understanding of Vulnerability in Rural Kenya.* Washington, DC: World Bank.

Conway, T. and Norton, A (2002) 'Nets, Ropes, Ladders and Trampolines: The Place of Social Protection within Current Debates on Poverty Reduction,' *Development Policy Review*, Vol. 20, No. 5: 533–40.

Cox, D. and Jimenez, E. (1995) 'Private Transfers and the Effectiveness of Public Income Redistribution in the Philippines' in D.van de Walle and K. Nead (eds), *Public Spending and the Poor. Theory and Evidence.* Washington, DC: and Baltimore, MD: Johns Hopkins University Press.

Cruces, G. and Wodon, Q. (2003) 'Risk-Adjusted Poverty in Argentina: Measurement and Determinants.' Paper presented at a WIDER Conference on Inequality, Poverty and Human Well-being, Helsinki, 30–31 May.

Cunningham, W. and Maloney, W. F. (2000) 'Measuring Vulnerability: Who suffered in the 1995 Mexican crisis?' Washington, DC: World Bank (mimeo).

Dercon, S. (2000) 'Assessing Vulnerability to Poverty' CSAE, Oxford University (mimeo). www.economics.ox.ac.uk/members/stefan.dercon/

Dercon, S. (1999) 'Income Risk, Coping Strategies and Safety Nets' (mimeo).

Dercon, S. and Krishnan, P. ( 2000) 'Vulnerability, Seasonality and Poverty in Ethiopia,' *Journal of Development Studies*, Vol. 36, No. 6, August: 25–53.

Ellis, F. (2000) *Rural Livelihoods and Diversity in Developing Countries.* Oxford: Oxford University Press.

Gibson, John (2001) 'Measuring Chronic Poverty Without a Panel,' *Journal of Development Economics,* Vol. 65, No. 2: 243–66.

Glewwe, P. and Hall, G. (1998) 'Are Some Groups More Vulnerable to Macroeconomic Shocks than Others? Hypothesis Tests Based on Panel Data from Peru,' *Journal of Development Economics*, Vol. 56: 181–206.

Glewwe, P. K. and Twum-Baah, K. A. (1991) *The Distribution of Welfare in Ghana 1987–88.* LSMS Working Paper No. 75. Washington, DC: World Bank.

Goldstein, M., de Janvry, A. and Sadoulet, E. (2002) *Is a Friend in Need a Friend Indeed? Inclusion and Exclusion in Mutual Insurance Networks in Southern Ghana.* WIDER Discussion Paper No. 2002/25. UN, Helsinki: United Nations University Press.

Grootaert, C. and Kanbur, R. (1995) 'The Lucky Few Amidst Economic Decline: Distributional Change in Côte d'Ivoire as Seen through Panel Data Sets,' *Journal of Development Studies*, Vol. 31, No. 4: 603–19.

Guillaumont, P. (1999) 'On the Economic Vulnerability of Low Income Countries,' CERDI-CNRS, Université d'Auvergne, France (mimeo).

Gunning, J. W., Hoddinott, J., Kinsey, B. and Owens, T. (2000) 'Revisiting Forever Gained: Income Dynamics in the Resettlement Areas of Zimbabwe, 1983–96,' *Journal of Development Studies*, Vol. 36, No. 6: 132–54.

Hoddinott, J. and Kinsey, B. (2001) 'Child Growth in the Time of Drought,' *Oxford Bulletin of Economics and Statistics*, Vol. 63, No. 4: 409–36.

Holzmann, R. (2001) 'Risk and Vulnerability: The Forward-Looking Role of Social Protection in a Globalising World.' Paper prepared for the Asia and Pacific Forum on Poverty — Policy and Institutional Reforms for Poverty Reduction, Asian Development Bank, Manila, 5–9 February.

Holzmann, R. and Jørgensen, S. (1999) *Social Protection as Social Risk Management: Conceptual Underpinnings for the Social Protection Strategy Paper.* Social Protection Discussion Paper No. 9904. Washington, DC: World Bank.

Jalan, J. and Ravallion, M. (1998). 'Transient Poverty in Postreform China.' *Journal of Comparative Economics*, Vol. 26: 338–57.

Jalan, J. and Ravallion, M. (2000a) 'Is Transient Poverty Different? Evidence from Rural China', *Journal of Development Studies*, Vol. 88, No. 6: 82–99.

Jalan, J. and Ravallion, M. (2000b) 'Behavioural Responses to Risk in Rural China.' *Journal of Development Economics*, Vol. 66: 23–49.

Kedir, Abbi M. and McKay, A. (2003) *Chronic Poverty in Urban Ethiopia: Panel Data Evidence'.* Paper prepared for International Conference on Staying Poor: Chronic Poverty and Development Policy, Institute for Development Policy and Management, University of Manchester, UK, 7–9 April.

Korboe, D. (1998) *Ghana: Targeted Poverty Reduction Project. Synthesised Report on the Ghana Social Assessment.* Study commissioned by the World Bank in collaboration with the National Development Planning Commission, Accra.

Kunfaa, E.Y. (1999) *Consultations with the Poor.* Ghana Country Synthesis Report. Washington, DC: World Bank.

Ligon, E. and Schechter, L. (2003) 'Measuring Vulnerability.' *Economic Journal*, Vol. 113 (March).

McCulloch, N. and Baulch, B. (2000) 'Simulating the Impact of Policy upon Chronic and Transitory Poverty in Rural Pakistan,' *Journal of Development Studies*, Vol. 36, No. 6: 100–30.

Norton, A., Bortei-Doku Aryeetey, E., Korboe, D. and Dogbe, D. K. T. (1995) *Poverty Assessments in Ghana. Using Qualitative and Participatory Research Methods.* PSP Discussion Paper Series No. 83. Washington, DC: World Bank, Poverty and Social Policy Department.

Pritchett, L., Suryahadi, A. and Sumarto, A. (2000) 'Quantifying Vulnerability to Poverty: a proposed measure with application to Indonesia.' Jakarta: Social Monitoring and Early Response Unit (mimeo).

Rosenzweig, M. and Binswanger, H. (1993) 'Wealth, Weather Risk and the Composition and Profitability of Agricultural Investments,' *Economic Journal*, Vol. 103 (January): 56–78.

Scott, C. (2000) 'Mixed Fortunes: A Study of Poverty Mobility among Small Farm Households in Chile, 1968–1986,' *Journal of Development Studies*, Vol. 36, No. 6: 155–80.

Seini, A. W., Nyanteng, V. K. and vanden Boom, G. J. M. (1977) 'Income and Expenditure Profiles and Poverty in Ghana', in Asenso-Okyere et al.

Sen, B. (2001) 'Risks, Vulnerability and Poverty Dynamics in Bangladesh,' Dacca: Bangladesh Institute of Development Studies. Paper presented at the Third Annual Global Development Conference, Rio de Janeiro, 9–12 December.

Sinha, S. and Lipton, M. (1999) 'Damaging Fluctuations, Risk and Poverty: A Review.' Background Paper for World Bank, *World Development Report 2001.*

Suryahadi, A. and Sumarto, S. (2001) *The Chronic Poor, the Transient Poor, and the Vulnerable in Indonesia Before and After the Crisis.* Indonesia: SMERU Working Paper.

World Bank (2000) *Dynamic Risk Management and the Poor. Developing a Social Protection Strategy for Africa.* Washington, DC: World Bank, Human Development Group.

**Appendix 14.1:   Regression Results**

| Variable | OLS | | FGLS | |
|---|---|---|---|---|
| | log (c) | Var (c) | log (c) | Var (c) |
| age head | −0.0005 | 0.0009 | 0.007 | −0.0003 |
| | (−0.87) | (1.93) | (7.82) | (−53) |
| hh size | −0.1146 | −0.0083 | −0.2274 | 0.0053 |
| | (−38.19) | (−3.12) | (−28.96) | 2.24 |
| sex head | 0.0124 | 0.0035 | −0.1806 | 0.006 |
| | (0.76) | (0.24) | (−6.84) | (0.44) |
| loc 2-2 | −0.1689 | 0.0075 | −0.2088 | 0.0013 |
| | (−9.40) | (0.47) | (−3.67) | (0.09) |
| region 2 | −0.2739 | −0.0298 | 0.0368 | −0.012 |
| | (−8.85) | (−1.09) | (0.59) | (−0.52) |
| region 3 | 0.1316 | −0.0669 | −0.034 | 0.0035 |
| | (4.23) | (−2.44) | (−0.50) | (0.17) |
| region 4 | −0.2462 | 0.0883 | 0.0988 | −0.0032 |
| | (−7.73) | (3.14) | (1.1) | (-0.09) |
| region 5 | −0.1911 | 0.1862 | 0.6245 | −0.0269 |
| | (−6.42) | (0.71) | (10.63) | (−1.04) |
| region 6 | −0.0039 | 0.0098 | 0.3249 | −0.0083 |
| | (−0.14) | (0.39) | (4.15) | (−0.35) |
| region 7 | −0.0816 | −0.031 | 0.0335 | −0.006 |
| | (−2.46) | (−1.06) | (0.43) | (−0.24) |
| region 8 | −0.4094 | 0.0785 | −0.4496 | 0.0077 |
| | (−10.56) | (2.29) | (−3.61) | (0.18) |
| region 9 | −0.593 | −0.1379 | −0.773 | −0.0077 |
| | (−10.46) | (−2.75) | (−7.97) | (−0.25) |
| region 10 | −0.8007 | −0.0966 | −2.216 | 0.0412 |
| | (−18.48) | (−2.53) | (−24.85) | (1.55) |
| seg. 2 | 0.0197 | 0.053 | 0.7609 | −0.0144 |
| | (0.49) | (1.48) | (11.77) | (−0.48) |
| seg. 3 | −0.1936 | 0.09 | 1.0241 | −0.0326 |
| | (−4.11) | (2.16) | (13.5) | (−0.78) |
| seg. 4 | −1226 | 0.0291 | −0.072 | 0.0087 |
| | (−3.15) | (0.85) | (−1.08) | (0.3) |
| seg. 5 | −0.3048 | 0.0726 | 0.4416 | −0.0123 |
| | (−9.99) | (2.69) | (6.97) | (−0.47) |
| seg. 6 | −0.0872 | 0.063 | 0.7048 | −0.0145 |
| | (−2.96) | (2.42) | (11.65) | (−0.62) |
| seg. 7 | −0.224 | 0.2226 | 0.756 | −0.0161 |
| | (−5.11) | (5.76) | (6.56) | (−0.26) |
| educ. 2 | 0.109 | −0.0391 | −0.5301 | 0.0237 |
| | (5.96) | (−2.42) | (−16.80) | (1.8) |
| educ. 3 | 0.277 | −0.036 | −0.2778 | 0.0207 |
| | (9.67) | (−1.42) | (−6.00) | (1.08) |
| educ. 4 | 0.38 | 0.052 | 0.502 | −0.0021 |
| | (7.75) | (1.2) | (4.12) | (−0.04) |
| constant | 14.903 | 0.2554 | 14.6128 | 0.9616 |
| | (301.3) | (5.85) | (134.84) | (6.43) |

*Notes:*   log (c) refers to log of consumption
var (c) refers to variance of consumption
t statistics in parenthesis

**Appendix 14.2:**     **Sensitivity Results of Vulnerability Headcount Rate**

| | Vulnerability Threshold (V) | | | | |
|---|---|---|---|---|---|
| | V = 0.3 | V = 0.4 | V = 0.5 | V = 0.6 | V = 0.7 |
| Total | 73.8 | 62.1 | 49.5 | 36.7 | 24.6 |
| ***Region*** | | | | | |
| Western | 85.0 | 74.4 | 63.7 | 51.4 | 35.4 |
| Central | 72.8 | 60.4 | 44.6 | 28.3 | 16.7 |
| Greater Accra | 61.9 | 45.5 | 28.3 | 17.0 | 6.2 |
| Eastern | 78.9 | 68.6 | 54.9 | 40.5 | 26.8 |
| Volta | 49.6 | 35.2 | 22.6 | 14.4 | 6.9 |
| Ashanti | 63.9 | 49.0 | 35.1 | 21.5 | 9.2 |
| Brong-Ahafo | 77.1 | 63.4 | 48.6 | 31.3 | 15.1 |
| Northern | 93.8 | 86.7 | 76.3 | 58.4 | 44.2 |
| Upper West | 98.4 | 97.6 | 94.9 | 88.6 | 74.7 |
| Upper East | 100.0 | 100.0 | 100.0 | 99.9 | 99.9 |
| ***Location*** | | | | | |
| Urban | 59.6 | 45.2 | 32.1 | 20.3 | 11.2 |
| Rural | 80.9 | 70.5 | 58.1 | 44.9 | 31.3 |
| ***Gender*** | | | | | |
| Male | 76.9 | 66.6 | 54.4 | 41.6 | 28.9 |
| Female | 65.7 | 50.1 | 36.3 | 23.0 | 13.2 |
| ***Occupation*** | | | | | |
| Public sector | 92.6 | 84.3 | 73.8 | 61.5 | 40.2 |
| Private formal | 48.7 | 30.3 | 18.6 | 8.3 | 1.2 |
| Private informal | 32.4 | 23.9 | 14.8 | 6.7 | 3.1 |
| Export farmers | 94.3 | 89.8 | 80.4 | 69.7 | 49.9 |
| Food crop | 81.9 | 72.0 | 61.7 | 47.5 | 33.5 |
| Non-farm | 65.1 | 49.4 | 31.7 | 18.6 | 11.1 |
| Non-work | 17.8 | 4.7 | 2.6 | 1.1 | – |
| ***Education*** | | | | | |
| None | 68.3 | 57.1 | 48.3 | 37.7 | 29.9 |
| Primary | 52.1 | 41.6 | 34.8 | 22.2 | 12.6 |
| JSS/Middle | 82.1 | 70.6 | 54.8 | 40.0 | 23.7 |
| Secondary | 72.6 | 58.5 | 44.7 | 32.7 | 22.7 |
| Tertiary | 37.3 | 23.5 | 15.7 | 9.0 | 4.9 |
| ***Ecological Zone*** | | | | | |
| Coastal | 64.7 | 50.1 | 35.3 | 22.3 | 11.6 |
| Forest | 70.8 | 58.2 | 44.5 | 31.3 | 17.7 |
| Savannah | 90.3 | 83.5 | 75.4 | 63.7 | 52.4 |

*Source:* Authors' computations.

# 15 Decentralization & Poverty Reduction

FELIX A. ASANTE
& JOSEPH R.A. AYEE

## 1. Introduction

Decentralization has been considered by many as one of the most important strategies on the agenda of public sector reform. This is because donors and governments in sub-Saharan Africa have considered decentralization as a strategy that will bring service delivery closer to consumers, improve the responsiveness of the central government to public demands and thereby reduce poverty, improve the efficiency and quality of public services and empower lower units to feel more involved and in control. In this connection, decentralization is linked to the concept of subsidiarity, that is, making decisions at the lowest feasible level. It is also meant to reduce overload and congestion at the centre and speed up operational decision-making and implementation by minimizing the bottlenecks associated with over-centralization of powers and functions at just one or two points in the hierarchy of a public service organization or ministry;[1] in other words, greater efficiency of public management, arising from improved co-ordination and shorter decision-making hierarchies ('less bureaucracy'), and improvements in political stability through the legitimization of differences in local needs and perspectives (pluralism). Consequently, decentralization seeks to increase the operational autonomy of line managers and agencies, leaving only broad policy guidelines to be worked out at the centre (Smith, 1985; Rondinelli et al., 1989; Mawhood, 1993; Crook and Manor, 1998; Wunsch and Olowu, 1995; Olowu and Wunsch, 2004).

---

[1] It has been pointed out that, in some respects, these arguments are simply restatements of traditional European ideas about the role of local government, many of which have been similarly invoked in recent European reforms, most notably the decentralization programme launched by Gaston Deferre in France in 1982. In much of Western Europe, decentralization has become a response to both political pressures and changing economic circumstances. Indeed, the principle of subsidiarity was incorporated within the European Union's Single European Act of 1987. In central and eastern Europe, the demand for local autonomy was a fundamental element of the political reform process of the late 1980s and 1990s. This resulted in the creation, or re-creation, of a large number of autonomous local government units, many of them very small (see Batley and Stoker, 1991).

This study concentrates on one of the most important reasons behind the implementation of decentralization programmes in sub-Saharan Africa, namely, the capacity of decentralized governments which, because of their closeness both institutionally and spatially to citizens in the rural areas, are more responsive to the needs of the poor than the central government and are thus more likely to formulate and implement pro-poor policies and programmes. Using the Ghanaian experience of decentralization, which started with the creation of 110 decentralized governments called District Assemblies in 1988/9, the study examines the impact of decentralization on poverty reduction.

The chapter is divided into five sections. Section 2 deals with the link between decentralization and poverty reduction and the conceptual framework for analyzing decentralization. Section 3 gives an overview of decentralization in Ghana by focusing on its objectives, successes and challenges. Section 4 evaluates the impact of the District Assemblies on poverty reduction based on the criteria of responsiveness to the needs of the poor, level and quality of representation and participation of the poor, and social and economic outcomes using the provision of basic services such as public spending on health and education. Section 5 is devoted to the linkage between decentralization and poverty reduction at the national level using the Ghana Poverty Reduction Strategy as a reference point. Section 6 highlights the lessons and their implications for poverty reduction.

## 2.    Linkages between Decentralization and Poverty Reduction

The virtues of decentralization, such as democracy, popular participation, responsiveness, accountability and equity have led to the belief that decentralization will lead to greater responsiveness to the poor. Since the poor have been excluded from politics and are therefore unable to access public goods and services, decentralization is seen as offering greater political participation to ordinary citizens whose 'voice' is more likely to increase with the concomitant relevance and effectiveness of government's policies and programmes, especially in poverty reduction (Crook, 2003; Crook and Sverrisson, 2001).

### *Decentralization: Definition, Benefits and Weakness*

The concept of decentralization defies clear-cut definition. Rondinelli (1981) defines decentralization as the transfer of authority to plan, make decisions and manage public functions from a higher level of government to any individual, organization or agency at a lower level. To Smith (1985: 1) decentralization means 'reversing the concentration of administration at a single centre and conferring powers on local government'. In the present study, decentralization is considered the opposite of centralization or concentration of power, and involves delegation of power or authority from the central government to the periphery.

In the study of politics, decentralization refers to the territorial distribution of power. It is concerned with the extent to which power and authority are dispersed through the geographical hierarchy of the state, and the institutions and processes through which such dispersal occurs. Decentralization entails the subdivision of the state's territory into smaller areas and the creation of political and administrative institutions in those areas. Some of the institutions thus created may themselves find it necessary to practise further decentralization (Smith, 1985).

## Benefits of Decentralization

The potential benefits of decentralization have been well documented in the literature. The majority of these benefits can be broadly classified as improved efficiency and effectiveness, governance and/or equity. These results, in turn, are often associated with economic development and poverty reduction (see Table 15.1). The realization of these benefits depends significantly on political decentralization.

**Table 15.1  Potential Benefits of Decentralization**

1.  Improved local economic development and poverty reduction through: (a) providing services that serve as production and distribution inputs for local firms and entrepreneurs; (b) contributing to a legal and institutional environment that is conducive to development; (c) co-ordinating key local public, private and community actors in creating partnerships that promote development.

2.  Improved governance because, if people see that their interactions with elected decentralized governments will lead to decisions that are more consistent with their wishes than those made by higher levels, they feel better connected to decentralized governments. Being able to influence public affairs in at least some modest ways that directly affect them empowers people, giving them a new sense of control and autonomy.

3.  Improved efficiency because decentralized governments are said to be closer to the people, have good access to local information and understand local context well. If so, they can better identify the mix and level of services that their constituents need than can the higher levels, thus improving allocative efficiency.

4.  Improved equity because if decentralized governments are familiar with local circumstances, they may be in the best position to distribute public resources more equitably and target poverty within their own jurisdictions.

5.  Improved responsiveness of government because local representatives are best placed to know the exact nature of local needs and how they can be met in a cost-effective way.

6.  Enhanced accountability because local representatives are more accessible to the populace and can therefore be held more closely accountable for their policies and outcomes than distant national political leaders (or public servants).

7.  Political equality from greater political participation will reduce the likelihood of the concentration of power. Political power will be more broadly distributed, thus making decentralization a mechanism that can meet the needs of the poor and disadvantaged.

8.  Political education teaches the mass of the population about the role of political debate, the selection of representatives and the nature of policies, plans and budgets, in a democracy.

9.  Training in political leadership creates a seedbed for prospective political leaders to develop skills in policy-making, political party operations and budgeting, with the result that the quality of national politicians is enhanced.

*Sources:*  Smith (1985: 18–30); Turner and Hulme (1997: 157); Smoke (2003: 9–10).

## Weaknesses of Decentralization

Although the demand for decentralization is strong throughout sub-Saharan Africa, there are serious drawbacks that should be considered in designing any decentralization programme. First, decentralization in practice runs up against objections at a political level. Indeed, it is felt that decentralization dislocates the nation, either by encouraging the appetites of certain regions for autonomy or by encouraging wealthier regions to operate as self-sufficient territories to the detriment of poorer regions. The problem of guarantees remains the issue that divides supporters and opponents of decentralization. What guarantees are there that decentralization will not encourage or endorse separatist or fissiparous tendencies? (Smith, 1985; Nzouankeu, 1994).

Secondly, as the wealth of a country is unfairly distributed, decentralization is likely to accentuate the already precarious imbalance within the state because the poor districts would tend to become even poorer. For poor districts and regions, therefore, autonomy would be void of meaning because they would continue to be dependent on the state. Moreover, decentralization is not always compatible with planning policies and strategic development projects (Nzouankeu, 1994; Prud'homme, 1995).

Thirdly, decentralization can lead to increased waste and squandering of public funds. The inexperience of locally elected representatives, coupled with the fact that they have had little or no training, gives rise to the idea that their ambitions attach more importance to their electoral preoccupations than to the interests of the people. Although there is an element of truth in certain of these objections, it should not be forgotten that waste is not confined to decentralized units and that the central government is also guilty of waste, often to a greater extent than decentralized authorities (Smith, 1985; Mawhood, 1993).

Fourthly, decentralization is not necessarily linked to democracy because the devolution of power may help to augment the dominance of those who, because of wealth or status, are already powerful at the local level. In other words:

> . . . it is conceivable, even likely in many countries, that power at the local level is more concentrated, more elitist and applied more ruthlessly against the poor than at the centre. As a consequence, therefore, greater decentralization does not necessarily imply greater democracy let alone power to the people — it all depends on the circumstances under which decentralization occurs (Griffin, 1981: 225).

Fifthly, decentralization might be accompanied by more corruption. If, as is likely, corruption is more widespread at the local than at the national level, then decentralization automatically increases the overall level of corruption. This outcome, incidentally, might not be bad in terms of redistribution, because the 'benefits' of decentralized corruption are probably better distributed than the benefits of centralized corruption. But it would certainly increase the costs in terms of allocative efficiency, because it leads to the supply of services for which the levels of kickbacks are higher (rather than those for which there is a demand). It is also costly in terms of production efficiency, because it leads to corruption-avoiding strategies that increase costs, favour ineffective technologies, and waste time (Prud'homme, 1995).

## Decentralization and Poverty Reduction

We may define poverty reduction as designing, implementing and targeting appropriate methods to ensure that scarce resources are allocated to activities that are likely to yield the greatest impact on the poor and to decrease their levels of deprivation and vulnerability (World Bank, 2001; Sen, 1999). Decentralization is seen by donors, governments and academics as one of the most important and appropriate strategies that will reduce the levels of deprivation and vulnerability of the poor.

There are three ways in which decentralization is linked to poverty reduction (Bird et al., 1995; Bird and Villancourt, 1998). First, as with many other public services, effective implementation of poverty reduction strategies often requires detailed and specific local knowledge which may be most readily obtainable through a decentralized and locally accountable system of governance. The right kind of decentralization will therefore enable local government units to have sufficient technical and financial capacity to carry out their assigned functions. On the assumption that people should get what they want — rather than what someone else wants them to want — poverty reduction programmes, like other programmes, should reflect local and regional variations in preferences where appropriate. From this viewpoint, decentralization in principle is good and this virtue depends upon political accountability and the inevitable need to strengthen local delivery capacity (Crook, 2003; Bird and Rodriguez, 1999; Crook and Sverrisson, 2001; Ayee, 1995; 1996).

Secondly, the design and implementation of the transfer of financial resources is an important influence, for good or for ill, on local spending decisions. Efficient assignment of revenue and expenditure responsibility to different levels of government invariably means that local government units as a group will depend to a significant extent upon transfers from the central government. From this perspective, decentralization does not mean that the central government plays no role in poverty reduction. Rather, what it means is that considerable thought, effort, and experimentation will be needed to develop a workable transfer system. Such a transfer should simultaneously accomplish the difficult objectives of providing localities with sufficient resources to do what they want to do, while ensuring that what they do is broadly in accordance with national priorities. The interaction between decentralization and poverty reduction emphasizes the importance of transfer design and the desirability of providing for periodic evaluation of that design (Bird and Rodriguez, 1999; Crook, 2003; Crook and Sverrisson, 2001; Ayee, 1996).

Thirdly, the relationship between decentralization and poverty reduction depends on the targeting of poverty-reducing public investment by local government units. Local government units implement the national poverty reduction policy, narrowly or broadly defined. A narrowly defined poverty policy uses transfers of income, in money or kind, to the poor. A broadly defined poverty reduction policy also encompasses policies intended to increase the productivity of the poor through the formation and maintenance of human capital — health and education — and improved access to markets and productive resources in general. Given the heterogeneity of resources, capacities, costs, needs and preferences that characterizes most countries, some local government units will need much more financial and technical support than others. If such disparities are accentuated, the greater is the direct access of local government units to their own fiscal resources, since those which have a tax base can get more revenue, while those which have not, cannot. Decentralized poverty reduction strategy thus inevitably requires some degree of 'equalization' — in the sense of larger transfers to poorer regions and not to poorer people as such — in fiscal transfers from the central government to localities (Bird and Rodriguez, 1999; Shah, 1994; Crook and Sverrisson, 2001).

## 3.   An Overview of Decentralization in Ghana
In 1988, the Provisional National Defence Council (PNDC) launched a major decentralization programme with the promulgation of PNDC Law 207. The initiative for the programme was inspired by the government's political philosophy of 'power to the people' and its structural adjustment programme (SAP), whose principles concern the role and responsibilities of the state and the expanding role of the private sector, both in the sense of private commercial entrepreneurship and of voluntary community initiatives (Ayee, 2003a; 2003b; 2004).

### *Objectives*
The 1992 Constitution, various legislation on decentralization[2] and government publications and donor reports[3] have articulated the objectives of decentralization.

---

[2] See the 1992 Constitution (Chapters 8 and 20); PNDC Law 207, 1988 which has been repealed by the Local Government Act (Act 462), 1993; the Civil Service Law (PNDC Law 327), 1993; Legislative Instrument (LI) 1514, 1991, which has been repealed by LI 1589, 1994; District Assemblies Common Fund Act (Act 455), 1993; the National Development Planning Commission Act (Act 479), 1994; the National Development Planning (System) Act, (Act 480) and the Legislative Instruments of 1988/89 that created the 110 District Assemblies (DAs). In addition to these, there are 8 administrative regulations, viz., the Financial Memorandum (Section 81) of the Local Government Act, (Act 54), 1961; Financial Administrative Decree (FAD), SMCD 221, 1979; the Financial Administration Regulation (FAR), LI 1234, 1979; bylaws of the 110 District Assemblies; Model Standing Orders for Municipal and District Assemblies, 1994; and Legislative Instruments of the Ministry of Local Government and Rural Development.

[3] Some of the government documents and donor reports in Ghana which have also addressed capacity, empowerment, transparency, accountability and effectiveness issues of decentralization include the following: *Constitution of the Republic of Ghana, 1992; Local Government Act (Act 462), 1993; Ghana Poverty Reduction Strategy, 2002–2004; Decentralization in Ghana: Implementation Status and Proposed Future Directions, March 2002;* the 2002 Budget Statement; President's 2002 Sessional Address; MLGRD's Network of Sectoral Co-ordinating Group on Decentralization in Ghana: *Issue Paper on Decentralization,* September 1999; MLGRD, *Ghana: The New Local Government System,* 2nd edn, November 1996; *Ghana Vision 2020: The First Medium-Term Development Plan (1997–2000);* GTZ, *PPR Programme for Rural Action (PRA) in Ghana, 1998;* GTZ, *Coordination Report: PRA Effectiveness and the Way Forward,* October 2001; GTZ, *Backstopping and Review Mission, Debriefing Notes for PRA,* November 2001; GTZ, *Project Planning Matrix, July 1999–June 2003;* KPMG, *Ghana Fiscal Decentralization Project, Design Report,* July 2001; IFES, *Civil Society and Local Government in Twenty Districts in Ghana: Surprises, Problems and Opportunities,* IFES Project ECSELL Baseline Assessment, March 1998; CIDA, *Final Study on the State of Decentralization in Ghana,* May 2000; UNICEF, *Supported Programme with MLGRD, District and Community Enhancement Programme,* 2001; World Bank, *Ghana and the World Bank, 2002: A Partnership for Progress,* March 2002; Organizational Capacity Improvement Consultants, *A Proposal to Build Capacity in Institutional Development/Organizational Development,* An OD Skills Training Programme designed for SNV (Netherlands Development Organization); *Ghana and German Technical Cooperation Agency (GTZ) — A Programme for Rural Action (PRA),* Ghana, April 2001; and Intersectoral Committee

In Chapter 6, 'Directive Principles of State Policy', of the Constitution, for instance, the government of the day is enjoined to make 'democracy a reality by decentralizing the administrative and financial machinery of government to the regions and districts and by affording all possible opportunities to the people to participate in decision-making at every level in national life and in government' (Ghana, Republic of 1992). The objectives of decentralization include participation, empowerment, accountability, decongestion of the national capital, effectiveness and checking the urban-rural drift. Specifically, the decentralization programme has been designed to:

i. devolve political and state power in order to promote participatory democracy through local-level institutions;
ii. deconcentrate and devolve administration, development planning, and implementation to the district assemblies;
iii. introduce an effective system of fiscal decentralization that gives the district assemblies control over a substantial portion of their revenues;
iv. establish a national development planning system to integrate and co-ordinate development planning at all levels and in all sectors; and
v. incorporate economic, social, spatial, and environmental issues into the development planning process on an integrated and comprehensive basis (Ayee, 1994; 2004).

In addition to these objectives, the individual Establishing Acts (Legislative Instruments) for each of the District Assemblies, which supplement the Local Government Act (Act 462), include a list of 86 specific responsibilities,[4] which include the following:

- to construct and maintain feeder roads, streets, parks and other public utilities;
- to build, equip and maintain primary, middle, secondary and special schools;
- to maintain as agents of the Ghana Highways Authority trunk roads lying within the boundaries of their areas of authority;
- to promote and safeguard public health;
- to regularly inspect the metropolitan area for the detection of nuisance or any condition likely to be offensive or injurious to health;
- to establish, install, build, maintain and control public latrines, lavatories, urinals and wash places;
- to establish, maintain and carry out services for the removal of nightsoil from any building and for the destruction and treatment of such nightsoil; and
- to provide, maintain, supervise and control abbatoirs.

---

on Decentralization, *Report on Decentralization Workshop,* held at the Marina Hotel, Dodowa, 14–16 July 2002.

[4] These responsibilities can be classified into three categories, namely, deconcentrated, delegated and devolved functions. For details see Ayee and Amponsah (2003); J. R. A. Ayee 'Decentralization and the Provision of Local Public Services in Ghana', in Karl Wohlmuth, Hans Bass and Frank Messner (eds), *Good Governance and Economic Development* (Hamburg/London: LIT VERLAG Munster, 1999), pp. 459–78.

Some of the objectives of the decentralization programme seem, however, incompatible. For instance, popular participation has been regarded as militating against local revenue generation and mobilization, on the one hand, and/or demands for increased expenditures on the other (Ayee, 2004).

## *Successes*

The successes of Ghana's decentralization programme can be measured against some of the main objectives for which it was implemented. One of the objectives of the programme is to ensure that people living in the rural areas have access to basic services and infrastructure. Indeed, the District Assemblies (DAs) have undertaken development projects such as the construction and maintenance of classroom blocks, feeder roads, clinics, public toilets, markets and the provision of street-lights in previously neglected rural areas which were denied access to these services. Some of these projects were sometimes undertaken in collaboration with local and international non-governmental organizations. The projects have in turn opened up development opportunities in the districts. The improved infrastructure development has improved the health and sanitation infrastructure and thereby removed some of the barriers to social and economic development. This notwithstanding, complaints have come from some rural people that most of these services and infrastructure have been concentrated mainly in the district capitals to the detriment of the rural areas (Ayee, 1992; 1996; 2003a).

Another main objective of the decentralization programme is to allow for the participation of the people in their own affairs and thus empower them. The activities of DAs have enabled the local people to show some interest in their affairs; a spirit of voluntarism and awareness to develop one's community was therefore created, especially at the initial period of the programme. However, people's interest declined when they realized that their expectations could not be fulfilled because of the incapacity of the DAs, which lacked the human and financial resources to implement the development objectives set. In addition, district plans are subjected as much as possible to public hearings at the sub-district level, but the hearings are not patronized by most people mainly because of apathy and the inability of the sub-district structures to be in place in some districts due to composition problems. In spite of these hiccups, the DAs have no doubt created a high level of political awareness, which has injected some political dynamism into some functionaries of the DAs and has led the electorate to demand greater accountability from the District Chief Executive and Presiding Member and DA members respectively (Ayee, 2004).

The issue of poverty reduction is central to the decentralization programme, even though there is the perception[5] on the part of some people that poverty reduction was not part of the original objectives of decentralization in Ghana but was rather a later objective forced on the government by donors. Given the central role of poverty

---

[5] This perception may be right or wrong. MLGRD (2002) does not mention poverty reduction as an achievement or problem of decentralization This notwithstanding, once the decentralization programme was meant to give 'power to the people' (empowerment) and redress the rural-urban drift, the element of poverty reduction could be seen as implicit in the objectives.

reduction in the decentralization programme, a number of poverty reduction strategies were introduced, including the Programme of Action to Mitigate the Social Costs of Adjustment (PAMSCAD)[6] in 1987, the Productivity and Income Generation Fund popularly called the 'District Assembly Poverty Alleviation Fund' in 1996 and the Highly Indebted Poor Countries (HIPC) funds in 2002. The Poverty Alleviation Fund, in particular, is to give the poor access to credit facilities to use in investment in job creation. Even though this is a laudable scheme and has assisted hitherto vulnerable groups like women in small-scale industries, it has not been well implemented for a number of reasons. First, the modalities for the selection of beneficiaries are not too clear. There is the perception, whether rightly or wrongly, that most of the beneficiaries are selected on the basis of their political affiliations and not on their levels of deprivation and vulnerability. Second, there has been a high default rate in the repayment of the loans given out because the beneficiaries have not invested them correctly to create the expected job but have rather regarded them as a windfall to meet personal commitments such as paying the school fees of children. In addition, apart from the smallness of the loan (¢500,000), the credit facility was not distributed on schedule so that, at the time people most needed it, it was not available. The problems faced in implementing the Poverty Alleviation Fund have been succinctly captured by former president Rawlings (1999: 5):

> The development import of the so-called 'Poverty Alleviation Fund' appears lost on some District Assemblies. The returns show that some District Assemblies have even failed to allocate funds. Despite unsuccessful attempts to politicize it, nobody who is seriously concerned about rural and urban employment and the need to increase and sustain national productivity would question the rationale for this Fund, especially for increasing rural productivity and generating urban employment through support to private sector small, micro, and medium scale enterprises. . . . It is important to remind ourselves that the 'Poverty Alleviation Fund' is the tax-payers money and it should be disbursed and recovered within the framework of the regulations that govern the use of public funds.

From the foregoing, it is clear that the decentralization programme has achieved marginal success. This notwithstanding, 51.6% of people in 12 districts[7] in Ghana have faith in the DAs not only as the appropriate institutions for solving community problems at the grassroots but also as holding the key to effective delivery of services (Ayee and Amponsah, 2003).

## *Challenges*
Since 1988, the challenges facing decentralization have been daunting in spite of the

---

[6] For a review of the PAMSCAD, see Eboe Hutchful, *Ghana's Adjustment Experience: The Paradox of Reform* (Oxford: James Currey and UNRISD; Accra: Woeli Publishing Services; Portsmouth, NH: Heinemann, 2002), Chapter 7, pp. 116–39.
[7] The 12 districts are Bolgatanga, Bawku East, East Gonja, Wa, Kintampo, Nkoranza, Kwahu South, Akwapim North, Mfantsiman, Kommenda-Edina-Eguafo-Abirem, East Nzema and Kpandu. They were the study districts in which pre- and post-district assemblies and unit committee elections surveys were conducted in July and August 2002, by the Department of Political Science, University of Ghana, covering 3,600 respondents.

efforts of successive governments to address them. In the Ministry of Local Government and Rural Development's 2002 *Status of Decentralization Implementation* paper there is a daunting list of constraints and challenges as well as a number of factors that have impeded previous attempts to strengthen local government capacities and performance. They include agitations for more districts which have led to the creation of a further 28 districts in addition to the current 110; sectoral conceptual differences in the interpretation of the decentralization policy and the transfer of powers, functions, responsibilities and resources; absence of maps to firmly identify boundaries that will enable DAs to plan for the development of their areas of jurisdiction; shortage of adequately trained human resources at the local level; inability to make the sub-district structures function because of their size and lack of funds to pay core staff; lack of participatory bottom-up planning; lack of fiscal decentralization as a result of the centralization of the management of public finance due to existing legislation (Financial Administration Decree, 1979 and Financial Administration Regulations, 1979) and administrative procedure on local government public finance; lack of management of the interface between decentralized public institutions, private sector enterprises and civil society, mainly because of the absence of clear-cut regulation, procedure and boundaries; and lack of good practices, consultation and communication on the roles of NGOs, CSOs and CBOs (MLGRD, 2002).

Apart from these constraints, a number of challenges face the decentralization programme.[8] They include the following:

- lack of strong leadership at all levels of decentralization; the absence of an authoritative responsibility centre for the decentralization process which plays the role of co-ordinating, overseeing and monitoring the individual and collective efforts of stakeholders across the government and plans and implements decentralization-related initiatives. This has also led to the lack of an authoritative common vision and plan for the decentralization process. In other words, there has not been a home-grown action plan to promote Ghana's version of decentralization. This problem may seem to have been resolved with the appointment of an 11-member Presidential Oversight Committee on Decentralization in November 2003.
- loss of institutional memory as a result of the change of government in January 2001, which resulted not only in a massive transfer of staff but also in the replacement of one-third of government appointees to the DAs. A further loss of institutional memory also occurred after the August 2002 District Assembly and Unit Committee elections. This shows the unpredictable nature of the process of capacity-building for decentralization.
- adoption by the New Patriotic Party (NPP) government of a stance which can be interpreted to mean that it would like to decentralize but cannot do so now because local capacities are so weak. Consequently, the government's performance

---

[8] For an extensive discussion of the problems and constraints see Ayee (2003a; 2003b; 2004).

with respect to decentralization may mean that it does not wish to commit to, or implement, a comprehensive decentralization programme. Knowing that decentralization necessarily involves major political and technical risks and trade-offs, the government as a whole may perhaps not be prepared to undertake in its first term extremely difficult and comprehensive reforms not considered to be essential in order to win a second term in office. From this perspective, the government's intention may be to be seen to be actively engaging (tinkering) in activities to strengthen the local government system without having to develop, and commit to, a risky and complex comprehensive decentralization programme.

• the District Chief Executives (DCEs) who are expected to be managers at the district level are not acting as such but rather are overloaded with workshops and meetings, most of which may not be productive or relevant to their managerial roles (Ayee, 1997a).

• unpredictability and lack of transparency of the District Assemblies Common Fund (DACF) and lack of discretion afforded to district authorities over the allocation of funds, coupled with the weak financial position of DAs vis-à-vis their 86 assigned functions (Ayee, 1995).

• non-partisanship of the DAs is a mirage. In actual practice Ghana's DAs are not free from partisan politics. This point was re-echoed by the former Attorney General, Nana Akuffo Addo, when he addressed the mid-year conference of District Chief Executives from the Southern Sector at Ho in the Volta Region at the end of June 2002. He charged District Chief Executives 'to ensure that the majority of elected assembly and unit committee members belong to the ideology and vision of positive change . . . district and unit committee level elections have always been partisan; consequently, DCEs must attach serious importance to it since it would be used to measure how the New Patriotic Party would fare in the 2004 general elections' (*Ghanaian Times,* 1 July 2002: 10). It is an open secret that in the District Assembly elections of 1994, 1998 and 2002, most, if not all, political parties either sponsored or supported individual candidates to win seats in the DAs, contrary to the Constitution. This is because the parties wanted to control the grassroots in order to boost their chances of winning the national elections. However, since this was unofficial and did not involve the public, the mobilizing role parties can play was not put into practice.

• the formal integration of the eleven line departments or organizations of central government at the district level into the decentralized local government system remains one of the unresolved issues that have stalled the implementation of Sections 37, 38 and 161 of Act 462. Associated with this problem is the apparent conflict between certain decentralized departments or organizations and the line departments or organizations, namely, the Ghana Education Service created by Act 506, 1995; the Ghana Health Service and Teaching Hospitals created by Act 525, 1996; the Ghana National Fire Service created by Act 537, 1997; the Forestry Commission created by Act 571, 1997; the Ghana Library Board established under Act 327; and the National Disaster Management Organization (NADMO) established under Act 517. All these services and organizations are listed among the decentralized departments of MDAs under Act 462. The apparent conflict between Act 462 and the enactments referred to raises issues of both policy and law — whether these services could and should be decentralized. The creation of these services seems to have undermined the speedy establishment of a Local Government Service, which Act was passed by Parliament in September 2003. It is a means towards re-centralization (Ayee, 1997b; Ayee, 2003a; 2003b).

## 3.    Measuring the Impact of District Assemblies on Poverty Reduction

### *Responsiveness to Needs of the Poor*
According to Alderman (1988), decentralization has shown that local government officials are likely to be well informed about the plight of members of their community and are therefore able to recognize those who are genuinely poor. Moreover, because poverty in one community may be characterized by different indicators from that in another community, a decentralized system may also increase the efficiency of access to public goods and services by allowing local authorities to determine the local eligibility criteria. Thus, decentralizing the responsibility to access the needs of communities to local administrators should be more accurate and cost-effective than operating through a central government agency.

The District Assembly (DA) system has greatly enhanced popular participation in local government, and has included greater numbers of previously excluded groups, but the responsiveness of the DAs to popular development needs and to those of the poor in particular has not been good (Crook and Sverrisson, 2001). In a survey of two districts by Crook and Manor (1998), 70% of respondents thought that the DA did not respond to their needs, and only 22% felt it was better than the previously unelected system. In the past, general development performance was disappointing, with recurrent expenditure dominating capital expenditure in real terms. Currently, capital expenditure overrides recurrent expenditure (see Figure 15.1) and so the DAs are beginning to be responsive to the needs of the communities.

The regional breakdown of local government expenditure in 1999 shows that Greater Accra, the richest region,[9] spent 56.0% of its local government expenditure on recurrent items and 44.0% on capital items. Similarly, Upper West Region, one of the poorest regions in Ghana, spent 77.2% of local government expenditure on capital expenditure and 22.8% on recurrent expenditure (see Table 15.2).

### *Levels and Quality of Representation and Participation of the Poor*
The 'poor and the unschooled' participate much more widely in village-level and contacting activities. As regards the 'gender balance', men are strongly dominant in contacting, but less so in the other activities. One area, however, where female participation is better than, or as good as, that of men is in the village-level unit

---

[9] The definition of the richest and poorest regions in Ghana is based on the fourth round of the Ghana Living Standard Survey carried out in 1998/9.

committee meetings (Crook and Sverrisson, 2001). In 1998 when the first Unit Committee elections were held (nine years after the DAs were set up), 65% of the elections were uncontested.

**Figure 15.1: Composition of Total Expenditure at the District Level, 1994–9**

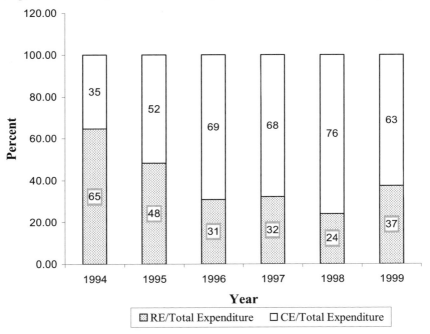

In order to understand the intensity and quality of communication between assembly members and their electorate, Asante (2003) carried out a survey of four districts.[10] This revealed that 51.3% of the respondents knew how decisions were made in their local community while 48.7% did not. About 90% of the respondents who knew how decisions are made actually participated in decision-making. On the issue of how often the community met to decide on developmental activities, 49.2% of respondents said they never met, while 14.7% said they met when the need arose.

## *Social and Economic Outcomes*

### *Basic Infrastructure and Services*
The District Assembly Common Fund (DACF) has enabled the districts to provide basic infrastructure in the fields of education, health and water and sanitation which

---

[10] The survey was carried out between July and September 2000 in Tamale, Sekyere East, Akwapim North and Awutu Efutu Senya Districts. These four districts were selected based on population classification by the MLGRD and the 3 agro-ecological zones (coastal, forest and savannah).

had been neglected in the past. Consequently, decentralization has caused an incremental access of people living in these areas to government resources and services.

**Table 15.2　Regional Expenditure Performance in 1999 (in million cedis)**

| Region[a] | Capital Expenditure (CE) | Recurrent Expenditure (RE) |
|---|---|---|
| Greater Accra | 18,196.53 (43.9) | 23,170.47 (56.0) |
| Western | 13,165.50 (68.8) | 5,962.60 (31.2) |
| Ashanti | 18,548.60 (72.3) | 7,116.00 (27.7) |
| Volta | 12,516.00 (72.1) | 4,852.80 (27.9) |
| Brong-Ahafo | 10,970.00 (59.9) | 7,353.50 (40.1) |
| Eastern | 11,490.60 (62.7) | 6,824.90 (37.3) |
| Central | 9,694.70 (62.1) | 5,910.00 (37.9) |
| Northern | 12,320.90 (75.9) | 3,912.57 (24.1) |
| Upper West | 5,003.3 (77.2) | 1,477.40 (22.8) |
| Upper East | 5,430.70 (64.5) | 2,992.53 (35.5) |
| Ghana | 117,336.83 (62.8) | 69,572.47 (37.2) |

*Note:*　a)　Regions are arranged based on poverty incidence from lowest or richest (Greater Accra) to highest or poorest (Upper East).

*Source:*　Data from Ministry of Local Government and Rural Development, Accra, Ghana.

Even though the DACF was to enable the districts to provide basic infrastructure and services, the survey by Asante (2003) in four districts revealed mixed results. When respondents were asked to compare the present quality/availability of selected public goods and services (education, health and water) with that of 1994 when budget allocation from the central government to the districts began, most of the respondents were of the view that the health sector had improved, while, in the water sector, there had not been any improvement (see Table 15.3).

**Table 15.3   Present Quality/Availability of Selected Public Goods and Services Compared with 1994 (% of Respondents)**

| Public Good & Service | Improvement | |
|---|---|---|
| | Yes | No |
| Education | 49.5 | 50.5 |
| Health | 53.0 | 47.0 |
| Water | 44.0 | 56.0 |

*Source:*   Asante (2003).

## Who Benefits from Public Spending?

Public subsidies for social services such as education and health care rest on two policy objectives — efficiency and equity[11] (Castro-Leal et al., 1999). Basic social services are essential in the fight against poverty, and for that, public subsidies on investments that enhance human capital must benefit the poor. To what extent has public social spending in Ghana been effective in reaching the poor? To answer this question, this section reviews the benefit incidence of government spending in basic education and health care in Ghana.

*Education:* Combining the unit cost of education with information from household surveys on the use of publicly subsidized education yields estimates of the benefit incidence of government education spending. Table 15.4 shows a comparison of the benefit incidence of public spending on education for 1989, 1992 and 1998.[12] Over the years the percentage of subsidy captured by the first quintile (poorest) has been decreasing, while that of the richest group has been increasing. Between 1989 and 1992 there was a slight increase in public primary school subsidies to the poor and a decrease to the rich. The situation changed between 1992 and 1998 when the percentage subsidy to the poor fell slightly and that to the rich increased. This resulted in an almost equal distribution in the quintiles in 1998. The table also reveals a favourable change in subsidies towards the rural population from the urban population.

Even though there were some unfavourable changes between 1992 and 1998, the primary education subsidies are not particularly pro-poor and on average serve children equitably. The decline between 1992 and 1998 of the benefit incidence of public primary school subsidies for the poor population (the bottom two quintiles) also reveals a deterioration in public primary education in recent years, and thus difficulty in reaching the poorest of the poor.

---

[11] Efficiency gains can be achieved when the subsidies produce external benefits or correct market failure. Equity is also important in the distribution of public spending.

[12] The years 1989, 1992 and 1998 correspond to the years of the Ghana Living Standards Surveys (GLSS) 2, 3 and 4 respectively.

**Table 15.4   Benefit Incidence of Public Spending on Basic Education, 1989–98**

| Welfare Measure | % of Subsidies Captured | | |
|---|---|---|---|
| (Quintile) | 1989 | 1992 | 1998 |
| 1 – Poorest | 21.2 | 21.8 | 20.4 |
| 2 | 22.1 | 23.6 | 20.8 |
| 3 | 22.2 | 21.7 | 20.9 |
| 4 | 20.3 | 18.8 | 20.9 |
| 5 – Richest | 14.3 | 14.0 | 17.0 |
| Urban | 29.4 | 29.9 | 25.2 |
| Rural | 70.6 | 70.1 | 74.8 |

*Note:*     1989, 1992 and 1998 correspond to the years of the Ghana Living Standard Survey
            (GLSS) rounds 2, 3 and 4 respectively.
*Sources:* For 1989 and 1992 see Demery et al., 1995 and Demery, 2000 and for 1998, see
            Canagarajah and Ye, 2001.

**Health:** As in the case of basic education, combining the unit cost of health-care
delivery with the use of publicly funded health facilities provides estimates of the
benefit incidence of government spending on health care. Table 15.5 reveals that
health spending in general is not well targeted to the poorest; it favours the richest
quintiles. There is a significant improvement in the middle expenditure group where
the share of health subsidy accruing to them rose from 17.2% in 1989 to 18.7% in 1992
and then to a high 25.7% in 1998. The high share of health subsidy to the rich,
according to Demery (2000), is due to dominance in the use of all health facilities by
the richest quintile. In 1998, there was a favorable change in public health spending
towards rural residents. This is likely to be the result of the current health reform
policy, which promotes basic health services in rural areas.

**Table 15.5   Benefit Incidence of Public Spending in Health, 1989–1998**

| Welfare Measure | % of Subsidies Captured | | |
|---|---|---|---|
| (Quintile) | 1989 | 1992 | 1998 |
| 1 – Poorest | 12.3 | 11.6 | 12.5 |
| 2 | 13.3 | 15.5 | 12.1 |
| 3 | 17.2 | 18.7 | 25.7 |
| 4 | 26.7 | 21.4 | 18.8 |
| 5 – Richest | 30.6 | 32.9 | 31.0 |
| Urban | 42.0 | 48.7 | 38.8 |
| Rural | 58.0 | 51.3 | 61.2 |

*Note:*     as for Table 15.4.
*Sources:* ibid.

## 5.    Linkages at the Policy Level

The potential benefits of decentralization can only be achieved — and the potential pitfalls can only be avoided — if policy design focuses on creating the appropriate institutional arrangement in which decentralization can occur. The policy of decentralization has never been seen as an end in itself but as a means to achieve strategic policy objectives. The linkages of decentralization at the policy level revolve around these questions: Is poverty reduction a motive or objective of the government's decentralization programme? How should linkages between decentralization and poverty reduction be conceptualized in national policies? Does national poverty strategy take account of the decentralization process?

### *Is Poverty Reduction a Strategic Objective of Decentralization?*

Views on the motives and objectives of the government's decentralization policy vary. The decision to engage in a process of politics and administrative decentralization has been driven by a number of different considerations (see Table 15.1). The current local government reforms and decentralization policy could be traced to many converging factors (GTZ/SNRD, 1996) including;

(a)    macroeconomic policies pursued under the Economic Recovery Programme (ERP);

(b)    urge of the international donor community to establish democratic structures and strengthen local government and bottom-up decision-making in order to achieve greater participation in the development processes;

(c)    demand (internal and external) for a devolution of power on a subsidiary basis;

(d)    shortcomings of the pre-and immediate post-independence local government systems (dual hierarchy model and single hierarchy model);

(e)    favourable political framework conditions, for example the government's genuine commitment to decentralization and grassroots participation in development activities.

While it was assumed that the reform process would ultimately result in improved living conditions at the local level, this linkage was seen as implicit in and secondary to other political and economic objectives.

Although decentralization was not launched with an explicit poverty reduction objective, policy documents leave no doubt that the decision to engage in the decentralization process was also driven by poverty concerns. The decentralization programme is aimed at addressing a number of political and institutional development constraints that were only later referred to more systematically as causes of poverty, such as the absence of opportunities for political participation by large parts of the population, especially in the interior of the country; the allocative inefficiency and low degree of needs orientation of a top-down command administration; and the absence of private initiative and self-help.

## *Conceptualizing the Linkages at the National Level*

Effective poverty reduction requires, among other things, increasing the poor's access to basic public and collective services, such as health, education, water, sanitation and transport, in order to enhance human capital, increase labour productivity (the principal asset of the poor) and foster access to economic opportunities (Asante, 2003): in other words, to improve the livelihood of the poor. Livelihood encompasses income, both in cash, and in the social institutions (such as family and relatives), gender relations, and the property rights required to support and sustain a given standard of living (Ellis, 1998). A livelihood also includes access to, and benefits derived from, social and public services provided by the state such as education, health services, roads and water supplies (Lipton and van der Gaag, 1993; Blackwood and Lynch, 1994).

The impact of decentralization on interregional and interpersonal equity can vary greatly, depending on institutional arrangements and policy design details (Litvack et al., 1998). If the central government makes no effort to redistribute resources to poorer areas, fiscal decentralization will result in growing disparities. Similarly, if districts do not redistribute within their jurisdiction, poor people may lack access to public services. Horizontal equity — that is, ensuring some level of comparability in ability to provide public services throughout the country — can be achieved through intergovernmental transfers that include equalization components.

Figure 15.2 shows the conceptual linkage between decentralization and poverty reduction. According to de Jong et al., (1999), decentralization is assumed to promote poverty reduction through the following positive linkages:

(i)   political devolution can aim at reducing poverty through empowerment strategy. This involves creating 'space' for people to participate effectively in the decision-making process;

(ii)   poverty reduction and decentralization might also be linked through a resource mobilization strategy. When people are given greater control over local statutory structures, they may be motivated to commit more assets to the common good; and

(iii)   decentralized government may also be seen as a more effective means of delivering basic social services, thus reducing many of the common causes of poverty such as illness, decrepit economic infrastructure and illiteracy.

## *National Poverty Strategy and the Decentralization Process*

In 2002, the government launched the Ghana Poverty Reduction Strategy (GPRS). This represents comprehensive policies to support growth and poverty reduction over a three-year period (2002–4). The preparation of the GPRS was preceded by two other national development strategies since the mid-1990s, namely, the Ghana Vision 2020: the first step (1996–2000) and the Interim Poverty Reduction Strategy Paper: 2000–2. The implementation of these two strategies met considerable challenges, in part due to weak national ownership, unrealistic implementation strategies and inadequate financing (Ghana, Republic of, 2002). The GPRS attempts to address these and other challenges, by instituting broad-based consensus-building among the government, civil society, the private sector and development partners on key issues and programmes for accelerated and sustained poverty reduction.

**Figure 15.2:  Linkage Between Decentralization and Poverty Reduction**

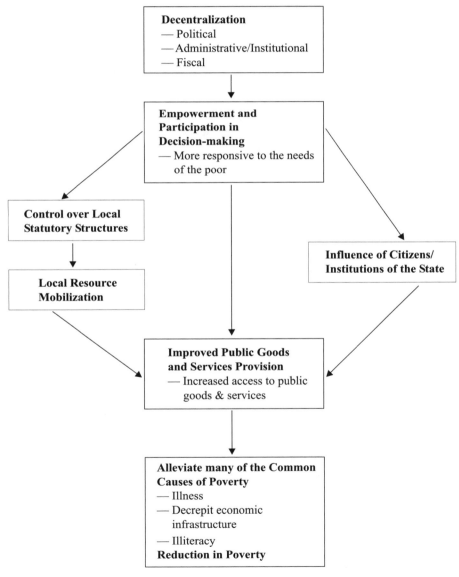

Source: Asante (2003).

The aim of the government with the GPRS is to create wealth by transforming the nature of the economy to achieve growth, accelerated poverty reduction and the protection of the vulnerable and excluded within a decentralized, democratic environment (ibid.). This goal is to be achieved by:

i.    ensuring sound economic management for accelerated growth;
ii.   increasing production and promoting sustainable livelihoods;
iii.  direct support for human development and the provision of basic services;
iv.   providing special programmes in support of the vulnerable and excluded;
v.    ensuring good governance and increased capacity of the public sector; and
vi.   active involvement of the private sector as the main engine of growth and partner in nation-building.

The GPRS will also ensure that all Ghanaians, irrespective of their socio-economic status or where they reside, have access to basic social services such as health care, quality education, potable drinking water, decent housing, security from crime and violence, and the ability to participate in decisions that affect their own lives. Two main activities of the poverty strategy in line with the decentralization process are:

i.    strengthening the leadership and capacity of District Assemblies through district elections, the exercise of traditional authority, local government service, the District Assemblies, financial management role and training and refresher programmes, among others;
ii.   deepening District Assemblies' association with civil society, by establishing a working partnership with NGOs and the private business sector.

## 6.    Conclusions: Lessons and Implications for Poverty Reduction

This study has sought to examine the impact of decentralization on poverty reduction. Even though it found that decentralization has an impact on poverty reduction, this impact is dependent on certain variables. It is not sufficient just to look at any type of decentralization, such as political decentralization, in isolation, when assessing the impact of decentralization on poverty reduction. Political, administrative and fiscal decentralization need to be considered simultaneously and the sequencing and pace of the different types of decentralization seem to play an important role.

The following lessons and implications for poverty reduction can be drawn:

i.    Poverty is closely linked to political factors, such as access to power and resources and the accountable and transparent management of local affairs. A genuine devolution of resources and authority can create openings for local communities, traditional leaders, private sector operators and non-governmental organizations to become more fully involved in local development processes. Thus, a democratically controlled local governance system is a precondition for poverty reduction.
ii.   An efficient local government can play a useful role as a catalyst and co-

ordinator of bottom-up development initiatives. A process of decentralization that best serves poverty reduction is one that combines the strategies of political empowerment, resource mobilization and enhanced service delivery in a coherent and balanced mix.

iii. The degree of responsiveness to the poor and the extent to which decentralization impacts on poverty are largely dependent on the relationship between central and local government and the commitment of the central government to poverty reduction.

iv. Removing social barriers and building social institutions for poverty reduction can only be addressed if the government has the political commitment and will to pursue decentralization to its logical conclusion, irrespective of its political and technical risks and trade-offs.

*Poverty, Education & Health*

## References

Alderman, H. (1998) *Social Assistance in Albania: Decentralization and Targeted Transfers,* Working Paper 734. Washington, DC: World Bank.

Asante, F. A. (2003) *Economic Analysis of Decentralisation in Rural Ghana.* Munich: Peter Lang.

Ayee, J. R. A. (1992) 'Decentralization and Effective Government', *Africa Insight,* Vol. 22: 49–56.

Ayee, J. R. A. (1994) *An Anatomy of Public Policy Implementation: The Case of Decentralization Policies in Ghana.* Aldershot: Avebury.

Ayee, J. R. A. (1995) 'Financing Subnational Governments in Ghana: the Case of the District Assemblies' Common Fund', *Regional and Federal Studies,* Vol. 5, No. 3 (Autumn): 292–306.

Ayee, J. R. A. (1996) 'The Measurement of Decentralization: The Ghanaian Experience', *African Affairs,* Vol. 95, No. 378: 31–50.

Ayee, J. R. A. (1997a) 'The Adjustment of Central Bodies to Decentralization: the Case of the Ghanaian Bureaucracy', *African Studies Review,* Vol. 40, No. 2 (September): 37–57.

Ayee, J. R. A. (1997b) 'Local Government Reform and Bureaucratic Accountability', *Regional Development Dialogue,* (UNCRD, Nagoya, Japan), Vol. 18, No. 2 (Autumn): 86–104.

Ayee, J. R. A. (1998) 'Decentralization in Sub-Saharan Africa: Lessons for the Future', *The LECIA Bulletin,* Vol. 4, No. 1: 1–21.

Ayee, J. R. A. (2003a) 'Local Government, Decentralization and State Capacity in Ghana', in Wisdom Tettey, K. P. Puplampu and Bruce Berman (eds), *Critical Perspectives on Politics and Socio-Economic Development in Ghana.* Leiden: Brill.

Ayee, J. R. A. (2003b) 'Towards Effective and Accountable Local Government in Ghana', in *Critical Perspectives* No. 13. Accra: Ghana Centre for Democratic Development (March): 1–27.

Ayee, J. R. A. (2004) 'Ghana: A Top-Down Initiative', in Olowu and Wunsch; Chapter 6.

Ayee, J. R. A. and Amponsah, Nicholas (2003) 'The District Assemblies and Local Governance: Reflections on the 2002 Local Elections', in Nicholas Amponsah and K. Boafo-Arthur (eds), *Local Government in Ghana: Grassroots in the 2002 Local Government Elections.* Accra: Department of Polical Science, University of Ghana.

Batley, R. A. and Stoker, G. (1991) *Local Government in Europe: Trends and Developments.* Basingstoke: Macmillan.

Bird, Richard, Litvack, J. and Rao, M. G. (1995) *Intergovernmental Fiscal Relations and Poverty Alleviation in Vietnam,* Policy Research Working Paper 1430. Washington, DC: World Bank, East Asia and Pacific, Country Department 1, Country Operations Division.

Bird, Richard and Rodriguez, E. R. (1999) 'Decentralization and Poverty Alleviation: International Experience and the Case of the Philippines', *Public Administration and Development,* Vol. 19: 299–319.

Bird, R. and Villancourt, F. (eds) *Fiscal Decentralization in Developing Countries.* Cambridge: Cambridge University Press.

Blackwood, D. L. and Lynch, R. G. (1994) 'The Measurement of Inequality and Poverty: A Policy Maker's Guide to the Literature'. *World Development,* Vol. 22, No. 4: 567–78.

Canagarajah, S and Ye, X. (2001). *Public Health and Education Spending in Ghana in 1992-98: Issues of Equity and Efficiency.* Working Paper 2579. Washington, DC: World Bank.

Castro-Leal, F., Dayton, J., Demery, L. and Mehra, K. (1999) 'Public Social Spending in Africa: Do the Poor Benefit?' *World Bank Research Observer,* Vol. 14, No. 1: 49–72.

Crook, R. C. (2003) 'Decentralization and Poverty Reduction in Africa: The Politics of Local-Central Relations', *Public Administration and Development,* Vol. 23: 77–88.

Crook, R. C. and Manor, J. (1998) *Democracy and Decentralization in South Asia and West Africa.* Cambridge: Cambridge University Press.

Crook, R. C. and Sverrisson, A. S. (2001) *Decentralization and Poverty Alleviation in Developing Countries: A Comparative Analysis or, is West Bengal Unique?* IDS Working Paper 130. Brighton: Institute of Development Studies at the University of Sussex.

Demery, L. (2000) *Benefit Incidence: A Practitioner's Guide. Poverty and Social Development Group, Africa Region.* Washington, DC: World Bank.

Demery, L., Chao, S., Bernier, R. and Mehta, K. (1995) *The Incidence of Social Spending in Ghana.* Poverty and Social Policy, Discussion Paper No. 82. Washington, DC: World Bank.

Ellis, F. (1998) 'Household Strategies and Rural Livelihood Diversification', *Journal of Development Studies*, Vol. 35, No. 1: 1–38.

Ghana, Republic of (1992) *Constitution of the Republic of Ghana, 1992.* Tema: Ghana Publishing Corporation.

Ghana, Republic of (1993) *Local Government Act (Act 462).* Tema: Ghana Publishing Corporation.

Ghana, Republic of (2002) *Ghana Poverty Reduction Strategy, 2002–2004: An Agenda for Growth and Prosperity — Analysis and Policy Statement.* 4 February.

Griffin, K. (1981) 'Economic Development in a Changing World', *World Development*, Vol. 9, No. 3: 221–6.

GTZ/SNRD (1996) *Decentralisation and Local Government in Ghana.* Working Paper No. 3. Accra: SNRD Working Group: Decentralisation and Rural Development.

Jong, K. de, Loquai, C. and Soiri, I. (1999) *Decentralisation and Poverty Reduction: Exploring the Linkages.* IDS Policy Papers 1/99. Helsinki: Institute of Development Studies and Maastricht: ECDPM.

Lipton, M. and van der Gaag, J. (eds) (1993) *Including the Poor.* Proceedings of a Symposium Organized by the World Bank and the International Food Policy Research Institute, Washington, DC. Washington, DC: World Bank/IFPRI.

Litvack, J., Ahmad, J. and Bird, R. (1998) *Rethinking Decentralisation in Developing Countries.* Sector Studies Series. Washington, DC: World Bank.

Mawhood, P. (ed.) (1993) *Local Government in the Third World: The Experience of Tropical Africa*, 2nd edn. Pretoria: Africa Institute of South Africa.

Ministry of Local Government and Rural Development (2002) *Decentralization in Ghana: Implementation Status and Proposed Future Directions.* Accra: MLGRD, March.

Nzouankeu, J. M. (1994) 'Decentralization and Democracy in Africa', *International Review of Administrative Sciences*, Vol. 60: 213–227.

Olowu, Dele and Wunsch, James (eds) (2004) *Local Governance in Africa: The Challenges of Democratic Decentralization.* Boulder, CO and London: Lynne Rienner.

Prud'homme, R. (1995) 'The Dangers of Decentralization', *World Bank Research Observer,* Vol. 10, No. 2 (August): 201–20.

Rawlings, J. J. (1999) Speech read on his behalf at Sixth Annual Conference of District Chief Executives, Ho, Volta Region, 5–10 September, published in MLGRD, *Selected Speeches and Papers,* Accra: MLGRD.

Rondinelli, D. A. (1981) 'Government Decentralization in Comparative Perspective: Theory and Practice in Developing Countries', *International Review of Administrative Sciences*, Vol. 47: 22–42.

Rondinelli, D. A., McCullogh, J. S. and Johnson, R. W. (1989) 'Analyzing Decentralization Policies in Developing Countries: A Political Economy Framework', *Development and Change*, Vol. 20: 57–87.

Sen, Amartya (1999) *Development as Freedom.* New York: Knopf.

Shah, A. (1994) *The Reform of Intergovernmental Fiscal Relations in Developing Countries and Emerging Market Economies.* Policy and Research Series 23. Washington, DC: World Bank.

Smith, B.C. (1985) *Decentralization: The Territorial Dimension of the State.* London: Allen & Unwin.

Smoke, Paul (2003) 'Decentralization in Africa: Goals, Dimensions, Myths and Challenges', *Public Administration and Development*, Vol. 23: 7–16.

Turner, Mark and Hulme, David (1997) *Governance, Administration & Development: Making the State Work.* New York: Palgrave.

World Bank (2001) *World Development Report, 2000–2001. Attacking Poverty.* Oxford: Oxford University Press for the World Bank.

Wunsch, J. S. and Olowu, D. (eds) (1995) *The Failure of the Centralized State: Institutions for Self-Governance in Africa.* 2nd edn. San Francisco: Institute for Contemporary Studies.

# 16 Technical Efficiency in Ghanaian Secondary Education*

KWABENA GYIMAH-BREMPONG
& ELIZABETH N. APPIAH

## 1. Introduction

This study uses panel data from school districts and a new panel data frontier estimator to investigate the effects of family inputs on technical efficiency in the production of secondary education in Ghana. It does this by estimating a translog stochastic frontier production function for education, calculating technical inefficiencies from the production function and using family inputs as correlates of the calculated technical inefficiency. It measures educational output as the proportion of students in a district passing the West African Examination Council's (WAEC) certification examination and estimates technical inefficiencies for two levels of education — Junior and Senior Secondary Schools — focusing on total technical inefficiency without decomposing it into its various components.

Education has always been important in Ghanaian life. Ghana was one of the first African countries to introduce free and universal primary education in 1960. This was followed by a rapid expansion of secondary and tertiary institutions under the Ghana Education Trust system, a process which continues today. For example, in 2001, there were about 3.5 million students enrolled in public Primary Schools, Junior Secondary Schools (JSS) and Senior Secondary Schools (SSS) in Ghana, a country with a population of about 20 million people (see Republic of Ghana, 2002). This indicates a high demand for education by Ghanaians. In addition, the government spends an enormous amount of resources to provide education. Indeed, the largest share of the central government budget is spent on the provision of education.

The importance of education in the development process is generally acknowledged in the literature. Apart from its contribution to growth, education, like health, is a

* The authors wish to thank Elizabeth Asiedu for assistance on the GLSS data. The research for this study was conducted while Gyimah-Brempong was Economics Programme Director at the National Science Foundation, Arlington, VA. The views expressed are those of the authors alone and do not reflect the views of the National Science Foundation or the United States Agency for International Development.

consumption good whose acquisition directly contributes to human well-being. It is partly for this reason that the United Nations Development Programme (UNDP) uses education as one of the components of its Human Development Index (HDI). While Ghanaian governments have expended a lot of resources on education, the level of literacy continues to be relatively low. Given the extreme scarcity of resources to provide education, it is important that education be produced efficiently. Some researchers, however, have argued that education provision in African countries is highly inefficient.[1]

Three approaches have been used to investigate the cognitive achievement of students: early child development, production function, and market structure.[2] These approaches focus on the importance of different aspects of education production — home environment, school inputs, and organization of the school system. Our approach is a combination of the first two approaches. However, instead of combining family inputs and school inputs in one regression, we conduct the research in two steps: we estimate the effects of school inputs on cognition and then investigate whether differences in efficiency in producing cognitive achievement are correlated with family inputs. This approach can illuminate the impact of omitted family variables on the educational performance of Ghanaian secondary school students.

The study is limited to public secondary schools for several reasons. First, public schools provide the overwhelming share of secondary education in Ghana. Second, we only have education data for the public schools. Third, while all secondary schools may have the objective of providing instruction in academic subjects, private schools may have additional objectives, such as religious education, that public schools may not be concerned with.[3] Finally, because private schools are free from the directions of central and regional education bureaucracies, they may combine school inputs in ways that may be different from those of public schools in order to achieve their objectives.[4] This means that the production technology in public and private schools may be different. Concentrating on public schools allows us to assume a given underlying production technology for all schools.

One may question our focus on technical efficiency if the objective of decision-makers is to produce secondary education in the most economically efficient way. Estimating economic efficiency would require us to obtain detailed cost and production data, that are not currently available to us. Estimating technical (in)efficiency in the production of education is important in itself. Technical efficiency is a *necessary*

---

[1] See Keller (2004) and McMahon (2000) for examples. Ghanaian students also performed poorly in a recently released international achievement test in basic science.

[2] We use educational output, educational outcome, and cognitive achievement interchangeably to mean the same thing in this study. While they may mean different things in the education literature, we use these terms to indicate that our measure of education output represents only performance in test scores.

[3] Public schools are, by law, not allowed to impose any religious instructions or practices on students who choose not to participate. This may not be the case with private schools.

[4] An example in the choice of production 'technology' is the use of adjunct instructors. While the private sector is free to use as many it likes, and often uses mostly adjuncts, the public sector is not free to do so, because of either contractual obligations with the teachers' union or the government's concerns about 'quality' control.

condition for economic efficiency, so finding that school districts are not achieving technical efficiency implies that they are not operating with economic efficiency. Also because production technology is almost the same in all public schools across the country, the most technically efficient school district may provide a benchmark for 'best practice' that other districts could emulate.

We find relatively large technical inefficiencies in the production of secondary education in Ghana, averaging about 11% for all subjects at both levels of education. Technical inefficiency varies with the subject taught, the level of education and the region. In general, technical inefficiency is higher in JSS than in SSS and also higher for General Science than for other subjects for both levels of education. We find that technical inefficiency in the production of education is significantly correlated with average household expenditure on extra classes, parental education, and the number of siblings in the household. Our results confirm the importance of both family and school inputs in the production of the cognitive abilities of Ghanaian secondary school students.

The rest of the study is organized as follows: The next section briefly mentions previous work on the topic and Section 3 introduces the stochastic frontier production function as well as the indices of inefficiency we estimate. Section 4 discusses the estimation method and the data while Section 5 presents and discusses the econometric results. Section 6 concludes the study.

## 2.    Previous Work

The literature on the economics of education is voluminous and growing rapidly. We shall therefore refer briefly only to studies that are relevant to this study.[5] The three approaches to the provision of education — child development, production function, and school 'market' structure — are identifiable in the literature. In the early childhood approach, family inputs and the social environment in which a child grows up are deemed to be the main determinants of cognitive achievement. The production function approach, on the other hand, stresses the relationship between school inputs and cognitive achievements, while the education market approach focuses on how the organization of the education system, especially competition in the provision of education, affects the cognitive skills of students. Clearly, elements of all three will affect the cognitive achievements of students, hence focusing on only one aspect to the exclusion of the others, requires very restrictive assumptions which could lead to biased estimates, as Todd and Wolpin (2003) point out.

The effects of school inputs on cognitive achievements are inconclusive in the literature. A significant number of studies find a positive and statistically significant impact of school inputs on student cognitive achievement (Krueger: 2003; Case and Deaton, 1999; Haegoland et al., 2005; Woβmann, 2005; Angrist and Lavy, 1999, among others). In part, they find teacher qualification and class size, as well as other complementary inputs, to have significant impacts on student performance. A large number of studies also find that school inputs have no significant impact on student

---

[5] For extensive reviews, see Hanushek (1986, 2003); Glewwe (2002); Lazear (2001).

achievement (Hanushek, 1986, 2003, for example); yet others find a negative relationship between school inputs and student performance.[6] This has led some researchers to argue that increasing the quantity and quality of school inputs will not increase the cognitive achievement of students; they point to the recent US experience for empirical support. If policy-makers are interested in increasing the cognitive performance of students, then they should look at other policies, such as increasing competition among schools. Dalton et al. (2003), using various approaches to the production of education, finds that student study time has a positive and significant effect on test scores. They also find that the effect is much stronger for the stochastic frontier model than either the IV or 'value added' model.

There may be several reasons why one may find no significant relationship between school inputs and cognitive achievements. Among these are the usually omitted variable bias and mis-specification generally. It is generally acknowledged that family inputs and student innate abilities as well as the trajectories of past input use have significant impacts on the cognitive achievement of students in the current period. However, data on these variables are not generally available to the researcher, who is then forced to ignore these variables and concentrate on school inputs only. Even when proxy variables are used for these variables, they could confound the results and increase the bias if the proxy variables are not 'close' to the characteristics they are intended to capture and if these proxies are not independent of other explanatory variables (Todd and Wolpin: 2003). It is also possible for families to substitute household resources for school inputs instead of complementing them. Das et al. (2004) find that families in Zambia tend to decrease their inputs when they expect an increase in school inputs. Only unanticipated changes in school inputs, they conclude, have significant effects on student cognitive achievements.

The foregoing implies that education production functions should include both school and household inputs in order to produce consistent and unbiased estimates of the effects of school inputs on cognitive achievements. Some researchers have included both school and family inputs in a single production function and have found both to be significant factors (see, for example, Gyimah-Brempong and Gyapong, 1991, 1992; Haegoland et al., 2005). The approach we adopt in the present study is to estimate a frontier production function for education using only school inputs as arguments. We then use family inputs to investigate the correlation of technical inefficiency with these inputs. We think of this approach as a diagnostic tool to answer the question: How important are omitted family inputs in explaining student cognitive achievements in Ghanaian secondary schools?

## 3. Model

We assume that school administrators maximize school output with a given set of inputs. We also assume that there exists a well defined, twice differentiable production technology of secondary education that underlies the stochastic production frontier. This production relation can be written as: $\mathbf{Q} = \mathbf{f}(\mathbf{X})$ where Q is the quantity of output

---

[6] Hanushek (2003) provides a summary of studies and the impact of school inputs they find.

and $\mathbf{X}$ is a vector of production inputs. Output may deviate from the frontier because of the usual stochastic error, hence the production function can be written as: $\mathbf{Q}^* = \mathbf{f}(\mathbf{X}, \mathbf{v})$ where v is the usual stochastic error term assumed to be independently and indistinguishably distributed, normally with zero mean and a constant variance $(\sigma_v^2)$.

In addition to the error term, it is possible for output in a particular school district to deviate systematically from the production frontier due to inefficiency. Define the measure of relative inefficiency for school district $i$ as $r_i = e - u_i$ where $u_i \geq 0$. We can then write an individual school district's output as: $\mathbf{Q}_i = \mathbf{f}(\mathbf{X}, \mathbf{v})e - u_i, u_i \geq 0$. If $u_i = 0$, then $Q_i = Q^*$, hence the school district produces on the frontier, whereas non-zero values of $u_i$ imply that the school district produces below the frontier. This interpretation implies that $\mathbf{Q}_i \leq \mathbf{Q}^*$. The equation can be written in the usual stochastic frontier production function specification as:

$$\mathbf{Q} = eX'\beta + Vi - u_i \tag{1}$$

where all variables are as defined above.

The functional form of the education production technology is an empirical issue. Several studies have used restricted functional forms, such as the Cobb-Douglas for the underlying production technology. Imposing such restrictive functional forms could result in biased and possibly inconsistent estimates, if such restrictions do not represent the underlying production technology. We use the transcendental logarithmic production (translog) function to represent the underlying production technology. The translog function is a second order approximation of an underlying production technology and is flexible enough to model a large number of production technologies through appropriate parametric restrictions.

The translog production function we estimate in this study is given as:

$$\ln Q = a_0 + \sum_i \alpha_i \ln X_i + \frac{1}{2} \sum_i \sum_j \alpha_{ij} [\ln X_i \ln X_j] \tag{2}$$

where all variables are as defined above We impose symmetry restrictions (i.e. $\alpha_{ij} = \alpha_{ji}$). Other production technologies as well as characteristics of the production technology can be obtained from the translog production function through appropriate parametric restrictions. For example, the Cobb-Douglas production technology is obtained when $\alpha_{ij} = 0$ for all $i, j$, and the production technology exhibits constant returns to scale if $\sum_i \alpha_i = 1$ and $\sum_i \sum_j \alpha_{ij} = 0$. The output elasticity with respect to a particular input, given by $\partial \ln Q / \partial x_i = \alpha_i + \sum_j \alpha_{ij} X_j$, is not constant but depends on the first order coefficient as well as the second order coefficients and the quantities of all other inputs. It is therefore possible for $\alpha_i$ to be negative but for the output elasticity of an input, $\partial \ln Q_i / \partial \ln x_i$, to be positive.

There are several possible ways to measure educational output. In this study, we measure educational output as the performance on national certification examinations at each cycle of the secondary educational level. Specifically, we measure educational output of a school district as the average passing rate of students in national certification tests conducted by WAEC. We consider two outputs — performance in the Basic Education Certificate Examination (BECE) for JSS and SSS Secondary School Certificate Examination (SSCE).

We use four inputs in the production of each output of education. These inputs pertain to the quantity and quality of teachers in a school as well as the physical capital in the school. We measure the quantity of teachers as the student/teacher ratio (*STRATIO*). Following earlier research (Woβmann, 2005), the proportion of teachers who are trained (*TRAINED*) and the proportion who are female (*FEMALE*) are used as our measures of teacher quality. The measure of physical capital we use is the proportion of school physical facilities that need major renovations (FREPAIR). We had no measure of students' innate abilities, such as IQ scores. For SSS, we use a two-year lag average performance on the BECE examinations to proxy students' innate ability. We do not have such a variable for the JSS sample, hence we do not include any variable to proxy student ability in the BECE equations.

We did not have data on *FREPAIR* for Senior Secondary Schools, so all SSS equations were estimated without this variable and its second order terms. We calculate the index of inefficiency from the stochastic frontier production function as $u_i = (q^* - q_i)/q^*$ or $1 - q_i/q^*$ where $q^*$ is output at the frontier and $q_i$ is a school district's observed output of education.

The focus of this study is on whether family inputs are significantly correlated with technical inefficiency in the production of secondary education in Ghana. A large proportion of students' education takes place outside the school environment in students' homes and communities. These non-purchased inputs, such as the availability of books at home, parental help with homework, and study skills, imparted by parents, are all crucially important in students' educational attainment. We postulate that the index of technical inefficiency in education production will be correlated with these family inputs, all things being equal. We therefore make technical inefficiency in education production a function of these family inputs. Formally we write the inefficiency equation as:

$$\mathbf{u} = \mathbf{u}(\mathbf{W}) \tag{3}$$

where **W** is a vector of family inputs.

There is no theoretical guidance on choosing these family inputs. Income summarizes a lot of socio-economic characteristics. However, what is important in our context is how much parents spend on educating their children, especially expenditure on 'extra classes'.[7] Hence we include total per child expenditure on extra classes in a household (*EDUCEXP*) as a regressor. Parental education has been found to influence cognitive achievement of students, so we include parental education (*DADEDU,*

---

[7] 'Extra classes' refer to tutoring outside the normal classes provided in the Secondary Schools. In Ghana, these extra classes are very widespread.

*MOMEDU*) as regressors. Finally, we include the average number of siblings in a household in each educational cohort (*SIBLING*) as an added regressor in the technical inefficiency equation. Educated parents are more able to help their children than uneducated ones, hence we expect a positive correlation between parental education and a child's school performance. Therefore, we expect a negative relationship between parents' education and technical inefficiency in the production of education.

We also assume that the larger the number of siblings in a given educational cohort in a family, the less time the family will have to devote to helping each child in their studies at home, all things being equal. We do not have any theoretical guidance on the functional form of the inefficiency equation. We therefore follow a simple specification and estimate it in the double log form. The inefficiency equation we estimate is given as:

$$u_i = \beta_0 + \beta_1 EDUEXP + \beta_2 PARENTED + \beta_3 SIBLING + \varepsilon_i \qquad (4)$$

where $\varepsilon_i$ is an idiosyncratic error term assumed to have a zero mean and a finite variance.

## 4.    Data and Estimation Method

### *Estimation Method*

The data we use to estimate the stochastic frontier production function are panel data with three years of data for each of the 110 education districts in Ghana. Panel data methods are therefore called for to take advantage of the time-series and cross-sectional dimensions of the data. The stochastic frontier production function has generally been estimated by Maximum Likelihood (ML) estimates. This will provide the correct results, provided the likelihood function is correctly specified and there are no measurement errors in the variables. When there are measurement errors in the variables and these are not taken into account in the estimation, the coefficient estimates will be biased, hence the frontier will also be measured with error. When the frontier is erroneously measured, the associated technical inefficiency measures will also be biased. It is therefore important to use estimation methods that are robust to the existence of measurement errors if one suspects the existence of such errors.

We are not confident that all the variables in our model are measured without errors. In particular, we note that some of the variables are proxy variables that we use in place of variables used in the production of education. For example, while student/teacher ratio and the proportions of teachers who are women or trained are likely to be correctly measured, it is unlikely that the proportion of school facilities needing major repairs will be correctly measured for obvious reasons. In addition, there are many school inputs, such as libraries, laboratory equipment, and school management, that we are not able to account for. Finally, the output variables are measured as performance in a particular subject, while the inputs are aggregates for all subjects. This means that all the productive inputs we use here are subject to measurement errors. It is therefore important that we use an estimation method that is robust to measurement errors in order to get consistent estimates.

Chen and Wang (2004) have proposed a two-step General Methods of Moments (GMM) estimator for panel data stochastic frontier functions when some of the variables are measured with error. The estimates from this two-step GMM estimator are robust to measurement errors.[8] This estimator is also appropriate for the estimation of panel data stochastic frontier functions. We used this panel data GMM estimator, programmed in STATA8, to estimate the stochastic frontier production function. In estimating this function, we included a regional dummy variable to account for regional effects.

A major problem with the production function approach is the possibility that the quantity of input used by schools (school districts) is itself endogenous, especially in countries where property taxation finances local school districts. In the case of Ghana, there are reasons to suspect that the problem of input endogeneity may be minimized. First, the inputs we use — teachers and physical capital — are generally provided by the central government through the ministry of education. While PTAs may provide additional resources, these are generally very small relative to the overall resources of the school, and they usually do not involve teachers or the construction of physical facilities. Secondly, for political reasons, the central government may not provide school resources that vary systematically across districts or regions, especially when measured on a per student basis. This implies that we could, potentially, treat the school inputs as exogenously determined.

We admit that it is possible that some schools in a region may get relatively large or higher-quality resources because the schools' administrations are more successful at lobbying the central government for resources or because central government decision-makers have some emotional affiliation with these institutions (e.g. they may be alumni of these schools). We also admit that schools in urban districts are likely to have more and better trained teachers than schools in rural districts because of the locational preferences of teachers. We believe the inclusion of a regional dummy variable may partly control for this endogeneity issue. Ultimately whether inputs can be treated as exogenous or not is an empirical question. We therefore use a Hausman test to check to see if we can treat the inputs as exogenous.

We had only one year of data for the family inputs we use to explain the sources of technical inefficiency in education production, hence we were not able to use panel data methods. In order not to discard any information in the estimation, we defined the dependent variable as the three-year average of the inefficiency index for each district. While we could use OLS techniques to estimate the determinants of the technical inefficiency equation, the technical inefficiency indicator is bounded at 0 and 1. Secondly, by construction, the most efficient districts have a technical inefficiency of 0; hence OLS will produce biased and inconsistent estimates, especially given that a relatively large number of districts were on or close to the frontier. We therefore use the Tobit estimator to estimate the coefficients of the inefficiency equation. Because the dependent variable is theoretically truncated at 0 and 1, we used the double truncated Tobit estimator to estimate the equation.

---

[8] We do not present the details of this estimation procedure here. Interested readers should consult Chen and Wang (2004).

## Data

We measure education output as the proportion of students who passed the WAEC certification examination in English, General Science, and Mathematics. For JSS, we measure outputs as the proportion of students passing the Basic Education Certificate Examination in English (BECEE), General Science (BECES), and Mathematics (BECEM) respectively. For Senior Secondary Schools, the outputs are the respective passing rates in the Senior Secondary School Certificate Examination in English (SSCEE), General Science (SSCES), and Mathematics (SSCEM).

Using cognitive achievement as the measure of output has its weaknesses. For one thing, examination scores are not the only outputs of the education system. Output may include character building, physical and spiritual well-being, as well as citizenship — outputs that examination scores do not measure. More important, this measure of output does not take account of the quality of the passing grades. For example, two school districts will be judged to have produced the same level of output when the same proportion of students in both districts pass a test, even if all the students passing in the first district received all 'As' while all the students passing in the second district received 'Ds'. We have no way of adjusting for these quality differences. On the other hand, this measure of output has its advantages. This examination is a national examination, so it provides a comparable way of evaluating the performance of school districts in the country.

Because school districts differ in size, we measure the quantity of available teachers as the student/teacher ratio (*STRATIO*). The lower the student/teacher ratio, the more time teachers can potentially allocate to each student, and therefore improve performance, all things being equal (e.g. Krueger, 2003). We measure teacher quality with two variables: the proportion of teachers in a school district who have the appropriate teaching credentials or are 'trained' (*TRAINED*) and the proportion of teachers who are female (*FEMALE*).

We had data neither on the services that flow from physical capital, libraries, laboratories, or ICT of schools, nor on the physical units of these inputs. However, we did have data on the proportion of schools in a district whose physical facilities needed major repairs (*FREPAIR*). Assuming that this is correlated with the useful physical capital services available to schools, we use this variable as the measure of productive capital for schools in the production of education.

Because this variable is negatively correlated with productive capital, given the stock of all capital available to the school, we expect it to be negatively correlated with school output. As argued above, we include the two-year lag of BECE scores in the relevant subjects as a proxy for student ability in the SSS equations. There are some inputs — such as school administration — that we do not have. If these omitted inputs are in any way correlated with the included inputs, the usual omitted variable bias problem is introduced.

*EDUCEXP*, parental education, and *SIBLING* are used as the proxies for family inputs to explain differences in technical inefficiency in secondary school production across school districts in Ghana. *EDUCEXP* is measured as the total expenditure of a household on extra classes at a particular cycle of education, divided by the number of students at that cycle in the household. Parents' education is measured as the average level of education in a district of mothers whose children are in a given educational (age) cohort. The *Ghana Living Standard Survey,* from which we obtained the family input data is detailed enough to allow us to construct these variables separately for JSS and SSS students. SIBLING is measured as the average number of children in a household who are enrolled in each cycle of secondary school. For JSS, we assumed that student ages were between 12 and 15 years, while for SSS, we assumed the ages to be from 16 to 20.[9] The age intervals for siblings in JSS and SSS were determined in a similar manner to those for parental education and *EDUCEXP.*

Data for the calculation of educational outputs (*BECEE, BECES, BECEM, SSSCEE, SSSCES, SSSCEM*) and school inputs (*STRATIO, TRAINED, FEMALE, FREPAIR*) were obtained from Ministry of Education (Republic of Ghana, 2002). The data are for all school districts in Ghana for 1999, 2000 and 2001, giving us a panel data set with 330 observations. While there are potentially 330 observations to be used in estimating the education production function, a few districts did not report observations for SSS in some years. In most cases, however, the number of districts not reporting was no more than 3 in a year; hence the minimum number of observations we had for the SSS sample was 321, while we had all 330 observations for the JSS sample.

Data for calculating the family input variables were obtained from the *Ghana Living Standards Survey* Wave IV, 2002 and the variables are for 1999. This means that there is a single cross-section data set for family input variables. There were a few school districts that were not covered by the *GLSS,* hence we have a total of 102 observations for the family input data. Summary statistics of the sample data are presented in Table 16.1. The data show that school resources in Ghana are relatively low. For example, the average student/teacher ratio in JSS is 19.1, while the proportion of trained (certified) teachers is only 62.9%. The proportion of JSS school facilities needing major repairs is 37%.[10] Not surprisingly, the average school output is low; barely 50% of JSS and SSS students, on average, pass these examinations. Fathers' education averages 2.5 years for both cycles, while mothers' education averages 1.5 for both cycles.[11] Household per student expenditure on extra classes averages ¢92,353.47 for JSS and ¢230,695.00 for SSS.

## 5.    Statistical Results

This section presents the statistical results. The first sub-section discusses the regression statistics of the estimates of the stochastic frontier translog production function as well as the indices of technical inefficiency calculated from these coefficient estimates. The second sub-section presents and discusses the correlates of technical inefficiency in the production of secondary education in Ghana.

---

[9] These age cut-offs were based on the idea that the average age of students taking the SSSCE was about 19 and those taking the BECE was 16.5.
[10] The numbers are even worse at the primary school level where the average student/teacher ratio is about 35.
[11] These are unweighted averages for JSS and SSS enrolments in a household.

**Table 16.1  Summary Statistics for Ghana Education Production Data**

| Variable | Mean[a] | Standard Error | Minimum | Maximum |
|---|---|---|---|---|
| JSS enrolment | 6560.988 | 7160.018 | 923 | 67840 |
| SSS enrolment | 1669.253 | 2618.777 | 0.0 | 18892 |
| JSS Female Teachers (%) | 18.6518 | 11.826 | 0.2 | 56.8 |
| SSS Female Teachers (%) | 12.371 | 8.4117 | 0.0 | 37.8 |
| JSS Trained Teachers (%) | 62.8912 | 40.9555 | 5.0624 | 92.8913 |
| SSS Trained Teachers (%) | 42.9952 | 28.7550 | 0.0 | 100.0 |
| JSS Student/Teacher ratio | 19.1333 | 3.7349 | 9.00 | 35.5 |
| SSS Student/Teacher ratio | 17.0936 | 8.7411 | 0.0 | 92.6 |
| JSS Fac. Repair (%) | 37.3482 | 11.9433 | 4.50 | 76.90 |
| BECEE | 49.2272 | 14.6422 | 17.9 | 89.6 |
| BECES | 52.4654 | 13.8956 | 21.3 | 93.5 |
| BECEM | 52.0897 | 13.9255 | 24.2 | 100.00 |
| SSSCEE | 41.9694 | 20.5220 | 1.51 | 92.6 |
| SSSCES | 35.1151 | 17.3857 | 0.51 | 85.1 |
| SSSCEM | 39.6473 | 17.3544 | 0.00 | 89.6 |
| DADEDU 12–15 | 2.0532 | 0.9547 | 1.0 | 5 |
| MOMEDU 12–15 | 1.655 | 0.5218 | 1.0 | 3.11 |
| DADEDU 16–20 | 2.5299 | 1.0899 | 1.0 | 5.2858 |
| MOMEDU 16–20 | 1.5727 | 0.6039 | 1.0 | 3.75 |
| EDUEXP 12–15 (Cedis) | 92,353.47 | 65,063.36 | 11,533.33 | 373,731.60 |
| EDUEXP 16–20 (Cedis) | 230,695.00 | 287,410.60 | 24,750.00 | 2,166,750.00 |
| SIBLING 12–15 | 2.1 | 1.582 | 1.0 | 5.0 |
| SIBLING 16–20 | 1.432 | 1.30 | 1.0 | 4.0 |
| N | 330 | 330 | 330 | 330 |

*Note:* a) These are unweighted means.

## Regression Statistics and Technical Inefficiency

We discuss the regression statistics of the production function in the first part of the sub-section, while the second part presents the indices of technical inefficiency calculated from the stochastic frontier production function.

### Regression Statistics

For space considerations, we do not report the coefficient estimates of the stochastic frontier translog education production function but discuss some regression statistics as well as testing for the structure of the underlying education production function.[12]

---

[12] The results are available upon request.

The stochastic frontier translog production function fits the data relatively well. All coefficient estimates are of the expected signs, as are the output elasticities with respect to all inputs. Likelihood ratio testing leads us to reject the null hypothesis that all slope coefficients are equal to zero at any reasonable confidence level. The likelihood ratio test to test whether the production technology is Cobb-Douglas produced $x^2$ statistics of 87.43, 67.38, 69.213, 83.94, 79.391, and 81.281 for BECEE, BECES, BECEM, SSCEE, SSCES, and SSCEM respectively. We therefore reject this

null hypothesis. Constant returns to scale (CRS) exist if $\sum_i \alpha_i = 1$ and $\sum_j \alpha_{ij} = 0$. The likelihood ratio test produced $x^2$ statistics of 89.32, 87.23, 76.82, 92.34, 88.13 and BECEE, BECES, BECEM, SSCEE, SSCES, and SSCEM respectively, so the null hypothesis of CRS production technology. We are not able to reject hypothesis that all inputs can be treated as exogenous, using a Hausman ....ty test.

The regression statistics also indicate that the stochastic frontier production function is the appropriate approach to use in estimating production of secondary education in Ghana. A disproportionately large share of the regression variance ($\sigma^2$), which is the sum of the variances of the two error terms, is accounted for by the variance of the inefficiency ($\sigma_u^2$). Indeed, $\lambda$ defined as $\sigma_u^2 / \sigma_v^2$, and which is a measure of the degree of asymmetry of the $v_i - u_i$ error term, is greater than 2.5 for all estimated equations, suggesting that an OLS estimation approach will not be justified in any of the equations. More important, the likelihood ratio test rejects the null hypothesis That there is no technical inefficiency in production ($H_0 : \sigma_u^2 = 0$) at $\alpha = .01$ for all subjects for both JSS and SSS.

## Technical Inefficiency

The main objective of this study is to investigate whether there are technical inefficiencies in the production of public secondary education in Ghana, and if so, whether they are correlated with family inputs. We used the estimated coefficients of the stochastic frontier production function to calculate indices of technical inefficiency for each school district. Regional averages of the calculated technical efficiencies are presented in Table 16.2.[13] Column 2 presents the technical inefficiency for BECEE, column 3 BECES, column 4 BECEM, column 5 SSCEE, column 6 SSCES, and column 7 SSCEM. The overall average indices of technical inefficiency are 0.102, 0.127, 0.091, 0.108, 0.118, and 0.087 for BECEE, BECES, BECEM, SSSCEE, SSSCES, and SSSCEM respectively. These averages, however, mask wide variances in technical inefficiencies across districts and across subjects. For example, the highest index of technical inefficiency in SSCES is 0.6367, while that of SSCEE is 0.4517. We note that the sa

Se

stand out. First, as indicated above, there is a wide variation in technical inefficiencies within subjects and across districts. Secondly, the calculated average technical

---

[13] We do not present technical inefficiency for each district for space considerations.

inefficiency varies by subject matter. Generally the calculated technical inefficiencies seem to be higher for BECES and SSCES compared with those for other subjects. This may be due to the unequal availability of qualified science teachers, laboratories, and equipment in all districts. Third, technical inefficiency seems to be higher in all subject areas at JSS level than in SSS, although the variance in technical inefficiency seems to be greater in SSS than in JSSS. This may be due to the fact that the system of admission to SSS tends to be based on students with superior capabilities and there are possibly, better quality school resources, especially in the non-science subjects, across school districts and regions at this level of education than at the JSS level for which there is less selectivity in admission. Student selectivity for SSS may combine with the possibility of wider differences in the quality of teachers to explain the relatively higher but variable efficiency in SSS relative to JSS. Finally, there are wide variations in technical efficiency across regions in all subject areas. In general, average technical inefficiency is lower in more urbanized regions than in rural regions.

**Table 16.2   Average Indices of Technical Inefficiency by Region**

| Region | BECEE | BECES | BECEM | SSCEE | SSCES | SSCEM |
|---|---|---|---|---|---|---|
| Ashanti | 0.1094 | 0.1543 | 0.0918 | 0.0963 | 0.1035 | 0.0663 |
| | (0.0620)[a] | (0.0637) | (0.0521) | (0.0621) | (0.1295) | (0.0933) |
| Brong Ahafo | 0.0827 | 0.1377 | 0.0990 | 0.0892 | 0.0752 | 0.0939 |
| | (0.0526) | (0.0545) | (0.0476) | (0.0549) | (0.1297) | (0.0983) |
| Central | 0.0937 | 0.1381 | 0.1110 | 0.0321 | 0.0502 | 0.0335 |
| | (0.0646) | (0.0671) | (0.0623) | (0.0438) | (0.0997) | (0.0851) |
| Eastern | 0.0609 | 0.1040 | 0.0828 | 0.0362 | 0.0237 | 0.0364 |
| | (0.0607) | (0.0628) | (0.0556) | (0.0945) | (0.0922) | (0.0908) |
| Greater Accra | 0.0112 | 0.0379 | 0.0295 | 0.0261 | 0.0518 | 0.0407 |
| | (0.0376) | (0.0427) | (0.0333) | (0.0873) | (0.0796) | (0.0581) |
| Northern | 0.0836 | 0.1345 | 0.0746 | 0.2903 | 0.3034 | 0.2128 |
| | (0.0626) | (0.0587) | (0.0605) | (0.1773) | (0.2422) | (0.2646) |
| Upper East | 0.0554 | 0.0965 | 0.0404 | 0.2023 | 0.1788 | 0.1236 |
| | (0.0389) | (0.0356) | (0.0396) | (0.1233) | (0.1799) | (0.0976) |
| Upper West | 0.0661 | 0.1040 | 0.0571 | 0.0841 | 0.0679 | 0.0636 |
| | (0.0262) | (0.0231) | (0.0228) | (0.1033) | (0.0907) | (0.1051) |
| Volta | 0.0782 | 0.1185 | 0.0835 | 0.0701 | 0.0427 | 0.0511 |
| | (0.0301) | (0.0312) | (0.0253) | (0.0651) | (0.0543) | (0.0714) |
| Western | 0.0824 | 0.1221 | 0.0737 | 0.0537 | 0.0827 | 0.0455 |
| | (0.0701) | (0.0713) | (0.0704) | (0.0728) | (0.1359) | (0.0988) |
| Overall Average | 0.102 | 0.127 | 0.091 | 0.108 | 0.119 | 0.089 |
| Maximum | 0.382 | 0.489 | 0.412 | 0.316 | 0.389 | 0.297 |
| Minimum | 0.00 | 0.00 | 0.00 | 0.00 | 0.00 | 0.00 |

*Note:*  a) standard errors in parentheses.

## Sources of Technical Inefficiency

What are the sources of the technical inefficiencies in secondary education production we presented in Table 16.2? We investigate this by regressing the three-year average index of technical inefficiency for districts on *EDUCEXP,* parental education, and *SIBLING* in order to find out the correlates of technical inefficiency in education production. The Pearson correlation coefficient between *MOMEDU* and *DADEDU* is .72, so, in estimating the equation, we used one variable in place of the other in different equations depending on the fit. All equations are estimated in the double log form, so we can interpret the coefficient estimates as elasticities. Coefficient estimates from the Tobit regression are presented in Table 16.3. Coefficient estimates for technical inefficiency for BECEE are presented in column 2, BECES in column 3, BECEM in column 4, SSCES in column 5, SSCES in column 6, and SSCEM in column 7. Regression statistics from the Tobit estimator indicate that the simple model fits the data relatively well. The likelihood ratio statistic as well as the $\chi^2$ statistic to test the null hypothesis that all slope coefficients are equal to zero rejects the null at $\alpha = .01$ or better in all equations. The pseudo $R^2$ is generally higher than 0.15 in all equations.

**Table 16.3  Correlates of Technical Inefficiency**

| Variable | BECEE | BECES | BECEM | SSCEE | SSCES | SSCEM |
|---|---|---|---|---|---|---|
| Constant | 0.1368 | 0.0302 | 0.1569 | 0.5761 | 0.6798 | 0.4017 |
|  | (2.085)[a] | (1.03) | (5.31) | (4.63) | (5.79) | (4.13) |
| EDUCEXP | −0.0070 | 0.0010 | −0.0078 | −0.0386 | −0.451 | −0.0221 |
|  | (0.84) | (1.30) | (1.88) | (3.58) | (4.35) | (2.58) |
| MOMEDU | – | −0.0609 | −0.0267 | −0.0734 | – | – |
|  |  | (1.93) | (1.85) | (2.18) |  |  |
| DADEDU | −0.0346 | – | – | – | −0.0331 | −0.0593 |
|  | (1.67) |  |  |  | (2.45) | (3.06) |
| SIBLING | 0.0241 | 0.0221 | 0.0141 | 0.0026 | 0.0214 | 0.0093 |
|  | (1.98) | (1.72) | (1.78) | (1.98) | (2.16) | (2.34) |
| N | 102 | 101 | 101 | 96 | 96 | 96 |
| Log Likelihood | 103.849 | 104.126 | 157.873 | 52.247 | 67.923 | 96.143 |
| PseudoR$^2$ | 0.155 | 0.245 | 0.187 | 0.2732 | 0.2377 | 0.0592 |
| $\chi^2$ [3] | 8.36 | 9.98 | 8.26 | 22.42 | 26.09 | 22.07 |
| sigma$^2$ | 0.0847 | 0.0863 | 0.0499 | 0.1054 | 0.0998 | 0.0851 |

*Note:* a) absolute value of 't' statistics in parentheses.

The coefficient of EDUEXP has a negative sign and significantly different from zero at $\alpha = .05$ or better in the BECEM, SSCEE, SSCES, and SSCEM equations. The coefficient estimate is negative but statistically insignificant in the BECEE and BECES equations. The negative coefficient of EDUEXP suggests that household expenditure on extra classes is negatively correlated with technical inefficiency in the production of secondary education. An alternative way to interpret this coefficient is that student cognitive performance is positively correlated with family expenditure on extra classes for students. The coefficient of DADEDU (MOMEDU) in all equations is negative, and statistically significant at $\alpha = .05$ or better, suggesting that parental education is negatively correlated with technical inefficiency in the production of secondary education in Ghana.

The coefficient of SIBLING is positive and significantly different from zero at $\alpha = .10$ or better in all equations, suggesting that, all things being equal, technical inefficiency in secondary school production is positively correlated with the number of siblings in a family. We do not interpret these coefficient estimates as causal because we have not provided any identification strategy that will allow us to interpret them as such. We only interpret them as correlational. Nevertheless, the positive correlation between technical inefficiency and the number of siblings is consistent with the idea that the more children a household has in school at the same time, the less time and resources it has to spend to help each student, all things being equal. This is likely to hamper the cognitive performance of students.

We make a few observations about the estimates presented in Table 16.3. First, the coefficient estimates of parents' education is consistently negative and statistically significant in all the equations, while that of EDUEXP is insignificant in the BECEE equation. The elasticities of parental education are also much higher and more precisely estimated than those of education expenditure. Secondly, the coefficient of SIBLING is positive and significant in all equations. The combination of the strong coefficients on parental education and SIBLING, on the one hand, and the weak performance of *EDUCEXP,* on the other, seems to suggest that, perhaps, non-purchased family inputs are more important than purchased family inputs in the production of student cognition in various subjects in Ghanaian secondary schools. Perhaps, educated parents are not only able to help their children at home, they are also able to point them in the right direction through their contacts for further help or to share their educational experiences, experiences and contacts that may not be available to non-educated parents.

A third observation is that, while parental education is an important correlate of technical inefficiency in secondary education, the roles of mothers' and fathers' education differ by subject and at different points in the cycle. Generally, fathers' education tends to matter more in the sciences and mathematics at the SSS level while mothers' education matters more in all other areas. Finally, the effects of family inputs (both expenditure and non-purchased) on technical inefficiency are much stronger and much more precisely estimated at the SSS level than at the JSS level. Perhaps, this is due to the nature of the Ghanaian educational system in which the more meritorious get to go on to higher levels in the secondary education cycle. The greater abilities of these students will imply that the productivity of family inputs is much higher than at the JSS level where the average ability may not be so high.

The conclusion we derive from this part of the study is that differences in family background and inputs partly explain differences in technical inefficiencies in the production of secondary education in Ghana. While we are not able to establish a causal link, the results suggest that family inputs should be included in education production functions as additional inputs. Our results suggest that both school inputs and family inputs are important determinants of cognitive performance in Ghanaian secondary schools. Perhaps, instead of the 'development approach' and the 'production function approach' going their separate ways, a more comprehensive framework that combines the two approaches is called for. Our results are consistent with the results of previous studies that find that both family and school inputs have significant impacts on the cognitive performance of students (Alderman et al., 1997; Brown, 2003; Case and Deaton, 1999; Dalton et al., 2003; Das et al., 2004; Filmer and Pritchett, 1999; Gyimah-Brempong and Gyapong, 1991; Haegoland et al., 2005; Krueger: 2003; Woβmann: 2005; among others). The results are different from those of studies that find that school inputs have no impact on student performance (Hanushek, 1997, 2003).

Our results should be interpreted with caution, as we consider this study suggestive rather than definitive. Besides the data problems, there are two specification issues that may have negative implications for our results. Greene (2004) argues that one of the major sources of technical inefficiency in production is the quality of managerial effort. We have no variables to proxy for the quality and quantity of management of schools. This could adversely affect our results. After all, the debate over school competition centers around issues of efficiency in managing schools. The second specification issue is that we have specified technical inefficiency as time invariant. Although we think that this is a reasonable assumption for this short series, one is never sure if that is the case.

Are there any policy implications that flow from our results? Given the preliminary nature of our study and the weaknesses inherent in our data, we hesitate to draw any policy implications from our results. The only thing we can point out is that our results suggest the importance of both school and family inputs in the production of cognitive achievements of secondary school students in Ghana. Policies to improve student performance should therefore target increases in the quantity and quality of both family and school inputs, among other things. Efforts, such as the adult literacy campaign, if combined with a campaign to educate parents on the importance of their role in enhancing their children's cognitive abilities, may be helpful in improving student performance.

## 6.   Conclusion

This study used panel data from school districts over a three-year period to investigate the existence of technical inefficiency in the production of cognitive abilities in Ghanaian secondary schools. We did so by estimating a stochastic frontier production function of the cognitive achievements of students in Junior and Senior Secondary Schools, calculating the technical inefficiencies from the production function, and using family inputs as correlates of technical inefficiency. Measuring educational output as the passing rate of students in three subjects — English, Science and Mathematics — in a school district, and using four inputs, we find that school inputs have significant impacts on the cognitive achievements of students in Ghanaian secondary schools. The underlying production technology is neither Cobb-Douglas nor constant returns to scale, as has been used in many studies. More important for the purposes of this study, we find evidence of the existence of technical inefficiency in all three subjects at both the JSS and SSS levels. The degree of technical inefficiency we find varies with the subject and also with the level of the secondary education cycle.

We find that the calculated technical inefficiencies are significantly correlated with family inputs, especially parental education. The estimates also suggest that parental education is more strongly correlated with technical inefficiency than family expenditure on education. The strength of the association between family inputs and technical inefficiency is higher at the SSS level than at the JSS level, suggesting, possibly, that the productivity of family inputs increases with student ability. The results of this study suggest that both school inputs and family inputs are important factors in the production of cognitive achievement in Ghanaian secondary schools. Policies to improve student cognitive performance should therefore aim at increasing the quantity and quality of both inputs. Our results should, however, be interpreted with caution.

## References

Aigner, D., Lovell, C. A. K. and Schmidt, P. (1977) 'Formulation and Estimation of Stochastic Frontier Production Function Models', *Journal of Econometrics*, Vol. 6, 21–37.

Alderman, H., Behrman, J. R., Khan, S. Ross, D. and Sabot, R. (1997) 'The Income Gap in Cognitive Skills in Rural Pakistan', *Economic Development and Cultural Change*, Vol. 46, No. 1: 97–123.

Angrist, J. and Lavy, V. (1999) 'Using Maimonides' Rule to Estimate the Effects of Class Size on Student Achievement', *Quarterly Journal of Economics*, Vol. 114, No. 2: 533–75.

Brown, P. (2003) 'Parental Education and Child Learning: Human Capital Investments in Time and Money'. Ann Arbor, MI: University of Michigan (mimeo).

Case, A. and Deaton, A. (1999) 'School Inputs and Educational Outcomes in South Africa', *Quarterly Journal of Economics*, Vol. 114, No. 3: 1047–84.

Chen, Y. Y. and Wang, H-J. (2004) 'A Method of Moments Estimator for Stochastic Frontier Model with Errors in Variables', *Economics Letters*, Vol. 85, No. 2: 221–8.

Dalton, P., Marcenaro, O. D. and Navarro, L. (2003) 'The Effective Use of Student Time: A Stochastic Frontier Production Function Case Study', *Economics of Education Review,*, Vol. 22: 547–60.

Das, J., Dercon, S. Habyarimana, J. and Krishnan, P. (2004) 'When Can School Inputs Improve Test Scores?' Washington, DC.: World Bank Working Paper (mimeo).

Filmer, D. and Pritchett, L. (1999) 'The Effects of Household Wealth on Educational Attainment: Evidence from 34 Countries', *Population and Development Review*, Vol. 25, No. 1: 85–120.

Glewwe, P. (2002) 'Schools and Skills in Developing Countries: Education Policies and Socioeconomic Outcomes', *Journal of Economic Literature*, Vol. 40, No. 2: 436–82.

Glewwe, P. and Jacoby, H. (1994) 'Student Achievement and Schooling Choice in Low-Income Countries: Evidence from Ghana', *Journal of Human Resources*, Vol. 29, No. 3: 843–64.

Greene, W. H. (2003) 'Simulated Likelihood of the Normal-Gamma Stochastic Frontier Function', *Journal of Productivity Analysis*, Vol. 19: 179–90.

Greene, W. H. (2004) 'Accounting for Unobservables in Production Models: Management and Inefficiency', Paper presented at the Australasian Meeting of the Econometric Society, 7–9 July, Melbourne.

Gyimah-Brempong, K. (1989) 'Production of Public Safety: Are Socioeconomic Characteristics of Local Communities Important Factors?' *Journal of Applied Econometrics*, Vol. 4: 57–71.

Gyimah-Brempong, K. and A. O. Gyapong (1992), 'Elasticities of Factor Substitution in the Production of Education', *Economics of Education Review*, Vol. 11, No. 3: 205–17.

Gyimah-Brempong, K. and Gyapong, A. O. (1991) 'Characteristics of Education Production Functions: An Application of Canonical Regression Analysis', *Economics of Education Review*, Vol. 10, No. 1: 7–17.

Haegoland, T,. Raaum, O. and Salvanos, K. G. (2005) *Pupil Achievement, School Resources and Family Background.* IZA Discussion Paper No. 1459. Bonn: International Centre for Labour Studies.

Hanushek, E. (1986) 'The Economics of Schooling: Production and Efficiency in Public Schools', *Journal of Economic Literature*, Vol. 24, No. 3: 1141–77.

Hanushek, E. (1997) 'Assessing the Effects of School Resources on Student Achievement: An Update', *Educational Evaluation and Policy Analysis*, Vol. 19, No. 2: 141–64.

Hanushek, E. (2003) 'The Failure of Input-Based Schooling Policies', *Economic Journal*, Vol. 113, February: 64–98.

Keller, K. (2004) 'Investment in Education by Education Levels and Effects on Growth', *Contemporary Economic Policy*.

Krueger, A. (2003) 'Economic Considerations and Class Size', *Economic Journal*, Vol. 113, February: 34–63.

Lazear, E. (2001) 'Education Production', *Quarterly Journal of Economics*, Vol. 116, No. 3: 777–803.

McMahon, W. (2000) *Education and Development: Measuring the Social Benefits*. New York: Oxford University Press.

Republic of Ghana (2002) *Education Indicators at a Glance*. Accra: Ministry of Education.

Todd, P. E. and Wolpin, K. (2003) 'On the Specification and Estimation of the Production Function for Cognitive Achievement', *Economic Journal* , Vol. 113: 3–33.

Woβmann, L (2005) *Families, Schools, and Primary-School Learning: Evidence for Argentina and Colombia in an International Perspective*. World Bank Policy Research Paper No. WPS3537. Washington, DC: World Bank.

# 17 Maternal Literacy & Numeracy Skills & Child Health in Ghana*

NIELS-HUGO BLUNCH

## 1. Introduction

One of the strongest and most consistent findings in development, health and labour economics is the positive relationship between schooling and child health. This empirical relationship has been confirmed in numerous studies across different time periods, countries and measures of child health.[1] These studies generally treat education as a 'black box', however. What is measured is not what a person has learned in terms of skills, such as, for example, literacy and numeracy but rather what level or grade has been completed. Two main issues are involved here. First, the link between schooling and child health really goes from schooling to skills to productivity to child health. As the link between schooling and skills is more tenuous in developing countries, due often to poor school quality, it is imperative that this part of the process receives particular attention in empirical analyses in this context. Secondly, policies focusing on education rather than on skills might be misdirected. With multiple paths to achieving skills (including formal education and adult literacy programmes) and with limited public budgets, cost-effectiveness of programmes is essential.

In response to these issues, I suggest that literacy, numeracy and other skills be viewed as intermediate outputs in a production process where the main inputs are formal (child) schooling and non-formal (adult) literacy course attendance. Subsequently, literacy, numeracy and other skills enter as inputs in a production process to generate the final outputs of child health.

* The author is grateful to Bryan Boulier, Donald Parsons, Claus Pörtner, David Ribar and participants at the Annual Meetings of the Population Association of America and the European Society for Population Economics, participants at the 'Ghana at the Half Century' conference in Accra and seminar participants at the George Washington University for helpful comments and suggestions on earlier drafts of this paper. Remaining errors and omissions are his own. The data were kindly provided by the Ghana Statistical Service. The findings and interpretations, however, are those of the author and should not be attributed to the Ghana Statistical Service.
[1] For comprehensive reviews see Behrman and Deolalikar (1988), Behrman (1990) and Strauss and Thomas (1995).

Building on the above sketched two-pronged production process, this study examines the relationship between maternal literacy and numeracy skills, formal education and adult literacy course participation and child health in Ghana. The health measures examined include child health inputs, namely vaccinations, pre- and post-natal care, and child health outcomes, namely, morbidity and mortality.

The rest of the study is structured as follows. The next section presents the conceptual framework of the study, while section 3 discusses estimation strategies and related issues. Section 4 presents the data, discusses sample restrictions and also provides preliminary, descriptive analyses of the interlinkages of mothers' literacy and numeracy skills, formal schooling and adult literacy course participation in Ghana. The multivariate econometric analyses follow in section 5, while section 6 concludes and provides directions for further research.

## 2.   Conceptual Framework

The interlinkages between skills and child health are examined in the context of Grossman's (1972) health production model. In the original model, an individual maximizes utility with respect to his/her own health and consumption. I extend the model by letting the mother also obtain utility from child health and by allowing the human capital effects to come from a set of individual skills, rather than from education *per se*. Furthermore, the skills effects run from the mother's skills to the child's health. While this model might be posed entirely in terms of a verbal description, a mathematical representation helps highlight some important issues and the latter will therefore be pursued in the following.

Specifically, I consider a two-person household consisting of a mother and a child in which the mother has preferences over the child's health $(Z_1)$ and other commodities $(Z_2)$. Alternatively, the set-up may be viewed as regarding a multi-person household, where the focus is on the interlinkages of mothers' skills, schooling, labour supply and child health investments and the resources of other household members enter the model through their added resources in terms of earned and unearned income (see below).[2] The utility of final goods is affected by three types of preference shifters: human capital skills, $S$,[3] observed family background including needs or fertility, ethnicity/tribal association, $B$, and unobserved characteristics including tastes, $\delta$, giving rise to the following utility function:

---

[2] Again, so as to focus on the main subject of this study, namely, the interlinkages of mothers' skills, schooling and child health investments, issues related to intrahousehold bargaining over resources are not explicitly incorporated here. A large literature, starting with Manser and Brown (1980) and McElroy and Horney (1981), examines issues related to marriage and household decision-making.  One of the main results from this literature is that the bargaining power over resources within the marriage (or household) related to, for example, child health depends on the opportunities outside of marriage (or the household). To the extent that bargaining power is correlated with mothers' skills and schooling, however, the analyses here will at least capture some elements of the bargaining structure within the household. For a review of family economics, including co-operative household models, see also Bergstrom (1996).

[3] S may be viewed either as a generic skill or alternatively as a vector of skills including, for example, literacy and numeracy skills.

$$U = u(Z_1, Z_2; S, B, \delta) \tag{1}$$

The utility function is assumed to exhibit the required desirable properties; most importantly it is assumed to be quasi-concave.

The household's utility maximization is subject to three types of constraints: technological, budget and time constraints. First, the technological constraints are given by the two production functions $f_1$ and $f_2$, which give output of child health and all other goods as functions of their respective inputs of a market good ($X$) and mothers' time ($T$), conditional on the mother's skills,[4] $S$, (both production functions) and the (unobserved) initial child health endowment, $\eta$, (only child health production) and community-specific health-related variable, $C$, which includes health infrastructure, treatment practices, and the disease environment (also only included in the child health production function):

$$Z_1 = f_1(X_1, T_1; S, \varsigma, C), \tag{2}$$

$$Z_2 = f_2(X_2, T_2; S), \tag{3}$$

The household's budget constraint defines the consumption frontier of the household as a function of its potential income sources. Specifically, the household may obtain income from engaging in labour activities, supplying $H$ amounts of labour at the rate $W$, which is affected by the vector of human capital or skills, $S$, and from other sources, $N$, including unearned income, transfers and remittances, which also depend on human capital or skills:

$$W(S)H + N(S) \geq P_1 X_1 + P_2 X_2. \tag{4}$$

Lastly, the maximization of Equation (1) is also subject to a time constraint:

$$T_1 + T_2 + H = K, \tag{5}$$

where $K$ is the maximum time available for home production and market work after accounting for time to eat and sleep, say, 16 hours a day (alternatively, it could be normalized to one).

The problem of the mother, therefore, is to maximize Equation (1) with respect to $T_1$, $T_2$, $X_1$, $X_2$ and $H$ subject to the constraints, Equations (2)–(5), that is, to decide the amount of time and goods inputs in the production of child health and other commodities and the amount of time devoted to market work so as to maximize utility, subject to the set of constraints.[5] Solving the model yields a series of market goods

---

[4] To simplify the discussion, skills are not modelled explicitly here. Following Blunch (2005), one might imagine skills being produced from time in child schooling, $T_1$, time attending adult literacy classes, $T_2$, the quality of these two types of education, $Q_1$ and $Q_2$, conditioned by a taste shifter, $\varphi$, capturing different tastes for education due to, for example, ethnicity and/or cultural norms and traditions in the community: $S = s(T_1, T_2, Q_1, Q_2, \varphi)$.

[5] The amount of time devoted to market work and one of the market goods inputs are redundant, due to the linear dependence between these variables.

demands and production time supply functions. The child health input demand function has our main interest:

$$X_1^* = x_1(W(S), N(S), P_1, P_2, S, B, \delta, \eta, C).$$  (6)

Substituting $X_1^*$ from Equation (6) into Equation (2) yields the reduced form child health production function:

$$Z_1^* = z_1(W(S), N(S), T_1, P_1, P_2, S, B, \delta, \eta, C).$$  (7)

The child health input demand function, Equation (6) and the child health production function, Equation (7), are what will be estimated in the empirical analyses.

From this discussion several issues with implications for the empirical analyses emerge. First, the reduced form child health input demand and child health production functions, Equations (6) and (7), suggest the variables that are potentially important determinants conceptually and therefore should be included in the empirical analyses. These variables include the mother's skills level and her wage rates as well as the prices of health care and time use of health-care services/child health production, needs and tastes. Secondly, several interesting research questions emerge from the model (I shall return to this after extending the conceptual framework a little). Thirdly, the reduced form (input) demand for child health market goods, Equation (6), and the reduced form child health production function, Equation (7), make it clear that human capital skills have both direct and indirect effects on child health input demands and child health production. May it be possible to disentangle the direct and indirect effects empirically? Equations (6) and (7) hint that it is: inclusion of skills will capture the direct effects, while inclusion of wages will control for indirect effects.

Lastly, the conceptual model outlined above also highlights the importance of unobserved heterogeneity and endogeneity for the subsequent analyses. From the presence of $\delta$ (unobserved family characteristics, including tastes) and $\eta$ (unobserved child health endowment) in both Equations (6) and (7), unobserved heterogeneity is seen to affect both child health input demand and the production of child health. Furthermore, the issue of endogeneity or simultaneity involved in an examination of the determinants of child health input demands and child health outcomes is also apparent from Equations (6) and (7): child health input demand and child health outcomes, which are chosen by the mother, both depend on skills and wages, which are themselves chosen by the mother also. In turn, these twin issues of unobserved heterogeneity and endogeneity/simultaneity highlighted by this model are something which needs to be dealt with in the empirical analyses.

Treating skills as one generic skill or vector of skills, $S$, simplified the presentation for the mathematical model above. At the same time, however, this simplified model helped bring out several important issues related to both the theoretical interlinkages of child health inputs and outcomes, mothers' skills and other variables and the subsequent empirical analyses. Conceptually, however, several extensions to the above model are warranted. First, where do skills come from? Rather than skills (implicitly) being obtainable via only one route, it is more realistic to consider several routes for achieving skills. In particular, I suggest that skills may be obtained either from formal schooling during childhood or from participation in adult literacy programmes during youth or adulthood. Secondly, while it seems intuitive that $S$ contains several skills (each of which is obtainable through one or both of the two alternative routes of achieving skills), which skills is it more precisely that $S$ actually contains? In discussing in more detail the exact nature of the different skills and the channels through which the different components of $S$ affect child health inputs and outcomes, I shall distinguish between direct effects on the mother's home productivity in child health production (working through her child health production function, Equation (2)) and other indirect skills effects.

Starting with the direct skills effects, there are several reasons why skills might affect the mother's home productivity of child health. First, the production of child health depends crucially on literacy and numeracy skills — being able to read and accurately follow prescriptions, for example. These are skills which are potentially obtainable from either formal education or adult literacy course participation, although the former appears to be much more efficient in generating literacy and numeracy skills in Ghana (Blunch, 2005). Secondly, health issues play a major role in education. In the formal education system, children learn about health-related issues from science classes,[6] for example, while in the adult literacy programmes 10 out of the total 28 topics taught in addition to literacy and numeracy skills include health-related issues, for example 'Family Planning', 'Immunization', 'Safe Motherhood and Child Care' and 'Safe Drinking Water'. Whereas literacy and numeracy skills may be regarded as more generally applicable skills, the latter may be viewed as a more specialized skill, which mainly affects the home productivity of child health. So how might increased efficiency in the (home) production of child health work its way through this modified Grossman health production model? Initially, (home) production will shift towards the production of child health, assuming that this is a normal good and that it is not relatively 'much' more time-intensive than other commodities. At the same time, however, there will be more time available for market work, which will enable the individual to purchase more of the market-good input for production of child health and other commodities. While this effect therefore depends on the relative time and goods intensities of the various commodities, intuitively, the net effect on the production of child health is most likely positive.

The indirect effects work mainly through the household's consumption possibilities. Most importantly, an individual's wages may increase from participation in schooling activities. This could be due to a direct productivity effect from literacy and numeracy skills or from socialization or discipline skills obtained from childhood schooling. Alternatively, earnings capacity may increase either from credentialism or signalling (Spence, 1973) obtained from childhood schooling or from participation in adult literacy programmes, where participants learn about income-generating activities

---

[6] Starting at the higher primary level, children have Integrated Science (Science and Agricultural Science), which at the junior secondary level subsequently is divided into Science and Agricultural Science.

and frequently engage in them directly under the direction of the teacher. The increased income potential of the household reduces the need to depend on children as a source of income, thus decreasing child labour. In turn, this will positively affect child health. Again, both substitution and income effects may be operating here; the net effect from these indirect effects, however, is likely to be positive. In addition to affecting the household's consumption possibilities, participation in schooling activities may also affect needs or tastes for child health. First, parents may become aware of the harmful effects of child labour on child schooling and child health. Secondly, the composition of the consumption basket may shift from predominance of food to include more non-food items, including child health-related items.

A few potentially important determinants are not included in the conceptual framework. For example, savings and assets are not included. Spillover effects from having other literates and/or literacy course participants in the household (and/or in the community) are also not included. While both of these factors might be considered, I choose to exclude these possibilities from the current analyses, hence focusing on the impact of the mother's skills and schooling.

## 3. Estimation Strategies and Issues

From the previous section skills directly affected child health outcomes by increasing the efficiency of household productivity, and indirectly affected these outcomes by increasing consumption possibilities and changing tastes. The empirical analysis will rely on linear specifications of the optimal intermediate and final child health outcome equations. These equations are written:

$$X_i = \alpha + \beta_1 S_i + \beta_2 E_{1i} + \beta_3 E_{2i} + \beta_4 W_i + \beta_5 F_i + \beta_6 A_i + \beta_7 P_i + \beta_8 C_i + \varepsilon_i, \qquad (8)$$

$$Z_i = \alpha + \beta_1 S_i + \beta_2 E_{1i} + \beta_3 E_{2i} + \beta_4 W_i + \beta_5 F_i + \beta_6 A_i + \beta_7 P_i + \beta_8 C_i + v_i, \qquad (9)$$

where $X_i$ is child health input (or intermediate child health output); $Z_i$ is final child health output; $S_i$ is literacy and numeracy skills; $E_{1i}$ is childhood schooling; $E_{2i}$ is adult literacy course participation; $W_i$ is the wage rate; $F_i$ is fertility; $A_i$ is access to health facilities (for example, health centre, midwife, doctor) in the community; $P_i$ is prices of health-related goods and services; $C_i$ is a vector of other controls, including the age of the mother (to capture experience and time having been of child-bearing age) and the child (to capture child needs and age-specific productivity effects in health production), geographical location, and ethnicity, and $\varepsilon_i$ is an error term capturing unobservables. Equation (8), therefore is a factor or intermediate output demand function, while Equation (9) is a commodity production function. In addition, I shall experiment with a combination of Equations (8) and (9), where (9) will be specified to include $X_i$ in a 'semi-structural' model. This is only possible for the case of child illnesses, however, since the other final child health outcome, child mortality, does not allow controlling for child health inputs (intermediate outcomes) such as vaccinations, since this is measured at the level of the mother.

First, I shall include only literacy and numeracy skills (and additional controls).

Secondly, I shall allow for an intermediating effect from literacy and numeracy skills on wages and fertility by including these additional variables in the regression. Thirdly, I shall include child schooling and adult literacy participation so as to test for the relevance of skills above and beyond literacy and numeracy.

## 4.    Data and Descriptive Analyses

The *Ghana Living Standards Survey* (GLSS) is a nationally representative, stratified multi-purpose household survey, carried out in 1987/8, 1988/9, 1991/2 and 1998/9 as four independent cross-section surveys. The most recent round of these (GLSS 4) is used for the analyses in this study. The household survey contains information on educational attainment, participation in adult literacy courses, literacy and numeracy, as well as information on background variables such as age, gender, tribal association/ ethnicity and region, which are also important factors in analyses of human capital processes. In addition to the household survey, each round also includes a community and a price questionnaire. The community questionnaire contains information on access to facilities, including schools, hospitals, markets, roads, public transportation and adult literacy programmes. Due to the difficulties involved in defining communities in urban areas, the community questionnaire was only administered to rural areas. The most important variables will now be described in turn, starting with the dependent variables.

### Child health outcomes

Five different child health outcomes from the GLSS 4 are examined in this study. They may be classified into intermediate child health outcomes (vaccinations, pre-and post-natal care) and final child health outcomes (child morbidity and mortality). The information is provided by the mother, except for the information on morbidity, which was provided by the head of household or another adult member (which may or may not have been the mother). Since these variables are crucial to subsequent analyses, I shall go through them in some detail, starting with the intermediate child health outcomes.

The intermediate child health outcomes are all based on information on whether the service in question was ever received by the child (vaccinations and post-natal care) or mother (pre-natal care). The samples subjected to the questions on vaccination and post-natal are children 7 years and under and 5 years and under, respectively, while the question on pre-natal care was only given to females, who were either currently pregnant or had been pregnant within the past 12 months (and were between 15 and 49 years old).

One problem with these measures is that it is not known when the service was provided. For vaccinations, for example, it is not known when a vaccination was provided, which type(s), and whether the full series of vaccinations for a given type was given (for example, polio and dpt vaccinations, to be fully effective, each require three consecutive vaccinations). Furthermore, it may be that the child will or will not receive a (the) vaccination(s) in the future. One way to address the latter issue, however, would be to choose a lower cut-off, but high enough that it would seem that children not vaccinated at this age would probably never be vaccinated, say, 3 years of age. Since this causes a large drop in observations, this strategy is not pursued here, however. Similar issues exist for post-natal care, except that the timing problem is reversed: post-natal care seems to be most relevant for younger children, so that here the issue is to choose an appropriate upper cut-off, say, two or three years. While timing problems do not appear substantial for the pre-natal care measure, the exclusion of mothers who are not currently pregnant or have not been pregnant within the past 12 months naturally limits the sample size considerably. Additionally, the pre-natal and post-natal care measures are potentially riddled with unobserved heterogeneity (or self-selection): mothers who have experienced complications with either their current pregnancy or past pregnancies would seem to be more likely to seek pre-natal care for themselves and post-natal care for their children. Vaccinations do not appear to be prone to these issues to the same degree, implying that this is a more objective measure of child well-being as related to the child's health.

Moving to the final child health outcomes, the information on morbidity is available for all household members and reveals whether an individual has suffered from an illness or an injury or both during the previous 2 weeks. While it therefore confounds factors that may be systematically related to the mother's education and literacy and numeracy skills (such as malnutrition or lack of preventive care, such as vaccinations and pre-natal care — which are *not* due to lack of resources) with factors that are not (such as accidents), in practice very few (less than 1%) answered 'both'. The child mortality measures are constructed from the fertility module, which includes information on the number of children ever born and ever died to a woman (15 to 49 years old) but not when, which is unfortunate: it would have been useful to be able to combine the information on child mortality with birth-spacing, since the latter may be an important determinant of child mortality. In addition, since it is possible that the child(ren) died far back in the past, the explanatory variables, which are current, may be poor predictors as a result. If a mother has recently participated in an adult literacy programme, for example, this of course has no impact on the past deaths. Similarly, high child mortality might have induced the mother to participate in the programmes in order to be able to prevent future deaths. With all its timing problems, however, it still appears fruitful to exploit this information. I therefore construct three measures of mortality based on this information: the total number of children ever died (preferred measure), as well as a binary measure for whether any children have died to a woman and a measure of the share of children died out of the children ever born. The two latter measures are included so as to evaluate the robustness of the results for the preferred measure.

As was also the case for the intermediate child health outcomes, the final child health outcomes are potentially prone to issues of unobserved heterogeneity (self-selection), as well. Again, this may not be equally relevant for all final child health outcome measures. Child mortality certainly leaves minimal room for subjective assessment, while this is not the case for child illnesses. Complicating the issue of subjectivity related to child illnesses, however, is the possibility that it may go either way: more educated mothers, while being more likely to be able to prevent their children's illnesses, at the same time would also seem to be more likely to be able to diagnose their children's symptoms properly as indeed a disease rather than, say, 'tiredness' or 'laziness'.

## Literacy and Numeracy

The information on literacy skills from the GLSS 4 include Ghanaian reading and writing proficiency and English reading and writing proficiency, while numeracy measures the ability to do written calculations. The question on English reading (writing) skills is: 'Can (NAME) read (write) a letter in English?', while the question on Ghanaian reading (writing) skills is: 'In what Ghanaian language can (NAME) write a letter?' (stating the one in which (NAME) is most proficient). The question on written calculations is: 'Can (NAME) do written calculations?' The respondent to these, as to most of the other questions in the survey, is 'preferably the head of household, if not available, any adult member of the household who is able to give information on the other household members'. While this may be an issue of concern, it is hard to correct. Since this is 'the' way these types of surveys are typically done, I shall therefore follow standard practice and assume that the individual who has answered the questions has sufficient knowledge of household members, i.e. that the data are reliable. Another concern, which may be examined a little further, is the subjective nature of the literacy and numeracy measures. In order to gain additional insights into this issue, and the extent to which it poses any problems in practice, educational attainment and skills proficiency for adults are tabulated in Table 17.1.

Three findings from the table indicate that such concerns may be unwarranted. First, the skill incidence does not appear heavily inflated. Secondly, literacy and numeracy rates increase with the level of education completed. Thirdly, few literates have not attended school (some of these may be genuine, however resulting from home-schooling or participation in adult literacy programmes).

**Table 17.1 Distribution of Self-reported Skills Across Highest Educational Level Completed**

|  | Ghanaian reading | Ghanaian writing | English reading | English writing | Written Calculations |
|---|---|---|---|---|---|
| Full sample | 0.435 | 0.400 | 0.498 | 0.519 | 0.609 |
| None | 0.060 | 0.046 | 0.038 | 0.033 | 0.132 |
| Primary school | 0.435 | 0.381 | 0.462 | 0.422 | 0.758 |
| Middle school | 0.741 | 0.689 | 0.875 | 0.846 | 0.960 |
| Junior Secondary school | 0.700 | 0.656 | 0.882 | 0.861 | 0.968 |
| Secondary and above | 0.874 | 0.841 | 0.999 | 0.998 | 0.996 |
| Vocational | 0.735 | 0.651 | 0.997 | 0.991 | 1.000 |
| Other | 0.937 | 0.885 | 1.000 | 1.000 | 1.000 |

*Note:* Sample is individuals 15-65 years of age who have answered whether they have attended an adult literacy course, yielding a total of 13,403 observations.

A related but somewhat different issue is the potentially high correlation among the four literacy measures and the numeracy measure empirically. The main issue here is that while conceptually the four literacy measures and the numeracy measures span five distinctly different dimension in the 'skills space', as it were, empirically the high correlation among the five measures may cause 'funny' results in terms of inference: statistically insignificant results of one or more of the measures and/or results of opposite directions of effects between sets of these variables, say, between English reading and writing skills.[7] The reason such correlation may come about is that when an individual can write, s/he will also be able to read and also tend to be able to do written calculations, although the association between writing and reading skills would seem to be somewhat stronger than that between writing (and reading) skills and numeracy skills. To examine this issue in a little more detail, consider the following correlation matrix for the estimation sample for the morbidity analyses (chosen since this is the largest of the five sub-analyses estimation samples and therefore likely to shed relatively most light on this issue):

**Table 17.2   Correlation Matrix for Full Set of Literacy and Numeracy Skills Variables**

|  | Ghanaian reading | Ghanaian writing | English reading | English writing | Written Calculations |
|---|---|---|---|---|---|
| Ghanaian reading | 1.000 | – | – | – | – |
| Ghanaian writing | 0.896 | 1.000 | – | – | – |
| English reading | 0.687 | 0.679 | 1.000 | – | – |
| English writing | 0.680 | 0.679 | 0.950 | 1.000 | – |
| Written calculations | 0.642 | 0.604 | 0.711 | 0.688 | 1.000 |

*Note:*    Sample consists of the 4754 mothers from the morbidity analysis sub-sample. All correlation coefficients are statistically significant from zero at 1%.

The results from Table 17.2 confirm that there is a high correlation between Ghanaian reading and writing skills, on the one hand, and English reading and writing skills, on the other, while the correlation between either of the four literacy measures and numeracy is somewhat smaller.

As a result of the high correlation empirically among the four literacy measures and the numeracy measure, I shall include only the two writing skills measures and the numeracy skills measure in the multivariate analyses. The motivation for this is that writing skills may be interpreted as the higher standard, relative to reading skills: if an individual can write, she can also read, while the opposite is not necessarily the case. While the correlation between writing skills and numeracy skills is also high, it is not as high as that between reading and writing skills and also may be argued to encompass skills which conceptually are quite distinct from either reading or writing

---

[7] Such results were actually obtained for preliminary analyses where all five skills measures were included simultaneously.

skills. It is therefore included in the multivariate analyses despite the sizeable positive correlation with the writing skills measures.

## Education Variables

Educational attainment is measured as the highest level completed, ranging from 'none' through 'university' and also includes vocational and technical training. Two sets of educational attainment variables are used: one in which the different levels are included as dummy variables and one in which the levels have been converted into years of schooling. Adult literacy course participation is a binary measure, stating whether an individual has ever attended an adult literacy course programme. A problem with this, of course, is that the time of participation is unknown. An individual may just have started attending a class, for example, in which case the impact from the programme will not yet have fully kicked in. Any impact from participation in an adult literacy course, therefore, is likely to be downwards biased. Furthermore, schools and adult literacy programmes are not homogenous. Specifically, school quality and content may be very different across areas or across time[8] (for example, in 1987 major schooling reforms aiming at improving the efficiency, quality and relevance of Ghanaian education were undertaken). Remote areas are also more likely to have fewer resources and therefore a lower quality of schools and instruction. In addition, private schools may be more effective than public schools in generating skills. Quality and content of adult literacy programmes may vary across time or across areas, as well, since these programmes are — and have been for a long time — offered by many different providers, including several different NGOs and the government. There is only information on whether or not an individual participated, however, and not on who the provider was.

## Economic Variables

The information on wages and earnings in the GLSS 4 is riddled with many zeros. For example, of the 4,406 mothers in the sub-sample for the morbidity analyses (the largest of the five sub-samples) almost 30% report zero earnings. Examining this a little further by cross-validating with these mothers' responses to the labour module of the survey, we find that these zeros are genuine in the sense that the overwhelming majority of these mothers, 99.6%, report not having done work in the past 12 months for which a wage or any other payment was received. Of the remaining 0.4%, half reveal themselves as economically inactive when answering the question on the main occupation during the past 12 months. In conclusion, 99.8% of the reported zero earnings are genuine. Even though the zero earnings responses are genuine, it still seems problematic to include them in the estimations, since the earnings distribution

---

[8] These factors are partially controlled for, however, by including age, rural-urban location and region of residence in the empirical analyses, as these variables capture components of differences in school quality related to cohort and geographical location. Note that the confounding of school quality and age and cohort effects among these variables is not a concern here, since the goal is merely to control for these factors so as to obtain valid inference from our main variables of interest — mother's literacy and numeracy skills and formal schooling and adult literacy course participation.

is so heavily skewed towards zero. I therefore run a Heckman selection model for (the log of) mother's (daily) earnings, using as identifying instruments marital status and the number of children born. For mothers where the observed wage rate is zero, the predicted wage rate is then imputed. Presumably, if a mother faces a higher (potential) wage rate, she will have relatively more bargaining power within the household (this is, of course, somewhat confounded with the skills and schooling of the mother, as well).

In addition, geographical variables (rural-urban location and region of residence) capture economic conditions specific to the area (as well as everything else related to rural-urban residence or the region in question).

### *Access to Facilities and Cost of Health Services*

While these variables are mainly included so as to ensure valid inference on impacts from the variables of primary interest, namely, mothers' skills, schooling and adult literacy course participation, their construction is rather tricky and therefore requires somewhat detailed explanations as compared with what one might initially think is warranted.

The natural first point when discussing the construction of community-level health variables would seem to be the community questionnaire. However, although the community questionnaire contains fairly detailed information on the availability of health personnel and facilities in the community,[9] there are several reasons to turn to the household survey for community-level health information. First, in the community questionnaire there is no information on prices of services (and in the price questionnaire there is only limited information on health-related items, such as aspirin, paracetamol and penicillin), so that the household part of the GLSS 4 would have to be consulted for that information, anyway. Secondly, due to the difficulty of defining communities in urban areas, the community questionnaire was administered only in rural areas. Using the information from the community questionnaire, therefore, automatically decreases the effective estimation samples substantially. I therefore construct community health information on facility availability and prices of services, using the information on actual usage of health services from the household survey.

Specifically, questions asked include whether an individual consulted a health practitioner or dentist or visited a health centre or consulted a traditional healer during the previous two weeks, type of health practitioner (traditional healer, doctor, dentist, nurse, and so on) and type of facility (hospital, dispensary, pharmacy, clinic, and so on). On the cost side, there is information on the fee paid for the last vaccination given to a child. For a child who has been taken for post-natal care during the previous 12 months there is information on whether or not there was a fee and, if so, how much

---

[9] This includes information on which types of facilities and health personnel are available in the community as well as the distance both in terms of physical distance and travel time. Facilities include hospital, drugstore/chemical store, pharmacy, maternity home, clinic or health post and family planning clinic, while health personnel include doctor, nurse, pharmacist, trained midwife, family planning worker, community health worker, traditional birth attendant, traditional healer and medical assistant.

is usually paid for one consultation. In addition, for women who were pregnant during the previous 12 months, and received any pre-natal care during this pregnancy, there is information on how much was paid for the first consultation.

This information may be used to create variables for access to and prices of health-care services in the community in a way such that these variables, by construction, are exogenous to the individual, even though they are based on information about actual usage. Specifically, based on the responses from individuals who have consulted a health practitioner within the previous 2 weeks, I create a binary access variable defined as one if at least one individual in the community (child or adult) has attended a health practitioner at a hospital and zero otherwise. Similarly, consultation cost may be constructed as the average cost for the given type of service. Missing observations quickly become an issue here, however, so I focus only on a few prices: cost of pre- and post-natal care consultations and vaccinations. To ensure exogeneity of the access and price variables, I calculate these variables for each household separately, omitting the contribution of the individual household from the calculations.

An important issue in these calculations is the level of aggregation. The sample contains 300 enumeration areas (clusters), covering 101 of the 110 districts in Ghana, both of which categories may be further divided into either one of the three ecological zones (Coastal, Forest and Savannah) or rural-urban locations. In principle, community averages could be calculated at a level of aggregation according to either of these variables (or combinations of these variables). However, the calculations face an obvious trade-off between including more observations in the analysis and losing variation in the calculated community access or price variable. Since these variables are only of secondary importance, and so as to include as many observations as possible, thereby possibly increasing the precision in the estimates of the parameters of particular interest, namely, the mother's skills, schooling and adult literacy participation, I chose the district level as the level of aggregation in the construction of these variables. In sum, the community-level information constructed includes availability of hospital and cost of vaccinations and pre- and post-natal care. The resulting variables are based on an average number of observations per district of 10.4 (access to hospital), 13.5 (vaccination cost), 15.1 (cost of post-natal consultation) and 9.3 (cost of pre-natal consultation), but with a somewhat wide range. For example, the minimum number of observations on post-natal consultation cost per district is 1, while the maximum number of observations is 100. While the range of the number of observations for the other measures is not quite as extreme, they all have at least one district with only one observation. The typical number of observations per district across the measures is about 8 or 9. Again, while these measures are clearly prone to criticism in terms of their precision (or lack of it), they are not essential to the subsequent analysis but are mainly included as additional controls so as to increase the validity of the inference from the skills and schooling variables.

## *Other Variables Related to Child Health Inputs and Outcomes*

Other variables related to child health inputs and outcomes not already captured by the previous groupings include the age of the mother and the child, the number of other adults and children in the household, fertility, water source and type of sanitation of the household.

The age of the mother proxies the potential general experience of the mother, while the age of the child proxies the needs of the child (the latter is only available for the vaccinations, post-natal care and morbidity samples, however, since the mortality and pre-natal care samples are at the level of the mother). For example, vaccinations are more needed at the earlier ages (and also mostly administered to young children, say below age three). Both of these are entered with a linear and a quadratic term to allow for non-linearities. The number of other adults (than the mother) and other children (than the child in question) indicates the availability of time resources for child care, while the latter at the same time also indicates needs in terms of other children in the household. Fertility may affect the health status and health investments in a child either positively or negatively. Since fertility is a measure of specific child experience, a mother with a higher fertility may have obtained more health knowledge than one with a lower fertility, for example as related to the benefits of vaccinations and pre- and post-natal care. On the other hand, a higher fertility also means that there will be fewer resources for the new child, both economically and in terms of child-care time. Which of these effects exerts the strongest effect on child health inputs and outcomes is an empirical question, however. I include the number of other children born to the woman as a measure of fertility. A problem with this measure is that not all women in the sample have completed their fertility cycle, so that the fertility measure will be downwards biased. Any measured impact will therefore provide a conservative estimate of the fertility effect.

In addition to these other variables related to the health inputs and outcomes the household survey includes information on the source of drinking water (indoor plumbing, public standpipe, rainwater, and so on) and type of toilet (flush toilet, pit latrine, and so on). This information is particularly relevant when examining morbidity and mortality determinants. For example, diarrhoea, which has been estimated by the World Health Organization to kill about 2.2 million people each year, mainly children in developing countries,[10] is thought to be caused mainly by contaminated water. The contamination may be caused by human faeces from municipal sewage, septic tanks and latrines, for example. It is more common when there is a shortage of clean water for drinking, cooking and cleaning. To capture these factors, I create a binary variable for whether the household has access to piped water and whether it has a flush toilet.

Lastly, ethnicity/tribal association, rural-urban location and region of residence may capture the taste for child health within the culture of origin and/or the culture of the local community. At the same time, however, these variables confound cultural factors with the economic conditions and experiences of different ethnicities and between different geographical locations. Again, since I am mainly interested in ensuring that valid estimates may be obtained for the skills and schooling variables and not in distinguishing between the relative impacts of cultural and economic

---

[10] http://www.who.int/water sanitation health/diseases/diarrhoea/en/

factors *per se,* the issue of confoundedness as it relates to these variables is not critical to the analyses in this study.

## Sample Restrictions

As was also apparent from the previous discussion on child health outcome variables, the way the questions pertaining to child health outcomes were administered in the survey implicitly gives some of the sample restrictions, while others are to be chosen. When analyzing the determinants of ever being vaccinated and ever having received post-natal care, the samples are therefore restricted to children in the relevant age ranges (vaccinations: 7 years of age or younger; post-natal care: 5 years of age or younger) for which information on mothers' literacy and numeracy skills, formal schooling and participation in an adult literacy programme is available. When analyzing the determinants of pre-natal care, the sample is restricted to women between the ages of 15 and 49 who were pregnant within the previous 12 months, while the determinants of child mortality are examined for all women between the ages of 15 and 49 years of age. To ensure consistency between the different sub-samples, the estimations involving child morbidity, vaccinations and post-natal care are restricted to children for whom the mother is between the ages of 15 and 49.

Moving to the explanatory variables, mothers should have had a chance to complete primary schooling, while at the same time being eligible for participation in adult literacy programmes (the lower limit). Also, individuals should not be 'too old', since then measurement issues start to kick in more (upper limit). Restricting the sample to women between the ages of 15 and 49 therefore remains a reasonable strategy. Lastly, some explanatory variables are missing for some observations, which causes a further drop in the sample sizes, though in most cases not substantial. Table 17.3 summarizes the sample restrictions and the impact on the estimation sample sizes for the various analyses.

**Table 17.3   Sample Restrictions and Impact on Estimation Sample Sizes**

| Sub-analysis | Sample | Initial sample | Estimation sample |
|---|---|---|---|
| (1) Ever vaccinated | Children 0–7 years | 4791 | 4406 |
| (2) Mortality | Females, 15–49 years | 4167 | 4144 |
| (3) Received pre-natal care | Females, 15–49 years, who were pregnant in past 12 months | 1142 | 1038 |
| (4) Ever received post-natal care | Children 0–5 years | 3588 | 3539 |
| (5) Morbidity | Children 0–7 years | 4821 | 4754 |

*Notes:*   Initial sample is sample for which information on the dependent variable is available and the mother is between 15 and 49 years old. Estimation sample is sample where all explanatory variables (gender and age of child, age, literacy and numeracy skills, formal education, adult literacy course participation and earnings of mother, rural-urban location, region of residence, ethnicity/tribal association and access to and prices of health-related services in the community, water access and sanitation of household) are available.

While the drop in observations from the initial to the estimation samples is not alarming, I nonetheless examine the impact of the sample restrictions on sample selection. This is done by tabulating the variable means for the initial and sample means and testing for statistical different differences between the two (see Appendix 17.A, Tables 17.A1 and 17.A2). Again, while there are statistically significant differences between the initial and estimation samples in some cases, the drop-out in absolute terms is quite low.

## Preliminary Analyses of the Determinants of Child Health Outcomes

In order to provide preliminary analyses of child health outcomes, these are tabulated across mothers' literacy and numeracy skills, school attendance and adult literacy course participation in Table 17.4. Again, while the reading skills variables are excluded from the multivariate analyses, it still seems worthwhile to examine the bivariate associations between these measures and the child health measures.

**Table 17.4   Children's Vaccinations, Mortality, Pre- and Post-natal Care and Illnesses Across Maternal Literacy and Numeracy Skills, Schooling and Literacy Course Participation**

|  | Full Sample Mean | Ghanaian Writing | English Writing | Written Calculations | Attended School | Adult Literacy Course Participation |
|---|---|---|---|---|---|---|
| Ever vacc. | 0.919 | 0.963*** | 0.968*** | 0.961*** | 0.948*** | 0.964*** |
| Number died | 0.536 | 0.323*** | 0.270*** | 0.316*** | 0.394*** | 0.669 |
| Pre-natal | 0.828 | 0.883* | 0.879* | 0.876** | 0.873*** | 0.778 |
| Post-natal | 0.394 | 0.409 | 0.443** | 0.433** | 0.419* | 0.449* |
| Ill | 0.319 | 0.305 | 0.308 | 0.315 | 0.327 | 0.375* |

*Notes:*   Samples are final estimation samples as shown in Tables 17.5 and 17.6 and contain children 7 years old or younger, except for (1) post-natal care, which is for children 5 years or younger, (2) pre-natal care, which is only measured for women who were pregnant within the past 12 months, and (3) mortality, which is measured for women between 15 and 49 years of age. Sample for literacy course participants is individuals who completed primary school or less. For presentation purposes the individual cell sizes for health variables have been omitted; they are available upon request.***: statistically significant from the reference category (not proficient in Ghanaian writing, English writing and so on) at 10%,**: statistically significant from the reference category at 5%,*: statistically significant from the reference category at 1%.

Judging from this evidence, there are major differences in child health outcomes across the mother's skills and schooling. First, mothers proficient in Ghanaian reading or writing, English reading or writing or written calculations experience lower child mortality and are also more likely to have their children vaccinated than both the 'average mother' (as measured by the sample means) and mothers who are not proficient in these skills. Secondly, mothers proficient in English reading or writing or written calculations are more likely to seek post-natal care for their children than are both the 'average mother' (as measured by the sample means) and mothers who are not proficient in these skills. Thirdly, mothers who have ever attended school are more likely to have their children vaccinated, seek pre-natal care for themselves and post-natal care for their children and also experience lower child mortality than are both the 'average mother' (as measured by the sample means) and mothers who never attended school.

I shall now examine these child health outcomes gaps (child health determinants) further, using multivariate statistical techniques.

## 5.    Multivariate Analyses

The multivariate analyses contain three specifications for each of the five child health measures, the last of which is the 'preferred' specification, and the first two are included for sensitivity analyses (Table 17.5). The first specification only includes mother's literacy and numeracy skills, formal education, adult literacy course participation and strictly exogenous variables such as gender, age and age squared of the child and the age and age squared of the mother. The second specification adds weakly exogenous variables such as health facility access, regional variables and cost of health services. The last specification adds potentially endogenous variables, including mother's earnings, water and sanitation of the household and fertility variables.

Judging from the evidence from the preferred specifications in Table 17.6, there seems to be some support of literacy and numeracy skills effects independent of the effects from formal education and adult literacy course participation for some of the child health measures. In particular, English writing skills have a negative and statistically significant impact on child mortality. This points to English writing skills being the 'higher standard' in terms of skills, as far as child mortality is concerned. Note, however, that this does not mean that English reading skills are not important: individuals who write must be able to read as well, and therefore that skill is implicitly included in English writing skills. For the unrestricted illness measure, the English reading and writing skills variables are both statistically significant but with opposite signs, indicating the existence of collinearity between the two variables. For vaccinations and number of children ever died, written calculations have a statistically negative and positive impact, respectively, for the initial specification, but it disappears after introducing more controls.

In accordance with the previous literature, formal educational attainment has strong and statistically significant effects in several cases, although the introduction of literacy and numeracy skills and adult literacy course participation seems to pick up some of the impact from formal education, so that there are not as many statistically significant formal education variables as one might otherwise have expected.

Adult literacy course participation is positively statistically significant for vaccinations and post-natal care, indicating the impact of the health knowledge, which is an integral part of the adult literacy course curriculum in Ghana (Blunch and Pörtner, 2005) on individual health-seeking behaviour. Again, had only formal educational attainment been included in the analyses, this important channel of health

**Table 17.5  Overview of Variables Included in the Different Specifications**

| (1) For all equations: | Model 1 | Model 2 | Model 3 |
|---|---|---|---|
| | Contains mother's skills, education and strictly exogenous controls: | Adds weakly exogenous controls: | Adds potentially endogenous variables: |
| **Mother's literacy  and numeracy skills:** | | | |
| Ghanaian writing | X | X | X |
| English writing | X | X | X |
| Written calculations | X | X | X |
| **Mother's education:** | | | |
| Literacy course participation | X | X | X |
| Primary | X | X | X |
| Middle/JSS | X | X | X |
| Secondary and above | X | X | X |
| Vocational and other | X | X | X |
| **Economic variables:** | | | |
| Mother's (potential) wage rate | | | X |
| Income of other HH members | | | X |
| **Access to facilities:** | | | |
| Access to hospital in community | | X | X |
| **Other variables related to child health inputs and outcomes:** | | | |
| Age of mother | X | X | X |
| Age of mother squared | X | X | X |
| Ethnicity/tribe of mother | X | X | X |
| Number of other adults in HH | | | X |
| Number of other children in HH | | | X |
| Access to piped water | | | |
| Urban-rural location | | X | X |
| Regional dummies | | X | X |
| **(2) For vaccinations, post-natal care and morbidity equations only:** | | | |
| Age of child | X | X | X |
| Age of child squared | X | X | X |
| Gender of child | X | X | X |
| **(3) For vaccinations, morbidity and mortality equations only:** | | | |
| Vaccination cost (cluster average) | | X | X |
| **(4) For pre-natal care equation only:** | | | |
| Pre-natal consultation cost (cluster average) | | X | X |
| **(5) For post-natal care equation only:** | | | |
| Post-natal consultation cost (cluster average) | | X | X |

**Table 17.6   Results for Preferred Specifications: Model 3 from Table 17.5**

| Dependent variable: | Vaccinations | Number of dead children | Pre-natal care | Post-natal care | Illness |
|---|---|---|---|---|---|
| Estimation method: | Probit | Ordered probit | Probit | Probit | Probit |
| Ghanaian writing | 0.085 [0.196] | 0.056 [0.081] | -0.02 [0.195] | -0.132 [0.098] | -0.083 [0.074] |
| English writing | 0.027 [0.209] | -0.259** [0.119] | -0.024 [0.185] | 0.169 [0.133] | 0.053 [0.100] |
| Written calculations | 0.099 [0.161] | -0.029 [0.093] | -0.096 [0.228] | 0.082 [0.110] | -0.005 [0.089] |
| Adult literacy course | 0.426*** [0.135] | -0.032 [0.100] | 0.069 [0.196] | 0.237** [0.101] | 0.178** [0.086] |
| Primary | 0.097 [0.131] | -0.057 [0.097] | 0.485** [0.205] | -0.005 [0.113] | -0.008 [0.083] |
| Middle/JSS | 0.315* [0.174] | 0.127 [0.118] | 0.383* [0.210] | -0.081 [0.130] | -0.003 [0.106] |
| Secondary and above | NA | 0.191 [0.231] | 1.584*** [0.463] | 0.263 [0.230] | 0.062 [0.226] |
| Vocational/other educ. | NA | 0.301 [0.208] | -0.626 [0.678] | -0.189 [0.261] | -0.237 [0.219] |

*Specification tests:*
(1) Hausman tests:

| | Vaccinations | Number of dead children | Pre-natal care | Post-natal care | Illness |
|---|---|---|---|---|---|
| Model 2 vs. 1 | $F_{(16, 270)} = 0.90$ | $F_{(16, 279)} = 17.39$*** | $F_{(15, 262)} = 0.60$ | $F_{(19, 274)} = 0.58$ | $F_{(19, 275)} = 1.53$* |
| Model 3 vs. 2 | $F_{(28, 258)} = 0.75$ | $F_{(28, 267)} = 18.09$*** | $F_{(27, 250)} = 0.74$ | $F_{(31, 262)} = 0.55$ | $F_{(31, 263)} = 0.48$ |
| Model 3 vs. 1 | $F_{(16, 270)} = 1.75$** | $F_{(16, 279)} = 28.28$*** | $F_{(15, 262)} = 1.17$ | $F_{(19, 274)} = 0.67$ | $F_{(19, 275)} = 1.23$ |

(2) Joint significance of additional variables:

| | Vaccinations | Number of dead children | Pre-natal care | Post-natal care | Illness |
|---|---|---|---|---|---|
| Model 2 vs. 1 | $F_{(12, 274)} = 2.34$*** | $F_{(12, 283)} = 4.97$*** | $F_{(12, 265)} = 1.22$ | $F_{(12, 281)} = 1.31$ | $F_{(12, 282)} = 3.48$*** |
| Model 3 vs. 2 | $F_{(2, 284)} = 4.70$*** | $F_{(2, 293)} = 255.94$*** | $F_{(2, 275)} = 5.53$*** | $F_{(2, 291)} = 4.48$** | $F_{(2, 292)} = 2.85$* |
| Model 3 vs. 1 | $F_{(14, 272)} = 2.14$*** | $F_{(14, 281)} = 46.02$*** | $F_{(14, 263)} = 1.98$* | $F_{(14, 279)} = 1.68$* | $F_{(14, 280)} = 2.98$*** |
| Number of observations | 4406 | 4144 | 1038 | 3539 | 4754 |

*Notes:* 'NA' indicates that variable dropped out due to being a perfect predictor, whereby the corresponding observation is dropped from the estimation, as well. Robust Huber-White Sandwich (Huber, 1967; White, 1980) standard errors in brackets. *: statistically significant at 10% **: statistically significant at 5%; ***: statistically significant at 1%. Since the asymptotic assumptions of the Hausman (1978) test are not satisfied when incorporating survey weights in the estimations, the Generalized Hausman test is applied here.

knowledge diffusion would have been overlooked. Somewhat puzzling at first, the impact of adult literacy participation on child illnesses is statistically significant and positive. One explanation for this is that participants in adult literacy courses may diagnose diseases more correctly, which would seem to inflate the self-reported child morbidity measure. This is supported by the results from the specification using the restricted child morbidity measure: when children have to stop their usual activities, the impact of adult literacy course participation is halved and is no longer statistically significantly different from zero. The intuition behind this is that when the illness is so serious that the child has to stop its usual activities, the health knowledge obtained from adult literacy courses is not 'necessary' in terms of assessing whether the child is ill or not.

Again, remembering the weaknesses of the various child health measures as discussed earlier, these results should be interpreted with care, especially in the cases of child illnesses, and pre- and post-natal care, whereas the results for child vaccinations and child mortality seem to hold up somewhat more strongly. Altogether, however, these results point to the importance of literacy and numeracy skills and adult literacy programmes for child health, two issues which have not received much attention in the previous literature on child health determinants.

## 6.    Conclusion

Viewing the accumulation of human capital as a two-pronged production process, where schooling produces skills, which subsequently enter as inputs (or intermediate outputs) to generate the final outcome of child health, this study examines the relationship between mothers' literacy and numeracy skills, formal education and adult literacy course participation and child health in Ghana. The health measures examined include child vaccinations, child mortality, pre- and post-natal care and child morbidity. The contribution of the study includes (i) analyzing the impact on child health from skills, including reading and writing skills and those for both English and indigenous languages, as well as numeracy and other skills, and (ii) including adult literacy course participation as a pathway for achieving skills — two issues which have not been addressed in the previous literature. The study considers how these skills affect the production of health, including mothers' pre-natal care and children's vaccinations and post-natal care, and how they affect outputs, including children's illnesses and mortality.

The results indicate some support for skills affecting child health outcomes independently of formal educational attainment. Most significantly, they indicate that the health knowledge skills obtained through participation in adult literacy courses significantly improve children's health in terms of vaccinations and post-natal care.

More research is required, however, in order to examine whether the link is causal, rather than merely indicating correlation. In particular, the current analyses implicitly assume that all explanatory variables are exogenous to child health outcomes. While that may not be too far off for some of the variables (gender, rural-urban location and region), for others this assumption is more problematic (maternal schooling, skills, earnings, water and sanitation). The many endogenous variables in this study and the resulting requirement for instruments appear to render instrumental variables methods infeasible as a means of addressing endogeneity. Future research should therefore address these issues by introducing — and hence controlling for — unobserved heterogeneity. This might be done by introducing a latent factor capturing unobservables such as 'type' or preferences, either assuming a specific functional form for the distribution of the factor or using the discrete factor approximation approach first suggested by Heckman and Singer (1984) and generalized by Mroz and Guilkey (1992). The latter is somewhat less restrictive but also entails a greater burden computationally.

## References

Becker, Gary S. (1965) 'A Theory of the Allocation of Time', *Economic Journal*, 75(299): 493–517.

Behrman, Jere (1990) *The Action of Human Resources and Poverty on One Another: What We Have Yet to Learn*. Living Standards Measurement Study Working Paper No. 74. Washington, DC: World Bank.

Behrman, Jere and Deolalikar, Anil (1988) 'Health and Nutrition', in Hollis Chenery and T. N. Srinivasan (eds), *Handbook of Development Economics*, Vol. I. Amsterdam: North Holland.

Bergstrom, T. (1996) 'Economics in a Family Way', *Journal of Economic Literature,* Vol. 34, No. 4: 1903–34.

Blunch, Niels-Hugo (2005) 'Skills Production and Education Sector Reform'. Washington, DC: George Washington University (mimeo).

Blunch, Niels-Hugo and Pörtner, Claus (2005) 'Adult Literacy Programs in Ghana: An Evaluation'. Washington, DC: World Bank, Human Development Network Education Department (mimeo).

Grossman, Michael (1972) 'On the Concept of Health Capital and the Demand for Health', *Journal of Political Economy*, Vol. 80, No. 2: 223–55.

Heckman, James and Singer, B. (1984) 'A Method for Minimizing the Impact of Distributional Assumptions on Econometric Models for Duration Data', *Econometrica*, Vol. 52, No. 2: 271–320.

Huber, P. J. (1967) 'The Behavior of Maximum Likelihood Estimates under Nonstandard Conditions', in *Proceedings of the Fifth Berkeley Symposium on Mathematical Statistics and Probability* Vol. 1, Berkeley, CA: University of California Press.

Manser, Marilyn and Brown, Murray (1980) 'Marriage and Household Decision-making: A Bargaining Analysis', *International Economic Review*, Vol. 21, No. 1: 31–44.

McElroy, Marjorie B. and Horney, Mary Jean (1981) 'Nash Bargained Household Decisions: Toward a Generalization of the Theory of Demand', *International Economic Review*,Vol. 22, No. 2: 333–49.

Mroz, Thomas and Guilkey, David K. (1992) 'Discrete Factor Approximations for Use in Simultaneous Equation Models with Both Continuous and Discrete Endogenous Variables'. Department of Economics, University of North Carolina, Chapel Hill, NC, (mimeo).

Spence, Michael A. (1973) "Job Market Signaling", *Quarterly Journal of Economics*, Vol. 87, No. 3: 55–74.

Strauss, John and Thomas, Duncan (1995) 'Human Resources: Household Decisions and Markets' in Jere Behrman and T. N. Srinivasan (eds), *Handbook of Development Economics,* Vol. 3A. Amsterdam: North Holland.

White, H. (1980) 'A Heteroskedasticity-Consistent Covariance Matrix Estimator and a Direct Test for Heteroskedasticity', *Econometrica*, Vol. 48, No. 4: 817–30.

**APPENDIX 17A   Comparisons of Means of Initial and Estimation Samples**

**Table 17A.1   Comparisons of Means of Initial and Estimation Samples: Vaccinations and Child Mortality**

| Sample/Dependent Variable | Vaccine | | | Mortality (all measures) | | |
|---|---|---|---|---|---|---|
| | Estimation sample | Excluded observations | Difference | Estimation sample | Excluded observations | Difference |
| Female | 0.497 | 0.508 | −0.010 | NA | NA | NA |
| Age, child | 3.567 | 3.141 | 0.427 | NA | NA | NA |
| Age squared/100, child | 0.180 | 0.149 | 0.031 | NA | NA | NA |
| Age, mother | 32.164 | 29.782 | 2.382 | 33.243 | 31.020 | 2.223 |
| Age squared/100, mother | 10.793 | 9.370 | 1.423 | 11.676 | 10.171 | 1.505 |
| Akan | 0.442 | 0.617 | −0.175 | 0.485 | 0.192 | 0.293*** |
| Ewe | 0.135 | 0.159 | −0.025 | 0.133 | 0.127 | 0.005 |
| Ga-Adangbe | 0.084 | 0.029 | 0.056 | 0.093 | 0.117 | −0.024 |
| Other ethnicity | 0.339 | 0.195 | 0.144 | 0.290 | 0.564 | −0.274** |
| Number children ever born | 3.644 | 1.953 | 1.691 | 3.978 | 3.190 | 0.788 |
| Access to hospital | 0.769 | 0.863 | −0.094 | 0.805 | 0.729 | 0.076 |
| Piped water | 0.245 | 0.251 | −0.006 | 0.337 | 0.118 | 0.219*** |
| Flush toilet | 0.030 | 0.030 | 0.000 | 0.056 | 0.027 | 0.029 |
| Urban | 0.251 | 0.204 | 0.046 | 0.339 | 0.318 | 0.021 |
| Western | 0.122 | 0.226 | −0.104 | 0.114 | 0.046 | 0.069* |
| Central | 0.086 | 0.056 | 0.031 | 0.092 | 0.014 | 0.078*** |
| Greater Accra | 0.082 | 0.083 | −0.001 | 0.120 | 0.115 | 0.006 |
| Eastern | 0.123 | 0.129 | −0.006 | 0.110 | 0.276 | −0.166 |
| Volta | 0.123 | 0.095 | 0.028 | 0.120 | 0.025 | 0.096*** |
| Ashanti | 0.155 | 0.172 | −0.018 | 0.170 | 0.098 | 0.072 |
| Brong-Ohofa | 0.083 | 0.035 | 0.048 | 0.091 | 0.224 | −0.132 |
| Northern | 0.149 | 0.103 | 0.046 | 0.108 | 0.162 | −0.054 |
| Upper West | 0.033 | 0.000 | 0.033 | 0.029 | 0.000 | 0.029* |
| Upper East | 0.045 | 0.102 | −0.057 | 0.045 | 0.042 | 0.003 |
| Number of observations | 4724 | 67 | | 4144 | 23 | |

*Notes:*   'NA': Information is not available in survey. ***: statistically significant at 10%, **: statistically significant from the reference category at 5%, *: statistically significant from the reference category at 1%.

**Table 17A.2   Comparisons of Means of Initial and Estimation Samples: Pre- and Post-natal Care and Illnesses**

| Sample/Dependent Variable | Pre-natal care | | | Post-natal care | | | Illnesses (both measures) | | |
|---|---|---|---|---|---|---|---|---|---|
| | Estimation sample | Excluded observations | Difference | Estimation sample | Excluded observations | Difference | Estimation sample | Excluded observations | Difference |
| Female | NA | NA | NA | 0.504 | 0.497 | 0.007 | 0.495 | 0.499 | −0.003 |
| Age, child | NA | NA | NA | 2.501 | 2.492 | 0.009 | 3.582 | 3.158 | 0.423 |
| Age squared/100, child | NA | NA | NA | 0.092 | 0.093 | −0.001 | 0.181 | 0.149 | 0.032 |
| Age, mother | 30.320 | 22.044 | 8.277 | 31.335 | 29.669 | 1.667 | 32.167 | 29.981 | 2.186 |
| Age squared/100, mother | 9.629 | 5.127 | 4.502 | 10.270 | 9.362 | 0.908 | 10.797 | 9.515 | 1.282 |
| Akan | 0.472 | 0.538 | −0.066 | 0.439 | 0.714 | −0.275 | 0.441 | 0.615 | −0.174 |
| Ewe | 0.132 | 0.128 | 0.005 | 0.134 | 0.085 | 0.049 | 0.135 | 0.170 | −0.034 |
| Ga-Adangbe | 0.095 | 0.143 | −0.048 | 0.085 | 0.039 | 0.046 | 0.084 | 0.029 | 0.056 |
| Other ethnicity | 0.301 | 0.191 | 0.110 | 0.342 | 0.162 | 0.180 | 0.339 | 0.187 | 0.153 |
| Number children ever born | 3.908 | 3.198 | 0.711 | 3.462 | 1.632 | 1.830 | 3.641 | 1.953 | 1.688 |
| Access to hospital | 0.764 | 0.812 | −0.048 | 0.762 | 0.908 | −0.146 | 0.767 | 0.864 | −0.097 |
| Piped water | 0.255 | 0.245 | 0.010 | 0.227 | 0.316 | −0.089 | 0.246 | 0.243 | 0.003 |
| Flush toilet | 0.028 | 0.066 | −0.038 | 0.025 | 0.041 | −0.016 | 0.030 | 0.030 | 0.000 |
| Urban | 0.261 | 0.273 | −0.012 | 0.237 | 0.264 | −0.027 | 0.252 | 0.196 | 0.056 |
| Western | 0.117 | 0.153 | −0.035 | 0.120 | 0.273 | −0.153 | 0.120 | 0.225 | −0.106 |
| Central | 0.097 | 0.064 | 0.033 | 0.088 | 0.086 | 0.001 | 0.086 | 0.055 | 0.031 |
| Greater Accra | 0.071 | 0.104 | −0.032 | 0.076 | 0.088 | −0.012 | 0.082 | 0.075 | 0.007 |
| Eastern | 0.123 | 0.123 | 0.000 | 0.126 | 0.079 | 0.047 | 0.124 | 0.139 | −0.016 |
| Volta | 0.143 | 0.146 | −0.003 | 0.125 | 0.106 | 0.019 | 0.123 | 0.094 | 0.029 |
| Ashanti | 0.151 | 0.263 | −0.112 | 0.156 | 0.155 | 0.001 | 0.156 | 0.172 | −0.016 |
| Brong-Ohofa | 0.102 | 0.022 | 0.080 | 0.081 | 0.037 | 0.045 | 0.082 | 0.034 | 0.047 |
| Northern | 0.127 | 0.098 | 0.029 | 0.149 | 0.087 | 0.062 | 0.149 | 0.103 | 0.047 |
| Upper West | 0.029 | 0.011 | 0.018 | 0.033 | 0.000 | 0.033 | 0.033 | 0.000 | 0.033 |
| Upper East | 0.040 | 0.018 | 0.022 | 0.046 | 0.090 | −0.044 | 0.046 | 0.102 | −0.056 |
| Number of observations | 1038 | 104 | | 3539 | 49 | | 4754 | 67 | |

*Notes:*   As for Table 17A.1

**APPENDIX 17B Sensitivity Analyses and Specification Tests**

**Table 17.B1 Results from Benchmark Estimation (Not Taking Endogeneity into Account): Vaccinations and Mortality**

| Dependent variable: | Vaccinations | | | Number of children ever died | | | Any children ever died | | | Share of children ever died | | |
|---|---|---|---|---|---|---|---|---|---|---|---|---|
| Estimation method: | Probit | | | Ordered probit | | | Probit | | | OLS | | |
| Model: | 1 | 2 | 3 | 1 | 2 | 3 | 1 | 2 | 3 | 1 | 2 | 3 |
| Ghanaian writing | 0.005 [0.186] | 0.078 [0.195] | 0.085 [0.196] | 0.059 [0.079] | 0.052 [0.078] | 0.056 [0.081] | 0.067 [0.085] | 0.045 [0.082] | 0.035 [0.085] | 0.012 [0.009] | 0.011 [0.009] | 0.011 [0.009] |
| English writing | 0.053 [0.201] | 0.053 [0.204] | 0.027 [0.209] | −0.346*** [0.116] | −0.317*** [0.118] | −0.259** [0.119] | −0.358*** [0.131] | −0.314** [0.134] | −0.252* [0.133] | −0.031** [0.015] | −0.027* [0.015] | −0.023 [0.015] |
| Written calculations | 0.206 [0.163] | 0.119 [0.161] | 0.099 [0.161] | −0.147* [0.075] | −0.098 [0.085] | −0.029 [0.093] | −0.069 [0.095] | −0.014 [0.103] | 0.066 [0.109] | −0.011 [0.013] | −0.006 [0.012] | −0.002 [0.012] |
| Literacy course | 0.445*** [0.138] | 0.422** [0.135] | 0.426*** [0.135] | 0.043 [0.081] | −0.025 [0.082] | −0.032 [0.100] | 0.143 [0.105] | 0.078 [0.108] | 0.078 [0.127] | 0.006 [0.013] | −0.001 [0.013] | −0.001 [0.014] |
| Primary | 0.179 [0.133] | 0.118 [0.130] | 0.097 [0.131] | −0.137 [0.094] | −0.127 [0.095] | −0.057 [0.097] | −0.203* [0.106] | −0.195* [0.108] | −0.146 [0.111] | −0.016 [0.013] | −0.013 [0.013] | −0.008 [0.013] |
| Middle/JSS | 0.442** [0.175] | 0.364** [0.177] | 0.315* [0.174] | −0.134 [0.108] | −0.103 [0.113] | 0.127 [0.118] | −0.166 [0.112] | −0.142 [0.116] | 0.04 [0.122] | −0.007 [0.015] | −0.004 [0.016] | 0.009 [0.016] |
| Secondary and above | NA | NA | NA | −0.438** [0.191] | −0.315 [0.209] | 0.191 [0.231] | −0.551*** [0.188] | −0.437** [0.199] | −0.009 [0.221] | −0.015 [0.024] | −0.008 [0.026] | 0.021 [0.027] |
| Vocational/other educ. | NA | NA | NA | −0.253 [0.201] | −0.061 [0.215] | 0.301 [0.208] | −0.23 [0.223] | −0.036 [0.240] | 0.285 [0.233] | −0.01 [0.023] | 0.006 [0.024] | 0.028 [0.024] |
| **Specification tests:** | | | | | | | | | | | | |
| (1) Hausman tests: | | | | | | | | | | | | |
| Model 2 vs. 1 | $F(16, 270) = 0.90$ | | | $F(16, 279) = 17.39***$ | | | $F(15, 280) = 2.78***$ | | | $F(16, 279) = 2.93***$ | | |
| Model 3 vs. 2 | $F(28, 258) = 0.75$ | | | $F(28, 267) = 18.09***$ | | | $F(27, 268) = 12.85***$ | | | $F(28, 267) = 2.63***$ | | |
| Model 3 vs. 1 | $F(16, 270) = 1.75**$ | | | $F(16, 279) = 28.28***$ | | | $F(15, 280) = 21.86***$ | | | $F(16, 279) = 6.40***$ | | |
| (2) Joint significance of additional variables: | | | | | | | | | | | | |
| Model 2 vs. 1 | $F(12, 274) = 2.34***$ | | | $F(12, 283) = 4.97***$ | | | $F(12, 283) = 4.07***$ | | | $F(12, 283) = 3.64***$ | | |
| Model 3 vs. 2 | $F(2, 284) = 4.70***$ | | | $F(2, 293) = 255.94***$ | | | $F(2, 293) = 170.15***$ | | | $F(2, 293) = 35.73***$ | | |
| Model 3 vs. 1 | $F(14, 272) = 2.14***$ | | | $F(14, 281) = 46.02***$ | | | $F(14, 281) = 28.54***$ | | | $F(14, 281) = 8.48***$ | | |
| No. of observations | 4406 | | | 4144 | | | 4144 | | | 4144 | | |

*Notes:* 'NA' indicates that variable dropped out due to being a perfect predictor, whereby the corresponding observation is dropped from the estimation, as well. Robust Huber-White Sandwich (Huber, 1967; White, 1980) standard errors in brackets. *: statistically significant at 10%; **: statistically significant at 5%; ***: statistically significant at 1%. Since the asymptotic assumptions of the Hausman (1978) test are not satisfied when incorporating survey weights in the estimations, the Generalized Hausman test is applied here.

**Table 17B.2  Results from Benchmark Estimation (Not Taking Endogeneity into Account): Illnesses, Pre- and Post-natal Care**

| Dependent variable: | Prenatal care | | | Postnatal care | | | Illness | | | Ill, stopped usual activities | | |
|---|---|---|---|---|---|---|---|---|---|---|---|---|
| Estimation method: | Probit | | | Probit | | | Probit | | | Probit | | |
| Model: | 1 | 2 | 3 | 1 | 2 | 3 | 1 | 2 | 3 | 1 | 2 | 3 |
| Ghanaian writing | -0.048 [0.189] | -0.013 [0.196] | -0.02 [0.195] | -0.13 [0.104] | -0.15 [0.100] | -0.132 [0.098] | -0.06 [0.073] | -0.083 [0.075] | -0.083 [0.074] | -0.05 [0.080] | -0.062 [0.084] | -0.068 [0.083] |
| English writing | -0.016 [0.172] | -0.006 [0.181] | -0.024 [0.185] | 0.154 [0.135] | 0.191 [0.134] | 0.169 [0.133] | 0.024 [0.104] | 0.039 [0.104] | 0.053 [0.100] | -0.005 [0.090] | -0.01 [0.094] | 0.007 [0.093] |
| Written calculations | 0.013 [0.229] | -0.074 [0.223] | -0.096 [0.228] | 0.152 [0.114] | 0.109 [0.108] | 0.082 [0.110] | -0.008 [0.086] | -0.006 [0.087] | -0.005 [0.089] | 0.041 [0.092] | 0.03 [0.091] | 0.037 [0.092] |
| Literacy course | -0.001 [0.205] | 0.063 [0.199] | 0.069 [0.196] | 0.244** [0.115] | 0.242** [0.102] | 0.237** [0.101] | 0.182** [0.086] | 0.183** [0.084] | 0.178** [0.086] | 0.034 [0.093] | 0.053 [0.093] | 0.044 [0.092] |
| Primary | 0.556*** [0.201] | 0.484** [0.204] | 0.485** [0.196] | 0.041 [0.115] | -0.001 [0.114] | -0.005 [0.113] | -0.023 [0.084] | -0.012 [0.083] | -0.008 [0.083] | -0.032 [0.086] | -0.015 [0.085] | -0.005 [0.092] |
| Middle/JSS | 0.468** [0.211] | 0.377** [0.209] | 0.383** [0.210] | -0.024 [0.131] | -0.066 [0.129] | -0.081 [0.130] | -0.026 [0.105] | -0.012 [0.105] | -0.003 [0.106] | -0.083 [0.113] | -0.062 [0.117] | -0.047 [0.119] |
| Secondary and above | 1.807*** [0.429] | 1.652*** [0.458] | 1.584*** [0.463] | 0.419* [0.248] | 0.363 [0.236] | 0.263 [0.230] | -0.073 [0.205] | -0.018 [0.212] | 0.062 [0.226] | 0.008 [0.233] | 0.038 [0.243] | 0.12 [0.259] |
| Vocational/other educ. | -0.371 [0.672] | -0.635 [0.685] | -0.626 [0.678] | -0.046 [0.261] | -0.133 [0.251] | -0.189 [0.261] | -0.342 [0.209] | -0.244 [0.215] | -0.237 [0.219] | -0.421* [0.241] | -0.354 [0.253] | -0.32 [0.255] |
| **Specification tests:** | | | | | | | | | | | | |
| (1) Hausman tests: | | | | | | | | | | | | |
| Model 2 vs. 1 | F(15, 262) = 0.60 | | | F(19, 274) = 0.58 | | | F(19, 275) = 1.53* | | | F(19, 275) = 1.05 | | |
| Model 3 vs. 2 | F(27, 250) = 0.74 | | | F(31, 262) = 0.55 | | | F(31, 263) = 0.48 | | | F(31, 263) = 0.28 | | |
| Model 3 vs. 1 | F(15, 262) = 1.17 | | | F(19, 274) = 0.67 | | | F(19 ,275) = 1.23 | | | F(19, 275) = 1.11 | | |
| (2) Joint significance of additional variables: | | | | | | | | | | | | |
| Model 2 vs. 1 | F(12, 265) = 1.22 | | | F(12, 281) = 1.31 | | | F(12, 282) = 3.48*** | | | F(12, 282)=3.51*** | | |
| Model 3 vs. 2 | F(2, 275) = 5.53*** | | | F(2, 291) = 4.48** | | | F(2, 292 ) = 2.85* | | | F(2, 292) = 3.42*** | | |
| Model 3 vs. 1 | F(14, 263) = 1.98** | | | F(14, 279) = 1.68* | | | F(14, 280) = 2.98*** | | | F(14, 280) = 3.47*** | | |
| No. of observations | 1038 | | | 3539 | | | 4754 | | | 4754 | | |

*Notes:*  Robust Huber-White Sandwich (Huber, 1967; White, 1980) standard errors in brackets.  *: statistically significant at 10%; **: statistically significant at 5%; ***: statistically significant at 1%. Since the asymptotic assumptions of the Hausman (1978) test are not satisfied when incorporating survey weights in the estimations, the Generalized Hausman test is applied here.

# 18

## Health-care Provision & Self-medication in Ghana*

G. J. M. VAN DEN BOOM, N. N. N. NSOWAH-NUAMAH & G. B. OVERBOSCH

## 1.    Introduction

Because of the relationship that exists between health, productivity and equitable development, health improvements form a key element of development. Since independence in 1957, the government of Ghana has implemented a number of policies aimed at improving the health status of its people. Its seven-year and five-year development plans in the early days of independence, as well as economic policies in recent decades, contain various measures to reduce the economic burden of disease, with a particular focus on morbidity, mortality and malnutrition among children. Indeed, the economic reforms and structural adjustment programmes that have been pursued since 1983 have gradually been accompanied by reforms in the health sector, which put more emphasis on primary health-care and stressed the importance of prevention of disease. The government of Ghana embarked on a health sector reform in the early 1990s to improve the accessibility and quality of services. The Health Service Act of 1996 and the Medium-Term Health Strategy based on Vision-2020 are further moves towards an efficient health-care delivery system (World Bank, 1997; MoH, 2000; GoG, 2003).

Over the years, several health indicators have shown positive trends. For example, the mortality rate of children under the age of five has successfully been reduced from 215 per 1000 in 1960 to 157 in 1980 and further to 112 in 2000 (World Bank, 2001; GSS and MI, 1999). Likewise, life expectancy at birth has increased from 45 years in 1960 to 53 in 1980 and further to 57 in 2000.

A comparison with targets of the Medium-Term Health Strategy indicates that successes have been mixed, however. Some targets remain far off (for example, maternal

*The authors acknowledge the foundation SADAOC (Sécurité Alimentaire Durable en Afrique de l'Ouest Central) Ouagadougou for co-financing the research, the Ghana Statistical Service and the Ministry of Health for kindly making the data available, and participants in the conference 'Ghana at the Half Century' for useful comments. The opinions expressed are those of the authors who remain responsible for any errors and omissions.

mortality more than doubled the targeted rate of 100 per 100,000 live births), others are fairly well met (for example, child mortality and life expectancy targets of 100 per 1000 live births and 60 years, respectively), and some are even surpassed (for example, 5% severe child malnourishment as compared with a target of 8%).

Notwithstanding the reforms and despite positive trends, the health situation in Ghana is still far from satisfactory. Recent figures still reflect poor average health conditions, and Ghana, like most developing countries, wants to move to better and more efficient health-care utilization. An extensive literature exists on how this could be achieved (Culyer and Newhouse, 2000). A major issue is how to promote competition in the health sector and take advantage of the allocative efficiency of markets. The efficiency of health-care markets in developing countries is hampered by factors such as the insufficient popular knowledge about diseases and treatment effects, and the external effects of communicable endemic diseases, HIV/AIDS, tuberculosis and malaria in particular. Furthermore, competition in health-care markets is hindered by set-up costs in both the training of health personnel and the construction of hospitals, clinics, and infrastructure for safe drinking water and sanitation. These set-up costs are particularly relevant in rural areas. In addition, health insurance on a scale much larger than the extended family is practically absent adding to the problem of efficient health-care provision.

For reasons of both efficiency and equity, there is ample scope for public interventions in health-care markets. Subsidized expansion of facilities, training of providers, health education, and health insurance could not only improve efficiency in supply, but also promote equity. In particular, rural health-care demand might be responsive to the proximity of providers, while extended insurance could account for care that would otherwise be unaffordable.

To foster the health of its population, Ghana has set up an extensive network of public facilities that offer subsidized care and health insurance in kind. But, current public provision is still biased towards hospitals in urban areas supplying curative care, and puts less emphasis on prevention and basic health-care in rural areas (Canagarajah and Ye, 2001). Local communities, however, become more involved through the direct provision of subsidized care to their members as well as through prevention and health promotion initiatives. Notwithstanding these efforts, many rural communities still experience high levels of morbidity and mortality due to lack of access to, and poor utilization of, health services, poor coverage of child welfare services and lack of technical support for initiating their own health programmes (Obuobi and Ahmad, 1998). In addition to supplying subsidized health-care, the government has recognized the importance of health education and insurance for an efficient and equitable access to health care. It has therefore implemented a School Health Education Programme and is currently exploring the possibilities of a National Health Insurance Scheme (GoG, 2003).

Within the low-income setting, health-care delivery in Ghana continues to face major challenges. These include lack of facilities and health personnel, limited supply of essential drugs, an unsanitary environment, and under-utilization of services due to insufficient knowledge.

To reduce the burden of health expenses on the national budget, the government introduced in 1985 user charges for health-care services and full cost recovery for drugs, popularly known as the 'Cash and Carry' system. These cost-sharing measures, consistent with the Bamako Initiative[1] (Ofori-Adjei, 1990), have increased the availability of medicines and probably removed apparent inefficiency, in particular in relation to the over-utilization of highly subsidized care. At the same time, however, they made orthodox health care less accessible to the poor. New types of behaviour and practices have emerged, such as delays in seeking care, joint purchases and sharing of prescribed drugs, and self-medication by way of using left-over drugs (Asenso-Okyere et al., 1998).

In the above perspective, and given its poverty reduction agenda in the area of health, the government considers an increase of health-care utilization a key development issue. The present study aims to contribute to the debate by presenting recent data on the supply and demand of curative health-care, and by an empirical exploration of equitable access opportunities.

The study is structured as follows. In Section 2 we describe the health-care system in Ghana, and present information on its utilization. Subsequently, in Section 3, we present a discrete choice model of health-care demand and consider the issue of imputing the cost of treatments not chosen. Data and results are discussed in Section 4. Special attention is given to access constraints and cost recovery through public-private insurance. In particular, we present two simulations, one that reduces the distance from orthodox providers, and one that replaces half of the private cost by a national health insurance with income-dependent premiums. The final section concludes and puts the results in a policy perspective.

## 2.    Curative Health-care Provision in Ghana

### *Characteristics of the System*
It is common to distinguish two broad groups of health-care providers, here referred to as orthodox and traditional. Orthodox providers have had a formal training in mainstream health-care practices as officially taught at universities, are typically clinic- or hospital-based, and prescribe modern medicines. Contrariwise, traditional providers derive their skills from tradition and informal training and, with few exceptions, do their work at their own or the client's home. Their treatment usually takes the form of herbs, plant preparations and prayers, though it is not uncommon to supplement traditional medication with modern medicines.

Table 18.1 lists the various health-care providers. The orthodox health-care comprises government health systems, as well as non-governmental organizations

---

[1] The Bamako Initiative was adopted in 1987 by African Ministers of Health at the 37th Session of the Regional Committee of the World Health Organization and the United Nations Children's Fund held in Bamako, Mali. The Bamako Initiative seeks to accelerate health for all through effective and effecient implementation of the primary health-care approach at the community level. It includes operational, technical and strategic support for community-based activities at the district, provincial and central levels.

such as the missions, and private non-subsidized practitioners. The government system is currently the largest provider, followed in importance by the missions and then the private practitioners. Health-care facilities can be distinguished in four layers, depending on the amenities available at the facility: village or community health posts, district clinics, regional hospitals and the two teaching hospitals. The village health posts predominantly provide preventive and primary health-care services, while the hospitals are the main providers of curative tertiary health care. In between, the clinics provide a mixture of preventive and curative care and use the regional hospitals for referrals. The regional and the teaching hospitals are usually perceived to be the providers of the higher and highest quality respectively. The village posts are staffed by nurses and midwives. Clinics also have medical assistants; urban clinics and hospitals also have doctors, while medical specialists work in hospitals only (Agyepong, 1999).

**Table 18.1  Overview of Health-care Providers in Ghana**

| Type of provider | Provider |
|---|---|
| **Orthodox**<br>(formal training;clinic/hospital based;<br>modern medicines) | Doctor<br>Dentist<br>Pharmacist<br>Medical assistant<br>Nurse<br>Midwife |
| **Traditional**<br>(traditional informal training; outside clinics;<br>traditional medication) | Herbalist<br>Spiritualist<br>Fetish priest<br>Traditional birth assistant<br>Unsupervised druggist |

Modern medicines are sold at pharmacies and by chemical sellers licensed by the Pharmacy Council who sell over-the-counter medication and non-prescription drugs. There are about 1,100 pharmacists and 6,000 chemical sellers in total (Nsowah-Nuamah et al., 2000).

The wide range of traditional practitioners is shown in Table 18.2. Traditional healers include pure herbalists applying preparations from leaves, roots, barks and other parts of plants, naturopaths and homeopaths, Muslim Mallams and priests who employ divination, and spiritualists using ritual manipulation in their healing. Unlicensed druggists and traditional birth assistants are also part of the traditional system, as well as a range of other specialized traditional practitioners (Anyinam, 1991; Obuobi and Ahmad, 1998).

**Table 18.2   Traditional Health-care Providers in Ghana**

| Practitioner | Activity |
|---|---|
| Herbalists | Persons versed in the knowledge of herbs and other natural products and their medical uses |
| Herbalists-cum-occultists | Herbalists also indulging in occultism in their dealings with patrons |
| Neo-herbalist | Herbalists with some education who operate in the urban areas |
| Priests, Muslim Mallams, spiritualists | Persons attached to a mosque, church or shrine of a minor deity who act as a medium or messenger for the deity |
| Traditional Birth Assistants | Usually old illiterate women (occasionally men) in a community with experience in conducting childbirth |
| Unsupervised druggists, medicine pedlars | Persons selling modern medicines without mediation of an orthodox practitioner |
| Other unorthodox practitioners | E.g. Bone setters who specialize in fractures, using herbs and other natural products; traditional male circumcisers (Wanzams); charlatans healing through various ways |

Frequently, when ill, Ghanaians also apply self-medication rather than consult a provider. The patient may go to a drug store or a drug pedlar and buy drugs on the advice of operators whose health-care knowledge is sometimes questionable (UNICEF, 2002). The patient may also opt for self-prescription and buy medicines on his own advice. Since the introduction of user fees in 1985, self-medication has become more popular among the entire populace as a means of economizing on consultation fees and transport costs (Asenso-Okyere et al., 1998). Though this might work in the case of endemic diseases such as malaria, the quality of the medicines is often doubtful.

Not all regions of Ghana are evenly covered by orthodox health care. Table 18.3 shows that Greater Accra and Volta Region seem best served. Many facilities are located in these regions, and also compared to their population size and area they are relatively better off. Least well covered by the orthodox system are the three northern regions. Especially the thinly populated Northern Region has the highest population per facility or public doctor, and the highest area per facility. This low supply level is also not compensated by a large number of outreach sites per facility.

## Incidence of Illness and Use of Health Care

As indicated in Table 18.4, of the respondents in a recent large-scale survey around one-quarter fell ill or suffered from injury over a fortnight period (GSS, 2000). The illness rate is highest in the rural areas of the forest zone, and lowest in the capital

Accra. About two-thirds of the ill or injured stopped their usual activities due to their health condition. Furthermore, the average length of a morbidity spell among ill adults is more than 5 days indicating that income reduction due to illness can be considerable (see also Schultz and Tansel, 1997). Remarkably, in the rural savannah area, which comprises the three northern regions with relatively poor supply of health care, prevalence of illness seems somewhat lower than average, while a greater share of the ill or injured continued their usual activities.

**Table 18.3   Health Infrastructure in Ghana by Region, 1999**

|  | Hospitals | Clinics and Health centres | Outreach site per facility | Population per facility | Area per facility (km²) | Population per public doctor[a] |
|---|---|---|---|---|---|---|
| Western | 20 | 180 | 6 | 10,000 | 143 | 25,600 |
| Central | 15 | 104 | 17 | 15,400 | 107 | 32,200 |
| Greater Accra | 13 | 249 | 21 | 11,900 | 50 | 6,200 |
| Eastern | 26 | 128 | 10 | 19,800 | 168 | 31,500 |
| Volta | 27 | 450 | 8 | 3,500 | 47 | 22,100 |
| Ashanti | 65 | 226 | 6 | 14,200 | 138 | 11,500 |
| Brong-Ahafo | 24 | 179 | 6 | 10,300 | 244 | 25,700 |
| Northern | 14 | 116 | 11 | 17,400 | 524 | 42,200 |
| Upper West | 5 | 51 | 14 | 12,900 | 105 | 35,900 |
| Upper East | 6 | 75 | 5 | 15,600 | 184 | 38,200 |
| Ghana | 215 | 1,758 | 9 | 11,000 | 142 | 15,800 |

*Note:* a)  Doctors working in the public health-care system provide some 70% of doctor's consultations. Thus, including private doctors, the population per doctor is probably some 30% lower.
*Sources:* MoH (2000); Canagarajah and Ye (2001); GSS (2001) and own calculations.

**Table 18.4   Prevalence of Illness and Injury, and Their Severity, Ghana, 1998/99, by Locality (%)**

|  | % ill or injured during last two weeks | % of ill or injured that stopped usual activities |
|---|---|---|
| Accra | 17 | 68 |
| Other urban | 26 | 62 |
| Rural coastal | 26 | 63 |
| Rural forest | 30 | 66 |
| Rural savannah | 24 | 56 |
| Ghana | 26 | 63 |

*Source:*   Computed from GSS (2000). Total sample N = 25,581.

The major cause of illness reported at the public health facilities is malaria, as shown in Table 18.5. Other infectious diseases and injuries are also major health problems in Ghana.

**Table 18.5    Incidence of Illnesses and Injuries Reported at Public Health Facilities, Ghana, 1994 (%)**

| | |
|---|---|
| Incidence of illness | 22.4 |
| — Malaria | 14.6 |
| — Upper respiratory tract infections | 3.0 |
| — Diarrhoea | 1.9 |
| — Skin diseases | 1.8 |
| — Intestinal worms | 1.1 |
| Involved in accidents | 1.7 |

*Source*: World Bank (1997)

The health-care utilization pattern is summarized in Table 18.6. The final column indicates that, when suffering from illness, 8% neither consult a provider nor buy any medicine. The figures further show that self-medication is nowadays by far the most common form of coping with illness. One out of two ill persons buys medicines without consultation. This high incidence of self-medication can partly be explained by the fact that patients might well recognize the symptoms in case of the most prevalent disease, malaria, and buy medicines without prescription (Asenso-Okyere et al., 1997). Note further that self-medication is more often chosen in rural areas.

**Table 18.6    Health-care Utilization by Ill or Injured People, Ghana, 1998/9 (%)**

| Treatment | Urban | | Rural | | All |
|---|---|---|---|---|---|
| | Stopped* | Continued | Stopped | Continued | |
| No treatment | 4.3 | 11.1 | 6.6 | 11.4 | 7.9 |
| Self-medication | 31.4 | 57.0 | 45.4 | 62.9 | 48.6 |
| Consulted health-care provider | 64.3 | 31.9 | 48.0 | 25.7 | 43.5 |
| — Doctor | 43.9 | 16.8 | 18.6 | 6.8 | 20.1 |
| — Medical assistant | 3.9 | 2.6 | 11.5 | 6.4 | 7.7 |
| — Pharmacist | 4.6 | 5.4 | 0.9 | 0.5 | 2.1 |
| — Nurse | 5.7 | 3.5 | 9.3 | 4.8 | 6.8 |
| — Midwife | 1.3 | 0.4 | 0.9 | 0.5 | 0.8 |
| — Traditional provider | 5.0 | 3.2 | 6.8 | 6.6 | 6.0 |
| | 100 | 100 | 100 | 100 | 100 |

*Note:* a)  Stopped=persons who stopped usual activities during illness or injury; Continued=persons who continued usual activities.
*Source:*  Computed from GSS (2000). N= 6621 persons ill or injured of total sample of 25,581.

Another salient feature of health-care utilization is the significant though modest role of traditional providers. Some 6% of those falling ill consult a traditional provider, as compared with 38% for orthodox providers. Traditional healers provide some 14% of all consultations, in accordance with the role commonly ascribed to them in Africa, for example 11% of consultations in rural Cameroon (Leonard, 2003).[2] Of the orthodox providers, doctors are most often consulted and provide the majority of consultations, in particular in urban areas.

The differences in behaviour between those who continue and those who stop their usual activities due to their illness are also remarkable. Consultations are much more common in the latter group, especially in urban areas where almost two-thirds consult a health-care provider (as compared with less than one-third of the persons who could continue their usual activities). In addition, those who stop their activities have a much higher propensity to consult a doctor, and again the difference is particularly significant in the urban areas. Conversely, those who are ill and continue their usual activities are more involved in self-medication and about 11% report no treatment at all for their illness, both in rural and in urban areas.

The apparent differences in health-care utilization suggest that health-care-seeking behaviour depends on the severity of the illness and the availability of providers. In urban areas, for example, three out of four consultations are with a doctor or pharmacist, rather than with other providers. As doctors and pharmacists are much more often posted in urban areas, their lower consultation rates in rural areas probably reflect their unavailability. Accordingly, medical assistants, nurses, and traditional providers are more often consulted in rural areas. Yet, as regards traditional healers, the remoteness of a doctor seems least important. Traditional care is also not uncommon in urban areas, where practically everyone lives within one hour's travel from a doctor (GSS, 1998).

**Table 18.7   Characteristics of the Place of Health-care Consultation, Ghana, 1998/9 (%)**

| Health-care provider | Public | Private | Hospital | Clinic | Other facility |
|---|---|---|---|---|---|
| — Doctor | 71 | 29 | 67 | 32 | 2 |
| — Medical assistant | 58 | 42 | 6 | 77 | 17 |
| — Pharmacist | 4 | 96 | 0 | 95 [a] | 5 |
| — Nurse | 55 | 45 | 12 | 73 | 15 |
| — Midwife | 30 | 70 | 17 | 39 | 43 |
| — Traditional practitioner | 2 | 98 | 0 | 4 | 96 |
| Average, all consultations | 53 | 47 | 35 | 45 | 20 |

*Note:* a) Pharmacy
*Source:*   Computed from GSS (2000). Total sample N= 2,877 consultations.

A little more than half of consultations take place in public health facilities, as shown in Table 18.7. In particular, the majority of doctors, medical assistants and

---

[2] Due to the activities of unlicensed druggists and medicine pedlars, this role might be somewhat underestimated and may include a part of the respondents classified here under 'self-medication'.

nurses are consulted in public facilities, though the share of the private sector is also considerable. From the last three columns of the table it appears that at the time of the survey 80% of the consultations took place in a hospital or clinic. The remaining 20% went to a variety of other facilities, most notably the maternity health centres to consult midwives and the private homes of traditional healers and their clients.

Consulting a doctor takes on average 4 hours including travel time, see Table 18.8. This is considerably longer than the average time spent for consulting other providers. Apparently Ghanaians find it worthwhile to spend more time on consulting a doctor. The average distance to a doctor is also greater than to a medical assistant or nurse. The average distances are quite large and hide a considerable dispersion. Ghanaians on average live about 16 km from a health-care facility where they can consult a doctor, but half of the population live within a 5 km radius. By the same token, the other half cannot consult a doctor within 5 km, which corresponds to a 1-hour walking distance, and one quarter even live more than 15 km from a facility where a doctor can be consulted. The situation might be even worse, because the figures include outreach facilities where doctors are only available part-time. One may further note that the rural population constitute two-thirds of the sample, while accounting for only one-third of the orthodox health-care use.

**Table 18.8  Characteristics of Private Costs of Treatment: Time and Distance, Ghana 1998/9**

|  | Consultation and travel time (hrs) | Distance to provider[a] (km) | Population within 5 km (%) | Population more than 15 km away (%) |
|---|---|---|---|---|
| Self-medication | – | 7 | 78 | 10 |
| Doctor | 4.0 | 16 | 55 | 24 |
| Medical assistant | 2.8 | 11 | 68 | 13 |
| Pharmacist | 1.3 | 26 | 44 | 38 |
| Nurse | 2.5 | 10 | 71 | 11 |
| Midwife | 2.7 | 14 | 69 | 12 |
| Traditional practitioner | 1.8 | 3 | 96 | 1 |

*Note:* a) The distance to doctors, medical assistants and nurses equals the distance to a facility where such health-care provider can be consulted, even when only part of the time.
*Source:* Computed from GSS (1998, 2000).

Within the same 5 km radius, medical assistants and nurses are more often available. Nonetheless, in rural Ghana more than a third of the population (37%) are still not well covered by the orthodox health-care system, and live more than 5 km away from a health facility where either a doctor or a medical assistant or a nurse can be consulted. In contrast, traditional health providers are present almost everywhere in Ghana, and chemical stores or drugstores are also widely available for the purchase of medicines for self-medication without prescription.

Household health expenditures are shown in Table 18.9.[3] The figures indicate that self-medication is by far the cheapest alternative and is estimated to cost less than ¢4,000.00 ($1.5). Consulting a provider cost almost ¢16,000.00 ($6.6). Visiting a doctor was the most expensive alternative, for all three cost items shown in the table, with an average cost of ¢23,000.00 ($10). Treatment by a medical assistant or midwife cost about half this amount, while consultation of a nurse or a traditional provider is the cheapest.

**Table 18.9   Characteristics of Private Costs of Treatment: Expenses (cedis), Ghana, 1998/9**

| Treatment | Consultation fee | Medicines | Travel cost | Total cost |
|---|---|---|---|---|
| Self-medication | – | 3,708 | – | 3,708 |
| Consulted health-care provider | 6,097 | 8,504 | 1,166 | 15,776 |
| — Doctor | 8,927 | 12,299 | 1,835 | 23,061 |
| — Medical assistant | 5,169 | 5,232 | 630 | 11,031 |
| — Pharmacist | 660 | 5,551 | 268 | 6,478 |
| — Nurse | 3,463 | 5,530 | 676 | 9,670 |
| — Midwife | 5,037 | 6,422 | 549 | 12,008 |
| — Traditional health consultant | 2,838 | 4,682 | 561 | 8,081 |

*Source*:   Computed from GSS (2000). Out of a total sample of 25,581 individuals, 6,167 fell ill or were injured, of whom 3,253 used self-medication and 2,914 consulted a health-care provider.

## Equitable Access

Over the past decades, a number of health indicators have shown positive trends in Ghana, despite the low-income setting and the structural adjustment policies. As a result of economic liberalization, public facilities now charge user fees for consultation and medication, while almost half of the consultations take place at private facilities. Private involvement and cost recovery have instigated competitive elements in health-care provision. In particular, while treatment costs reflect provider credentials, the variation in fees among providers of given credentials might well reflect the amount of care offered, both quantity and quality.

The Ghanaian health system continues to face major challenges. First, despite a fair overall number of facilities, a considerable part of the rural population have only limited access to health care. More than a third of the rural population lack access to a modern health-care provider within 5 km and more than two-third lack access within 5 km to a doctor, which is the preferred health-care provider when available. Clearly, for equitable access the number of health workers and facilities would need to be augmented, in particular in rural areas.

---

[3] Note that in 80% of the cases, the head of household pays for health expenses, while another household member pays in 16%. Sometimes a relative pays (3%), while finance through employers or other non-relatives is very exceptional.

Secondly, health-care costs for households are significant and show large variations. For severe illnesses or bad injuries, treatment might easily be too expensive for the poor, who often resort to self-medication. Equitable access could be improved through the certification of commonly used medicines and through public health insurance that reduces the cost of certain treatments at an affordable premium. The currently subsidized health-care facilities can be regarded as an attempt at such equitable access, but they suffer from incomplete geographical coverage, while the subsidies tend to favour relatively expensive tertiary care in the main cities.

To study these problems of equitable access, we proceed with an investigation into the question of the extent to which health-care use might be improved by means of proximity of health-care providers and through public insurance. We first specify a commonly employed multinomial model. Next we use the survey data to estimate its parameters and simulate the effect of reducing the distance to orthodox providers, and of replacing half of the private health costs by a national health insurance with an income-dependent premium.

## 3. Health-care Utilization Model

### *The Choice Model*

In health economics it is common to employ multinomial models to explain the utilization of curative health care (see, for example, the survey by Jones, 2000). Consider a Ghanaian suffering from illness or injury. Treatments are indexed j and we let $j = 1$ refer to non-treatment or self-medication, while $j = 2, 3, 4$ refer to treatment by a doctor or pharmacist, by a medical assistant or nurse or midwife, and by a traditional health practitioner, respectively. Treatments include both the consultation (if any) and the medication (if any).

The well-being of a person treated by provider j is denoted by $U_j$ and presumably depends on his consumption $C_j$ of non-health goods and services, on his health $H_j$, and on the proximity $a_j$ to the particular health-care provider.[4] This relation is represented by a utility function u.

$$U_j = u(C_j, H_j; a_j) \qquad (1)$$

Suppose further that the person's health $H_j$ depends on the treatment $c_j$ received from provider j and on individual characteristics z that are independent of the type of treatment (e.g. gender, age, education, type of illness, urban-rural locality).

$$H_j = h(c_j; z) \qquad (2)$$

Now let m be the person's total income, which defines his net income $m_j$ available for

---

[4] Typically, proximity is inversely related to distance and travel time to the provider and accounts for the time savings of travelling to and from the place of consultation and the positive effects of the timeliness of a treatment.

non-health consumption $C_j$ after payment of the cost $e_j = p_j c_j$ of treatment j.

$$m_j = m - e_j \tag{3}$$

Conditional on the choice for health care j and provided that he can afford the chosen treatment ($m_j > 0$), the demand for other goods and services $C_j$ derives from the maximization of utility $u(C_j, H_j; a_j)$ subject to the budget $P C_j = m_j$, where P is the price of non-health consumption. By implication, non-health consumption $C_j$ when treatment j is chosen will equal

$$C_j = m_j / P = (m - e_j) / P \tag{4}$$

Accordingly, the equation $V_j(P, m_j, H_j; a_j) = u(m_j / P, H_j; a_j)$ defines the conditional indirect utility functions $V_j$, and ill persons will choose the treatment with the highest value for $V_j$.

$$\textit{maximize} \ \{V_1, V_2, V_3, V_4\} \tag{5}$$

By their discrete choice nature, health-care demand models like Equation (5) can only identify the relative propensities of choosing one of the alternatives. Consequently, a normalization rule is needed. We follow common practice and use self-medication j = 1 for this purpose.

## Specification
To apply the multinominal model, we employ simple semi-logarithmic forms for the utility and the health production function of Equations (1) and (2).

$$U_j = \beta_C \, log(1 + C_j) + H_j + \beta_A \, a_j \tag{6.1}$$

$$H_j = \beta_{0j} + \beta_H \, log(1 + c_j) + \beta_j \, z \tag{6.2}$$

with normalization $\beta_{01} = \beta_1 = 0$.

The forms are linear in the parameters, which are presumably expected to be non-negative, except for the treatment-specific effects $\beta_j$ that represent health differentials due to individual characteristics z. Substituting for optimal non-health consumption $C_j$, see Equation (4), and adding a disturbance term $e_j$, specification (6) leads to the following indirect utilities:

$$V_j = \beta_{0j} + \beta_C \, log[1 + (m - e_j) / P] + \beta_H \, log(1 + c_j) + \beta_A \, a_j + \beta_j \, z + \varepsilon_j \tag{7}$$

Adding the subscript i for individuals where appropriate, this equation reads

$$V_{ij} = m_{ij} + \varepsilon_{ij} \tag{8}$$

where $m_{ij}$ is the expected utility of client i when choosing alternative j

$$\mu_{ij} = \beta_{0j} + \beta_C \, log[1 + (m_i - e_{ij}) / P] + \beta_H \, log(1 + c_{ij}) + \beta_A \, a_{ij} + \beta_j \, z_i$$

Accordingly, the propensity for a sick person i to choose the treatment k is described through the probability $\Pi_{ik}$ that the utility $V_{ik}$ exceeds the utility $V_{ij}$ of any of the alternative treatments j. Clearly, this probability depends on the distributional assumptions of the disturbance $\varepsilon_{ij}$. For example, when $\varepsilon_{ij}$ are identically and independently distributed according to the Weibull extreme value distribution,[5] the difference between two disturbance terms will be logistically distributed, leading to the popular easily computed multinomial logit model.

$$\Pi_{ik} = exp[\mu_{ik}] / \Sigma_j \, exp[\mu_{ij}] \tag{9}$$

In empirical health-care literature this is by far the most frequently estimated specification (see Jones, 2000). Yet, the logit model implies restrictions on the changes in utilization patterns $P_{ij}$ caused by changes in the expected indirect utilities $m_{ij}$ from various treatments. In particular, the logit model assumes that all alternatives are equally uncertain and equally affected by unobserved heterogeneity (homoskedastic disturbances), and that the relative preference for any couple of alternatives is independent of the characteristics of the remaining treatments (uncorrelated disturbances). The latter implies that a change of any treatment will only affect the preference for the particular treatment, leaving unaltered the relative importance of the unchanged alternatives. By the same token, when a new treatment becomes available, the logit model assumes that the utilization of all alternatives is decreased in a proportional manner.

To allow for a more flexible response, alternative probability distributions have been proposed that allow for heteroskedastic disturbances, correlated disturbances, or disturbances that are both heteroskedastic and correlated. The latter includes the multinomial probit model, which is considered the most flexible specification.[6] According to the probit specification, the probability that a person chooses the treatment k equals

$$\Pi_{ik} = \int_{A_{ik}} f(\varepsilon, \Sigma) \, d\varepsilon \tag{10}$$

where $A_{ik}$ is the area where alternative k yields highest utility

$$A_{ik} = \{\varepsilon \mid [\varepsilon_{ij} - \varepsilon_{ik}] < [\mu_{ik} - \mu_{ij}] \text{ for all } j\}$$

---

[5] The Weibull distribution derives from the cumulative density function $F(\varepsilon_{ij}) = exp[exp(-\varepsilon_{ij})]$.
[6] Other distributional assumptions that generalize the logit model include the nested logit model that allows for correlated disturbances between groups of alternatives, and the generalized logit model with heteroskedastic variances that follow from the cumulative density $F(\varepsilon_{ij}) = exp[exp(-\varepsilon_{ji}/\lambda_{\varphi})]$. For a further discussion on these and other alternatives, see Powers and Xie (2000).

and f is the density of the multivariate Normal distribution with zero mean and (co-) variances $\Sigma$.

Clearly, the estimation of probit model (10) is computationally much more demanding than the estimation of logit model (9). The required multidimensional integration has hampered application, and numerical algorithms for fast and adequate approximations of probabilities (10) have only recently been developed and tested (Geweke et al., 1994; Hajivassiliou et al., 1996; Bolduc et al., 1996; Powers and Xie, 2000). Here we estimate discrete choice model (8) under the two alternative distributional assumptions (9) and (10), the multinomial logit and probit model, respectively. But, first, we turn to a commonly encountered data issue.

## Imputed Cost of Treatments not Chosen

Model estimation requires information on health expenses $e_{ij}$ and health consumption $c_{ij}$ for all individuals i and for all possible treatments j. In most cases, and the *Ghana Living Standards Survey* is no exception, such information is restricted to the chosen alternatives, while the cost of treatments not chosen must be imputed. It is common practice to compute these imputations either directly from data on official fees for particular providers (Mwabu et al., 1993) or indirectly from the estimation of hedonic price equations based on the characteristics of the sub-sample of ill persons who were treated by a particular provider (Lavy and Germain, 1994; Bolduc et al., 1996). These approaches assume that heterogeneity of treatment cost stems primarily from heterogeneity of patient characteristics (e.g. age, gender, illness) and provider credentials (e.g. doctor, nurse). Accordingly, for the chosen alternatives, one would expect that the regression of actual health expenses on official fees and on instrumented treatment cost would give a good fit. But this is generally not the case. Instrumented treatment cost generally leaves unexplained the lion's share of the variation in the actual cost (Propper, 2000).

Indeed, we find a very low fit of actual health expenses on instrumented cost ($R^2 = 0.1$). This may negatively affect the precision of parameter estimates (Bound et al., 1995). Moreover, for the health market in Ghana, it might well be that similar patients pay different prices at similar providers for the reason that those who pay more are probably the ones who receive more and better care, i.e. have shorter waiting time, longer consultations, a more experienced practitioner and better medicines. This importance of quality as an explanatory variable is increasingly recognized (Lavy et al., 1996; Collier et al., 2002; Leonard et al., 2002).

Given the low fit of actual on instrumented prices in our sample, and given that observed health-care expenses in Ghana might partly reflect competitive market conditions, we propose an alternative approach to impute the cost of treatments not chosen. Imputation is done by multiplication of the relative cost of alternative treatments (i.e. the average cost of the provider divided by the average cost of all providers: trained providers offer more or better treatment) and the intensity of the chosen treatment (i.e. the patient's expense divided by the average expense of patients choosing the same provider: patients paying more get more or better treatment).

Following the notation above, we let $e_{ik}$ be the health expenses of client i who actually seeks treatment k, and $e_{ij}$ be the imputed expenses if the client had sought the alternative j, j ≠ k. Furthermore, let $p_k$ and $p_j$ denote the average health expenses of all persons who chose treatment k and j, respectively, and, finally, let p denote the average health expenses of the entire sample. Then, $e_{ik} / p_k$ could be interpreted as patient i's use intensity with respect to the observed treatment k and which will be assumed to be representative of i's use intensity if the patient had sought one of the other treatments j. Accordingly, the amount $e_{ij} = (e_{ik} / p_k) p_j$ will be used to estimate the imputed health-care expense of patient i, if he had chosen an alternative treatment j, j ≠ k. Next, to estimate the imputed amount $c_{ij}$ of health-care consumption, we assume that the overall average health expense p reflects the scarcity of health care. The diversity of health-care providers and the competitive elements of the health-care provision system in Ghana suggest that price differences among providers are probably indicative of service quantity and quality. Under these assumptions, the imputed consumption $c_{ij}$ of patient i, if he had chosen an alternative treatment j, j ≠ k is defined as follows.

$$c_{ij} = (e_{ik} / p_k) (p_j / p) \tag{11}$$

This imputation preserves the variation in observed expenditures $e_{ik}$ and avoids problems related to the low fit of hedonic price equations. Moreover, the assumptions that use intensities are similar across treatments and that health-care markets are fairly well integrated would seem reasonable in the Ghanaian context.

## 4. Data, Estimation and Simulation Results

### Ghana Living Standards Survey

This study is based on data from the recent 1998–9 round of the *Ghana Living Standards Survey* (GLSS), a series of large-scale representative household surveys conducted by the Ghana Statistical Service (GSS, 2000). The survey provides detailed data on various dimensions of living standards in various parts of the population, at individual, household and community level. It consists of both a household questionnaire and a community questionnaire, and we combine data from both of these.

### Description of Variables

Equation (8) defines the discrete choice model to be estimated. As already mentioned, we distinguish four treatments, starting from non-treatment or self-medication j = 1, while j = 2, 3, 4 refers to treatment by a doctor or pharmacist, by a medical assistant or nurse or midwife, and by a traditional practitioner, respectively. The explanatory variables include income $m_i$, provider-specific costs of treatment $c_{ij}$ and provider characteristics $a_{ij}$ reflecting the effort required for obtaining the treatment, and, finally, client characteristics $z_i$ that do not vary with the type of treatment. Table 18.10 gives a brief description and summary statistics of the data.

For income $m_i$ we take the total bi-weekly expenditure per adult equivalent, expressed in January 1999 Accra prices. We refer to GSS (2000) for the methodology used to estimate the various components of household expenditure. The average indicates that those reported ill during the GLSS-4 have an income of some ¢3,740.00 per adult equivalent per day, which is about $1.6 and only slightly more than $1 per capita per day (using the average equivalence scale of 0.78 and the exchange rate of 2,400 from GSS). The average income of the ill is close to the average of the entire GLSS-4 sample and reflects the generally low standard of living in Ghana.

**Table 18.10   Description and Summary Statistics of Variables**

| Variable | Description | Mean | Standard deviation |
|---|---|---|---|
| Response profile[a] | | | |
| j=1 | self-medication | 0.54 | |
| j=2 | doctor | 0.24 | |
| j=3 | medical assistant/nurse | 0.15 | |
| j=4 | traditional | 0.07 | |
| Explanatory variables | | | |
| mi | expenditure per adult equivalent (1000 cedis) | 52.38 | 46.96 |
| ei1 | (imputed) health expenses: self-medication | 3.69 | 5.83 |
| ei2 | (imputed) health expenses: doctor | 17.26 | 18.12 |
| ei3 | (imputed) health expenses: medical assistant/nurse | 9.52 | 12.15 |
| ei4 | (imputed) health expenses: traditional | 7.64 | 10.25 |
| di1 | distance to facility: self-medication | 5.53 | 15.02 |
| di2 | distance to facility: doctor | 14.82 | 20.57 |
| di3 | distance to facility: medical assistant/nurse | 5.34 | 12.91 |
| di4 | distance to facility: traditional | 1.46 | 10.29 |
| ti1 | time to facility: self-medication | 0.55 | 1.04 |
| ti2 | time to facility: doctor | 1.31 | 1.71 |
| ti3 | time to facility: medical assistant/nurse | 0.65 | 1.21 |
| ti4 | time to facility: traditional | 0.14 | 0.55 |
| age | age in years | 33.48 | 20.88 |
| female | gender (=1 if female) | 0.58 | 0.49 |
| sch yrs | years of schooling | 4.38 | 3.93 |
| days ill | days suffered | 6.01 | 3.92 |
| stopped | had to stop activity | 0.64 | 0.48 |
| commun. | included in rural community questionnaire | 0.67 | 0.47 |

*Note:* a)   This response profile is slightly different from the corresponding profile in Table 18.6 due to the focus on persons aged 6 and over.

*Source*:   Computed from GSS (2000) for the 4,800 persons aged 6 and over reported ill during past two weeks.

Provider- and client-specific treatment cost $c_{ij}$ is imputed from Equation (11) as the product of the observed use intensity ($e_{ik} / p_k$) and the observed relative prices ($p_j / p$) of the alternatives. Expenditures $e_{ij}$ have already been discussed in Table 18.9 and comprise amounts paid for consultation, medication, and transport.

As regards access to providers we use the information on distance and time collected in the rural communities.[7] The average distance and the average time to reach the various providers are not particularly high, but note the standard deviations of Table 18.10, which reflect large differentials. Access is generally good in urban areas, but the proximity of health-care providers in rural areas is much less. For example, more than half of the rural population live outside the 15 km radius of a doctor and have to travel more than 3 hours for a consultation. We use the distance and time data to construct two variables $a_{ij} = (a^1_{ij}, a^2_{ij})$. To reflect the idea that the role of distance and time is particularly significant when a provider in neither very close nor very remote, the distance variable is transformed into a logistic curve. The proximity indicator ranges between zero and one and was specified as $a^1_{ij} = 1/[1+exp(\beta * d_{ij} - \alpha)]$. For example, letting a = 3 and b = 0.2, the indicator takes the value 0.95 when the particular provider is immediately available, and values 0.5 and 0.05 when the distance is 15 and 30 kilometres, respectively. Indeed, compared with the specification with proximity decreasing linearly with distance (i.e., $a^1_{ij} = -d_{ij}$), the logistic transformation gave better results. The second access variable was defined as the reported speed to reach the provider, i.e., $a^2_{ij} = d_{ij} / t_{ij}$. Those who have to travel to a provider report an average speed near 15 km per hour with considerable variation.

Finally, as regards client characteristics $z_i$ that do not vary over treatments, we include age, gender, years of education, number of days ill, necessity to stop usual activity and locality as explanatory variables. The inclusion of these variables could pick up unobserved heterogeneity due to the type of health problem, the reason for non-consultation, and the quality of the facility (availability of drugs, staffing, community population per provider). We thus control for various circumstances when estimating the price and income effects (as reflected in the coefficients $\beta_c$ for $[m_i - e_{ij}]/P$ and $\beta_c$ for $c_{ij}$) and the access effect (as reflected in the coefficients $\beta_d$ for $a_{ij}$).

## Results

Parameter estimates of discrete choice model (8) under the two alternative distributional assumptions (9) and (10) are listed in the Appendix as Table 18A.1. In terms of sign and significance, the results are generally satisfactory, both in the more restrictive logit model (9) and in the computationally demanding probit model (10)[8]. Controlling

---

[7] By type of provider and by type of facility, the chief of the community and other prominent members were asked: 'Is there a . . . in this community?' And if the answer was negative: 'How far from here is the nearest . . .' and 'How long does it take to get there?' The distance to a provider is set equal to the minimal distance to any facility where they have been consulted. This distance is sometimes smaller than the distance to a resident provider, since it is not unusual to consult a non-resident travelling provider at a local facility.

[8] Whereas it takes only seconds to estimate the multinomial logit model, estimation of the probit model requires 20 to 40 minutes. Also, probit estimates could only be obtained with restrictions on the covariance matrix and disturbances were assumed to be either homoskedastic or uncorrelated.

for client characteristics, both the proximity to providers and the treatment cost appear to have a notable impact on health-care utilization. Moreover, the effects of client characteristics have a comprehensible interpretation.

For example, the estimated age effects indicate that the elderly in Ghana tend to favour self-medication rather than consult a medical assistant or nurse, while women more often than men choose self-medication rather than consult traditional practitioners. On the other hand, those who are educated have a clear preference for orthodox health care, and seem indifferent between traditional practitioners and self-medication. The strong effect of schooling on choosing a doctor, medical assistant or nurse is consistent with the idea that education allows people to make better use of modern health care (Mwabu et al., 1993; Bolduc et al., 1996). The coefficients of the number of days ill and the halting of usual activities indicate that those severely ill tend to turn away from self-medication. Finally, the locality effect suggests that unobserved heterogeneity of the demand for doctors' consultations is correlated with urban localities, while the logit model indicates that there is a similar pattern in rural areas as regards the preference for using medical assistants and nurses. The latter is, however, not confirmed by the probit estimates.

The alternative specifications have in general the same qualitative implications, though the magnitude of the coefficients differs, and, occasionally, an effect that is significant in one specification is not so in the other. Whether or not these differences dominate the quantitative consequences of reforms in the health sector will become apparent when considering utilization patterns under alternative policies, to which we now turn. Considering options for equal access, we look at the effects of removing some of the apparent disparities. In particular, we present the results of three simulations that look at the impact of more proximity in rural areas (expanding the network of facilities), the impact of more insurance (financed through a flat rate tax), and a combination of these two, respectively. Simulation results are summarized in Table 18.11.

In the first simulation 'Proximity' the distance from orthodox providers in the rural areas is reduced so that everyone can consult a medical assistant or a nurse within a distance of 5 km, while a doctor is assumed to be available within 15 km. The second simulation 'Insurance' deals with the introduction of a national health insurance with an income-dependent premium. Here part of the private cost of the orthodox health care is replaced by a subsidy, financed from a flat rate tax.[9] The simulation presumes that half of the private cost reported in the GLSS 4 is brought under an insurance scheme, and a premium of 1.6% on expenditure would be necessary to finance that scheme. Finally, the third simulation 'Combined' combines the effects of reducing the distance in rural areas and insuring half of the private cost of treatment by orthodox providers.

---

[9] Letting $\theta_j$ be the subsidy rate on health-care expenditure $e_{ij}$ at the j-th provider, i.e., $e_{ij} = p (1 - \theta_j) c_{ij}$, the flat rate tax rate can be computed as $\tau = \Pi \Sigma_i \Sigma_j \Pi_j \theta_j e_{ij} / \Sigma_i m_i$, where $\Pi$ is the overall probability of falling ill and $\Pi_j$ is the average probability of an ill person choosing the j-th provider. Letting $\theta_2 = \theta_3 = 0.5$ and using the sample probabilities gives $\tau = 0.014$. However, this rate does not account for the induced increased use of orthodox care. Since this increase is some 5–15%, we took $\tau = 0.016$.

**Table 18.11    Impact of Proximity and Insurance on Health-care Utilization Patterns in Ghana**

|                                     | self-medication /no treatment | doctor | nurse medical assistant | traditional provider |
|-------------------------------------|-------------------------------|--------|-------------------------|----------------------|
| Sample probabilities                | 0.545                         | 0.240  | 0.147                   | 0.068                |
| Simulated probabilities             |                               |        |                         |                      |
| Logit model                         |                               |        |                         |                      |
| *Proximity*                         | 0.531                         | 0.250  | 0.153                   | 0.065                |
| *Insurance*                         | 0.511                         | 0.277  | 0.150                   | 0.062                |
| *Combined*                          | 0.496                         | 0.288  | 0.157                   | 0.060                |
| Correlated probit model[a]          |                               |        |                         |                      |
| *Proximity*                         | 0.534                         | 0.251  | 0.149                   | 0.067                |
| *Insurance*                         | 0.523                         | 0.273  | 0.138                   | 0.066                |
| *Combined*                          | 0.512                         | 0.284  | 0.140                   | 0.064                |
| Heteroskedastic probit model[a]     |                               |        |                         |                      |
| *Proximity*                         | 0.531                         | 0.250  | 0.152                   | 0.067                |
| *Insurance*                         | 0.517                         | 0.274  | 0.142                   | 0.066                |
| *Combined*                          | 0.504                         | 0.284  | 0.146                   | 0.066                |

*Note:* a) See Table 18A.1 for estimated variances and covariances of the probit specifications.

Simulation outcomes appear to be rather insensitive to the distributional assumptions of the logit and probit specifications. According to the 'Proximity' simulation, improved access to orthodox health care in rural areas increases the consultation of doctors, medical assistants and nurses by a modest 3–4%. Clearly, this increase is entirely located in rural areas, where the treatment by doctors, medical assistants and nurses increases by more than 10%. The 'Insurance' simulation indicates that a national health insurance covering half the current private expenses could increase the demand for doctors by some 15%, whereas there is little effect on the consultation of medical assistants and nurses. In combination, improved access and limited insurance lead to a simulated increase of 10–15% in total demand for orthodox health care, which is almost entirely due to decreased self-medication in favour of a 20% increase in the use of doctors. The simulations further indicate that the choice of traditional practitioners might not be responsive to changes in the access to orthodox health care.

## 5.    Conclusion

### *Overview of the System*
Self-medication appears to be the predominant form of curative health care in Ghana and is used by about 50% of those falling ill in the GLSS 4 sample. Also, at 8% and 6%, respectively, no treatment or the consultation of traditional practitioners occurred regularly. The consultation of doctors, nurses and medical assistants was limited to

less than 40%, i.e., 22%, 8% and 7%, respectively. This utilization pattern varies considerably over population groups.

The overview of the health-care system illustrated the need for more providers in rural areas, in particular for doctors, who are already the preferred providers in urban areas. The population per doctor in the public sector averages around 16,000, a figure that reduces to some 11,000 when private doctors are included. The location of doctors at public facilities shows a clear urban bias, and the location of private doctors is most likely to show a similar bias. Health staff are generally reluctant to be posted to more remote, thinly populated and poor areas (Agyepong, 1999; Hammera and Jack, 2002). The shortage of doctors is thus felt in the rural areas in particular, which is confirmed by the large distance to a doctor found in the survey.

Another feature of the health system that stands out is the significance of the private contributions. The level and variation of the cost of treatment suggest that the poor, when ill, cannot afford the necessary care. It has therefore been suggested that the financing of health care should be reformed and a national insurance scheme introduced (Asenso-Okyere, 1995; GoG, 2003).

### *Simulations*

To investigate such issues we presented a health-care choice model and estimated its parameters with recent data from Ghana (GSS, 2000). In the spirit of most previous applications, we first estimated the multinomial logit version of the model (Mwabu et al., 1993; Asenso-Okyere et al., 1998; Propper, 2000; Jones, 2000). To relax the assumption that utilization patterns are homoskedastic and uncorrelated, we also estimated a probit version (Bolduc et al., 1996).

The direct imputation of the cost of treatments not chosen was a distinct feature of our approach. We based the imputation on the use intensity of the chosen treatment and the relative cost of alternative treatments. In this way the full variation in the health expenditures observed could be preserved, and problems related to the low fit of hedonic price equations could be avoided (Gertler et al., 1987; Bound et al., 1995; Propper, 2000). Moreover, the approach reflected the fact that health-care markets in Ghana have become fairly competitive, with prices that are indicative of the quantity and quality of the service provided.

Estimation gave satisfactory results in terms of the sign and significance of the effects, both in the (more restrictive) logit and in the (computationally demanding) probit specifications. Probit estimates differed considerably from logit ones, though the results from the simulations were similar. In both models, the simulated effects of improving the proximity to orthodox health care in rural areas (medical assistants and nurses within 5 km; doctors within 15 km) or insuring half of the private cost (financed from a flat-rate tax) led to modest increases in the use of orthodox care. When combined, the utilization of orthodox health care increased by 10–15%, almost entirely due to decreased self-medication in favour of an 18% increase in doctors' consultations.

Thus, the results corroborate that the proximity to providers and the cost of treatment have a significant impact on health-care utilization in Ghana. The equitable-access policies discussed could thus improve health-care use. By the same token, the proximity of providers has been found to enhance sufficient use of ante-natal care (Overbosch et al., 2003). Equitable access could further involve coverage of priority treatments (Ministry of Health 2000; World Bank, 1997), while charges for non-priority treatments could be increased.

Nonetheless, the results suggest that relatively cheap self-medication remains the predominant type of health care. The widespread use of modern care would therefore require more than just equitable access. At the current stage of development, the provision of timely and affordable health care for all Ghanaians remains a formidable challenge. One option would be to put more emphasis on the quality of self-medication, say through certification and by the training of chemical sellers, traditional healers, unsupervised druggists and medicine pedlars. Training could focus on a limited number of commonly used drugs commonly sold without prescription.

## *Role of Private Contributions*

A comparison at the national level of official figures (MoH, 1999, 2000) and figures derived from the GLSS (GSS, 2000) pointed to certain ambiguities as regards the functioning and financing of health care. Survey figures suggest markedly higher levels of health-care utilization and private financing. Almost 10% of the persons in the survey had consulted an orthodox provider during the previous two weeks, of whom some 60% went to a public (or quasi-public) facility, with some 10 % of them admitted overnight. If these figures were representative of the population at large, they would imply 2.5 outpatient visits per year per person, or 1.5 consultations at public facilities — much higher than the average reported by the Ministry of Health (0.4 visits; 6.6 million outpatient visits in 1998). A similar discrepancy concerns hospital admissions, which in the survey would be almost six times higher than the official figure (3% of the population; 482,000 hospital admissions in 1998).[10] Outpatient visits are targeted to increase to 1 per person, while hospital admissions are targeted to rise to 5%. The GLSS data suggest that these targets may have been met long ago. Nonetheless, considering the lack of facilities in rural areas and the large private cost in the absence of insurance, it can be argued that current health-care use is still below efficient levels.

Analysis of the GLSS further indicated that the official figures might underestimate the role of private expenses and that an evaluation of the health-care system could benefit from improved accounting. Health care is highly subsidized in Ghana. According to the Ministry of Health, the payments by households ('Internally Generated Funds') amounted to only 33 billion cedis or 13% of the total recurrent costs in 1998. Estimates on the basis of the GLSS suggest that the private contributions are much more significant. We find that households spent on average ¢2,750.00 per person for health care in a fortnight period, corresponding to an estimated ¢72,000.00 cedis per person per year, the equivalent of almost $30, of which about one-seventh concerns consultation fees at public facilities. Accordingly, households would have

---

[10] Note, however, that here the estimate might be imprecise, due to the small sample size (180 hospital admissions in a sample of over 26,000 persons).

paid some 200 billion cedis for consultations at public facilities. Even when corrected for inflation, for regional variation of cost, and for local administration cost, this amount far exceeds the official figure. A similar discrepancy has been observed by Nyonator and Kutzin (1999) for the Volta Region and by Canagarjah and Ye (2002) for the country as a whole. The former study finds that locally administered fees barely apply the official exemptions and are much higher than the official fees which were nominally fixed in 1985. The latter study contains the results of the Ghana Public Expenditure Survey, which estimates that 60% rather than 13% of treatment costs is paid for by patients. Our findings are in line with these studies and indicate that the private contributions to the performance of the health sector in Ghana might be much more significant than the official figures indicate.

414 Poverty, Education & Health

## References

Anyinam, C. (1991) 'Modern and Traditional Health Care Systems in Ghana', in R. Akhtar (ed.), *Health Care Patterns and Planning in Developing Countries*. New York: Greenwood Press.

Agyepong, I. A. (1999) 'Reforming Health Service Delivery at District Level in Ghana: The Perspective of a District Medical Officer', *Health Policy and Planning*, Vol. 14: 59–69.

Asenso-Okyere, W. K. (1995) 'Financing Health Care in Ghana'. *World Health Forum*, Vol. 16: 86–91.

Asenso-Okyere, W. K., Osei-Akoto, I. and Adukonu, A. (1998) 'Cost Recovery in Ghana: Are There Any Changes in Health Care Seeking Behaviour?' *Health Policy and Planning*, Vol. 13: 181–8.

Asenso-Okyere, W. K., Dzator, J. and Osei-Akoto, I. (1997) 'The Behaviour Towards Malaria Care: A Nultinomial Logit Approach'. *Social Indicators Research*, Vol. 39: 167–86.

Bolduc, D., Lacroix, G. and Muller, C. (1996) 'The Choice of Medical Providers in Rural Bénin: A Comparison of Discrete Choice Models'. *Journal of Health Economics*, Vol. 15: 477–98.

Bound, J., Jaeger, D. A. and Baker, R. M. (1995) 'Problems with Instrumental Variables Estimation when the Correlation between the Instruments and the Endogenous Explanatory Variable Is Weak'. *Journal of the American Statistical Association*, Vol. 90: 443–50.

Canagarajah, S. and Ye, X. (2001) *Public Health and Education Spending in Ghana 1992–98: Issues of Equity and Efficiency*. Washington, DC: World Bank.

Canagarajah, S. and Ye, X. (2002) *Ghana: Tracking Public Resource Flows in Schools and Clinics*. Washington, DC: World Bank.

Collier, P., Dercon, S. and Mackinnon, J. (2002) 'Density versus Quality in Health Care Provision: Using Household Data to Make Budgetary Choices in Ethiopia', *World Bank Economic Review*, Vol. 16: 425–48.

Culyer, A. J. and Newhouse, J. P. (eds) (2000) *Handbook of Health Economics, Vol. 1A and 1B*. Amsterdam: North-Holland.

Gertler, P., Locay, L. and Sanderson, W. (1987) 'Are User Fees Regressive? The Welfare Implications of Health Care Financing Proposals in Peru', *Journal of Econometrics*, Vol. 36: 67–88.

Geweke, J., Keane, M. and Runkle, D. (1994) 'Alternative Computational Approaches to Inference in the Multinomial Probit Model'. *Review of Economics and Statistics*, Vol. 76, 609–32.

Government of Ghana (2003) *Ghana Poverty Reduction Strategy: An Agenda for Growth and Prosperity*. Accra: Government of the Republic of Ghana.

GSS (1998) *CWIQ Core Welfare Indicators Questionnaire Survey, 1997*. Accra: Ghana Statistical Service.

GSS (2000) *Ghana Living Standards Survey: Report on the Fourth Round, April 1998–March 1999*. Accra: Ghana Statistical Service.

GSS (2001) *2000 Population and Housing Census*. Accra: Ghana Statistical Service.

GSS and MI (1999) *Ghana Demographic and Health Survey 1998*. Accra: Ghana Statistical Service; Calverton, MD: Macro International Inc.

Hajivassiliou, V., McFadden, D. and Ruud, P. (1996) 'Simulation of Multivariate Normal Rectangle Probabilities and Their Derivatives: Theoretical and Computational Results', *Journal of Econometrics*, Vol. 72: 85–134.

Hammera, J. and Jack, W. (2002) 'Designing Incentives for Rural Health Care Providers in Developing Countries', *Journal of Development Economics*, Vol. 69: 297–303.

Jones, A. M. (2000) 'Health Econometrics', in Culyer and Newhouse.

Lavy, V. and Germain, J-M. (1994) *Quality and Cost in Health Care Choice in Developing Countries*. LSMS Working Paper 105. Washington, DC: World Bank.

Lavy, V., Strauss, J., Thomas, D. and de Vreyer, P. (1996) 'Quality of Health Care, Survival and Health Outcomes in Ghana', *Journal of Health Economics*, Vol. 15: 333–57.

Leonard, K. L. (2003) 'African Traditional Healers and Outcome-contingent Contracts in Health Care', *Journal of Development Economics*, Vol. 71: 1–22.

Leonard, K. L., Mliga, G. R. and Mariam, D. H. (2002) 'Bypassing Health Centres in Tanzania: Revealed Preferences for Quality', *Journal of African Economies*, Vol. 11: 441–71.

Ministry of Health (1999) *Health Sector Five-Year Program of Work 1997–2001, 1998 Review*. Accra: Ministry of Health.

MoH (2000) *Medium Term Health Strategy Towards Vision 2020*. Accra: Ministry of Health.

Mwabu, G., Ainsworth, M. and Nyamete, A. (1993) 'Quality of Medical Care and Choice of Medical Treatment in Kenya: An Empirical Analysis', *Journal of Human Resources,* Vol. 28: 838–62.

Nsowah-Nuamah, N. N. N., Appiah-Kubi, K., Asante, F., Asenso-Okyere, K. and Afari, E. (2000) *Situation of Health and Nutrition in Ghana.* Legon: Institute of Statistical, Social and Economic Research, University of Ghana.

Nyonator, F. and Kutzin, J. (1999) 'Health for Some? The Effects of User Fees in the Volta Region of Ghana', *Health Policy and Planning,* Vol. 14: 329–41.

Obuobi, A. A. D. and Ahmad, O. B. (1998) *Health Delivery and Private Sector Participation.* New York: United Nations Development Programme.

Ofori-Adjei, D. (1990) *Baseline Survey for the Implementation of the Bamako Initiative in Ghana.* Bamako Initiative Technical Report, Geneva: UNICEF.

Overbosch, G. B., Nsowah-Nuamah, N. N. N., van den Boom, G. J. M. and Damnyag, L. (2003) 'Determinants of Antenatal Care Use in Ghana', *Journal of African Economies,* Vol. 12, No. 4.

Powers, D. A. and Xie, Y. (2000) *Statistical Methods for Categorical Data Analysis.* San Diego, CA: Academic Press.

Propper, C. (2000) 'The Demand for Private Health Care in the UK', *Journal of Health Economics,* Vol. 19: 855–70.

Schultz, T. P. and Tansel, A. (1997) 'Wage and Labor Supply Effects of Illness in Côte d'Ivoire and Ghana: Instrumental Variable Estimates for Days Disabled', *Journal of Development Economics,* Vol. 53: 51–86.

UNICEF (2002) *The State of the World's Children 2002.* Geneva: UNICEF.

World Bank (1997) *Republic of Ghana Health Sector Support Program.* Staff Appraisal Report No. 16467-GH. Washington, DC: World Bank.

World Bank (2001) *World Development Indicators 2001.* Washington, DC: World Bank.

**Appendix Table 18A.1**    **Parameter Estimates of the Health-care Utilization Model, Equation (8), Ghana 1998/9 (4800 ill persons aged 6 and above; multinomial logit and probit specifications; t-value in parentheses)**

| | Logit Uncorrelated, homoskedastic | | Probit Correlated | | Probit Heteroskedastic | |
|---|---|---|---|---|---|---|
| **Income-price effects $\beta_C$ and $\beta_H$** | | | | | | |
| Non-health consumption | 0.378 | (9.53) | 0.197 | (6.34) | 0.200 | (5.98) |
| Health consumption | 0.555 | (4.33) | 0.138 | (1.56) | 0.263 | (2.89) |
| **Proximity effects $\beta_A$** | | | | | | |
| Distance | 0.805 | (6.96) | 0.497 | (5.92) | 0.472 | (5.61) |
| Speed | 1.099 | (5.17) | 0.656 | (4.46) | 0.629 | (4.47) |
| **Provider-specific constant $\beta_{0j}$** (j=2=Doctor; j=3=Medical assistant/Nurse; j=4=Traditional) | | | | | | |
| cst2 | −2.188 | (14.21) | −1.448 | (12.37) | −1.321 | (8.73) |
| cst3 | −2.640 | (15.45) | −1.597 | (12.86) | −1.185 | (12.60) |
| cst4 | −3.141 | (14.03) | −2.491 | (13.23) | −8.402 | (0.92) |
| **Provider-specific effect of individual characteristics $\beta_j$** | | | | | | |
| age2 (Age) | 0.159 | (0.82) | −0.259 | (1.80) | −0.152 | (1.25) |
| age3 | −0.847 | (3.77) | −0.501 | (3.34) | −0.360 | (3.24) |
| age4 (Female) | 0.114 | (1.43) | 0.103 | (1.77) | 0.063 | (1.25) |
| sex3 | 0.083 | (0.93) | 0.085 | (1.35) | 0.047 | (1.07) |
| sex4 | −0.337 | (2.75) | −0.226 | (2.58) | −0.845 | (0.83) |
| edu2 (Years of schooling) | 0.070 | (6.84) | 0.057 | (7.48) | 0.046 | (6.48) |
| edu3 | 0.044 | (3.71) | 0.045 | (5.67) | 0.031 | (5.36) |
| edu4 | 0.001 | (0.05) | −0.003 | (0.24) | −0.039 | (0.49) |
| ill2 (Days ill) | 0.123 | (11.90) | 0.086 | (10.87) | 0.079 | (9.32) |
| ill3 | 0.055 | (4.62) | 0.058 | (6.29) | 0.044 | (7.18) |
| ill4 | 0.118 | (8.10) | 0.075 | (7.29) | 0.206 | (1.06) |
| stp2 (Stopped activity) | 1.226 | (13.81) | 0.969 | (15.54) | 0.814 | (11.68) |
| stp3 | 0.988 | (9.97) | 0.868 | (13.64) | 0.631 | (13.44) |
| stp4 | 0.462 | (3.62) | 0.271 | (2.32) | 0.455 | (1.45) |
| rur2 (Community survey) | −0.900 | (10.36) | −0.579 | (8.93) | −0.515 | (6.93) |
| rur3 | 0.439 | (4.14) | −0.139 | (1.48) | −0.061 | (1.00) |
| rur4 | 0.089 | (0.64) | 0.177 | (1.67) | 0.710 | (0.66) |
| **Co-variances $\Sigma$ (probit specification)** | | | | | | |
| var2 | | | | | 0.646 | (5.19) |
| var4 | | | | | 4.585 | (0.90) |
| cov32 | | | 0.791 | (9.49) | | |
| cov43 | | | −0.530 | (0.68) | | |
| Log Likelihood | −4946 | | −4932 | | −4934 | |

# Index